PETTY TYRANTS
&
FACING THE UNKNOWN

The Wave or Adventures with Cassiopaea by Laura Knight-Jadczyk

Riding the Wave (vol. 1)
Soul Hackers (vol. 2)
Stripped to the Bone (vol. 3)
Through a Glass Darkly (vol. 4)
Petty Tyrants & Facing the Unknown (vols. 5 & 6)
Almost Human (vol. 7)
Debugging the Universe (vol. 8)

Other books by Laura Knight-Jadczyk

The Secret History of the World and How to Get Out Alive
9/11: The Ultimate Truth (with Joe Quinn)
High Strangeness: Hyperdimensions and the Process of
  Alien Abduction

volumes 5 & 6 of
LAURA KNIGHT-JADCZYK'S
THE WAVE
OR ADVENTURES WITH CASSIOPAEA

PETTY TYRANTS
&
FACING THE UNKNOWN

NAVIGATING THE TRAPS AND DIVERSIONS
OF LIFE IN THE MATRIX

Red Pill Press

TABLE OF CONTENTS

PETTY TYRANTS

CHAPTER 33
INTRODUCTION

AN EXERCISE IN SEEING

At this point in this series of volumes, I find that I must change direction again. What you are going to read from here on, was not originally part of *The Wave Series* as it was published on the Internet beginning in spring of 2000. What happened was that writing and publishing *The Wave* apparently made waves in certain circles and it seems that I was marked for destruction for daring to reveal the truth about so many esoteric subjects. But, I will come to that. First, I would like to make some general background comments.

The reader who has read this far in *The Wave* has surely come to the conclusion that what I am saying is "nothing is as it seems and never has been," including the many religions and methods of ascension promoted down through the ages.

But what is lacking is a clearly defined *way* that might give guidance to the seeker in his quest for the keys to his own salvation in whatever terms he might define it. I have worked on presenting the Way in this series by sharing my own experiences and what I have gleaned from much study and research, but some readers are put off by material that deals with all the lies and deceptions that we face in our reality and simply want to read something uplifting. It doesn't seem to occur to them that one cannot be "uplifted" as long as one is mired in quicksand. What seems to be true is that we live in a world of lies – ruled by lies and stealing – and that human beings lie because it is impossible for them to do otherwise. Without a Way, that is.

As a result of our own searching and questing for answers, the repeated trying and testing of sources and materials, little by little we have come to the idea of what *not* to do. But again, there has not been a whole lot about what *to do*.

The Cassiopaeans have indicated certain pathways to follow, but as always, we are more or less on our own in acquiring the knowledge and learning how to apply it – and for good reason, as the reader may know.

So it was that I began to write *The Wave*, little knowing that the act of writing it would bring to me my most important lessons; the lessons that would enable me to see, and to describe in detail, the most important issues facing all of humanity.

One of the main things I learned through this process is that any individual who wishes to pursue esoteric studies ought to have a clean and fully functional – and most of all *healthy* – psyche before he goes wandering off into unknown realms. After all, if your psychological state is such that you cannot deal effectively with your everyday life, how can you possibly trust such a psychological state not to mislead you in studies where you have fewer solid landmarks or feedback mechanisms to guide you?

And so, it strikes me that the very *first* order of business in any esoteric work is to get psychologically healthy. That's basically what the Gurdjieff "self-remembering" and Mouravieff "introspection" and Castaneda "recapitulation" is all about.

Sure, it can be referred to in nebulous ways such as "the work of sorcerers" and "recapturing energy" and "crystallizing a soul" and so on, but it can also be talked about in very practical, scientific, modern terminology with definite examples and techniques for accomplishing this important work of knowing your machine, cleaning and adjusting it so that it works properly, and preparing oneself for more interesting esoteric work.

Recapitulation as formulated by Castaneda was, I think, a take-off on Gurdjieff's self-remembering. The words self-remembering as Gurdjieff used them are, however, somewhat nebulous. Boris Mouravieff states the matter in a rather more practical way:

> *Homo Sapiens* lives immersed in his everyday life to a point where he forgets himself and forgets where he is going; yet, without feeling it, he knows that death cuts off everything.
>
> How can we explain that the intellectual who has made marvelous discoveries and the technocrat who has exploited them have left outside the field of their investigations the ending of our lives? How can we explain that a science which attempts everything and claims everything nevertheless remains indifferent to the enigma revealed by the question of death? How can we explain why Science, instead of uniting its efforts with its older sister Religion to resolve the problem of Being – which is also the problem of death – has in fact opposed her?
>
> Whether a man dies in bed or aboard an interplanetary ship, the human condition has not changed in the slightest.
>
> Happiness? But we are taught that happiness lasts only as long as the Illusion lasts … and what is this Illusion? Nobody knows. But it submerges us.

If we only knew what Illusion is, we would then know the opposite: what Truth is. This Truth would liberate us from slavery.

As a psychological phenomenon, has Illusion ever been subjected to critical analysis based on the most recent discoveries of science? It does not seem to be so, and yet one cannot say that man is lazy and does not search. He is a passionate searcher ... but he misses the essential; he by-passes it in his search.

What strikes us from the very beginning is that man confuses moral progress with technical progress, so that the development of science continues in dangerous isolation.

The brilliant progress that has come from technology has changed nothing essential in the human condition, and will change nothing, because it operates only in the field of everyday events. For this reason it touches the inner life of man only superficially. Yet from very ancient times it has been known that the essential is found within man, not outside him. ...

Esoteric philosophy concerns man as he is: the investigator is the object of his own studies. Starting from the constatation that man is unknown, his target is to make himself known to himself – as he is, and *as he might become under certain conditions.* (Mouravieff 2002, xxiii)

Gurdjieff had his methods and Boris Mouravieff, as noted, wrote about these methods in a slightly different way.

As it happens, during our research into Boris M., we discovered that he was being soundly lambasted by William Patrick Patterson in his book *Talking With the Left Hand* in which he accuses Mouravieff of stealing his ideas from Gurdjieff. Patterson is the author of four highly praised books on spiritual development and is a longtime student of John Pentland, the man Gurdjieff chose to lead the Gurdjieff Work in America.

Just in case the reader is not familiar with Gurdjieff, let me give a little background. Dating from his first lectures in Moscow and St. Petersburg in 1912, George Ivanovich Gurdjieff attracted the attention of occultists and many Western aristocrats. His teachings (often referred to as the "Gurdjieff Work" or "Fourth Way") became widely known through the writings and lectures of his pupil, the famous Russian mathematician and journalist Pyotr D. Ouspensky, and were later propagated by Alfred Orage, John G. Bennett, Rodney Collins, and Dr. Maurice Nicoll.

Gurdjieff himself admitted that he was utilizing "stolen" teachings from a wide range of groups that he had encountered (including the Yezidis, the Russian Orthodox Church, and Sufi "Bektashi" and "Naqshbandi" sects in the Hindu Kush and Pamir regions) in his world travels. A deep study of Gurdjieff's work shows that he was obviously experimenting with his own ideas on how to utilize bits and pieces from these different teachings to create a system that would enable individuals to overcome ingrained cognitive defects, become more conscious, and awaken the Higher Self's "Objective Conscience."

At a certain point, it seems that Gurdjieff realized that he had undertaken an impossible task since nearly all of his students "heard" only what they wanted to hear. He closed his school and concentrated on putting his ideas into allegory in his book *Beelzebub's Tales To His Grandson* (1950), which also incorporated and developed additional esoteric themes into his ideas.

Many of Gurdjieff's concepts have profoundly influenced our present culture due to the fact that some of his followers were famous and wealthy and had the means to promote them to others in the upper classes. After his death in 1949, Gurdjieff's legacy was disseminated through many people, and much of his work has been passed on through fragmentation of the many groups into something akin to secular denominations. One of the biggest problems with what happened to Gurdjieff's work – what seemed to be a sincere attempt to help humanity – was further obscured by the formation of what can only be called personality cults and identifications with Gurdjieff at the expense of his ideas. It seems that Gurdjieff himself saw this coming at the end of his life.

Groups that are offshoots of Gurdjieff's teachings have been known to use all kinds of things to reprogram their members, including isolation, group think, authoritarian power structures, and other psychological methods designed to unmask or break down the personal ego. But, what seems clear is that, in the case of Gurdjieff, no one group can claim the whole cheese since he was curiously selective about what he told whom, and even those who were closest to him obviously misunderstood what he was trying to convey, as evidenced by his own statements about this factor towards the end of his life.

The fact is, Gurdjieff faced great difficulties at the point in time when he sought to experiment with waking up humanity. As noted above, it was "Mission Impossible." However, what he and his followers did manage to do was to slash a trail through a jungle of lies and disinformation. It is not appropriate for his followers to insist that this bare trail is all there is and that there is no more. Rather, it is only logical to widen the trail, to pass through the gate revealed at the end of the trail, and discover what lies on the other side.

Mouravieff certainly had his own issues and of the two, I would rely on Gurdjieff before Mouravieff, but Mouravieff did do a service by transmitting a most ancient esoteric tradition. As long as he was writing about the tradition, he was being helpful. When he began to add his own ideas or interpretations, he exposed his ignorance and failure to understand the very material he was conveying.

Castaneda either borrowed many of these ideas and re-framed them in a Southwestern shamanic context with his own spin, or actually found traces of the same ideas there. I tend toward the former supposition based on the timing and several insightful discussions with someone who knew him personally.[1]

Our own approach, guided by the Cs, is more strictly along the lines of Gurdjieff and Mouravieff and a bit of Castaneda with a kick. Gurdjieff and Mouravieff and Castaneda all talk about a man needing to know himself, to know his "machine," to observe it, to engage in introspection or recapitulation or self-observation and so on and so forth. We have taken this to the next logical step and utilize the terminology of modern psychology. In our searching for validation of these ideas, we have found that there are actually studies and books written about various aspects of human psychology that service these very ancient traditions remarkably.[2]

Gurdjieff talked about "buffers" and how they are created. It's clear that Castaneda's recapitulation was supposed to be a means of dealing with buffers though Castaneda's presentation of many things was sorely lacking in clarity. He tended to mystify the whole thing. That is unfortunate. A lot of people follow after the Castaneda way because of this very mystification. It sounds so – well – esoteric and they don't want to accept the simple fact that the first order of business is to deal with your own psychology in a very basic and practical way.

Have a look at what Gurdjieff had to say about buffers and keep in mind that he is talking about the many "programs" or thought loops that become inculcated into us from childhood due to our experiences and familial and social conditioning. These programs, or thought loops, are the same thing that Castaneda refers to as the "Predator's mind."

> You often think in a very naive way ... You already think you can do. To get rid of this conviction is more difficult than anything else for a man. *You do not understand all the complexity of your organization* and you do not realize that every effort, in addition to the results desired, even if it

---

[1] In 2008, years after this volume was written, William Patrick Patterson published a book, *The Life & Teachings of Carlos Castaneda*, in which he shows that Castaneda had indeed adapted the teachings of Gurdjieff for use in his books. Patterson also analyses Castaneda/don Juan's major themes in relation to Gurdjieff's teaching and terminology. [Editor's note.]

[2] 1) *Trapped in The Mirror* by Elan Golomb, 2) *Unholy Hungers* by Barbara Hort, 3) *The Myth of Sanity* by Martha Stout, 4) *The Narcissistic Family* by Stephanie Donaldson-Pressman and Robert M. Pressman, 5) *The Mask of Sanity* by Hervey Cleckley, 6) *Without Conscience* by Robert Hare, 7) *The Sociopath Next Door* by Martha Stout, 8) *Snakes in Suits* by Babiak and Hare, 9) *Political Ponerology* by Andrew Lobaczewski.

gives these, gives thousands of unexpected and often undesirable re-sults, and the chief thing that you forget is that *you are not beginning from the beginning with a nice clean, new machine.* There stand behind you many years of *a wrong and stupid life, of indulgence in every kind of weakness, of shutting your eyes to your own errors, of striving to avoid all unpleasant truths, of constant ly-ing to yourselves, of self-justification, of blaming others,* and so on, and so on. All this cannot help affecting the machine. The machine is dirty, in places it is rusty, and in some places artificial appliances have been formed, the necessity for which has been created by its own wrong way of working.

These artificial appliances will now interfere very much with all your good intentions.

They are called 'buffers.'

'Buffer' is a term which requires special explanation. We know what buffers on railway carriages are. They are the contrivances which lessen the shock when carriages or trucks strike one another. If there were no buffers the shock of one carriage against another would be very un-pleasant and dangerous. Buffers soften the results of these shocks and render them unnoticeable and imperceptible.

Exactly the same appliances are to be found within man. *They are cre-ated, not by nature but by man himself, although involuntarily.* The cause of their appearance is the existence in man of many contradictions; contradic-tions of opinions, feelings, sympathies, words, and actions. If a man throughout the whole of his life were to feel all the contradictions that are within him he could not live and act as calmly as he lives and acts now. He would have constant friction, constant unrest. We fail to see how contradictory and hostile the different I's of our personality are to one another. If a man were to feel all these contradictions he would feel what he really is. He would feel that he is mad. It is not pleasant to any-one to feel that he is mad. Moreover, a thought such as this deprives a man of self-confidence, weakens his energy, deprives him of 'self-respect.' Somehow or other he must master this thought or banish it. He must either destroy contradictions or cease to see and to feel them. A man cannot destroy contradictions. But if 'buffers' are created in him he can cease to feel them and he will not feel the impact from the clash of contradictory views, contradictory emotions, contradictory words.

'Buffers' are created slowly and gradually. Very many 'buffers' are created artifi-cially through 'education.' Others are created under the hypnotic influence of all surrounding life. A man is surrounded by people who live, speak, think, and feel by means of 'buffers.' Imitating them in their opinions, actions, and words, a man invol-untarily creates similar 'buffers' in himself. 'Buffers' make a man's life more easy. It is very hard to live without 'buffers.' But they keep man from the possibility of inner development because 'buffers' are made to lessen shocks and it is only shocks that can lead a man out of the state in which he lives, that is, waken him. 'Buffers' lull a man to sleep, give him the agreeable and peaceful sensation that all will be well, that no contra-dictions exist and that he can sleep in peace. 'Buffers' are appliances by means of which a man can always be in the right. 'Buffers' help a man not to feel his conscience. (Ouspensky 1977, 154–155)

We have found that dealing with the issues of narcissism and psychopatholgy in our world is the clearest and most direct path to dealing with programs, buffers or the Predator's mind in man. Most human beings in the world are narcissistic and most of us are raised by narcissists. The world itself – society, culture, science, religion – is heavily influenced by psychopathic influences and these influences are one of the reasons that most potentially healthy people become narcissistic – it is a defense – a system of buffers.

And so, as we are raised in a psychopathic/narcissistic world, we also grow these buffers that separate us from our true self and that force our machine to use up vast quantities of soul energy just to keep running at all.

And so, we approach the problem in a very pragmatic and practical way. A person can do nothing until they are psychologically healthy and this means removing buffers, mentally going over the machine in a careful and thorough way, cleaning it, re-wiring it and most of all, having new experiences that help with this re-wiring process in an environment where this is possible.

Then, of course, you need to really understand how the world got to be the way it is, and that involves the study of psychopathy. Studying psychopathy is useful for another very good reason: when you finally clearly see the traits of the psychopath writ large, it helps you to identify traces of such influences in your own make-up. Psychopaths are like caricatures that help you recognize something by its most pronounced features, just like the drawing known as a caricature.

Perhaps the most destructive, and thus most important, of the relationships that must be parsed is interaction with psychological deviants in our society. In the past few years, as a result of the experiences that were triggered by the writing of *The Wave* (which I am about to recount), we have done much research on the subject, finding such indispensable works as Robert Hare's *Without Conscience*, Martha Stout's *The Sociopath Next Door*, Hervey Cleckley's *The Mask of Sanity* and Andrew Lobaczewski's *Political Ponerology*. As we did more research we discovered just how many people are affected by these intraspecies predators. The problem is truly epidemic, and as researchers like Robert Hare and Andrew Lobaczewski demonstrate, the effect psychopaths have on normal people of conscience inevitably leads to tragic results. A person's moral and logical reasoning abilities are numbed and distorted. They, in essence, become what has enslaved them. It is only by rigorously analyzing these dynamics that we can protect ourselves.

One of the concepts that seems to be integral to the idea that knowledge protects is that saving energy will enable us to grow and become more aware of higher levels of consciousness. It is this growth of awareness that binds us and makes us eligible to graduate as a result of the coming Wave, or Macrocosmic Metamorphosis.

According to the Cassiopaeans, our third density world consists of what we can know within third density parameters – it is our third density awareness that binds us to it. When that awareness grows, we are able to bind with higher levels of reality. Don Juan says that all that we know as humans, and can describe with words, is a very small part of what actually exists. It is an island upon which we pass the whole of our lives.

What lies beyond?

The Cassiopaeans say that it is a hyperdimensional state of existence, partly physical and partly ethereal, with a greater balance of these elements than what we have here, where the physical dominates. This physical aspect is what don Juan says is controlled by the Predator, and that we, ourselves, as physical beings are controlled by the Predator's mind. The process by which the Predator gives us its mind has since been scientifically described in *Political Ponerology* as that of ponerization – the effect on normal people of the Predator's almost-human interface: psychopathy.

From don Juan's perspective, what lies beyond the borders of third density is an unfathomable mystery that cannot be understood verbally, but it can be witnessed, and experienced by anyone *with enough energy*. By integrating the known with the unknown, an integration of the self occurs. When the individual begins the process of integration, they begin to realize that the reality of the world is merely a matter of perception. And when they begin to become aware of this, one of the results is that their perception changes.

The Cs have made it clear that we are "food" for self-serving beings at higher levels, and that they feed on our energy, for the most part, but in some cases may actually feed on our flesh. Don Juan points out that they keep us in this chicken coop by controlling our thinking. The Cs say essentially the same thing. Gurdjieff talked about it in terms of being mechanical and "food for the Moon" and the movie *The Matrix* presented a similar idea, stating that the basis of the Matrix is "rules."

Our bodies are fields of energy that are constantly affected by other fields of energy – from planets, to the human beings in our lives – whether they are physically present or merely connected via psychological strands of etheric energy. All of these fields affect us, and the Cs have pointed out through the many answers to my questions about my own relationships and interactions with others, that these interconnected fields are the means by which our energy is either "eaten" or augmented, depending on the nature of the interaction.

INTRODUCTION

Don Juan taught Carlos that foreign energy can distort our own energy fields for years as a result of our interactions with those we encounter during our lives. By the same token, we can have a distorting effect on the energy fields of others. Don Juan said that this distorted energy holds us back, holds us under some dark spell because it interferes with our daily living by draining our energy. What is easy to see is that he was attempting to convey the fact that these distortions can create energetic links by which the Matrix, or Predator, drains our energy continuously. These ideas are a recurring theme in literature.

"Our lives are merely strange, dark interludes in the electrical display of God the Father," or so wrote the playwright Eugene O'Neill. In its time, *Strange Interlude* achieved a success no other American play had ever equaled. The published play became a national best seller – the first time a drama had attained that honor – and O'Neill received his third Pulitzer Prize for the work.

The reviewers of 1928 weren't crazy about it, calling it naïve in its use of psychological theory in an attempt to represent the point made in the title line, delivered by the heroine of the play, Nina. But to the public, it was clear that a deep chord of resonance had been struck, and they responded to this exploration of reality with enthusiasm.

Strange Interlude appeared as a work which dealt seriously with facets of human nature not yet fully explored. It attempted to establish a kind of primer of new ways of understanding human drives and motivations. O'Neill himself, in his *Memoranda on Masks* wrote of using masks to "express those profound hidden conflicts of the mind which the probings of psychology continue to disclose to us." At the same time, he spoke of masks as providing "a chance for eloquent presentation, a new form of drama projected from a fresh insight into the inner forces motivating the actions and reactions of men and women – a drama of souls."

In the context of what I am about to disclose, a series of behind the scenes views of the dynamics of channeling and the necessary human interactions, there is an echo of the ideas of *Strange Interlude* which O'Neill was never quite able to sufficiently delineate. In the present series, the reader will note that a tension is suggested between that which is purely psychological and that which is mystical and abstract. The astute reader will perceive a theologically oriented drama of souls. In this sense, we come to the realization that the human masks are just the surfaces of the dramas of higher levels of being, and that the psychological layer is merely the immediate subsurface. We hope that the reader will be able to see even deeper, and discover what it is that the Cassiopaeans have tried to convey to us and through us about the nature of the Matrix reality in which we live.

In fact, the movie, *The Matrix*, is the next level of revelations beyond that approached by O'Neill in *Strange Interlude*. It is also an excellent metaphor for the drama we have lived, are living, and which others live, though often unbeknownst to themselves. It is our hope that the experiences we will be describing here, our learning to see the unseen, in terms of penetrating not only beyond the masks of the physical symbols of reality to the psychological substrate, but even deeper to the theological drama of souls, will be useful to others in terms of navigating the Matrix-like reality in which we live.

In addition to providing a map for others, what I will be disclosing to the reader is also an act of recapitulation. According to don Juan, recapitulation is an exercise to recall, review, release, and recharge energy lost in this drama of souls. It rids a person of assumptions and preconceptions. It frees locked energy and restores balance. The chief thing about recapitulation that seems to not be clearly stated by the so-called Toltec teachings is that what it really does is increase awareness by increasing knowledge, and with increased knowledge and awareness, the individual is able to employ will to choose to act differently; to cut the connections between the self and those who drain us.

Life is lessons. It's that simple. We "pass" these lessons by learning to see the hidden dynamics of our interpersonal relationships. Once we understand these dynamics we can learn to put an end to the destructive and emotionally draining ones. If what the Cs have said about the Wave is true, then it is by learning these simple karmic understandings that one can learn the lessons of third grade. Therefore, the process of recapitulation is one of great importance. By having an understanding of our past mistakes we can apply our understanding in the present, thus protecting ourselves for the future. We can truly self-remember, as Gurdjieff says, and utilize the present for whatever aim we have set for ourselves.

Carlos Castaneda's teachings about warriors and sorcerers seem to suggest that the only option to really become free is to cut all connections, and to isolate the self psychologically and even, in some cases, physically. He did not seem to be aware that there was another option. The Cs, on the other hand, suggest that there is another way: that of networking in a manner aligned with service-to-others.

The hidden key in the teachings of the Cs, don Juan, and Gurdjieff, is that human beings may, indeed, be what they are because of genetics, but they can *change* this – to some extent – by what they *learn*. Perhaps we ought to pause for a moment to consider how this is possible.

A sea slug is a pretty basic creature. It cannot migrate, communicate, fly, or think. It exists in a life of eating and sex. That's about it. *But*, if a jet of water is blown on its gill, it withdraws the gill. If the jet of water is repeatedly blown on the gill, the withdrawal gradually ceases. The sea slug stops responding to what it now recognizes as a false alarm. It habituates. This is learning. Maybe not algebra, but learning nevertheless.

If the sea slug is given an electric shock once, before water is blown on the gill, it learns to withdraw its gill even further than usual – it is sensitized. It can also be conditioned to withdraw its gill when it receives only a gentle puff of water if that puff is paired with an electric shock, after which only the puff is present, stimulating the behavior. This is associative learning.

The thing is: the sea slug does not use its brain. *The changes occur in the abdominal ganglion.* Since sea slugs have pretty large and simple neuron complexes, they are easy to study, and scientists were able to determine what, exactly, occurs in the process of learning. When an electrical nerve signal reaches a synapse, it must transfer to a chemical signal, like a train passenger having to catch a ferry across a sea channel before getting back on another train. Learning seems to be a change in the properties of the synapses. Either the synapse is weakened or strengthened, and the whole operation centers around a molecule called cyclic AMP.

A series of chemical reactions occurs which leads to the activation of a protein called CREB. Animals which lack the activated form of CREB can learn, but cannot remember. This is because CREB, once activated, starts *switching on genes*. The genes switched on are called CRE genes and are "cyclic AMP response elements." The human CREB gene is on chromosome 2, but a crucial component is also found on chromosome 16. It now seems that a further component is on chromosome 21.

In fruit flies the cyclic AMP system seems to be especially active in brain regions called "mushroom bodies." They are toadstool-shaped extrusions of neurons. A fly that has no mushroom bodies in its brain is generally incapable of learning. CREB and cyclic AMP do their work in these mushroom bodies. (Now, think of the mushroom imagery of the ancients! Mycenaea – the place of the mushroom. Of course, the occultists would have us believe that they were all slurping *amanita muscaria*, but were they?)

Deep in the base of the brain is a structure called the hippocampus (Greek for *sea horse!*) and a part of the hippocampus is called Ammon's horn, or the *Ram*. In the Ammon's horn, there are a large number of *pyramidal* neurons which gather the input of other sensory neurons. A pyramidal neuron is difficult to fire, but if two separate inputs arrive at once, their combined effect will fire it. Once fired, it is much easier to fire, but only by one of the two inputs that originally fired it, and *not* by another input. Thus, for example, the sight of a pyramid and the word Egypt combined, could fire the pyramidal cell, creating an associative memory. This means that things that occur together in time can "potentiate" associative learning.

What resides in and near the hippocampus is the mechanism for creating long-term memory. The cells there transmit the newly formed long-term memory to where it will reside in the neo-cortex. People with small hippocampuses can form procedural memories – that is, they can learn to do things that require skill, like reading and writing, and diagramming sentences, teaching English and literature, performing rituals and collecting data of all kinds, and even aping scholars to a sufficient extent that the non-discriminating observer is easily fooled. If, however, there are lesions in this region of the brain, or genetic malformation, the likelihood is that such individuals have no real ability to associate so as to do anything that is truly creative or new.[3]

This means that they cannot and do not learn from their experiences if it requires the extraction of a principle and applying it to other situations in the realms of pure thought. As Gurdjieff noted, even great literature can be written altogether mechanically.

This, of course, makes me wonder if part of the STS problem is hippocampus-related, since semantic aphasia seems to be one of the chief clues that we have noticed in dealing with such individuals, and since psychopaths are remarkably inept at learning from experiences what behaviour is self-destructive in the *long*-term. But, I am getting ahead of myself.

Getting back to recapitulation. It seems that, when utilized correctly, it is a process of "thinking with a hammer," and *making associations*. Recapitulation can be a tool by which awareness is enhanced. According to don Juan, it consists in hashing over and reliving one's experiences. One must attempt to remember every possible, minute detail. When this is done within a group, it becomes the essence of what Paul wrote when he said "confess your sins one to the other," keeping in mind that Gurdjieff referred to the Fourth Way as "Esoteric Christianity." The Cs say "network" and "air it out." The result seems to be that recapitulation increases awareness, which then enables us to apply what we are now aware of in practical ways, and thus, we are enabled to begin

---

[3] "Psychopathy and the posterior hippocampus," Laakso MP, Vaurio O, Koivisto E, Savolainen L, Eronen M, Aronen HJ, Hakola P, Repo E, Soininen H, Tiihonen J. – "The regional volumes along the anteroposterior axis of the hippocampus were correlated with the subjects' degree of psychopathy as evaluated by the Psychopathy Checklist-Revised. Strong negative correlations, up to -0.79, were observed, among the study subjects, between the psychopathy scores and the posterior half of the hippocampi bilaterally. These data are in accordance with experimental studies proposing that lesions of the dorsal hippocampus impair acquisition of conditioned fear, and with theories on psychopathology according to which one of the central features in the birth of psychopathy is a deficit in acquisition of conditioned fear."

the process of reclaiming our energy, and making better choices about who or what we connect to, or associate with, in terms of our interactions with people and situations that we encounter in our daily lives.

The way this may work is that, by recapitulation, we are discovering principles. We are looking at an event in the real world, considering the psychological, "real" reason, and associating it to the theological reason. This means that we are firing the pyramidal cells in the hippocampus because we are coming at the issue with numerous inputs at once. This then ships the information off to the neo-cortex where more synapses are formed, and more thinking capacity results, establishing a positive feedback loop.

According to don Juan, recapitulating an event starts with one's mind arranging everything pertinent to what is being recapitulated. Arranging means reconstructing the event, piece by piece, starting with recollecting the physical details of the surroundings, then remembering the person with whom one shared the interaction, and then proceeding to the examination of the self and one's own feelings. This is extremely important, and the reader will recognize echoes of Gurdjieff's self-remembering and will also see the associative properties of creating the multiple inputs for the hippocampus.

While don Juan taught that recapitulation ought to be accompanied by deep breathing and slowly moving the head back and forth, we are dealing here with a form of recapitulation that includes a network, so we have to sort of wing it and figure out the process as we go along.

As a general rule, our reality discourages recapitulation. It teaches us to "forgive and forget" and "make nice" and think in strictly third density terms. We are beginning to realize that this is a program, and it is the main reason so many of us suffer for so many years: we are trying to "make nice" when things clearly are *not* nice.

And how easily we are persuaded to *stop* seeing, to stop thinking, to stop examining, and to most definitely *not* make any choices based on any such perceptions. We have already mentioned the fact that we are programmed to *not* do post mortems on our relationships because it is considered to be gossip. We are discouraged from talking about our ongoing interactions and the clues we see, because it is "not nice" or it is "two-faced" or whatever. In hundreds of different ways, we are programmed to not examine our interactions, and most especially our own take on things at one time as opposed to another.

Those who constantly seek to understand their experiences may find themselves accused of being inconstant in their opinions. Well, heck, nobody wants to be accused of being flaky or inconstant. In this way, a "paramoralism"[4] is used as a weapon against us, to keep us as food.

Most importantly, the Matrix, the Predator, or the fourth density STS controllers,[5] do not want us to govern our lives by what we see when we recapitulate. They do not want us to "spot the program" and refuse to run it. They do not want us to see the small clues that our energy is being drained, and learn that it is not only okay to disengage from association with such individuals, it is required.

It is okay to figure out that somebody is not what we thought they were. It is okay to decide that we don't have to continue in a relationship with that person because we know from our experiences, from our recapitulation, that there is so little possibility that they will change that it is almost not worth considering. It is okay to admit we were evaluating or making choices based on limited information that has now been superseded by deeper or more accurate information. It is okay to simply come to the realization that we have been slowly manipulated into making one choice after another that we didn't really want to make, and now we have decided that we don't want to be manipulated anymore.

We are allowed to change our minds as often as our minds change. And if our minds are open, and in tune with the infinite possibilities of the cosmos, that can be rather frequent.

At one point during the events I am about to recount, I received an email from a correspondent. In this email, he told me some really ugly things about an individual he recently realized was a psychic vampire in his own life. He described a meeting where he and this psychic vampire were having a discussion with two other men, one of them a writer and film producer, and expert on "sacred geometry" and mysticism in general. The correspondent described how this well-known man excused himself about ten or so minutes into the discussion, and left. A few days later, he called my correspondent and told him that there was something *very* wrong with the psychic vampire and that he would not be willing to work with my correspondent in any way as long as interactions with the psychic vampire were a part of the deal.

---

[4] The conviction that moral values exist and that some actions violate moral rules is so common and ancient a phenomenon that it seems to reside in man's instinctive psychological substratum. At the same time, this conviction represent centuries' worth of experience, culture, religion, and socialization. Thus, any insinuation closed in moral slogans can by psychologically suggestive and manipulative, even if the "moral" criteria used are just an "ad hoc" invention. Any act can thus be labeled immoral or morally proper by means of such paramoralisms.

[5] The concepts of Service-to-Self (STS) and Service-to-Others (STO) are introduced and discussed in the previous four volumes of the Wave series.

My correspondent said that the only reason he disregarded this warning was because *"I am a man of my word. I had made a promise."* He then ended up spending several years being manipulated, drained of energy, drained of cash, suffering losses to his reputation, and finally being stabbed in the back by the psychic vampire. In fact, we were taken in by the very same psychic vampire, as I will shortly recount.

In short, he had warning. Not just his own instincts, because he confessed that he was uneasy about this collaboration, but another person clearly and plainly told him, "I can't associate with you as long as you associate with him." And the guy who said this was obviously somebody who knew about energy and how it is drained, and how to spot such people and decline to interact.

And that is what we need most desperately to learn.

What was it my correspondent said? "I am a man of my word. I had made a promise." Well, guess what? This is a paramoralistic program. In this case it plays on what we have been programmed to think is "moral" and what is not. How can you consider yourself obliged to keep your word to an individual who has obtained your word by fraud? If a person obtains a promise from you that you will give him money by claiming that he is broke, and you then find out he is a millionaire scrooge, are you going to give him your money anyway? We begin to get a niggling suspicion that this was the real reason that Jesus taught that a person ought not to swear about anything; because new information can, at any moment, change the perspective, the reality, and our lives. We ought to always be free to change our direction at any moment, the same way the pilot of a ship makes constant corrections in the heading based on the different external influences such as the wind and sea currents.

Life is like that: there is wind, there are currents, and it is somewhat chaotic. If we do not examine it, stay alert to these things, we will end up far off course and never reach our destination.

Much of this book is a recapitulation. It is the performance of an act of power. But it is not just *my* recapitulation; it is the recapitulation of a much larger group and soul dynamic. It is the act of opening doors to other realities because, as I proceed, as I think back and study what I remember, attempting to be as accurate as possible, why I did what I did, how I felt, how the different people acted or reacted, as I search through the transcripts to jog my memory – because the transcripts are mostly a diary of my personal life and thinking – I am finding that much of the material from Cs that never made complete sense before is now beginning to fit together in a surprising way.

I am also seeing something else: In every case where I have held back telling anything, I have done so for the very reasons cited above: I was acting according to the rules, out of courtesy, or because I was "giving the benefit of the doubt," or "turning the other cheek," or making nice. And, as the Cs have pointed out, expecting something to turn out differently from what it is at the moment of realizing what the program is, is wishful thinking. And wishful thinking is the essence of service-to-self.

At the time that many of the attacks I am going to disclose were going on, we did not write about them, we did not share them, we tried to keep them private for the sake of giving more chances for the others involved to do something else that would heal the breach. We were always expecting them to just wake up and see that we are not their adversary, that we do not want to interfere in their lives, that we simply and only want to have the right to our own choices, even if those choices include *not* associating with them in any way. We wanted them to understand that we had realized that our mutual energies were obviously not in sync, so "let's have a parting of the ways." At each stage of the process, we waited and hoped that this realization would arise in their minds. But it seems that such things never occur to people who are filled with their own self-importance. Such individuals become furious when their self-importance is provoked. They talk themselves into a state of righteous indignation that anyone would dare to refuse to associate with them; that anyone would dare to assert the right to their own space, be it real or virtual; that anyone would dare to make them look like a fool.

And then they go out and make themselves look like fools.

And here we come to the primary issue: When we identify the fact that our energy fields are not compatible with some other individual or that there is a drain, we have the right to choose to disassociate ourselves. We have not only the right, but if we are truly seeking higher knowledge, it is a necessity.

As we have quoted don Juan, recapitulation is an exercise to recall, review, release, and recharge energy. And so it is, what we are about to recount is a series of encounters with what don Juan called "petty tyrants." But, before we do, I would like to present don Juan's story of his petty tyrant from Castaneda's book *The Fire from Within*. It is a delightful, hilarious account of deep and important principles of awareness and energy conservation, and I recommend the reader to read the chapter in its entirety. Every time I read it I laugh with glee to see the very situation we will be discussing here so humorously depicted, petty tyrants who attempt to annoy us to distraction. As don Juan has said, "the warrior who stumbles on a petty tyrant is a lucky one … because if you don't, you have to go out and look for one." The objective is, of course, that if an individual can "hold their own in facing petty tyrants, they can certainly face the unknown with impunity, and then they can even stand the presence of the unknowable." In other words, we are enormously grateful for the petty tyrants in our lives. That we have them, and so many, indeed, gives me great hope that this very process of recapitulation, undertaken with self-restraint, will achieve the very pragmatic goal of serving others.

Castaneda's chapter on petty tyrants (pp. 11–30) begins with don Juan telling Carlos Castaneda that they must go for a walk to "sit down and talk". La Gorda, another of don Juan's students, upon overhearing that don Juan wishes to speak with Carlos in private, assumes that they are going to talk about her behind her back. Don Juan replies that she is correct, and he and Carlos leave to talk.

When alone, don Juan tells Carlos that he "told her that just to pro-voke her enormous self-importance. And it worked. She is furious with us. If I know her, by now she will have talked to herself long enough to have built up her confidence and her righteous indignation at having been refused and made to look like a fool. I wouldn't be surprised if she barges in on us here, at the park bench." He elaborates, saying, "Self-importance is our greatest enemy. Think about it – what weakens us is feeling offended by the deeds and misdeeds of our fellow men. Our self-importance requires that we spend most of our lives offended by someone."

When Carlos compares ridding oneself of self-importance to the Church's dictums on the evil of sin, don Juan replies, "Warriors fight self-importance as a matter of strategy, not principle. Your mistake is to understand what I say in terms of morality." He explains that what Carlos perceives in him as "morality" is really his impeccability, or his proper use of energy. By properly identifying "behavioral patterns that are not essential to our survival and well-being", like the activity of self-importance, one can eliminate what is unnecessary and draining. "One of the first concerns of warriors is to free that energy in order to face the unknown with it."

The process of rechanneling this energy involves six interplaying el-ements, five of which are called the "attributes of warriorship" – control, discipline, forbearance, timing, and will. While these apply to the inner world of the warrior, the sixth applies to the external world: the petty tyrant. "A petty tyrant is a tormentor. Someone who either holds the power of life and death over warriors or simply annoys them to distraction." Commenting on the irreverent humor with which the "new seers" classified their petty tyrants, don Juan tells Carlos:

> The new seers, in accordance with their practice, saw fit to head their classification with the primal source of energy, the one and only ruler in the universe, and they called it simply the tyrant. The rest of the despots

and authoritarians were found to be, naturally, infinitely below the category of tyrant. Compared to the source of everything, the most fearsome, tyrannical men are buffoons; consequently, they were classified as petty tyrants, pinches tiranos.

He said that there were two subclasses of minor petty tyrants. The first subclass consisted of the petty tyrants who persecute and inflict misery but without actually causing anybody's death. They were called little petty tyrants, pinches tiranitos. The second consisted of the petty tyrants who are only exasperating and bothersome to no end. They were called small-fry petty tyrants, repinches tiranitos, or teensy-weensy petty tyrants, pinches tiranitos chiquititos ...

He added that the little petty tyrants are further divided into four categories. One that torments with brutality and violence. Another that does it by creating unbearable apprehension through deviousness. Another which oppresses with sadness. And the last, which torments by making warriors rage ...

"My benefactor used to say that the warrior who stumbles on a petty tyrant is a lucky one. He meant that you're fortunate if you come upon one in your path, because if you don't, you have to go out and look for one."

He explained that one of the greatest accomplishments of the seers of the Conquest was a construct he called the three-phase progression. By understanding the nature of man, they were able to reach the incontestable conclusion that if seers can hold their own in facing petty tyrants, they can certainly face the unknown with impunity, and then they can even stand the presence of the unknowable.

"The average man's reaction is to think that the order of that statement should be reversed," he went on. "A seer who can hold his own in the face of the unknown can certainly face petty tyrants. But that's not so. What destroyed the superb seers of ancient times was that assumption. We know better now. We know that nothing can temper the spirit of a warrior as much as the challenge of dealing with impossible people in positions of power. Only under those conditions can warriors acquire the sobriety and serenity to stand the pressure of the unknowable."

It was only after dealing with the conquering Spaniards of the Conquest that the seers of that time were capable of facing anything. Luckily, in a time without petty tyrants of that scope, a "king-size one" found don Juan. At the time, however, don Juan found it hard to consider himself fortunate.

Don Juan then tells Carlos a story of his own petty tyrant. When barely twenty years old, he was essentially sold into slavery, although he was under the impression he was getting a well-paying job on a rich family's land. A self-described "lowly ignorant Indian" with no immediate relatives, the foreman of the ranch on which he was to work thought him the perfect employee! Don Juan knew soon after arriving at the ranch that he had to escape, but was threatened with a gun at his first attempt to flee. He worked three weeks doing strenuous labor, with the ever-present boss bullying him under the constant threat of a number of weapons.

Upon realizing that the foreman was in cahoots with the man at the sugar mill, where don Juan had previously worked, to sell Indians into slave-labor, don Juan went on a rampage through the kitchen and out the front door. But the foreman was too fast, shooting don Juan in the chest and leaving him for dead. Luckily don Juan's benefactor found him and nursed him back to health. As don Juan told Castaneda, "When I told my benefactor the whole story he could hardly contain his excitement. 'That foreman is really a prize,' my benefactor said. 'He is too good to be wasted. Someday you must go back to that house.' He raved about my luck in finding a one-in-a-million petty tyrant with almost unlimited power. I thought the old man was nuts. It was years before I fully understood what he was talking about." Don Juan then tells Carlos that he did go back to the house, three years later. His benefactor "developed a strategy using the four attributes of warriorship: control, discipline, forbearance, and timing."

> Don Juan said that his benefactor, in explaining to him what he had to do to profit from facing that ogre of a man, also told him what the new seers considered to be the four steps on the path of knowledge. The first step is the decision to become apprentices. After the apprentices change their views about themselves and the world they take the second step and become warriors, which is to say, beings capable of the utmost discipline and control over themselves. The third step, after acquiring forbearance and timing, is to become men of knowledge. When men of knowledge learn to see they have taken the fourth step and have become seers.

Teaching Carlos the importance of petty tyrants, don Juan told him that "the idea of using a petty tyrant is not only for perfecting the warrior's spirit, but also for *enjoyment and happiness*." In fact, don Juan's boss was nothing compared to the tyrants of the Conquest.

> Don Juan explained that the mistake average men make in confronting petty tyrants is not to have a strategy to fall back on; the fatal flaw is that average men take themselves too seriously; their actions and feelings, as well as those of the petty tyrants, are all-important. Warriors, on the other hand, not only have a well-thought-out strategy, but are free from self-importance. What restrains their self-importance is that they have understood that reality is an interpretation we make. That knowledge was the definitive advantage that the new seers had over the simple-minded Spaniards.

After building up his strength, don Juan managed to get the same job unrecognized by his former employers.

The same routine took place. The strategy, however, called for refusing payment to the foreman from the outset [for his 'service' of providing the new job]. The man had never been turned down and was taken aback. He threatened to fire don Juan from the job. Don Juan threatened him back, saying that he would go directly to the lady's house and see her. Don Juan knew that the woman, who was the wife of the owner of the mill, did not know what the two foremen were up to. He told the foreman that he knew where she lived, because he had worked in the surrounding fields cutting sugar cane. The man began to haggle, and don Juan demanded money from him before he would accept going to the lady's house. The foreman gave in and handed him a few bills. Don Juan was perfectly aware that the foreman's acquiescence was just a ruse to get him to go to the house. ...

"As soon as we got there, I ran into the house to look for the lady. I found her and dropped to my knees and kissed her hand to thank her. The two foremen were livid.

"The foreman at the house followed the same pattern as before. But I had the proper equipment to deal with him; I had control, discipline, forbearance, and timing. It turned out as my benefactor had planned it. My control made me fulfill the man's most asinine demands. What usually exhausts us in a situation like that is the wear and tear on our self-importance. Any man who has an iota of pride is ripped apart by being made to feel worthless. ... "

This time, instead of feeling sorry for himself, don Juan controlled himself while he worked on finding the boss' strengths, weaknesses, and personal quirks. While his strengths were his daring and violent nature, his weakness was that he liked his job – he couldn't kill don Juan on the compound or he might lose his position. He was also a family man, with a wife and child living near the house.

Having *forbearance* meant being patient for the right time to act, all the while enduring the tortures of slave labor and playing the role of ignorant worker to perfection.

He also employed his benefactor's method of *systematic harassment*, by taking cover under the "higher order" of the Catholic church, as his forbears had done during the Conquest. He daily kneeled before the lady of the house, calling her a saint and asking for a medallion to pray for her. The foreman was livid upon learning that not only had she given it to don Juan, but don Juan had got the other servants to pray with him at night.

"Daily he shoved me into the stallions' stalls hoping that I would be crushed to death, but I had a plank of heavy boards that I braced against one of the corners and protected myself behind it. The man never knew because he was nauseated by the horses – another of his weaknesses, the deadliest of all, as things turned out."

Don Juan said that *timing is the quality that governs the release of all that is held back*. Control, discipline, and forbearance are like a dam behind which everything is pooled. Timing is the gate in the dam.

Don Juan found the perfect moment to neutralize the man's violence under the cover of the watch of the other workers. He insulted the foreman by telling him to his face that he was afraid of the boss's wife. The man went into a rage, but by then, don Juan was "solicitously kneeling in front of the lady."

Don Juan said that when the lady went inside the house, the man and his friends called him to the back, allegedly to do some work. The man was very pale, white with anger. From the sound of his voice don Juan knew what the man was really planning to do. Don Juan pretended to acquiesce, but instead of heading for the back, he ran for the stables. He trusted that the horses would make such a racket the owners would come out to see what was wrong. He knew that the man would not dare shoot him. That would have been too noisy and the man's fear of endangering his job was too overpowering. Don Juan also knew that the man would not go where the horses were – that is, *unless he had been pushed beyond his endurance.*[6]

Don Juan jumped into the stall of the wildest stallion, hiding behind the boards he had prepared. The petty tyrant foreman charged into the stall blinded by rage and was killed with one kick of the stallion.

Don Juan told Carlos, "My benefactor explained something very interesting. Forbearance means holding back with the spirit something that the warrior knows is rightfully due. It doesn't mean that a warrior goes around plotting to do anybody mischief, or planning to settle past scores. Forbearance is something independent. As long as the warrior has control, discipline, and timing, forbearance assures giving whatever is due to whoever deserves it."

Carlos asked don Juan what measured defeat in an encounter with a petty tyrant. "Anyone who joins the petty tyrant is defeated," he replied. *"To act in anger, without control and discipline, to have no forbearance, is to be defeated."*

What is important about this subject is that the petty tyrant dynamic is the fundamental feeding mechanism of third density, and as such, is the real reason, or the psychological reason, that is the interface between the theological drama and the events of our lives. Don Juan has just told a story that caricatures the interaction so that we can recognize the chief features easily by association.

Just to review the classifications of petty tyrants, don Juan tells us that the primal source of energy, or the ruler of the universe, is The

---

[6] Which the insult was intended to do …

Tyrant. This resonates with Gurdjieff's Sufiesque idea that our world is run by an "Evil Magician." It also fits with the Gnostic Demiurge, and the Cs' presentation of the STS hierarchy that dominates our world from fourth density. It is in comparison to this Matrix Control System, The Tyrant, that even the worst of the despots and authoritarians of our reality are petty tyrants. These petty tyrants would be someone such as Adolf Hitler, Josef Stalin, Torquemada, and others with the power of life and death over other people. Below them are the "minor petty tyrants" who do not have the power of life and death over others, but who do persecute and cause misery, or who are exasperating and bothersome, as Castaneda phrased it. These are "little petty tyrants" and "teensy weensy petty tyrants."

Don Juan then tells us that the "little petty tyrants" are further subdivided into four additional categories: one that torments with brutality and violence, another that does it by creating unbearable apprehension through deviousness, another which oppresses with sadness, and the last, which torments by making warriors rage. What we will be noticing is that the same petty tyrant can, at different times, operate through any of these modes.

The purpose of the petty tyrant in our lives is to teach us detachment. It is a challenge to deal with impossible people, but by doing it, we acquire sobriety and serenity. In short, out of the fire comes light.

Don Juan described the steps of utilizing a petty tyrant to achieve a state of expanded consciousness. The first step is to consciously decide to seek Truth. As Gurdjieff noted, the question must be a "burning one." Neo, in *The Matrix*, had a "thorn in his mind." The Cs have said that it is a result of being "at that point on the learning cycle."

The next step is to change one's views about themselves and the world. This means to no longer accept the party line of the Matrix, and to begin the work of digging beneath the surface. This process reveals to the seeker that there is evidence everywhere of the hyperdimensional reality in which our own is embedded. Once this realization is made, the individual must decide if they wish to access that reality, or if they are simply content with the present one. *The Matrix* presented this as choosing whether or not one wishes to take the red pill, or the blue pill.

This is, essentially, the choice to become a warrior. A warrior, in mythical terms, is an individual who is capable of self-discipline and control over himself because this is what is necessary to take the next step of becoming a person of knowledge. This is knowledge that is only accessible by integration of the higher mind into the third density reality. This then becomes the mustard seed of the growth of the self *into* fourth density whereby the knowledge can be directly accessed. Unfortunately, this understanding has been seriously derailed by many New

Age teachings wherein the "intelligence of the heart" has been completely twisted to mean feelings or emotions or indiscriminate "love."

Gurdjieff describes this process as "fusion." He remarks that inner unity is obtained by means of "friction," by the struggle between "yes" and "no" in man. And this is where we find the usefulness of the petty tyrant. Petty tyrants produce friction in our lives. They are annoying, irritating, aggravating. They can drain our energy with their demands on our time and attention through the hooks of pity and manipulation. They can lie about us, have fits and give performances of righteous indignation that is based only on their own illusions, violate our privacy, our free will, and just a host of fun and games. But, what is important is that they are like sparring partners who teach us forbearance and timing. Of course, that is not their intention. But as Mephistopheles told Faust, "I am he who constantly intends evil, yet does good."

The machinations of STS in our world are like that: the Matrix, the Predator, the Evil Magician, the fourth density STS Control System, entropy; by whatever name you call it, it functions by draining us of our energy, uses us for food, and manipulates us for further purposes unknown; and it is done via agents, vectors of direction, sirens: psychopathic petty tyrants.

If we practice against the petty tyrant successfully, we are enabled to take the fourth step: to become *seers*. And here we don't mean a psychic who looks into a crystal ball; the meaning is one who *sees* what is real.

And so it is that when we discover a petty tyrant in our lives, a strategy is necessary to induce them to spar with us, a systematic harassment that not only engages them, but also causes them to expose themselves for what they are to other people. In this way, not only are they helpful in honing our skills, they are rendered unable to inflict their tyranny on others. That is, of course, another purpose of this public recapitulation.

A key fact to remember is this: in the deepest sense, we are *not* sparring with an individual; it is with a program, with "agents of the Matrix," the "mechanicalness" of the world, or the fourth density controllers pushing the buttons and pulling the levers behind the scenes. As the Apostle Paul wrote: "For we are not wrestling with flesh and blood, contending only with physical opponents, but against the despotisms, against the powers, against the master spirits who are the world rulers of this present darkness; against the spirit forces of wickedness in the heavenly, supernatural sphere … " (Ephesians 6:12)

And in the dynamic of Castaneda's account of dealing with the petty tyrant, we discover how it is that Knowledge Protects. Give the lie what it asks for: Truth.

OUR VERY OWN PETTY TYRANT

We come now to the story of making waves by writing *The Wave*.

In response to many questions and requests for more information about the Cs material, which was all I had put up on the Internet, in the spring of 2000, I began to write *The Wave Series*. This attracted a great deal of attention, mostly positive, though it also attracted the personal attention of what seem to be some extremely dark forces.

In order to explain this adequately, we have to back up to the spring of 1999, when I was put into contact with a fellow named Vincent Bridges. He immediately showed interest in my ideas regarding the Rennes-le-Château phenomenon, and we exchanged a fair number of emails on the subject, all of which are available on our website.[7] During our exchange, Bridges represented himself as an investigative journalist who was an expert on New Age/Occult matters, and with connections to all the big names. He was, he said, writing a book on the subject of Alchemy and Fulcanelli and he wanted to get as much information from me as possible to help with his analyses. Unfortunately, I was taken in immediately by this flattery. After all, here was a real, bona fide journalist and expert who was actually interested in what I thought about a subject that had received such wide publicity. I was a nobody! I was so happy that, finally, here was someone who was pursuing the same lines of research, and he was so charming and knowledgeable! Little did I know at the time that it was all an act.

When his book was finally finished in the fall of 1999 (and I had been waiting with baited breath to read what I was sure was going to be the best analysis of alchemy and Fulcanelli that had ever been written), to say that it was anti-climactic is an understatement. He sent me a copy and I read it with a growing sense of frustration and disappointment. Not only was it naïve and shallow, he had taken a great deal of the material I had sent him and had twisted it all out of recognition for some obscure purpose. I began to wonder if we were even talking the same language. There were a few more or less desultory exchanges for the next few months. I believed that he was sincere and even told myself that he was right not to trust the Cs – or any channeled source – without doing the research, but the issue of where and how the ancient sources he relied on got their knowledge was still not resolved.

At this point, I decided that probably the best way to explain all the ideas, experiences and material that combined in my thinking was to write it up for the website. I began a series on the subject of the Holy Grail.[8]

---

[7] http://cassiopaea-cult.com/the-bridges---jadczyk-correspondence-part-1
[8] http://cassiopaea.org/category/volumes/the-grail-quest-and-the-destiny-of-man/

I wanted to be as helpful to Vincent as possible because even though we did not agree on several issues, I did not see it as a serious thing. I believed that if he had all the data I had collected, we would be more in agreement. To that end, I found a small part in his book that I felt I could quote in my writings on the web (*The Grail Quest*), and did so, giving a link to his book.

Things continued on in this way for several months until I just didn't see much point in continuing the correspondence. I was busy writing and gardening, our discussion group had begun as a result of people writing to ask questions about the website, and things were just stable, as one might say. I published my exposé of the Rennes-le-Château, then, along came a totally bizarre email that actually frightened me a bit. This prompted me to re-activate my correspondence with Vincent because I was sure that he would have some knowledge about the occult language that was being used in the email. Of course it never occurred to me that he, himself, had sent the email for that express purpose.

In the fall of 2000, "Frank Scott" (pseudonym) – a long time member – left the working group. In the same period, Vincent Bridges initiated a discussion with me in which he claimed to be a struggling new publisher needing good authors – with an offer to publish my work with his company, Aethyrea Books.

Being overwhelmed with the work of keeping up with the discussion group, answering questions, editing the transcripts, researching clues from the material, and writing articles for the site, I thought Vincent was a godsend! Having corresponded with him for almost two years, even if we did not agree on everything, I felt I could trust him, and I turned over to him unpublished material, confidential materials that he suggested he would help to edit, and believing that my life's work was in good hands, I settled down to concentrate on getting the book ready.

We began working on this project in the early part of 2001. It wasn't long before I invited Bridges to become a member of our discussion group. So, throughout the spring and summer of 2001, there was very intense and regular interaction.

The summer of 2001 … I'm sure that a great many people wish we could all go back to those last few weeks before 9/11 changed our world.

In any event, also in the summer of 2001, the Cassiopaeans initiated a daring plan that can only be seen in retrospect, setting up the conditions for me to experience a direct visual representation of Vincent Bridges. What I saw stunned me. His mask was so effective and convincing that I could hardly believe that what I was seeing was true. After all, this was not just a matter of deciding you didn't like someone and didn't want to associate with them for one reason or another. The fact was, just as I had liked Frank Scott very much, I also liked Vincent

Bridges and where both of them were concerned, had spent many enjoyable hours in conversation with them. This was seeing on a whole new level and I had many, many doubts about what I was seeing. It was actually painful to contemplate the necessary response to the understanding. If knowledge really did protect – but only if applied – Ark and I had to apply what we knew.

We discussed the matter for weeks seeking hard data – evidence. It was not lacking, certainly, but it was always possible to give the benefit of the doubt and overlook the subtle clues. A hypothesis was formed, a series of tests were devised, and – once again – the Cassiopaeans were proven correct – with a twist. It seems that this experience was the opening of the door to one of the most advanced lessons of adeptship available to the ordinary human. It was also, obviously, a test of sorts.

The facts of the situation are as follows:

While Bridges and his wife were allegedly getting my book, *The Noah Syndrome*, ready for publication, he proposed an idea for a conference in September of 2001. Our regular policy at the time was not to do any conferences. Bridges knew this, but we agreed to do it as a favor to him, to help his "business" sell our books that he was preparing to be published (which, as it turned out, were not even ready in time for the conference, nor did Bridges even have a real publishing company as he claimed!). However, in the time leading up to the planned dates for the conference (Sept 21-23, and 9/11, had we only known it), several strange things converged on us simultaneously with the information received from the Cs about Bridges.

First of all, we received a lot of emails from readers who were concerned about our public association with Vincent's so-called Fifth Way Mystery School. I had only read Vincent's articles on subjects dealt with in his book, like the Grail legends, the Rennes-le-Château mystery, and Fulcanelli. Vincent himself had told me that he was an investigative journalist and repeatedly expressed doubts about the Cs, so I had been reassured that he was a rational person and certainly wasn't into anything weird. I was wrong. After reading the emails from readers, I went and had a look for myself.

I was a little upset at what I found on the Net, considering the subject matter we had discussed. Vincent had many articles on the subject of his Enochian magick, and all the so-called workings or rituals that go along with it. Here's a sample:

> The Apocalypse working completed, perhaps for the first time since its transmission in the 16th century, the Enochian or Ophanic astral communication device. This structure included the basic forms necessary to harmonize the on-coming galactic alignments. ... A little more than a year later, the Ophanic Intelligences announced that projecting the Tree

of Life on the Celestial sphere on the equinox for the next ten equinoxes was the simplest way to align with the energy shift of the Great Cross. ... It was indeed the OI angels that gave me the clue.

The second thing brewing in the summer of 2001 was that we were being accused of belonging to a Nazi black magic cult and, lo and behold, Vincent just happened to have pages on his website that could easily be interpreted as being such. In fact, in retrospect, it seems like a definite set-up. We in no way wanted to be associated with black magic, Nazis, or any such mumbo-jumbo. In addition, we had learned of the perceived connection between these groups and anti-Semitism. It should also be mentioned that many of Ark's professional colleagues were – and are – Jewish.

There seemed to be two ways to look at the problem we were confronted with. The first thing was our responsibility to our readers to live what we talked about, and the second was whether we could trust what we were sure we were seeing behind the scenes even if there was no overt evidence of bad intent from the side of Vincent Bridges?

We knew that there was really no way we could continue to be associated with the ideas that Vincent Bridges was promoting; we knew we had to make that a reality if nothing else. So, we posted a disclaimer in latter part of July about our appearance at the conference on our website, stating that our presence there did not mean that we advocated the ideas of the promoters or other presenters. Since Ark has attended and organized many scientific conferences, we thought that this would be enough.

We also decided to give Vincent the opportunity to make his own position clear. We asked him, for the sake of our reputation, our work and even safety (the attacks against us relating to the charges of being associated with Nazi black magic and anti-Semitism were really getting intense to the point that we were receiving death threats), to remove the "magick" material from his website and to disassociate himself from such ideas publicly so that we could continue our work together. He refused.

So when Vincent refused to dissociate from his magick, we decided to dissociate from him and decided to cancel our attendance due to these issues. We cancelled our book publishing agreement. We obtained legal advice on how to do this since, at the time, we didn't know that the agreement had been made with a non-existent company!

In the world of conferences, if an invited speaker cancels, for whatever reason, it is the responsibility of the organizers to find an acceptable replacement, if such is needed. At this point we discovered that the conference attendees were almost exclusively our readers and discussion group members. In short, we were the lynchpin, the attraction, the goose that was supposed to lay the golden egg. When we cancelled, nearly all attendees also cancelled and requested refunds of their deposits or payments. But keep in mind, this was still over six weeks before the dates of the conference. At that point, we had our own private 9/11, Vincent aimed for us like a jumbo jet sailing into the Twin Towers: flames and defamation, libel, and so on.[9] That is what baffled us. We could not understand how an individual who claimed to be so esoterically knowledgeable, so psychically advanced, so full of the milk of human kindness and understanding, could behave like a low-life guttersnipe and write the filthy, disgusting, libelous things that he and his friends began to spread around the web about us. It not only baffled us, it got our attention. Since we could see quite clearly that he had no regard whatsoever for facts or truth, it made us begin to question everything he had ever said to us before this parting of the ways. And so, after suffering in silence from August until November, we finally decided to try to find out the truth.

On a practical level, my questions about the matter were put to rest when the Perseus Foundation research group undertook an investigation of Bridges – including a professional private investigator's report – in the fall of 2001. To my chagrin, it was revealed that Bridges was little more than an ordinary con artist. Not only was his entire published resume a complete fraud, he had a history of attaching himself to individuals – to ride on their coattails, so to say – in hopes of stealing their work, their money, or both.

Even though there was a history of fraud, Ark and I were reluctant to publish the report on Bridges. However, it finally became necessary to respond publicly to the many attacks Bridges made on us in response to our attempts to simply disassociate ourselves from him. It was certainly clear that there was something very, very wrong with the interaction, and only much later was it realized that the entire dynamic was a crucial lesson.

As it turned out, learning about Vincent Bridges through personal interaction produced a question that needed an answer. And the seeking of the answer resulted in developing the necessary tools and insight to move the Cassiopaean work to the next phase – the Quantum Future School.

Mr. Bridges reacted to the data presented in the report as expected: at all costs he wanted it removed, and since he could not force us to remove it legally (truth is not libel or slander), he resorted to attempted blackmail and extortion to try to force us to remove this report.

Not only did we discover that Vincent was trying to use us to make money at a conference to promote our books (supposed to be pub-

---

[9] The reader can access all information, including emails, etc., by starting here: http://cassiopaea-cult.com/category/the-defamers/vincent-bridges

lished by *his* company), we discovered through the tax collector's office, as well as the Secretary of State's office in North Carolina, that he did not even own a legally registered company and therefore, any of his representations as being a publisher were fraudulent and misleading. His co-author, Jay Weidner, later filed the corporation papers on Aethyrea Books, LLC, and this was the first time that it had existed as a legal corporation.[10]

At some later point, Mr. Weidner described in detail how he had been defrauded by Vincent, including the fact that Bridges claimed to have written a novel for DAW books, articles for Rolling Stone, Cream, and Newsweek magazine. Weidner felt that Vincent had made these claims in order to establish credentials and convince him that he was a legitimate writer and that Mr. Weidner could feel confident in working with him as a co-author. Vincent posted on the Internet in numerous places that we had blackmailed Jay into writing the letters that said these things.

Mr. Weidner then detailed several items relating to the hows and whys of his having been defrauded by Vincent and the fact that he had actually paid for the initial publishing of their co-authored book. He pointed out that the book was, indeed, published with the Aethyrea Books, LLC logo. He pointed out that not only had he not received repayment for the monies he spent on their research trip, but that he had also never received any monies from the sale of the books that Vincent was marketing under Aethyrea Books, LLC.

Mr. Weidner next wrote that he feared that his work was being "destroyed by Vincent Bridges' dishonesty and misrepresentation." He then announced that Vincent and his wife, Darlene, "commited [sic] fraud. Not just with me but with several other potential authors." He announced that he was preparing a lawsuit against Vincent and Darlene for "misrepresentation."

Several letters were published by us, on behalf of and at the request of Jay Weidner, in our ongoing effort to expose what we then understood to be a serious Internet predator who has a history of theft, lies and fraud.

We discovered, to our chagrin, that Vincent Bridges seems to be unable to comprehend the difference between lies and truth. The Perseus Foundation report was researched thoroughly, and by accusing it of being false, he is accusing a lot of people of being liars who clearly have no reason to lie. His story changed time and again *after* the truth was exposed, and never did he say a single thing that addressed the fact that his original bio and credentials were *all lies*.

---

[10], See Appendix A for documents showing that Aethyrea Books, LLC was not incorporated until January 2002 (also: http://www.secretary.state.nc.us/corporations/Corp.aspx?PitemId=5415984).

He has since then repeatedly – for over 6 years, on dedicated websites and wherever he can obtain a dupe to believe him – accused us of "libel, slander, defamation of character, cyberstalking," etc., in the true manner of the psychopath who always accuses their target of what they themselves are doing. When he began to accuse us of blackmailing his former co-author, Jay Weidner we should have known that *he was effectively announcing his next maneuver.*

At one point, Mr. Bridges declared in several places on the Internet that he was going to "publicly address the Cassiopaean Cult issue and tell the real, unedited version of the story." He then announced that he was going into the business of distributing our copyrighted work free to anyone who wanted it. This was accompanied by nonsensical lies that only *he* understood how to interpret it, and the further claim that we were deceptively "altering" the text and had been doing so "from the beginning." Well, since he is not in possession of either the tapes, or the notes, we wondered on what "facts" he based such claims.

There were other follow up posts, but I won't bore the reader with the endless lies and nonsense. The bottom line was this: Vincent Bridges published the complete unedited transcripts without any care or concern for any of the private individuals who had attended sessions, many of whom had specifically requested that, at any point in time when the material was published, their names and identities should be disguised.

As we noted on our own page where the transcripts were available, it was the work of removing names and sensitive items that proper respect and regard for other human beings mandated, that held up the publication, along with the necessity of going back and checking the transcribed material with the notes and tapes to ensure its accuracy. It was and is an enormous job. In some cases, we have done global file replacement, which has resulted in areas of file distortion, but in no case is this intentional obfuscation. Little by little, we have been working to correct the errors in the transcripts, and this takes time. We are also entitled, as the owners of the material, to not publish those portions of it that are personal.

So, the point was not the distribution of the material, which we give away free on our own website, the point was concern for the privacy of people who had entrusted their privacy into our care, as well as our legal right to ensure that the transcripts are accurate, or to make sure that appropriate notes or comments are appended when we are not sure.

Knowing that it was futile to appeal to Vincent Bridges to have concern for other people's privacy, we directly addressed the owners of the server where Bridges had parked the pirated transcripts via email and fax.

In response to our request to the server that the transcripts be removed, Mr. Bridges sent the following email which included a startling email from "Frank Scott":

Date sent: Thu, 10 Jan 2002 13:06:34 -0500
Subject: FW: Permission Granted!
From: Vincent Bridges <...@ac.net>

Unless you want the entire sordid saga published, you might think of taking my name down.
Vincent

Date: Mon, 7 Jan 2002 04:15:49 EST
To: ...@ac.net
Subject: Permission Granted!

Hi Vincent:

I will now make the following statement on your behalf:

My name is [Frank Grant Scott]. I give full and complete permission to Vincent Bridges to publish in full or in part the Cassiopaean transcripts in the way that he chooses and for whatever purposes that he deems appropriate.

I participated in all of the sessions that took place between July, 1994 and November, 2000. My participation in the channeling sessions was to an extent as great as or greater than that of any and all other participants.

Thank You,

[Frank Grant Scott]

Aside from the fact that Frank's claim that his participation in the experimental sessions was "to an extent as great as or greater than that of any and all other participants," is an outright lie (and there were, in fact, sessions in which he did *not* participate), the legal fact is that the transcripts have been copyrighted by me from the day that I transcribed and printed out the first copy back in 1994. That is the *legal* fact.

Any and all witnesses (of which there are *many*), as well as the hard evidence, shows that Frank's "permission to publish" is as valid as permission from Garfield the Cat. He does not, and *never did*, have any copyright rights. All of the experiments were conducted in *my* house, on *my* equipment, recorded by me personally, *my* voice. I own the tapes, I transcribed nearly every word, I burned the CD that Vincent Bridges pirated, that he was no longer entitled to have once we had terminated our relationship and requested return of same.

In short, Mr. Scott's presence at the sessions was the *only* thing he *ever* contributed, and there were a lot of other people present at different times. Being a guest in our house does not constitute owning what we produce there! By Frank's standards, any other guest would also have the right to grant permission to publish. In point of fact, dealing with Frank throughout the entire period of time, was problematic at best as those who have read *Amazing Grace* already know.

But what is a more serious matter, as it turns out, is the fact that Vincent Bridges has, by writing the above email, attempted to blackmail us, to extort and coerce us. Blackmail consists of two elements:

> a) extortion or coercion by threats especially of public exposure or criminal prosecution
>
> b) the payment that is extorted.
>
> Example from a real court case: SS threatened to expose MD on the Travis Carroll & Justin Show. This exposure would have harmed Dubose's career and most likely his future emloyeement. In return for silence, SS was trying to coerce MD into turning down one offer *with the expectation* that JS would accept another, thereby giving SS greater job security.

You have coercion, threat of exposure and expected payment. Vincent Bridges wrote: "Unless you want the entire sordid saga published, you might think of taking my name down." He is threatening to publish the unedited transcripts with names and personal details, and he expects a return – payment in the form of us removing our articles about his fake bio and phony credentials, and psychological terrorism.

Even though Mr. Bridges was clearly attempting to blackmail us, and we knew it, we were only concerned about the innocent people who wished to have their identities and personal information removed. What was more, the remark about the "entire sordid saga" didn't really apply to the transcripts alone; it didn't make a lot of sense so we dismissed it.

As it happens, the Universe was on the alert. Later that day, another email came from Jay Weidner.

From: Jay
Date sent: Thu, 10 Jan 2002 22:24:15 EST
Subject: Re: VB again
To: Laura Knight-Jadczyk

[Vincent and I] exchanged a couple of very bitter emails. I told him he was a sociopath and that I couldn't sue his book company because it does not [legally] exist. This is his reaction. I will not be emailing him anymore so maybe it will go away.

By the way he says that he has 'proof' that you attempted to murder someone. [...]

INTRODUCTION

Well, well, well. It all became chillingly clear. I instantly understood that it was, indeed true, that Frank had written the above letter (which I had initially doubted because I was quite certain that Frank knew enough about the law to not do something that stupid), and why.

Those readers who have read *Amazing Grace* will surely recall the chapter where I describe Frank's long years of embezzling funds from his former employer which, at the end, caused his father's death by suicide. For those of you who have not read it, you may wish to have a look at the chapter entitled "That's Hollywood!"

The chapters subsequent to that explain how I reconciled myself to Frank's perfidy, how I explained it away, and essentially put full confidence in Frank that he had learned a significant lesson, and that he needed to be trusted in order to be trustworthy. After all, that is what we are taught, isn't it? So, I trusted him. And I confided in him a number of things, including the story I am about to tell.

Even though Mr. Bridges thinks that he has discovered a "major skeleton" in the closet, it just so happens that this event is something that journalist Tom French duly investigated and decided not to write about since it was essentially, not significant to the story. Some may think that he should have, because the fact that women are sexually assaulted with alarming regularity gets far too little attention as it is. But he was correct in his decision, in my opinion, because to tell it would have taken up space in a story that was, essentially, focused on different issues.

Nevertheless, when Tom interviewed me, even though I was very reluctant to talk about something so distressing, I did tell him everything. As every other woman who has ever been through a similar experience will agree, it was so unpleasant that I have spent over 30 years trying to forget it. And Tom agreed with us that it ought to just be left in the past. Because, in the end, it was proven to be a very similar event to what Mr. Bridges is attempting to do now: coercion, blackmail and extortion. As one reader has noted: "Anyone who would attempt to blackmail you with this incident falls into the same category as the person who committed the initial assault. Such people view others as prey. They assess all those that they wish to prey upon as vulnerable and methodically proceed to search for a weak point and then attack." And sometimes they take years to do it, as is proven in the case of "Frank Scott".

When I received the email from Vincent's former friend and co-author remarking that Vincent Bridges "says that he has 'proof' that you attempted to murder someone," along with Bridges' simultaneous attempt to blackmail us by saying he was going to tell "the entire sordid saga," what I realized was the utter and absolute perfidy of Frank behind it – that he was, effectively, party to yet another criminal act that is almost the same as the embezzling he did from his former employer – because *only* Frank could have been the one to share this information with Bridges. What was more, Frank was being touted by Bridges as the "Cs authority," who is claiming in a libelous way that we have been "altering the texts" of the transcripts from the beginning. We find this to be more than odd, since one of the early things we noted about Frank was the fact that he never seemed to be aware of what the Cassiopaeans said, and would discourse for hours about issues in which everything he said was in complete contradiction to their messages. At one point, I provided him with a printed copy of the text so he could read it, but it became apparent that he was either not reading it, or that he could not comprehend it, because he continued to pronounce "knowingly" on many subjects from a totally opposite viewpoint. It was clear that the communications from the Cassiopaeans were *not* coming from Frank.

The long and short of it was that Frank claimed to be *the* channel, and the *only* channel, and repeatedly wanted us to convert the experiment from using the board to direct trance channeling with *him* as the only source. On the several occasions we tried it, we found that the personality and feeling of the contact was so distinctly different – and, in fact, repellant – that we realized that this suggestion was the maneuver of the STS forces to take over the work completely.[11]

Just as it had been with his former employer, Frank did as little work as possible, and thought that he was entitled to a whole lot more than he actually earned, and just decided to write himself a weekly check. In relation to the Cs, Frank is trying to write himself another check on somebody else's account.

Considering the evidential fact that he has now chosen a path of deliberate disregard for the legal rights of others, his participation in an attempt to blackmail, extort, and coerce us, any further statements from Frank Scott must be considered to be emanating from the same source as Vincent Bridges. Bridges has demonstrated total disregard for the truth, for the free-will rights of others, and he has clearly established that he believes that the readers are too lazy to check things for themselves. He has also made it evident that his philosophy is the bigger the lie, and the more often it is repeated, the greater the likelihood that the public will believe it. In short: they have nothing but contempt for other human beings.

---

[11] A sample of Frank's "direct channeling on his own" is available here: http://www.cassiopaea.org/cass/dante.htm

If, at any point, Frank Scott becomes the "authority of dirt" to back Bridges up, promoted as the "witness who knows the truth," *caveat lector*, is all we can advise.

Having this realization, and putting it together with all the odd remarks the Cs had made about Frank through the years, we realized that there were many mysterious pieces of the puzzle finally coming together. We decided to have an unscheduled session and find out exactly what was going on. And then, even though there were a dozen other tapes that still need to be transcribed and posted at the time, I decided that I had better put everything else aside, transcribe this one, and post it.

From what the Cassiopaeans told us that night, it now all begins to make sense – it's sick, but it makes sense. I never could quite put together *why* the Cs would slip through those cryptic remarks about Frank, and why they would refuse to answer certain questions when it was *only* me and Frank at the board. It seems that there was a lot of information that could *not* be given with Frank present, and while I created many theories about this, it never, ever occurred to me that it was because I was being protected from Frank!

Well, all speculation aside, read what Cs said about the whole situation:

January 10, 2002

Q: (L) Hello.

A: Hello.

Q: And who do we have with us this evening?

A: Fiaage.

Q: And where do you transmit through?

A: Cassiopaea.

Q: As you know, we have become aware this evening of Frank's extraordinary conversion to the dark side. Is that an accurate way of perceiving it?

A: Close enough.

Q: Quite a few years ago, there were several remarks made on two or three occasions regarding Frank's battle with the dark forces, and the issue of whether or not he would be able to resist their domination. Was it always known that he would fail?

A: He is not a failure.

Q: What do you mean?

A: From the perspective of STS he is a success.

Q: Why was it that we were able to channel STO material, with Frank being so borderline regarding this ultimate choice between STS and STO?

A: He was programmed for the specific purpose of "downloading" from you secrets coded into you before birth of your present body. He failed because you were incorruptible. He is now charged with the mission, in concert with Vincent Bridges, of destroying your ability to accomplish your mission.

Q: Well, that means that there is a strong possibility that the material that came through while Frank was a participant was very likely corrupted. Is that why you gave the figure of 72 percent purity of the material regarding those sessions?

A: Yes.

Q: So, are you saying that Frank's presence produced that 30 percent corruption?

A: Yes.

Q: What was the form that most of that corruption took? Can we identify it?

A: Predictions and terror tactics.

Q: What is the advisable course of action to take at this point in time? Shall I stop what I am doing and take time to deal with the issues that have come up as a result of this action by Frank and Vincent?

A: Good idea to deal with it A.S.A.P.

Q: Should we also pursue legal action?

A: Yes, in terms of copyright.

Q: What about the stalking, harassment, defamation, blackmail?

A: It will be handled at the proper time by you, and you will know when to do it.

Q: (A) Why isn't ignoring them completely not the answer?

A: Because they are not affected by being ignored. And your reality is such that lies and liars have prevailed in violating Free Will for millennia. They do this most effectively by programs that are designed to perpetuate it, such as "Turn the other cheek," and "If you ignore it, it will go away." Give what is asked for by a lie: Truth.

Q: (L) So, it comes back to balance. In the face of a lie, balance is only restored by truth. Well, now, let me ask this: did Terry contribute positive energy at the board?

A: Most of the time.

Q: Was that the reason that you encouraged Terry and Jan to be present? To counterbalance Frank's negative energy?

A: Yes. Frank would have killed you with his STS draining rather soon otherwise.

Q: Is that why I (and everyone else) always felt so tired after some sessions and he always felt so energized?

A: Yes.

Q: He was literally sucking my energy out of me?

A: Yes.

Q: Is that why I had so many health problems during that period of time?

A: Yes.

Q: Well, yes, the evidence was all there. The problem was, not being able to interpret it. Of course, one believes the lies, and Frank was very good at it. He was a consummate liar. And I already had the evidence of what a capable deceiver he was from observing his interactions with NE and other people, including his embezzlement of funds. But I chose to ignore it because I thought I could help him. I thought that our mutual interest in this project would help him as much as it would help me. And you are saying that the whole thing was set up, with all the synchronicities at the beginning, just for the purpose of getting me involved in this channeling experiment, to make the channeling experiment 72 percent positive, so that I would be encouraged to continue it, so that Frank could, more or less, vacuum out of me, from some level of consciousness, other information, and kill me. Is that what we are getting at here?

A: Pretty much.

Q: That's depressing. Why do all these people hate Ark so much?

A: Because Ark won't allow them to regard you as an object to use for their own nefarious purposes.

Q: In other words, it looks like Frank dropped out just as the time that Bridges moved in. Bridges was the new "agent." He spent his time getting close so that he could come and attempt to extract the same information that Frank had failed to get, only the new plan was to try to use hypnosis. Is that what the plan was?

A: Yes.

Q: Who is pulling the strings behind this whole thing?

A: It is better not to know specifics. But a clue: STS Consortium.

Q: I would really like to have some knowledge that would protect in this situation. I would like to know what actions to take, some inside information, something that would help us. Here we are, these guys keep us just constantly upset. Is this the way it is going to continue to be from here on out?

A: Not to worry, reinforcements are on the way.

Q: I sure wish they would show up now! We could use the cavalry. I mean, here we are, the wagon train is drawn up in a circle, we are surrounded by outlaws, we are down to our last few silver bullets; you keep telling us that we aren't supposed to worry, that reinforcements are on the way, and so forth, and we just keep hanging in there, working, working, working, and I don't see anything materializing here. I think we ought to just sell the house and retire.

A: Not yet!

Q: (A) I want to ask about my theory about why walking is so important – that when one thinks while walking, one is able to evade mind control signals which are directed or reinforced when one remains static. Is there anything to this?

A: Close.

Q: (L) I want to know what caused my ear infection?

A: Stress.

45

Q: Should I continue to keep Frank informed in an effort encourage him to see the hole he is about to fall into? I can't help but feel sorry for him.

A: He is going to fall in the hole anyway. So, why prolong the agony?

Q: What hole do you mean?

A: Suicidal thoughts; since he does not have the STO motivation to help others without an agenda, which gives staying power to those of the STO persuasion to survive great troubles.

Q: Well, then it seems to me that he ought to avoid getting into such troubles.

A: He can't.

Q: Why?

A: Drives.

Q: What kind of drives?

A: Programmed in by parental abuse and neglect.

Q: Well, if you could say anything to Frank just now, would you want to?

A: No.

Q: But ought I not to feel grateful to Frank for his participation, helping me groove the channel?

A: That was not his agenda.

Q: (A) We would like to know if it is recommended that we transcribe and publish the "mirror session" with Vincent Bridges, as part of the truth that needs to be made known?

A: Yes! All Truth is beneficial and promotes balance in a world dominated and run on lies.

Q: (L) Yes, but when you start telling the truth in a world dominated and run by lies, the liars go absolutely crazy in trying to destroy you! That is the plain hard fact that we have been facing. It is unbelievable to strip away the lies; layer after layer of lies, the liars themselves, impossible to conceive how they can lie the way they do; I am just utterly astonished by it.

A: Yes. It is part of your mission.

Q: (A) Well, I am wondering if the way I am managing these attacks is the proper STO approach? For example, I have blocked his access to the website. I have removed his entries to the guestbook. I have removed him from the egroup. I am just simply making his mission of spreading lies difficult. But I am not completely sure if this is an STO approach?

A: It is.

Q: (L) Well, I think he has the perfect right to tell all the lies he wants in the places where lies are wanted and asked for. He does not have the right to trespass on our space and tell lies because we do not ask for lies, we don't want lies, and it violates our free will to try to discover truth in our space. He has the Matrioshka list that obviously wants to hear his lies. They make no effort to discern truth in any way, and they certainly got very upset when Ark posted truth on their list, which only gave

them a small sample of how it feels to have your free will violated. He can tell all the lies he wants where they are wanted. Any other suggestions?
A: Just persist and be patient.
Q: Is there anything we can do to accelerate the receiving of assistance?
A: It is on the way.
Q: [laughter] I know that time does not exist on sixth density. However, all these months dealing with these lunatics seems like six years, or six thousand years. Well, I'm just whining.
A: Either way it will come. "Miles to go before you sleep." Keep on going. Destination will be reached.
Q: Anything else we ought to know that we haven't asked?
A: Not for now. Goodnight. [End of Session]

Now, I am going to reproduce here an account of the incident that Vincent Bridges and Frank Scott attempted to use as blackmail. This account is the one that I wrote for Ark when we first met. Just as I told it to Tom French who was entitled to know everything about me, I also told it to Ark from the very beginning. Unfortunately, at some point, I also told Frank Scott.

When he began to investigate the matter, Tom French told me that the public records on the event are so old that they don't even tell the disposition of the case. Tom French had to search out the attorney based on my information, to interview him and the private investigator in order to get all the details.

In order to provide the "bona fides" behind the story, I searched for an email from Tom that I thought existed, but only later remembered that, after he had talked to Joe Aloi, the investigator, and Brian Hayes, the attorney, that he had called me to tell me how glad he was that everything was exactly as I had said it was, even adding that these two gentlemen who were truly STO angels in my life, had sent their best wishes to me and were very happy to know that I was okay.

So, not having anything in writing, and knowing how difficult and costly such record searches can be, I decided to just call Brian Hayes and talk to him about the situation. In any event, Brian and Joe were very happy to provide letters about the case.[12]

---

[12] Brian's letter is available at http://cassiopaea-cult.com/its-your-word-against-his. It reads:
In re: State v. Laura Knight
In the Spring of 1970, in Tallahassee, Leon County, Florida, I was serving as Assistant Public Defender. I represented Laura Knight of Aripeka, Florida, who was then a teenager and was charged with an Aggravated Assault on an employee of the Florida Legislature. I attempted to locate a newspaper clipping from the "Tallahassee Democrat", but could not locate it, and my file has long since been destroyed.
However, the result of the trial was clear in my memory. Laura Knight was found Not Guilty on all charges, fully exonerated, and costs were taxed against the State of Florida. A check of the Public Records in the Circuit Court of Leon County, will verify

Without further ado, here is the dreadful story about how Laura Knight, at the ripe old age of 18 years and 2 months, in Vincent Bridges' words, "attempted to murder someone."

My mother was a bookkeeper who had contracted with several local businesses to do their books. One of these businesses was owned by a man who was also something of a local politician. He ran for a State office and was elected, so spent much of his time in Tallahassee, the State Capitol. Mother ran his business for him.

He was sort of like a local big wig who had a home in the county, and an apartment in Tallahassee. When he was in residence here, he would come to the house and discuss the business with mother and drop off and pick up the accounting and checks and deposits and so forth.

During this time, I was spending many hours a day practicing the piano. I would practice in one room while they would spread out papers on the table in the other room.

One day mother announced that this man had expressed an interest in me and wanted to send me to school in Tallahassee where he could oversee my care. She thought this was wonderful and a great opportunity!

It was agreed that this plan would be put into action, but I had to finish school first. So, I attended locally from September 1969 to December 1969. At that point, the plan was that I would go to Tallahassee and finish high school there in an accelerated class, and then be enrolled at the University. So, in January I went.

An apartment had been reserved for me in the same building this man lived in when he was there doing his legislative duties, whatever they were. Everything had been arranged. So, I went to school, met new people, and things were fine for a few months – through April. The apartment building had a nice pool, and I enjoyed studying by the pool... or, for me, at least reading. A friend of mine came to stay with me because I was lonely and her mother knew this man also and thought this would be fine for her as well.

One night he came to our apartment and asked me to come down so he could talk to me privately since he had something very special to tell me and it was a surprise.

So, in an hour, when I was done with my homework, I walked down the outside walkway and knocked on the door. He answered wearing a robe and smoking a cigar and with a glass of liquor in his hand.

---

this recollection, or Joe Aloi, who was then a part-time investigator for the Public Defender's Office, is also available to corroborate this statement. His telephone number is: 850-575-6265 listed under the name of Aloi-Williams Bail Bonding.
Very truly yours,
Brian T. Hayes

To make a long story short, it became clear that the man expected payment for his help. I was so dumb that I actually thought that he was just being a nice guy with a fatherly interest in me. But that wasn't the case.

When I said "no," he got rough. When he got rough, I fought back. When I fought back, he became enraged and started choking me. Since we happened to be standing in the kitchen, and I was being pressed back against the counter and was starting to lose consciousness, I threw my hands back to grab the counter to keep from falling. When I did, my hand landed on a heavy object with a handle. I grabbed it and hit him with it. He loosened his hold momentarily, but then started squeezing again and I hit him again, only harder this time since I had been able to get a breath. I hit him again in the head, and it was sort of a nightmare where he was totally enraged and I was totally determined to hit him until he let go of me.

At this point, he was bleeding on me, still refusing to let go, so I hit him again. I think I must have landed about four or five good ones before he let go to try to protect his head from another, and when he did I ran like hell. I was sure that he was after me, and I made it to my apartment, banged wildly on the door for my friend to let me in. She did and was utterly horrified. We were both just hysterical.

She was hysterical at the blood all over me and we didn't know what to do... so she made me take off my clothes and go take a shower... then, while I was in the shower, still shaking with the thought that the man could force his way into the apartment, she told me that police cars and an ambulance were in the parking lot outside. Apparently the man had gone out to the balcony and yelled "rape" or some such nonsense, and someone heard him and called the police. I was dressed and shaking violently when the knock came at the door. He had made a statement to the emergency crew that I had attacked him for no reason after coming on to him sexually!!

I told them what really happened, and they were satisfied but told me not to go anywhere for a while until they investigated further.

And, seemingly the incident was closed. But, three days later, I was called out of my English class to find a message that the police department wished to ask me a few more questions. So, after school, I took the bus to the police headquarters. When I walked in, expecting to answer questions, handcuffs were immediately place on me and I was arrested for "Assault with a Deadly Weapon with Intent to Commit Murder." The guy had created a fantastic story in which he was the "innocent" victim of a crazed teenager.

And I was taken and locked in a cell.

There is no way to describe such a transition. None. If a person is of a nature that they deliberately break laws, there is some idea in their mind that this could be a result. But, for a person who has, essentially, done nothing wrong but be stupid and naive, someone who has been betrayed by someone she trusted, who has been viciously attacked, and then, instead of anyone realizing that I was the *victim*, I was put in jail on the word of a psychopath and charged with trying to murder him! All women who have suffered this way understand that such an event is in a class by itself especially when the realization comes that grandfather cannot fix it, mother cannot fix it, no one can fix it. And, when the realization came that this was a "capital crime" and just having someone come and pay money to get one out of jail was not possible, well... just imagine it.

A week later I was taken, in handcuffs, to court and stood before a judge who read the formal charges. I was just 18 years old, and I had to walk down a public street, between two policemen, in chains.

The judge asked me if I had legal counsel. I started to cry and said no. But, a man sitting in the row of attorneys jumped to his feet and came forward and said: "Yes she does, your honor! I am offering my services!" He then asked me if I would accept him as my attorney and I said yes. So that was settled. I had an attorney. His name was Brian T. Hayes. He was assisted by a cracker jack Private Investigator, Joseph Aloi, and both of them were literally Knights in Shining Armor.

What they discovered about my "benefactor" was shocking. It seems that I had been the prey of a very sharp operator who had been trying to gradually draw me into a very ugly operation. (Sounds a lot like the situation with Vincent Bridges, eh?) And only my instinctive refusal to be used had saved me. Indeed, my resistance had plunged me into a somewhat serious problem, as it has repeatedly in my life. The Powers of Darkness don't like it when you resist their attempts to control you or draw you into their plans. It is the same now as it was then.

You see, as a minor government official, my benefactor had a little side-line: he made home movies used for blackmail. Apparently, he had plans for me. He wanted to use me as the star in movies that would be filmed by a secret camera set up in an A/C vent. These movies would then be used to extort money, favors, and probably even for a special brand of lobbying.

All of the evidence of this little "business" was discovered while the guy was in the hospital, desperately trying to lie his way out of the mess he was in. He even tried to change his claims that I had assaulted him for no reason, he was so desperate to avoid scrutiny. But it was no go. Once the State decides to prosecute, it doesn't matter if someone who formerly claimed to be a victim has now changed his mind. The State is a juggernaut, and the trial *did* take place.

Well, the bloodbath in the courtroom was actually worse than the one at the time of the incident. The guy, like all true psychopaths, lied himself black in the face, even when confronted with hard evidence of his intentions, his actions, his perfidy – in his own writing – and the end result was a resounding return of the verdict of "Not Guilty by Reason of Self-Defense." And the only reason he wasn't prosecuted for his own crimes was that he was so pitiful and swore he had learned his lesson, and also because he still had a few people in government offices who would go to bat for him (probably because he was blackmailing them).

In short, I was acquitted of any and all charges, exonerated, proven guiltless of any crime except protecting my honor and reputation, a situation I find myself in again and again.

And in the present situation, we find almost the exact same situation. Vincent Bridges has reacted against my refusal to be psychologically raped as violently as the benefactor of my youth. He has told the same kinds of lies. He has tried the same maneuvers. In fact, the entire scenario is something of a repeat.

You'd think those guys would learn.

The Forces of Darkness don't like Truth. They don't like people who resist their control and manipulation. And they will do anything, use anybody, tell any lie, stoop to any degradation, to try to force their control on other people.

And it seems that, by communicating a twisted version of this incident to Vincent Bridges, Frank Scott has firmly and definitively chosen which side he is on.

It was in January 2002 that Frank Scott joined forces with Vincent Bridges to discredit the Cassiopaean experiment, to label the members of the Cassiopaea discussion list as members of a cult, obviously in a concerted effort to put an end to the experiment itself.

Even though I had kept the door open for Frank to return to the group right up to the moment of his public attacks – just as I had hoped that Vincent Bridges would demonstrate that he was not as he had been revealed to be – I had to acknowledge the fact that two people I liked very much, whose companionship I enjoyed immensely, and who I felt could have been the most marvelous of co-experimenters had they chosen to release their egos and stop trying to manipulate, control and lie, had simply chosen the other path.

I was heartbroken. My health deteriorated rapidly, and in January of 2002 I suffered a life-threatening illness. After I had recovered enough to sit at my desk, I did the only thing I knew to do with what I had learned: I sought daily to understand the dynamic I had been shown through research and then, shared it with others by writing the present volumes, an account of the events and dynamics.

Day after day I struggled to make sense of what was happening in my life. As it turned out, my act of converting my suffering to sharing led to some profound revelations regarding the nature of our reality. Seeking to understand the inexplicable perceptions and capacity for deception of Vincent Bridges, Frank Scott, and others involved in the attacks, I searched and probed and tested on the daily public stage of the Internet. The search for answers led to revelations about psychopaths, which opened the door to our understanding of Organic Portals. Without this understanding, it would be almost impossible to comprehend the events on the world stage, most particularly including the behavior of George Bush and his gang.

Once I had escaped Bridges' clutches and foiled his plans to associate me with such material (which I later learned are typical COINTELPRO tactics), then the next level of COINTELPRO was activated: libel, defamation, fake emails, the whole nine yards.

One of Vincent Bridges' main rants was about our books. First he wanted to publish them. He couldn't say enough nice things about our work as long as he was trying to maneuver our books out of our control so *he* could make money from our labor. After he had spent so much time trying to get control of them, only to shoot himself in the foot, he then did an about-face and began ranting, "You're just trying to make a buck on lousy books ... "

Another of the rants of the Bridges gang was the typical COINTELPRO accusation of "cult! cult!" This was actually pretty rich because becoming free of cultic thinking is one of the main objectives of the Quantum Future School, and that is exactly why Vincent Bridges was kicked out: he couldn't let go of his cultic thinking and manipulation. In short, creating a cult was exactly what Vincent Bridges wanted to do, and most of all, he wanted to do it in the Quantum Future School, with himself as the head guru.

It is also notable that he had a Fifth Way Mystery School formed up and waiting for his cult following long before our closed discussion group came to the idea that it was a genuine anti-cult school. The problem Bridges had was that he couldn't get a following, and wanted to subvert our readers to his own benefit. And when he was removed from the group, his main rant was that we were trying to "suppress free speech."

Well, things just got worse and worse as time went by. More death threats. My dog (offspring of the one that had died after the UFO sighting) was poisoned and died, my oldest daughter was run off the road three times by what seemed to be road rage-infected lunatics. The third time resulted in a serious accident that totaled her car. My second daughter was poisoned at a gathering of kids and spent three days on life support – nobody thought she would live. Our names and addresses were posted on an ADL group (the anti-Semitism label was being widely used by Bridges and his cohorts), and it was suggested that anyone in our area should "take care of us," and on and on and on. False police reports were filed against us for abusing our children (thankfully, the police chief in our town knew us and just warned us that this was being done) and so on.

Bridges even called Tom French to repeat his filth to him. Tom wrote and told me about it. We complained to the FBI, the FDLE, etc. The special agent for FDLE told me on the phone that they could do nothing because it was "out of their jurisdiction," since it was being done from another state. He then suggested that if I didn't like what was being done to me that I ought to stop doing what I was doing that set Bridges off!!! In other words, Bridges could do whatever he liked, including filing false police reports, stalking, harassment, defamation, libel, slander, coercion, etc., and their answer was: "Well, give in to him."

And so it is that this volume opens on the day that I discovered that Frank Scott, former Cass group member, had made a dark alliance with Vincent Bridges, COINTELPRO psychopath.

CHAPTER 34
THE CHANNEL

Having begun writing about the matters contained in this volume, we have received many emails from readers who have thanked us for bringing these issues to the fore. As one reader pointed out, for those who resonate strongly with *most* of the material, this now gives a platform from which they can "revisit the concepts with a mental filter allowing for new interpretations." I have noted before there are many instances when the experiences behind the scenes had a great deal to do with the direction of the questions, and now we begin to understand exactly how the internal drives of the participants could act to skew that 30 percent of material that felt "off" even to the casual reader. On August 8, 1998, an interesting series of remarks were made that seem to be almost a prediction about the present events:

> Q: We have been discussing the strange visitors to our website. [This referred to an extremely high number of .mil and .gov organizations. We tried to just pass it off as the fact that even people who work for the military and government have interests in channeling, but this really didn't explain the daily visits from certain sites, and even from some sites that had IP numbers that resolved into servers where public access to information about them was restricted.] It seems that there is a lot of interest from groups that are connected with intelligence and military organizations. Can you tell us what their interest is in our material?
> A: Material is largely accurate.

Notice that above, Cs are pointing out that it is only "largely" accurate, and this is the statement upon which the next comments are predicated.

> Q: Do they understand that this material is largely accurate, and is this the reason for their interest?
> A: Yes.
> Q: Do we have to be concerned about any ramifications as a result of their interest?

A: If so, the need for concern began with your respective births!

Q: Why did the interest begin with our births?

A: Not interest we speak of; destiny.

This remark refers specifically to me (Laura) and Ark, since the question related specifically to our efforts to publicize the material on the website. The Cs repeatedly, throughout the sessions, talked about a certain "destined" activity for the two of us in concert with others we had yet to meet. I once asked specifically about this destiny and the answer was very curious, especially the reference to Frank's role:

August 31, 1996

Q: (L) What do these guys [the folks in the underground bases and laboratories with designs on taking over the world] plan on doing?

A: This is where "The Master Race" is being developed.

Q: (L) And what is the timeframe they have planned for this activity?

A: Never mind.

Q: (L) Is Ark going to be able to help us with technology, to help other people, or to protect ourselves in some way? In this really bizarre stuff going on on our planet?

A: Too much, too soon, my dear. Curiosity killed the cat.

Q: (L) Well, satisfaction brought him back!

A: Not in this case!!!

Q: (T) You've got to let this go along. It's picking up momentum every day, it seems. So, just let it roll along and let it see where it goes. (L) All right, let's ... (T) He's coming to protect you. That's what he said.

A: Maybe, but there is so, so, so much more in store than that!!!!!!

Q: (L) Stop! ... Is that an ominous, "maybe, but there's so, so, so much more in store?" Or is that a positive, "there is so, so, so much more in store?"

A: Why would you think it ominous?

Q: (L) Well I don't know ... because I'm scared of what I don't know! (T) Faith, we're back to faith again.

A: What have we helped you to discover so far? Would you rather discontinue this operation?

Q: (L) Oh, hell no! (T) After two years, you know she's always going to ask those kinds of questions!

A: Not two years, eternity. [...] We have helped you build your staircase one step at a time. Because you asked for it. And you asked for it because it was your destiny. We have put you in contact with those of rare ability in order for you to be able to communicate with us. Again, because you desired it, in order to realize your path. By now, you should recognize the signs ... Those who display thinking patterns which in many ways deviate from that which is considered ordinary. The more unusual, the more telling. They have past lives on 3rd density earth, but not recently, but for this one. And they are not oriented to the earth frequency vibrations.

The remark about being put in touch with those of "rare ability" (clearly plural) undoubtedly referred to Frank with the agenda of his controllers to extract information and destroy, *and* Terry with his role as protector *and* Ark with his role in the mission. It is quite clear that even though the agenda of those operating behind Frank was not favorable, as noted in the January 10 session, the effect was to "wake me up." I am still somewhat uncertain about the last remark: which individuals are the Cs referring to as not having had a recent past life on third density earth? Ark, or Frank or Terry? We had started out discussing Ark's role in the mission, and the Cs brought up the issue of their having put me in contact with those of rare ability in order to communicate, and then they came back to "recognizing signs … " which takes us back to Ark. For the moment, my interpretation is that Ark is the only one with a recent past life on the earth, and that of the three, neither Terry nor Frank had recent past lives *on earth*.

> Q: (I) … It is destiny for you to find out what your path was, you had to make this contact, because it was what you were supposed to do. (L) Are we not talking about Frank in terms of being put in contact with someone who enables me to communicate with you, so you can put me on my path, which is building the staircase, etc., etc.? Is that not what we've got going here?
>
> A: He is one, but not the only one, just the one who awakened your sense of recognition.

So my question as to whether Frank was the channel was effectively answered. The material that came through when Terry was present to counterbalance the negative agenda of Frank was obviously far more reliable, and we will encounter this factor more than once as we go along. Going back now to the prediction given in August of 1998:

> Q: Well, since we have revamped the website, there has been a huge amount of interest, so we have decided that it would be a good idea to get a book out since I can already see signs of plagiarism on other sites, and they are taking whole chunks of our material and passing it around on some of the news groups. I need to put the whole thing together. Any advice about the book? Anything you would like to add or suggest?
>
> A: Be careful to make attributions valid.
>
> Q: I don't think that will be a problem. Anything else?
>
> A: Resist urge to place credit/onus on yourself. E.G. if "you know what hits the fan," do you wish to be in the line of fire?

Now, the interesting thing about the website at this particular point in time, i.e. 1998, was that we carefully avoided any distinction of persons in talking about the work of the Group. At this point in time, we simply referred to the Cassiopaean Group, with no distinction as to persons, and certainly no hint that all of us felt funny about Frank's claims and participation. I refused to make any one person the "source," referring to it always as a group, and that irritated him to no end. Frank had been agitating a very long time for us to proclaim him as *the* channel, and to attribute all of the material to him. This process had been an ongoing theme of manipulation on his part for several years, at that point, and I strenuously resisted making the Cs a cult of personality for Frank, which he clearly resented, but attempted (ineffectively) to conceal. There were numerous instances in the transcripts where it was his agenda, or the agenda of his controllers, to proclaim him as the channel, but usually this occurred when Terry was absent, or when there were not sufficient others of positive energy present in the room to counterbalance what we now see was a very powerful STS force.

In the above excerpt, it seems that there is a hint of an accusation that we are taking credit away from Frank, and that is certainly the way Frank felt; but his view was largely constructed in his own mind and had no basis in reality. Since he did not have a computer, he did not have an opportunity to view and read the website (though we often suggested to him that he ought to do it at our house, and even write and contribute to it, which he never did because it took time away from his watching of sports on television). The facts were that no one individual was being credited with the Cs material. It was presented as a group effort. That was all. So, at one and the same time, we see a personal prejudice of Frank's skewing the response, but the Cs managed to turn it into a save by inserting the word "onus" and giving the warning about something "hitting the fan."

I ought to make it clear that my own view of Frank was very sympathetic. And that is one of the chief things that can be learned from this account that I am sharing. The fact is, *those with powerful STS agendas* can and do *utilize all kinds of ways and means of manipulating emotions and perception in order to make themselves appear to be helpful, benevolent, giving, kind, and usually to evoke pity and sympathy.* They can speak or channel truth in order to insert a single twist that leads the uncritical thinker off-track, and that is why we have always promoted the idea of critical channeling.

We received a post from an individual who says that telling the story of the behind the scenes dynamics "discredits the entire channeled material from beginning to end." And such a view, of course, relates directly to the Cs remark above: "Resist urge to place credit/onus on yourself. E.G. if 'you know what hits the fan,' do you wish to be in the line of fire?"

By "saving" the remark this way, the Cs were warning us that there would be an operation put in motion to discredit that portion of the material that was "largely accurate," as they put it. And this is most certainly what has been identified as the current activity of Bridges and

Williams and Co. And indeed, by *not* telling this story of the background earlier, we have most certainly left ourselves open to these attacks.

The Cs are very precise in their use of words, and the remark included the word "onus." This is a word that generally refers to a dirty task, or a burden or the burden of proving something. The evidence will show that we certainly were not claiming credit for the material ourselves, but we were most definitely protecting Frank by not sharing the issues that we are now discussing. In this way, we had taken upon ourselves the onus of defending corrupted material that was indefensible. And, by taking on ourselves the burden of this defense, by *not* dealing with the issue of what we already suspected to be a source of corruption, by continuing to keep the door open for Frank to make a different choice, even though, by that point in time, we knew that his days with the group were numbered, we still continued to protect him. This protection even extended to the point of giving him a pseudonym in *Amazing Grace* so that I could compromise between telling the story as accurately as possible, and still protect Frank. As one observer on the sidelines once remarked (and it incensed me greatly because I was protecting Frank), "Frank plays on your sympathy like a Stradivarius."

As to whether our decision to try to give Frank every chance possible to make a different choice was the correct one, and whether the present "hitting of the fan" of the operation suggested by the Cs in the above excerpt will permanently damage and discredit *all* of the material, will have to be up to the reader. We think that telling the truth is the only way. It is then up to the reader to decide what he/she wants to credit and what not. One learn lessons, one learns truth, and one tells truth. That is how we see it. We do believe that the truth will survive the attacks.

Getting back to the August, 1998 excerpt, since I had been so careful to *not* make the material a cult of personality, I simply did not see what the Cs were trying to tell me. I brushed aside their remark about something "hitting the fan" if I did not make clear who was doing what in the project.

Q: I don't think that's a problem either.
A: Oh, but it could be!

And regarding how I ought to deal with telling the story, the Cs clearly said: "Tell the story as it happened." This made me a little uncomfortable because I knew that I would have to tell about the many issues with Frank, and I tried to squeak out of doing that:

Q: I had thought that I would limit the story and concentrate on the material.
A: The material is part of the story. So are the participants.

And that was the thing that the Cs wanted me to tell: the whole story, and the material as part of the story, and the dynamics of the individuals in the interaction of bringing through material that was "largely accurate," needed to be told "as it happened." Thus I began to write the Wave series. And oh, did the stuff hit the fan. But, I am getting ahead of myself here. Let's go back and pick up some threads that need to be discussed before we get to the events that led to the writing of this recapitulation.

As the readers who have read *Amazing Grace* know, I pretty much left off at the point when the Cassiopaeans first made their debut. It was my intention to continue the story in two more volumes; the second one would cover the period from the beginning of the Cassiopaean Transmission to the point in time when Ark arrived on the scene. This is a period of only two years, but it was so full of lessons and experiences that seem to have been activated by the contact itself, and some plan or destined mission, that it would take an entire book to tell it all. Jan used to joke about having to raise the bizarre bar daily to accommodate the truly weird things that happened in the lives of all of us involved in this project. The third volume was to include our many experiences, research, and what we have learned since Ark's arrival. Again, it would take an entire volume to tell it all!

Since the present circumstances are not at all out of sync with previous attacks, and merely represent the ramping up of what has gone before, I will try to cover that period quickly, briefly, and with some links to other pages where some of the matters have already been discussed to save time.

As it turned out, interacting with the Cassiopaeans has been a lot like Neo and the cookie-baking Oracle in the movie, *The Matrix*. It seems that, very often, in order to not only preserve free will, but also to circumvent the activity of Agents of the Control System, many strategies must be developed and utilized, and some of them are as fun and interesting as the double and triple reverse psychology of a spy thriller. In fact, it may turn out to be the grandest spy thriller of them all because it has operated at several levels of density at once, across years into the past and future, and most certainly involving time loops, changing of the program, and a whole host of fun maneuvers to deceive and beguile the most perspicacious of Grail Questors!

Having said all that, let me go back to where I left off in *Amazing Grace*. At the time of the second Cassiopaean Contact, the following exchange occurred.

July 22, 1994
Q: (L) What is causing the earth changes?
A: Electromagnetic wave changes.

Q: (L) Can you be more specific?

A: Gap in surge heliographic field.

Q: (L) I don't understand.

A: Put Frank on processor channel open.

Q: Do you mean that Frank can channel on the computer?

A: Yes. Do it now.

Considering what I already had learned about channeling, and how easily it was taken over and corrupted, I did not see this as a viable suggestion. In fact, I recognized it as one of the first attempts at corruption. Just to prove my point, we did try it and it was nonsense. In light of all that has occurred since, my conclusion that this was an attempt at sidetracking the process has proven to be correct.

A little further on in the same session, the next attempt was made:

Q: (L) What is the Zindar Council?

A: Two cycle exchangers mission.

Q: (L) What does that mean?

A: References vast. Use Laura channel computer.

Again the computer and direct channeling was being suggested, only this time it was specifically addressed at me. But, I wasn't buying it. Yes, I had experienced some stupendous success with the information that had been received about Cosmic Metamorphosis that led to the research I did to write *Noah*, but I knew that even deeper and more accurate information was needed, and that the developing of the unconscious circuit to access those layers required time and effort *and* strengthening.

The issue of Frank himself was, of course, an interesting one. Having observed him for some period of time, I knew that he was emotionally arrested in his development. I'm not claiming to be a psychotherapist with this remark, and in my own description of his makeup that was written in *Amazing Grace*, I relied heavily on his own descriptions and assessments. His major claim was that his birth had been a mistake and that he really did not belong in this world because he was, effectively, just too sensitive and spiritual. He couldn't have normal relations with other people because they "didn't understand" him. The reason they didn't understand him was because he was "spiritual" and the mass of humanity was not. At least not spiritual enough to appreciate *his* spirituality. He couldn't work at a "real job" because he was "too sensitive" and he couldn't tolerate pressure. It was unfair of ignorant, unwashed hoi-polloi to put expectations on him to perform a job, when they were so un-spiritual and did not grok his truly superior spiritual nature. His parents were horribly abusive (according to him), and he spent endless hours describing in great detail how much he despised his parents for what they had done to him. Again, this was because they did not recognize his superior spirituality.

Well, naturally, I was moved by all of this pain and suffering that he described and I was determined to make a place for Frank to express the one thing that he claimed he was good at: channeling. As he repeated over and over again, it was the one thing he could do, that he wanted to do, that he was comfortable doing, and which did not seem to require any great effort on his part. Because, in the end, it was effort that he could not tolerate. It required effort to get along with other people. It required effort to work at a job. It required effort to understand that parents generally do the best they can with what they know, and to be able to adjust our own thinking so as not to carry so much anger for the fact that they do, often, unconsciously hurt us.

As I wrote in *Amazing Grace*, it's not likely that my own mother will ever wake up and figure out how her own emotional actions and reactions were so hurtful to me and other people. But I am not angry at her, I still maintain relations with her, and if she had a need I could fulfill, I would do it without question. But all of that requires effort. And Frank did not seem to have anything inside him that could result in externally directed effort. He never had a girlfriend, he never dated (he claimed to have had one experience with sexual intercourse that was so disgusting that he vowed never to repeat it), he had very few friends, and his main activity outside of his telemarketing job that he took after the embezzlement episode, was watching football on television.

I had the idea that being accepted for himself would lead to Frank being able to blossom as a human being. I was always making suggestions that he ought to become more socially active, to go back to college, or do some writing (since he had such an excellent command of language). All of these suggestions were met with, "You just *don't* understand! I *can't* do any of those things!" And this was followed by a monologue on how spiritual he was and why being spiritual and a highly developed being prevented one from being capable of interacting with ordinary human beings in normal ways.

At one point I asked him if he thought that a highly developed spiritual being ought to be defined as one who had mastered the lessons of this human level. He hesitantly said yes. I then asked him why, if such a being had mastered such lessons, that being would be unable to just handle ordinary life as easy as falling off a log? It seemed to me that if a college graduate knows the ABC's, it should be so easy for them to recite them that even if it was boring, it should certainly not be stressful to do it.

He had no answer.

What was even more disturbing was his view of humanity as a whole. He had nothing but contempt for other human beings who were not as spiritual as he was. This, of course, led back to his claims that his birth was a mistake, and that then, of course, led to the idea that this mistake was easily corrected by suicide. Naturally, I was horrified and spent hundreds, if not thousands of hours, pouring energy into preventing him from doing this. I didn't realize at the time that it was merely a means of draining my life force.

But, the suicide issue led to a series of exchanges in which I asked Frank if he thought that it could really be a mistake that he was born? And if so, how could such a mechanism operate? He described a "psychic memory" of a harsh voice commanding him to "Go!" and a pointing finger that forcefully ejected him from the delights of the higher levels of ethereal existence into incarnation in the present body.

I didn't say so at the time, but such an image was very troubling for a lot of reasons, not the least of which was what kind of higher being would act in such a way as to forcefully eject an innocent soul from realms of bliss into incarnation? The bottom line was this: I saw Frank as a soul crying out for help, and I was going to be the one to help him. The channeling project was going to be the platform for me to do this.

There had been so many synchronicities that popped up when we met, and I naturally thought that this was a positive thing. After all, Frank's middle name was "Grant" and that had been the name of my first boyfriend. I just ignored the fact that the boyfriend had created so much turmoil and destruction in my life. (As it happens, the "friend" with whom the first boyfriend interacted that caused me so much extreme grief had the last name "Bridges," though it was her married name. Another item I ignored in giving people the benefit of the doubt. Those of you who have read *Amazing Grace* will know exactly what I am talking about.)

The first thing on my mind was to settle the issue of abduction, since Frank incessantly talked about his abductions by aliens and how his parents had never believed he was being tormented this way and failed to protect him. I truthfully didn't see how any parent could have been blamed for such a failure since any such activity is most definitely not considered to be a reality in our culture. But, the fact was, Frank had conscious memories of many abductions. In my own case, even if there is some circumstantial evidence of possible abductions, there was most definitely no conscious memory, and to this day, I cannot say that I have ever seen an alien in any sort of conscious state, nor in any way that could not be explained as a dream, or the result of hypnagogic or hypnopompic states. Having said that, let me add that I do not subscribe to the view that just because such things *can* be explained in such ways, that they ought to be. There is too much evidence that something strange is going on to do that. But the point is, one has to be very careful in this kind of research.

So, dealing with Frank's abductions seemed to be a natural issue to discuss with the Cassiopaeans. We asked about the numbers of times we each had been abducted and received different answers on different occasions. (I considered this variance to be evidence of attempts to corrupt the information.) On the first occasion the question was asked, the answer was:

July 16, 1994
Q: (L) How many times?
A: Frank-57 ... Laura-12.

Over two months later, we asked about Frank again and the answer was four less than the first answer:

September 30, 1994
Q: (L) How many times has Frank been abducted?
A: 53

A week or so later, I asked again about my own purported abductions:

October 9, 1994
Q: (L) How many times have I been abducted?
A: 17
Q: (L) How many times have they abducted Frank?
A: 53
Q: (L) Why have they abducted Frank more than me?
A: You fight it.

Now, in this last instance, the number given for me is five more than previously stated, though the number given for Frank is the same as the number given the second time, which was four less than the first answer. However, even this number is suspect because two years later, more specifics were given, and in this case, they matched real life clues, so this next figure regarding myself, if it is true at all, might be the correct one.

April 24, 1996
Q: (L) Can you tell me what ages?
A: 2, 4, 7, 10, 17, 22, 44

Now, if we consider the fact that, as I described in Grace, the incident when I was four was a human abduction, and that at the time of the first answer, I was not yet 44 years old and the last figure in the above recitation would be necessarily deducted, this means that this last figure of only five instances is probably accurate regarding myself.

Regarding Frank, in all cases, whichever number we accept as the correct one, his experiences are five times as frequent then, and probably since. And the answer as to why he was abducted more frequently was very telling *and* disturbing: effectively, he was abducted more because he did *not* fight it. And that means, he either accepted it out of weakness, or agreement.

And here I want to make it perfectly clear that I am not talking about conscious agreement by any stretch of the imagination. A person can be paralyzed and brutalized (or so they say) in an abduction, and be completely helpless. There is obviously some other quality or quantity of something that makes one person more or less susceptible than another. Why else would the Cassiopaeans have made such a remark? I am certain that if I was abducted (and there is certainly circumstantial evidence that it was so), I never managed to stop it because I "fought it." (Until, of course, the last attempt which is recounted in my book, *High Strangeness*). But clearly, something in me fought it at some level of which I was (and am) completely unaware. And this is most definitely something we need to research for the sake of others who have similarly fought such battles, with greater or lesser success.

Frank, of course, was certain that these abductions were what gave him his "channeling" ability. We discussed it and decided to ask if this was the case: that he had been programmed to be a channel. In the session of October 9, 1994, I asked:

Q: (L) Is Frank's mind programmed?
A: Yes.
Q: (L) To do what?
A: To be an open channel.
Q: (L) By whom?
A: Us.
Q: (L) You said one other time that he was also programmed by the Grays.
A: Yes.
Q: (L) To do what?
A: To destroy himself.
Q: (L) Is this why it is important for him to channel?
A: Yes.

The above remarks, of course, raise the all-important question as to *who* was giving the answer. We certainly know from the vast body of material that the Cassiopaeans do not "program" anybody. So it seems fairly obvious that this response, due to the wishful thinking of Frank, either drew in a corrupting energy, or was answered by Frank himself.

Throughout this period I was, of course, doing all of my testing of the source, and asking of wide ranging questions on hundreds of subjects. The information was checking out and I was becoming more convinced that we had most certainly achieved a significant contact and so I asked:

October 16, 1994

Q: (L) Why did it take so long for us to get a good source through this medium?

A: Too many interactions with channel cancellers.

Q: (L) Who are the individuals who are channel cancellers?

A: It would not be our way to name names.

Q: (L) Do you mean people we have had involved in our lives?

A: Yes.

Q: (L) Does it have anything to do with our activities?

A: No.

Q: (L) Does it involve other entities that have tried to come through that have blocked the channel?

A: Yes.

Q: (L) Are they Lizards?

A: No.

These remarks were most revealing to me though, as usual, I kept my deeper speculations to myself. When discussing it with Frank, his answer was, of course, that all "channel cancellers" were individuals he did not like or who didn't like him because they were repelled by his disdainful and superior attitude. As usual, I always put the most positive spin on this, giving Frank the benefit of the doubt and attributing this behavior to a defense mechanism. I knew perfectly well that many people who act superior only do so because they are covering up deep inferiority feelings inside, and again, I had the idea that Frank was certainly a person with many talents and abilities and that helping him was a good thing to be doing.

Through all these months, Frank regularly repeated the claim that the only reason the Cassiopaeans were able to communicate was because of him. I was certainly open to this possibility, and the possibility of further tuning as a trance channel, since that was what he was pushing for so regularly and repeatedly. Even though I pointed out to him that trance channeling, by definition is disabling, and therefore pathological, he was anxious to work on it and presented arguments that it was not disabling if it was the only thing a person could really do in life, and if it was what they had been born to do. These were compelling arguments, so reluctantly, I agreed to the experiment.

The trance material was very good, of that there was no doubt. There were several problems, however, that were disturbing. The first one was the "air" that was emanated by Frank when channeling from a trance. There is no way to describe this other than to say it felt very uneasy, faintly repellant or "off" in some way. Even though the words were high sounding, and the information was good, the sensation that I had was unpleasant.

Another factor was a sort of resistance to freely answering questions. There was an obfuscatory action that was in play, utilizing a lot of words to avoid exactly direct answers. I had seen this in so much other channeled material that I knew that it was bordering on a source that rambles on and on with many words and little content. In short, the word density deteriorated when Frank channeled from a trance.

I decided to ask about this the next night at a board session, and this was the very first clue that Frank was *not* the channel.

October 23, 1994

Q: (L) Was Frank operating as a clear channel last night?

A: Partly.

Q: (L) What was the nature of the interference?

A: Static electromagnetic.

Q: (L) What was the origin of this static?

A: Various. Channels must be grooved as this one has been.

Q: (L) Is it correct that we should persist with practice for him to become a clear channel?

A: Yes.

Q: (L) How often should we do this?

A: Open, but one time per week would work.

Q: (L) How long will it take to "groove" or clear the channel?

A: Open.

When the Cs said "channels must be grooved as this one has been," it certainly could have referred to the board channeling. There is also the possibility that the "grooved channel" that the Cs were referring to was simply me, as other comments later indicated. In any event, it was already becoming clear to me that the Cs were communicating against some sort of block, and I was pretty sure it wasn't me. And, if no one else but Frank was present, who else could it be? The one thing that was certain from these remarks was: Frank was *not* the Cassiopaean channel in the exclusive way that he was repeatedly trying to suggest.

At about this point in time, I visited a local lady psychic with a friend who praised her abilities to the skies. She wasn't a professional, and didn't charge anything, but she did have a study group and a small local following, so I was reassured that this was not going to be another psychic scam. She was very nice, and we visited around her kitchen table. She told me many accurate things about my then-current situation which I have long since forgotten. The most remarkable and surprising thing she said was that she saw a little red-haired girl following me around and she believed it was representative of the soul of the next baby in my life. The funny thing was, this was merely a reiteration of the same thing that several other psychic friends had said to me.

Well, at that point in time, having another baby was not something I wished to contemplate. My health had been so seriously compromised in that respect that I knew another pregnancy would just kill me. (Yeah, I know, a little dramatic, but the ladies will understand!) Of course, I couldn't wait to ask the Cs about *that*! (And of course, I did not want to be too specific since Frank knew nothing about this visit to the psychic and I wanted to see what the Cs would say without any leading.)

October 28, 1994

Q: (L) Now, several people have told me that there is a small child who is with me constantly. Who is she and why is she here?

A: Next in line.

Q: (L) Next in line for what?

A: Birth.

Q: (L) Am I going to have another child?

A: Maybe.

Q: (L) How many are there in line?

A: One.

Q: (L) Male or female?

A: Female.

Q: (L) Is this to happen within the next year?

A: Open.

Q: (L) I am 42 years old. If I were to get pregnant would I be able to have a normal pregnancy and produce a healthy infant?

A: Yes. Your consciousness will soon give you spectacularly sharp, exact and correct information.

Q: (L) Will this be due to ingesting the Melatonin?

A: Partly.

Q: (L) Is soon within a month?

A: You will know.

Q: (L) I get the feeling that this has a lot to do with trusting my own intuition.

A: Yes.

Q: (L) What occurred to make my pool clear up?

A: You restored your own energy.

Q: (L) And it had nothing to do with rituals?

A: Correct. In spite of rituals but you were lucky could have gone the other way.

Q: (L) What prevented this from happening?

A: Divine intervention. [energy surge]

Q: (L) Well, my life seems to have been full of incidents of divine intervention. Is this true?

A: Yes.

Q: (L) What is the purpose of this intervention?

A: To preserve and prepare you for work.

Q: (L) What is this work?

A: You are extremely valuable to all on your planet.

Q: (L) What particular value? Is this common to all people?

A: No.

Q: (L) Is this something meaningful? What is the mission?

A: Faith in your opening channel you will learn as you go. We cannot tell you all at once.

This bit of dialogue was very interesting and very troubling at the same time. First the Cassiopaeans were indicating that asking questions as we were at that point was only a step in a process, the end result of which would be that "your consciousness will soon give you spectacularly sharp, exact and correct information." Of course, I was thinking that this would be just some sort of magical "opening up of awareness," and asked if it would be because of taking melatonin.

Because I had relied upon this intuition regarding the Green Pool affair, it was only natural to ask about it in the context of developing psychic awareness. I most certainly did not expect the answer that came about divine intervention. The energy surge that is noted in brackets related to the fact that the planchette began to move very fast and actually nearly flew off the table. It seems that opening the door to that subject by asking the question, allowed me to receive a real surge of positive energy.

I knew I was treading on thin ice when I asked why divine intervention would be activated on my behalf and frankly, I didn't put a lot of stock in the answer that I was "extremely valuable to all on your planet." That struck me as an ego hook, and I was really wary of such things. The only thing that restored my confidence at that moment was the fact that the Cs wouldn't tell me the answer. How many people are led astray by being told that they are here to save the world or some such nonsense! For all I knew, the value of my life consisted in being burned at the stake or something gross like that. Nevertheless, in response to the question "what is the mission," again the Cassiopaeans slipped something past Frank that obviated his claim to be *the* Cassiopaean channel: "Faith in your opening channel you will learn as you go.

We cannot tell you all at once." And I knew for certain that there was a problem in working with Frank. The Cs were declaring as clearly as they could, that they would tell me many things in bits and pieces via the current medium, and that the opening channel was something deep in me. Further, that it would only be from my own consciousness that the ultimate answers would come.

But, as was usual, I shoved it under the rug. At the same session, another very interesting series of remarks was made:

> Q: (L) Since the energy is high at this time, we would like to know if you have anything to give in the form of a teaching.
> A: Not ready for that yet; establish clear channel and forum first; one step at a time.
> Q: (L) What is the forum?
> A: What do you think?
> Q: (L) Do you mean that we need to bring more people into this work?
> A: Close.
> Q: (L) We need to create a forum.
> A: Yes. A direction will open if you persevere.
> Q: (L) So things will be brought to us and happen for us if we just persevere?
> A: Soon expect big opportunity.
> Q: (L) I assume that we are not to ask what it is, we are to have faith, is that correct?
> A: Yes. Danger you may misinterpret opportunity.
> Q: (L) Should we all three be able to realize in congruence whether the opportunity is good?
> A: Varying degrees.
> Q: (L) If there is a danger we may misinterpret the opportunity, could you give us a couple of clues so that when it occurs we won't miss it?
> A: At least one of you will have instant recognition but others may not. Wait and see.

The first remark was that we needed to establish a clear channel first. This related back to the immediately previous remark about having faith in my own opening channel, that "your consciousness will soon give you spectacularly sharp, exact and correct information." I didn't realize it at the time, but the Cassiopaeans certainly knew in advance how the drama would play out, and no clearer evidence of this, as well as their refusal to interfere with free will and my own need to learn things by experience, could be given. When I asked about a "forum," naturally, I was thinking in small, local terms. A forum to me was something like a study group or a minimal number of people who would meet to discuss things. What was most curious was the remark about a "big opportunity" that there was some danger of misinterpreting on the part of all of those present except for one person.

As it turned out, this opportunity was meeting Ark. And it was certainly true that it was misinterpreted by everyone but me. I had "instant recognition" to a depth and extent that can barely be explained or expressed. Frank, on the other hand, literally spent days trying to convince me that I ought *not* to communicate with Ark, that he was a spy or KGB agent sent to kidnap me and use me for vile purposes. (Funny how real agents always accuse others of what they are doing themselves.) What was more, he managed to convince other members of the group that Ark was a danger to the all of us, and I basically had to stand alone against them repeating to me over and over again that I was falling into a trap.

But because the Cs had cleverly used the exact phrase that would communicate to me the essential thing to know – that there would be instant recognition – I knew that Ark was the One, and that his coming and importance to the mission had been known and predicted 21 months in advance.

But I still had 21 months of serious learning ahead of me before I would even be ready for Ark, and the Cassiopaeans must have been smiling all the while at what was waiting for me at the end of what I could only describe as a long tunnel of suffering.

Not too long after the above session, Terry and Jan became regular members of the group. The Cassiopaeans were almost overjoyed at their presence, and it is only in retrospect that the reasons become clear. Nevertheless, they willingly and readily put in many hours of labor on analyzing and collating material.

Frank continued to ask that we convert the channeling process to the trance method with him as the subject/channel. With Terry and Jan present, we experimented with it a number of times. I didn't express my own feelings about it in advance since I wanted them to witness it without prejudice, and it turned out that their reaction was exactly the same as my own. In fact, it almost seemed that the repellant aspects of the voice and presence of Frank's trance source was amplified with the three of us on the other side. It was this experience that prompted us to discuss at some length the role that Frank played in the process. It was also this that prompted us to devise ways and means of wording inquiries so that we could bypass Frank's "controller" as well as whatever programming he was operating under. There are quite a number of questions in the transcripts that are asked, seemingly about someone else, when a prearranged agreement was made that these questions were inquiries about Frank himself. In some cases these questions were about Terry and in other cases, they were about other individuals. In later sessions, Ark and I used this same method. In the course of this series of articles, I will reveal where and what these questions are, what the circumstances were that prompted them, and what the coded answers meant.

But again, the bottom line was that, despite the fact that we knew we had to find ways to circumvent the corruption that was evident in Frank, we all saw Frank as a valuable human being who had been abducted and kidnapped as a child, and that his free will had been violated, and we felt that if we continued to work with him, to encourage him, that something of strength and true STO will would grow in him. I clung stubbornly to the belief that Frank was, at the core, an STO being who had just been presented with so many challenges that he needed help to meet them. It took us a long time to fully realize that when such things happen, the soul is not an infant. If I could resist or fight back as a child so could Frank; only he didn't. And ultimately, that was an expression of his soul choice.

Over the next six years, the Cassiopaeans gave clue after clue about many things, including Frank himself, that were delivered to us based on a secret signal system that was unknown to Frank, and is only now being revealed. And this, of course, leads to another reason why we did not choose to publish all the transcripts at once, unedited, and without commentary. Without this background, without the information about the code and the questions that were asked in code and answered in code, there is no way that the casual reader can fully realize the truly amazing nature of the transmissions.

What is more: we wanted to wait for the "rest of the story." Right up to the very last minute, we left the door open for Frank to make a different choice.

CHAPTER 35
A STRANGE INTERLUDE

The *Matrix* comparison is not only useful in describing our global reality; the story of the group who are working to circumvent the Matrix, to wake people up, is entirely synchronous with our own experiences, right down to each and every character! In the case of Frank, we find the classic role of Cypher in action. In his repeated claims that his very birth was a mistake, we hear Cypher saying: "You know, I know what you're thinking 'cause right now I'm thinking the same thing. Actually, to tell you the truth, I've been thinking the same thing ever since I got here. Why, oh why, didn't I take that blue pill!?"

We next see Cypher in a fancy restaurant sawing a steak while the voice of Agent Smith asks: "Do we have a deal, Mr. Reagan?" And Cypher tells us even more:

> You know, I know that this steak doesn't exist. I know that when I put it in my mouth, the Matrix is telling my brain that it is juicy and delicious. After nine years, do you know what I've realized? Ignorance is bliss. ... I don't want to remember nothing. Nothing! You understand? And I want to be rich. Someone important. Like an actor. You can do that, right?

And Agent Smith tells him: "Whatever you want, Mr. Reagan."

From my own perspective, I understood Frank's desperate need to be all-powerful and in control of something – anything. Throughout all of the past nine years, I hoped that if we persevered in our acceptance of him and his many quirks, that he would eventually learn by osmosis to just be himself as a part of a group of friendly souls who neither wanted to control, nor be controlled. I also thought that he wanted to know the truth more than he wanted to live in illusion. I believed that this love of truth, whatever it turned out to be, and however painful it might be to face it, even if it meant completely eliminating our own personal wants and desires, would win in the end; that Frank was as motivated as I was to discover it.

Because of the fact that I knew Frank was under almost constant internal attack, I became very protective of him, constantly looking for ways and means to encourage him to branch out a little in the real world and try something new. I wanted to see him have positive experiences, to develop a new circuit where he could regard other human beings as equal seekers on their many paths; to stop having to feel so defensive. It was this defensiveness that led to the endless hours and hours of descriptions he would give of how horribly he had been treated by this person or that person. Most of these issues had to do with what can only be described as severe homophobia. Frank was utterly convinced that people thought he was gay, and this enraged and horrified him.

While there was certainly some truth to this idea, as the reader of *Amazing Grace* will already know, I decided that if Frank was afraid of it, if it was a problem in his own mind, then certainly we could find a way to deal with it effectively. We had many discussions about it, all of which centered on the fact that Frank had seen himself in a video, and it had been a shock for him to realize that many of his gestures and movements were obviously feminine. Once he came to that decision, he became even more self-conscious and attempted to compensate for it, which only resulted in worsening the problem because then he became unnaturally stiff and jerky in his physical motions which was jarring to strangers. All of this contributed to his reclusive nature, the many, many hours spent alone, or watching football or videos, during which he brooded on the unfairness of his existence in the world.

I was worried. I wanted to help.

Over and over again I was being subjected to Frank's lengthy diatribes about how cruel his life was and how abominably he was treated. The thing was, there really wasn't much in the way of real evidence that this was so. He had all the advantages of an upper middle class family, he had been given opportunities I never had; he had most certainly never been hungry, cold, or without a home; he had never suffered the helplessness of watching someone he loved in pain or sitting up all night with a sick child, or rocking a loved one who was dying of cancer. But I pushed such thoughts away, and took his word for it that he was suffering, and gave endless support, sympathy, and suggestions.

After one particularly grueling session of complaints from Frank about how the world simply was not ready for his presence, his high spiritual nature, and how awful it was to be so spiritual in such a revolting world, I decided to ask the Cassiopaeans about it:

November 2, 1994 – Frank, Laura and V**

Q: (L) Why was Frank in such a state last night?

A: Because his life is difficult.

Q: (L) What is making his life difficult?

A: Destiny.

Q: (L) Is it his destiny for his entire life to be difficult?

A: Open.

Q: (L) Is that choice up to him?

A: No.

Q: (L) Well then, why is it open?

A: Will dark or light forces win?

Q: (L) Win what?

A: Battle.

Q: (L) Battle where?

A: All.

Q: (L) Well, I thought you said that the forces of light were definitely going to win? Is that not correct?

A: Too simplified.

Q: (L) Is there anything Frank can do in this battle to assist getting over this problem?

A: Fight.

But, as we already know, Frank was not fighting.

Nevertheless, in a sort of desperation, I gave him more and more time and support in an effort to help him fight, or to develop the will to fight. It was not lost on me that the Cassiopaeans were clearly saying that there was a very good possibility that the dark forces would triumph in Frank's case, and I most certainly did not want that to happen.

I started reading book after book about different kinds of therapies that might be helpful for him to try. I came to the idea that all of the torment he had described as having been inflicted on him as an infant had locked up the natural flow of energies in his body, and if he could do some body work, it would free up this energy, and he would be more at ease with himself, and therefore, better equipped to interact with the real world, and be as successful as he most evidently deserved to be. He had so many gifts, it seemed quite unfair to me that he was not in a position to develop them, and have others appreciate them or benefit from them. As a result of this course of reading, I explained to Frank one night the different theories that I had encountered, and how evident it was that he most certainly could deal with this problem effectively. I didn't realize that Frank didn't *want* a solution; that the act of complaining and ranting about the unfairness of the world was what he wanted to do because it was a means of holding me captive as audience and sympathizer, and sympathy was what he wanted, because it was energy.

The end result of all of it was that since I had proposed a solution to his problem, Frank announced that his problem was not *his* problem. The problem was with the rest of the world, none (or few) of whom were spiritually advanced enough to understand that he was an advanced spiritual being, and that his was the body mode of the future.

Following this discussion, in which every proposal I made was countered by a reason that it would not work for *him*, I insisted that we ask the Cs about it. And it is a certainty that this exchange was somewhat corrupted by the working of Frank's own prejudices:

November 6, 1994

Q: (L) Have you been listening in on our discussion?

A: As always.

Q: (L) In this particular discussion we have been talking about freeing up life energy which can be blocked by emotional traumas and so forth, and that, according to this book I read, you can tell the life energy is blocked by the way a person holds or moves their body. From this information I think that Frank's life energy is blocked. Am I correct?

A: No.

Q: (L) Then why is Frank so ill at ease in his body?

A: Book not entirely incorrect but remember not to take anything entirely on face value.

Q: (L) Is there some part of that idea that would benefit Frank and help him to feel more at ease?

A: Frank is ill at ease because most others are ill at ease with him.

Q: (L) Well, who started out being ill at ease, him or others?

A: Others.

Q: (L) And why were they ill at ease with him?

A: Sensed differences.

Q: (L) If Frank were to do some bodywork and bring his energies into focus where his physical sensations are concerned, would this, in some way, help to overcome this particular difficulty or situation?

A: Won't work.

Q: (L) Is there anything Frank can do to free up his energies and to become more at ease with himself?

A: He is more at ease now than before because he no longer listens to others' criticisms.

Q: (L) Is Frank correct in saying that his body and mode is that of the future?

A: Closer. But not there yet.

I wasn't entirely comfortable with this answer. But, since the Cs were saying so many other things that were not part of our general understanding that *did* prove to be accurate upon deeper inspection, perhaps this was another unknown factor that I would have to deal with? Perhaps Frank was right? Perhaps Androgyny was the mode of the future? It had certainly been hinted at by other sources from time to time. Nevertheless, we can revisit these remarks with better perspective here and see quite clearly that, even though there was an intent to corrupt and slant the meaning, the Cs still managed to get across a message for those with eyes to see and ears to hear.

At this point, I shifted gears and referred back to a comment made on October 19, 1994, where we had been encouraged to persevere through a series of financial setbacks that were creating severe stress in our lives. The Cs had said that all would be well if we kept pushing forth and if we would "coordinate each other's input equally."

The reason I wanted to ask about this question was quite simple: at this point, I was doing all the work and Frank was claiming all the credit. I wanted to know if this was "equal input?" Was it possible that his claim to be the channel was true, and that this meant that all other work that fell to me was "equal input." In a sense, it was sort of a trick question that was asked suddenly and out of the blue.

Q: (L) There was a comment made in an earlier reading when we were told we needed to coordinate our input in this project. I am curious as to the exact meaning of equalize the input? Does that refer to use of the board or what?

A: Many meanings. One must not dominate decision-making. Be open all ideas and input. Once we have made financial arrangements that will be your cue to dedicate full time efforts to this endeavor.

It was comforting to think that some of the financial pressures on my life might be relieved, but I wasn't putting anything in the bank on it!

As we continued to chat with the Cs, I was paying acute attention to every movement and sensation. I noticed that Frank often seemed to sink into a bored, half-sleeping state while the planchette moved, and that it was during those periods when the energy of the information was most comfortable. This was an awareness that only grew gradually, but I was very soon employing this knowledge in a protective way. I would begin a series of questions, about which Frank had no emotional prejudices, and once he had become completely bored with my questions (most of the time), I would ask the question that concerned me most.

November 9, 1994

Q: (L) Having you as communicants, does this protect us from the intrusion of earthbound spirits?

A: Earthbound spirits yes but others no.

Q: (L) What others do you mean?

A: Aliens.

Q: (L) So your presence protects us from earthbound spirits but other aliens can come through if they choose?

A: Not through while with this connection but around.

Q: (L) They are around?

A: Not now.

Q: (L) Have they been around on other occasions when we were communicating?

A: Yes.

Q: (L) Have they ever, on any occasion, contaminated or corrupted our channel?

A: Tried but failed because you recognized it the one time.

Q: (L) When was the one time?

A: Several sessions ago.

Q: (L) Is that one of the sessions on tape? What was the name of the individual that came through that time?

A: Not named.

My intent with the question about "other occasions" was directly concerned with the issue of trance channeling as opposed to working with the board. I wanted to get a definite identification, but failed. But I did manage to get confirmation that my questioning and awareness during the trance session had gone a long way toward preventing major corruption. The important point was that others could not come "through" when working at the board, but that they were definitely around and could skew the information. And the reference to "this connection," in the above context, was clear: as long as Frank was "connected" to me, to my intent to receive truth, the worst that could happen was skewing. On his own, he was subject to directly channeling STS. It was obvious that as I got close to the issue of the trance channeling, Frank woke up and "blocked." I shifted gears again.

Q: (L) In this book I am reading it talks about knowledge that is only given to the elect and that certain things are passed down through secret organizations. Most people think this organization is the Illuminati and that they hold many deep, dark secrets. Is that true?

A: Close. But now there is a knowledge explosion. The Illuminati is no longer exclusive; but they still think they are.

Q: (L) Compared to the big high mucky mucks in the Illuminati, what percentage of their knowledge do Frank and I possess?

A: 2 per cent.

Q: (L) You mean they know 98 per cent more than we do? That's depressing! How much knowledge, relative to the Illuminati, does the average college graduate have?

A: 0.02 per cent.

Q: (L) Is there any one person who holds a major chunk of knowledge on this planet?

A: By this time next year you will have 35 per cent as much.

Q: (L) That means I have to work hard!

A: No. It will flow into you. Stop listening to those that block.

Q: (L) Who in my life is blocking me now?

A: Can't say. You must find this out.

Q: (L) Is it myself?

A: Only through others.

In response to my question about any *one* person holding a big block of knowledge, it was odd that their response did not designate both of us, but was predicated on the platform of one person, and that this knowledge would flow into me if I would stop listening to those that block. The only problem was: at this point in my life, the *only* person I was really listening to was Frank! Of course, at that point in time, I never would have believed that Frank was the block in that sense. In my mind, he was a good soul that was struggling to overcome terrible programming, terrible suffering, and even though I knew I had to work with his psychological issues and strong emotional prejudices, that he might be blocking the inflow of knowledge was a preposterous idea. And when I asked "who?" their non-violation of free will response was classic: "You must find this out." What is funny is that I naturally took the onus upon myself, blamed myself for any shortcomings of the material, and the Cs made it clear that if I was blocking myself, it was only "through others." And again, the only possible "other" at this point in time was: Frank.

Not too long after, an extremely curious event occurred which demonstrated this blocking. I had been reading abduction cases, trying to sort it all out and come to some idea about the nature of the interaction, how controls of abductees might be put in place and utilized, and how the emotional feeding or "uploading or downloading" of information to or from the abductee took place. I had the idea that it was partly technological through implants, but I also realized from some of the descriptions of abductees that there was something much deeper to this issue than met the eye. It was in asking this little series of questions that a very strange thing occurred.

December 3, 1994

Q: (L) In the establishing of an ongoing connection between an abductee and the abductor, what methods or techniques are used? Is it a psychic bond?

A: Close.

Q: (L) Is it formed technologically?

A: Partly.

Q: (L) There are so many stories of the gazing process where the alien controls that abductee by staring into their eyes and the abductee feels full of love and harmony and thereby thinks that the experience is beneficial. This makes me wonder just exactly what is the purpose of this gazing?

A: Hypnotic.

Q: (L) Does it also form a bond?

A: Yes.

Q: (L) What is the substance of this bond? Is there a psychic cord or connection and is it true that the same …

A: Channel wavering …. [planchette spinning around board]

Q: (L) Is that all you are going to say on that?

A: Please say good night.

It seems that I was moving into areas that the STS controllers did not want to discuss, and they exerted extra blocking energy to halt the receiving of answers. The Cs said "Channel wavering … " Similar events occurred later on, when Ark pressed for certain information that could not possibly be construed to violate free will, but which obviously approached subject matter that was directly concerned with the control system and how it operated directly on human beings. They couldn't send a lie through, but they could block transmission by static discharge through Frank. The "Powers That Be" clearly did not want us to learn how this process worked, and I have thought since then that if we had learned this at that point in time, it would have been indicative of how Frank himself operated in vectoring our thoughts, as well as blocking the transmissions from the Cs on occasion.

A couple of days later, a friend of mine was present for the session. There is a long story about her that goes in a direction that is not pertinent to the current issue except to say that Frank rapidly developed an extreme distaste for her presence and spent many, many hours ridiculing her simple approach to life, which included a naturally giving nature. (And here I want to note that "simple" does not relate to intellect in the case of V**, but rather the fact that she was a person who was emotionally reactive and wore her heart on her sleeve.) On this particular evening, she and I had been playing around with the board for a few minutes to see if the Cs would say anything before Frank arrived. He came in the house without knocking (as was usual), almost out of breath as if he had been in a big hurry, and he walked in on us doing this. It was evident from the look on his face that he was angry. He rapidly regained his composure and sat down at the board and the following message came out:

December 5, 1994 – Frank, Laura, V**

Q: (L) Hello.

A: Hello.

Q: (L) Celestial dudes! [Laura and V** had been trying to make contact prior to arrival of Frank and were commenting on the fact that not so much as a nudge came from the planchette.]

A: Look upon that as a sign.

Q: (L) A sign of what?

A: Kindly remove ridge from board. [adjustments made] Move board away from center of table. [further adjustments made]

Q: (L) Is that better?

A: Okay.

Q: (L) Now, look upon what as a sign?

A: Channel.

Q: (L) Channel? How is that a sign channel? I don't get it?

A: Who? [draws large question mark]

Q: (L) Who?

A: Is.

Q: (L) OK, you mean who is the channel?

A: Yes.

Q: (L) They are trying to tell us Frank is the channel. Who do we have with us tonight?

A: Urua.

I didn't really think about the fact that Frank was in an emotional state that could easily skew the material, I just figured that since he said it so often and with such conviction, perhaps it was so and this was just a little confirmation? In any event, we went through some personal issues, the Cs came across as rather irritated which was not inspiring to say the least, but eventually the energy of Frank's anger dissipated, and he finally settled into his bored half-sleep. And it was at this session that the remark about getting on the Internet was made. The curious thing about it was that, even though they had insisted repeatedly that they did not wish to discuss personal matters, my question about a dream I had was not considered to be "personal!" Whatever it was that was skewing the reception at that point, melted and talking about the dream was encouraged. In retrospect, it's easy to see that the controllers wanted to see what I had dreamed, if it was of any significance, but the result was that by removing their blocking efforts, the Cs were able to tell me something of great significance: to get on the Internet, and that my life would change suddenly and dramatically!

Q: (L) What a relief! A concession! OK, I had a dream last night, I dreamed about large mechanical flying V's that had flapping wings like metal bat boxes. They scared me. Then, I was with my family and we were going to see my cousin who is deceased and she had just had a baby. The baby was walking and talking and quoting Shakespeare. My Aunt got very upset and said it was unseemly because the baby was illegitimate and she walked out. The baby was only 10 days old. My aunt ran out the door and said it was evil.

A: Suggestion, get on computer net ASAP.

Q: (L) In other words, I really need to take my computer down and get the A drive fixed etc. and log onto the network?

A: Yes.

Q: (V) What does that have to do with the dream? (L) I think it relates back to when Terry and Jan were here and we were talking about dreams and the suggestion was given to hook up to the network and discuss and share dreams. Like a dream forum kind of thing. Is there any significance to the ten days in this dream?

A: When you network, your entire life will dramatically improve immediately! See, sometimes we do advise when appropriate.

As the reader may have guessed, my computer really wasn't up to doing the Internet in any big way. It was already several years old, and this was 1994, remember? It was a Packard Bell 386 with two 40 megabyte hard drives. I couldn't install any software because the floppy drive wasn't working.

Based on this advice, I broke down and called the repair guy who worked out of his home. He came by a day or so later, and discovered that our youngest child had inserted a business card into the floppy drive. After all, it was a nice slot just sitting there, and she knew I was always inserting things in it, so why couldn't she? I laughed with relief that it wasn't serious, and told him that she had also recently inserted a peanut butter sandwich in the VCR. Thankfully, there was no peanut butter on the business card!

So, there I was finally, two days before Christmas: Have computer, will travel! With an AOL free trial diskette in my hand, I was ready to rock and roll! I was going to change my life suddenly and dramatically! I was ready! Enough of this nonsense! Let's find out what's going on out there in cyber land!

I followed the directions (keeping in mind that my computer was, at this point, merely a glorified word-processor) and soon found myself in the world of America Online. The only thing I could figure out how to do was check out some chat room where they were discussing channeling and the paranormal. It didn't look too promising, and I didn't have time to do more than introduce myself and sign off. I had Christmas preparations to take care of. What was more, my best friend was in the hospital, and I wanted to spend some time with her as soon as I had the holiday matters under control.

The following day, Christmas Eve, after rushing around all day, baking and cleaning, I borrowed my ex's truck to drive to the toy store to pick up the bicycles that they were holding for me until Christmas Eve. I was going to fetch them home and conceal them under a cover in the back yard, and then drive to the hospital to visit Sandra and take her some things to cheer her up.

While waiting at the intersection to make a left turn onto my street, I was struck from the rear at speed by a guy who said in his statement to the police that I was *not* there. And frankly, even though my eyes were on the big side view truck mirrors that show everything in the rear, I didn't see him either. Since he never "saw" me, he never slowed down. The impact was serious enough that his entire car was destroyed.

It would be three years before I recovered from the injuries received in the accident. But in a way, it was the best thing that ever happened to me.

Indeed, my life changed suddenly and dramatically.

CHAPTER 36
A VILE SUPERSTITION

As we proceeded with our interaction with the Cassiopaeans, we slowly, but surely, came to the idea of the Matrix reality. Of course, in those early days, we had no metaphor for what we were learning, and we certainly were charting little-known territory of soul dynamics. The idea of a theological drama between the gods or higher level beings of both the positive and negative orientation was the major theme.

Certainly, this is not an entirely new idea, but it was being expressed to us in scientific terms of hyperdimensional physics and we were being encouraged to explore and perceive it for one very simple reason: awareness. The Cassiopaeans had told us that it was awareness that binds us to our reality, and by becoming aware, interactively, with the higher reality, we are stretching beyond our normal human limitations. And, when we expand our awareness, as well as act upon higher awareness, we are nurturing that part of ourselves that ultimately grows to "fit" the higher levels, and we then graduate.

Someone once said that there are two reasons a person does a thing: the reason they give, and the real reason. We had some idea that there was actually a deeper reason beyond the psychological one, and that this was, so to say, the theological reason, which manifested and utilized the real reason, and we were seeking to penetrate to that theological reality.

All the members of the group were widely read in the various subjects of metaphysics, philosophy, and even science to some extent, and all of us felt that there was some significant piece missing that would be the key to unlock our understanding. We were searching for that key. We knew that when a person views any given situation from the strictly human perspective, without considering psychological dynamics, they are subject to the pitfalls of "the real reason." We knew that the teachings of love and light had been promulgated for a very long time, but for some reason, such ideas only seemed to lead to more and greater misery.

It was actually in terms of principles that we gradually learned to discern the theological drama, and at this point, we have certainly learned even more, and quite deeply at that. That there were psychological issues where Frank was concerned was always apparent to all of us. We didn't think too much of this except in terms of sympathy and learning to interact with it, and our own as well. The idea that Frank's issues were clues to his core being were just simply not part of anything we wished to consider, and in that respect, we were acting out an obsession, a refusal to see the truth.

Learning to navigate the labyrinth of human relations, to be able to discern the real reason behind the actions of those people we interacted with, was an early concern. Unfortunately, as already noted, this was often skewed by Frank's powerful negative reactions to many people, and, for the most part, such direct questions about anyone he either disliked or favored ought to be discarded. A prime example is Richard Hoagland.

By this time, all of us had read the Ra Material, suggested very early by the Cs, though in a session that was neither recorded on tape nor in notes, so I can't reproduce the exact remarks here. It had been indicated that this was a primer and would save a lot of time if we could grasp the essential concepts about service-to-self and service-to-others. In this seemingly simple concept, we began to discern the reason behind the real reason, or the manifestation of the theological drama.

We began to realize, slowly at first, that a person could have psychological issues, and still be oriented to service-to-others. They could also be oriented to serving self. By the same token, a person could appear to have no disabling psychological issues at all, and be completely oriented to serving the self. We began to learn that closing our ears to the words that other people use to beguile us, and observing only the actions, was the key to discernment.

These terms, "service-to-others" and "service-to-self", are inextricably mixed up with the idea of love. On an individual basis, we may say that we love this or that person, and want to serve them, but then the question arises: *which part of them* are we serving? The higher part that seeks spiritual growth and union with God, or the lower part that seeks survival in the flesh? When we help someone who keeps making the same mistakes over and over again, we are clearly interfering in their lessons. What, then, are we serving? Most likely ourselves because we are then able to "feel good" that we are so "long suffering" and "patient" and "self-sacrificing," because we can certainly see, from the evidence of our eyes, that the other person isn't making any progress by virtue of our efforts. And, it may be a far more difficult thing to deny assistance, to refuse association with them, particularly when it is someone we love, because it "hurts us to see them hurt." Yet, that may be the very thing needed in order for them to grow – to be left to their own suffering until they have had enough so that they will begin to see their own way out of the difficulty, thereby building soul strength and accessing their own powers and inner potentials.

But, we run into a problem of judgment here: aren't we judging whether the person is really asking from the soul level or the level of the flesh? And, can't we be wrong?

How do we know when our giving is violating another's free will? Well, we *do* have a little bit of a clue in many ancient teachings about "asking." The stories say: "ask and you shall receive." But, if you study this idea, you find that what they really say is "ask and keep on asking, and it shall be given you; seek and keep on seeking, and you shall find; knock and keep on knocking, and the door will be opened to you."

There are a number of Jesus' parables that illustrate this point, particularly the "Friend at Midnight," found in the Gospel of Luke 11:5–13. The same teaching is standard procedure among the yogis of India and Tibet. A sufficient effort must be made by the supplicant before a response is made. In some cases, it takes *years* of asking! So, a good general rule to follow is that *true* asking is accompanied by sincere effort on the part of the one asking, and they must have done all that is in their power to achieve that for which they are asking.

And so we began to learn that sometimes, serving others, in the human sense of the word, is merely the serving of the STS part of the person, the third density aspect of the flesh, and is *not* true STO in the sense of achieving higher balance. If you give a child candy every time they ask for it, because you "love" them, or seek to "serve them" by meeting their every request, are you truly "serving" them? Even if their constant diet of candy leads to their ultimate physical death from diabetes? If you intercede for your child every time he misbehaves in life, and prevent his experience of the consequences, how will he grow up?

Another aspect that needs to be understood is this: In third density, we are *all* Serving Self in one way or another. We cannot, by our very nature of existence in the flesh that must consume to survive, be pure STO beings. That's the bottom line. And, it is in the understanding of this, the acceptance of it and then focusing on learning the lessons of this estate in which we find our being, becoming, at the very least, aware, and acting on that awareness to whatever extent possible, that we have the chance of becoming "STO candidates."

And that is accomplished by becoming aware of the soul dynamics which express the battle between the higher-level beings of both the STS and STO orientation, and then *choosing* which dynamic one wishes to align with, and *acting* on that choice. The Cassiopaeans say knowledge protects, and from their perspective, it is not knowledge until it is applied – before that, it is merely a collection of data and facts.

And so we come to the idea that if a person is viewing this present situation we are discussing from a strictly human view, without considering the soul dynamics involved, then it certainly would seem to be merely a "tempest in a teapot" or a "petty squabble" or even a "lack of harmony." From the human perspective, most of what occurs in interpersonal dynamical interactions is so judged. It is that very human judgment that we are being challenged to see through! It is in seeing the unseen that we become aware of higher levels of being; it is in ordinary human interactions that we experience the battles between the forces of STS and STO! And it is most definitely this factor that the Matrix Control System vigorously attempts to conceal!

About these times in which we live, and these very matters we are discussing, Jesus said, "Be careful that no one misleads you ... many false prophets will rise up and deceive and lead many into error ... for false Christs and false prophets will arise, and they will show great signs and wonders so as to deceive and lead astray, if possible, even the elect. See, I have warned you beforehand" (Matthew 24:4, 11, 24–25). "Do not think that I have come to bring peace upon the earth; I have not come to bring peace, but a sword. For I have come to part asunder a man from his father, and a daughter from her mother, and a newly married wife from her mother-in-law; and a man's foes will be they of his own household" (Matthew 10:34–36).

The apostle Paul wrote in Ephesians 6:11–12: "Put on God's whole armor, that you may be able successfully to stand up against all the strategies and the deceits of the devil. For we are not wrestling with flesh and blood, contending with physical opponents, but against the despotisms, against the powers, against the master spirits who are the world rulers of this present darkness, against the spirit forces of wickedness and the heavenly sphere." Hebrews 4:12: "For the word that God speaks is alive and full of power; it is sharper than any two-edged sword, penetrating to the dividing line of the breath of life and the spirit, and of joints and marrow, exposing and sifting and analyzing and judging the very thoughts and purposes of the heart."

Those of you who have read Fulcanelli and other alchemical works will immediately recognize the elements of the Great Work revealed in the above quotes from "Jesus" and "Paul."

Such passages in the Bible have generally been utilized by various Christian religions to justify murder and war. But this is exactly the problem we are dealing with here. They were read and interpreted in the STS version of physical swords and hate, giving themselves the authority to arbitrate who was saved and who was not. And of course, all of those who were "saved" and under the aegis of the church, must then subscribe only to the "peace and harmony" and "love and light" teachings: turn the other cheek, or "ignore it and it will go away," or "it's just a squabble." Choosing truth means choosing to take responsibility for one's self and one's own actions. The ordinary human interpretation that is generally put on such things is a mechanical reaction from the why-can't-we-all-just-make-nice-and-get-along school of thought. And that is precisely what the Matrix Control System promotes.

Since the church was promoting a religion of passivity, with themselves as the beneficiaries, it is not likely that they would have left the above sayings (and similar ones) in the Bible unless they were widely known, and people would have noticed their absence. What is certain is that they made no effort to have them be understood in their proper context of learning to be aware of the hyperdimensional realities, and to act on the clues of this higher truth.

When we understand that sword, in the terminology of Jesus, meant truth (or word of God), then it makes more sense. When we understand the hating of the father or mother in the context of refusing to be controlled or manipulated even by family members, because they may, indeed, be representatives of the forces of the STS alignment, it puts it in an entirely different context.

The Cassiopaean presentation of our reality as being a Control Matrix that keeps us in a prison, and uses us for food or energy, was naturally distressing. This was not a new idea to me, because, of course, I was entirely familiar with the teachings of Gurdjieff on the subject, but having such a clinical description of it, the pointing out of the mechanism and how it works through our very human interactions, was almost unbearable. I hadn't yet read Castaneda, so I didn't realize that, in his last book, he would reveal much the same thing, which he had not made entirely clear in his earlier work. I also had not read Fulcanelli and discerned his own teachings on the subject. Each of them, in their own time and context revealed this apparent truth in the best way they could, considering the dangers to which they were exposed by the very system they sought to reveal. But it was in the teachings of Jesus that I was most surprised to discover that he had most likely been saying the exact same things the Cassiopaeans were saying.

When we examine the New Testament, when we remove the obvious gloss of the Egyptian resurrection myth, we are left with the clearly gnostic teachings that the "God of this world" is an "evil magician!" When the reader is fully informed about the variations on these two themes, it is almost pathetically easy to read the New Testament and see what might be original to "Jesus," and what was added by the creators of Christianity as we know it. I will refer the reader to chapter five of my book *The Secret History of the World* for a more in depth discussion of the early Christians.

The medieval Cathars appear to have been carriers of part of the original ideas taught by the man we have come to know as Jesus. Curiously, their view on marriage seems to have been that if you bring a child into the world, you are perpetuating darkness because this world is ruled by beings that can invade the mind, and thereby further entrap the soul. This idea has recently been brought forward in a most interesting way. Dr. David Jacobs, professor of History at Temple University (Dr. Jacobs wrote his Ph.D. thesis on the history of the UFOs) wrote about his extensive research into the alien abduction phenomenon. Dr. Jacobs says that now, after all of these years of somewhat rigorous research that he knows what the aliens are here for and he is afraid. David Jacobs says that producing offspring is the primary objective behind the abduction phenomenon. And we might suspect that producing offspring that are more nutritious would be similar to our own breeding of cattle to be meatier or hybridizing of plants to be more productive per acre, is a good comparison. As above, so below, in more ways than we ever suspected.

We find here a strange and frightening connection between the alien abduction phenomenon and the teachings of the Cathars. And, if it is so that the Cathars were following a form of Christianity that was closer to what the real Jesus taught, then the entire mystery begins to make sense. Apparently what "Jesus" taught was the reality of hyperdimensional beings who can travel in time, invade and control the mind, and whose primary source of nourishment is human beings – either physically or mentally or emotionally. Don Juan said: "They took over because we are food for them, and they squeeze us mercilessly because we are their sustenance. Just as we rear chickens in chicken coops, the predators rear us in human coops. Therefore, their food is always available to them." And how did don Juan say they can do this and get away with it? Because they "gave us their mind."

What is this Predator's mind that don Juan talks about?

When you put the various pieces of the puzzle together, what you find is that the Predator's mind, the "hypnosis" that Gurdjieff talked about, the Matrix Control System interface with our bio-cosmic computers, our bodies, is our DNA which is controlled and restricted by the generation of specific brain chemicals via the control of our emotions. This is what determines the way our brains and nervous systems are set up, which includes certain early periods of imprinting (this subject will be discussed in a future volume of *The Wave*), which establishes our circuitry and thinking processes at an age and under conditions over which we have no control. And once those circuits are set up in a certain way, they can almost never be changed without a major melt-down, and they determine forever after how all incoming information is categorized. Indeed, we all have reptilian DNA. But we also have avian DNA. In fact, we are a veritable smorgasbord of DNA from all that exists around us. Nevertheless, something is going on that puts the reptilian DNA in control, and it is in that context that don Juan means that the "Predator gave us his mind."

Also, that these Control Programs, these chemicals of feeding, can be and *are* stimulated and perpetuated through our interactions with other human beings, most especially those closest to us, is a cold, hard fact of science.

About 50 percent of the consciousness of the All consists of the thought of *not* creating, *non*-being. In the emergence of this thought, necessitated by the definition of All, which includes *all*, including the thought of non-being, service-to-self becomes the pathway to "sleeping matter" with which the creative Spiritual half plays. This means that in the cycling of consciousness, some matter is "spiritualized" and some consciousness is "matterized."

Consciousnesses that follow the path of STS and do not choose to spiritualize, have chosen to be matterized – it's a choice, and it's free will, and does not require our forgiveness or our judgment that it is wrong or that it needs to be fixed in that other person. However, as we already have seen, that matterizing consciousness tends to be moving in the direction of the "black hole" thought center. And it is this Preda-tor's mind that teaches a form of "love" that is based on the STS principles of deception, manipulation, control, and subsumption to a single individual so as to fulfill the function of the black hole reflection of regeneration of primal matter. And that is our problem. When we dance with it, there is the danger of our being matterized also. We lose virtue in such interactions … and I use the term in its original sense.

Those folks who choose the path of matterizing of consciousness become less and less conscious of *what is* and more and more focused on their wishful thinking and warping of reality around their own ideas. And as we have learned from Jesus, Gurdjieff and the gnostic Sufis, Castaneda, and the Cassiopaeans, the rules of this world in which we live were set up and are controlled by this STS hierarchy and have been for a very long time. Each and every time the revelation of this Control System is attempted, the Matrix goes into overdrive to destroy it. And it is clear that this is the present situation.

In other words, we are not just talking about a petty dispute, we are talking about a battle of forces at other levels, manifesting – as *always* – in human dynamics.

Thus, at this crucial level of existence, where the choice must be made as to whether or not the path of matter or spirit is followed, clear boundaries must be set and, in actuality, those sayings of Jesus that were quoted above relate to this problem.

It seems to be our greatest task to determine from the clues we can glean from our reality exactly who is or is not of the alignment we choose, and to *act* upon that knowledge. It is up to us to decide who or what we dance with because there are many invitations to dance with the devil.

It is in this sense that Castaneda discussed what he called systematic harassment of the petty tyrant. Once the individual has a small clue, or set of clues, that they are dancing with the devil, they need to really know for certain if it is so, or if it is merely another deception of the Matrix. And so, systematic harassment is the key to discovery. If an individual is, truly, of the STS persuasion, this activity, described in some detail in the book *The Fire From Within*, outlines the strategy for both identifying and becoming free from the feeding of the STS hierarchy acting through human beings in our dynamical relationships.

Unfortunately, just as the church misrepresented – deliberately – Jesus' words about swords and hating one's family members, so do very few people today fully comprehend the principle of systematic harassment as a tool for becoming free of control. They know the words in the context of matterizing, but are not able to perceive the spirit – because it is not in them. But, we will come to that soon enough in this narrative.

It is in the details that we are writing about here that the reader will learn the essence of becoming aware of the theological drama that is enacted in our lives. And it is in this awareness, and acting on the awareness of the spirit, and not the common definition of words and deeds, that we establish a bond to the higher realms, and thereby become a candidate for graduation.

CHAPTER 37
CRITICAL CHANNELING

Working with a board-type instrument is both a very positive thing as well as problematical. In the early sessions, as I have noted, we were not taping, so reconstructing them was done based on scribbled notes and memory. Sometimes, those notes were being written in my lap with one hand, while the other hand was on the planchette! On better occasions, there was a sufficient number of people present that one of them could devote their attention to taking notes. But this produced its own problems as the reader will see.

With a board and a moving planchette that has not yet been fully tuned, it is often difficult to determine if a stop indicates a cessation of flow in the transmission or if it is designating a letter or sign on the board. I tried to faithfully call out all apparent letters, numbers, or stops, whatever they might appear to be, and often had to cancel the call because it became apparent that it was only a pause and not an indication of a letter or number. To add to this problem, if a third party was taking the notes, they would often misunderstand what was being called out, or transpose letters, numbers, or misplace decimals if they were given, and otherwise unintentionally contribute to the loss of fidelity of the material. It was only quite a bit later in the process, after many hundreds of pages had been received, that we began to work with ways to increase our accuracy in recording both via tape and handwritten notes. As with anything, practice improved performance.

There was another curious problem that the many people who have sat in on sessions have experienced first hand. I would warn them, but they really didn't have any idea of what I meant until they experienced it for themselves. Everybody has a tendency to want to anticipate a word or phrase – to complete it according to what they think it will be once they have heard the first couple of letters. Sometimes this is helpful and speeds up the taking of notes, but more often than not, the anticipated word ended up being incorrect, the person taking the notes would have to switch mental gears in mid-word, after having already written the wrong word, and would then entirely lose their place and fall behind, rushing madly to catch back up with the letters being called out. This would only compound the problem. Our notebooks are *full* of crossed out anticipated words and loss of context because the person taking the notes tried to think ahead of the Cs, made an incorrect assumption, and fell behind or rushed to catch up, leaving out entire words or letters. In some cases, a word was written in anticipation, and even though a different word was spelled out on the tape, the incorrect word was left because that is what the individual heard.

At the same time, we were very anxious to get the transcripts typed up just for the simple reason that we wanted to read them as soon as possible, and thus, many of these errors were included in the original typescript, along with standard typos, all of which require enormous work to weed out.

At the present moment, the Cassiopaean transcripts consist of 634 pages, set up in 3 columns in 10 point Ariel font. This equals 699,056 words, 122,719 lines, and 3,742,197 characters. And I can guarantee you that I typed nearly every word of it, with later help from Jan when she and Terry were finished with their project of sorting material by subject matter.

There are some people who look upon our attempts to go back and discern where these errors occurred, or even to try to discern the true intent of the earlier sessions, or obviously skewed sessions, based on later information that was clearer, more precise, and being transmitted at a point in time when the static and other difficulties were more fully understood and dealt with, as some sort of maneuver to misrepresent what the Cs have said. Nothing could be further from the truth. Aside from the fact that such critics certainly have made no years-long efforts to produce anything similar of their own, upon which foundation they might have the right to consider themselves some sort of expert.

As we have repeatedly said, it is our project, and we have the right to determine how we analyze the data, evaluate the results, retest that which does not stand up, and make those corrections and addenda that are deemed necessary based upon our long experience in translating. This is, in fact, the deeper issue concerned with channeling and doing the work necessary to penetrate to the deeper levels of understanding. I understood from the outset that what I was trying to do had seldom, if ever been done. And it must be clear from the very outset that the idea was mine, the theory behind how it worked was mine, the drive to do it was mine, and the driving force stimulating any participation from anyone else, was mine. And most of the time, I worked against enormous resistance, obstructions, and through hardships that would have stopped about anyone on the planet; and that is not an exaggeration.

Recently I came across the work of Professor Douglas Robinson at Ole Miss, a professor of English, and an expert in translation. I was surprised to discover that translation was a science, with experts and theory. But I was gratified to learn that some of the ideas I had about channeling related directly to translating, and that someone was considering these problems far more thoroughly and competently than I was. What was even more surprising was that Prof. Robinson had suggested outright that an analogy can be drawn between the function of a translator and the channel or medium. It is the work of the channel-as-translator to use every means available *to convey the fullest intention* of the original author to a new audience that might never hear it because they do not know the language. Prof. Robinson points out that, in the ordinary sense, translation is done merely across linguistic or cultural barriers, but when channeling is involved, it is done across temporal, consciousness, or even *hyperspatial* barriers.

In the present day of techno-marvels and instant gratification, the idea that anyone can just sit down and begin to channel Jesus, aliens or even the Host of Heaven seems to me to be very similar to the idea that translation can be done by machines with no human interface. This is a very subtle point and I know that it might seem that it is the reverse, but bear with me. In terms of a computer program that translates from one language to another, we see that the program attempts to execute an algorithm, or series of algorithms that consist of gathering intelligence, charting a course of action, giving a series of commands, and carrying them out. *The results are only as good as the algorithms.* And we see, from the literature, that the channeling phenomenon as it is widely practiced, *omits reason from the algorithm.* There is no feedback mechanism, and thus no possibility of accurate tuning. This means that it does not allow for an algorithm that can handle the fact that there may be competing forces inside the channel's head – or, in the case of a group, the competing forces of different individuals and intentions. Excluding reason and the possibility of competing forces is not very professional translating. It's like a person who attempts to translate a book on physics when his competence in the language only suffices to ensure that he can order a meal in a restaurant, get directions to the airport, and distinguish between the ladies' room and the men's room.

In the case of board channeling with a group, these factors become all important. The work of gathering material together that is related to a given subject, analyzing it, understanding that part of it was being translated at a stage when language competence was minimal, is the greatest part of the work we have had to do with the Cs material. And it is very likely for that precise reason, because we know the conditions under which we are working, and understand the task before us, that we *are* the ones receiving the material, and are charged with its conservation. If someone else were actually more capable of the task, it is a certainty that they would be receiving the material. We find, again and again, that the critics who have received no material, who have no context in which to evaluate it, and who most certainly have no experience and have not spent years studying the language, seem to be the most vocal in their criticisms. Their comprehension of the material and their understanding of the task at hand is equivalent to the mental capacity of a person who would accept a computer translation of French poetry into English and believe that it was entirely adequate.

The fact is, machine translation researchers haven't had a whole lot of success with programming a machine to produce a good translation without human assistance. In the same way, it is likely impossible to produce channeled material of any usable quality without full consideration for the competing forces as well as the application of *reason* in dealing with them. Without application of knowledge and direct, rapid feedback, the material that will be produced will be about equivalent to a machine translation of a technical text. And if the reader has read any of these kinds of things, they will surely know how funny some of them can be.

As Prof. Robinson points out, in the end, those machine translation systems that do work are, effectively, *cyborg translation systems*: they all require *a human-machine interface.*

The point I am trying to make is that by the use of prosthetics, we are in a position to *employ an algorithm that includes reason and feedback!* According to Prof. Robinson, translators must be trained; they must not only know the other language, they must know "how to regulate the *degree of fidelity* with the source text, how to tell *what degree and type of fidelity is appropriate in specific use contexts,* how to receive and deliver translations, how to find help with terminology, and so on." All of this suggests a long period of training and preparation, study, analysis, and correcting those translations done when competence was insufficient.

Adapting Prof. Robinson's ideas to the subject at hand, it seems that a translator-channel is someone who has studied these things, who knows these things, and who, most importantly, *governs their channeling-translating behavior in terms of this knowledge.* This knowledge is ideological. It is controlled by *cosmic ideological norms.* To know, via reason, *what those cosmic norms prescribe and act upon them is to submit the work to the intent of the original author.*

If you want to become a translator-channel, you must submit to the translator's role of learning the language in an expert way; you must submit to being directed by what the cosmic ideological norms inform you is the true spirit of the source author, and to channel that spirit into the target language, constantly utilizing research and reason in the rapid feedback loop.

For the period of training, of learning the cosmic language in an expert way, the use of a board-type instrument combined with long study and analysis of the material is essential. It is a prosthetic device that allows constant feedback between the algorithm of machine translation of the subconscious/unconscious, and the human interface of the conscious mind which must constantly employ reason for tuning. This is possible only with a board due to the fact that the channel is using both the conscious bypass for reception, while at the same time is able to maintain constant conscious integrity. By being, at all times, in full possession of their own mind and having the ability to observe, control and direct acceptance or rejection of any material or sensation at any time, reason is brought in as part of the algorithm.

Of course, as we have seen, the problem is compounded by the consideration of the effect of conflicting forces at higher levels and how they can and do utilize their human tools in our reality. This brings us back to the human dynamics themselves, the expressions of the battle between the forces of Darkness and Light.

At this point, we need to briefly visit one of the side issues between Frank and the previously mentioned individual, V** which demonstrates part of the problem. As I already mentioned, I had the idea that positive experiences in his interactions with people would reframe his view of the world, strengthen his will and potential toward serving others, and get him off the suicide rants that were draining me almost daily. With my struggles to recover from the accident consisting of therapy three days a week, five very active children, a house to run, all the transcribing and research on the subjects the Cs had covered, I was running out of energy and the demands made on me by Frank were becoming insupportable even if I refused to admit it.

For the most part, he seemed to be entirely oblivious to the effect he was having on me, but I continued to excuse it because he said all the right things about his aspirations for "doing good" or "helping others" or whatever. Besides, he had said he was a higher spiritual being so often, and had certainly demonstrated time and again that he was so different from most people, that I had come to think that it may very possibly be true. And that meant, of course, that it was doubly important for me to help such a being adjust to life in this reality where everything was so extremely difficult for Frank.

On New Year's Eve of 1994/95, we had our standard New Year gathering in spite of the fact that I was trying to recover from the accident. I couldn't disappoint all the people who had been planning on attending no matter how bad I felt, and the children all agreed to help with getting the house ready and managing the affair. There were about 20 people in attendance, and we decided to have a session so that the Cassiopaeans could "attend the celebration" as well. It was a festive occasion, and Frank, as the center of attention, was having a great time. I was very pleased to see it, since the past few months had been a truly dreadful series of his episodes.

Everybody took turns at the board, and at one point, it was Frank and two other men, and the planchette kept flying around faster than anyone could keep up with. Nothing that was especially "Cassiopaean" was said, and Frank became more and more expansive as the guests oohed and aaahed over his abilities as a channel. Everybody except V**. At one point she noted rather sarcastically that a comment the Cs made was strangely similar to a remark that Frank had made to her not too many days before. I jumped immediately to his defense because I most definitely did not want anything to take away from his experience of being positively received by others.

> January 1, 1995
>
> Q: (V) That kind of smacks of Frank's "When did you ever see this in Half-Moon Bay, V**?" (L) Where do you think Frank is getting it from? (V) Aren't we all being enlightened? (T) Is this …
>
> A: Frank is channel. Others are grooving rapidly.
>
> Q: (T) Others of us?
>
> A: Yes. Forming conduit.

Terry had been carefully examining the material in the previous weeks since he and Jan had become regular members of the group. He was certain, based on the passages I have already quoted, as well as on-the-scene observation, that Frank was not the channel in the sense that Frank claimed. In the above excerpt, the reader will also note that Terry started to ask a question about this, and was interrupted by the clear statement that "Frank is channel. Others are grooving rapidly."

The fact that this contradicted previous remarks that had been made under more controlled or balanced circumstances than a New Year's Eve party where half the people were well on the road to inebriation was not lost on me, but I was so desperate for Frank to have some feeling of self-esteem about something – anything – that I allowed it to pass without comment. For all I knew, it was true. It was most certainly true that the speed and ease of transmission was very good with Frank present.

We also notice in the above excerpt that V** had to be ridiculed for her lack of belief in Frank as the channel. Nevertheless, she had seen something, and it wouldn't go away.

The day following the New Year's Party, you would think that, after his triumphant display and reception, Frank would have been exultant. But not so. Obviously, V**'s remark had embarrassed him and he launched yet again into a painful diatribe about his sufferings and how unfair the world was, and how he was simply too good to continue to exist within it. I persuaded him that we ought to talk to the Cs about it. I simply couldn't understand, if Frank was the channel, as had been unequivocally declared the previous night, and if he was constantly channeling the Cassiopaeans, as he was now claiming, why he could not access the information that would assist him in dealing with all the issues that he dumped on me with such agonizing regularity.

January 2, 1995

Q: (L) Have you been listening to Frank talk about his woes and miseries?

A: Yes.

Q: (L) What do you have in response to his woes and miseries, since he is the primary channel, it seems to me that it ought to behoove you to give him some kind of a word on this matter …

A: Open.

Q: (L) What do you mean it is open? Is he going to …

A: Is under attack, as previously described.

Q: (L) Well, would it not behoove him to not respond negatively in thought, word or deed and to take care of business as best he can and trust that it will all work out? Because, by becoming all discombobulated, he is giving off negative energy …

A: His methods accomplish the task.

Q: (L) So, in other words, it is alright for him to get all emotionally wrought up and to spout off all these violently …

A: That repels attacking forces because they thrive upon blasé passivity.

Q: (L) Well, we are not talking about passivity here. Are you sure you are a Cassiopaean? It sounds to me like you are saying he ought to be giving off … I think we are pulling in Lizzies because of your negativity …

A: Incorrect, you have your "way" of repelling attack, and Frank has his.

Q: (L) Well I just don't see how a whole bunch of negative energy in thought and word can repel beings who thrive on negative energy. I mean, they should be just rolling in joy that they are making him so miserable that he has to carry on that way which then makes me miserable.

A: Not miserable when repelling.

Q: (L) Well, then, the problem here is that when he does this, everybody else he does it around, it makes them miserable, so, what's the deal here?

A: Subjective, your methods can cause perception of upset too.

Q: (L) Yes, I know this, but I am working on being totally unmoved by attack, isn't that the whole point here?

A: If it ain't broke, don't fix it.

Q: (L) So, I should continue, when I get upset or attacked, to just rave and rant and yell and scream and carry on?

A: You don't, you attack back, externally. Frank attacks back internally. The external manifestation is merely overflow and harmless if recognized correctly.

Q: (L) My understanding is that service-to-others involves complete lack of concern for self. Therefore, the objective is to have complete lack of concern for self, therefore one would be in such a state of lack of concern for self that when one feels oneself to be under attack, so to speak, or being baited or jabbed, one would simply utterly and entirely disregard this and continue on in a peaceful way. Now, am I misapprehending this in some way?

A: Not misapprehending, misinterpreting.

Q: (L) So, I misinterpret Frank's lack of regard for my feelings because he spouts off and upsets me … that's really a service-to-others activity and it is only my subjectivity that makes me get upset, therefore, I should eliminate my subjectivity as a service to him so that he can continue to spew off and therefore not upset me, is that what we are getting at here?

A: Off base.

Q: (L) Well, that is what you are saying.

A: That's what you want to believe we are saying, but we are not we are saying all should strive to be objective.

Q: (L) Well, I don't think it is being objective for every little sling and arrow of misfortune to throw somebody into a tailspin. I think part of the whole process is to learn how to go smoothly through all this stuff. And, what you are saying here is don't worry about going through stuff, just dump …

A: You are all learning, including Frank.

Q: (L) Well, let's drop it … I want to ask: the other night Frank read my palm and gave me several bits of information. When he reads palms does he direct channel this information?

A: Some.

Q: (L) Where does the other information come from when he is reading palms?

A: Varied.

I had a powerful sensation of unease about this session, though I couldn't put my finger on it. The reader will note that even though the Cs remarks seem to be merely a defense of Frank's extreme, virulent negativity, they were delivering a deep message about him! Nobody with any grasp of the principles of STS and STO could possibly construe the answers about Frank to be describing an STO individual. From the point of view of describing the STS reality, the answers were exactly correct! It was, indeed, a description of the STS mode of handling things, and the Cs were, indeed, communicating the message that this was Frank's path, though I was too dense to see it at the time.

I then shifted the line of questioning to Frank's palm-reading talents, since I was beginning to formulate the idea that he was merely downloading, and that his palm reading had nothing to do with reading palms, but with the fact that he could connect to the individual and more or less act as a speaker to their radio receiver, and that this was the correct interpretation of his function. In other words, his activity at the board was exactly similar to his activity when reading palms which was, in fact, his most amazing talent.

After the session above, and my sense of unease about it, I sat down with Frank and went over many of these clues about the channeling with him, pointing out the discrepancies in his own view, and what the Cassiopaeans had said, and how I thought the phenomenon actually operated. I also made it pretty clear that I was becoming exhausted carrying the load of my own life, and his inability to adjust to this reality as well. I urged him to make more positive efforts, to think about the many positive experiences he had had, and to try to help me by helping himself. I pointed out how much work I was doing, and how little he was doing, and that if we continued on this way, I would soon run out of gas and then nothing would get done. Terry and Jan added their input to the situation, and it seemed that, with their presence, Frank stabilized somewhat.

We knew that he had a problem with "dark forces" battling for control of his mind, and I pointed out that this was obvious evidence that he was a higher spiritual being otherwise they wouldn't be fighting so hard to take over his mind. With this encouragement, he appeared to renew his commitment to fighting them in a more productive way.

The sessions themselves reflected this temporary defeat of the dark forces, producing material of much greater clarity and validity.

January 11, 1995
Q: (S) Why are you choosing Laura and Frank to transmit this information?
A: Because balancing fields are correct. [...]
Q: (B) Is this channeling going to go beyond the primitive method of one letter at a time, or is it going to go into the method of writing or typing or direct channeling consciously or unconsciously?
A: Can now, less danger of corruption through this method.

In retrospect, the remark about balancing fields being correct is rather curious if balance means half STS and half STO. There is also the possibility that this remark reflected the presence of Terry as a member of the group, as well as the fact that I had taken steps against Frank's continued manipulations. I was also becoming far more vigilant about potential corruption, taking greater care with framing my questions, and just generally employing reason and perspicacity in the feed-back loop.

At this point, things took an interesting turn. Tom French entered the picture. As I have written elsewhere, the story goes like this:

> Back in 1995 I gave a little talk to the Clearwater, FL, MUFON group (was invited, did not solicit them) and, in the audience, was a *St. Pete Times* journalist, Thomas French, who was, apparently, quite taken with both myself and what I had to say. He was looking for something "new and different" to write about, and I just sort of "fit the bill." As he described it to me, he was "falling asleep" through all the speakers before me, and when I started to talk, he "woke up, for sure!" He approached me after the meeting and pretty much pleaded with me to give him an appointment to talk to me.
>
> I was *extremely* reluctant, as you might guess, knowing what kind of treatment folks who have the courage to ask questions generally get from the mass media. He promised fervently that I would have some considerable degree of input into what was published – that he would certainly go over everything with me prior to publication, and work with me on any objections and concerns. He further urged me to read some of his previous work to get a feel for how he approaches his subjects. I did, and he seemed to have a deft and sensitive touch.
>
> After some lengthy negotiations, I agreed to let him follow me around with the intent of my story being a single thread of a 7 part series that he thought might even ultimately be a book as well. There were 7 subjects: a homicide detective, a doctor/director of an AIDS clinic, a preschool for children from Cambodia and Laos who had been rescued out of the horrors of revolution and violence, a single mother raising children in a drug- and crime-infested slum, a fundamentalist preacher, myself, and Tom French, himself, who is the grandson of a Freudian psychoanalyst.
>
> Presented in this manner, as a single thread among many, I thought it would be a unique approach as a part of a whole work whose subject was more or less good and evil in different contexts.

Now, what I did *not* write about in the above passage was the effect that this event had on Frank and why there was the need for "lengthy negotiations" and why I was so reluctant, and just a whole host of interesting little things behind the scenes.

Terry and Jan, being the editors and publishers of a regional MUFON journal, had been instrumental in arranging for the little talk at MUFON. Terry was pretty excited about the Cs' take on the alien abduction issues because it had been an area in which he had invested a goodly amount of time in hard research and where he had access to materials through MUFON that were not ordinarily available to the average person. He knew that something was going on because the Cs seemed to know things that were not in the public domain. And so, even though it was a channeled source of information, he thought that the material itself stood on its own.

But, since MUFON is mostly a nuts and bolts organization, we discussed it and agreed that we would try to limit what was said to mostly nuts and bolts events, such as the sighting of the "Black Boomerangs," the work with abductees, and with just an aside mention of the Cassiopaean contact. We had discussed privately who ought to be the one to give the little talk and I was elected because we all were aware that Frank, even though he had a nice speaking voice, tended to be long-winded and to get sidetracked on irrelevant issues. There was also some concern that he would turn people off with their perception that his manner was "superior." We knew that he couldn't help acting this way, but we also knew that a lot of people weren't as willing as we were to accept Frank as he was.

Terry and Jan both gave a short talk each, and then introduced me. I only spoke briefly; pretty much giving a report of the UFO sighting I had experienced myself, and listing some of the things that had been revealed to me by abductees under hypnosis. It really wasn't much of a talk, for sure, and the only time I had ever spoken in public before was a speech contest in high school (which I won, though I don't, to this day, remember what I said), and I just took Jan's advice and found a person to the front of the audience to "speak to," and pretended I was talking to that person alone. Aside from some difficulty breathing, I survived.

When Jan introduced me to Tom French after the meeting, and he indicated he would like to interview me, I thought that it was the group he was interested in, and I was excited for the Cs. I said something about the fact that we were all together on Saturday nights, and that would be the best time, but he insisted that he would call me and make an appointment later in the week.

Frank was, as might be expected, utterly ecstatic that Tom was interested in writing about us. He just knew that this was the door to fame for the Cs, and him by virtue of association! He told me to be sure and call him the instant the interview was scheduled. He would take time off from work, if necessary to be there.

When Tom French finally called, he made it clear that it was me he wanted to talk to — alone. I was confused and felt just a little trapped because without Frank and Terry and Jan there, what was I going to say? I certainly couldn't make any kind of commitments for them without them being there. I even outright suggested that they ought to be present, but Tom was firm. He wanted to talk to me, and not the group. Reluctantly, I agreed.

When I told Frank that the journalist didn't want to talk to him — at least not yet — he became very sour and critical. He spent hours and hours giving me instructions on what I was supposed to say, how I was supposed to act, and the image I must convey to Mr. French in order to make him understand just how important the Cs (and Frank, by default) were to the world. Most of his comments were aimed at undermining my confidence. He described in great detail all of the people in my position who had been interviewed by journalists and that, without exception, they had been ridiculed and made to look like fools. He outlined exhaustively the detrimental effects this would have on me, my children, and life in general and specific. And of course, the problem was that I was just simply too naive to know how to talk to a journalist and not get taken in by conniving and trickery. All journalists were the scum of the earth, and I was going to get slimed.

By the time he was done, I was ready to call Tom French and cancel the whole thing. But, before I did, I wanted to discuss it with the Cs. In their responses, it is clear that Frank's attempts to undermine my confidence were skewing the flow. He was emoting to the max!

March 7, 1995

Q: (L) OK, there is a journalist coming here on Friday who wants to talk to me …

A: Be open in your mind regarding the flow of the situation. You have a tendency to forget that all do not share your ability to expand consciousness so easily.

Q: (L) So, you mean he is going to be a real skeptic and I am going to have to deal with validation issues?

A: That is not the point. The audience will be looking for flaws in the materialistic reference point, so you must be cautious, lest you be made to look irrational.

Q: (L) Well, then I guess I better not talk about exorcisms or anything like that.

A: Balance.

Q: (L) OK. I will try to stay balanced. I don't want to have to leave the country.

The fact is, no one but Frank has ever suggested that I discuss metaphysics and the paranormal in any kind of irrational way. No one but Frank has ever suggested that I forget the limitations of my audience. In fact, in retrospect, it is singularly curious that as long as he thought that he was going to be interviewed, he was extraordinarily enthusiastic about the idea. The instant he realized that it was me who was going to be interviewed, it became the Titanic of ideas: doomed to hit obstructions and sink unless I listened to Frank and managed to convince Tom of how the story ought to be told, which was, of course, as Frank wanted it to be told. After his hours and hours of indoctrination, Frank was finally assured that I would do as he wanted – that I would convince Tom of the importance of writing about the Cs group, and then, being reassured, he again became enthusiastic about the idea. I would be the public relations agent, and fame was only a hop, skip and a jump into the future!

At that first interview, Tom made it pretty clear that he was not particularly interested in the Cs material – or channeling in general, or Frank in specific – he was only interested in the fact that I was interested in investigating unusual things while still being a more or less ordinary wife and mother. I admit that I tried every way I could to turn his interest to the Cs, and by default, Frank. I failed. He had an idea, a plan, and I was part of it; but most definitely he was in charge of the execution and he was confident that he knew what he was doing, how to do it, and what his audience liked and expected. In the end, he turned out to be right. But that didn't stop me from trying regularly and repeatedly to shift the attention to the Cs, and the group, and Frank.

Aside from the shocking effect of this revelation – that anyone would be interested in my very mundane life of struggle and worrying about how to make ends meet – my very first thought was, "Oh, no! How am I going to tell Frank?!" How was I going to tell Frank that Tom French was not really interested in the channeling except insofar as it was one of the tools I was using to pursue my interests while raising a family? Frank was so sure that this was going to be the opening of the door to fame and glory! Frank was so excited that now, people would finally see that he was a force to contend with – a channel – and one that had attracted the attention of a real journalist at that! After all his excitement, after all of his hours of instruction to me about how to conduct myself in the interview so as to place him and the work in the proper light, how was I going to tell him that Tom French was more interested in an overweight, stressed-out, middle-aged housewife, than in a brilliant, highly developed spiritual being who was channeling sixth density light beings such as himself? Frank had placed so much confidence in me to be able to turn Tom French's attention toward him, and I had failed. It was going to be a negative experience, and I just couldn't figure out how to tell him without triggering another series of suicidal rants.

Fortunately, I didn't have to deal with the issue the next Saturday night, because that was the day we took the Cs out of the closet for a public test drive at another MUFON meeting. It wasn't until the following session, on March 18, that I broke the news.

The reader who is astute will notice that, up to this point in time, we had sessions very frequently – usually more than once a week, but certainly every week. However, we now encounter an anomaly: there is a break here – the next session in the file listing is April 15, almost an entire month later. And therein hangs a most interesting tale.

Because Terry and Jan had brought a guest with them to the March 18 session, they left early. Frank wanted to do what he usually did after a session which was to hold court and discourse for several hours about whatever came to mind. The rest of us had endured this a sufficient number of times that, after awhile, we had a sort of unspoken agreement to not ask a question, because asking Frank a question meant that he would talk for at least another hour. These sessions drained everyone, and no matter how many times anyone hinted that they were exhausted, Frank would brush their need for sleep or getting home before the sun rose aside with an insouciance that was completely incomprehensible. I wrote it off to his arrested emotional development, that children don't think about the needs of others, and since I had sort of "taken Frank to raise," I tolerated it as best I could.

The only person who seemed to be able to stand up to Frank in these late night marathons was Terry. Jan and I would sit there like zombies throughout these dialogues, voicing our quiet requests for sleep at periodic intervals, ignored by Frank, and with Terry refusing to leave until Frank had, so it was often a standoff. And for the reader who thinks that it should have been a simple matter of just asking Frank to go home, believe me – I did that over and over again. His answer to that was, "Just five more minutes! You can give me that! After all, I have listened to your problems before!" And the five minutes would turn into an hour. If I reminded him of the instant when the five minutes was up, he would suggest that I was not being a very giving person if I was not willing to listen to him when he needed someone to talk to. Never mind that it occurred over and over and over again. After a certain number of these experiences, a discussion about it came up with Terry and Jan and they agreed to not leave without helping me to launch Frank out of whatever chair he had taken possession of, and maneuver him to the door.

But, on the night of the incident we are approaching, Terry and Jan had to leave right away to take their guest home. That left Frank, S** and myself, and I knew I was in for a long night. After my explanation about Tom French's lack of interest in the Cs (which is still his position, as he stated just the other day), Frank's mood was brittle and artificially bright. He was behaving in a way I had never seen before, and it seemed almost bellicose. I was tired and in no mood to sit up until 4 a.m. discussing just anything and I suggested repeatedly that I was exhausted and would like to close up the house and go to bed. S** was exchanging light banter with him, also suggesting that the two of them should leave so I could go to bed, and to this day I can't remember exactly what was said, either by the two of them, or myself, other than that it was in the light banter mode of trying to convince Frank that it was time to say goodnight – a difficult task under any circumstances. I may have teasingly threatened to turn him into a pumpkin or something equally silly. The only thing I *do* remember is that what he said next was so completely out of context and out of proportion to anything that I had said, that I will never, ever forget it. He said: "Well how about this: I'm going to tell [your daughter] that [her father] isn't her real father!"

Doesn't sound like much, does it? But the point was that, of all the private things I had ever confided to Frank, this was the one thing that he knew would hurt and upset me the most. As a mother, I am a tigress, and it is a very dangerous thing for anyone to threaten to hurt one of my children, physically, mentally, emotionally, or any way.

As those who have read *Amazing Grace* know, my first child was adopted as a baby by my first husband after we married. She never knew any other father, and as far as the two of them were concerned, he was her father. Of course I realized that, at some time in her life, we would have to tell her the facts, but at that particular moment, it was *not* the time to do it and I had made the big mistake of confiding my concerns about it to Frank.

My daughter was, at that point, in the midst of a teen-age crisis. It wasn't unusual or overly serious in any sense, but she is a very sensitive child, and was particularly vulnerable.

Yes, I am familiar with all of the pro and con arguments about how to handle such issues with children, and in the end, I believe that it is up to the judgment of the parent who, after all, knows the child best. And in this case, I had already clearly expressed the opinion that it was not the time to tell her; that it would be a disaster because her own emotional development was at a delicate stage, and Frank knew all of this. He had gone to great lengths to inquire about what was bothering me, to pretend sympathy and interest in order to extract the details from me. And here, now, for the first time, I clearly saw *why* Frank spent so much time pretending interest in certain people. Indeed, with his rant about being so spiritually superior, his interest was projected like a benediction of approval, but the now obvious *true* motivation was revealed: he pretended interest, not because he was really interested in the person, but because it was his agenda to extract information that he could later use to control the person. He was nothing more or less than a common con-man, and I use the term in its original meaning as one who gains the confidence of another in order to get something from them.

With stunning clarity, I saw that the embezzlement episode wasn't just a glitch in his life, an act of desperation in a difficult situation. I saw that he had not, indeed, been taken advantage of by "Dane" or anyone. I saw him clearly and without blinders or wishful thinking. He was not a pitiful, damaged soul who needed to be helped; he was a predator. Nothing more, nothing less.

And he chose to try to control and hurt me for no reason other than the fact that he believed that I had turned Tom French off to the idea of writing about the group (mainly *him*), and focusing on me. And it was totally untrue. He was jealous, and felt that he was entitled to what he had not worked for, and if he couldn't have it, he would hurt me through my child.

I was almost speechless. I calmly told him that I could not believe that he was such a low-life as to do something so despicable as to hurt my daughter. He stuttered out a protest that he had only been joking, that it just jumped out of his mouth and he didn't mean it. And I replied that it was "out of the fullness of the heart that the mouth speaks." Obviously he would never have said such a thing if he had not already thought about it in those terms. And then I told him (rather calmly, which surprised me), that he had better go home and do it *now*, and spend some time thinking about what he had just said.

He left.

S** and I sat there, speechless, and just looked at each other. Neither of us could believe this revelation of Frank's viciousness and meanness. Finally, S** tried to smooth things over by saying that Frank obviously wasn't himself. He was under stress. He was overtired. It was late. All kinds of excuses.

But nothing could excuse the fact that, in his anger at me, justified or not, Frank had expressed the idea that he would willingly harm an innocent person I loved because he knew that this was the most direct and vicious way of hurting me. And nothing is more despicable than that. The only kinds of people I have ever heard of who consider such actions to be acceptable, are the lowest criminal types who are even despised by other criminals. Felons who hurt children are often placed in solitary confinement in prisons because the other prisoners will try to kill them. Hurting a child to hurt the parent is an unspeakable act of cowardice and depravity.

In the days following this event, I was rather startled at the view of Frank that was opened to my mind. All of the aspects of Frank that I had been ascribing to the possibility that he was, truly, a higher spiritual being who was just having a battle with dark forces – and the battle was explainable because he *was* a higher spiritual being – were now perceived as simply expressions of a very narrow, selfish, conniving, manipulative, and fundamentally mean character. I could see nothing positive in him at all and I marveled that this was so.

I was not as aware of the chemistry of the brain then as I am now, and I was very curious about this effect. How could it be that the mind can shift so instantaneously from one perspective to another? How completely the light had changed on my perception of him, and all of the things I had formerly excused, shoved under the rug, giving a positive spin, or taken his word for, now appeared to me in an altogether different context. Had I really been wearing the proverbial rose-colored glasses all that time? Or was what I was thinking *now* the distorted view?

In retrospect, I realize that I was, in fact, having a serious lesson in how our thinking is controlled or clarified by our chemistry. As I now know, when a shock is received, or a threat of danger, the mind becomes acutely clear and lucid and what *is* becomes evident to the extent that every nuance of reality is exposed to view with a clarity that is stunning. I suppose that this is a condition of evolutionary advantage; the creature that cannot see clearly when in danger does not survive. And I suspect that the same is true whatever the soul orientation. Any individual, when shocked, will suddenly see who is and is not "like them," and thus a danger to their existence.

Because I was so furious, I didn't trust myself to speak to Frank. But I certainly had plenty I wanted to say. I decided to write a letter to him, since I was still too distraught to speak to him. I still have the notes of the quotes I used in this rather lengthy missive wherein I itemized his every flaw in excruciating detail, even pointing out that I could see his disdain for normal human relations as supreme selfishness. I realize now that I was hoping that Frank would respond by saying, "Indeed, I agree with all you wrote, and I am truly all those things, it was just a momentary lapse, please accept my apology," and so forth. Among the quotes I included in my letter:

Master K'ung said: There are three sorts of friend that are profitable, and three sorts that are harmful. Friendship with the upright, with the true-to-death and with those who have knowledge is profitable. Friendship with the obsequious, friendship with those who are good at accommodating their principles, friendship with those who are clever at talk is harmful.

Confucius: People of superior refinement and of active disposition identify happiness with honour …

Aristotle: But to die to escape from poverty or love or anything painful is not the mark of a brave man, but rather of a coward; for it is softness to fly from what is troublesome, and such a man endures death not because it is noble, but because he is afraid.

Sir Thomas Malory: Ever will a coward show no mercy.

Confucius: To see what is right and not do it is cowardice.

Montaigne: Cowardice is the mother of cruelty.

From Emerson: Persons with character are as easy to spot as if they were a different color. Self-trust and the perception that virtue is enough is the essence of character. It is the natural tendency to defy falseness and wrong. It speaks the truth, and it is just, generous, hospitable, temperate, despises pettiness, and is scornful of being scorned. Character persists when the mood has passed in which the decision to act was made. Character displays undaunted boldness and a fortitude that does not wear down or out.

When the soul is not master of one's reactions to the world, then that soul is everyone's dupe. The person of character is not for sale. He does not ask to dine nicely and to sleep warm. He does not need plenty; he can lose with grace. Character is persistent. The person of character makes a choice based on honorable considerations and sticks with it and, no matter what, does not weakly try to reconcile itself with the world.

Most outstanding of all is the good humor and hilarity of the person of character. The great will not condescend to take anything seriously. The heroic soul is not common nor can the common be heroic. The person of character always does what he is afraid to do. Greatness ignores the opinions of others.

The person of character knows that he is born into a state of war and his own well-being requires that he should not go dancing for peace. Knowing this, he collects himself and neither defying nor dreading the thunder, he takes both his reputation and his own life in his hand, and, with perfect calm and politeness, dares the hangman and the mob by the absolute truth of his speech, and the correctness of his behavior. Toward all external evil, the person of character affirms his ability to cope single-handedly with an infinite army of enemies. To this military attitude of the soul we give the name of heroism.

Heroism is self-confidence which ignores the restraints of prudence, because of the natural energy and power of the belief that it can repair any harms it may suffer. The hero possesses a mind of such balance that nothing can shake his will. Pleasantly and merrily, he marches to the beat of his own drum no matter what disasters or dissolutions take place around him. He is in the world, but not of it. He does what he does because it is the thing to be done at the moment and he is present and capable of doing it. There is a quality in him that is negligent of expense, of health, of life, of danger, of hatred, of reproach, and knows that his will is higher and more excellent than all actual and all possible antagonists.

His victories are by demonstration of superiority. The most violent or conniving person learns that in this person there is resistance on which both impudence and terror are wasted. This resistance is faith in fact and right. The natural power of the heroic character is like light and heat, and all nature cooperates with it. The reason why we feel one man's presence, and not another's is as simple as gravity. Heroic characters are the conscience of the society to which they belong.

No change of circumstances can repair a defect of character. The heroic character does not accept the conventional opinions and practices. He is a nonconformist. Acquiescence to the establishment indicates lack of character which must see the house built before they can comprehend the plan.

There is a class of individuals which are endowed with character, heroism, insight and virtue. They are usually received with ill-will by the masses. No one can use common beliefs to understand these characters. They cannot be judged from glimpses. They need perspective, as a landscape. You cannot understand them by popular ethics nor by simple observation of their actions. It is said that He who confronts the gods knows heaven. This is the nature of the person of character.

In past times of violence, every person had many opportunities to prove his worth; therefore, every name that has emerged from the masses can teach us something of heroism, character, and manners. Personal force never goes out of fashion. Persons of valor become known and rise to their natural place. In any milieu, heroes and pirates are worth more than talkers and clerks.

The heroic character perpetuates good breeding. Good manners are a spontaneous fruit of the heroic character. The heroic character is a person of truth, master of his own actions, and expresses that mastery in his behavior, not in any manner dependent and servile either on persons, or opinions, or possessions.

People of character are an energetic class, full of courage and of attempts which intimidate their paler brethren. Being up to the demands of their very nature, they can out pray saints, out general veterans and outshine all courtesy. They are comfortable with pirates and scholars. Persons of character sit carelessly in their chairs and are too excellent to value any conditions.

Money is not essential to the aristocrat, which is the true class of those of heroic character. Society among aristocrats is mutually agreeable and stimulating. By swift consent, everything superfluous is dropped, everything graceful is renewed. Good manners are a formidable defense against the common people.

The manners of the aristocrat are aped by the commoners, but never understood.

Aristocrats never do as the common people do when following fashion. They understand that "fashion" is virtue gone to seed. Aristocrats are sowers, people of fashion are reapers.

Each person's position in life depends on some symmetry in his inner makeup. A natural aristocrat will find his way to those of his own kind. Those of good breeding and personal superiority readily find each other. A person should not go where he cannot carry his whole sphere with him. A defect in manners or character is usually a defect in perceptions. In addition to personal force and perception, an aristocrat is also good natured, generous and obliging.

Times of heroism are generally times of terror, but the day never dawns in which this element is without value. Latent inner power is what we call Character, a reserved force which acts directly by presence, and without means. It is conceived of as a certain indemonstrable force, a Familiar of Genius, by whose impulses the hero is guided, but whose counsels he cannot impart. Character is of a stellar and indiminishable greatness.

I lambasted him up one side and down the other. I told him in no uncertain terms that, if what I had seen on the night of March 18 was the *real* Frank, then he was not any of those things that we had discussed so many times. I wanted the real Frank to please stand up. Tell me one way or another. And if you say one thing with your words, and behave another way in your actions, how can I believe what you say?

What happens after such a "seeing" is that the chemistry of the "shock" begins to dissipate, and the normal chemistry resumes, and the ability to see and think with such clarity recedes. I began to doubt what I had seen. I began to doubt my perceptions. The rose-colored glasses of giving the benefit of the doubt went back on, and my mind began to work on the problem of how to reconcile. Because, after all, if I wasn't there to help Frank, to make a place in the world for him, who would do it?

As I said, at the time, I didn't know how subtly our thinking can be controlled by our chemistry. I only knew that I wanted to find out if I was making a big mistake; was I misjudging Frank because of emotion? Was I being unfair? Shouldn't I discuss it with others and discover if my thinking was askew? It was so shocking a thing to be going along one day thinking that a person was a higher spiritual being having trouble adjusting to the real world, and in a single instant, suddenly seeing everything completely differently.

Naturally, Terry and Jan and S** were anxious for Frank and me to reconcile. While they were very shocked by the turn of events, like all of us, they encouraged forgiveness and forgetting. And truthfully, I was beginning to believe that this was the proper course of action myself. After all, it is what we are raised to believe in. The "normal" chemicals began to take over, and being reminded by my friends of all the good times we had experienced, it was easy to begin to forget that moment of clarity.

But, meanwhile, just in case, we decided to continue the sessions without Frank even though we knew we would have to go through the tuning process again to some extent. These sessions were not included in the transcripts because they were, for the most part, about Frank (naturally). And even though they were not as smooth as we would have liked, having become very accustomed to fast paced dialogues with the Cs, it was clearly evident that the ability to make the same connection was present. And again, we were confirmed in our opinion that the Cs and Frank were not one and the same.

During the course of this experimental work, we received what I perceived to be a frightening message from the Cs telling us that there was grave danger around Frank and that agents of some kind were involved. It was difficult to determine from the responses if the danger came from Frank, or if the danger was to Frank. Because of the return of my rose-colored glasses, I decided that it was most likely that Frank was in danger, that he was being stalked and/or used by agents unknown, and that his very life was in peril.

Well, that was all it took to galvanize me! Even if I was mad at him, I had spent so much time and effort keeping him alive that I wasn't going to let anything happen to him now! I asked S** to deliver a message to him to call me since he no longer had a telephone where I could leave a message. I heard nothing for several days, and my concern mounted by the hour. I was practically frantic to make sure Frank was okay. Finally, I asked S** if she had actually even talked to Frank and after some very confusing exchanges, Frank arrived at my door and was welcomed like the Prodigal Son.

We all sat around and discussed the matter at some length, the end result being that Frank noted that S** had been the only one present at the time he acted strange. He then claimed that he had, indeed, sent a conciliatory message to me through S**. This was troubling, because I had never received it. Frank's conclusion was that there was some controlling influence there, and the implication was, of course, that S** was to blame for the problem!

I didn't see how it could be possible, but I wasn't in the mood to doubt Frank now! S** was such a simple soul, always helping out and with a truly generous and giving nature. But there it was. I had sent a message, she had not delivered it as I sent it (or so Frank claimed), and he had sent one back (he claimed), that had not been delivered to me, of that I was certain. I was really becoming confused and uncertain. Just what was going on here? And naturally, we decided to ask the Cs.

April 15, 1995 – Frank, Laura, Terry and Jan
Q: (T) Good evening. Who do we have with us tonight?
A: Good evening!
Q: (L) Who do we have with us tonight?
A: Shoura.
Q: (L) And where are you from?
A: Not from, but you know as Cassiopaea.
Q: (L) Alright. Long time, no see!
A: Oh yes!

Q: (L) Did we communicate with you when it was just S**, Terry and Jan and I?

A: Fragmented.

Q: (L) But it was you, fragmented?

A: Some.

Q: (T) Not all of it was you?

A: Like conflicting signals on radio.

Q: (T) Should we continue working with changing people on the board so that we can all work on the channel so that the channel will open for all of us?

A: Vague.

Q: (J) Do you recommend switching people on the board?

A: We recommend that which you feel is best.

Q: (L) Now, the pressing question: What has been happening to us?

A: We have warned repeatedly of attack!!

Q: (L) Was this ordeal we have just gone through an attack?

A: Of course.

Q: (L) What made us vulnerable?

A: Your work.

Q: (L) Was there anything having to do with any one of us contributing to this vulnerability?

A: Open.

Q: (J) Was anything that happened conscious with anyone?

A: Is this your inquiry?

Q: (J) Yes.

A: Then answer from within.

Q: (L) That doesn't help. A** said that, even as a kid, she could have straightened it out between us without even trying. (J) Well, maybe S** just wasn't cut out to be a mediator.

A: Okay.

Q: (J) What were the intentions of this attack?

A: S** is insecure. Have you not noticed?

Q: (J) Yeah. (T) But insecurity is not a problem as far as that goes.

A: Problems are according to circumstances.

Q: (L) Well, that still leaves us in a bit of a quandary …

A: Do you employ a maid to fly a passenger jet?

Q: (T) So, the wrong person was doing the wrong thing. It wasn't her fault.

A: But relaying of messages is sensitive issue.

Q: (J) There is a clue there. Who indicated that she should relay messages between you and Frank? (L) Nobody, I guess.

A: Was spur of moment "flow." Plot course carefully, so as not to run aground.

Q: (T) We are doing Chinese fortune cookies tonight. (L) Well, I still feel a little bit hurt that everything I said was simply not understood and that the things Frank said, had they been conveyed exactly as he said them, would have brought the problem to an immediate halt. What should have been repeated was not and what should not have been repeated was.

A: True. Attack is most purposeful! Watch all portholes.

Q: (L) So, in other words, S** may have been an instrument of attack unwittingly?

A: Close. [...]

Q: (L) The other night when we were working without Frank, we got some information that indicated that Frank was in danger via the government. Is that true or was that true?

A: Partly.

Q: (L) What is the source of this danger?

A: Source?

Q: (L) I mean like, the IRS, the FBI, the CIA, or what?

A: Not initialed as such.

Q: (L) Is this physical danger or just harassment danger?

A: Mind attack for purpose of self-destruction.

Q: (L) Is there anything that can be done to shield against this kind of attack?

A: Yes.

Q: (L) What can be done for shielding?

A: Knowledge input on a continuous basis.

Q: (L) And what form should this knowledge take? Does this mean channeled information, books, videos, what?

A: All and other.

Q: (L) A specific other?

A: Networking of information now, warning!!! All others will very soon experience great increase of same type of attack, two of you have had episodes in past from same source for similar reasons, but now your association puts you in different category!! Remember all channels and those of similar make-up are identified, tracked, and "dealt with."

Q: (T) Which two have experienced similar types of attack?

A: Up to you to identify for learning.

Q: (J) I'm pretty sure I'm one of them because I have been way down mentally and emotionally. (T) Is Jan one of the two? (J) I know I'm one.

A: Suicidal thoughts?

Q: (L) Have you had suicidal thoughts? (J) No. (T) Not me. (F) I have had them constantly. (T) Laura, did you? (L) I was pretty damn low. I wasn't contemplating suicide, I was just thinking how nice it would be if we could just turn out the lights and end the illusion. (T) OK, so we have identified the two, you and Frank. (L) So, in other words Jan, it is going to get worse. (F) Didn't they say two others? (L) I guess they are saying that a similar thing can happen. (T) If we don't work together on this, we are going to lose the whole thing. (J) OK, ask about the card reading Terry did tonight? (T) Was it accurate?

A: Close.

Q: (T) Was the reading referring to the same thing you are now referring to?

A: Close.

Q: (T) So, we have the knowledge and all we have to do to prevent the attacks from being nasty?

A: You do not have all the awareness you need! Not by any means!

Q: (J) Is one of the reasons why this whole thing between Frank and Laura happened to show us that we could establish, albeit a very weak and very jumbled, connection with the channel without Frank's presence? A sort of verification of the channel's integrity. Was that one of the byproducts of this, or one of the purposes of it?

A: Byproduct is good way of putting it. Remember, all there is is lessons.

Q: (L) The attack was more internal in terms of doubt, not only of the channel and the information, but of the very foundations of existence. I mean, the realization that we may not be at the top of the food chain was shattering. (T) That snowballed on its own once the initial conflict was established. (J) Maybe the way to look at it is: yes, we went through all this crap, and you and Frank went through all this anguish, but maybe one good thing that came out of it, and maybe wasn't intended, was the fact that yes, we were able to see that there is a channel separate and distinct from all of us. It is not dependent on any one of us to be present. Yes, we do need to have all of us together for optimum contact …

A: All are able to channel, but practice is required to establish the same extent of grooving but be aware of ramifications!

Q: (L) What ramifications?

A: Observe Frank.

Q: (T) We are observing you. (J) Yeah. And? (F) I think what they mean is, when you can channel as I can, because I channel almost continuously, this has a good side and a bad side. Now, the good side you know. The bad side you don't know. The bad side is very hard to live with. I cannot even describe the state of my mind. (L) I would like to have practical advice and guidance on what we can do to fend off or prevent psychic attack. We know that knowledge and awareness is important, but any words of wisdom or advance things that can be given would be appreciated.

A: Daily prayer helps. […]

Q: (L) Is there anything you wish to tell us before we shut down for the night?

A: Reread information given about attack warning and discuss amongst yourselves for strengthening of learning and knowledge base for purposes of protection and ultimately, survival!!

The fact that the responses relating to S** did not conform to Frank's opinion of the situation, suggests that the session was uncorrupted by his emotional input. Even if we were discussing human relations which was a subject so often skewed by his emotional prejudices, he was contrite and subdued. What went right over our heads, however, was the fact that the Cs gave us the answer right there and then! They said: "Attack is most purposeful! Watch all portholes. All others will very soon experience great increase of same type of attack, two of you have had episodes in past from same source for similar reasons, but now your association puts you in different category!! Remember all channels and those of similar make-up are identified, tracked, and "dealt with." All are able to channel, but practice is required to establish the same extent of grooving but be aware of ramifications! Observe Frank."

Frank had, of course, quickly identified himself as having had suicidal thoughts. But in retrospect, the context of episodes in the past, as it applied to myself, was a very long time in the past – many years previous. And in fact, as we later discussed this, it turned out that very much the same type of attack in the past had occurred to Terry. In point of fact, Frank's claims to be suicidal were, for the most part, if not entirely, a means of controlling others.

"Attack is most purposeful. Watch all portholes. Practice is required to establish the same extent of grooving. Be aware of ramifications. Observe Frank."

And we didn't even see it.

CHAPTER 38
THE FEMININE VAMPIRE

It's difficult to describe the state of my mind after the return of the "Prodigal Son." All of my do-gooder programs had been effectively activated in a powerful way in by the perception of physical and spiritual danger to Frank. My rescue program, mother program and save-the-lost-and-heal-the-wounded program – all were on hyperdrive with one object: Frank. His plight had been so eloquently described when he said: "I think what they mean is, when you can channel as I can, because I channel almost continuously, this has a good side and a bad side. Now, the good side you know. The bad side you don't know. The bad side is very hard to live with. I cannot even describe the state of my mind."

I realized at this point that what had been done to Frank as an infant and a young child, was that he had been programmed or engineered to be a channel, in the sense of being almost empty inside of anything that was essentially "him." It was almost as though he had been drilled through, like with a well digging machine, cored out and reconfigured. I began to understand that, in this sense, he was "the channel," in the same way a pipe that is sunk into the ground is a channel for the water or oil to be extracted. I also understood that it depended entirely upon who or what he was connected to, as to what was drawn through this pipeline.

In a sense, my perception of him was that he was as helpless in his dilemma as a newborn baby.

My idea at this point was rather simple: obviously, Frank very desperately needed to be connected to me in order for the Cassiopaeans to be the well from which the information he channeled was drawn, and it was crucial to his development and survival that this connection be sustained and further developed. I had the idea that, just as a pipe is made wet by what passes through it, the more he channeled the Cassiopaeans, the more saturated he would be with the STO messages, and the more likely it was that the healing of his own soul would take place.

His free will had been so violated, so decimated, that the only way to rebuild it, to restore it, to restore his soul, so to speak, was to channel with me as regularly and as often as possible. Just as a mother feeds a baby so he will grow, I committed to "feeding" Frank so that he would grow into the great soul that I was sure he was capable of becoming. Whether or not he had been a higher spiritual being who had become helpless by agreeing to be born, and who had afterward been attacked and manipulated by dark forces to create this condition, didn't really matter. I was committed anew to "helping" him. And I was committed with full heart and soul and mind.

Frank, on the other hand, having been exposed as being something other than the higher spiritual being that he had so repeatedly claimed – having acted in a way that belied such a claim and in fact, having given evidence of very dark self – had to reorganize himself as well.

Now, it would be rather easy for me to just write it all off as having been victimized by a conscious con-man, and that is always a possibility. But the fact seems to be that in human dynamics, each participant in a drama is, at some level, firmly convinced of the rightness of their view and perceptions. The test is, of course, how closely their views align with factual data and observable evidence.

As we have just seen, chemistry can play a huge role in our perceptions. What we view for all of our lives in a certain way, can be changed in an instant of soul-shock. And most often, after the shock wears off, the programmed or accepted view, gradually displaces the clarity and we go back to sleep in our illusions and narcissistic constructs of reality. This is why the Cassiopaeans repeatedly encourage us to dig, dig, dig for facts and evidence. Don't listen to opinions; check the facts.

We have explored, to some extent, the idea that the psychological make-up of an individual can be the real reason they do something or behave a certain way. But beyond that, what we were in the process of learning from the Cassiopaeans was that this so-called psychological dynamic was *merely the tool* with which battles between forces are fought in hyperdimensional realities. The significance of this point cannot be overemphasized, because until the individual fully grasps the idea that their very thoughts, emotions, and perceptions can be *augmented* by external forces – which can include brain chemical alteration – and how drastically this can change their perceptions, they have no possibility of developing the ability to truly act with free will.

As I have said before: any woman who has experienced PMS knows how changes in chemistry can so completely alter perception and thinking, that it is utterly terrifying to think that this might be the constant state in which we live: a bag of hormones and brain chemicals that keep us connected to the Matrix as food.

I had, of course, gone back to sleep in my narcissistic images of myself as the rescuer and do-gooder and healer of all wounds and mother to every lost child; images that had been inculcated into me from childhood, as the readers of *Amazing Grace* already know. That's the real reason of the psychological substrate. The theological reason was, of course, that, utilizing such programs as the tool, I was most definitely set up to be energetic food.

The question arises at this moment as to why I would refer to such seemingly positive self-images as narcissistic? Aren't people who rescue and do good and heal and function as mothers pursuing paths of service to others?

Indeed they are. The difference is: are they functioning from a position of truth or wishful thinking? And this is, ultimately, the difference that I was about to learn, even though it took me another year to get even the first phase of the lesson under my belt. It's an ongoing project!

All of us here in this reality are, to one extent or another, predators or prey. The husband who is energetically fed upon by his employer cannot refuse because he would lose his job. So, he goes home and feeds on his wife. The wife is afraid to refuse because the husband might leave and she is helpless and must care for her children. But she is deficient in energy and she must get it somewhere, so she manipulatively indulges her children so that they will give her praise and love, and thereby feeds on them. She may also abuse them psychologically to feed on their suffering. She doesn't see that she is feeding on them; she is behaving mechanically according to the programs of the Matrix which keep the whole machine complex running to constantly siphon energy off and pass it up the line to – well, to whom?

Our fourth density STS hyperdimensional Controllers of the Matrix, perhaps?

It is in this context that the theological reality becomes all important. Aside from just thinking or talking about the psychological substrate, the tools of the battle, we need to see the clear distinction between the forces. As above, so below.

In an STS hierarchy, as described above, there is an ultimate feeder, or recipient of the energy that is gathered and passed along through the interstitial spaces of our reality – the threads of consciousness that connect us to our family, friends and associates. In the case of the STS reality, this is a Thought Center of Non-being which is where consciousness goes that has been ultimately matterized. Because, consciousness that is being drawn to the idea of non-being cannot actually become nothing, or die, but it can go to sleep for a very, very,

very long time. In short, consciousness that is subsumed into the STS hierarchy ultimately becomes primal matter.

In some philosophies, this truth that a certain pathway will lead to matterization is openly taught – at least in the inner circles. To achieve this "oneness of eternal sleep" is the primary objective. Exercises and tasks of almost superhuman darkness are undertaken in order to be granted this eternal rest. The problem, however, as the higher teachers of this pathway very well know, is that in order for this oneness to be achieved, *as they desire it*, all else in the cosmos must be brought to a halt – the eternal expansion and cycling of creation must be ended – God must be killed, or at least effectively put back to sleep.

What this means is that the idea of "being" must be destroyed. Like a snake that attempts to swallow its tail in order to end its own existence, the STS pathway seeks to swallow all of creation into the sleep of non-being.

When we wake up and realize that we feed on those below us, and are in turn fed upon by those "above us," we naturally want to ask what is the alternative? And the Cassiopaeans have presented an alternative: STO, something that is hardly conceivable in our reality, a circle of symbiotic giving and support where no violation of free will occurs, and where the energy commutates and expands for All, instead of disappearing along an ever-narrowing, one-way street to the top of an STS pyramid.

It is in the gaining of knowledge about how our archetypal images are twisted so that we are manipulated to feed the STS pyramidal hierarchy that we have the chance to become free of it and join the STO circle of commutating, shared energy and joyful creation.

In other words, when we are locked in a dynamic that is fundamentally STS, there is no equal sharing of energy. One or the other participants is the predator and one or the other is the energy food, and the energy of both is being drawn off to some higher being who is manipulating the situation for this very purpose. And it is not always easy to discern this unless we are fully aware of the theological reality and learn to read the very small signs. The Matrix is cleverly designed to conceal itself, but as all mechanical systems, it is not perfect. With careful attention and awareness, the man behind the curtain can be seen.

What this means is that when my images of positive orientation were activated, they were activated narcissistically so that I thought I was doing all those good things for another soul that was truly asking. But the truth was, that other soul was not asking; I was being manipulated to give my energy of helping, mothering, healing, doing good, to the STS dynamic which ultimately seeks to kill all of those things by draining the energy of those who are configured that way. And I was being tricked to do it by the activation of my illusions about how these things operate rather than keeping my eyes open to the truth that I had already seen.

Frank had also experienced a shock, I am sure. I can only speculate that he may have perceived the darkness within which was revealed by his behavior. There is altogether the possibility that he was so locked in his narcissistic image of himself as a higher spiritual being who was simply too good for this earth that even this revealing event could not penetrate that shell of illusion. What is certain is that he was at least aware that the members of the group, and probably society at large (at least those members of society who ascribe to truth, honor, courage, decency), would view his little lapse as a clue to a hidden persona of darkness. There had been a serious crack in the image he presented of himself, and it had almost resulted in the complete loss of his ostensible quarry.

What was his quarry? What did Frank want?

Well, the evidence of the many clues scattered throughout the text, as well as the observations of the other participants and witnesses, was that his psychological make-up drove him to seek fame and fortune – with a strange twist: he felt he was entitled to it, that he deserved it and ought to have it, but had no intention of doing any work for it. He was, essentially, a coat-tail rider. But the Cs have said that there was another reason: "He was programmed for the specific purpose of "downloading" from you secrets coded into you before birth of your present body. He failed because you were incorruptible. He is now charged with the mission, in concert with Vincent Bridges, of destroying your ability to accomplish your mission."

That, then, becomes the theological reason behind the real reason.

But, as we have noted, there was another dynamic at work that the Cs have identified:

Q: Was that the reason that you encouraged Terry and Jan to be present? To counterbalance Frank's negative energy?
A: Yes. Frank would have killed you with his STS draining rather soon otherwise.

And here is where we arrive at the crux of the matter: Because of my lack of awareness of the theological reality, I had fallen victim to what is called in Jungian psychology the "feminine vampire." This designation is not really gender oriented in the sense that a woman preys on a man. The archetype is that of the person of power or force or energy who is victimized or fed upon by an individual who seems to be completely disempowered. Allow me to quote from Jungian psychologist, Barbara E. Hort's book *Unholy Hungers*, keeping in mind that the dynamic she describes is the real reason, and behind it is the theological reason.

She tells the story in terms of a knight rescuing a damsel in distress, but more often than not, in our world, the opposite is true: women rescue men due to their mother instinct which is precisely the same dance.

It may seem incomprehensible that a powerful person could be victimized by a psychic vampire who seems to be completely disempowered. Yet there are few lures more potent for a powerful champion than rescuing a grateful waif in distress. How exciting it is to save someone from the jaws of tragedy, particularly if the recipient is adoring and appreciative! You, the noble champion, journey alone down the desolate nighttime road, when there appears by the wayside a sweet little mist who is weeping in loneliness and alluring despair. Ah, you think, here is a perfect chance for me to put my sword to its proper use! Here is someone to save! And how charmingly pathetic she is! Perhaps there will be some love for me at the end of the heroic rescue!

Your sword flashes up, and you dash to her aid – slaying all foes, fixing all woes, and paying each bill that she hands you. You parry and thrust, parry and thrust, cutting off hundreds of dragon heads, past the point of exhaustion, for two adoring eyes are watching and their owner must not be let down. Onward you march, beyond fatigue, beyond all means, until your every resource is spent. But still you fight on, despite your depletion, to rescue the sweet, helpless mist, for how could you let down the poor little thing? Whatever would become of the helpless mist without you and your sword to defend her against the cruel world?

The dance between an empowered masculine victim and the feminine vampire who hides under the veil of vulnerability may be the most insidious vampiric duet of them all. So many of us have gone to our physical, financial and spiritual graves never realizing that we have been duped, never relenting in the deployment of our swords, never stanching the flow of our blood, and all for the sake of a pitiable feminine vampire? How can we be so powerful and yet so blind?

But really, our gullibility is no mystery. When we embark on the path of the Champion, when we don the armor of empowerment, we expect our vampires also to be draped in the cloak of power. We never suspect that a vampire might veil itself in the guise of weakness and vulnerability. What's more, when the Champion Archetype is active in our psyche, we strive to serve those less fortunate than ourselves, so when we come upon the sweet mist by the side of the road, is it any wonder that we bleed on its behalf? What a cruel ruse this is, for in fact the mist is a vampire who will feed on us by exploiting the very nobility of which our Championhood is based.

...

In the beginning, the man was happy to rescue the pathetic damsel, who, coincidentally, had just one or two more little traumas that she hoped he would be kind enough to rectify. Thus began a long series of heroic rescues, each one of which was appreciated by the woman only long enough to resuscitate her hero before she needed his next valorous deed. ...

She is Spider – the incarnation of the Terrible Mother as a devouring weaver of fate and bringer of inevitable death. ...

... In *A Dictionary of Symbols*, J.E. Cirlot interprets the image of the spider at the center of her web to represent the Gnostic notion that "evil is not only at the periphery of the Wheel of Transformation but in its very centre – that is, in its Origin." The image of the Great Spider on her web is symbolically synonymous with another ancient image of the negative Feminine, one that is found at the center of many web-like labyrinths. The image is that of the Gorgon Medusa ...

Why is it so difficult for us, even when we are empowered, to kill the feminine vampire? One reason may be that the ethic of nobility asserts that the strong should protect the weak. ...

In all cases, the empowered victim perceives that life has bestowed on him or her some opportunities that the feminine vampire never had. For the pitiful vampire's sake, the victim strives to excel in ways that are not personally meaningful, because he is made to feel that turning aside to more meaningful pursuits is a deadly abandonment of the poor, disadvantaged vampire. Clearly, this vampiric duet is insidious and pervasive which is why a model for its deactivation is very important to our psychic health. ...

Because the archetype of Medusa, like that of the feminine vampire, is as complicated as it is dangerous ... the creature that best embodies the inner nature of the feminine vampire is the needle-fanged, cold-blooded, venom-spewing serpent. ...

... The Medusan vampire slithers up in silent hunger behind her unwary prey, freezing her target with her stare (pitifulness and wiles of the damsel in distress), and then sinks her fangs into the petrified victim, spitting out the venom of her embittered rage, and then leaves the lifeless body behind as she gathers her sinuous coils of deceptive lethargy and sniffs the air for the scent of hot blood, waiting for the next victim who will prolong her life ... The Medusan vampire relies on snakelike subtlety to capture her prey. ...

[The true hero] must be able to sense the Medusan viper who lurks under the veil of imploring vulnerability ... note the term "sense" rather than "see." The myth tells us that it is extremely dangerous to look directly on the truth of this entity, for the vision will immobilize and destroy us.

This means that the key to our approach to the Medusan vampire is to do it reflectively. If we have spent time in the company of someone who is a feminine vampire, we already have some Medusan behavior on which to reflect. By engaging in reflective exercises, we can safely bring the light of our consciousness to bear on the monster we wish to deactivate, without looking her full in the face and risking petrification [by the pitifulness of her projected situation]. ... Have we been pulled by our compassion to give more to this pathetic being, who seemed to be suffering unfairly? [Have we felt guilt at the thought of abandoning her when the problems seemed too great? Has she induced guilt by claiming how worthless she is, so that you, fair champion, can assure her that she is not, indeed, worthless, but merely disadvantaged or in need of rescue?] If the answer to any of these questions is yes, then we are probably dealing with a feminine cvampire [a Medusa who is slowly turning you to stone].

If [this individual] evokes your compassion, remember that Medusa's story was pathetic, too, but that did not lessen her dangerousness. Whenever we feel the itch of the pity for a feminine vampire, we would be wise to recall the image of Perseus as he backed slowly toward the Gorgon ... we must hold the image of Perseus close to our hearts and remember that if he had dropped his guard, let his attention waver for a moment, or glanced backward out of guilt or compassion, then we would have been transformed into yet another of Medusa's yard ornaments.

An awareness of the feminine vampire's nature is critical to her deactivation, but it is not sufficient. In the stories of Perseus and Oedipus, the call of greater deeds and a higher good kept the champion from yielding to the ruses of the feminine vampire. (Hort 1996, 113–114, 134, 136–137, 143–144, 146–147)

Where Frank was concerned, I admitted him into my life out of courtesy and compassion. He was so desperately lonely and "different" and in need of help, companionship, acceptance and true self-esteem. He used all the words at his command to produce the belief in me that he was an empathic soul, striving for resonance with other souls. He was very interested in me and my life, and I perceived this as part of his seeking of resonance.

At first, all of his questions about me and my experiences seemed to be sincere interest, and I answered them and indulged his need for information. It is also true that, at the beginning I experienced surges of uneasy suspicion. Very often, his questions were entirely too personal, too probing, too hungry for information that was private. But I was trying to be polite, to accommodate him in a courteous way, and I discarded these suspicions.

Frank made detailed inquiries about my thoughts, my health, my life, my state of affairs. It was as if he were conducting an in-depth interview with an important person. No one in my experience had ever been really interested in what I thought about anything, nor had they made me feel that anything about my life was important, and so I answered the questions about my thoughts, and soon found myself answering all the other questions as well.

The skill of guileless cross-examination is the chief tool of the feminine vampire, because information is power; when you have information about people, you have a means of exploiting them, which is, after all, the primary objective of the vampire.

I didn't realize that my answers were like money in the bank to Frank – hoarded, to be used later for manipulation.

At the point of the almost breakup, I had come to the realization that Frank's interviews were followed by his demand that I listen to his litany of woes and the favor of my time to the point of utter exhaustion. Since he had been so concerned about *my* well-being, asking such careful and detailed questions, how could I be so discourteous as to refuse to listen and comply with his need for time and energy?

The end result was, of course, that I was hit with a double whammy. Not only did I feed Frank with my energy, I also gave him information that he could use to exploit and control me.

Of course, it is true that a vampire does not become a vampire without having been bitten and infected. The Jungian psychologists would like to think that the infection is passed on from parent to child, that this condition results from early childhood victimization by the parents. It certainly seems to be true that parental programming of a child is part of the means by which the infection is spread, but it also seems that there is something far more insidious at work here: hyperdimensional beings, literally the archetype of the ancient vampire.

Frank's conscious memories of his abductions and torment at the hands of aliens as well as the fact that he did not fight back were all clues. But there were many more clues that developed over the next couple of years.

There is, of course, in any such person, some sort of vestigial soul. It may be a soul that is growing and which will, at some point in the future – perhaps another lifetime – begin the process of spiritualizaton of its matter environment. On the other hand, it may be a soul that is diminishing, or in the process of matterization, compaction, or subsumation of consciousness to the STS hierarchy. It's really hard to tell. My guess – and it's only a guess – is that at this point in history, the types of souls that will be incarnated are not so much the immature kind as they are those that are potentially at the point where this all-important choice is being made – to choose the wishful-thinking, STS path of ultimate matter, or to choose the STO path of spiritualizing matter.

The STS choice is, essentially, the default choice of this density. And, by being the choice that is presented as natural by the Controllers of the Matrix, it is generally the easiest. It is the path of least resistance, most especially in terms of giving ourselves up to our emotions or intelligence of the heart, as it is being promoted nowadays. It is also, very often, the obvious choice, or the sensible choice or even the logical choice. This "obviousness" and "sensibleness" and "logicalness" are, of course, based on the rules of the Matrix that dominate our reality.

The STO choices, on the other hand, are far more difficult to see, and thus, more challenging to make and follow. We have already looked at a couple of examples of this in our little exploration of what

Christianity may or may not have originally taught, as well as the fact that many individuals lack the ability to comprehend the deeper meaning of systematic harassment as Castaneda explicated it. Thus it seems that one of the symptoms of those who consistently make STS choices, is that they develop a kind of semantic aphasia. They may be able to grasp a certain, limited, literal meaning of a word or a concept, but they are simply unable to think any higher than that. I have observed certain people who certainly had the intellectual capacity to do so, but they didn't have the drive. This is the result of the fact that as the STS mind is fed, the person becomes less and less able to grasp the deeper meanings of things, the hidden reality that is exemplified by the alchemist Fulcanelli in his exposition on cabala, or the "language of the birds." At the same time, those who are making the STO choices become more and more able to reach into these higher realms of pure thought.

What seems apparent to me is that this is not just a single choice, it is a daily choice, a moment-by-moment choice and that once an individual wins just one little battle against the mechanical nature of the STS reality and default choices, and moves even momentarily into that STO realm, it strengthens the ability, however incrementally, to make the next STO choice that is presented. And, for the most part, these choices have to do not only with seeing what *is*, but in choosing how to respond to it: creatively or destructively, with truth or wishful thinking and narcissistic personal opinions.

Thus it is that a person who chooses to understand Castaneda's term systematic harassment in a materialistic way, as opposed to the deeper perception of the theological reality behind it and the example he gave, has effectively made the choice for the default mode of STS understanding or what is "obvious, sensible and logical," based on the rules of the Matrix-reality language structure. Such choices of perception, made over and over again, result in a sort of hardening of the categories, or being matterized. The point is that as long as there is life, there is hope, and even if the surface appearance of the events would suggest that I had been victimized by a conscious psychopath in my interactions with Frank, I tend to think that we ought to give a certain amount of the benefit of the doubt, within limitations, to anyone we encounter. There may, indeed, have been some part of him that was truly asking, and I was giving to that part as well as the part that was manipulating.

In a very real sense, the psychic vampire, or the STS feeding machine, is very well described in terms of criminal psychology. The chief traits of the criminal personality are weakness, immaturity, and self-delusion mixed with a strong desire to deceive other people. The weakness is an important factor because it seems to be the root of the inability to "think higher" beyond the Matrix reality. Such thinking requires great effort of a certain kind, and many individuals simply do not want to do it. It's too much like work. Even people who can do enormous physical work, do not seem to have the ability to understand what work is truly valuable. They may spend days, weeks, months, looking up endless words and permutations in dictionaries, but the ability to push into the deeper reality, that comes from a certain strength of the soul, is simply not in them.

Such individuals have amazing skills at self-justification and rationalization for what they do. They are also masters at appealing to the sympathies and emotional triggers of other people. They also, most definitely, have a well-developed ability to shut off what they do not want to see or admit to. They are generally cowards, but with a twist: their greatest fear is that others will see them as weak, so they create a persona of bombastic strength and power that simply does not exist.

Criminals are also hypersensitive to what is said to *them*, and will become angry all out of proportion when they perceive that they are being put down, but are also completely insensitive to the feelings of others to whom they may address great cruelty. Of course, when someone can be used by them, they take great pains to pretend sympathy.

In the words of one criminologist, the criminal mind suffers from a series of faulty blocking mechanisms. In other words, in the terms of the Cs and the STS reality: wishful thinking. They are blind and deaf to anything that contradicts their view of themselves and the world. They literally *see* things differently.

Now, it is obvious that we are all in this condition to one extent or another. And it is this very wishful thinking that keeps us in the Matrix. As strange as it may seem, studying the criminal mind has the same effect on us that the ghosts of Christmas had on Ebenezer Scrooge – it makes us more aware of the reality we ignore.

Vampires that are not fully formed may desperately try to cover up the growing vampire seed within by doing good deeds. This isn't done consciously, mind you. At this point, the narcissistic view of the self is so powerful that looking in the mirror and seeing the true emptiness of the soul is impossible. Such an event would result in the total meltdown of the entire personality structure, and the subconscious defense mechanisms won't allow that.

Rather than facing and dealing with the real issues, acknowledgment of the darkness within, acknowledging mistakes and lies and manipulations of others, being truly sorry, and truly asking for help such people desperately seek to eradicate what they subconsciously suspect about themselves in any way they can. The chief method is by doing good deeds through projecting the darkness in their own soul onto someone else.

Of course, that is just the psychological real reason, and not the theological reason. The archetypal forces will use this mode of behavior – will stimulate such thinking – in order to accomplish their own goals. The individual will be persuaded in their own mind that, by following a certain course of action, they can – little by little – eradicate the dreaded shadow that haunts their mind. And of course, the darkness is "out there." But this then becomes the tool of the head vampire at the top of the food pyramid, to both enhance feeding potentials, as well as to destroy any threat to the status quo.

Vampire lore tells us that holding up a mirror to a literal vampire is a dangerous task. In psychological terms, holding up a mirror to a person in whom the vampire archetype is active is also problematical at best. It is at such a moment that the individual can make one of three choices: denial, growth, or despair. In criminal psychology terms, they have the choice to continue their criminal behavior with the strong likelihood of ultimate destruction; to radically change; or just commit suicide and get it over with. The individual who chooses to not change and grow, to not acknowledge the emptiness of the soul, effectively chooses to become a full vampire. Such a person has no capacity for true human compassion, but they have endless forms that they may take on to pursue the goal of obliterating the threat to their survival as a vampire.

Such a person, faced with such a revelation about themselves are most often completely unable to give up their illusory perfection and celebrity status. They cannot disentangle themselves from the programmed illusion and delusion of the narcissistic self-created in a fake bio and credentials. They *must* believe that they are the fake self, because in the deepest recesses of their subconscious minds, they feel that they are nothing at all. And in the theological reality, that is what they are making true. By being controlled by this psychological program, they utilize their energy to manifest that archetype.

The Matrix supports such behavior. The illusion, the wishful-thinking reality in which such a person lives, consists of a firm conviction that they are, indeed, of the light – a higher spiritual being – and that they must destroy that which has mirrored back to them the horrible truth of their lies and imperfection – a truth that is backed up by evidence and witnesses. They galvanize all their energy to strike and destroy; to banish the darkness, so that they can live in the everlasting light that is promised them for their "service."

The pernicious vampire who has had a glimpse of himself and his emptiness, and has projected this emptiness onto another, knows instinctively that he needs to utilize his "other forms" to survive and ultimately destroy the threat to his being. These other forms can consist in what may seem, initially, to be changes in behavior. This manifests, again, in the psychological belief of the individual that by doing good deeds he can vanquish the vampire "out there." He will do favors for others, believing that this is a good, compensatory deed that will earn him salvation. But in his heart of hearts, he knows that the person he is doing the favor for is someone he has wronged. In fact, he believes that by doing something for someone he has wronged without confessing that wrong, or even acknowledging it, that it is all that much more a good deed.

The pernicious vampire will give time and energy to a group or a cause that he really holds in contempt. He will do things for people he secretly disdains, and he will do it all the more sweetly if he thinks it will strengthen his chances for survival. Such a vampire who has gone deeper under cover will patronize people who he is really, secretly, exploiting. And he will most certainly proclaim that he is a follower of beliefs that he secretly desecrates, and his actions will most ultimately demonstrate that he is not truly an advocate of such ideas in his soul.

In some cases, when the darkness in a single person becomes too great to bear, he or she will project it onto a whole group of human beings. They will then go and seek out a group of neighbors and friends with similar darkness that they want to unload, and they form an agreement about what group they want to project their multiplied lawlessness and iniquity onto. In this way, they don't have to hide their darkness because they can join together in a public orgy of projection. They believe that if they can destroy whomever they have collectively projected their darkness onto, that they will be collectively purged and will all be fresh and new and perfect together. The only problem is: in such a dynamic, the individual and collective darkness only grows in this miasma of vampiric revelry, and as it grows, they must project more and more to cleanse themselves. What they do not realize is that they are, step by incremental step, killing their own souls. Because by feeding the vampire inside the self, that vampire archetype grows stronger and stronger, and this is a manifestation of the eating of the soul of the infected victim by the hyperdimensional vampires, and thus represents the theological reality.

Of course, as noted already, this is an incremental process.

When a con-artist deliberately deceives someone, he keeps his human feelings separate – compartmentalized. He may be, essentially, two people: a human being to his wife and family and friends, and a criminal to his victims. All psychological studies show that if he continues on such a path long enough, he ultimately becomes less and less human with everyone. Like Dr. Jekyll and Mr. Hyde, each time the STS behavior or wishful thinking is indulged, each time it is not resisted and overcome, it becomes stronger and stronger. And its ultimate objective is to destroy its victim who, in the throes of his own destruction, reaches out to try to save himself by destroying others.

In the most mundane sense, this manifests in our real world as people who have no manners, who have no class, who have no nobility of soul and who are incapable of recognizing it, nor do they understand that they don't have it. They then attempt to compensate for their lack by declaring it to be of no value, therefore not having it does not diminish their value within the structure of their wishful thinking. In addition, because it is something not possessed, they must attack it and those who possess it.

Getting back to the matter at hand, Frank tried to obliterate the darkness within by a course of good deeds, or more precisely, by curtailing some of his previously draining activities, including his regular rants about committing suicide. He became more helpful and generous in his words, to me at least. He never did – nor could he, it seems – actually overcome his lethargy long enough to do anything physical for any of the group.

But what is most important at this point is the fact that Frank had most definitely begun the process of projection. And the objects of this projection were varied, but most particularly Terry and Jan and S**, all of whom actually did a lot of work for and with the group.

And me? Well, I was as easy to manipulate as any doting mother of a brilliant, helpless child. Fortunately, as we will soon see, the Cs were not so easy to manipulate.

CHAPTER 39
THE COURT OF SEVEN

It is important to remember, in the telling of the present story, that what we are talking about here is where the rubber hits the road. That is: our ordinary relationships with other people. It is in the context of human behavior that we either attract or repel higher influences. It is in the reality of our daily lives that we either manifest this archetype or that one, depending on our choices.

There is a very important thing that I am trying to convey, something that I have said before, but which bears repeating: it is in the context of our ordinary lives that the Universe answers our questions. Learning to read the symbols of reality includes examining our experiences and extracting the "juice" from it so as to progress along our path of learning. If we keep making the same mistakes over and over again, can we say we are learning? And we notice that the kinds of mistakes that people make most often, the kinds of mistakes that cause the most suffering at all levels of society, are the mistakes of relationships with others.

In writing about these things, I am trying to describe the events as they unfolded and what the meaning was that I found in them, both at the time (which was sometimes right, sometimes wrong), and in retrospect. The greatest thing a person can do is to give something to another that helps them have a better experience in life. Unfortunately, the human being is not born with an instruction manual, and most of the ones we have at the present time seem to be written to deliberately obscure the matters of most concern to us: how to not suffer over and over again by making the wrong choices in relationships.

But if our energies are truly what is at stake in our relationships, and if it is true that only when we recoup a sufficient amount of energy, are we able to grow, then it becomes of paramount importance who we do or do not interact with in a close, psychologically connected way.

And that just flies in the face of the teachings of our society. We are supposed to forgive and forget, give the benefit of the doubt, compromise – "Let's all get along," "I love you, let's work it out," and so on and on. But what if all of that is designed to keep us in relationships that make us food? What if that is designed to keep us from having enough energy to grow?

Writing about most of this is very painful. Living many of these experiences was very painful. I know from direct discussions with others that they, too, have had similar painful experiences. Nearly everybody has. But for some reason, it is deemed taboo to discuss it. It is considered to be gossip or petty or "why don't we all kiss and make up?"

The same people who give such advice are generally the ones who have had half a dozen partners who beat them up, or ran around on them, or spent the grocery money on drugs, or they are the psychiatrists or doctors whose livelihood is dependent upon us being sick either in mind or body.

We are discouraged by our culture from talking about these things. To do a post-mortem on a relationship in order to come to some idea of what kinds of clues or signs we ought to look for in order to keep ourselves from making the same mistakes over and over again; to relate the information about how brain chemicals can – and most of the time do – control our thinking, and thus our choices and consequent experiences, is verboten. And it is most especially forbidden to come to the understanding that our world is embedded in a hyperdimensional reality, and that the chief meaning of our lives seems to lie in the fact that we are not just "strange, dark interludes in the electrical display of God," but that our relationships and interactions, personally, as individuals, and groups, and cultures, and even globally, may actually represent a *projection* of a cosmic drama, a drama that is essentially a representation of a battle between forces at higher levels.

In such a case, our ordinary choices take on a whole different meaning.

All alone, Susy Smart's choice to go back to her abusive boyfriend because the Bible teaches her that forgiveness is all important, and her therapist tells her that compromise is essential, certainly can't mean much in the Grand Scheme of Cosmic things, can it?

But when it is multiplied millions of times each day, and the end result is that Susy continues to be food in the Matrix, it becomes a matter of some concern in the global sense.

Every human being who continues to make choices based on the lies of the Matrix, continues to interact with others in ways that serve the STS hierarchy by feeding it, contributes to its existence and domination of our reality. The battle between forces for the control of our planet takes place *through us!* It's that simple.

So, being able to analyze and identify these things can be thought to be quite important.

The Sufis say that "the words of God are the entities of His existent things. … Meanings, which have no form, assume forms within the reality. … The reality of an existent thing/being is not what we see of it, but its immutable entity which is seen only by God and certain of His friends. … Each creature is a word of God. The life of a single man is a book" (Chittick 1989).

It is in discovering the reality, the deep inner nature of what we experience, including our relationships and the people with whom we interact, that we reach into the realms of pure thought – the awareness that will bind us to the higher levels of being.

As human beings, it seems that an essential part of our nature is to feel that there is more to life than the immediately apparent material world. We don't like to think that our lives are a game of chance played by the gods. Yet, we can observe that the heartless randomness of the world is at odds with the religious views of a loving, caring God.

The eighteenth century Icelandic mystic, Jon Jonsson said "God plays at *Forkjaering* with man in this world." *Forkjaering* is a dice game. Later, Albert Einstein said "God does *not* play dice" with the universe. I think the truth is somewhere in between. We *are* pawns in a game, only the players are, in some sense, ourselves. And we are pawns so long as we don't know the rules of the game. Once we have served our apprenticeship as playing pieces, we then are able to take our place with the players.

I once read a saying that goes: "A bird doesn't fly because it has wings; it has wings because it flies." That is to say: a bird is the incarnation of "Bird-ness," which includes flight and, in many species, song. Human beings, individually and collectively, are the incarnation of specific ideas as well.

We have a clue then, that we can learn a great deal about ourselves, our reality, our destiny, and our proper response to our environment by studying our relationships and experiences. But, it is not just observation of the outer structure that we are after; it is the discovery of the inner nature, or the Idea of a thing. Here I would like to quote from volume three of this series:

> In a general sense, to almost everyone, including yours truly, the very idea of time-traveling, mind-marauding, hyperdimensional beings with full powers to create and maintain a reality of illusion and restriction in which we are confined like sheep, waiting daily to see which of our number will be "taken" for their wool, skins, or flesh, is so horrifying a concept that accepting it as a real possibility, is tantamount to being stripped of all hopes, dreams and comfort.

Like many of you, I began this work full of frustration with teachings that don't work or don't make sense when compared with honest observation of reality and experience. There was such a labyrinth of contradictions everywhere I searched, and I *knew* it was necessary to go beyond everything hitherto known or tried. I did have the idea that this knowledge had been available in ancient times, judging by the evidence of the megaliths and other incomprehensible structures all over the globe, but whether or not it would be possible to rediscover this path was uncertain.

It was *very* clear that there was a serious discrepancy between the observable reality and some "deeper reality" from which, presumably, ours derives something of its form and structure, but I knew there was something that separated "us" from "them." And again, when searching for answers, it always ended in a maze of insupportable assumptions and irreconcilable facts.

But when the Cassiopaeans began to communicate, to say things that *did* explain the problems I was finding in science, religions and philosophies, and those things they told us were *not* part of my expectations, I became furious and railed at such a bleak picture of our existence. I had already gone through some of this process in earlier years while reading Gurdjieff and Ouspensky, but I found that what the Cassiopaeans were saying was far more dispiriting than I was prepared to receive. I rejected ideas that suggested our "fairy tale" beliefs just *might* be imposed on us to keep us asleep and unaware because I didn't like them either! As time went by and evidence from other sources mounted, I raged at lessons that drove home these points in my personal life; and I have wept oceans for the loss of my innocence. So, believe me when I say to those of you who write to me struggling to grasp this, trying to reason and rationalize some way to hang on to the old, false belief systems – I *do* understand!

But, when all is said and done, I think I wept even more for all the years wasted in stupidity and blindness. After a time, I realized that we are only stupid and blind exactly as long as we *need* to be stupid and blind, and not one second longer. I am enormously grateful for all those experiences because they *did* teach me in a very deep way.

If it is true that humans are being bred and raised like cattle in a global stockyard and fed upon both psychically and sometimes even physically, we have a truly serious situation going on here, to put it mildly. As I have explained before, I have *never* seen a "Drachomonoid" being except in dreamlike states or almost hypnopompic semi-sleep states. So, when the Cassiopaeans began to talk about them, it was truly "Twilight Zone" time, in my opinion!

I have also stated that, whenever the Cassiopaeans have told us anything, I work very hard to discover if there is any form of what I call vertical or lateral corroboration. Vertical data is that which is located in history at any point different from the present. Lateral data consists of collecting reports, witness information, and other data that amounts to circumstantial evidence from the present time. It is always better if the two types of data "cross" or intersect. But it is still not the same as having a smoking gun. When you are dealing with hyperdimensional realities, smoking guns are not very likely to be found.

In the case of the idea of man being food for hyperdimensional beings, there is an enormous amount of both vertical and lateral corroboration of *all* kinds. So much so that, in fact, it is almost impossible to understand why it is not generally known. Clearly, there have been deliberate efforts to hide this fact, and the fact that it is hidden may itself tell us something.

The point is, when don Juan and Gurdjieff and the Cassiopaeans (and others) tell us that our religions, our social structure, our values, our beliefs about our spiritual nature and condition have been *deliberately created to perpetuate the illusion that we are free*, that we are (or can be) "special and adored children of a loving God"; that we are or can be co-creators with God, that we can *do* anything at all of a positive and powerful nature, we need to carefully examine this issue!

But it is *work* to examine it objectively. It is *hard work* because it consists of long and difficult self-examination in order to be able to overcome the emotions that prevent us from discovering what illusions we are hanging onto, what illusions are preventing us from seeing and acting in such a way as to *become free*.

And yet, we *can* see that *something* is evolving here! With the maturation of the group mind, the stakes get higher and the deceptions deeper!

For many centuries, millennia even, simplistic religions and social dynamics were dominant over most of the world. This was possible because even when there was an intrusion by one of these hyperdimensional beings into our reality, when they did drop in for dinner, so to speak, it was easy to conceal because of the lack of communication between tribes and peoples.

When we sit in our comfortable homes and look at our reality, including that which is outside our windows, we see a stable front. Cars pass on the street taking people to and from their homes in their varied daily activities. The sun shines, children pass by, talking and laughing. Everyone is involved in their life in an immediate and identified way, believing that this life they are involved in is what *is*.

But, once in a while, something bizarre happens to someone and they struggle to deal with this anomaly in the space-time continuum. Usually, it is sufficiently minor that they can damp it and forget about it; which they *must* because it is too aberrant in the normal accepted course of events. It must be shoved under the rug and hidden.

Once in awhile, bigger things happen in the reality – evidence of the hyperdimensional control system intrudes, or the screen breaks down in some way – and it becomes news and gets reported. Charles Fort spent many years collecting these types of things from the newspapers and magazines all over the world.

When this happens, the accepted belief system hurries to damp down the item so that everyone can go along in their respective and collective illusions. And, since the events are localized, it is easy to cover it up. And, in the past, this was a *lot* easier than it is today.

When you read the collected information of Charles Fort, you see that the alien reality that is so widely reported today was just as active then as it is now. In fact, you see that it may even be somewhat cyclical. Just as we have cycles of food production, planting, growing and harvesting, so may hyperdimensional beings harvest us according to some seasonal rule.

But, in any event, in the past it was a lot easier to keep the lid on the matter. But then, people began to become literate. Books and papers and magazines were published and distributed. Travel became easier and information from around the world about these odd intrusions into our reality could be collected giving an overall pattern that something was not right.

Before Charles Fort, there were some few people who already smelled a rat. But, Mr. Fort kindly shoved it right under our noses and the reaction has been quite interesting. The cover-up machine went into *full* operation through the most effective vectors of mainstream science and religion.

But, the rat had been smelled and some people couldn't just shove it back under the rug. The stench kept wafting in the window that had been opened.

And so, certain people began to start searching for the source of this stinky rat. They began to gather knowledge and information.

We can even note *how* the coverup machine began to do this damage control. When you study the history of social and religious movement and change, you can see the control mechanism morphing with every discovery or realization made by human beings. As they outgrew the old religions, the simplistic explanations, new religions were put in place. At exactly the right time – the period of scientific expansion and growing knowledge of the nature of reality which brought the old religious views into serious question – the whole spiritualist movement began, leading to channeled information that was designed to patch up the holes in the control net. Newer and more elaborate explanations of the higher realms came into our reality. And, with each new question, the control system had a new answer to help everybody calm down, relax, and stop asking questions!

At the present time, this is even more amazingly evident. A few years ago, when we first began sharing the Cassiopaean information, many of the issues we dealt with were not even addressed by these other sources. But, with everything we release, the other side brings some new candidate forward with new explanations to patch the holes we are tearing in the fabric of reality.

While we never had considered it as a possibility before the recent revelations, the idea that Frank was the mole from the very beginning is not really too hard to comprehend when one considers all the hyperdimensional factors. Heck, if I was one of those 4D movie-makers, I'd have thought of it myself! What a plot twist!

And so it is, regardless of how painful these events are to recount, they are presented as lessons, as ways to derive knowledge.

As I am going through my memory of the events of the past nine years, gathering the threads together that are, in truth, the pathways of some of the most important lessons we have learned from the Cassiopaeans, I keep hearing Frank's former "employer's" words at the time of the discovery of the years-long embezzlement operation Frank had been engaged in. In my efforts to try and determine if the man was truly as evil as Frank painted him, I discussed the matter with him, pointing out how many years of "faithful service" Frank had given him, how much work Frank must have done, and how, even just considering the time Frank gave him, he most certainly deserved *some* compensation!

The man snorted at my suggestion – practically choking – and when he had regained his ability to speak just said: "You have no idea about Frank. What Frank did here could not conceivably be called "work." In fact, he was more of an annoyance. I only let him hang around out of pity. The fact is, he was about as useless as [anything.]" (Actually, the direct statement was a rather graphic reference to genitalia being useless to nuns and priests.)

I was, of course, pretty incensed that he would say something so nasty about Frank. I also took into consideration the fact that the man was generally hostile at the moment. The Frank I knew had a wonderful voice, an amazing command of the English language, and could discourse for hours on many interesting subjects, pulling all sorts of facts and figures right out of his head almost like an idiot savant who can memorize train schedules or batting averages.

But, the fact is, the man had many years of experience with Frank, and after our own experiences with Frank, looking back and recapitulating all of it here, it seems that "Dane" was not too far wrong.

It is, of course, in retrospect that we certainly are better able to piece things together and come to some better understanding of the dynamics at work, both in psychological terms as well as in the terms of the theological reality. I have said that I was "as easy to manipulate as any doting mother of a brilliant, helpless child." But, as any such mother will tell you, even if they dote, or allow themselves to be manipulated, they are not completely blind nor are they complete fools; only partial fools!

From my own perspective, I no longer was susceptible to Frank's claims to be a higher spiritual being in the terms he would have preferred it to be understood. I certainly never discarded it as a possibility, but it was one of those things that I held close and pondered in my heart. There was certainly awareness on his part that we were all scrutinizing him closely with this question uppermost in our minds, and we certainly discussed it at some length many times when he was not present, trying to work out a theory as to how such a dynamic could manifest. The idea we finally formulated was that if it was indeed true, then it was likely that Frank had been a soul that had received special attention from the negative forces in a very detrimental way. Of course, that led back to the idea of how important it was for us to continue to work with him, give him support, and try to make it possible for the damage to be undone.

Considering the fact that there was amplified scrutiny of his conduct and function at the board, it seems that whatever negative forces had been in domination had subsided to a great extent – at least in terms of doing anything to excite our suspicions. This was something we were to learn about as time went on: the principle of mental blocking via awareness. It seems that our heightened state of alert could literally block such energies and the sessions reflected this defense system. On the other hand, such interference may have subsided for the simple reason that the controllers were intent on vacuuming out of me some specific information they were after, using the Frank-as-a-well-pipe analogy. In this case, it could be said that unless Frank's emotions of ego were excited, the Cs transmissions were, from here on out, mostly uncorrupted. The following excerpt, from a session where only Frank and myself were present, demonstrates this quality.

As I already mentioned, Frank had hinted that S** was the source of the energy that had caused him to act out. He suggested that she was an agent of the aliens in some sense. I argued this point since S** was really a very simple and giving person who was always being helpful and concerned about others. (And when I say simple, I mean a person who is uncomplicated and does not deceive others. It is *not* a reference to intelligence.) I simply could not see how she could be an agent. Because of my new awareness, I framed my questions carefully so as not to trigger any emotional response in Frank which would have skewed the reception.

April 18, 1995

Q: (L) … Is it all right if we ask some questions about the situation that has transpired here over the last month or so?

A: Yes.

Q: (L) OK, is there anyway I can access the information I need because we need to make some kind of assessment of what occurred here?

A: Open.

Q: (L) Have we ever had a person in our group or in our room here, who was sent here deliberately to break up our interaction?

A: If so, that is for you to discover for purposes of learning and growth.

Q: (L) Is that part of what has been taking place here?

A: Good chance.

Q: (L) Well, that is getting close.

A: Remember one can be manipulated by another.

Q: (L) In this case, who was the one being manipulated?

A: We mean that one can appear to be an "agent" when in actuality, control is originating elsewhere, this is especially true when the apparent "agent" is one of a good and simple and seemingly stable nature.

Q: (L) OK, you are saying the control could be originating elsewhere. Is that correct?

A: Yes.

Q: (L) Would that control be third density or fourth density?

A: Either, or elements of both.

Q: (L) In this particular case, I would much prefer to think that someone was being used or manipulated by other forces. But, in that case, that could be a loose cannon, so to speak. Am I correct?

A: Up to your discretion.

Q: (L) Can we identify the source of control in this particular case?

A: We mentioned discovery and learning earlier.

Q: (L) So, we have to figure this one out?

A: Will benefit you greatly in "future" to do so.

Q: (F) Why is that?

A: In order to recognize "symptoms," which may be common occurrence.

Q: (L) In this case, we have discussed it, and it seems that it has already become a common occurrence. Persons come in and are all excited and they put in energy or money or whatever, and they are all gung-ho, and then they become a disruption.

A: Yes. You are already learning.

What are we to make of this somewhat mysterious exchange? The first remark "Remember one can be manipulated by another," would seem to suggest that Frank's claim that he was acted on by an agent was correct. But the problem was obviously much more complex and the Cs added: "One can appear to be an "agent" when in actuality, control is originating elsewhere, this is especially true when the apparent "agent" is one of a good and simple and seemingly stable nature."

This last seemed to negate the idea that S** was an agent, unless she was being utilized in some way to deliver a signal of some sort that did, in fact, affect Frank. But in that case, the signal would only have served to activate a trigger that generated a response from him that was pre-coded, so to speak. In other words, he could not have been triggered if

138

the program was not already there. This was one of the early points when I realized that the Cs were talking to me, via the well-pipe analogy, but that they had to be extremely careful both due to considerations of free will, and the issue that for some reason, some things could not be told with Frank present. But again, I kept these thoughts to myself and just simply continued to observe.

Importantly, what *never* occurred to me from the above exchange was the idea that Frank could be the one doing the manipulating, that S** could be being made to look like an agent because Frank was the origin of the manipulation. And I was certainly so sure that I was aware of Frank's little manipulations, which I considered to be just quirks of his personality and only required humor to deal with, that the idea that a far deeper manipulation was taking place was not even considered.

Terry's presence at the board, making it a three way operation, in retrospect again, seems, to have brought a significant balance to the effort. It was certainly true that *if* there was any possibility that Frank was directing the planchette, it was a lot harder with the three of us. What is more, the energetic response of the movement and flow when Terry was present was truly astounding. People (including us!) were utterly amazed at the speed and precision of the delivery of the material. The planchette would run away from us, often zipping around the board so fast that I had difficulty keeping up with calling out the letters, and Jan had as much difficulty writing them down that fast. The Cs, it seemed, just *loved* Terry. And they also apparently had a message to convey to us about him and his role in the session about the perpendicular realities on April 29, 1995.

The first unusual thing about this session was the fact that the Cs initiated the subject matter by asking: "Terry, was it October, 1964?"

We were all rather taken aback by this opening remark. On this particular night, I was in terrible pain. The strange thing about it was that it was the other arm, and not the one that had been injured in the accident! I had received a shot of cortisone directly into the joint just a day earlier, and it was almost as though the pain had then just jumped to the other side. I was having a lot of trouble concentrating and even just sitting there at the board required a supreme effort. I didn't want to disappoint anybody by canceling the session, but I wanted to get through the list of questions that had been prepared in earlier discussions so we could shut down early. But the Cs had something they wanted to talk about, and they pressed on.

The Cs' agenda seemed to be to awaken a memory in Terry that would lead to a realization. The focus seemed to be his role in group activities in his youth, and that now, the training of that time was coming into play. He had been at a crossroads, and in our group, the connection was completed. In other words, the training then was being utilized now.

In working through the issue, the following exchange occurred:

> Q: (T) Does it have to do with the fact that I am saying certain things to people at work, or wherever I can, when I talk about events that are happening these days and trying to raise their level of thinking on these things?
>
> A: Yes, now, let's explore your friends and relationships and experiences in the years immediately following the event to see if we can "dig up" something of startling significance!!!

A major clue was Terry's remark "trying to raise their level of thinking on these things," which was followed by an affirmative response from the Cs.

In fact, the person whose awareness Terry was trying to raise was *me*. And the subject of that raising of awareness was Frank! The Cs drove this point home with the remark, "let's explore your friends and relationships ... to see if we can 'dig up' something of startling significance!!!"

We went through a tiresome series of false clues until finally, we arrived at this:

> Q: (T) Is it the fact that I am able to form relationships with vastly different types of individuals?
>
> A: All originate from same "plane."

Followed by another:

> Q: (L) Do they all share a common origin?
>
> A: Yes.
>
> Q: (L) And what is that origin?
>
> A: Neormm. [...] Closest English equivalent. [...]
>
> Q: (T) Is this a star? All of us are from another star that I've formed relationships like that; the special ones that I would consider lasting?
>
> A: In perpendicular reality.

The key terms in the above remark was "special relationships" that were "lasting."

> Q: (L) All right! Where are we now? We have discovered that Terry has a perpendicular reality that has been running through his life and probably is an ongoing thing, is this correct?
>
> A: Yes.
>
> Q: (T) What is a perpendicular reality? ...
>
> A: Intersection is at realm border. [...] They merge. [...]
>
> Q: (L) Well, I am just trying to understand what this whole thing is all about. What are we getting at here?

A: Then learn from what we communicate to you and what you already have "locked up" inside of you i.e. time to get the key! [...]

Q: (L) In which case, what alternate reality do we share or do we share no alternate reality and are each representatives of an alternate reality different from each other and are a connection point?

A: Latter concept is exactly correct! [...] What did we say about increasing power? [...]

Q: (L) I have heard the concept, written or talked about, that certain people, or perhaps everybody, have locked up inside themselves pockets of energy or knowledge as in electromagnetic patterning in their fields ...

A: Like putting together the pieces of the puzzle.

Q: (L) Are we ultimately going to have seven spokes?

A: Yes.

Q: (T) Are the five of us here, five of those spokes?

A: Open.

Q: (T) That was diplomatic, wasn't it? Is there more to this concept?

A: Of course!

Q: (L) Once the seven spokes are in place in terms of persons, is that going to increase our power/knowledge exponentially?

A: Explosively.

Q: (L) Is this why there has been so much attack and so many attempts to stop this process?

A: Partly.

Q: (T) OK, we have the image on the paper with seven spokes. What do we do with it next?

A: Open.

Q: (T) OK, this is just this lesson. (L) What is in the center of the circle?

A: Will fall into place, now you must ponder the significance and we must say goodnight!

Now, there are several important clues in the above passage that the Cs declared would lead to us being able to "dig up something of startling significance." As usual, they were giving us clues that only have begun to make any kind of sense in the present time, after the learning experiences of the past couple of years. Let me just connect some other excerpts from the transcripts together for the reader to gain a deeper understanding of the information above, as well as how the Cs worked to deliver it in pieces throughout time so that, once certain lessons were learned by us, we could them begin to assemble it.

First of all, there is that most mysterious word "Neormm." It would be two years before I came back to ask about this word. As it happens, this later question was during the period of time that Frank was most diligently seeking to demonize Terry because Terry most definitely had stopped even considering the possibility that Frank was a higher spiritual being. After a couple of years of observation of Frank, he had come to the conclusion that Frank was running some sort of operation, but he wasn't sure what. I, of course, continued to defend Frank as I could, wanting to give him endless chances to prove himself. Since Frank was claiming that Terry was the fly in the ointment, repeatedly and tediously, and Terry was just simply fed up with Frank from long experience, and didn't even want to discuss it anymore, at the time of the following excerpt, I had thought of a way to ask a question that might settle the issue.

> June 7, 1997
>
> Q: In a previous session where you introduced the concept of perpen-dicular realities, you stated that Terry was connected to a particular reality called "Neormm." You also designated the "thought center" of STS as Ormethion. I noticed the similarity of the names. Is there a rela-tionship?
>
> A: The Orm is close to orimulsion. Look it up.
>
> Q: Well, what I am asking is about the possible relationship between Neormm and Ormethion ...
>
> A: Our answers have meaning best not to presuppose!

The Cs pretty effectively shot down any such connection. And as I read over the text, I have the strange feeling that "The Orm" might have been intended to be "Theormm." One of the problems of this type of channeling is that we have to put in the word breaks ourselves. All the letters are delivered in a rapid, endless stream, unmarked by any point where one word ends and another begins. Sentences are desig-nated, and other punctuation is handled by the Cs themselves, but not word breaks.

But I was given a clue: orimulsion. What in the world is orimulsion? "Orimulsion is a Venezuelan boiler fuel made up of natural bitumen (70%), water, and an emulsifier."

Now, look again at this:

> Q: (T) Is it the fact that I am able to form relationships with vastly dif-ferent types of individuals?
>
> A: All originate from same "plane." [...]
>
> Q: (L) Do they all share a common origin?
>
> A: Yes.
>
> Q: (L) And what is that origin?
>
> A: Neormm. [...] Closest English equivalent. [...]
>
> Q: (T) Is this a star? All of us are from another star that I've formed re-lationships like that; the special ones that I would consider lasting?
>
> A: In perpendicular reality.
>
> Q: (T) What is a perpendicular reality? ...
>
> A: Intersection is at realm border. [...] They merge.

And now look at this from January 10, 2002:

Q: Was that the reason that you encouraged Terry and Jan to be present? To counterbalance Frank's negative energy?
A: Yes. Frank would have killed you with his STS draining rather soon otherwise.

And we begin to understand the symbolism of a blend of bitumen and water with the aid of an emulsifier. Frank and I were like oil and water. But there is much more than that. The Cs also made strange allusions to "digging up" something which was connected to individuals who have "secrets locked up inside them" and to a group of seven which would form, like pieces of a puzzle, which would lead to "explosive learning." They also made reference to keys in the context of "unusual persons."

So, we come back to this:

February 24, 1996
A: Oh Laura, my dear, seems you need a refresher course in the transcripts. Maybe suggest you read them and relax and privately listen to the ones you have not as of yet transcribed a little more. This would be extremely helpful in your many and increasing communications via the "net" as well. Remember, we help you to unlock answers that have been placed in your superconsciousness files from before the "time" of the birth of your physical body.

And this:

April 15, 1995
A: You are in pain, my dear, and when you hurt, all others do too!

In the context of the following:

August 31, 1996
Q: (L) Is Ark going to be able to help us with technology, to help other people, or to protect ourselves in some way? In this really bizarre stuff going on on our planet?
A: Too much, too soon, my dear. Curiosity killed the cat.
Q: (L) Well, satisfaction brought him back!
A: Not in this case!!!
Q: (T) You've got to let this go along. It's picking up momentum every day, it seems. So, just let it roll along and let it see where it goes. (L) All right, let's … (T) He's coming to protect you. That's what he said.
A: Maybe, but there is so, so, so much more in store than that!!!!!!
Q: (L) Stop! … Is that an ominous, "maybe, but there's so, so, so much more in store?" Or is that a positive, "there is so, so, so much more in store?"
A: Why would you think it ominous?

Q: (L) Well I don't know … because I'm scared of what I don't know! (T) Faith, we're back to faith again.

A: What have we helped you to discover so far? Would you rather discontinue this operation?

Q: (L) Oh, hell no! (T) After two years, you know she's always going to ask those kinds of questions!

A: Not two years, eternity. […] We have helped you build your staircase one step at a time. Because you asked for it. And you asked for it because it was your destiny. We have put you in contact with those of rare ability in order for you to be able to communicate with us. Again, because you desired it, in order to realize your path. By now, you should recognize the signs … Those who display thinking patterns which in many ways deviate from that which is considered ordinary. The more unusual, the more telling. They have past lives on 3rd density earth, but not recently, but for this one. And they are not oriented to the earth frequency vibrations.

[group discussion ensued on last response]

Q: (T) … It is destiny for you to find out what your path was; you had to make this contact, because it was what you were supposed to do. [And here, I had to jump in to defend Frank's role as the channel so he wouldn't go into a blue funk.] (L) Are we not talking about Frank in terms of being put in contact with someone who enables me to communicate with you, so you can put me on my path, which is building the staircase, etc., etc.? Is that not what we've got going here?

A: He is one, but not the only one, just the one who awakened your sense of recognition.

Not only did they *not* confirm his role as the channel, which I suggested, they seemed to be deliberately minimizing his role. He was certainly never told he had "keys" locked up inside him, nor that he had "answers locked up" in his "superconsciousness" that were placed there before birth of his physical body.

Q: (L) I know this is probably not the time to ask this question; this is the kind of discover, open, find out, open – that kind of thing, but it seems to me almost that you are leading up to say something, so maybe I can help you along by asking, what is this staircase, what is this destiny?

A: Discover.

Q: (L) I knew it was coming! (T) Why don't we ask who else is involved. (L) You ask, I'm trying to … (T) Well, if Frank is one, who else is involved?

Here, Terry is also trying to give Frank some importance so he wouldn't go off on an emotional roller coaster. But the Cs have something most interesting to say about Frank.

A: We have given the signs, but they are not necessarily the same with each individual.

Now, how are we to understand this last remark? That the signs are not the same with each individual? Yet, they have just given the signs for recognition, so that can't be it. The only way to understand it seems to be that the signs do not mean the same thing with all individuals with the signs. I puzzled over this a great deal trying to understand what was being hinted. But the idea that the remark, "Those who display thinking patterns which in many ways deviate from that which is considered ordinary. The more unusual, the more telling," could be used to identify both STO and STS individuals never occurred to me. I had the idea that if a person was "not oriented to the earth plane" that it naturally meant STO.

> Q: (T) Let me ask this. All this work you've been doing, all this nurturing you've been doing, is Laura a keystone to whole project that you're working on?
> A: We suggest you avoid anticipatory exercises, as realization comes after the fact.
> Q: [Frank complains because Laura keeps taking her hand off the planchette and resting it in her lap.] (L) Well, I'm in pain, Frank, it's hard for me to sit here. Appreciate the fact that I'm in pain!
> A: Appreciate the fact that you have been given the keys to end all this pain.
> Q: (L) When you say, "end all this pain," it sounds a little more inclusive than just my shoulder hurting! I mean, that sounds rather suggestive.
> A: Yes.
> Q: (L) To end all this pain …
> A: It all goes hand in hand.

The very instant that the Cs said "you have been given the keys to end all this pain," a vision and a sensation came over me, the likes of which I had never experienced before. In ordinary slang, you could say it was a body rush, but it was far, far deeper than that. But ego is a terrible thing, and of all things, I have tried to be vigilant against the traps of ego. So I asked. We will see, further on, Ark's "Bird's Eye View" of such things, and our understanding of how small acts that are not based on any egoist idea of saving the world can benefit many people over time. That is still our perspective, and it is why we work so hard in our small ways. We have no desire or intent to make a big splash, or start any kind of movement. We think that incremental, nonlinear efforts that are cumulative over a long time are far more likely to be helpful.

Regarding the remark "hand in hand," there are many things that this might allude to, not the least of which is the use of the board which is a multiple hand activity. Nevertheless, as it happens, on that particular day, Ark and I had discussed combining our efforts to discover the proper way to serve humanity/Creator, and the key phrase had been that we will work "hand in hand." I had another body rush from this remark because it was a certainty that no one else in the room had been privy to that information. But, let's go back to the issue of Neormm.

The first thing we notice about the word is that it is similar to the word "Neo," as in the hero of *The Matrix*. We then think about this in terms of a perpendicular reality composed of seven people who originate from same plane, share a common origin, which intersects and merges at the realm border.

Which relates to an interesting exchange relating to the possible function of the "group of seven":

June 14, 1997

Q: (C) Thinking is electrical. Does a person leave an electrical echo and can certain combinations produce harmony which is cumulative and exponential, thereby certain groups thinking can produce more than others, or individually?

A: Close. Now, for C**. Suggestion: Combine frequencies to witness the development of a directed wave effect; packs a potent "punch."

Q: (C) And is this related to the group of seven? Seven pieces of pizza?

A: Certainly! See what letting it flow does, C**?

And of course, "packing a potent punch" takes us directly back to the role of Neo in the movie, *The Matrix*. And here we come to a most cryptic series of remarks. As the readers know, Ark was "looking" for me for many, many years – his entire life, in fact. He seems to have been born with an awareness that there was someone he had to find, that he had a mission to accomplish, and this person was essential both personally and to the mission itself.

At the same time that the Cs were urging me repeatedly to network on the computer, in conjunction with the remark that this would lead to an opportunity that only "one" of the group would "recognize," Ark was thinking that the Internet might be the way to "find" what he was searching for, and was working on getting a website set up.

At the same time that the Cs were urging me to investigate unstable gravity waves, Ark was writing about them in his journal as being a key to a certain problem. At almost the same moment in time, we were both on the hunt for information about unstable gravity waves, our paths converged, and his website was instantly recognized by me, and the rest is history. But, the point was, even with the deepest knowing imaginable, that something of great significance was in process, my conscious mind continued to doubt, to try to reason, to demand answers according to the normal view of the world. I didn't want to make a fool of myself, and I certainly didn't want to fall into a trap as Frank was regularly and repeatedly saying was going to happen! And so, I tried to get the Cs to give me some straight answers. But, on this subject, there was only a single clue:

August 3, 1996

Q: (L) Before I give up the floor to everyone else, I would like to know if you have any comment about AJ? My experience here is so strange, and I don't want to be caught in a trap …

A: New.

Q: (L) New what? What does that mean?

A: What it is.

Q: (T) New as in "renewed?"

A: Yes.

Q: (L) Beginning?

A: See how one simple word causes you to use your minds?

Q: (T) Yes.

A: And if we had given you a long and eloquent response, as you desired, you would not have!

Q: (L) Any more words on this subject?

A: No, thank you!

Here I would like to point out some of the ways the Universe utilizes the phonetic cabala, or Language of the Gods to send us messages if we are alert enough to pay attention. I was very deep in a study of the Rennes-le-Château mystery as introduced to the world by Henry Lincoln *et al.*, at the very time that Ark first wrote to me. We note the most interesting fact that he goes by "Ark," and I had already channeled the ideas of Quantum Cosmic Metamorphosis in 1985, centering around the subject of the Flood of Noah. The book was, in fact, entitled "Noah," which is very close to "Neo," or "New," and the theme was discovering the true meaning of the Ark. The second interesting fact is that his full name is Arkadiusz, or the Polish variation of Arcadia, and the central mystery of the Rennes-le-Château affair happens to be a painting entitled "The Shepherds of Arcadia."

Since Ark was back in Europe at the time of the above session, he was asking his questions via computer. He had written a little synopsis earlier in the day; what he called a "Bird's Eye View" of the situation. He wrote as follows:

Some thoughts.

Before I go on to study all these Celts and Cathars and Templars and grails and bloodlines and dna and gold and mercury and oaks and …

Before all this let me try to formulate my present view of the situation. It will be a kind of bird's eye view; from a distance when details are unimportant. So I will pick up SOME themes that seem to me important. There will be several of these themes and they will be discussed separately.

1. I take it as a hypothesis which perhaps is true and perhaps not, but I take it to be true unless proven otherwise: that for you and for me nothing happens by mere accident. All that happens has a meaning and purpose. It is hard work for us to find out what is this purpose exactly and to an extent we are also the creators of this purpose.

Thus it is not an accident that you are who you are. It is not an accident that I am a physicist. It is not an accident that we are separated for a while. It is not an accident that we have had our lives the way we had. It could be little bit different, or it is a little bit different in some parallel realities, but we are now concerned about our reality, our present and our future.

2. Thus every book that you ever read was not an accident and every conversation that you ever had; even those silly books and conversations were lessons. The same with me.

3. We are both searching for something and it was clear that we would never find it in this lifetime while alone. There was ONE who you saw somehow in your imagination. There was also my thoroughly repressed idea of having an "American wife". Somehow it was coming to my head, but I was instantly repelling it as a completely silly thought. But it was knocking. This way I was being "prepared" because otherwise I was/am very conservative.

Anyhow we have found each other and there is purpose in that. I take it as possible that you/me – we are connected to the Creator and are distant parts of it so that we are His tools and we are responsible for something, this something being the whole universe and its fate. This is not a crazy idea. It can be explained in completely plain terms. You/me – we can discover something, a formula or an idea that will change the future development of humanity – even if a little, it will magnify after years and years so that world will be "saved" by it. This is what we learned from the concepts of chaotic mechanics. There are systems, if sufficiently complex, such that a little change now leads to a dramatic change after a time.

Now the universe is not only a complex system but also it has intelligence in it. It may well be that an "intelligent" change that we do now will change completely the fate of the universe. Instead of dying a thermal death it will flourish forever …

My whole life I have lived with this feeling of responsibility. It was a recurring theme in my journal. If we accept the hypothesis that nothing happens to US by chance then there is a purpose in this feeling too.

4. So we you/me are responsible. We accept it. That is clear. Now, from Cs we know you have "all the keys". In a sense we find it in Pleiadians or in the Bible that everybody has the keys. But in too many these keys are broken, destroyed, desynchronized, detuned and hard or impossible to make them work. We do not know how many people there are on this earth who have keys and how many of them are already using these keys or assisting other people in using them. And for a while it does not matter. All is lesson – we accept it – and we have our homework. Neither you nor me have a wish "to be told".

5. So you have the keys and we were brought together. Now, I am a physicist and know the math which is the universal language. On the other hand you know and like all these funny stories that merge history/alchemy/whatever. These are all words while math is all logic. While physics is testable and helps us to build technologies, this stuff of grail and Templars and Rennes is somewhat unsharp and for those who have no math, can lead nowhere ...

But NO! If nothing with us happens accidentally, then the fact that you are interested in what you are interested is also not an accident. So what can be a purpose of all that? A purpose can be that the KNOWLEDGE is not just math and equations but it is also intelligence and consciousness and mind and idea. Because equations DO NOTHING alone. So we need both. There were many that perhaps followed the path of technology and are working underground doing "great physics" or "great math". But this is not what we are about. We do not want to sell our souls like Faustus. We do not serve to the dark. Therefore we need knowledge. And the more knowledge we have the more protected we are. This point is again easily understood in plain terms. Once we play not only with TDARM's and time machines and gold making but also with ouija boards and history and templars and Arcadian shepherds and all this funny stuff – we are not considered as dangerous because we clearly are not after power. Neither do we want to take power FROM somebody.

Our goal is all different. We have our personal mission to fulfill: External dark forces being dispersed by multiplicity of our frequencies – so to say.

6. But why ARE all these Templars and Rosicrucians important? Because it is all knowledge. Pieces of knowledge from here and there. We are not gonna use or try to use this knowledge. But somehow it is necessary for us to know this so as to find out the best possible use of this knowledge.

7. I think this IS true that the only limits that we find are those imposed by our own minds and thinking habits. Thus we must be more and more bold in our thinking. On the other hand we need always to go step by step. Otherwise there is danger.

8. Is the life sufficiently long? We take it as a working hypothesis that yes, it is. Because it depends only on us how long it is gonna be. There is a great work that is in front of us and this work includes rethinking and rearranging our cellular structure. We believe it can be done even with the presently known (secret) technology. The fountain of youth, and such things, but also what we know from Cs and Pleiadians and alchemical texts etc. all point to it. It is possible. But the point is of course what purpose one is using it for. If just for prolonging one's own life – well ... But we have something different in mind because we are service-men here for the Creator, to whom we return.

9. So we continue. I do my math but also I have to learn a lot of stuff. Not only I NEED TO LEARN, BUT ALSO I NEED TO HELP YOU AND WE ARE SUPPOSED TO ACT TOGETHER!

Now, we come to the session on July 12, 1996, wherein Ark, writing from Florence at the time, wanted me to ask about this "Bird's Eye View" of the situation. I didn't read it aloud or share it with the group, wanting to prevent any "leading" in the answer.

> Q: OK, here is Ark's first question: if the general view of the situation that I wrote you, "bird's view" is correct?
>
> A: Why not? The thought would not be so "nagging" if were not so!
>
> Q: Or, perhaps, I am missing some important point(s), and if so what is(are) this point(s)?
>
> A: When one is on a quest for true learning and higher knowledge, there are no "missing points," only those not yet discovered!
>
> Q: How "long" will they still be able to use the Cassiopaean transmitter, should we start to take some steps thinking of the future when the transmission point will have to be moved? Or, perhaps, this is not something we have to worry about in advance? I would like to know … I do not like to be taken by surprise …
>
> A: No need to worry!
>
> Q: Is there anything that you can say to help him with his worries? He is probably gonna worry anyway …
>
> A: "If one has the will of a Lion, one does not have the fate of a mouse!"

In the following segment from the session, the question about the event referred to a period of several hours on the 9th of July, when we experienced a break in computer communication, accompanied by several glitches in our own understanding of what the other was saying. It was as though the reality had shifted and something was not quite in sync. It had upset me and my first thought was that some sort of wave or frequency was being picked up by one or the other of us, leading to some confusion. There was a severe storm in Florence, and three mild earthquakes in the region. What we didn't know at the time was that a flood was beginning in Poland that was going to directly affect our own affairs. Since we were at the end of our questions, before stopping for the night, I tossed in the question about the event just to see if my idea about some frequency in the air was correct.

> Q: What was the influence that caused our little "event" of the past few days?
>
> A: S waves.
>
> Q: What is an S wave?
>
> A: Look it up.
>
> Q: Who was being subjected to the S waves?
>
> A: Ark.
>
> Q: Was this having an effect because of the events in Dijon? [He had spent a few weeks visiting University of Dijon before traveling to Flor-

ence, and had there suffered from insomnia at night, and overwhelming sleepiness in the day time. The Cs had said that there were 4D influences in operation, connected to the Max Planck Institute which was directly across the street from Ark's office, two months before, in Göttingen.]

A: Semi.

Q: Well, what other factor is involved?

A: Arkadiusz is strong willed. Must be to be seeker of worlds. To paraphrase: "I am become ONE ... Creator of worlds." And, on that contemplative note, good night.

So, regarding Ark and his "Bird's Eye View," the Cs had said: "If one has the will of a Lion, one does not have the fate of a mouse!" ... Arkadiusz is strong willed. Must be to be seeker of worlds. "I am become ONE ... Creator of worlds."

All of which takes us back to the perpendicular realities converging and merging at the realm border, a group of seven, "packing a potent punch" to "pierce the spider," and Neo/Noah/New. Which brings us to this:

August 17, 2000

Q: Our little egroup discussion list is growing. Everyone is talking about the Wave: what does it mean, what is it, when is it coming, how are we going to be able to tell, and so on. I have been collecting the material and getting it in shape. I have been learning a lot as I go along as well. It isn't finished, but as I go along, I do have some questions. We would like to have a little bit of a clue about the progress of the Wave. I would also like to know if this Wave is sort of like the recompiling of a computer program, with the universe as the program? What is the progress, and is it going to recompile the program of our universe?

A: So many questions rolled up into one. But, one way it might go is that all of a sudden, everything that ever was is new, everything that IS is new, and everything that will be is new. Programs change, oh we suppose, what an awesome event indeed!

Returning now to the present situation, the tempest in a teapot, so to say. As we are beginning to suspect, there are theological dynamics being expressed in our world via the psychological expressions of human beings across the globe. Our own piece of the puzzle is only one part of it, which may or may not be significant in the sense that Ark has described it in his "Bird's Eye View" of the situation. Only time will tell. There are certainly forces acting to negate any such possibility of our small, local activity in the universe having any positive nonlinear effect.

We are not the only ones experiencing such attacks. We have received many emails from people who say that something very strange happened to our world on September 11. Many people feel that the universe changed in some way, exactly as it was described in the movie, *The Matrix*, where the controllers "change the program." Many, many people are experiencing similar dynamics, or the struggle between forces at higher levels, *manifested in their daily lives*, their human interactions, their relationships, and so forth. What can all of this extreme polarization – these pockets of chaos – represent? Has the world gone mad?

In this book, I don't intend to go through the entire transcripts to exhaustively examine each and every related reference. With what I have described thus far, the reader will probably have sufficient tools to do that themselves and draw some meaningful conclusions about the behind-the-scenes events that led to any particular series of questions. But, there is a small series of connections that I still must present before we move on to the present situation in some greater detail.

This next excerpt, from June 9, 1995, was a sort of emergency session with just myself and Frank in order to ask about an exorcism I had just recently performed which literally would have peeled the chrome off a car bumper. What was also on my mind was the fact that Frank had become so lethargic and tired since the group had gone back to regular and frequent sessions. Before our "episode," Frank had always been charged up by the sessions, and now he was complaining regularly of being exhausted. I was concerned for his health.

Q: (L) Why is Frank so tired lately?
A: Depression.
Q: (L) Is there anything I can do to help?
A: Let it "run its course," karmic in nature.
Q: (L) Well, Frank has such a lovely aura, how can he have such icky karma?
A: Not "icky" karma, has to do with adjustment factors.
Q: (L) As soon as he adjusts in some way, he will stop having these depressions?
A: Not point.
Q: (L) What is the point? I mean, he is suffering. It is awful to have to spend so much time suffering.
A: Adjustment process.
Q: (L) What is he adjusting from to?
A: Not to be answered at this point.
Q: (L) Edgar Cayce said you could just stop karma at any point by opening your awareness and making a decision. Why can't Frank do that? Can anybody do that? Can you just say: "I've had enough," and stop it?
A: No, because not usual circumstance.
Q: (L) Is Frank's karma "special" karma?
A: Subjective. Different.

Q: (L) Different from the usual. Is there any thing that he could do to make it better? Any clue? Any word of encouragement?

A: Won't change until environment does.

Q: (L) Do you mean the environment as in the whole planet, or his personal environment?

A: Former.

Q: (L) Does this mean he is going to have this until we all go to fourth density?

A: Until status quo is abridged.

Q: (L) What is the status quo?

A: Self explanatory.

Q: (L) So, it doesn't mean going into fourth density necessarily, but until the status quo of the planet is abridged, or some change occurs in the status quo?

A: Yes.

Q: (L) So, when some sweeping changes in the status quo of the planet occur, Frank will "come into his own?" Is that correct?

A: Close.

Q: (L) Is this going to happen soon?

A: Open.

Definition of status quo: the existing state of affairs. "Temporal," perhaps? Abridged: to lessen, reduce in scope; lessen or curtail rights or authority.

As most of us realize, the status quo of the planet was "abridged" in a big way on September 11, 2001. It was a watershed event and our lives will never be the same again. National Guard units patrol airport terminals and our nation's Capitol, the Senate office building is closed because of the threat of anthrax. Barricades block streets leading to the White House. The FBI is detaining hundreds of suspects, the recently passed "Patriot Bill" (H.R. 3108) suspends important provisions of the Bill of Rights, the Office of Homeland Security has been established, and the The Model State Emergency Health Powers Act will soon become the law of the land. Most people accept what is happening because they've been told we must change our way of life and accept more government surveillance to preserve our liberty. Nothing could be further from the truth. The new measures are designed to restrict our freedom, undermine our Constitution, and usher in the New World Order.

Why did the Cs give a sort of "prediction" that Frank's "different karma" would not be evident until the environment on the planet was "abridged?" My question as to whether Frank would "come into his own" at that point in time was answered with "Close." So why is it that Frank's life would change and become *less* difficult when the status quo is abridged? Could it be because, in some way, he is a part of the forces that are abridging the status quo?

I couldn't figure it out. What's more, I also missed the clues about Frank's depression and adjustment. The Cs did not want to answer the question about what he was adjusting from and to, but it is obvious in retrospect. At this point in time, what Frank was adjusting to was the increased scrutiny of the group members regarding his claims to be the channel, and a higher being. With this added vigilance, he was obviously no longer able to use the sessions to drain energy from me. But there is a lot more in the above session than meets the eye and I am sure that the reader will catch it without me spelling it out.

Looking back at events then and currently, it is rather amazing that the Cs chose that exact word to describe Frank coming into his own, so to say. "Abridged." A Bridge? Bridges? Again, the phonetic cabala, the Language of the Birds, or the Language of the Gods is part of the clue system. As I noted previously, the combination of a "Grant and a Bridges" in my early life (recounted in *Amazing Grace*) nearly drained all life force from me, resulting in my vulnerability to an attempt to take me out of the picture. This was, of course, after the attempt to remove me from the scene in many other ways had failed, including the incident in Tallahassee when I was 18. It is obvious in retrospect that all of these were deliberate setups of interpersonal relations designed to do just that. In the present moment, we seem to have another Grant and Bridges combo with a far more insidious purpose.

There are several other places in the transcripts where the word abridge is used, and it is interesting to notice that it is in the context of abridgment of free will. The Cs say: "Free Will could not be abridged if you had not obliged," referring to the human race's Fall from Eden. And as the Cs pointed out:

> March 11, 1995
>
> Q: (T) We were third density STO at this time. Was this after the battle that had transpired? In other words, were we, as a third density race, literally on our own at that point, as opposed to before?
>
> A: Was battle.
>
> Q: (L) The battle was in us?
>
> A: Through you.
>
> Q: (T) The battle was through us as to whether we would walk through this doorway ... (L) The battle was fought through us, we were literally the battleground. (T) I got that, but I want to get back to this analogy to make sure where we are in the overall picture. The battle was going on when the door was opened. Was the battle over whether or not we walked through that door?
>
> A: Close.

Q: (T) OK, we were STO at that point. You have said before that on this density we have the choice of being STS or STO.

A: Oh Terry, the battle is always there, it's "when" you choose that counts!

And of course, we see that this relates directly to Frank's choice. The Cs said that his life was hard, because his mind was a battleground, and that the question was: would the dark or light forces win? And then, at a certain point, they mentioned that he was suffering depression – anger turned inwards – because he was having "adjustment" problems. They then said that his suffering would end when the status quo was "abridged," and we are now in that time. I am not certain that the Cs were predicting that choice, though it seems that way. As always, any of us can change our minds at any moment in "time," as the Cs pointed out to Terry. But there may be some factor involved in this abridging of the status quo that locks a person in to whatever choice is made in this, our present period of chaos which is an expression of the cosmos asking the individual to *make that choice*. Everyone is currently facing this choice. The battle has been entered; it is taking place *through* us, at this point in time.

And that brings us back to the more recent times when the following was said:

July 15, 2000

Q: Well, Frank felt that the attack would come through Constellation, but I guess if Ark was sick, that would be sort of true, because then, he couldn't work. Is that why Frank picked it up that way?

A: Partly, but other complications lurk … Jealousies building with one who has a name with a "B."

Q: Any particular action to take to forestall that one?

A: Be on alert to conferences with others.

Question is: how does all of this fit together? The "abridged status quo," the karmic destiny of a soul that would only come into his own comfort zone when forces of darkness began to rampage on the planet, the person with the letter "B" in the name, and conferences?

As it happens, there are a number of people in the drama who have the letter "B" in their names. And just "who is on first" has been a subject of some discussion. The answers may be surprising.

Knowledge Protects.

CHAPTER 40
SECRET AGENTS FROM ALPHA 1

The reader should keep in mind always that when we are talking about petty tyrants, we are talking about agents of the Matrix in almost exactly the same terms described in the movie. In other words, anyone can – in an instant – receive the "download" of an "agent program" and begin to function as a petty tyrant for the very first time. By the same token, when an agent in a certain quarter is no longer needed, he/she can be turned off and the individual will go along living a peaceful life, never bothering anyone unless – and until – they are needed as an agent again. And truthfully, any of us can, at any time, be activated as a petty tyrant in someone else's life! However, once one has entered the path of the warrior or STO candidate, as the Cs describe it, that is less likely. The reason for this is that the awareness and acknowledgment that it is always possible contributes to the warrior's defenses against such manipulation. As don Juan suggests, one of the chief traits of the warrior is self-examination. A warrior is self-oriented, not in a selfish way, but in the sense of a total and continuous examination of the self. Warriors continuously take strategic inventories in an effort to eradicate their own self-importance which is what makes human beings vulnerable to being used as agents in the Matrix.

The story I am going to recount in the upcoming pages will seem unbelievable, I can assure you. If we had not lived it ourselves, we wouldn't believe it either. But since we are both pack rats and save every email we have ever received, every scrap of paper, every note, and Ark has 30 years worth of journals, all of the evidence that every word is true is easily available. And as we go along, I will use excerpts from some of these sources, if not entire emails. What you will begin to see, as I describe the events, is the mechanism of the Matrix exposed. It is both frightening and liberating. What is more, you will notice certain names and connections that will pop up again and again in relation to certain activities.

When the Cassiopaeans arrived on the scene, I had no idea that this was part of what I would be learning. It's really a good thing that I learned the principle before *The Matrix* came out or I would have never believed it! But, by early 1996, I had the principle in my grasp, and, as it happens, the Universe immediately challenged me to utilize what I had learned. The main petty tyrant in my life at that point was my ex-husband. Even though I had not yet even read *The Fire From Within* at that point, I employed a similar strategy to that outlined by don Juan, and escaped from that situation without ever wishing any ill-will toward my ex, which is, in the end, the objective: to not become like the petty tyrant – full of anger, resentment, self-righteous indignation, and other energy-draining emotions. I wasn't much of a warrior at that point because it nearly killed me to deal with that one, and he was only a teensy, teensy, weensy petty tyrant. This may have been due to the fact that he was, and is, essentially a decent, caring person. He had his programs, and it is a certainty that my energy was nearly drained out of me to the point of death, but he was never mean or vicious. He was only unaware. But it is those who are unaware that can most easily be used as agents. Anyone who denies the possibility is a dangerous companion to one who is aware. They can be turned on or off in an instant.

Meanwhile, Ark had his own petty tyrants to deal with – far more than I ever would have dreamed of since he was an administrator at a University with a staff and a budget under his control, and a chain of command above and below him. He was also married to one of the great petty tyrants of all time, so it took some doing to strategically deal with that situation. His skills had been honed, however, by long years dealing with the tyranny of life behind the Iron Curtain, so he learned the Art of Stalking from masters. He just didn't know about fourth density stalking.

Once the Cs had brought us into contact with one another, the Matrix, the Evil Magician, the fourth density Control System, went into hyperdrive to prevent us from ever actually joining forces. We have already noted that the role of petty tyrant can rotate and shift, and that it is merely the tool of the theological reason for the events in our lives, and here is where we are going to see this in action. Most of this had to do with the legal system in Poland, and Ark's efforts to obtain a divorce there, which we finally gave up and he obtained his divorce in America. But there was a lot of agent activation in his life, most of which could be explained in completely mundane ways.

There are, of course, many people who would suggest that it is all a part of a vast, human conspiracy, and that the individuals involved were conscious or in contact with one another. But I am sure that the reader will see that this would pre-suppose a network of conspirators that is simply impossible to conceive. I had a vision of how it works once. In the image in my mind, I could see a fourth density controller sitting at a big computer console with buttons and levers and dials. He had a screen on which he watched human affairs, and all he had to do was sort of lock in the target on a particular person displayed on the screen, and begin pushing buttons and levers, and turning the different dials to put certain inputs into the situation. These machinations produced frequencies that stimulated certain chemicals in the bodies and brains of the individuals displayed on the screen, and there were nearly infinite possibilities of manipulation available just through this kind of activity. I laughed at this vision, of course, because it was almost like a comic strip character. But I was later to learn how much it really does seem like this is the real way it works.

At the same time, however, there were also active positive influences that seemed to be operative. It is in observing the activities of the various players in action that the theological drama reveals itself.

So, where were we? Oh yes, physicist meets channel and they each discover that the other is the One they have been looking for. However, in order for the physicist to be able to do what needs to be done, if anything needs to be done, he can't just ditch his job, leave the country, and toss caution to the winds. He must proceed through channels. Everything must be arranged in proper order for the safety of both parties, as well as their future success.

The reader who has read *Amazing Grace* might recall the bizarre little episode of the "two "Wilburs." For those who haven't read it, let me quote that short passage from Chapter 42 here before coming back to the matter at hand which ties it together:

> At this time, events began to converge rapidly in a strange synchronicity. Random threads from the past, in the space of a few weeks, began weaving together in a coherent design in ways that astonished me.
>
> The phone rang one day with a call from my Private Investigator friend. We'd cooperated on the 1993 child murder investigation. He had a question about something unrelated to that case. At the end of our exchange, he asked me about a conversation I had with a certain law enforcement employee. Well, this conversation had never happened.
>
> "What are you talking about?"
>
> "I called you back in October when he was here in the office with me," my friend said, "and one of your kids said you were in the hospital. I left his number and a message that you should call him. I was sure you had by now."
>
> I never got the message. The kids must have forgotten. I called the number and left a message.
>
> I'll call him "Marion Wilbore". I knew that "Marion" was fairly common as a man's name in the past, but it was unusual now, so I

thought it odd. Also, Wilbur was the name of my brother and grandfather.

Two days later, Marion Wilbore returned my call. I thought it was most curious this guy should call on my Grandfather's birthday, February 11th. Two "Wilburs".

Then the phone rang again. This time, it was "Marion Wilson," the owner of a local used book store, calling to tell me that she had a copy of Velikovsky's *Worlds in Collision* that I could have for seven dollars. I was so excited that I told her to put a "sold" tag on it and I would be right down. I'd been searching for this book without success for two years.

It wasn't until I hung up that I realized the pattern. "Marion Wilbore? Marion Wilson? Two Marions? Two Wilburs? What is going on here?!"

The phone rang again. I almost didn't answer it, but decided I'd better. It was Sam, my cousin, whom I'd met for the first time at the MUFON meeting. Sam is the one whose name is my grandfather, Wilbur's middle name. He, too, was calling to announce that he had just found a copy of Velikovsky's *Worlds in Collision* in a box of books in his garage. He knew I had been looking for it, and it was mine if I wanted it!

Well, that was just TOO much! Two "Marions," two Wilburs on Wilbur's birthday, two last names beginning with "Wil," two copies of Velikovsky after two years of searching, one of them from a guy who had Wilbur's middle name as a last name.

All within about half an hour!

I mean, what were the chances of two completely unrelated people named "Marion," with their last names beginning with "Wil" – for God's sake! – calling me within a few minutes of each other? And what were the odds, within the same few minutes, of having two people offer me a specific book after two years of trying to locate it?

What were the odds of the whole rest of the deal?

I shook my head to clear the cobwebs, sure that I was being taken over by "magical thinking". I knew things were getting weird, I just didn't know how weird they were gonna get.

As it happens, I had been to see my brother, Wilbur (he goes by the name Tom), on the day Ark first read a transcript from the Cs and decided to write to me. He actually wrote the next morning, which happened to be my brother's birthday, July 5th. That's one Wilbur.

Then, on July 16th, *eleven* days later, which also happened to be the *two*-year anniversary of the first transmission from the Cs, a very strange thing happened.

Ark was at a conference in Goslar, Germany. He was trying to think of how to come to Florida within the parameters of the system in which he had to function. It seems that the Cs must have been active. He wrote to me:

Date sent: Tues, 16 Jul 96 08:41:24
From: "ajad@physik"

Dear Laura,

Yesterday there was a party and I met a colleague physicist from Gainesville and he will invite me to Gainesville somewhere next year for a month or two. We will see what will happen. In fact I was supposed to go there two years ago and I had even booked a plane, but then, on a hunch, I canceled all. Till recently I did not understand the reasons. Now I understand. I have now more reasons to come. It is not that far from Gainesville to New Port Richey.

I go to prepare my talk.

ark

As soon as his series of conferences that summer were over and he had returned and settled back in to work at the Institute, Ark began the process of negotiating the visit through the proper channels. It was several months before all the paperwork was done.

From: "ajad@physik"
Subject: news
Date sent: Mon, 25 Nov 1996 11:34:49 +1

All good news.

Talked to the Rector. They will help me – no problem! There will be no money problem and there will be no visa problem. And as you know by now, John will also help.

The arrangements were made between the two institutions, and a firm date was set for our first meeting. Ark would arrive in Tampa on February 11, my grandfather's birthday. The second Wilbur. And here is when it begins to get really weird. Exactly two days later he received the following, suddenly and out of the blue.

Date: Wed, 27 Nov 1996 03:12:03 +0100
To: Arkadiusz Jadczyk "ajad@ift"
From: "L E. S**" "*****"**
Subject: Space, Time and Matter

Dear Professor Jadczyk,

I have read your papers on *Event-Enhanced Quantum Theory*, which I liked very much. I am offering you the following: The Central European University of Budapest will hold a workshop on philosophical questions of physics. I wonder if you would be interested to participate! [...] Wednesday, 22 January:

All of your expenses, of course, will be covered by the CEU.

Sincerely yours,

L****

Aside from the curious date of the conference, 1-22, Ark had never heard of the Central European University. Who were these people, and why were they writing to him all of a sudden and offering, on what is really short notice in such things, to pay him to come and sit around and talk? He wasn't even being asked to give a talk. Just hang out. And when the specific terms later were specified, it was something of a surprise. Who were these new kids on the block with so much money to hand out?

The Central European University was established in 1989, funded by George Soros, a philanthropist billionaire with very forward-looking ideas. Much of his philanthropy is aimed at improving networking between those countries formerly behind the Iron Curtain, and the West. As it happens, Central European University is also chartered in the State of New York, and has the status of Publicly-Supported Educational Institution Granted by the IRS – 501 (c) (3), the most favorable tax-exempt status, that of a publicly-supported educational institution.

After we had researched it, we didn't see any reason for Ark *not* to go. Besides, I wanted pictures of Budapest. The money wasn't bad either. Nothing like getting paid to take a little vacation and stay in a fancy hotel.

And here we come to the strange event in Budapest. Yes, it's already just a tiny bit strange to get the invitation two days after arrangements are confirmed to come to the U.S. for two months; it's even stranger the circumstances under which the invitation came, not to mention the lure of the bux that was dangled, but all of that can be shoved under the rug. Who knows the ways of the Universe, right?

Ark took a train to Budapest, and when he arrived he was met and taken to a very nice hotel in the city. As soon as he had settled in, he called me and gave me the number there. The university was all the way across town, and there was no Internet access from the hotel, so there are only a few emails from this period. Most of what happened was discussed over the telephone.

Ark was already in bed on the evening of the 23rd when a call came from the hotel management. The clerk asked him, "Are you Dr. Jadczyk?" Ark said yes. He was asked several other interrogatory questions, and then asked to please get dressed and come downstairs.

When he got downstairs, he was asked again if he was Dr. Jadczyk. After saying yes, he was asked if he was missing any papers. He was sure he was not because he kept his papers, his passport and wallet and credit cards, in a belt pack when traveling.

But the clerk, after hemming and hawing around, produced both his passport *and* his wallet with credit cards and all. It was claimed that someone had found them in the computer lab at the University and had turned them in to the hotel management.

Well, this was so unlikely a story that Ark could hardly believe it. He retrieved his possessions, went right upstairs and called me. The whole situation was perfectly ludicrous. In the first place, if someone found the papers in the computer lab, and knew enough about to whom they belonged to convey them to the right hotel, why didn't that person just call Ark on the phone and say they had found his papers? The hotel clerk refused to identify who had found them, and that was suspicious also.

But that didn't even come close to explaining how his papers were removed from his belt pack. He was absolutely certain that he had the belt pack on the entire time, had not opened it in the computer lab, had not had any reason to open it at any other time before he returned to the hotel, and the only possible time it could have been removed from his person was during the ride back to the hotel on the public trolley. He had stayed behind that day to write an email to me from the computer lab at the University when all the other conference participants had been transported back to the hotel, so he had to go back alone on the public transportation. It had been crowded, so it would not have been impossible for a skillful pickpocket to have filched the papers.

But why would they return them? And why not just take them up to the room and deliver them? Why the big official drama about getting dressed and coming downstairs to identify what the hotel management *must* have known was his property. After all, he had checked in, they knew his name and room number.

The whole thing stunk to high heaven. I decided to ask Cs:

January 25, 1997

Q: (T) Is the government watching [Ark]?

A: Yes. [...]

Q: (T) Is the U.S. government watching him? Or at least have taken note of his actions? Think about it; he was invited to the conference.

A: That may be true long before any of this!

Q: (T) They're watching him because he's a top-rated European scientist; they watch everybody. But, just think; he was invited to the conference, and you asked why was he invited to the conference, besides for his expertise?

A: If you beg for advice in this matter, we will say only this: perhaps best to concentrate all, and we do mean all, energies upon this matter and the seriousness therein during communications. There will be "time" for matters more akin to the "future," and of the heart, at a later juncture. Needs to understand the dangers that lurk, and that are potentially extreme, once and for all!!!!! [...]

Q: (T) The Feds, and the scientific community want to make sure that Ark's not doing something behind their back that they should be aware of at this point. Are we right about the papers, and the passport and the credit card?

A: Partially.

Q: (L) What happened to the passport and the credit card?

A: Examination, encoding, and alteration for purposes of monitoring.

Q: (L) Where did they remove them? Where were they taken? Where was he when they were taken?

A: Seated in crowded setting.

Q: (J) When were they replaced? (L) They weren't replaced; they were given back to him at the desk. (J) Oh, that's right! (L) Who took them? (J) Who returned them?

A: Agent from Alpha 1.

Q: (T) Probably a government program. (J) Theirs, or ours? (L) They're all the same.

A: Both.

Q: (L) OK, would it be advisable for him to try and have these cards replaced?

A: No!!!

Q: (T) It won't matter. Besides, if he does that, then they'll know he knows! Then, they'll just give him another set that's marked!

A: Knowledge protects and … ignorance endangers!

Q: (L) And what else was it about that whole situation that we wanted to know? Was Ark trying to communicate to me that he was in danger when he was telling me about the cards and paperwork, or that he was aware of the situation?

A: Sensed something awry, but misdiagnosed, partially.

Q: (J) Why was the phone call to him in his room so interrogatory?

A: To gauge awareness.

Q: (L) Are they monitoring my phone calls to him there, every day?

A: Yes.

Q: (T) They even monitor phone calls to Canada and back, and we're buddies. We're all the same country, it's across-border, and they monitor them. (J) Are they monitoring all your phone calls? (L) Probably.

A: Sometimes "they" even monitor these communications. Long ago, we told you how technology now existent makes such things as phone taps, for but one example, totally, completely, and ridiculously obsolete.

Q: (L) Should I try to tell him anything, either by the phone, or by e-mail, about this?

A: Pointless.

Q: (T) You don't have to. He has to be aware of it on his own, and from what you've already told us, he's aware. The scientology thing has to have really blown him away … where would that come from?

A: Assumptions. Awareness needs to be increased. And, we must tell you that "secret world government" technologies are approximately 150 years in advance of anything that you have access to.

Q: (L) Why is it pointless for me to try to communicate any of this to him? Why did you reply "pointless" to that?

A: Not what we said. It is not pointless to warn him to smarten up on the vigilance and caution scales. Just pointless to try to direct him with details, or practice "subterfuge." After all, when your mind can be read like the morning newspaper, what is the point?

And so, even though it was a small, strange incident, we had our first real in-your-face clue that somebody really was watching, and that there were, indeed, strange things going on behind the scenes. And it was going to get a lot uglier. There were petty tyrants everywhere.

The sparring match had begun.

CHAPTER 41
THE REALM OF ARCHETYPES

At this point I would like to divert back into the past again for a little bit in order to discuss some of the background issues that are important to this process of recapitulation and revealing the Matrix.

Over the course of the past few days we had a meeting of members of the group, past and present, in order to discuss Frank-as-Cypher-in-the-Matrix. One of the many subjects that was put on the table was the issue of Frank's direct channeling, as well as several instances in which group members had strong, instinctive negative reactions to the material, none of which made sense until now. In a very real way, Frank has done all of us a favor by revealing his true agenda and orientation. This has made it quite easy to spot when Frank's controllers or Franks emotions were in motion, skewing the material.

Of course, all of us were just smacking ourselves in the forehead that we didn't think of it before. But Frank was very, very good at it. He's probably a lot better than his present *compadres* realize. After all, he spent years embezzling from a guy who is said to have been one of the smoothest operators in the business.

As I mentioned before, when Frank channeled directly, there was a repellant air that emanated from him. We discussed this at length, those who had experienced it attempting to describe it in words for those who had not. A couple of members proposed the idea that the directly channeled sessions ought to be completely disregarded as being entirely corrupted. I pointed out that, in all fairness, even if the material was subject to being skewed by Frank's emotional or programmed agendas, he was still able to be very accurate due to the well-pipe analogy. As long as he was in the physical presence of the individual asking the questions, he could tune into that person's mind to some extent, most particularly when the questions were personal. In this way, under hypnosis, he was quite able to channel via a sort of telepathy, the same way he was able to accurately read palms. He simply connected to the individual asking the questions and sort of vacuumed the information out and verbalized it, as long as they were physically present. At the same time, it seems pretty obvious that even if Frank claimed that he channeled "all the time," whatever he was channeling on his own, out of our presence, was very likely being beamed from a satellite at the very least, or downloaded from fourth density STS at most.

Another point we discussed was the fact that even things that may seem to be negative occurrences from one perspective, can be very positive from another. We have already noted the fact that STS-oriented individuals have a sort of semantic aphasia – likely a consequence of wishful thinking, and even when an obvious truth is right in front of their faces, they cannot see the range, depth, or associative properties of the principle. It was in this sense that Frank was quite able to participate in the delivery of material of a very STO orientation, because he simply could not understand what it really meant.

So it is that, in the present instance, Frank's declared alignment with the forces whose origin and activities are under discussion, we now have a much better handle on understanding some of the formerly puzzling elements from certain sessions that were so completely out of character for the Cs. As we revisit the transcripts with Frank's exposed agenda and assignment to download, steal, drain, and then destroy, we are better equipped to recognize that activity and to literally spot Frank in action when his STS agent mode was activated! Fortunately, as the Cs themselves denoted, it was only 30 percent corruption.

It wasn't just the direct channeling that suffered from Frank's manipulations, or from Frank being manipulated, whichever the case may be. Even with the presence of Terry, there were instances of the bleed-through of something – either from a higher density STS source or Frank's psychological agenda. As we have already speculated, the latter is the tool of the former, so it's difficult to separate the two.

I would like to discuss here several session excerpts. In the first one, Terry announced at the beginning of the session that he was low on energy, and we can now recognize that this might have tended to reduce the shielding effect. If Terry was low on energy, it would mean that Frank's negative agenda would be more able to manifest, as was, indeed, the case. What made the session even more problematical was the presence of guests – this was the first session attended by Tom French.

I was pretty happy that Tom had decided to attend a session. I was absolutely certain that he would see that the group was far more interesting than I was. I hoped that the result would be that he would then want to interview the other members and that the focus might shift to the group and away from me, individually and specifically.

When he scheduled his attendance at this session, Tom had specifically asked that we should not do anything in any way different from
any other session – he just wanted to be a fly on the wall, so to speak. I
promised that would I try to make everything as "normal" as possible. I
decided not to notify any of the group members in advance that Tom
would be at the session. I wasn't being discourteous by springing something on them that they might not find agreeable, because all of them
had already said that they hoped he would attend a session soon. As I
saw it, Tom's attendance would be a surprise, but a nice one. At the
same time, I was keeping my promise not to do anything different.
Now, let's look at a few specific remarks from that session:

> June 3, 1995
> Q: (L) Hello.
> A: Hello.
> Q: (T) I'm running on low energy. […] (L) We have guests this evening;
> this is Tom and Cherie.
> A: Hello Tom and Cherie.

The session went along rather normally, with the standard kinds of
questions we ordinarily asked, and nothing particularly different in any
way. Anyone can read the sessions and determine that this is so, which
is what made the remark so surprising.

> A: This is more complex than your queries allow.
> Q: (L) In other words, our questions are not complex enough to get the
> answer?
> A: You are "rushing it" due to company present, now please relax and
> just behave as always.
> Q: (J) She's trying to show off! (L) I am not! (SV) That's what they said!
> (L) That's not what they said, and I am not the only one asking ques-
> tions. (T) Let's start over with something simple. We are talking about
> the aura or something similar. The planet's aura.
> A: Yes.

I was more than a little stung by such a remark, followed by Jan's
declaration that I was showing off. What was more, as I pointed out at
the moment, I wasn't the only one asking questions, nor was I in any
way rushing anything. A bit later, the Cs made the comment: "You are
drifting and there is much too much thought fragmentation tonight."
We can now recognize that the suggestion that the subject was too
complex for the board would have lead to the suggestion for Frank to
channel directly. If anything would have turned Tom French off to the
Cs, that would have done it. So, even though Jan's teasing remark focused the attention in her direction, we can now see that it was a
diversion away from Frank's agenda. The remark that there was too

much thought fragmentation was a warning from Cs that something was going on, and in retrospect we think that it was a sort of "battle of forces." What happened toward the end of the session was also rather strange:

Q: (L) Let's go onto something else that is more simple. The other night the children saw some lights in the sky. I went out to see what they were talking about and at that point there were no moving lights, but there was a single, pulsating, red light about ten degrees to the right of Jupiter. My initial reaction to it was that it was atmospheric twinkle of a large red star or the planet Mars. There was nothing there the following night. What was it the children saw?

A: Children saw planes and a helicopter.

Q: (L) Well, what was it I saw when I saw this red, pulsating light which did not move for quite some time?

A: Mars.

Q: (L) It was not Mars because it wasn't there the next night.

A: Clouds.

Q: (T) Yeah, there were clouds on Mars that night. (J) Well, let's move on. (L) Well, I thought it was Mars. (J) You were right.

A: You were right.

The only problem was, it could not have been Mars. And at that moment, I knew it couldn't have been Mars. But rather than argue the point, I decided to let it drop. I was hugely disappointed that the session had not been like so many of the others, full of fun and lively exchange and accurate information. Of course, that may have been partly due to my own wish that the group would "shine" and demonstrate that it would be far more interesting for Tom to write about *all* of us, than just me. But there had been a distinctly unpleasant sensation in the air at the time, and I wanted to know why. Jan had drawn attention to herself by saying, "She's just trying to show off," and that was very hurtful, most especially when it wasn't true. In fact, the opposite was true. I wanted to know what had happened, why the energy had been so unpleasant. So, Frank and I had a session a few days later to ask about this. In retrospect, this wasn't a very good idea because it gave Frank the opportunity, as occurred on many other occasions, to divert attention and suspicion away from himself, and plant it on others.

June 6, 1995

Q: (L) Hello.

A: Stop.

Q: (L) What does that mean? (F) Don't ask me! (L) Hello!

A: Hello. Azoref from Cassiopaea.

Q: (L) Who was it that said stop?

A: Static.

Q: (L) There was static?

A: Yes.

Q: (L) What was the source of the static?

A: Not important, static always present to some degree.

Q: (L) I want to ask some fairly quick questions.

A: Okay.

Q: (L) With whom were we communicating on Saturday night?

A: Cassiopaea.

Q: (L) Was there any corruption in Saturday night's session?

A: Maybe.

Q: (L) Well, I am not looking for a maybe. I felt somewhat offended by the atmosphere that was generated. We had guests and it was important …

A: If corrupted, came from 3rd level.

Q: (L) Can you only identify the corruption that comes from your level?

A: No.

Q: (L) Was there an element of … I don't want to lead here … my impression was that the group was in a state of tension, is this correct?

A: Yes.

Q: (L) Why?

A: Jan was unhappy because of guests.

Q: (L) Why?

A: Not notified ahead. […] If there is strong prejudice by any member or members of level three channel participants it may cause messages to be altered at the point of reception.

Q: (L) […] I spent a lot of time preparing questions and it seemed that whatever was making it through the "prejudiced channel" did not even want to deal with questions that were quite similar to many we have asked in the past – so it seems that the prejudice came through toward me in a specific way.

A: Yes.

Q: (L) Well, if people can be so easily subjected to prejudice and emotional thinking, would that not be considered psychic attack?

A: Result of. Careful not to make hasty moves based upon events which may be transitory in nature.

Q: (L) Well, I feel like we have all been under attack …

A: Attack does not emanate from Terry and Jan.

Q: (L) Well, the whole session seems ruined. Even the answer about the lights in the sky was verifiably wrong. You have said that the channel is grooved and cannot be corrupted, yet obviously wrong answers were given, and it seems that you are saying that the attack is "through" Terry and Jan and the garbled emotions they are experiencing, correct?

A: Yes.

Q: (L) Well, even the answer about the lights in the sky. Mars is 120 degrees away from Jupiter …

We can note a very strange thing in the above remarks: first, Jan is being blamed for the emotional prejudice that poisoned the atmosphere of the session, and at the same time, it is being said that the attack does not emanate "from" Terry and Jan, which suggests that it was "through" them rather than originating there.

And I missed the clue. It never would have occurred to me that Frank, himself, was the vector of attack, that he could possibly have been emanating the energies that affected Jan, as well as the rest of us in the room.

Nevertheless, after this incident, Frank renewed his campaign to do the direct channeling, and so the group discussed it and decided we would give it another try. I started off with my question about the session itself that had been described by me as "corrupted," and that wrong answers had been given as a result of this corruption, to which the Cs had given assent that my analysis was correct.

June 10, 1995

Q: (L) The first question I have is concerning last Saturday night's session, which nobody seems to have been happy with. We would like to understand why the information seemed to be so garbled and distorted and, quite frankly, incorrect.

A: What makes you feel it was incorrect?

Q: (L) Because one of the answers was that what I was seeing outside was the planet Mars. It could not have been the planet Mars because Mars was 120 degrees away from the planet Jupiter.

A: Perhaps the question was posed in such a way as to receive that response. Suggest you check the material more closely.

The reader can look at the question and response above and see quite clearly that the question was not posed in such a way as to "lead" the response. And, in fact, when I pointed out that the light could not have been Mars because it wasn't there the next night, the answer was that I couldn't see it because of clouds, which was also incorrect. I couldn't see it the next night because it wasn't there. There were no obscuring clouds.

Q: (L) It was also said that the children were seeing airplanes and helicopters. When I went out, what I saw was most definitely not a helicopter or an airplane and was only ten degrees away from the planet Jupiter, and was a red, pulsating light. Can you tell me what I saw?

A: Well, if you desire to believe that what you saw was something other than any response given, that's perfectly acceptable. But, when inquiring upon such things as visual reference, one must be prepared for any and all answers.

Q: (L) That seems to be rather evasive.

A: Evasiveness may also indicate a desire to help one learn about one-self and one's environment.

Q: (L) What I saw out there was not an airplane or a helicopter; it was also not the planet Mars. Whatever it was, it was not there the following night or any night subsequent to that. Therefore, it was some sort of object that wasn't of a sort that we usually see, and it baffles me as to why it would be conducive to learning for me to …

A: May we ask a question?

Q: (L) Sure.

A: When seeking to identify visual reference, would it not be wise to be patient with the outcome of the analysis?

Q: (L) Well, sure.

A: You state that what you saw was not a plane or a helicopter. We are interested to know how you can be certain of that?

Q: (L) Because I stood and watched it for a considerable period of time and it never moved.

A: Does that indicate that it was not a helicopter?

Q: (L) Yes, because even helicopters, when they hover, there is some lateral or horizontal movement or motion, and they also have different kinds of lights on them. They don't sit there and look like a single, large, reddish orange, glowing light that pulsates.

The subject was changed right after the above because none of us saw any point in pursuing it. All the while these words were coming out of Frank, we were all looking at each other and silently signaling each other that this was most definitely *not* the Cs talking. I was embarrassed for Frank. He had no idea how pompous and condescending he sounded or that he was being viewed as a poseur by the other members of the group. I continued to have faith that his "talent" could be developed, but I knew that he needed more exposure to the Cs by group channeling before we tried trance channeling again. What is more, I protected him. I didn't want to undermine his confidence by telling him that everybody felt just plain yucky in his presence when he channeled on his own. After all, his claim to be able to channel was the only thing he had. How could I take it away from him?

Frank's controllers' efforts to subvert the channeling to direct channeling through him came up at sporadic intervals such as the following clip from November of '95. At this point in time, I decided that, for Frank's sake, I needed to gently approach the issue of the flavor of the trance channeling, in hopes that I could get the issue on the table without triggering Frank's emotional responses based on his belief that he was the channel. I should have known that the very fact that direct channeling was being pushed indicated that the controllers were already skewing.

November 4, 1995

Q: (L) Is there anything about these bases and this subject matter that you wish to teach us further at this time?

A: Suggest direct channeling for this subject.

Q: (L) Well, you know how we feel about the direct channeling, that there is too much personal filtering involved. This way, none of us knows anything …

A: Faith must enter the picture somewhere, lest you fall behind. Some subjects are too complex to be properly discussed through this medium.

Q: (L) OK, we'll save this discussion of the bases for a direct channeling session. The only thing is, in a direct channeling session it is … There are some things about it that are disturbing. It tends, after doing it several weeks in a row, to become, it begins to sound pompous. (SV) Let's ask. (L) Why is it after doing it several times in a row, it begins to sound pompous, information begins to get skewed, why is that?

A: Perceptions are a fun challenge.

Q: (L) That's easy for you to say, because, when the answer comes back that … (J) You're not "perceptually challenged!"

A: It is easy for you to say many things.

Q: (L) Well, the thing is, when absolutely incorrect information comes out, I have a difficult time dealing with that.

A: How do you determine correctness?

Q: (L) Well in that particular instance, I was told that a certain thing that I saw in the sky was the planet Mars, and the planet Mars was so far away from that spot, that it was absolutely incorrect. I mean, the planet Mars was 120 degrees away from Jupiter. And yet, you said that they were 10 degrees apart; that what I saw that was 10 degrees away from Jupiter was Mars. Unless Mars traveled 110 degrees across the sky in one day, then that was incorrect information. There's no two ways about it!

A: Wrong!!!

Q: (L) No, it's not!

A: It is!!!

Q: (L) What is wrong? That Mars didn't travel 110 degrees? Because that is exactly what you said, that it was Mars. I went back, I read over the session!

A: You were in a 4th density flap.

Q: (L) Well, fine and dandy! If I'm in a fourth density flap, that's an easy answer for … any answer that seems to be at variance with what's happening here. I mean, do you get my point here?

A: Yes. But you are still mistaken.

Q: (L) Why am I the one that's mistaken? Why can't you be mistaken?

A: We can, but not on this one! Remember, you felt strange during this experience. And besides, you asked us for the information, we must present it to you as it is.

Q: (L) You're saying that I felt weird or strange or unusual at that occasion. I don't remember saying that I felt strange or unusual. Are you trying to put words in my mouth?

A: Who said that? You said that.

Q: (L) OK, you didn't say that I said that. You said that I said that I felt strange or unusual. I don't remember that I said that. I don't remember feeling strange or unusual.

A: OK.

The reader may want to look again at the clips from the sessions where the light in the sky was brought up to see that I most certainly did not say anything about feeling unusual during the experience, nor, more importantly, *did* I feel unusual during the experience. I simply saw something inexplicable. I watched it for a sufficient length of time to be certain that it was not an airplane or helicopter, and I just wanted to ask a simple question and get a simple answer. So why was this issue so touchy? Why was such a block being placed in front of it so that, under no circumstances, was I able to get a straight answer? It was pretty obvious that it had become an emotional issue for Frank, and the answer might be as simple as that.

The fact that we were not giving him acceptance and kudos as the channel seems to have begun to prey on Frank's mind at some point. All attempts to move the channeling to that format were rejected, though we most certainly gave it a spin a few times. Our vigilance kept the material uncorrupted for the most part even when he was direct channeling. The only problem was the repellant nature of the personality that came through Frank. It was like Frank himself to an exponential power. There was such an attitude of superiority and even contempt for human understanding completely out of keeping with the kind and patient responses of the Cs that there was no comparison.

Another example of this that deals directly with Frank's growing resentment that he was not being given top billing is the next excerpt. We had gotten into a discussion about it because he had started another of his "pity me" rants and I had just told him in a joking way that if he started on that again I was going to throw something at him. He became all upset that I had used a word describing a physical act of violence. I pointed out that the violence was only words spoken in defending myself against his words which were, effectively, doing violence to me because they were draining my energy. What was more, it was merely a metaphor, and he knew I really wasn't going to throw anything at him. But he just wanted to argue, so I suggested that sometimes, one had to do or say something to make the point. What is interesting about this one is the fact that the following excerpt generally contradicts the information given in the session about Frank's many rants as being his way of "fighting back." Of course, as I have already mentioned, the truth was coming through then, though it was being skewed by Frank's agenda. The same is true in the following:

June 1, 1996

Q: (L) Frank and I would like to have a comment on our dispute.

A: Ask.

Q: (F) I don't know what to ask. (L) Well, Frank says that violence is *never* an appropriate response to words.

A: Okay.

Q: (L) I say that under some circumstances, it may be the only response.

A: Why do you say that?

Q: (L) Because there do exist situations where words are used repeatedly to harm another. One example is the Nazi propaganda machine. If someone had shot Goebbels, it might have saved a lot of people from dying.

A: No.

Q: (L) Well, of course. There would have been someone else. Still, the point is, words can be used to destroy, and words of power can be used to kill. Sometimes words can be a lot more hurtful to the soul than physical acts.

A: Not directly.

Q: (L) Well, directly, or indirectly, it still amounts to the same thing.

A: No.

Q: (L) Well, I know you are not going to agree with me.

A: This is a subject that demands further exploration, in order to bring about a definitive answer.

Q: (L) Go ahead. Explain it to me.

A: Words only have power if the receiver believes they do.

Q: (L) But, in many cases, that belief exists.

A: The power to control belief lies exclusively within the receiver.

Which, of course, begs the question of why it was okay for Frank to fight back with words, but it was not okay for me to do it! In another sense, however, if Frank was already marked as an STS individual, then the answers then and in this particular session were exactly correct, only I was seeing them from the idea that Frank was seeking to serve others.

Q: (L) Let me put it this way: Frank often says things that are not precisely soothing to the soul, to say the least. Most often, I ignore them. But, sometimes I am not in an ignoring mood, and my response is no more violent toward him than his toward me. I merely speak metaphorically. When I do, I am only saying, "Stop doing that!" in a figurative way. But, he finds this to be as irritating to him as what he says that irritates me …

A: And …

Q: (L) Well, that is about it. I have lately been verbally attacked by numerous individuals … so I am not in a mood to tolerate much in this line from those around me.

A: And if this irritates you, it is because you allow it to.

Q: (L) Fine and dandy. And it is true, and I know it. Which is why I am beginning to think that I ought to simply do nothing, because my feelings are too sensitive.

A: And do you really believe that that is an unalterable condition?

Q: (L) Well, why should I be the one who is obliged to become less sensitive, and other people are not obliged to become more thoughtful about what they say?

A: You cannot control others.

Q: (L) I don't want to control anyone. I am just saying that the obvious thing is for me to simply withdraw into my own little world of reading and thinking and writing, and if nothing ever comes of any of it, it is utterly immaterial to me.

And here we see Frank's powerful emotional reaction. There I was, suggesting that we give the entire project up, forget about the Cs, forget about making Frank a star, and just go back to doing what I enjoyed doing where I certainly didn't have to put up with Frank or the various types of nastiness encountered on the Internet, from Frank, and elsewhere.

A: That is your choice, but not a wise one!!!

Q: (L) Well, you say that, but it is, as several people have pointed out to me, only since we have begun this channeling project that all these dreadful things have happened in my life. My life is a shambles!

A: "Dreadful is subjective."

Q: (L) I would say that the physical things that have happened to me, the collapse of my marriage, the things that have happened to my children, are pretty damn dreadful, subjectively or otherwise!

A: Before these changes began to manifest, you were deeper into the "deadly illusion" than you are now. Emergence is, by its very nature, uncomfortable. But, it has and will, empower you, we promise!!!!!!!!

Q: (L) It is a very trying time now. I am having a difficult time just coping.

A: And there have been others, and will be others, but that does not mean that the rewards will be slight.

Q: (L) Well …

A: You are on a path of destiny, and there is no turning back now.

Q: (S) What happened in specific? (L) Well, I was trying to explain some of the material to several people, and the end result was that they decided that I was possessed and that the Cs were evil because they say that we have to figure things out ourselves in order to graduate to the next level. Including my husband.

A: Why does this bother you? It does not bother us. They can all decide that we are the "Queens of Satan," if they wish. It is free will.

Q: (L) I don't like the implied hardness … I am not a hard person.

A: It is not hardness. The "feelings" you describe are related to ego, and by relation, pride, two things that were deliberately implanted into the 3rd density human psyche by the 4th density STS 309,000 years ago, as you measure time. Refer to the transcripts with regard to DNA alteration and the occipital ridge. Believe it or not, you, Laura, will be rid of these, eventually. It is not what some individuals respond to you that matters. It is sharing the information that counts. Also, remember, these persons do not perceive your feelings and sensitivities as keenly as you do, nor do you perceive theirs, likewise.

That was all fine and good, and I certainly couldn't argue with it in principle. However, I was having some difficulty understanding how feeling hurt after being attacked for sharing some of the Cs material was related to ego and pride. What is more, this didn't seem like the Cs I was used to. Indeed, there comes a time when a person needs to toughen up, but considering the beating I had been taking for so long, these remarks were singularly cold.

Yes, they offered the carrot that "you are on a path of destiny," and "rewards" that were not slight were indicated. But as a general rule, I am on guard against such lures, considering them to be ego hooks. I realize in retrospect that yes, it may be true that there is some destined activity, but the entire interaction with Frank was designed to divert that destiny to some other agenda, and to prevent the real destiny, if there is one, and whatever it may be. But it was the next segment that was so completely untrue that I was shocked. I thought that the Cs (even if skewed by Frank) were finished and I started to ask a question for someone else. I was about to find out that the Cs were not only being cold, they were being completely inaccurate and making assumptions that were untrue!

Q: (L) There is someone who wants to ask some questions …
A: We are not finished with this subject. Also, it is important to note that, in most cases in which you have suffered "attack" from those on the Internet, you were not directly conveying the information we have given to you. You were presenting thoughts that you claimed as your own, or knowledge that you have gathered strictly through your own efforts, thus, it was responded to in kind. This you must expect if you are going to plant the bulk of the credit upon yourself, then you open up yourself to direct criticism. This is not wise if you are not prepared for negative reactions. Third density beings will always perceive knowledge that is being given to them before they are ready to receive it as "preaching," and they resent this because of the very same ego related issues we discussed earlier. So, suggestion: better to frame knowledge transference with a preamble such as, "this is what was given to me, it is up to you to decide for yourself whether or not you are comfortable with accepting it, or not."

What was so shocking about the above remarks was that it was entirely and altogether untrue. In fact, it had *always* been as a direct result of presenting the *raw* material that I had suffered attack! I was most definitely directly conveying the information, and I was most definitely *not* presenting thoughts that I claimed as my own!!! And that's a cold hard fact because I still have the emails and message board discussions from that period. There is no doubt whatsoever that this was Frank using the board to express what *he* believed to be true. He felt that he was not being sufficiently revered as the channel, and this led him to create wild theories in his mind that everyone was conspiring against him to "cut him out" of something, including credit for being the channel. What is more, for a very long time I presented all material as simply from the Group, with *no* names designated at all. I was so stunned by this attack from the C's, that I knew it was not them at all and I terminated the session.

Q: (L) Well, that is *not* true, by *any* stretch of the imagination. I don't want to talk about it anymore with you. You are being completely wrong! Talk about assumptions! [End of Session]

But again, let me point out to the perspicacious reader that, even though there was skewing, again, there were remarks that were made that were right on the money, most especially those comments about DNA alteration and our need to hone our skills as warriors by divesting ourselves of self-importance in the sense of being subject to offense. Indeed, when I am offended, it is an effect of self-importance. But in the above case, I was most definitely not guilty of the offenses for which I was being blamed.

By now the reader may be getting the idea that sometimes the transmissions were like trying to watch television while someone runs the vacuum cleaner (no pun intended!). The degree of interference can vary by the position of the vacuum relative to the television, as well as other factors including the strength of the broadcast signal. So, even though the picture might get very snowy or distorted, the real picture can still be seen and interpreted. The best pictures came when the vacuum was turned off, and Frank practically dozed at the board from boredom. For the most part, when I was off on my cosmic questions, my questions about history and the nature of reality, he practically went to sleep.

There is another consideration that would negate the assumption that, just because the material was delivered by Frank in trance, that we ought to just toss it out. As the Cs themselves once said when we asked a question about a similar situation:

March 18, 2000

Q: Whitley Strieber and Art Bell have published a book about a "global superstorm." Is any of the information they have given in this book fairly accurate?

A: Derived from non-human sources known for stark accuracy, when convenient.

Q: What makes it convenient at the present time for them to be "starkly accurate?"

A: Fits into plans.

This now brings us to a particular session, one that was direct channeled via Frank when the entire group was present. This session was one that demonstrated the superior, condescending attitude so sharply that it is even obvious in the text. Many people have written to ask me if I was sure that we were talking to the Cs on this one. However, even though repellant obfuscation and avoidance of the issues by a lot of words that said little was apparent, there was so important a message conveyed in this session that it deserves attention. In this particular case, I don't think it was the Cs, and I don't think it was the STS controllers speaking; I think it was a simple matter of Frank tuning into me telepathically, or was acting as the well-pipe, and the information was being drawn directly from my unconscious mind. One thing I do know is that, in retrospect, the way I received the information, and the way I ultimately acted on it, was one of the keys to unlocking the destiny and changing my reality completely.

The therapy I was receiving for the injuries sustained in the accident some seven months earlier wasn't helping me very much, to put it briefly. At some point, another X-ray was made by the chiropractor, and he noted a strange shadow that looked like a metal pin linking the 5th and sixth cervical vertebrae together. He referred me to a neurosurgeon who ordered a series of MRI's.

On the night before I was scheduled to have these films made, I woke up suddenly, as though I had been thrown off a cliff, my heart pounding, choking and gagging on something thick in my throat. My entire mouth and throat, going deep inside, was in horrible pain. I felt as though my tongue had been torn out by the roots and I was strangling on it.

I ran to the bathroom and tried to spit out what was choking me, and it was a big clot of blood. The only explanation I could think of was that I must have bitten my tongue in my sleep. I examined my throat, and it was torn, red and swollen way in the back, beyond my teeth, slightly to one side of the back of my throat. The bleeding redness extended down into the recesses of my throat where I couldn't see it all. There was no way I could have bitten myself there! When I tried to wake my husband up to help me, I was unable to rouse him, and he had *always* been a light sleeper. This disturbed me very much. My throat and the side of my face swelled up and stayed swollen for over a week and I had difficulty eating and talking, much less swallowing.

The bottom line was: whatever had been seen by the chiropractor on the X-rays was no longer there. But I did have a bulging disk that was pressing on the spinal cord and the neurologist felt that this was the source of most of the pain. He wanted me to see a surgeon. The films were sent over and I was given an appointment.

Surgery was not the best option because I have a congenitally narrow spinal canal. But the same thing that made surgery problematical, made it likely that I would suffer constant pain and occasional paralysis for the rest of my life. What was more, with the vagaries of spinal impingement, it was hard to tell where I was going to hurt or experience the paralysis from one day to the next.

Having suffered so much pain for so long, I was rather depressed by this news. I mean, what else can go wrong?

The attorneys for the fellow who hit me wanted my MRI's to send out for a second opinion, but they had "disappeared." All the efforts of two doctor's staffs as well as the staff at the medical center where they were taken, were unable to produce them. It was a big mystery. The staff at the MRI unit were so upset that they undertook to do hand searches in relays to try and find them. They were under a *lot* of pressure to find them because, otherwise, they had to do them over again without charge, and it was a very expensive set of films. After almost two weeks of searching, the MRI staff finally admitted defeat. I was scheduled to come in to have another set made.

The night before the new pictures were to be made, I was worried about being able to go to sleep due to the strange events surrounding the loss of my films as well as other matters. After lying down, I was just trying to be still and calm down the pain, knowing I wasn't going to be able to go to sleep. I was right in the middle of puzzling over those blasted MRI's, when the next thing I knew there was a sort of momentary blank-spot and I came to myself, only to discover that I was being floated out of bed, feet first, by three or four spidery creatures who had me by the ankle and were "pulling" on me.

I was struggling and resisting and apparently had been doing so even while asleep because I found that my paralyzed arm was extended up over my head and was locked on the brass headboard in a death grip and the bed was shaking and bouncing with the efforts of my resistance. It was virtually a tug of war and I wasn't going to let go!

I looked at them and the creepy little spider guys realized that I had awakened. One of them put its hand on my head and I felt a paralysis coming over me. I became very angry. I wanted to curse them. But it was impossible to resist this paralysis and that made me even madder! I was determined that, even if they had technology that could overcome all of my efforts of resistance, that at least I would give them a piece of my mind! I was going to have my say!

With enormous concentration, I was able to utter a strangled sound. It was not the defiant curse I was working on in my head, but anything was progress against the frozen sensation of my entire body. And, it had a startling effect! As soon as I uttered this incomprehensible, cave person-type sound, they dropped me like a hot potato and began sort of flitting and chattering like a nest of birds with a cat climbing the tree. They huddled together and sort of melted into a shimmery curtain thing alongside my bed. It was much like the mirage effect one sees on the road ahead when driving on a hot day.

My heart was pounding from real exertion. I can't say that I was terrified because such a thing is beyond terror. And, I have always been a person who acts cleanly and efficiently in a crisis, so this was no different in that respect. What had been most useful was that I had the information from the Cassiopaeans because that certainly had a lot to do with not feeling terrified which is more often a reaction to the unknown. At least, to some extent, I had an idea of what I was dealing with, even if I preferred to believe that it had been a hypnagogic nightmare.

At one point, while I was fighting them, while the bed seemed to be bouncing and jerking, I was very conscious that it was not waking my husband up, and after the creatures had melted away, when I had turned to work at peeling my paralyzed hand away from the headboard, I was startled to see and feel three distinct, wave-like shudders pass through his body starting from the head and moving down. After the third one, he took a deep breath, and began to snore suddenly and loudly as though he started right in mid-snore.

What was troubling me was that he was not been moving at all, not even to breathe. It struck me with horror that he seemed to have been "turned off" in order to prevent his intervention. That he *could* be turned off scared me half to death! I had *no* protection at all! Not only that, when I tried to tell him what had happened, he thought I was imagining it. I can assure you, it was *not* Imagination, though it may indeed have occurred in a hyperdimensional reality, and had not been a material event as we understand them.

As I lay there, trying to figure out whether the event had really happened, or if it had just been in my own head, I realized that the evidence that something had happened was that my partially paralyzed left hand was holding the headboard. Heck, I couldn't even lift that arm, much less hold anything with my left hand. And that I had been gripping and struggling for some time was pretty certain because of the way the hand refused to come open. I lay there trying to figure out what the heck had happened, while cradling my arm that was still screaming in pain and jerking spasmodically. What was more, I couldn't understand how my ex-husband could have slept through all of that rather violent struggle! I was pretty sure that, even if nothing had been physically manifested in the room, at least I had been struggling.

I got out of the bed and sat up the rest of the night in a recliner, thinking and smoking. Early in the morning, the girl from the test center called, and in a shaking voice, told me that when she had come in that morning, my file with all films intact, was on the reception desk. No one admitted to finding it and placing it there, and she had been the last one to leave the office the night before and the first in the office that morning and had unlocked the doors herself. It was a mystery that has never been explained.

That gave me even more to think about, but I will leave the speculation to the reader. I can only recount what happened. Because of the exhausting, obfuscatory nature of the following session during which I wanted to ask a few simple questions about this event, I was never able to ask about the films, and never came back to the subject. Another important point: I had not discussed the event with the group before asking the questions. The reader will notice that I do not initially even describe or name the event in order to not lead the answers. Also, I have edited out the tedious rambling around of Frank and have retained only those questions and answers bearing on the event itself. The interested reader can go to the sessions page and read the entire session and see what I mean by "tedious."

July 23, 1995

Q: (L) Toren, the first thing on my mind is an experience I had several nights ago. It seemed as though there was some sort of interaction between myself and something "other." Could you tell me what this experience was?

A: Was eclipsing of the realities.

Q: (L) What is an eclipsing of the realities?

A: It is when energy centers conflict.

Q: (L) What energy centers are conflicting?

A: Thought energy centers. [...] Therefore, energy centers conflicting involve thought patterns. You could refer to it as an intersecting of thought pattern energies. [...]

Q: (L) Well, it seemed to me that something happened to me that blanked out a period of my experience, and you say this was an eclipsing of energies caused by an intersecting of thought centers. Now, this in-

181

tersecting of thought centers, did this occur within my body or within my environment?

A: They are one and the same. […]

Q: (L) Alright. I was lying in bed worrying about being able to get to sleep. The next thing I knew, I came to myself feeling that I was being floated off my bed. Was I?

A: No. When you say "I" you are referring to your whole person. There is more than one factor involved with one's being to any particular definition.

Q: (L) Was some part of my being being separated from another part of my being?

A: Yes.

Q: (L) Was this an attempt to extract my soul or astral body?

A: Attempt is not probably the proper term.

Q: (L) In other words …

A: It is more just an activity taking place. Attempt implies effort rather than the nature present in a conflicting of energies and thought centers.

Q: (L) I also seemed to be aware of several dark, spider-like figures lined up by the side of the bed. Was this an accurate impression.

A: Those could be described as specific thought center projections.

Q: (L) I seemed to be fighting and resisting this activity.

A: That was your choice.

Q: (L) Was I successful?

A: Now, we are back to leading again.

Q: (L) Alright, was this the ending of an abduction that had already taken place?

A: Not the proper terminology. It was the conclusion to an event, not necessarily what one would refer to as an abduction, but more what one would refer to as an interaction.

Q: (L) What was the nature of the interaction?

A: The conflicting of energies related to thought center impulses.

Q: (L) Where are these thought centers located?

A: Well, that is difficult to answer because that is assuming that thought centers are located. And, of course this is a concept area in which you are not fully familiar as of yet. So, an attempt to answer this in any way that would make sense to you would probably not be fruitful. We suggest slowing down and carefully formulating questions.

Q: (L) At what level of density do these thought centers have their primary focus?

A: Thought centers do not have primary focus in any level of density. This is precisely the point. You are not completely familiar with the reality of what thoughts are. We have spoken to you on many levels and have detailed many areas involving density level, but thoughts are quite a different thing because they pass through all density levels at once. Now, let us ask you this. Do you not now see how that would be possible?

Q: (L) Yes. But what I am trying to do is identify these conflicting thought centers. If two thought centers, or more, conflict, then my idea would be that they are in opposition.

A: Correct. […]

Q: (L) OK, you said I wasn't abducted, that an event of some sort occurred. What was the event?

A: We have already described this, but the problem that you are having is that you are assuming that the description we are giving is more complicated than this. It is not. […]

Q: (L) OK, in the experience I felt a paralysis of my body, what caused this paralysis.

A: Yes. Separation of awareness. Which is defined as any point along the pathway where one's awareness becomes so totally focused on one thought sector that all other levels of awareness are temporarily receded, thereby making it impossible to become aware of one's physical reality along with one's mental reality. This gives the impression of what is referred to as paralysis. Do you understand?

Q: (L) Yes. And what stimulates this total focus of awareness?

A: An event which sidetracks, temporarily, the mental processes.

Q: (L) And what event can sidetrack the mental processes to this extent?

A: Any number.

Q: (L) In this particular case, what was it?

A: It was an eclipsing of energies caused by conflicting thought centers.

Q: (L) What energies were being eclipsed?

A: Whenever two opposing units of reality intersect, this causes what can be referred to as friction, which, for an immeasurable amount of what you would refer to as time, which is, of course, nonexistent, creates a nonexistence, or a stopping of the movements of all functions. This is what we would know as conflict. In between, or through any intersecting, opposite entities, we always find zero time, zero movement, zero transference, zero exchange. Now think about this. Think about this carefully.

Q: (L) Does this mean that I was, essentially, in a condition of nonexistence?

A: Well, nonexistence is not really the proper term, but non-fluid existence would be more to the point. Do you understand?

Q: (L) Yes. Frozen, as it were?

A: Frozen, as it were.

Q: (L) Was there any benefit to me from this experience?

A: All experiences have potential for benefit.

Q: (L) Was there any detriment from this experience?

A: All experiences have potential for detriment. Now, do you see the parallels? We are talking about any opposing forces in nature, when they come together, the result can go all the way to the extreme of one side or all the way to the extreme of the other. Or, it can remain perfectly, symmetrically in balance in the middle, or partially in balance on one side or another. Therefore all potentials are realized at intersecting points in reality. [...]

Q: (L) Was one of the thought centers me?

A: That is presupposing that you, what is defined as you, or how you define yourself as "me" is of and by itself a thought center.

Q: (L) Well, I am trying to find this out by asking these questions. I am not presupposing here, I am just trying to find out what is going on here!

A: Part of what is you is a thought center but not all of what is you is a thought center. So, therefore it is incorrect to say: "Was one of these conflicting energies or thought centers me?"

Q: (L) Was one of these conflicting thought centers or energies some part of me?

A: Yes.

Q: (L) And was it eclipsed by interacting with a thought center energy that was part of or all of something or someone else?

A: Or, was what happened a conflicting of one energy thought center that was a part of your thought process and another energy thought center that was another part of your thought process? We will ask you that question and allow you to contemplate.

Q: (L) Was it?

A: We will ask you that question and allow you to contemplate.

Q: (L) Does it ever happen that individuals who perceive or think they perceive themselves to have experienced an abduction, to actually be interacting with some part of themselves?

A: That would be a very good possibility. Now, before you ask another question, stop and contemplate for a moment: what possibilities does this open up? Is there any limit? And if there is, what is that? Is it not an area worth exploring?

Q: (L) OK, help me out here ...

A: For example, just one example for you to digest. What if the abduction scenario could take place where your soul projection, in what you perceive as the future, can come back and abduct your soul projection in what you perceive as the present?

Q: (L) Oh, dear! Does this happen?

A: This is a question for you to ask yourself and contemplate.

Q: (L) Why would I do that to myself? (J) To gain knowledge of the future.

A: Are there not a great many possible answers?

Q: (L) Well, this seemed to be a very frightening and negative experience. If that is the case, then *a*: maybe that is just my perception, or *b*: then, in the future I am not a very nice person! (J) Or maybe the future isn't very pleasant. And the knowledge that you gained of it is unpleasant.

A: Or is it one possible future, but not all possible futures? And is the pathway of free will not connected to all of this?

Q: (L) God! I hope so. [...]

Q: (L) OK, when this experience occurred, am I to assume that some part of myself, a future self perhaps, of course they are all simultaneous but just for the sake of reference, came back and interacted with my present self for some purpose of exchange?

A: Well this is a question best left for your own exploration as you will gain more knowledge by contemplating it by yourself rather than seeking the answers here. But a suggestion is to be made that you do that as you will gain much, very much knowledge by contemplating these very questions on your own and networking with others as you do so. Be not frustrated for the answers to be gained through your own contemplation will be truly illuminating to you and the experience to follow will be worth a thousand lifetimes of pleasure and joy.

To say that I was puzzled and confused is putting it mildly. But there was still something else about the event that was bothering me: the fact that my husband had been "turned off." For some reason, I had the idea that this was connected to another event that had occurred several days previously. So, trying to be discreet, I asked:

Q: (L) OK, just a few days prior to this experience, I experienced a couple of headaches brought on by marital interactions. I would like to know what was the source of this sudden, extreme pain.

A: Have you not answered that for yourself already?

Q: (L) Not satisfactorily.

A: No. It is that you perceive it as being not satisfactory.

Q: (L) Well, I have a couple of choices and I haven't selected one as being the one.

A: Well, then select one.

Q: (L) What if I select the wrong one?

A: You won't.

And this brings us to the crux of the matter at this point, the very thing we have been discussing: our relationships in terms of theological realities and conflicts between forces at higher levels.

If all of existence is consciousness, if alternate universes are different individual or mass consciousness trajectories, then it must be very much like a tree.

When we look at a tree we notice that some branches start to grow, but for some reason, they become stunted and die and fall off. Others will grow for a little way before doing so. Still others grow strong and get all the "juice" and develop, and more branches grow from them, and so on.

In terms of alternate dimensions, its all too easy to use it as an excuse for any lie to be accepted as truth, and this is why I sat back to think about this idea a little more carefully.

As soon as the Many Worlds theory of physics was dropped into public awareness, the New Age grabbed it and it became *the* new explanation for everything weird. If a source was caught in a lie, it was easy to explain that it "happened in another dimension."

My guess is that the real world of third density/dimensions, is a collapsed wave function reality. It is like the branch of a tree. At certain nodal points, there are other branches that have the possibility of "getting all the juice" and becoming the dominant branch, and what determines which it is depends on many factors.

But, once one bud begins to dominate, the others become smaller and smaller and fall away eventually for lack of "juice." There is only one "real" reality. The others are only ghost or potential realities. Like a tree, with gazillions of branches, each individual's reality grows in this way. At certain points, there *are* alternate realities. But, depending upon choice, attention, and other factors, those realities that are undesirable can be "pruned" or deprived of sap so that they wither and fall away.

At the same time, each individual being their own "branch," has a slightly different reality from every other individual, and some responsibility for the way their branch grows. But it is all from the same tree, and thus has a more or less single reality. If their choices are "diseased," their branch will grow in a way that causes it to be pruned, or wither, or face some interference even from other branches, perhaps.

So, in a certain sense, at the nodal point, many possibilities may exist, just as several buds may put out on the end of a branch, but not all of them will continue the process of branching, and at such points, we have some freedom to choose, individually or collectively, depending on the nature of the branch.

It is my thought that, at this time of eclipsing of realities, a very interesting thing had occurred: the energies of awareness I had been acquiring for almost a year had brought me to a point where the nascent Thought Centers of STO and STS each had an equal possibility of becoming the dominant branch. If the Cassiopaeans were one Thought Center of a different reality, me in the future, so to speak, but a future that was not yet "firm," it was only a budding branch on the tree, and the abducting critters originated from a different "me in the future," of another branch. At this moment, the energies were equal, and something tremendous hinged upon my choice. And that choice had consequences relating to my marriage.

I began to understand that our reality is masked as a medium for growth. What we are growing is our Will which, when aligned with a given Thought Center, allows that Thought Center to manifest its Will in our reality to the extent we are in alignment and can be amplified! To be in alignment with the STO Thought Centers results in an increase of spiritual consciousness and a diminishment of the "sleeping" consciousness of matter. To align with the STS Thought Centers, as we *are*, results in an increase of the sleeping consciousness, or wishful thinking of matter, and a diminishment of spiritual consciousness.

Every situation or dynamic in which we find ourselves demands a *response*. To not respond is, of course, a choice to accede to the dynamic as *it* is. This means that the only true response we can give is to *be* more fully and strongly what we have chosen. Consciously. And only by doing this do we progress to the next level.

We come then to the problem of how to do this and I realized that it was a matter of growing stronger in terms of polarity/orientation. At the level of third density, the animal man is far stronger than the spiritual man. Third density is the point at which the process of division into those that will follow the unification into Oneness that leads to the "new" descent into primal matter, and those that will follow the unification into Oneness that will be the consciousness that will "play" with this clay, losing itself in it for the joy of creation and learning and experience.

It was at this point that I began to understand the principle and purpose of the petty tyrant. Even though I hadn't read Castaneda at this point, I knew that there was a moment in which I had received a warning that my ex-husband was draining my energy to the point of death. And after the two experiences, where I realized that he might actually be the one whose energy was utilized to interact with me – that it was through him, as a portal, that such beings were enabled to enter my reality – it was a terrible thing to face. I was seeing the theological reality, the eclipsing of realities, that my real choices in real life, regarding real people, reflected some higher realm of existence. And all the niceness in the world wasn't enough to make this one go back under the rug.

In dealing with my ex as a petty tyrant, I had achieved a certain level of modification that allowed me to hold my own in the face of the unknown. Combined with knowledge from research and information from the Cs, I hadn't run screaming in terror; I hadn't collapsed in horror; I hadn't allowed myself to be a victim. Even though I had the idea that such beings might have more power than me, I refused my permission. If they were going to do it, if I couldn't kick and scream, I would think the loudest yells at them imaginable. And they knew it somehow. Remember what don Juan said?

> He explained that ... if seers can hold their own in facing petty tyrants, they can certainly face the unknown with impunity, and then they can even stand the presence of the unknowable.

"The average man's reaction is to think that the order of that state-ment should be reversed," he went on. "A seer who can hold his own in the face of the unknown can certainly face petty tyrants. But that's not so. What destroyed the superb seers of ancient times was that assump-tion. We know better now. We know that nothing can temper the spirit of a warrior as much as the challenge of dealing with impossible people in positions of power. Only under those conditions can warriors acquire the sobriety and serenity to stand the pressure of the unknowable."

I vociferously disagreed with him. I told him that in my opinion ty-rants can only render their victims helpless or make them as brutal as they themselves are. I pointed out that countless studies had been done on the effects of physical and psychological torture on such victims.

"The difference is in something you just said," he retorted. "They are victims, not warriors."

And that was the key. I began to grow a branch of the tree that went in a different direction, toward a different future; a future wherein I was no longer willing to be a victim.

The branch grew slowly, of course. It would be 8 months before there was enough growth to stand the pressure of the unknowable – and then, only to a certain extent. But everything hinged on recouping my energy, and I knew that I must concentrate everything on this task.

This idea, this principle, that close association with an individual who is on a path to a certain future, a person who is growing the branch of a certain Thought Center, being united with such a person as in a marital relationship, is a crucial element of the theological reality. They may be on the same branch for a long time, but when a new bud begins to grow, there is a choice. This fact is disguised from us in myri-ads of ways all engendered and supported by the theories of psychology promoted by the Matrix control system.

And the same is true for all our many relationships. Each and every encounter with a petty tyrant will ultimately bring us to a point of eclipsing of realities wherein we can make choices. There are any num-ber of futures, but they are ghost futures; potential futures; you can build up your energy and choose which branch grows. But only at those points where you have done a certain amount of work that "seeds" the new branch. And when it is ready, it will let you know.

And based on those choices, the entire universe can be changed.

CHAPTER 42
THE TRADITION

During the course of our experiences with the Cassiopaeans in the two years before Ark's arrival on the scene, we had many other experiences with attack that resulted from our association with individuals who were what we had begun to call agents. I have recounted some of these in the Wave Series, including the research I was doing at the time which, little by little, made me aware that something seriously interesting was going on with this communication with Cassiopaea.

Up to this point in time, there were a number of esoteric traditions that were available to seekers of higher knowledge, all of which emanated from secret societies, and groups that required oaths of secrecy, rites and rituals, or periodic or permanent withdrawal from the world in order for a person to achieve higher consciousness – which was, of course, promulgated as the means by which the ultimate goal was achieved; this goal being either power over the forces of life, or escape from life itself.

Ark and I both have investigated these paths to some greater or lesser extent through our searches, but neither of us ever felt sufficiently inspired by their exoteric cloaks to do more than give them academic interest. "Control over the forces of life" via magic and ceremony never appealed to either of us, and abdicating responsibility to life and other people also never appealed to either of us. What we had both independently recognized was that George Gurdjieff had brought to the world "fragments of an unknown teaching" that resonated deeply in our souls.

Gurdjieff's work is evidently deeply rooted in an ancient tradition that predates all other known teachings promulgated by any of the so-called secret societies. Some have suggested that it points toward Egypt, but we believe that we clearly demonstrate in our book, *The Secret History of the World*, that its origins are precisely where Gurdjieff said they were: deep in Central Asia.

Even though he had received his initiations in the Tradition of the Ancients, Gurdjieff was clearly breaking with the tradition by opening it up to the world at large. No one has any clear answer as to whether he was charged with this mission, or whether he decided on his own to take the responsibility for gambling on awakening mankind at large, but the result was that he came under intense criticism and castigation by both initiates and the uninitiated.

Interestingly, in his last book, *Life is Only Real Then, When I Am*, Gurdjieff makes a very revealing statement. He describes certain abilities of the mind which he possessed directly relating to "the power of telepathy and hypnotism." He voluntarily gave up the use of these abilities to manipulate others, but also "made a reservation that my oath should not concern the application of it for scientific purposes. For instance, I was very much interested then, and even now my interest has not entirely vanished, in increasing the visibility of *distant cosmic centers* many thousand times *through the use of a medium* ... " Relating this to what we have said about Thought Centers in the previous chapter, we begin to see that Gurdjieff was engaged in activities and goals very similar to our present work.

Gurdjieff seemed to be acutely aware that the conditions of life had become so abnormal that only a desperate gamble might avert a certain catastrophe. He introduced a practical esoteric method into a system of initiation that taught that life itself was the great initiator. He hoped that he would be able to stimulate enough people to undergo the adventure of self-awakening so that the world as we know it might not be destroyed.

Gurdjieff himself said that "the teaching whose theory is here being set out is completely self-supporting and independent of other lines and it has been completely unknown up to the present time."

That does not, of course, mean that it did not exist for millennia before Gurdjieff was charged with its exposition in these times.

The significant things about what came to be known as the Fourth Way was that it was not a religion, there was no dogma, no belief system, every idea and practice was to be verified by one's own intentional observation and experimentation. What was essential to it was not devotion or belief, but effort, self-study, self-sacrifice in the true sense of the word, and understanding. What was more, the effort had to be *completely voluntary*.

The central theme of Gurdjieff's work was that the individual could awaken through special efforts, utilizing the uncertainty, shocks (to one's beliefs, preconceived notions, and habitual ways of thinking, feeling, and behaving), suffering and negativity of real life, to produce the ability to extend intentionally the inner processes of the conscious absorption of impressions for the purpose of stimulating and enhancing awareness at multiple levels of being. This effort was aimed at developing a special quality, a wading through the processes of the psychological and organic self with a view to preparing the ground for the development of the higher self that was more than the sum of its parts. This quality that was sought was that of the higher mind that could impartially observe the self *as it is* – not as it was imagined to be, or wished to be – so as to "grow the mustard seed" of the essence so that a higher-being body could be formed and a soul crystallized.

Observation of the self, and the world, *as it is*, brings a kind of suffering that only impersonal truth can evoke. And doing it repeatedly can crack the shell of the Matrix.

Castaneda had obviously either read Gurdjieff's work, or had tapped into a similar current either through his own psyche, or literally through the teachings of a group of seers, or Naguals, as he claimed. Dr. C. Scott Littleton, Professor of Anthropology at Occidental College, Los Angeles (author of *From Scythia to Camelot*), with whom I have personally discussed the issues of Carlos Castaneda, wrote to me:

> Yes, I'm convinced that there was indeed a prototype of don Juan & that he was probably a Yaqui who moved rather freely between the Tucson area and northern Sonora. I also recall Carlos telling me that he never saw the guy again, at least in the flesh, after he, Nestor & Pablito jumped off the Ixtlan cliff at the climax of their initiation. He also said that his mentor died shortly thereafter.
>
> I did hear through the grapevine that FD conned him into believing her account of her relationship with a South American shaman & managed to get him to write the foreword to her book, which, I've been told by persons I trust, is pure BS. Actually, this credulity on Castaneda's part is thoroughly believable. He was a "trickster" who often tricked himself into accepting other people's lies. ...
>
> I do know that in the late '80s & early '90s Carlos & his disciples, most of them Indians in the country illegally, were engaged in collective dreaming experiments from their base in the Mojave Desert. These included "voyages" to "planets in nearby star systems," as he described it in the last guest lecture he ever gave to one of my UCLA Extension classes, ca. '89. ...
>
> Finally, as I've said before, I suspect that most of the guy's experiences reflect a UFO connection, despite the absence of clear-cut UFO imagery in his writings. ... Yes, I did raise this possibility with Carlos on several occasions, and he told me that he'd "look into it." Whether he ever did is a moot point.

In other words, hyperdimensional teachers may not be so crazy an idea. And if so, the Cassiopaeans seem to be of the same extremely ancient "Tradition" of Gurdjieff, and to some extent, Castaneda.

It is truly only in this sense that the Cassiopaeans can be understood. Their method of teaching, frustrating and trapping us in reactions, all the while urging us to not identify, to become free of our reactions, is a mode of self-development of conscience and understanding and true individuality that enables one to become free of the service-to-self hierarchy.

Gurdjieff taught that, since we are all One, what each of us does for ourselves in terms of self-development and awakening, we do for others, because when we withdraw from the feeding dynamic, we are then able to assist others to withdraw. We are the protectors of our inner life, the essence of the Divine, and as we protect it from the predations of those who would seek to devour it, to use it, to abuse us, we are protecting and defending that Divine spiritual part of us that seeks full manifestation and "birth" into this world – *thy will be done on Earth, as it is in Heaven.* This Divine self, this essence of God that is the seed of the soul, is hidden, buried in a shell of false personality that consists very often of "niceness" and seeing only "good" all around, when in fact, the reality is one in which very little of "goodness" is truly manifested because it is a Matrix control system that feeds on the energy of suffering that comes from beliefs in such illusions that are regularly and repeatedly violated.

The Matrix teaches us to be long suffering and to never revolt against the control system, to turn the other cheek. It teaches us to be food. Since we are all one, each time we allow ourselves to be violated, we are allowing all others and life itself to be violated. Each time we placate the Predator, we are feeding it not only with our energy, but enabling it to continue to consume others. Each time we keep silent or turn away from confronting lies, we feed the predator and we enable it to feed on others. Each time we are not truly ourselves, each time we do not choose from a position of freedom, because we are unaware, so are all others to whom we are connected and responsible deprived of free will. *"Use the present to repair the past and prepare the future,"* Gurdjieff said. And this is exactly what we have learned from the Cs.

For people who have a serious interest in the path of awakening and becoming free according to this most ancient teaching that has been hidden for long ages until the present time, there is no clear and explicit source of information. Because of its very nature, it has no center, no lectures, no seminars and those that have been formed since the death of Gurdjieff are, like any teaching that becomes codified, somewhat suspect. Gurdjieff himself said, *"Since I had not, when in full strength and health, succeeded in introducing in practice into the life of people the beneficial truths elucidated for them by me, then I must at least, at any cost, succeed in doing this in theory, before my death."* He had dissolved his school, and devoted himself to writing. He finished the final draft of his manuscript of *All and Every-thing* before 1930, but he would not authorize its publication until 1950. Four years later Fulcanelli authorized a second edition of his *Le Mystere* with the added Hendaye chapter. My guess is that the two events are not unrelated.

The point here is, however, if Gurdjieff was unable to succeed in transmitting the system, or inspiring awakening by direct teaching, do we suppose that second-hand sources are doing a better job than he did himself?

That was, of course, our own dilemma. As I have noted elsewhere, Ark sought out Henri Tracol in order to determine whether or not he ought to join with such a school as those formed by some of the students of Gurdjieff. He realized after an hour of conversation that there was simply no point.

At the present moment, we have a large body of text, delivered for the most part as a direct interaction between myself and the Cassiopae-ans. As I have noted, I had come to the same conclusions that Ark did, that there was no other place on the planet where the deepest teachings that fed the soul of those seeking to be free could be found. And so, I formed the theory of accessing the information directly. The theory, the drive, and the dedication to bring it into this reality was mine, and the presence of Frank was almost immaterial. If it had not been him, it would have been someone else. If it had not been done the way it was done, it would have been done another way. As the Cs themselves not-ed:

> Q: (I) After two years, you know [Laura's] always going to ask those kinds of questions!
> A: Not two years, eternity. [...] We have helped you build your staircase one step at a time. Because you asked for it. And you asked for it be-cause it was your destiny. We have put you in contact with those of rare ability in order for you to be able to communicate with us. Again, be-cause you desired it, in order to realize your path. [Frank] is just the one who awakened your sense of recognition.

And Frank had an agenda. His psychological agenda was to become a rich and famous New Age star, with me as the beast of burden doing all the work. The theological reality behind him was that of self-serving forces which sought to distort and corrupt, steal or destroy this work. And at the present moment those forces are active in pursuit of this goal. The Evil Magician-Matrix will do anything and everything to put the sheep back under hypnosis so he can take their skins and flesh whenever he likes, even including hypnotizing agents and convincing them that they are eagles, or channels or magicians.

We come back now to Ark in Budapest. He spent a week there and as soon as he returned to Poland, he began his final preparations to come to the U.S. As the day we would finally meet in the flesh came closer, I thought I would be a nervous wreck. But, in actuality, I was quite calm. I did have all the concerns as to whether we were making a big mistake, and all the rational excuses that the mind constructs as defenses, but the Cs had said that I had nothing to worry about, so I just didn't worry. What I was worried about was my house being clean. I had heard that Polish ladies were outstanding housekeepers and I was terrified that my housekeeping would be found lacking. I was pushing myself daily to clean places in my house that hadn't been cleaned since we bought it and did all the cleaning before moving in when there was nothing in the house to get in the way. As a result of this activity, I fell three times, under strange circumstances. These falls aggravated my already compromised physical condition, and I was having some difficulty functioning.

Ten days before Ark was to arrive, we had a session in which a completely strange remark was made. It was attended by the regular group, with the addition of V** who only was occasionally present due to her class schedule as well as that undercurrent of antagonism toward her from Frank. At this session, a series of rather disturbing comments were made by the Cs that only recently, with Frank's revealed agenda, became clear in their intent.

We had been sitting around before the session discussing new information that Terry had obtained about future plans of the Secret Government for the institution of a global control system, the so-called New World Order. I was having a hard time concentrating on such topics when my whole personal life was sort of in a major transition, but the Cs evidently wanted to communicate something extremely important.

February 1, 1997

Q: Have you been listening to our discussion?

A: Yes.

Q: Do you have any commentary you would like to make on the subject?

A: Well, more specific than that, please!

Q: Well, I'm not going to ask any questions about munitions. I don't know anything about munitions, and I couldn't ask any intelligent questions …

A: Your conversation covered a whole lot more than just munitions.

Q: Yes, it did. Now … (T) What did they ask? What did the discussion cover? (J) … our conversation "covered a whole lot more than munitions." (T) Yup, it did! (L) OK, well, if we've got these … these … well, I don't even want to get on the subject, because I just … it … (T) Then, well, let's talk about something else.

A: Yes, we do suggest you do get on to the subject.

Q: (L) All right, then, you guys go ahead and ask your questions, because you know what to ask … They want you to get on to the subject …

A: No, Laura, you do too!

Q: (L) Well, I don't …

A: You don't know anything about Illuminati? Or secret government? Or future plans to institute changes?

Q: (T) Yep, that's what we were talking about …

A: Or, how this may, let us make that, *will, affect you?!?* It would be wise to learn, discuss, and network quite a bit about this, for your own good!! Especially since we have noticed a distinct change in your "tone" since Arkadiusz came into your life … you have become somewhat "euphoric" about this turn of events, and your perspective on the prospects for your future. But it would be most decidedly unwise to let your temporary feelings obstruct the bigger picture, especially since *the addition of Arkadiusz will have a stunningly profound effect on the course of events and all that implies with regards to the coming of the Wave and the turmoil that will precede it!!!*

This was a startling remark. How in the world could our little group, our little reality, our insignificant lives have a "stunningly profound" effect on the course of events? Oh, indeed, they had hinted about many things, but I always just took them with a grain of salt, and tried to avoid ego hooks of thinking that anything we did was so tremendously significant. As the group discussed it, we naturally tried to minimize it to merely a local significance.

Q: (T) [A]nd it's not that we're anchoring it in New Port Richey … (L) It's the planet … (T) … we're anchoring it to the planet. And, there are other groups, anchoring frequencies. Maybe different frequencies, maybe the same frequency. They alluded to that, too, they said that there were other groups … (V) Yes, that's something I was wondering about, for the last month, was one of the first times that I sat with you and Frank, they had said, what, that there were about ten people on the planet, that they were … (L) They said about 100. And they said that 10 were getting similar … (V) I was wondering whether that's grown in the last two or three years … (J) Good question! (T) Well, I think the Gulf Breeze Six people were hooked into it and they didn't make it. A lot of the groups are not going to make it. (V) Well, a good way to gauge is to the interaction (T) They can't depend on just one group to do it. They've got to have a whole bunch of different groups trying to do it. That way, at least one will make a connection. The more the merrier. The more groups, the stronger it becomes. (L) The whole thing is, is to survive. I mean, after we've had some of the bizarre things …

A: Start the flow again, Laura.

Q: (L) Which flow?

A: You don't know?!? They said, incredulously …

Q: (T) The frequency, the flow, what we've just been talking about. (L)
OK … (T) Start the flow again. Is that what you're talking about?
A: Yes.
Q: When Ark gets here, this particular group is going to increase …
A: We meant to restart questions …
Q: (L) OK, start the flow …
A: … regarding the subjects at hand.

It was definitely startling that the Cs were suggesting that the flow was dependent on me. But, it certainly fits with Frank-as-the-well-pipe analogy.

Q: (L) OK, they want me to start the flow again … (T) Start the questions … (L) All right. To start the flow of the energy, let me ask this: You have said, on a number of occasions, that somehow, some way, what we are doing is going to play some role in these upcoming changes, turmoil, etc. And then, you've also, on other occasions, made allusions to secret government, and to the Illuminati, and so on and so forth. And you have also said that our knowledge is going to increase to, I think it was 30 to 35% of what the Illuminati possesses, but that would be like individually, each of us individually, so added together, it would be a lot more than that. Can we think, or ask, if there's going to be a general tendency for our activities to be more closely scrutinized in the not too distant future?
A: What do you think?
Q: (L & T) Of course! (L) Let me ask; is there going to be any attempt to further attack or harm us in any way?
A: Well, let us put it this way: the future is fluid, as you know. Knowledge protects you. But, it would be wise to picture these letters appearing on a screen somewhere, at the same moment that they are uttered!
Q: (L) Is it the uttering that … (T) Uttering, or spelled on the board? (L) … "the moment they are uttered" … is it the uttering that is the key?
A: Does not matter, in all reality. The key is what the expectation is as to how they are intended to be put to use.

And of course, we didn't even get it. The use of the term "utter" was curious; but again, it makes sense with Frank as the well-pipe, attempting to extract information from me. The fact that it was given in response to the question about whether or not there would be any attempts to attack or harm us, the key being how the words that are "uttered" were intended to be used, suggested that now that Ark was becoming involved, we might be considered as more problematical to the "powers that be."

Naturally, in later times Frank opined that the remark was made in reference to Terry and Jan. Since it was impossible for me to consider the possibility that it might be Frank himself, I was willing to entertain the possibility, so we decided to ask about it over a year and a half after the above remark, in August of 1998. The Cs basically nixed the idea that Terry and Jan were the monitors, and the way the answers were delivered is truly strange in light of recent events.

> August 15, 1998
>
> Q: (A) I want to ask whether this channel is being monitored, and if so, by whom?
>
> A: Only effective monitoring so far is by direct 3rd density observation and enticing some to share data, then "spill their guts" with "shaky" correspondents.
>
> Q: (L) So, it's only when I get enticed to share what ought not to be shared, or when someone is present who is a monitor, that we have been monitored?
>
> A: Close. It can be monitored in other ways, but so far, *these have been only seldom necessary.* All STS always seek the path of least resistance first.

Naturally, I had the immediate idea that I was the guilty party since Frank had repeatedly told me that the only reason I was ever attacked was because I shared too much of the information with others. He wanted to keep it secret so that people could be induced to pay for it and it aggravated him to no end that we were giving it away for free. What is even more amazing is the fact that there were segments of the transcripts that the Cs suggested we ought not to share for safety reasons. Yet, in recent times, Frank, claiming to be the channel, has illegally claimed that he has the right to authorize Vincent Bridges to publish *all* of the material, including personal names and the passages that the Cs specifically said ought not to be shared. If anything ever demonstrated that he is *not* in any way the channel of the Cassiopaeans, that act alone clinches it. If he were, as he claims, the "authorized representative," one would think that the directions given by the Cs would be honored. That he has neither honored the free will of those present at the sessions to not be identified, nor the request of the Cs that certain material not be published, completely invalidates his claim to be the channel. His behavior and actions are so out of range of the Cs' teachings that there is no longer any realistic basis on which he can stake a claim to any of the material whatsoever.

At the time, I was feeling that maybe the remark was meant for me, but we now see that the precise way the Cs described it: "Only effective monitoring so far is by direct third density observation and enticing some to share data, then "spill their guts" with "shaky" correspondents," applies exactly and precisely to Frank in the current time. The further remark that other ways than direct third density monitoring could be used, but "so far, *these have been only seldom necessary.* All STS always seek the path of least resistance first," was a dead giveaway! Since we already know that Frank's mind was the battle where it was in question as to whether the dark forces or the forces of light would win, it's pretty obvious that Frank was *always* the path of least resistance for purposes of monitoring. He had been programmed for it; specially prepared for it. And it was probably only during those few times when he was blocked by our efforts from his link to the STS forces, that other means of monitoring had been utilized.

> Q: (L) You once said when Terry and Jan were here that we should imagine the words appearing on a screen somewhere as they were being delivered on the board. Now you say that this is not necessarily the lengths to which they [meaning the controllers] have gone. Was that because they were present?
> A: Seldom does not mean never.
> Q: (L) If such a thing was to happen, would it be because of the presence of someone, such as when you said PZ was a monitor?
> A: PZ, yes definitely!

Returning to the February 1st session when the idea of a monitor being present in our midst was first proposed, we find even more clues pointing in Frank's direction.

> Q: (T) Remind me, I've got another observation to make about the people on the other end ... (L) Is there an internal configuration or frequency level that makes it so that the persons who are selected to do this monitoring, or to be involved in any of this kind of activity, such as you have described, as in the words appearing on the screen, etc., so that they are definitely selected because of their STS orientation?
> A: *This process takes place naturally.* Now, a warning for you. Frequency resonance modulations of vibration rate can be altered or modified from outside if one is not cautious and/or aware enough, and thus takes necessary precautions.

We were not quite sure what this last remark meant, but it was a warning clearly directed at me, personally.

> Q: (L) Well, OK, we know that. So, in other words, not only the information channel ...
> A: Yours can, ours cannot! [tape off]
> Q: ... and they're letting them go and do it, because they figure it's going to be great, because everybody'll think it's just TV, it's just phony. And they are hoping it won't go. The whole thing all goes together. It's all linked together. Somebody's watching this stuff, it's disseminated through their organization, too. (L) I want to ask a question ...
> A: Now, remember technology can be used to "zap" you in a number of ways. For example ... beware of any episodes of sudden storminess that may occur between you and Ark.

As it happened, one of the first things Frank tried to do after Ark had arrived was to plant seeds of division between us. So, again, we see that the Cs were telling us things that we never thought to apply to Frank, yet all the time, Frank was the spider at the center of the web. At this point, I wanted to get in a quick question about my falls that were so very strange.

> Q: (L) Let me ask this quick, before anything else happens, just hold everything. I want to get it in. I have had, in the last couple of weeks, three very difficult falls, almost as if something was done. Now, Ark and TA perceive this as a deliberate attack on me physically. Is it, in fact, an attack on me physically?
>
> A: Yes.
>
> Q: (L) What is the purpose of these … well, it's pretty obvious. It's to put me out of commission. Is this the chief way that I generally get attacked?
>
> A: Yes. And we are warning you now!!! Do not get distracted any further by worrying over details of preparations to this house for Arkadiusz's arrival. This is ridiculously unnecessary, and furthermore, diverts your energy and awareness to such an extent that it can leave you open to even the ultimate "hit"!!!!

I was just a trifle unnerved to think that somebody out there wanted me dead.

Ark's arrival in the U.S.A. on my grandfather's birthday – the second Wilbur – was exactly two years to the day from the episode of the "Two Wilburs" and the two copies of Velikovsky. We had two months to be together before he had to return to Europe to fulfill a series of obligations that had long been in the planning stage. During this two months, he was required to be in Gainesville doing research. This presented certain difficulties for us since it was only natural that we wanted to spend as much time together as possible.

My mother lived with us, and this ameliorated the problem somewhat. Without her presence with the children, it would have been impossible for me to even consider spending several days a week away from home. We worked on the schedule and it was set up so that we could go to Gainesville on Monday mornings or late Sunday nights, and then drive home on Thursdays or Fridays, depending on the activity. One of the first items we had on our list of things to do was to buy my eldest daughter a car so that during any period of time that we were gone to Gainesville, there would be a car at home for the use of the family.

We had promised my daughter that she would receive a car as a graduation gift. She had worked very hard, and completing her first year of college classes at the same time that she finished her last year of high school under a special program for gifted students. She had also held down a job for the same period of time, so she had more than proven her responsibility. We went car shopping.

Since we aren't rich, we had set a limit on how much we were going to spend, and we wanted to find the best buy for our money. We also wanted to make sure that whatever we found, we could buy it outright because I didn't want her to be burdened with making a big car payment every month. She had worked hard enough that I thought she ought to be in a position where she could just finish college and not worry about having to work full time to pay a car loan.

We had already been looking and test-driving cars for weeks before Ark arrived and had narrowed our search down to a couple of dealers who seemed to be where the best buys were to be found. As it happened, on this particular day when we were ready to make a purchase, they had just put a nice little candy-apple red Volvo out on the lot. My daughter fell in love with it. The only problem was, after we dickered through the cash bargaining process, it was still half again as much money as I had allotted for the purchase of a car. Ark thought she ought to have it and so he paid the difference out of his own pocket.

Fine, everything was settled. And it was a good thing, because as things turned out, the attack forces began to try to hit us through the children. The Volvo saved my daughter's life. But, we will get to that.

Having spent over two days on trains and planes to get here, Ark was totally exhausted, but we decided to have a session anyway. Ark wanted to "meet the Cassiopaeans." It was also my 45th birthday. Frank was in rare good humor when he arrived; Ark's presence was a confirmation that the Cassiopaeans were a valid source, and of course, this was going to contribute immeasurably to his cachet as a New Age star once everyone acknowledged him as the channel. Of course, I only see this in retrospect. At the time, I just thought he was happy that the group was expanding in such an amazing way.

Whatever Frank's motives and agenda, the Cs themselves were happy that Ark had finally made it through the red tape to get here. Ark, on the other hand, was the scientist examining up close a new phenomenon about which he was very curious, but regarding which, he also had many doubts.

February 12, 1997
Q: (L) Alright, questions …
A: You are the one has the questions!!
Q: (L) Me?
A: Did we mean singular? Or plural?
Q: (L) Ask a question. (A) Me? I didn't think about a question … I can't think of one …

A: Arkadiusz, you have racing thoughts, thus making you tired and wide awake at the same "time."

Q: (A) Yes …

A: We see those thoughts … Be not reluctant to seek relief. A question not asked leads to a problem unresolved, as all your many years of training, education, research, and networking have taught you.

Q: (A) My first question is: I want to understand what is this "predestined mission," what it consists of?

A: It consists of following the path that has confronted you.

Q: (A) OK …

A: We do not tell you of your predestined mission, because then it is no longer "predestined." You learn by experience, and as you sense, you are on the threshold of a rather profound experience.

Q: (L) What kind of experience? (A) Yes! What kind?

A: We could well ask you the same!

Q: (A) So, we don't know what kind of experience …

A: Yes we do!!

Q: (L) We who? We here or we/you on sixth density?

A: What do you think?

Q: (L) Quit teasing me! (A) What do I think? OK … (L) Is this experience going to be something that involves interacting with external sources, an internal experience, a learning experience, can you give me a hint here? (A) Yes …

A: We would prefer Arkadiusz ask these questions … We were always most impressed with his skills in this area. Do you remember being caught in a cold rain on the "long walk," and how through your upset, you had an insight that "opened a new door?" We remember 1966 as a turning point. Well, this is another, Arkadiusz, and the emotions feel strangely familiar, but this time you have the aid of others on 3rd density.

Q: (A) Um hmm. I would like to know if physics is of any use, or if this is something completely different. I am supposed to concentrate upon what *we* are supposed to concentrate on, and does this require abilities in physics or some completely different abilities?

A: Can you not combine?

Q: (A) OK. I could combine. But what are the other abilities? I have no idea.

A: Not so, my Arkadiusz. You have reluctance, much like a small child learning to walk. But no lack of ideas. Before, when fear crept into the picture, you had the wisdom not to "look back," even though you had the temptation to do this. Look what has happened!

Q: (A) OK, I don't believe there are any dangers because I think I know how to avoid danger; I think they are illusions. I don't want to be … I just … I don't believe them. I'm safe. I don't believe that there are dangers which I do not see. Now, are there any dangers that I am not aware of? Something new?

A: It would be nice if those on third density could always be aware of all dangers which exist, but, then again, the learning would be hindered, would it not?

Q: (A) OK. It is nothing. Essentially nothing. They are just avoiding answering questions. This much I could explain myself. I asked if there was anything new, anything that I am *not* aware of!

A: You are presently in less danger because of your physical locator.

Q: (A) OK, so that's new. Why?

A: Why, you ask? Well, because the grooved vectors of attack for you lie in the locators where you have established your principle connections.

Q: (A) I want to know if they can tell me what I should really do during these two months that I am supposed to be here? That I should work on this problem of phase of the wave ... of whatever wave ... electromagnetic or gravity or whatever ... phase ... phase ...

A: The answers for this connection will come to you with surprising clarity, and will "unfold in front" of you with greater and greater intensity with each passing day.

Q: (A) OK. Very good. This is something that will be going on. (L) Then why did you ask? (A) Because I thought that there would be ... (L) Because you thought they were going to just hand it to you on a little silver tray ... (A) No, no, no! I wanted a hint! But there is no hint! (L) Well, they did say "unfold" and "in front of you." (A) Sure! In front of me and not behind me! (L) Well, let me ask: is there a hidden meaning in those terms? Unfold in front?

A: Maybe.

Q: (A) There are clues in front of me. Waiting for me. Very good. Perhaps I should not ask any more. OK, I pass. Because there is nothing complete ... I mean this was a complete question. I thought that there would be a complete answer.

A: You hold back questions which you would love to have answered. The clarity of the response is based upon the level of specificity of the question!

Q: (A) So, they are asking me what are these questions. Genes, unified field theory, relativity and time. OK, those are the questions. What else? On the one hand, it looks like that what one needs is to do something clearly spiritual, to be spiritual and one doesn't do this by equations and mathematics. And the suggestion was, and what I understood was, that there is no use for physics or mathematics ... (L) Who said that? Not the Cs! They have said that mathematics is *very* important! (A) Yessss ... okay. This is what they said. But when I asked them what kind of mathematics ... they said something which ... I mean, the technical answer to this question ... (F) Well, maybe if they gave you answers that did not make sense at first, you ought to examine it further and you may discover something important lying under there. It's like a treasure hunt. Buried treasure. We don't learn if they just give us answers. Yes, they may be very specific, and maybe more specific than we think. But, the answers in and of themselves have to be examined very closely. (A) Um-hm. (L) Let me ask a question. Earlier they said something about being on the threshold of an experience. And now they say something is going to unfold in front of you. Are the two response "threshold" and "unfold in front of you," connected?

A: Of course!!!

Q: (L) OK, he is on the threshold of some kind of experience. Is there some way that we might identify this experience? Is it going to be so outstanding that you can't miss it? Or, is it going to be something that you have to pay attention to or you might miss it?

A: What does "threshold" imply?

Q: (L) Well, a door. It's a door. Does this mean he is going to go through a door, psychically, spiritually, physically? Going to someone's house?

A: It does not just imply a "door," but also one's positioning, and a sense of inevitability.

Q: (L) Is there something I can do to help?

A: Have you not helped already?

Q: (L) But, I mean specifically in this "threshold" and "unfolding" experience?

A: Yes! And, by the way, Arkadiusz, science is most spiritual indeed!

Q: (L) Well, considering certain other elements, I was just wondering if our pathways are supposed to now be parallel or diverge ... how they relate from this point ...

A: Seems to us that your pathways are intertwining!

Q: (L) The use of the word "intertwining" is curious. You used that in regard to the relationship between EM and gravity. Is there a parallel?

A: If you wish.

Q: (L) Well, I am tired, Ark is tired, so is there anything further you would like to tell us this evening?

A: Combine energies in pursuit of answers, and the rest falls into place.

Q: (L) One last question: you say "combine energies." Is there any reason why this will facilitate the pursuit of answers?

A: Complementary souls.

The last two answers say it all: "Combine energies in pursuit of answers, and the rest falls into place. [This will facilitate the pursuit of answers because the two of you are] Complementary souls."

In retrospect, it is clear that this was the beginning of the implementation of the learning that would lead to the unfoldment of the mission, whatever it is and however it is supposed to manifest. It is also clear in retrospect that the Cs intended for us to understand that Frank was not a part of it, that his function of "awakening my sense of recognition" had been fulfilled, and it was time to move on.

But neither of us was wanted to do this. We continued to try to shove it under the rug and maintain the status quo. I wanted Frank to be happy with us, to have a place in our lives and work. But over the next two and a half years, the Cs repeatedly gave hints and urged us on to other things, and only in retrospect do we understand what they were trying to tell us. For example, just ten days after the first session where Ark was first physically present, the following remark was made:

February 22, 1997

A: Bio and cyber/genetic humanoid types now increasing exponentially in general population. You may have already encountered one or two during the past 10 days.

Q: (L) You, who? You, as in me, you as in Frank, who?

A: Reflect upon activities, and power and influence centers for answer.

In its context, there is no other explanation than that the Cs were referring to Frank and had used this mode of delivery to try to alert us, even if we would only realize it now. The exact number of days between the sessions was ten, and the Cs specified the ten day period. When we reflected on our activities and "power and influence centers," there was no real-world application for this remark. But in retrospect, Frank's behavior as a channel, in terms of the well-pipe function, acted as an agent for STS power and influence centers, and our activities in interacting with him during that period of ten days (the two sessions), is the only thing that fits. The only question in my mind is: does this mean that Frank is a cyber/genetic humanoid? As we go along, I will show where the clues were given that this is, in fact, the case. But one step at a time. We were learning, and it took time.

Little by little, step by step, the seeds of the clues were being dropped into our minds. But for the moment, we were only interested in that very short two month period that we had to be together before a six-month separation that I knew was going to seem like six years.

CHAPTER 43
THE HEAD OF BRAN

The two months that Ark was here in early 1997 were packed with interesting events which slowly began to reveal a strange situation that made me rather nervous and still gives me the willies when I think back over it. The Hale Bopp comet was in the sky heralding mass suicide, UFOs were hovering over Arizona, strange people with strange agendas were trying to lure us into traps, and the Cs were dropping hints and clues all over the place.

For the first month of his research in Gainesville, we rented an efficiency apartment that specialized in providing housing for visiting professors and researchers. With the USF libraries so handy, I spent most of my time doing research on things the Cs had indicated would lead to revelations, keeping a research journal of my findings and thoughts as I worked.

Ark was assigned an office in the Mathematics building, just a hop away from the offices of the colleagues with whom he was working. One of them lent him a bicycle so as to solve the parking problem (there were generally no places to park!) and he enjoyed cycling around the campus for exercise and reflection.

The second month, we were offered a chance to share a larger house that was made available as accommodation for visiting professors. It was located in a wooded area that was very quiet, and this was the primary attraction. The apartment had been in a very noisy location.

There were several other visiting researchers in the math and physics departments, and our host very much enjoyed taking us around to the various restaurants where everyone talked physics and math, and I mostly just listened.

At one point, our host decided that we should all go canoeing on the Ichetucknee river, one of Florida's most scenic rivers with giant Cypress and Live Oak tress, many types of water birds and turtles, and undoubtedly a few alligators lurking, though we didn't see any. Since Ark had spent many hours kayaking when he was growing up, and canoeing had been a popular activity when I was a teen-ager, we found that we were a great team in a canoe, and I am happy to report that we didn't capsize even once! Afterward, we all visited my aunt and uncle who have a large farm near to the river. They were happy to set a table for a phlock of physicists, and the foreign guests very much enjoyed good Southern food and hospitality. On the drive back to Gainesville that evening, we stopped on the side of a dark country road and got out to gaze at the Hale Bopp comet. It was magical.

Meanwhile, strange things were brewing. The Matrix was locked on our frequency and began firing weirdness like heat-seeking missiles.

Out of the many strange emails Ark received, among the strangest was one from something called The Institute of New Physics, which proposed to finance Ark to do research in nanotechnology. The email had been sent to his institute in Poland from an individual named Sue Brana.

March 1, 1997

Q: (L) Now, Ark got an email from some organization called the Institute of New Physics, informing him they were financiers, and was he interested in joining? Could you tell us who or what is behind this Institute of New Physics?

A: Well, perhaps it would be better to help you to tell yourselves. Where did the message come from?

Q: (L) We don't know ... (A) No, there is something, because there is, some info – GAIN – and I looked on the Web, and there are many institutions which have "Gain," you know, in their name. And I don't know if this is just one ... (L) Well, don't you think it's kind of funny that it has "gain" in the name, and you're in Gainesville? (J) Yes, that's what I thought, too ... (T) WWW dot ... well, no it's email, so it would be ... (J) Oh, "gain," and they're financiers ...

A: What do financiers do?

Q: (L) What do financiers do? They give you money. They finance you ... (J) They help you "gain" ... (L) Yes.

A: Do they do this for no reason ... ?

Q: (L) Of course they don't do this for no reason! They have an ulterior motive. They want something.

A: AHA HAH!

Q: (L) Ahah!? (T) Yes, they're the money store! (L) Well, all right. We'll play it by ear, and see what they want ...

A: Do they have an agenda?

Q: (L) Of course! No doubt, they have an agenda. Everybody that's been writing to us lately has an agenda! You know, we've been getting these ...

A: What may this be?

Q: (L) Well, their agenda ... (J) They want something from him, obviously. (A) When I get back to Poland, they said that they will have some printed material on this New Institute ready, that we could read, that they will send it to me ... (T) Where is the New Institute located? They didn't say? (A) No, they didn't say. (J) Ohh, I think you have a right to know that! (L) Well, I'd say, just let it float, and see what they say ... (J) They had to wait until you were back in Poland before they'd send you anything? (A) Well, if this is just in the stage of organization, so perhaps, it's a big something, which until now, was working in a certain field, getting money from, I don't know, from something, and now, they want to expand and to invest in nanotechnology, or whatever.

A: When you are getting close to something, there are always those who wish to distract, disrupt and track for later plans ... Anything worth getting must be sought.

We decided that we needed to dialogue with Sue Brana a bit more. During the course of these exchanges, she revealed that one of the groups she represented had financed the writing of the book *Angels Don't Play This HAARP*, by Nick Begich. It seems that this was shared in order to suggest to us that they were "good guys" and definitely open to unusual thinking and approaches.

Ark decided that openness and directness were the best policy, so he told her that he was not much interested in doing nano-tech, but that he was very interested in funding for crop circle research. She seemed to be interested in this, suggesting that it might lead to some kind of technological applications.

But having been warned by the Cs, we continued to dig. At that particular time, my daughter worked for a private investigator, so we handed what info we had over to her and she discovered some rather disturbing things about Gain Systems, the company that was supposed to be financing The Institute for New Physics. It seems that the whole company was a front. But a front for what? Indeed, the California Department of State had the corporation filings, with contact addresses, and there were several layered corporations, but all of them led back to a single individual: Sue Brana.

It became clear, after a bit, that Sue Brana may have thought that Ark was still in Poland because all of the exchanges were made through his email address at the Institute there. She wrote that she would be attending a meeting in Poland because her group was planning on investing in hemp farming, and when she was there, could they meet?

At this point, we were just simply interested in getting to the bottom of this mystery. Just because the Cs warned us about it, didn't mean we were not going to check it out as far as we could go.

Ark let her know that he was in the States, and since she was in California, it might be easier to arrange something sooner that would be more convenient. As soon as Ark wrote that, talk about your fast back-pedaling! All of a sudden the schedule was very tight. Sue Brana would *only* be able to meet with Ark in Poland. This struck us as singularly odd. Nevertheless, since we were trying to find our way in terms of being able to do the necessary research, we certainly did not think that we ought to discard what might be a legitimate opportunity. And, since she had brought up the fact that she had been instrumental in financing the book about HAARP, surely there would be interest in a similar research project into Crop Circles? We decided to ask some more questions:

March 29, 1997

Q: (L) All right, now, let me get my questions. The first question I want to ask tonight is about SB who has been corresponding back and forth with Ark … OK, what is the source of the funding behind them?

A: We know this, but, any guesses?

Q: (L) OK, they want us to play 20 questions. Do we have any guesses?

A: Ask Lindemann.

Q: (L) Well, we know who's behind it now … Rockefeller! So we're talking Rockybucks and his bunch.

A: Are we? Or, is that unsubstantiated rumor?

Q: (L) Well, yes, it could be unsubstantiated rumor, we don't know that it's the Rockefellers behind Lindemann. OK, let me ask this. Is it the United States government?

A: There is no such.

Q: (L) Well, let me try this another way. Is this SB a legitimate source of funding for …

A: It is "legitimate," as it can indeed provide unlimited funds. But, the real question is: Do you want to take advantage?

Q: (J) What is the price tag attached?

A: Depends upon results of experimentation.

Q: (L) No, I asked what's the price tag? Does it depend upon the results of our experimentation, or theirs?

A: Ours.

Q: (L) Yes.

A: If you discover something truly "earthshaking," well …

Q: (L) In other words, if we discover something truly earthshaking, the price might be very high. Is that it?

A: Maybe. Or, you could be sequestered.

Q: (T) In other words, put out, taken away … caged and used! (A) Anybody can be sequestered away from what is necessary …

A: It is possibility.

Q: (L) OK, do you have any other comments to make about SB? What did they say now, that maybe the same funding as Lindemann was behind them also? How about, what would you call it … the Quorum. Is the Quorum behind it?

A: Yes.

Q: (L) OK, is the Quorum the group we're supposed to be looking for? (I') We have to go back and ask about the Quorum. We've got so many characters, it's worse than *X-Files!*

A: No, more interesting.

Q: (I') Yes, it is, definitely!

A: World banking conglomerate.

Q: (I') World bank. (L) I do not wish to be "owned" in that way …

A: Not easy to avoid.

Q: (L) Well, I know it's not easy to avoid.

A: Will become even more difficult soon.

Q: (L) Well, they didn't say impossible … they just said difficult. But, on the other hand, I don't know if I want to do "more difficult" … well, we've got so much difficult … (I') … that it's easy now!

A: Many interesting things to happen.

Q: (L) To happen? Where, when, how, why, and to whom?

A: You. And everyone else in your realm … Expect revelations.

Jumping ahead just a bit, after Ark had left to go back to Poland, I had the idea that names might lead to some sort of understanding about people in a subliminal way, or might show some relationship to the hyperdimensional reality. Just to see if anything synchronous would turn up, I decided to search for the word "brana" on the Internet. I came across a lot of strange things, the most interesting being related to a Swedish bioengineering company that did genetics research. Other searches turned up mythical relationships to Celtic gods, an area I hadn't studied, and that is one of the things that opened the door to my realization that the grail stories were just redacted tales about the "head of Bran." Well, of course, I was pretty excited with this information, not realizing that anybody who was really familiar with those themes already knew it!

April 12, 1997

Q: (L) One of the things I was doing last night was a little web search on the word "brana," because we have a particular interest in finding out if there is any significance to this. I found some very interesting things about this word. I discovered that it was an Old English word for a blackbird or crow. It can also be a name in Yugoslavia and Russia. It was also the name of a great Irish king. Anything further you can add to that list?

A: What does this tell you?

Q: Well, that maybe the source of funding is not in this country. Maybe Russia?

A: Beware of unexpected assistance.

Q: We can be wary and still utilize it, can't we?

A: Up to you.

Q: If, in fact, there is a power mad clique running the world, what difference would it make if you got money from one country or another?

A: That is not the point: who is "running" the "power mad clique?"

Q: (L) So ... (V) The Lizzies, the Lizzies ...

A: Okay ...

Q: So you are essentially indicating in a roundabout way that we ought to ditch this offer?

A: Not so. We are indicating in a straightforward way that you should strive for objectivity at all times, and especially at junctures such as this, and not let subjectivity or emotions or hastily thought of ideas or decisions rule you!

Q: Could it also be possible that this source, this "brana," is in contact with the alleged Orion group?

A: Excuse us?

Q: I mean the Quorum as you have described?

A: Always be vigilant so as not to perceive a tangled web as a neatly constructed loop.

Q: The suggestion was made in another session that we need to devote some time and energy to the crop circle problem.

A: Yes ...

Q: And finding funding to do this in the correct way, as in networking and so on, is difficult, to say the least.

A: Patience pays ... "Haste makes waste."

Q: Well, we would not be doing it primarily to develop technology, but for information of a more cosmic or theoretical nature. Now, whether that would lead to technology is another question.

A: Review from whence and how this offer originated before you "leap into it," lest you become the fish that is attracted to the really shiny and tasty looking lure!

Q: Well, then ...

A: Review for insight ... it will come!

Just to see what would come out of it, Ark did agree to meet with Sue Brana in Poland on April 22nd. He described Ms. Brana as tall and blonde, nervous and talkative, and most definitely playing games with words. After he explained to her the needs and costs of the kind of research we were proposing, including the fact that we would not agree to a proprietary contract, Ms. Brana said she had to think about it and call him later. Ark wrote to me about the meeting:

Subject: yesterday's talks

Date sent: Tue, 23 Apr 1997 07:35:37 +0100

Honey,

I do not like "I will call you later" – I expected to have a definite answer now. And in fact it seems to me that I was close to getting it – but it was like that: warmer, colder, warmer, colder … We will see. She brought me a book by Schnabel on remote viewing and *Discover* magazine. I was completely open with her – so she knows the essentials of our story. She can be a banker (most probably she is), a spook, a representative of a secret government or an alien. This I do not know. She knows surprisingly many things. Around 4th May she will be back in States and then we will know more …

As there was also talk about quantum theory – there is a chance that before (or instead…) of venturing into CC research we can get a grant for writing a book on EEQT with nice computer software … I can't say now what will be the result …

Ah, and apparently she is investing millions into "industrial hemp" in Poland. […]

Two years ago, when I had described this little episode to some friends, one of them did a little research and found the following interesting item:

Western Producers, March 16, 2000

Little Homework Done on Hemp Company

By Roberta Rampton, Winnipeg Bureau

The hemp industry should have done more homework before doing business with Consolidated Growers and Processors Inc.

That's the opinion of Gero Leson, an environmental consultant from Berkeley, California, who was CGP Inc.'s first president. CGP recently closed its offices in Winnipeg and announced it intends to declare bankruptcy.

Leson said he knew little about Susan Brana, the majority shareholder and chair of CGP Inc., before he went to work with her in 1997. "I'm to blame, and so is everybody else," he said in an interview at the recent Hemp 2000 conference. Leson first became involved with industrial hemp when he helped organize an international symposium on the crop in 1995.

Brana contacted him the following year as a venture capitalist interested in funding hemp projects. She hired him to do some consulting work, and paid him for his work, Leson said. Together with Winnipeg hemp store owner Martin Moravcik, Brana and Leson formed CGP Inc. in the summer of 1997. The goal was to jump-start hemp production and processing, Leson said, and to take the company public to make money.

The emerging industry was short of capital, he said, and he thought the economies of scale Brana sought would be a good idea. But over time, Leson said he came to realize Brana was most interested in profits from company shares. She wanted to promote the company's big vision, but Leson said he was uncomfortable with hyping too much, too quickly. "Sue Brana thought I was too negative," Leson said.

By April 1998, Leson wanted to leave, but couldn't agree on terms with Brana, and was fired. A difference in management philosophy and style helped lead to his departure, he said.

Brana has not responded to repeated requests for interviews. Throughout CGP's time in the spotlight, Brana did not give interviews to reporters. Brana, 46, grew up on a farm in Ohio, and still keeps a residence in the state, according to sources. Her biography in CGP documents lists experience with several banks between 1975 and 1989.

More recently, Brana ran a stock broker/dealer firm called Alt Capital Inc. out of an office in Los Angeles. The office address and phone number were shared by Gain Integrated Systems, a shell company owned by Brana.

The same address was used for CGP Inc., along with a North Hollywood address for Dugan and Associates Construction Management Inc. The North Hollywood address was also used for Ntech Corp., a start-up nanotechnology development company with which CGP had joint venture projects.

Persuasive Personality: Brana was convincing in her vision to increase hemp acreages quickly, said Leson, even though he believed she tried to grow CGP Inc. too large, too soon. "You never quite knew if you were right, or if Sue Brana had found somebody to buy 10,000 pounds of oil," Leson said. "You always think maybe there's something you just don't know."

Since his time with CGP, Leson said he has learned about the obstacles for hemp in the pulp and paper and textile sectors. "It's much more complicated to get into those markets." He was alarmed when he learned last summer how much hemp CGP had contracted for 1999. "I thought it was misleading to do that."

Leson said Brana gave the impression through anecdotes that she had considerable experience starting and running businesses. Not all her stories were rosy, said Leson, making her track record seem realistic.

Leson said he doesn't believe CGP was a fraud or a scam. But he does think industry leaders, including himself, should have done more checking into Brana's work experience. "I think we're all to blame on not really insisting on seeing a résumé."

Pretty interesting, eh? And we see that, but for the grace of the Cs, we would have been sucked into a rather embarrassing series of activities. All things considered, it seems pretty obvious that Ms. Brana was a front for somebody, otherwise she wouldn't have been spreading so much cash around; the only question is: who? And why were we targeted for the dangling of a lure of big bucks to do something that really wasn't an area of particular interest to us, and would most certainly have diverted our time and resources, if not resulting in being totally discredited? Another good question is: what was the deal with the HAARP book?

Yes, we found out that they did finance Nick Begich. But that begs the question: *to what purpose?* Who are these people and what are they trying to do? All of the current ideas about HAARP are "out there" as a result of Begich's book, and he was *paid to write it* by this same group. Just like these folks wanted to pay us to do their idea of research on crop circles and possibly technology derived from it and they kept trying to plant ideas in our heads about it and point out this or that person who they thought was on the right track, and we could see that they weren't, perhaps the same is true about HAARP as presented in Begich's book?

Well, things proceeded on their very weird course. Jan kept joking that we had to raise the measure of bizarreness daily in order to keep up with it.

At this point, something rather strange began to occur. Right up to this point in my life, I had always been a deep sleeper. I would not only sleep deeply, I rarely moved or changed my position during the entire night. If I did become uncomfortable and needed to shift my posture, I always woke up briefly, made the adjustments, and then could go immediately back to sleep. Noises – unless they were extreme – did not bother me. Lights didn't bother me. Once I was asleep, I was asleep and that was that. Of course, sometimes I did have trouble getting there since my thoughts were always entertaining and were often difficult to slow down so that I could go to sleep, but over the years, I had developed strategies to deal with this, and unless I was extremely stressed, I could manage to go to sleep within 20 or 30 minutes of lying down, and stay asleep through all kinds of things.

I never talked in my sleep, I never did anything unusual.

But now, all of a sudden, that changed. Within a week or so of our taking up residence in the private home in the wooded area of Gainesville, something began to disturb my sleep. I was fighting and struggling in my sleep, and Ark was having a time soothing this disturbance and getting me to wake up from these events. For about a week or so, he spent a lot of his sleep time staying awake and watching over me so that he could intervene at the first sign of stress.

Right at the point that this problem began, we brought it up at a session that was mostly taken up with discussions of subatomic particles But, a peculiar thing happened right in the middle of this session that later connected in a funny way.

March 15, 1997

Q: So, a proton is a little manifestation of the consciousness of God?

A: No.

Q: Well, that would be what I would understand as the ultimate sense. Correct me please.

A: Too complex.

Q: (L) OK. (F) Spider! (A) Indeed! A spider! [It seems that at this precise moment, a spider descended from the ceiling on a thread.] (L) Teensy weensy spider … (A) It's a spy! (F) Yes, but a second density one. (A) But it has a lot of protons! (F) That's its connection with seventh density. [The spider is rescued and put elsewhere.] (L) Now, back to the questions. […] (L) The last few nights I have been having very strange things happening to me while I sleep. Waking startled or fighting or feeling something touching me … What is going on?

A: Burial ground.

Q: You mean the place we are staying used to be a burial ground?

A: 400 years ago.

Q: Swell! Just what I needed to hear! Is there anything I can do to limit this activity?

A: No.

Q: Is it particularly harmful or just annoying?

A: More the latter.

Q: (L) How come it bothers me and not Ark?

A: Sensitivity profile.

As it happened, though we were not aware of it, at precisely the time of the descent of the spider, during these same days of sleep disturbance, something strange was happening out in Arizona. There were multiple UFOs in the sky over Phoenix. The image that came to my mind when I later learned about these sightings was the part in the television movie series *V*, where the alien ships are approaching earth, and all the animals that are normally preyed upon by serpents were going crazy in their cages. Later still, I read a book by a woman name Marcia Schafer, wherein she promotes what amounts to a reptilian agenda. She reported a major abduction at around the same time I was having my extremely unusual sleep experiences, and I decided to bring it up at a session (though this was much later).

August 28, 1999

Q: Aside from most of the absurdities in this book, there was one thing that did disturb me: On March 19, 1997, she says that she had a major abduction. She remarks that "I recall being present at a meeting with hundreds of other humans. In retrospect, this bothers me. We were told that we were being tested to see how well we could recall specific training we had been given over our lifetimes to work their technology. Each of us had a partner and we were assigned to activate small 3-seater spacecraft. I don't know what the other people were told, but I do recall what happened to me. They had a lot of information and it was given in pieces. I was informed that I would no longer be allowed to dismiss or repress my work with others not of this planet. They said that the time had come, and I must have complete recall. They showed me a life review. They revealed all the visits and interactions I had in this lifetime. As they were about to start this, I recall arguing heatedly with them. In fact, I remember saying, 'No f***ing way! I'm not going through this.' In retrospect, I find this kind of funny in a juvenile type of way, that I swore at them. I received back the telepathic response: 'Way!' In other words, I had no choice and this was going to happen. Generally my wishes were respected in things of this matter. But, not now; they said it was 'time' and I was being brought into 'full activation' in accordance with schedule, whatever that means."

It just so happens that this event occurred at about the same time of the major UFO sightings out in Phoenix, and, if I remember correctly, you commented at the time that things were really getting ready to heat up, though we were unaware of these sightings then, being so busy with traveling back and forth to Gainesville. You did indicate that this had something to do with the fact that Ark and I were together, finally, and the beginning stages of some grand destiny were falling into place.

[We had a session on the night of the 15th, and I asked the question about what had made me so violently sick the previous night, and for several nights previous to this, I had awakened startled and fighting, feeling presences in the room and things touching me. Also, on the night of this session, the spider descended on the table in the middle of asking our questions about protons.] Is there any relationship between what was occurring with this Marcia Schafer, and what was occurring with us?

A: Well, best to consider this book, and the author, as an amalgamation of things read and things imagined.

That didn't really answer my question about my own experience, though it gave us a clue about the disinformation of this "Galactic Anthropologist." A bit later, the situation must have changed because the Cs brought up the subject again in a curious way at the end of a session.

March 29, 1997

Q: (L) Anything that you wish to convey to us, consider the question asked!

A: Energies at your Gainesville locator.

Q: (T) What about the energies there?

A: Negative.

Q: (L) Yes, it's pretty and all, but ...

A: No. The house!

Q: (T) What's causing the negative energy at this house?

A: Poltergeist.

Q: (L) Will we be all right for the little time we have left?

A: Maybe.

Q: (A) Yes, but the last time we asked about that, they said that it was an old cemetery, but that it was not important. (J) Ask if that has changed.

A: Yes. Beware of possible leg fracture.

Q: (L) For whom?

A: Laura.

Q: (L) Well, obviously, it's not going to be you, Ark! I'm the one that's always falling! So, it's obviously a good idea for me to go and stay in the office all day long.

A: It is a good idea for you to watch yourself!!

As it turned out, the man who owned the house we were staying in came one day while everyone was out and was doing some repairs. He fell and broke his leg. This was the second time that the Cs had mentioned a health issue in relation to me, that later manifested in someone else with whom I was in contact.

During the same time period, Tom French and Cherie Diez, the journalist and photographer, had been up in Ohio, I believe, doing some wrap-up interviews with the man who had been the husband and father of the three women who had been murdered several years earlier. This was one of the threads in Tom's project – the Rogers Murders – and when he later decided to write about it separately, it won a Pulitzer Prize.

But, strangely enough, it happened to be right at this point in time, after their trek to Ohio, that they came to Gainesville to spend some time with us, and the subject of the Rogers case was discussed briefly. Both of them were somewhat overwhelmed with all the depressing information they had gathered on this story, and as he often did during this period, when the stress of the subject matter became too much, Tom would find out where we were, and visit for a sort of "recharge" of his batteries.

On that same night we had a discussion of the crop circle-type image that had appeared in my ex-husband's driveway many years before. For some reason, I connected it to all the strange things that had happened when we lived out there in the woods. I had the idea that it was a sort of warning sign, though I was unable to formulate any clear idea about it.

One of the many synchronous things that had happened during the years Tom was gathering his material to write about us was the fact that all three of us (including Cherie) went through similar divorces at precisely the same time. It was actually sort of comical in retrospect, since Tom had been afraid to tell me that he was getting divorced. I actually dreamed about it just before Christmas of 1995, and told him about my dream. I'll never forget the strange look on his face. But, even at that moment, he didn't say it was true or not. It was only after I told him that I had made the decision to divorce myself that he heaved a sigh of relief and 'fessed up. I think he had the idea that I would judge him in some way, and nothing could have been further from the truth. But, after that, when Cherie also announced her intent to divorce, we all found it so odd that each of us, for different, yet similar reasons, were going through the exact same traumas at the exact same time. And all three of us had been, prior to our decisions to divorce, fully and completely committed to commitment. That is what made it so traumatic. Three people who believed in True Love, and full commitment, and who weren't cry babies by any stretch of the imagination, facing the same hard lesson that sometimes, love isn't love, and quite often, love isn't enough.

So a sort of bond was formed, and we mutually supported one another through the process. It was a rough ride, but we all made it through.

Tom and Cherie attended the last session with Cs before Ark returned to Poland and some of these threads all sort of came together at that point.

Another curious thing happened in March of 1997. On March 25th, Ark and I took the afternoon off to go to a local Gainesville park and hike about for some much needed relaxation. The park's claim to fame is something called the Devil's Millhopper, and is a huge sinkhole surrounded by trails, and wooden walkways, and a little bridge over the stream that runs out of the enormous depression in the ground. It seems that we were there alone, and as we strolled about, we came to the bridge and I recounted to Ark some marriage customs I had been reading about where one of the requirements are that the couple must stand in water while saying their vows. Ark pointed out that we weren't exactly standing in water, but we were standing over water, would that do? It did.

The next day there was the shocking news of the mass suicide of the Heaven's Gate cult members, and I was just furious with all the people I knew on the Internet who had been so busily promoting the Hale Bopp affair as the precursor to a mass landing of aliens, or the harbinger of the Alien Rapture. We had been interviewed about it by a little ezine put out by a guy named Jason Dunlap, and he was not happy that we flatly stated that it was all rumor mongering and hysteria. Ark had even taken the trouble to contact a professional astronomer, a friend of a friend, for the inside scoop, and we asked the Cs about it, and repeatedly called attention to what they said about it, as well as the results of our own investigations. But we simply were fighting a forest fire of rumors with only a single bucket of water.

When we arrived home late that Friday, my daughter excitedly announced that a reporter from the *New York Times* had called and wanted to interview me about the Hale Bopp affair. I was completely taken aback. Why would anyone want to interview me about it? What's more, even if somebody did, how did they get our phone number? At the time, the phone was unlisted, and the account was in my mother's name. I asked if she had taken a number, and she said that when she offered to have me call him back, he said "no thanks," he would call back himself.

But, that wasn't the only mystery. At the time, our "website" consisted of just a few articles that Ark hosted on the Institute server in Poland. Every weekend he would access the server and download all the statistics logs of visitors and what they were reading. So on the weekend after the Hale Bopp suicides, we were simply taking care of business and we noticed something very startling: the visitors to our site had not just doubled, they had increased quite literally a thousand percent! What's more, nearly every one of them was either from a .gov, .mil, or industrial aviation site, as in Boeing. There were also a large number of visitors from that very strange bioengineering site in Sweden that I had discovered when I was searching the term "brana." But what was strangest of all was the fact that the peak had been hit the *day before* the Hale Bopp suicides. What's more, the term did not even appear anywhere on our little collection of pages at that time. So we wonder, just what the heck was going on?

For Ark and me, our time together was racing by, and we avoided thinking too much about the fact that Ark would soon have to get on a plane and we would be separated for six months. The closer the day approached, the more my sleep was disturbed, only now it was happening at home. All Ark's research was done, and we had a few days to relax before he had to leave. At this point, I had the "experience."

I was fighting and struggling and Ark had awakened and was talking to me through my sleep, asking me to describe what was happening, what I was seeing and experiencing. I could hear his voice as though it were coming to me from the top of a very deep well. I was way at the bottom of the well, and I knew that there were important things buried at the bottom of this well, and that when I rose up out of it, I would not be able to remember since the properties of the place were necessary to comprehend what was there.

But I desperately wanted to remember, and I knew I needed some sort of device, or clue, and that if I could bring that back with me, I could follow it to the answers. I struggled with all my might to be able to speak from the depths of the well, to communicate from that place before I left it, and I managed to utter "Three Dominoes. Don't let me forget! Three Dominoes." And I shot up out of the well like a rocket and woke up with Ark holding me and asking what had happened.

THE HEAD OF BRAN

April 5, 1997

Q: A little change of subject. Last night I had a bizarre experience, I don't think I would call it a dream, but it was similar to what happened a couple of weeks ago. Out of this experience, I was only able to bring up two words: three dominoes, which seemed to be extremely important. But now, they make no sense at all. Could you give me some clue as to what the three dominoes means and what these experiences are that I am having?

A: One possible meaning: 3 Dominos pizza outlets in Gainesville!

Q: All right, what is another possible meaning?

A: Three dominos missing from your dominos set.

Q: OK, another one?

A: Your turn!

Q: Whatever it was, it was from a very deep level of the subconscious and I knew that if I did not get it out, I would lose it. OK, when these events occur …

A: Not an important dream, Laura.

Q: Well, maybe it was not an important dream, but it was accompanied by some very serious … what was I doing? (A) You were fighting. (L) And that was what I was doing before. Struggling and fighting. And, to my knowledge, I have never done this before in my life. I am considered a monophasic sleeper. (A) How do you know? (L) Because I have been told. I used to go to sleep in one position and wake up in exactly the same way, and not even the covers would be messed up.

A: House is "affected."

Q: This house is affected?

A: No.

Q: The house we were in at Gainesville?

A: Yes.

Q: Did it carry over from there?

A: Yes.

Q: What is it related to?

A: Oakwood Drive.

Q: The house we used to live in out in the country …

A: Turned around in bed.

Q: That refers to the night I woke up and found myself reversed in the bed, my nightgown wet from the knees down, and there was simply no way I could have turned around because I was sleeping against the wall and there just wasn't enough space. Are you saying I am having memories of this coming to the surface?

A: Motor memories.

Q: Memories in the body?

A: Close.

Q: Ark and I were talking the other night about the symbol that appeared in [my ex-husband's] driveway many years ago.

A: Winged Sceptor.

Q: (A) We wanted to know why you related it to Grays, but would not say whether an abduction had taken place, and later you said that L [my ex-husband] had never been abducted. So, how does that relate? What is the connection?

A: Connections are not necessarily "time tracked."

Q: Well, Ark remarked that it may not have related to L at all, but that was a message to us in the present. What was the message and who was it for?

A: Not a message. A marker.

Q: Is this a marker in the same sense as you described relating to memory awhile ago?

A: Close.

Q: Who was this marker supposed to affect?

A: Not correct concept.

Q: What is the correct concept?

A: All events are synchronous only when perception becomes a catalyst for learning.

Q: (TH) What is the meaning of synchronous in this context?

A: Only discovered when the lesson is completed.

Q: (TH) Do they mean that all events exist somewhere outside of time and that we just experience them sequentially?

A: Close, Tom.

Q: And why were we discussing that particular item at that house in Gainesville ... [TF's notebook computer indicates that its batteries are getting low by saying: Hasta la vista, Baby!] (TH) There's your answer! Deus ex machina! (L) Why did the discussion of this symbol come up, and more or less synchronistically related to my battling dreams, and then you mentioned motor memory and the incident at Oakwood Drive ...

A: Contemplate. Please do not leave just yet, Mr. French!

Q: Why do you not wish Tom to leave?

A: We may have some things to say to him.

Q: What?

A: Not yet.

Q: Cherie is the one who has to go. She is having allergic reactions to smoke.

A: Really? What do you feel about things, about changes we referenced for you in our last communication to you?

Q: (TF) It was necessary. Glad that it ... that last year's over.

A: It is not over.

Q: (TF) Yes, there are some more things to do ...

A: There are many changes yet to come.

Q: (TF) That's true. (L) Is Tom going to feel positive about at least 50% of them?

A: About 100%. When the conclusion is reached you see, Tom, this "struggle," or "challenge," relating to the perceptions of the coming ending/beginning of the millennium, was really a doorway opened by your subconscious to begin the necessary process of examining the metamorphosis of your own being.

Q: (TF) So, I had subconscious motivations of my own when I decided to follow this subject? It was for me?

A: Yes.

Q: (TF) Well, there has certainly been a lot of pain involved.

A: With pain comes renewal.

Q: (TF) What about the sickness I had at the beginning of the year?

A: Purging of built up "poisons" of an emotional/spiritual nature.

Q: (TF) I can certainly see that! Yes, that's very true. But, you have indicated more. What more can happen?

A: Now, finally, you will be able to move ahead and make significant progress, including ways not yet imagined!

And indeed it was true. Tom didn't know it then, but the Pulitzer was in the not-too-distant future, and I suspect that there is more to come.

The day finally came when we had to get up in the morning, knowing that every minute had to be concentrated on preparations for Ark to leave. We both knew that we were going to have a difficult time of it. Two months after a lifetime of looking just wasn't enough. And even though we had our plans made, that it would only be a temporary separation, we both knew that many things can happen and we might very well never see each other again.

I wept as I packed for him, tears splashing on everything I put in the suitcase. I had washed all his clothes and packed them carefully. He had a tape I had made for him on which I sang some of his favorite songs. There was a large envelope full of photographs of me and the children. Some of them were the only copies in existence. I packed his current journal on top, and some papers of the correspondence between him and Ms. Brana. I packed his vitamins and whatever little things I could think of to tuck in so that when he unpacked, he would have surprises. Finally, I made sure his passport and tickets were all in order in his jacket pocket, and that he had plenty of cash for any incidentals on the way. We loaded everything into the van, everybody kissed everybody goodbye, and he drove us to the airport. I tried not to think about having to drive home alone.

I watched him through the boarding trolley until he turned one last time to look at me, and was out of sight. I rushed up to the roof of the airport to watch the plane itself and when it lifted off the runway into the air, I burst into tears right there. Finally, I was able to calm down and drive home. It was terrible, but I had promised not to cry every day, and I meant to keep my promise. I had resolved to do as much research as possible to fill my time up, and I already had a calendar set up to cross off the days. Each day had a number on it telling how many days I had to wait.

Of course, things got weird right away. Ark had to make a connection in the States to fly to Frankfurt, Germany. From Frankfurt, he made another connection to Warsaw, and from Warsaw, he was booked on a train to Wroclaw. When he arrived in Warsaw, for some reason, his luggage had disappeared.

After doing all he could to get them to locate it, he left his contact information and took the train to Wroclaw where he called me and explained the situation. I immediately got on the phone to the airline and started jacking them up from this end. Suddenly, they "located" his bags. The explanation was that they were put on the wrong flight from Frankfurt and came in on a later plane, but I didn't buy it. They were going to fly them to Wroclaw and have a courier deliver them to Ark, and he explicitly told them to bring them to the Institute. They didn't. They delivered them to his estranged wife. And when I say "estranged," I do mean estranged!

I need now to give just a little background about the situation over in Poland. I can't talk about his ex-wife because I never knew her. I only knew her by what she had done, and much of that is personal, so I won't go into it. But the reader may have some idea of what kind of person she is by the fact that, two days after he told her he wanted a divorce, she went to the bank where all their money was and drew it all out, and it has never been seen since.

Now, we aren't talking about just a little bit of money here. The reader should remember that Ark spent most of his career traveling and working at some of the world's most prestigious European universities. He was well paid, and expenses in Poland were low (as was the pay). He habitually lived economically so that he could put as much money in the bank as possible, often existing on hot dogs and instant potatoes for weeks on end to save money. Because of the favorable exchange rate, he managed to accumulate what amounts to a considerable fortune. He paid for an apartment in a high-rise, had two cars, and essentially was considered to be a wealthy man. On top of all that, he was awarded a Humboldt Prize in 1995, and it was a significant chunk of cash.

And it was all gone. She didn't say a word, simply went to the bank and took everything. When he went to the bank on his lunch hour to cash a check for pocket money, he was told that he no longer had any accounts, no CD's, nothing. All gone.

Well, naturally he was curious and wished to know where 30 years worth of money accumulated by his self-denial and careful management had gone. She told him that she gave it all to the church to pay for masses for his soul since he was being evilly influenced to ask for a divorce. No mention was made, of course, to any of her contributions to his desire for a divorce. She had always been perfect. So I won't describe the 30 years of entries in his journal that chronicle her behavior, except to mention the fact that she hired a private detective to follow their daughter's husband around because she didn't like him and wanted to discover something that she could blackmail him with in order to force him to agree to divorce her daughter so she could resume control of the daughter's life. We'll just leave it at that.

In any event, Ark was without money, and she worked herself up to such a state of frenzied violence that he knew (from experience) that she was going to begin mutilating herself so she could run outside and scream that he had beat her. So, to forestall that possibility, he knew that he must never, ever, be in her presence alone. He left with the clothes on his back, and went to live with his mother. From that point on, his ex-wife refused to appear in court when over half a dozen hearings were scheduled. She refused to hire an attorney. She repeatedly sent doctor's notes that she was "unwell."

You can't divorce somebody you can't get into court. And without getting her into court, nothing could be decided about the equitable division of property. Ark was advised by his attorney to press criminal charges against her because her theft of his money was a crime. Since he had announced his intention to divorce, it had been illegal for her to take anything until the court ruled on who got what. Ark couldn't do it. As he said to me, it was worth a fortune to find me and escape from her. He had spent the entire winter before he came to the States, trudging through the snow while his soon-to-be ex-wife drove by in the new car he had bought just a few months earlier. She even refused to allow him to retrieve any of his clothes. So that is where the matter stood when he returned to Poland.

And the airline delivered his luggage to his old home address on file when the tickets were purchased.

April 12, 1997
Q: Who was responsible for the lost luggage?
A: Polish authorities.
Q: Let me go back to the luggage. The Polish authorities, as in which branch?
A: Secret police.
Q: What were they looking for? Just anything?
A: Yes.

223

Q: Did they satisfy themselves that there was nothing subversive in there?

A: Yes.

Q: Why, then, did they cause the luggage to be delivered where it was?

A: Honest mistake.

Q: (L) Was this mistake stimulated by the Lizzies?

A: In that vein, there is little in your STS locator that is not, ultimately.

Q: What was the reaction of the recipient of the luggage?

A: Stunned.

Q: Was I correct when I thought that there was rushing off to find someone to translate the tape?

A: Well, it was more like rushing off to "find my lawyer."

Q: Is this information going to be used in a detrimental way against him?

A: Yes.

Q: Is the luggage going to be returned?

A: Wait and see … "Stay tuned, fasten your seat belts," etc. …

Q: Anything further you can give to help me sleep tonight?

A: Ask …

Q: Is it going to prolong the proceedings?

A: Open.

Q: Will she show up at the hearing?

A: Will most likely ask for a delay, based upon "new information," to be entered into evidence.

Q: Would it be a good idea for him to suggest that he can get an American divorce?

A: Good idea!!

Q: Should it be let out so that she will hear of it?

A: Why not proceed discreetly?

Q: Would it be advisable to pursue the money issue?

A: It might be advisable for A to simply concentrate upon his new beginning as opposed to the old, dead past …

Q: Does that mean that he will not be able to get the legal affairs straightened out in Poland?

A: This is a complicated situation which will unfold in a proper way if handled in a positive, forward looking manner.

Q: Forward looking would be looking to the future?

A: Yes.

Q: Does that mean looking out for some of his interests?

A: See previous response.

Q: My original thought was that he should just walk away from it, let her have it. There are other opportunities.

A: Look ahead, not back.

Q: I think that the pictures and tape will be gone when he gets the luggage back.

A: Wait and see. [I was right.]

Q: Why was she stunned at what was in the luggage?

A: Think of all that was in the luggage, and you will know the answer to that question.

Q: Was it the pictures?

A: See previous answer, obsession aideth not, my dear!

Q: I am not obsessed! I am curious.

A: Worry not, just sit back and enjoy the show!

Q: I can't enjoy myself if I think she is going to make him suffer!

A: No more on this!

It was two days of phone tag before he discovered what had happened. He knew that he had to retrieve his luggage, and he made arrangements with another professor and friend at the institute to accompany him to get his possessions.

After an unpleasant scene, he was finally able to open his suitcase and unpack. The customs seal was intact, so it was a certainty that no one had opened the bag. Yet, the tape, the journal, the manila envelope of photographs, and the pages of correspondence with Sue Brana were all missing.

And the Cs were right on the money. The next hearing was scheduled for June 17, on the very day Ark was scheduled to leave for Dijon, followed by a stay in Gottingen, and then on to Florence. But even before that, he was scheduled to spend two weeks in Bielefeld. Meanwhile, he was working very hard on the details of the upcoming Xth Max Born Symposium that he was organizing with two colleagues, sponsored by a list of luminary organizations in Poland, Great Britain and Germany. He certainly had his hands full with such an exhausting travel schedule, and every day was an uphill battle to keep the ship of the upcoming conference on course. With 25 of the world's most eminent physicists scheduled to speak, coordinating the schedule, arranging for their travel and accommodations, making sure everybody's needs would be met, was an overwhelming task. Ark delegated as much as possible to his staff, but in the end, he had to make the call on the big decisions.

When the day of the hearing finally arrived, again, the soon-to-be-ex-wife did not appear. Again she sent a letter asking for a delay. However, the court was getting rather impatient with these manipulations. Ark described the event in an email:

Subject: news

Date sent: Tue, 17 Jun 1997 09:52:06

A did not appear. She sent a letter and asked for 4 months of delay because of "psychic health" reasons. The Court did not agree arguing that everybody divorcing suffers psychic tensions. Rescheduled for July 22 when the session will be held even in absence of A.

A admitted on paper that she has the Journal and tapes!

Her letter states, in part, that I have been taken over by a mind-control cult because of my "interdisciplinary interests," i.e. anything she thinks is "strange." She wrote:

"These interests (my interdisciplinary) in recent times, i.e. since June 1996, through the Internet, became continuous contacts with a group of people which, as they claim, have contact with extraterrestrial civilization, that is with Cassiopaeans. In this way he got to know a woman, named Laura, and he remains under her influence.

"From this time on he tells his colleagues about his love for Laura, his plans of living together with her. He says that he wants to have a child with her and also take care of her five children.

Proof: [names of witnesses]

"In his journal he describes his emotional states and his supernatural love which he feels towards Laura. He seeks advice from her, she is giving him horoscopes, sends him cassettes with "motivating" recordings. From his notes it also follows that he is financing enterprise of this Laura and the group of people contacting the Cassiopaeans."

Proof: [journal from October-November 1996]

My God!

Bernard, his wife and two other friends will witness for A that I was proposing to give her apartment and car and half of the money if she agrees to the divorce.

Then she argued (on paper) that she stole the money to save it from being given to a "group" ...

Somehow she is totally unaware that the fact that she has taken these things from my luggage makes her guilty without any doubt to everybody including her attorney. And that alone is a sufficient reason to ask for a divorce. She seems to be also totally unaware (and her attorney was not able to explain it to her) that the fact that she prevents me from spending my part of the money however I wish is another sufficient-in-itself reason to ask for a divorce.

Marek noticed these two things instantly.

I believe the judges also noticed. The main judge was very nice, flatly dismissing the demand to wait for four months.

And so the next hearing was scheduled for July 22, come Hell or High Water.

As it happened, both came.

CHAPTER 44
THE CRANE DANCE

Any reader who goes through the Cassiopaean Transcripts with care will come to the realization that, more than anything else, the dialogues represent a personal diary of my life. They will also realize the level of trust I placed in Frank at certain points to have him present during so many very personal discussions. The reader may also realize the reticence I felt about publishing the entire transcripts, considering these factors.

Aside from the very personal element of the transcripts, as I pointed out in Chapter 41, there are many segments in there that the Cs specifically instructed us *not* to publish – for particular reasons. Then, there are the people who specifically did not wish for their private affairs to be aired, at least not with their names revealed. And then, of course, there were particular segments that I was not publishing out of consideration for Frank. However, having been placed in a position where full publication was necessary, we realize that it was certainly the right thing to do especially in consideration of Frank's recent choices. Because, in point of fact, the transcripts themselves are the testimony of my life as I struggled against Frank's losing battle with the dark forces. And now that they are published, there is no longer any possibility of protecting Frank.

The reader will notice that throughout the transcripts, against all evidence to the contrary, I continued to have faith that Frank would win the battle that the Cs had indicated was taking place in him, that he would undertake the necessary self-examination that would enable him to become free of these forces.

In addition to the fact that the majority of the over three million words of the transcripts being a personal diary of my external life, they are also a diary of my spiritual life and a record of my initiation. As the Cs said themselves, Frank was "just the one who awakened your sense of recognition." That they were distinctly *other* than Frank was made clear when they noted, "We have helped you build your staircase one step at a time. Because you asked for it. And you asked for it because it was your destiny. We have put you in contact with those of rare ability in order for you to be able to communicate with us. Again, because you desired it, in order to realize your path."

Frank's ability was, indeed rare. At a later point in time, an individual asked if he might contact the Cs himself. Frank's role was clarified:

Q: (BRH) Is there any way I can contact you guys directly?
A: Well, D**, only if you present yourself into the presence of these 3rd densities here. Remember, their request was hard earned, and one of them has been channeling throughout this incarnation, much to his detriment. Those neighborhood kids usually do not respond favorably to psychic awareness, now do they? Another one here has literally turned the world upside down in search of the greatest truths for all of humanity, much to her potential peril. And the third one here had to endure almost unimaginable hardships and tests of stamina in order to realize his destined path of bringing your 3rd density realm to the brink of 4th density transitional adjustment. So, the path is open to you. Wanna follow?!?

We notice immediately the curious way Frank's ability to channel was described as being "much to his detriment" because "neighborhood kids do not respond favorably to psychic awareness." Again we see a clue to the well-pipe analogy. Wherever he is, whoever he associates with, to a great extent, that is what Frank channels. It is undoubtedly true that he suffered the torments of the damned as a channel.

There are a number of people currently researching the elements of the Matrix and how it utilizes individual human beings as the playing pieces in the war games of the theological reality. The following account is extracted from *Amazing Grace*, based entirely on Frank's own descriptions of what occurred to him as he grew up.

I spent quite a number of years in a very close interaction with Frank, engaged in thousands of hours of conversation, and interacted with his family. Frank's father was a physician. During his childhood, they lived in Chicago. He was brought up in an upper middle class neighborhood where he never, then or since, suffered lack or deprivation of any material sort. His family environment placed great emphasis on logic, monetary value, and scientific transactional approaches to life. In his family cerebral and academic excellence was an expression of superiority; a means to an end. And the "end" was generally to live well, be rich, or even to be famous.

Frank's mother was the child of immigrants from a Scandinavian country. She had experienced a very unhappy first marriage which produced a daughter, and after a bitter divorce, had married Frank's father, who was quite a bit older than she was. She was artistically gifted in a conventional way.

228

Frank's father was quite set in his ways at the time he married a divorcee with a young child. As a man of scientific background, Frank's father was steeped in the child-rearing theories of his own generation rather than the more modern conceptions of nurturing the psyche. His ideas related to hardening the body and toughening the will and cultivating the mind.

Frank's mother, with her immigrant background, supported the same concepts since they were a part of her heritage, but she had also been brought up to serve and support the will of her husband and children. She was, in this drama, the slave to her husband, as well as the slave of her children, and that is a situation which can lead to great conflicts when the natural manipulations of children go against the will of the husband.

I don't think that Frank was ever physically abused in any serious way, though he did claim on a number of occasions that his father "knocked me across the room." Such incidents were, I think, rare.

What Frank complained about most was the fact that his father, finally having a son, needed so desperately for his son to be strong, to be manly and to be the All American Boy. This included not just academic and moral strength, but also athletic excellence. To this end, Frank said he was subjected from a very early age to various "programs" designed to produce this paragon of American virtue. But Frank was not the least bit inclined to want to play baseball, go camping with a scout troop, or exert himself in activities demanding interaction with the world at large.

As infants and toddlers, we all feel that we are the center of the Universe, that we are omnipotent and omniscient beings. In the beginning, we perceive our parents as merely extensions of ourselves in the sense that when we are uncomfortable in any way, these shadowy figures, the landscape of our universe, act on our behalf. Thus it is that, at the earliest stages of development, the response of the universe to our needs becomes our deepest belief about life itself – a belief inculcated before verbal skills are developed, and therefore, hardly amenable to psychiatric exploration in the ordinary sense.

If, when we are hungry or cold or too warm, or lonely and in need of touching and comfort, the Universe-as-mother responds immediately with the appropriate solution, our earliest and deepest sense of existence tells us that the Universe is safe, that it is good, that it is responsive to us. This becomes the fundamental platform from which we operate throughout our lives. We have learned that the Universe is safe, that it is good to us, that we can reach out or cry out and the Universe and all within it will provide.

When a child is treated, at the very earliest stages, as an object to be molded and shaped by regimentation, a dreadful crime against the essential self, at the deepest levels of being, is committed. A child who is left hungry because it is not the scheduled feeding time will be conditioned to believe the Universe does not provide nourishment in response to his cries. A child who is not picked up and comforted when he is frightened, startled, or simply lonely and in need of being touched, is conditioned to believe that there is no point in reaching out or interacting with the Universe in any way. So it is that a child raised according to the Cartesian "man as machine" model has no sense of safety or sufficiency.

An infant subjected to abrupt and arbitrary schedules, promoted by parents who, convinced by "medical and psychiatric theories," believe they are doing the "right thing," end up producing intense injuries to the infant's tender, budding self-esteem. Such injuries can be severe and irreversible.

The empathic support of our Primary Objects, the parents, is crucial at these early stages. In its absence, our sense of self-worth and self-esteem in adulthood tends to fluctuate wildly between over-valuation of ourselves by regressing to the infantile narcissistic mode, or devaluation of ourselves as the helpless child slave of a sadistic, even if well-meaning, parent.

Such a child can grow up with a heavy sense of bitter disappointment and radical disillusionment with the Universe as a whole. They are often unable to accept self-limitations, disappointments, setbacks, failures, criticism or disillusionment with grace and tolerance. Their self-esteem is inconstant and negative. There is a tendency to believe everything that happens to them is the result of outside events, or that everything is their fault, in some way. In my own case, Larry took the former approach, and I took the latter! A child may think that if they only give more or do more, or find the flaw in themselves, they will be able to "fix everything." Such a view is growth inducing. If they cannot tolerate the stress of the feeling of being wrong, they often choose a growth-denying mode of reversion to the narcissistic phase of infancy. This was my mother's choice, Larry's choice, and Frank's choice.

Since his father, aided and abetted by his mother, worshipped the external self, how Frank appeared to others became a chief concern. The constant pressure to be a certain way, that is essentially artificial, by default convinces the child that what is inside him is not acceptable. His parents believed in a peculiar mix of the child as a blank slate and the "natural child" as a dirty and ignorant animal in need of training. In short, as a soul with specific inclinations and tendencies requiring delicate handling, Frank never had a chance.

Frank's experiences as a child were, in many respects, similar to my own. His father, supported by his mother like a Greek chorus in the background, put him down and disregarded him and his feelings. The most poignant story he told me about his childhood concerned a time when he was left, before he was two years old, with an uncaring baby-sitter while his parents went on a two week vacation. Frank's father was certain that a child so young couldn't possibly have any awareness of a caretaker or any capacity to feel more than basic instinctive drives and programs. It was his father's intention to toughen and condition Frank. Unfortunately, Frank was not only cognizant of what was being done, he never forgot it.

At the same time, Frank was being tormented by more than a "Face at the Window." He was being regularly and repeatedly "visited" by what he came to know as aliens. He believed that he was regularly taken by them, and tortured by them, and all his efforts to communicate this to his parents were ignored and disregarded. He lived under siege with no one to turn to for protection.

He was utterly terrified to be left with strangers (not a surprise). On one occasion, he discovered that his mother had left him with a children's play group without telling him, in a moment when he'd been distracted. He cried so bitterly that the teacher forced him to stand up in the middle of the group and "tell his name." He was naturally paralyzed and incapable of doing so. Frank remembered all the other children staring at him in his misery, laughing and pointing at him.

The next day, when he realized he had to go back again, he resisted and delayed getting dressed and ready. Finally in the car and on the way, in desperation he grabbed the door handle and told his mother that if she didn't stop the car and turn around and take him home, he would jump out that very instant and kill himself. He was only four years old.

Frank's mother stopped and turned around. Frank had learned the secret of controlling others to do his will. His mother's submission was probably the first time in his short life that he felt any power in his environment at all. This became a seed later to bear bitter fruit for all of them.

I have most definitely experienced that feeling of being paralyzed and unable to act. More than once. But in thinking these things over, I realize my own good fortune in the fact that my choice in every such situation has been to take some sort of definitive action to solve the problem, and that I am basically fearless in all cases. So, somebody must have done something right when I was an infant. Whatever it was, it wasn't done for Frank.

In the end, it seems that Frank's efforts to deal with the "unfriendly universe" created by his parents had failed repeatedly and consistently. My own experiences had been similar, and I was learning a different way to cope. I wanted to help Frank break out of his loop also.

The contrast between the fantasy world of the omnipotent four-year-old who threatened his mother with suicide to obtain relief from external pressures, and the real world in which he was continuously frustrated, was clearly too painful to deal with. At that age, or perhaps even earlier, this dissonance may have caused him to make an unconscious decision to live in the fantasy world where he was omnipotent and omniscient. In his private world, he felt special and entitled to things for which he had not worked nor put forth the effort expected of ordinary human beings. And it was from this platform that the next interesting phenomenon developed.

As he grew older, Frank learned a curious trick. He discovered that a sort of rhythmic dancing and creation of vibratory sounds and sensations enabled him to enter and sustain this fantasy existence to an extraordinary degree. In this trance, he was the only occupant of the universe and he was entitled to all its secrets and lore. The way he did this was to perform a sort of "crane dance" while beating the ground with a stick. He once demonstrated this for me and it was, as close as I can describe it, a shamanic performance of pure instinct.

The soothing effect of retreating into this trance state was so effective that, in the same way some people become addicted to other things, Frank became addicted to being in a trance. He had discovered the ultimate means of retreating into what was, effectively, a pre-birth state of nonexistence.

It is likely that the first time he achieved this state, it was accidental. He described it as having occurred after one of the episodes where he reached out to his parents for love and acceptance and, instead, received a lecture which included a list of all his faults and failings. He went out to the back yard and picked up a stick and began to pound the ground with it. As he did so, he became fascinated by both the vibratory sensation traveling up the stick from the impact, as well as the sound itself. He then began to experiment with different rhythms, most likely in an idle way, and then found himself entranced. At that point, the trance dancing began.

Thus he learned a trick that provided comfort.

Frank began to stimulate the trance state habitually in order to derive pleasure and gratification in a world that was not very friendly to his real self. The fact that this self-gratification was so easy to produce, rapidly conditioned him to prefer it. This, of course, produced another effect: laziness. But, this was not laziness in the ordinary sense of the word. Frank became lazy in the psychological sense because he learned that fantasy land was preferable to investing efforts in reality where failure was assured. Frank became just like a rat with an electrode implanted in the pleasure center of the brain, repeatedly pushing the button that induced ecstasy in preference to real life.

And here we have an important clue as to how and why Frank also developed highly specific abilities that enabled certain results to transpire in my interactions with him.

Frank was performing this ritual stick dance so often that his parents became concerned and, at a very early age, they labeled him as "sick" and called in a psychiatrist.

This shamed his father terribly and only added to the demands being made on Frank to "toughen up" and "be a man." Frank reacted by intensifying his "ritualistic" behavior and time spent in a trance, though he learned to hide it better.

Frank had acquired the gift of the Crane Dance. At what cost, we can only guess.

We can surmise that the crane dance was Frank's manifestation of soul inversion, but that the total "auric death" may not have occurred until recently. And we will eventually come to the reason for it, but for now, let's return to the more or less chronological account of my initiation and growing awareness of the reality of the Matrix Control System, with some diversions to provide background.

In retrospect, it is obvious that the Cs' primary objective was to initiate me into literally becoming unified with myself in the future. At the time, I didn't spend too much time thinking about the fact that by asking the questions that were compellingly interesting to me, I was activating that "destined" activity of accessing more and more of myself. But, with the clues they gave and the events that have interacted with the clues, it is clear that this was the process.

June 22, 1996

Q: (L) How come I am always the one who gets assigned the job of figuring everything out?

A: Because you have asked for the "power" to figure out the most important issues in all of reality. And, we have been assisting you in your empowerment.

Shortly after Ark had first written to me, triggered by this contact, I found myself at the center of a maelstrom of awakening psychic awareness, memory, and recognition, and the following little exchange took place:

July 27, 1996

Q: (L) Is there anything I can ask? What is going on with me? I am an emotional wreck … Is the past life connection that I perceive part of this?

A: Do you learn when we lead you by the hand? You have all the necessary tools to discover this.

Q: (L) Well, I thought *you* were one of those tools! That you are here to help us …

A: But not by giving the answers to "Level One" questions.

Q: (L) Just one thing I would like to know is, what is the source of this emotional energy that is practically tearing me apart? Is it coming from outside or inside me?

A: The one thing we would like to know is: how much transcribing have you been doing?

Q: (L) I have been going through the notebooks and reading, I have been sorting things … I am getting ready to start typing …

A: The "answers" are there.

Q: (L) Well, one thing I came across was a mention almost two years ago that something would happen, and one would have instant recognition but the others may doubt. For me, it was instant recognition. But, recognition, by definition, is to know someone again. So, I think maybe that you were using the term recognition because you were talking about a person and not an event, necessarily.

A: And learning helps you in immeasurable ways.

233

The remark the Cs made about "transcribing" was directed at the fact that, at this point in time, I was backed up in the transcribing process, and there were about 60 tapes sitting in a box waiting to be done. Because of illness and the depression I had been going though prior to, and during, the ending of my marriage, I simply had not had the energy or motivation to transcribe.

At this point, because Ark wanted to read every word of the transcripts, I was motivated to set to work getting the job done. It was a long and agonizingly painful process. I did receive some help from Jan, but she and Terry had a business to run and many of their own projects sorting and analyzing the material that had already been transcribed, so for the most part, I had to do it all myself. Frank had already declined to help in any way, giving as an excuse that he didn't have a computer. When I suggested that he could spell me on my computer, he didn't have time, or he was too tired.

It was during this period of getting all the later material transcribed that I discovered the clues. But in order to explain it, let me back up and gather the threads together that will bring us back to Ark in Dijon and the realizations that followed.

On October 20, 1994, as part of my rapid fire testing questions, I threw out the following:

Q: Who built the city of Baalbek?
A: Antereans and early Sumerians. We meant Atlanteans. [Who are the Antereans?] [...]
Q: What technical means did they use to cut the stones and transport them?
A: Sound wave focusing.

On October 23, 1994, in response to another question, a similar answer was given ... with something added:

Q: (L) Who built Stonehenge?
A: Druids.
Q: (L) Who were the Druids?
A: Early Aryan group.
Q: (L) How did they move the stones and set them up?
A: Sound wave focusing; try it yourself; Coral Castle.
Q: (L) Who taught the Druids to use the sound waves?
A: They knew; handed down.
Q: (L) What was Stonehenge built to do or be used for?
A: Energy director.
Q: (L) What was this energy to be directed to do?
A: All things.
Q: (L) Was the energy to be directed outward or inward to the center?
A: Both.

Q: (L) Does this sound come from our bodies?
A: Learn. Laura will find answer through discovery.

Well, *that* was a pretty cryptic remark, that I would learn something about this through a discovery! And the comment about the Coral Castle intrigued us as well. Even though I live in Florida, I had never been to see this purported marvel and the only things I knew about it were what I had learned by watching a television program about it on *Unsolved Mysteries*, I believe.

As it turned out, I was invited to give a talk to a UFO group in Orlando the following February. I had no idea what I was going to say, how open this group was going to be, or anything about the participants at all.

On the drive over (about 100 miles from my home), accompanied by two of my children, my daughter asked me what I was going to talk about. I told her that I didn't really know because I didn't know if this group was really ready for what the Cassiopaeans were saying about the UFO phenomena and the alien presence on the planet. She replied: "Well, Mom, you don't have time to break it to them gently!"

So, I didn't. I talked for an hour and a half or longer about the phenomena preceding the Cassiopaean communications followed by a synopsis of the different players as described by them, particularly the Grays and Reptoids.

The reception was underwhelming to say the least! One lady in the audience came up afterward and offered to use her "contacts with the Pleiadians" to "heal me" of the injuries received in the automobile accident several months prior to this time. Another offered to interpret our reality according to his Kabalistic training, and so on. They gathered around me with faintly pitying looks on their faces! How could I be so deluded as to think that aliens were not the saviors of mankind?

However, there was a funny old man who came up to me with a big grin on his face, grabbed my hand and shook it vigorously and said to me with a faint accent, "Ya know, I've been studying this UFO business for over 40 years – I talked with Dr. Hynek and Major Keyhoe and all that – and you are the first person I have ever heard who has gotten up in public and described it as it really is! I have some material you might be interested in. You should come and see me some time!"

Well, I thought he was just an old guy with a lot of time on his hands who needed company and might be using this as an excuse to get it. I thanked him and edged away to the host of the event who was chatting with several other people who were, apparently, from out of town, and were inquiring about the various tourist attractions. The host was telling them about the many interesting sites, and then he said,

"And you might want to go down and have a look at this Coral Castle, too!"

"What is that?" one of them asked, and the host proceeded to recap the *Unsolved Mysteries* presentation. Then he said, "You can ask Hilliard over there," pointing at the old man who knew Dr. Hynek. "He was a close friend of the guy who built the Coral Castle."

Well, needless to say, after hearing this, I remembered what the Cassiopaeans had said that I would "discover" something about this "sound-wave focusing" in relation to the Coral Castle and I eased back over to the old man and said, "I hear you knew the guy who built the Coral Castle?"

"Ayup! Sure did! Knew him for years! I was stationed over there in Homestead area after the war and got to know him pretty well."

I asked, "Did he ever tell you how he did it?"

"Nope. He never would tell anybody. He would always say that he knew the secret of how the pyramids were built, but nobody ever saw him do it. I have some ideas about it, though, and I wrote a little book about him and my experiences and observations. You know, it's a shame that the television program didn't give the real story! All that nonsense about "Sweet Sixteen" and a "broken heart" and so on! What a lot of crap! Sure! If you come to visit, I can show you what I *do* know! Do ya know something? I am the only person Leedskalnin ever let come inside his home! Ayup! He was a real loner!"

And so on. I was already making plans for this visit! Just before the visit, the following clues were giving:

March 4, 1995

A: Enough said, remember, you have been learning slowly that personal issues hold minor significance. Terry's dream was significant, however!!!!! And Frank has been sent same message as well.

Q: (L) Did you have a dream or message, Frank? (F) That's true. I did have some funny feelings. Just the same kind of thing, that there is something that we are missing in all of our questions. (T) OK. We are missing a key topic or issue, here, that's true.

A: 4th level STO! You have only thought of 4th level STS.

Q: (L) Ahhh! What S*** was talking about, we need to ask about the good guys.

A: They are the only ones who can help you defend yourselves against 4th level attack!!!! We give you information which is invaluable in nature, but remember we are 6th level STO, Beings of light, and on this density level there simply is no interference with free will no matter how detrimental to you!!!

Q: (T) Fourth-density STO beings can actually help in a meaningful way! We knew there was both sides, but we never asked. We have been concentrating on finding out about the Lizards. Who are these fourth-density STO beings that we need to contact? Obviously we need to talk to them because they can talk to us. Sixth-density "Us" can't.

A: Orion Federation.

Q: (L) And who are the members of the Orion Federation? What can you tell us?

A: You have asked us to protect you, it is important for you to under-stand that we are beyond that!

Q: (T) We understand that you, at sixth density, can't interfere with free will on either side. Well, you said that knowledge protects. You have been providing knowledge.

A: Indirectly. We are providing invaluable information which becomes knowledge, but you are under attack, therefore, you could maybe use some direct power from the same density as the attack is coming from.

Q: (L) OK, guys, what do we need to do here?

A: Find a "Nordic." They are on Earth posing as humans.

Q: (T) They are fourth density.

A: Yes.

Q: (T) I thought that fourth density couldn't hold the frequency that long and that is why the Lizards have so much trouble. (J) They're STS.

A: Not STO!

Q: (T) Very good, Jan hit it as they said it. The STS can't stay, only the STO.

A: Yes. Discover, remember these are among your protectors and Laura and Frank know what level one attack is like, Terry, Jan and S** are perilously close to finding out!

Q: (L) Well, should we wear something special like a red scarf so they can find us in the crowd?

A: Not needed at all, just be open and aware!!

A few days later, I visited Hilliard. Following this visit, on March 11, 1995:

Q: (L) I want to ask about the fellow with the Coral Castle. We went over to see Hilliard, as you know. When we were talking to Hilliard, he told us about the man who built the Coral Castle, his habits and so forth. He was very ascetic and thrifty. He didn't have many friends and there was a part of the place that was his private residence where no one was allowed to go. Except Hilliard. According to Hilliard, this fellow had, apparently, in his private quarters, three objects: a bed, a table, and a swing made of an airplane seat suspended from the ceiling by a chain, complete with seat belts. Is this …

A: You got it right because you are learning and rebundling DNA as a result of this and other activities.

Q: (L) Well, you didn't let me finish! OK, so the things S** and I were discussing, this mystery, the understanding of how this man performed these remarkable feats of engineering and construction, is correct?

And right here, the Cassiopaeans *changed the subject!*

A: Hypnotize S** if you wish. What do you suppose has happened to S** in her life, and why does she have nagging thoughts about her personal reality which she chooses not to disclose?

This was a peculiar thing to say. Well, clearly we had been pushing things a little too hard, and it was very curious that the Cassiopaeans did not want to continue to discuss Hilliard and the Coral Castle and deflected the subject to S**. But, as the reader now knows, this was just shortly before the event that revealed Frank's hidden persona, and this was connected to the interaction with S** which later brought us back to the subject of the Nordic Covenant, as the reader will soon see.

Several months later, again as a result of people I met because of the MUFON talk, a local woman called me on the phone and said that she had heard that I was interested in starting a magazine.

This was true. I was looking for a venue for the Cassiopaean material and I had mentioned it to a local bookstore owner who often hosted various speakers and seminars in her store.

The woman on the phone said that she had been publishing a small metaphysical newsletter for over two years and was ready to give it up and I was welcome to her subscription list and various accoutrements of her project if I wanted to take it over. We decided to meet to discuss it.

When we did, it was a funny trigger for a variety of things. She was Jewish and almost immediately began talking to me about her past life in Nazi Germany and how she had been experimented on by Dr. Mengele and had died as a result. There was an instant rapport between us, and she was interested in attending a session.

Right after this meeting and before her attendance at a session, I had a dream. In this dream, I was the bride and was wearing a wonderful dress with flowers in my hair and there was a limousine waiting outside to take me to my "wedding." I didn't know who the groom was, but there were a lot of people around me encouraging me to "get in the car" and go to "meet the bridegroom." For some reason, I was filled with happiness and the joy of those around me was contagious, so, overcoming my hesitations, I went to the car, got in and was taken to the place of the wedding. I was aware that the date was a Saturday, and it seemed to be the 14th because something was said about Friday the 13th having been the day before.

It turned out to be a big restaurant with a wonderful feast prepared and waiting. It was all decorated with flowers and streamers everywhere and many, many people were gathered in a happy and joyful crowd who cheered me as I got out of the car.

The "bridegroom" came forward to take my hand and we walked through the crowds of people to stand in front of a priest-like person who married us. I was overcome with happiness even though I could not see the groom's face!

As soon as we were married, the music began to play, and he took me out onto the middle of the floor where everyone had cleared a space, and we began to dance. It was like flying and we whirled and spun. It was happiness such as I had never experienced in my entire life and I awoke bathed in a sensation of ecstatic joy!

A few days later, my new Jewish friend, RC, came to a session and several strange remarks were made by the Cassiopaeans. RC wanted to ask about the feeling of rapport between us but I wanted to get in a quick question about my dream.

September 16, 1995

Q: (L) I dreamed the other night that I got married, and there was a big party, dancing, the limousine and so on ... flowers, happiness. In my dream, I heard a voice saying that the wedding would be on a Saturday the 14th, following Friday the 13th, could you tell me anything about this dream?

A: No.

Q: (RC) What is my relationship to Frank and Laura from any past life connections? Did we know each other in Germany?

A: Maybe. Discover.

Q: (L) Now, I was looking at the charts, just to see what kind of matches there were and it was a lot. (RC) According to astrology, that shows a past-life connection.

A: Who were you?

Q: (L) You mean me?

A: Yes.

Q: (L) I was just German woman ... (RC) I was wondering about Egypt?

A: But we are still in Germany!

Q: (L) All I know was that I committed suicide, name was Helga, I think ...

A: Who was your husband?

Q: (L) I don't know. He was Jewish. Is that what you are getting at?

A: Okay. Who were your children?

Q: (RC) They asked who were the children. Was I one of your children?

A: Discover. When we say discover, we mean for you to use your given talents to learn, not to have us lead you by the hand every step of the way. If we were to do that, we would cheat you out of an opportunity to gain knowledge, and more importantly, understanding. Thus, we would be abridging free will!

It struck me as strange for them to be directing me to think about this in this way in response to my dream of getting married. They were not answering my question, but they were trying to get something across without violating free will. Then, they said this:

A: We are receiving strong wave pattern surrounding subject we chose to cover, thus we interrupted inquiries! Moshe in Israel.

Q: (RC) Who is Moshe in Israel?

A: Moshe is IN Israel.

But we could get no more that made any sense.

The following week, with RC present, another strange series of remarks were made. I had been doing research on secret societies which included the Rosicrucians, Masons and others, and had ended up deep in a study of alchemy. The Cassiopaeans had mentioned a super-secret group once before, called the Quorum, and I was on the trail. And, we had recently been introduced to the work of David Hudson and his monoatomic gold. I was struggling to put the pieces together and find out just who was "on first."

September 24, 1995

Q: (L) OK, square one: Is the Quorum composed of humans who have been alchemists, who are presently in possession of a substance called "the elixir of life" and which David Hudson calls monoatomic gold?

A: And much, much more! Monoatomic gold is but one minor issue here. Why get lead astray by focusing upon it solely. It would be akin to focusing on the fact that "Batman" can fly! Is that the only important thing that "Batman" does in the story? Is it?

Q: (L) Of course not! (RC) Batman fights crime!

A: What we mean is that alchemy is but one minor piece of the puzzle.

Q: (L) OK, I understand. But, understanding the alchemical connection, and its potential for extending life and opening certain abilities, makes it more feasible to think of a group that has been present steadily and consistently for many thousands of years on earth.

A: They are not the only ones!

The night of this session was very strange. After RC and her husband went home, I went to bed in a strangely excited state. I knew it was going to be difficult to get to sleep, so I began to practice meditative breathing exercises to relax myself. Suddenly, I saw a face right before me! It was as clear and real as if someone had entered the room! It is difficult to convey to anyone how truly solid and three-dimensional this face was. I did not know this face, but it was a man with light hair and glowing eyes and he looked at me so kindly and lovingly before he vanished like a popping balloon! I was so startled that I nearly lost my breath altogether, but with firm effort, I resumed my meditation and soon went to sleep.

THE CRANE DANCE

In December of 1995, we discovered that the Gulf Breeze UFO conference was going to be held in the spring of 1996 rather than the fall. This was rather startling since, the previous February, the Cs had made a remark about going to Gulf Breeze in the spring. What was even more interesting was that this remark had come immediately following a mental question that I had asked about some thoughts I was having. I didn't want to share those thoughts with anyone, nor did I want to ask the question aloud. However, in light of recent events, I can now tell the reader what it was after giving the background information.

As the readers of *Amazing Grace* know, Frank's father committed suicide to avoid becoming a burden on his family as a consequence of declining health. Up until the time of Frank's embezzlement debacle, he had been in extraordinarily good health for a man of his age. In fact, he didn't look his age at all, which surprised me when I first met him because Frank had spent so many hours ranting about how terrible it had been to grow up with an "old father." He was sure that all the neighborhood kids laughed at him behind his back because his father was not young and virile and whatever. I wasn't terribly sympathetic to his description of how he had suffered so much because of this since I would have been happy to have such a father at any age.

Nevertheless, the old gentleman went into a sudden, precipitous decline following his arrangements to keep Frank out of jail by paying back the money that had been embezzled. Within less than six months, he went from swimming laps in his pool every day, to being unable to rise from his chair unassisted.

Frank blamed the decline on the medications his father had been given while hospitalized for an infection, and there is certainly much evidence to suggest that the American Medical system had a hand in the deterioration. I certainly agreed with Frank that a more holistic approach to the health issues might have saved his father's life. But when we consider holistic medicine, we also have to consider the stresses that bring on illness. It certainly seems that his shame over Frank's illegal activities contributed enormously to his vulnerability to illness which then necessitated hospitalization. The bottom line was, he was a courageous man, and he could see that his decline in health would soon lead to a drain in finances and other resources, and he chose to end his life before he became a burden on anyone else.

It was a strange event. At the exact time that Frank's father was setting out the important papers for the convenience of his survivors to manage his affairs after he was gone, following which, he went outside and selected a spot where there would be no muss or fuss and did the deed, I was overcome with an irresistible urge to sleep. And in my sleep, Frank's father appeared to me and we talked for a very long time. The only problem was, I couldn't remember what was said when I woke up. I woke up to the phone ringing, and it was Frank calling to tell me what had happened.

Just a couple weeks prior to this event, Frank and I had asked a few questions about any past-life connections.

January 5, 1995

Q: (L) When was the last lifetime Frank and I were together?

A: 1700's.

Q: (L) Who was Frank in the 1700s?

A: Bavarian landowner's son.

Q: (L) Who was I in this lifetime?

A: Daughter.

Q: (L) I was Frank's daughter?

A: No, sister.

Q: (L) Was this the same lifetime when I was married to G**?

A: No. Spent 3 lifetimes in what is now Germany.

Q: (L) Was my mother with me in that lifetime?

A: No.

Q: (L) In that lifetime as Bavarian landowner's children, what was Frank's name?

A: Heinrig.

Q: (L) What was my name?

A: Sheila.

Q: (L) What did we do in that lifetime? Argue?

A: Were sheltered.

Q: (L) Any exceptional talents or abilities?

A: Piano and harp.

Q: (L) So, all I did was sit around and play the piano and harp all the time?

A: Close.

Q: (L) And read books? What did Frank do, smoke cigars and gaze out the window?

A: Read.

Q: (L) Must have been nice, Frank. What area of Bavaria was this?

A: Muenchen near. South of there. On Braunau.

Q: (L) Was this a very large house?

A: Castle.

Q: (L) Sounds better all the time. Is the castle still standing?

A: Yes.

Q: (L) Would we know that castle by name?

A: No.

Q: (L) What was our last name, surname, family name?

A: Von Endersohn.

Q: (L) Did we live long and fulfilling and happy lives?

A: Open.

Q: (L) Did we experience tragedy?

A: Was turbulent era.

Q: (L) Well, how old was I when I died?

A: 43.

Q: (L) How old was Frank when he died?

A: 43.

Q: (L) Were we twins?

A: No.

Q: (L) Who was older, me or him?

A: Year apart.

Q: (L) What did he die from?

A: Heart attack.

Q: (L) What did I die from?

A: Pneumonia.

Q: (L) Did we die still living in our castle?

A: Yes.

Q: (L) Did either of us have any children?

A: No. Were sheltered from turbulence directed at wealthy.

Q: (L) How were we sheltered from this turbulence?

A: Kept isolated. Never married.

Q: (L) Well, I guess that is one way to shelter yourself from turbulence, just never go out. We just sat around, played the piano and harp and read books. That sounds like a pretty ideal existence to me. Did we ride horses too?

A: Yes.

Q: (L) I guess we worked hard to entertain ourselves. (F) That must be why we both yearn for security, peaceful reading and so on. (L) I have always wanted to live in Europe. Would I be happy doing so?

A: Up to you.

Q: (F) Well, that is probably why you yearn to live in Europe, because you spent 3 lifetimes in that area. (L) If I used hypnosis, could I improve my piano playing? Also, would I be able to automatically play the harp?

A: Open.

Q: (L) Has it ever been done before?

A: Yes.

It's another of those very strange synchronicities that these questions were brought up just prior to an event that seemed to trigger the memories of that life. I had no idea that my view of that period as being so simple and peaceful and sheltered was about to crash and burn. The reader of the above passage would probably not see anything strange or horrifying in the simple exchange above. But having asked the question, the door was opened, and I was about to remember. It began on the day Frank's father committed suicide.

February 22, 1995

Q: (L) OK, I am not going to ask about things I can figure out myself, but I am going to ask about something I don't know: as you know, Frank's dad passed away about two weeks ago. From that day to this, everything has seemed to be different in terms of dynamics and energy, and this is not just with Frank and his family, but also with myself. I am curious as to why I feel so different. I cannot put a word to how different I feel … it is definitely a feeling, an emotional sense, why is this?

A: Let us just refer to this as a steppingstone or "milestone," if you prefer.

Q: (L) OK, it is a milestone, but why should this … I wish I could convey to you all how strange I have been feeling … (DM) Can you specify strange? (F) See, I don't even know … (L) Is Frank's dad earthbound?

A: Partially.

Q: (L) Is he trying to communicate through me?

A: Maybe.

Q: (L) Why, on the day and at the time that Frank's dad decided to make his transition, was I overwhelmed with the need to go to sleep?

A: Connection.

Q: (L) Connection to what? (DM) You mean he was connecting with Laura?

A: Close.

Q: (SV) She was connecting to him?

A: Close.

Q: (DM) Were they mentally entangled.

A: No, you are drifting.

Q: (F) Let Laura ask the question. (L) Did he basically come to me at another level …

A: Yes.

Q: (L) He came to me at another level. Why me and not Frank?

A: He always trusts others to be more qualified.

Q: (L) So, he was trusting me to be more qualified than Frank, to advise him in his new estate, is that it?

A: Yes.

Q: (F) Well, that certainly fits his personality. (L) What does he want from me now?

A: Nothing specific, but open channel and see.

Q: (L) Can we address Frank's dad directly through the board?

A: Laura can meditate on an individual basis, this is the chosen mode.

Q: (F) That is probably why you are feeling so weird is that you haven't opened to channel on your own. (L) Yeah, and it's driving me nuts.

(DM) It's interfering with your thinking processes. (L) Does Frank's dad need me to help him to release into the light?

A: Open.

Q: (L) Well, it has definitely been a problem, but I'll deal with it. [...] OK, anything further on this matter that you can give me to ease the situation?

A: No.

Q: (L) One of the things that has been been brought to my mind continuously and repeatedly since that time has been the memory of the lifetime that Frank and I explored before, where we were brother and sister in Bavaria, and I am wondering if there was some connection with Frank's dad in that time, and is that why it is being continuously shoved in my face?

A: Why not check it out? You are good at that, when you want to be.

Q: (L) Obviously you want me to check it out through my own head, right?

A: Yes.

Now, first of all we have the remark that this was a "steppingstone," and that I should "open the channel" myself. This was followed by "Laura can meditate on an individual basis, this is the chosen mode." The reader may also note that my remark about the past life that was constantly being brought to mind was a bit negative. I described it as being "shoved in my face."

So, what exactly was going on that I didn't want to talk about except in allusions and veiled questions?

First of all, indeed, the channel had been blown wide open in me. The only way I can describe this feeling is that it was like having a huge opening right in the solar plexus through which emotional energy poured like water exploding through a collapsed dam. And each of these emotions was connected to a memory, and as they rushed in, the memories were activated and I re-experienced every single one of them like a concentrated, fast forward review. And I remembered every single detail of this former life with Frank.

Indeed, we were children of a powerful man, though I cannot say if there is any accuracy to the name the Cs gave. And when our father died, he left me in the care of my "brother." However, Frank, as the "brother" of that lifetime was what was called in those days "dissolute" and self-indulgent to an extreme degree. He was weak and inconstant and the only object over which he had complete control was me. And he exercised that control with fiendish depravity.

I will spare the reader the Marquis de Sade-type scenes I was witnessing in my own head, accompanied by horror and sick revulsion, and will only say that after it was all over, I had to find some way to reconcile this truly wicked and corrupt Frank with the current Frank who repeatedly expressed extreme distaste for normal human sexuality.

Frank's rejection of this side of himself – his complete denial of any sexual nature at all – had been something of a puzzle anyway, and now I had a perfectly reasonable theory as to why this would be so. I concluded that he had felt so much remorse in the afterlife state that he resolved to come back and atone for his sins by repressing and suppressing any such inclinations. In this way, I was able to justify Frank's views, all the while ignoring the hints that were given here and there that he engaged in vicariously prurient activities. I was able to shove under the rug the remarks he had made on numerous occasions indicating a more-than-casual acquaintance with literature sold from behind the counter, in plain brown wrappers, as well as dark smoky dives where, as he once remarked, one had to be careful where one stepped to avoid having one's shoes stick to the floor. When I asked what that meant, he guffawed at my ignorance and refused to explain it. It was only much, much later that someone else did.

But we believe what we choose to believe. And I chose to believe that Frank was on the road to atonement, and learning, and balancing his karma. Just because I remembered how horribly I had been treated by him, didn't mean that I had to bring it up and blame him now.

Nevertheless, these events are what bring us to the question I asked the Cs in my mind which led to such a strange answer that contained within it an amazing prediction. Before we diverted to the story of Frank's father, the issue was the UFO conference in Gulf Breeze that was to be held rather soon. We were talking about attending and distributing our magazine, the *Aurora Journal*, and I was reminded of the fact that the Cassiopaeans had suggested going to a Gulf Breeze conference "in the spring" at a time when the Gulf Breeze conferences had always been held in the fall.

Now, this is one session that I believed to be corrupted. The woman, D**, was the probable cause, but there was also a *strong* conflict between her and Jan. There were *many* peculiar things about this whole session. The whole "personality" that came through in occasional surges *was* D**, as we were to find out later. But, also, there *was* some of the Cs energy coming through. I think the first clue I had was when they abbreviated the word "Cassiopaea," which was odd … almost as though it were a clue that I was only going to make a partial connection.

The first peculiar remark was strange – as though my mind was being read. I was most definitely concerned about the recent experiences of remembering this past life and all the terrible turmoil it was causing in my thinking and emotions.

February 18, 1995

A: Forget it, Laura, it was just only one of many, many learning experiences! They all enriched us tremendously.

Q: (L) What am I supposed to forget that was the learning experience?

A: Lifetimes of "woe."

Q: (T) Is this one of her/your lifetimes of woe?

A: They all are if we choose to view them thusly. [...]

Q: (L) Well, I just want to say something ...

A: Okay, Laura, ask it if you must.

Q: (J) I want to ask about ...

A: Laura first, we/she is about to jump out of her/our skin.

Q: [laughter] (T) Ask away, my dear. (L) I wanted to ask, now you guys are going to be mad at me because I am going off on a very serious tangent ...

A: We know, just ask it, already!!!! [...]

Q: (L) As you know, I am reading this book about Holocaust victims reincarnating and remembering their experiences at this time. The question is, on one occasion you told us that the Jewish people, as a racial group, were Atlantean descendants, is that correct?

A: Some.

Q: (L) There is some. Can you give us that some?

A: No.

Q: (L) Is there some karmic element that was fulfilled by the Holocaust?

A: Of course.

Q: (L) Could you tell us what karma was being expunged in that activity, and what group the Jews represented?

A: This is not germane, but it was Atlantean overseers "expunging" guilt from that life experience.

Q: (L) So ...

A: So what?

As the reader can guess, I was not very pleased with this communication. Neither were Terry and Jan, and it showed. We tried to be "light" and have a little fun with it, but the "off" flavor and texture of the contact made it clear that something was going on, and it was only right at the end that the clue was given as to what it was. The woman, D**, was feeding Frank energy that empowered the STS-force connection to him. Based on the remarks, he was obviously able to vacuum out of me many details of what was in my thoughts and experiences of the past weeks. The information given was, indeed, "starkly accurate" in that respect. And there is clear evidence that my own foreknowledge of coming personal events was being tapped. This is also one of the few sessions in which Frank was actually active.

Q: (L) Alright, I want to ask what it was that I went through about a week ago when I felt like I was getting all kinds of stuff pumped into my system that I did not seem capable of coping with in terms of emotional control. What was going on?

A: Answered about one half hour ago as you/us measure time. [...]

Q: (L) What are you talking about ... the past life business?

A: Yes.

This refers to the remark at the very beginning about "lifetimes of woe." This had been brought up spontaneously, with no question asked, which was another bit of evidence that Frank was "vacuuming" *a la* STS.

Q: (L) Well, what precipitated that activity?

A: Ions charged by awareness opening in window of EM envelope, used to precipitate physical trauma in immediate surroundings. "Used to" refers to past tense.

Q: (L) OK, so in the past, this kind of opening of a window in the EM envelope ...

A: You have elevated.

Q: (T) You made a connection with other life experiences, and you were able to experience them in another way. (L) Well, it had some damn strange effects, that's all I've got to say about it! I wasn't very happy about it. (T) Will she be experiencing more of this now that she's made this elevation?

A: Yes. Each episode will be easier and easier.

Q: (L) Thank God! When do these guys get to enjoy that particular ... (T) We haven't gotten to that point yet, or we may experience it in a different way. Is that it?

A: Sort of, each has their own issues.

Q: (T) Well, we are all doing different things as we move forward. (J) We all have different issues to work through.

A: Why wish agony upon another?

Q: (L) I don't wish agony upon another, I just want you guys to appreciate the utter agony ... (T) They do appreciate ... (J) And we do too ... They went through it with you. You didn't go through it alone! (T) They are you!

A: Why wish agony upon another, all have personal trials, would you/us like to share?

And here, there is the most curious "dig" about the event which clearly indicated some awareness of the nature of it and the memories that were revealed. Of course I was not going to share such revolting information about Frank!

Q: (L) In other words, be grateful that it wasn't worse. (D) I would like to ask a question because you probably understand it and I do not. If we are sixth and we are also third, in the future, will we be another third and another sixth … (F) In our third-density perception, since our time is linear and we are looking at us in the future, talking back to us in the present, but it is all happening at once because there is no real time. And, probably, I guess this also means that one day, which is also today, we will be sixth looking down here … (D) We will be doing the same thing over and over? (F) Sort of yes and no … I don't think we can quite grasp the whole thing … (T) The problem is …

A: You will grasp it when at 6th level!!! So, rejoice in the "here and now!"

Q: (T) Even at fourth we will understand more than we do now. They are giving us concepts that are beyond third level. They are working with us to prepare us so that when we move into fourth we will have a head start on what's going on. They are bringing us up to where we already are because we came from fourth level to come here to do this originally, to set the frequency and hold it so that others can move to fourth level. We came from fourth density to do this. They are trying to give us enough information so that we will remember. It is kind of like Hansel and Gretel going into the forest and leaving a trail of crumbs so that they can find their way out. We came back from fourth to third to do what we've got to do and we're going back to fourth but we've got to leave a trail for us to keep connected to where we came from … something similar to that, in any event. Is your mind exploding, D**? We, where we are now, don't grasp all this because we are not supposed to at this level.

A: Learning. Laura just gained one more strand, that is why it was so painful, okay?

Q: (D) Say! Congratulations! (T) Yup, she gained another strand and made Reiki Master! (L) I am in a bear of a mood! (T) Mirth! You in sixth density are enjoying the hell out of you now. We are going to take a break. (F) You gained a strand of DNA?

In any event, after a break in which Terry and Jan and I consulted in the kitchen while Frank regaled D** in the living room with tales of his feats of channeling derring-do, we came back to the table, aware and alert, and the rest of the session was far more stable, even if there were a couple of quirky moments of skewing and a couple of attempts at "time-anchored predictions," which was always a dead giveaway that STS forces were trying to horn in.

It is also at this point that I asked the question. After pondering the idea that the events of the past weeks had been related to DNA, I came to some sort of idea that I had been inspired to undertake the channeling project as a means of this very DNA activation that had resulted in this awakening, or quickening, and that ultimately, my entire life would completely change as a result, and I was asking mentally if this was true, and if so, how would it manifest?

Q: (L) Alright, I want to ask a question. This is a trick question. It involves mind-reading. Please answer the question I am thinking.

A: Your dreams are valid.

Q: (D) My dreams are valid?

A: No.

Q: (T) Laura's dreams?

A: Yes.

Q: (T) What dream? (D) Your dreams are valid, Laura. (T) Was that your question? (L) Well, sort of. It could apply. (T) They answered your question before you asked it. (L) Yeah. I wasn't going to ask it out loud, anyway. (T) If we could just get them to skip the questions and go to the answers, we would make a lot better time here.

A: Have.

Q: (L) In other words, my impressions of the ultimate outcome of this DNA switcheroo is …

A: Yes!

Q: (T) Any other questions?

A: Go to Pensacola.

Q: (L) Who wants to go to Pensacola?

A: I do, I do. [laughter]

Q: (T) Is something going to happen in Pensacola?

A: Conference. Increasing activity in Florida panhandle, vortex. If you go to Pensacola you will see UFOs of all origins including yours truly.

Q: (T) Oh! It's your conference! And we've been invited!

A: Okay.

Q: (T) When is it that we are supposed to go. Is it that whenever we go, then will be the conference?

A: May.

Q: (T) Is there something in May? In Pensacola? (J) Project Awareness is in May but that's in Tampa. Are you talking about the conference in May that is being put on by the Pensacola group?

A: Look and see.

Q: (T) OK, in May we should go to Gulf Breeze?

A: Yes.

Q: (T) OK, the conference in Gulf Breeze is going to be in Tampa in May.

A: Do a session and monitor the skies at the same time. Have someone posted outside with a video camera!! Let's try to steer all these "Ufologists" in the right path. […]

Q: […] (D) You guys, I am getting very, very weak.

A: Obvious.

Q: (L) Let's shut down for the night, I am pooped.

Now, the strange thing about this UFO conference that we were talking about was that the normal schedule was for the spring conference to be held in Tampa and the fall conference to be held in Gulf Breeze.

As it turned out, that very year the fall Gulf Breeze conference was nearly canceled because of a hurricane! That, in itself, was an extremely interesting event. We had been planning on attending this particular conference and Terry and Jan had already made the reservations. Hurricane Opal was spinning around in the Gulf and everyone was waiting to see where it would come ashore:

October 7, 1995

A: Review: what did we say about weather. Why do you suppose "Opal" occurred at time, place reference point?

Q: (L) To put a stop to the UFO conference in Gulf Breeze? Does this mean we ought to stay home?

A: Up to you, but, suggest deferment, we could tell you of titanic battle!!!!

Q: (L) So, hurricanes are a reflection of battles at higher levels? Did the good guys win?

A: Yes, but not concluded, and we fear for those drawn to locator because of sinister plans by 4th-density STS.

Q: (L) Plans such as what? More weather phenomena or something more direct?

A: Both, several options open to them, and in works; monstrous hurricane to hit during conference, or tornado strikes Embassy Suites hotel, or bomb blast levels conference center, or mass abductions and mental controls initiated in order to cause dissension and possibly violence, followed by extreme factionalization.

Q: (L) So, there is the possibility that something really positive could come from the connections made at the conference and, to prevent this possibility, the fourth-density STS are taking steps?

A: Yes, why do you suppose it has been disrupted as of now? And have you noticed that the hurricanes have been increasing in October, rather than decreasing as would normally be true?

Q: (L) Well, then, I guess we will be staying home.

A: Free will.

So, we canceled our reservations. As it turned out, the hurricane did hit Gulf Breeze almost dead on, and the conference was moved to Mobile. Clearly, there was no bomb blast or tornado so if any of the above mentioned possibilities did play out, it would seem to have been mass abductions and mental controls initiated.

As a result of this hurricane, the organizers of the conference decided to switch the schedule around so that *the Gulf Breeze conference was held in the spring* the following year, 1996. But, *not* in May. In March. So, even if the Cassiopaeans were picking up something about this specific switch, it was not a bull's eye exactly. Another thing that has happened since that hurricane is that the organizers of the conference *broke up their organization and reformed*. They no longer hold UFO conferences, but rather focus on metaphysical/New Age assemblies. So, it may be that there was a mass abduction and mental controls that initiated dissension, but it would be difficult to make Ufologists any more fragmented and factional than they already were and are!

But, getting back to the UFO conference that we learned was going to be held in the spring, right after we had made the arrangements to take over RC's magazine:

December 2, 1995
Q: (L) This year the UFO conference in Gulf Breeze is in the spring. Is this the one we are supposed to go to?
A: Yes.

All of the strange elements came together at the UFO conference in the spring of 1996. And looking back, the answer to my silent question: "Your dreams are valid," was directly related to this event. Not only had I had the dream about getting married immediately after meeting the woman who wanted to transfer her magazine to us, but as soon as that project was underway, I had the vision of Ark's face. At Gulf Breeze, I had another dream, and indeed, the Cassiopaeans were there. Just not the way we expected, as we will see.

One of the main reasons we wanted to go to the Gulf Breeze conference was because of the magazine. It was hoped that it would be an organ for the Cassiopaean material since I could really think of no other affordable way to make the material available. We planned to print a thousand copies and take them to the conference with us and give them away with a subscription form attached inside.

As you might expect, the events surrounding the work on the magazine, *The Aurora Journal,* took on a Twilight Zone like quality. The Matrix again went into overdrive to prevent the plan from being brought to fruition.

One of the first things I wanted to do was to find a printer who would do a nice job for me at a reasonable cost since I was paying for it out of my own pocket. There was a print shop near the chiropractor I was still seeing three times a week for therapy, and I decided to stop in and find out what my options were and how much I could do myself to keep the costs low. At the same time, I had printed up a large volume of the Cassiopaean material and thought that it might be cheaper to have it copied, so I hauled it in with me.

The young lady at the counter quoted me a very reasonable price for the copying but said that she couldn't tell me anything about doing a magazine layout because she was just there in a clerical capacity and I would have to come back. I left my material with an order for three copies, bound in a plastic spine.

Several days later I went back to pick up my copies. As the girl was getting them from the back, a woman emerged from the shop area, grinning widely, and said, "I *thought* that was you I heard out here!" I looked at her blankly because, frankly, I had *no* idea who she was! She realized that I didn't recognize her and she said "Pam! You remember! I came to you for hypnosis!"

And then I realized who she was! She was the woman I had hypnotized back in 1993 the night the Flying Black Boomerangs were sighted over the three-county area. She had been so upset by the idea of an alien abduction lurking in her subconscious that she never came back for any further sessions. I had always wondered what had happened to her since, and it was very curious to find her in this print shop since she had told me back then that she was in real estate. It was even stranger when you consider that I had selected this print shop over any other simply because it was en route between my house and the chiropractor I was seeing every other day as a result of an accident that I was certain was a deliberate attempt on my life by hyperdimensional forces. Not only that, I was in the print shop for the very purpose of having copies made of material that related to the events in which Pam had been involved at the very beginning. Further, that I was planning on inquiring about the printing of a magazine that was an offshoot of those same events.

I was shocked. She looked like she had aged about 20 years in the almost three years since I had seen her! As it turned out, Pam had recently bought the print shop as a business venture for her kids. She invited me into the back of the shop for coffee and we brought each other up to date on what had been happening in our lives since the incident of the UFOs. That event had upset her so badly that she completely retreated into denial and the "normal life" routine. I told her how that event had done just the opposite for me – I had been catapulted into a series of learning experiences that had completely shattered my previous world, and made it seem like I was on a continual roller coaster ride. I told her, "Honey! If you had any idea of the stuff that has happened to me since you were at my house and opened the door to those damned aliens, you would *not* believe it!" And we both laughed.

So, we spent an hour or so catching up. Pam was fascinated by the story of how the contact with the Cassiopaeans had developed the year following her hypnosis session and wanted not only to read the material, but to attend a session. It turned out that she was very interested in mysteries, or so she claimed. It never occurred to me to wonder why she wasn't interested in her own mystery!

I was, of course, thinking to myself how serendipitous this was for Pam to own this print shop since it just *might* mean that I could get my magazine printed at a really reasonable price.

As we talked, Pam began to reveal things about her past that were beyond strange. When she had come to me for hypnosis, she was working in real estate and caring for her retired and dying husband who had been a former government employee. That was basically all she had said at the time. I had never asked her if her husband worked for the post office or any other specific agency, not realizing that it *might* be important.

Now she was telling me that he was a physicist who had worked at various government labs, including JPL on the Mars Observer, and had spent most of his time working in an underground laboratory some- where in Maryland or thereabouts. She was telling me so many things that I found it difficult to assimilate all of it. It was as though, in the years since the door to the idea of aliens had been opened in her mind, all sorts of associations had come together. It never occurred to me that this might be bait to attract my interest.

On top of her husband's work, Pam, herself, had a high security clearance and had spent years working (or so she said) in certain office positions that gave her access to highly sensitive information. Finally I thought I understood why Pam may have been abducted. If her hus- band was a scientist and she had a security clearance, that might explain it. I shared with her that I had learned that families of government em- ployees generally seem to be abducted more than the average person. She thought this was interesting, but still didn't think that it applied to her specifically.

I was pretty excited by all of this. A real, potential witness to weird- ness! What a find!

We discussed the magazine, finally, and she agreed that if I would come into the shop and physically help assemble it, in addition to hav- ing camera-ready copy, she would be able to give me a considerable discount. So, I left feeling like the fates were in my corner and all was going to be right. I also thought that this was a *big* opportunity – per- haps the one the Cassiopaeans had mentioned when they had said back in October of the previous year:

Q: (L) We need to create a forum.

A: Yes. A direction will open if you persevere.

Q: (L) So things will be brought to us and happen for us if we just per- severe?

A: Soon expect big opportunity.

Q: (L) I assume that we are not to ask what it is, we are to have faith, is that correct?

A: Yes. Danger you may misinterpret opportunity.

Q: (L) Should we all be able to realize in congruence whether the opportunity is good?

A: Varying degrees.

Q: (L) If there is a danger we may misinterpret the opportunity, could you give us a couple of clues so that when it occurs we won't miss it?

A: At least one of you will have instant recognition but others may not. Wait and see.

My first interpretation of this opportunity was the fact that RC wanted to dump her magazine. She did claim to "recognize" me as a connection from her past life, though I can't say that I had similar recognition. A magazine was a "forum."

The next interpretation I put on it was that Pam had "instantly" recognized me, but I hadn't recognized her. And having an inside line to printing, especially since we were planning a journal, was definitely a "big opportunity" in terms of "creating a forum," one would think.

Earlier, I had joined Mike Lindemann's ISCNI forum on AOL and had been invited to chat live, online, with his group in a sort of question and answer session. I felt sure that this, also, was part of the "forum" and might be the "big opportunity."

But, the fact that, in none of these instances had there been "instant recognition" by any of the group, with the others "doubting," still bugged me. What other big opportunity could there be?

So, it's funny how we anticipate things in ways that never quite fit, and yet how desperate we are to make them true.

And this is where we find me in the early months of 1996 … moving slowly and inexorably to the threshold of the unknown; my conscious mind fighting tooth and nail against the forces of my own higher self, ignorant of the Predator's mind, ignorant of the Matrix, learning by experience and direct, painful interaction. There was the world of practical events in which this drama manifested; there was the underlying psychological drama, and there was, apparently, another reality – the theological reality – from which the energies emanated.

And learning to see this other reality and to be able to respond to it with no apparent proof seemed to be the big test.

CHAPTER 45
THE GULF BREEZE

The trip to Gulf Breeze was all Frank could talk about. I had the idea that we would drive up in my van, split the expenses three ways, and we could park the van on one of the great beaches up there and camp out with sleeping bags. Frank would have none of that! He would have a hotel room or nothing.

OK. Well, I couldn't afford a hotel room. But Frank pointed out that S** could. She had a large inheritance from her father, and Frank decided that she ought to fund this trip. As he pointed out, S** had certainly been providing printing supplies, paper, ink, and tapes to me for the sessions and printing excerpts and copies of sessions. Why shouldn't she pay for a trip to Gulf Breeze?

I didn't like it, but Frank said, "If we don't go in style, I ain't goin'!" And I most definitely wanted Frank to go! "Just let me handle S**," he assured me.

I didn't want S** to have to discuss this with Frank alone, since I was already certain that she couldn't see through his little manipulations that I generally swept under the rug when he tried them on me, and made every effort to protect other people from them. (Again, I was waiting for Frank to come into his own, and I tolerated his flaws until he did, which I was sure he would eventually!)

After Frank had made his proposal to her in a more or less direct way, which could not have been faulted, I mentioned the fact that my idea had been to drive up and camp out to save money. S** thought my idea was more fun, but Frank again interjected that he wasn't going to go if he couldn't stay in a hotel.

So, S** said, "Sure! That would be fun! We can just all share a double room!"

"Nope!" Frank declared. He would not go if he couldn't have his own room. I could see the chances of going to the conference and distributing the magazine dwindling. But S** agreed. Sure, she'd pay for two rooms if that would make Frank happy.

However, that wasn't all that Frank wanted. Now he announced that it would undoubtedly be cheaper all the way around if we were to fly up instead of drive. I could see the chances of going to the conference and distributing the magazine dwindling. But S** agreed. Sure, she'd pay for round-trip tickets for the three of us.

And Frank just beamed with delight.

At some point during the magazine preparation period, S** made an offhand remark about her relations with several people that I knew to be deeply involved with ritual magic and other unsavory activities. I was surprised. After all we had learned so far, didn't she think it was a bit dangerous to be hanging out with those people? S** explained that she really wasn't hanging out with them, she was being paid to do therapy with them. It was purely and simply a business relationship.

But she knew that this was the same group of people who had previously tried to harm me,[13] and I felt a tremendous sense of betrayal. I knew I couldn't ask her to give up a massage client in solidarity with me, but I certainly hoped she would.

Having this sudden revelation just before our trip did not make the prospects all that pleasant for me. But, I was committed to getting the magazine out, and that was that.

In addition to the storm that was brewing in regard to S**, it was becoming very evident that our involvement with Pam was far more complicated and problematical than I had ever anticipated. We had started the project at the beginning of January, and already I was becoming unwillingly embroiled in Pam's control games with her children and her dying husband. The whole family dynamic had presented itself in the beginning as so very charming and loving. As I spent more time with them on the magazine project, more and more secrets – *ugly* secrets – bubbled to the surface.

It became clear that Pam had bought the print shop business in order to be able to totally dominate her children. It was also clear that her children, aged 20 and 17, were completely and totally irresponsible and undesirous of being dominated. With a dying husband and mounting medical bills, Pam had also endeavored to exert controls on her children by buying both of them expensive new cars as well as a 40K sports car for herself so that they could maintain their images as "business owners." Patrick and Shayna, the children, thought that the print shop was their personal bank and that it was supposed to finance their every whim – even without completing the many orders that were placed by their customers. They would take initial payments on large

---

[13] See volume two of *The Wave* for details. [Editor's note.]

business orders, close the shop and go out to eat and party and sometimes not return to the shop for days.

Pam laughed at this in an indulgent way for a while. But then the bills began to pile up, the investment income from her other sources began to dry up, and her husband's pension and inherited trust fund payments were not nearly enough to keep up the car and insurance payments.

And, angry customers became more and more frequent, making Pam embarrassingly aware of what her kids were doing when she wasn't watching.

Pam was at her wit's end. She would be at home, caring for her husband, and would call the shop to see how the kids were managing things, and find that it was closed and they were gone. Little by little she confided to me her concern over Patrick and his apparent substance abuse problems as well as her perception of her daughter, Shayna, as a flighty, promiscuous borderline mental case. Pam was constantly dragging Patrick to doctors for mind-controlling drugs such as Prozac and other antidepressants. She was convinced that if he failed to take his medication he would turn into a monster, and he would certainly fail to take his medicine if he did not have his mother's constant attendance.

I was unsure why she felt this until she began to reveal that he had violent tendencies and had physically attacked both his parents on occasion, even throwing his father's oxygen tank into the swimming pool. Pam had to call the police several times, but each time, she refused to press charges when Patrick would beg her forgiveness as soon as the police were at the door. On one such occasion, he had stormed out of the house and had taken her car and disappeared for two weeks along with her credit cards. It turned out that he and a friend had been partying in New Orleans, visiting whorehouses and eating in fine restaurants. She attributed all of this behavior to his failure to take his medication, and she was determined to keep him under her thumb; thus, she bought the print shop after he had expressed interest in the printing business.

Shayna, a more-than-plain girl with little but air between her ears, was proving to be a teenaged slut of the first order. She had picked up a very sleazy boyfriend at a nightclub who glommed onto her because of her fancy car and access to fast, easy cash. More than once I observed him brazenly opening the cash drawer in the shop and taking out money for dinner and movies for himself and Shayna, who was simply gaga that such a slick guy would pay her so much attention; never mind that he was doing it with the customers' money and no work was getting done for that money!

Pam tried to control all of them and get the print shop to run, but it was a losing battle. I was practically desperate to get the magazine finished and Pam began to manipulate *me* to that end. She couldn't get to my magazine (which had been paid up front), until *other*, even older, backed up orders were finished so I ended up spending many nights in the shop helping her get the orders out. But, we could only do that if Patrick showed up in condition to run the presses, which was problematical at best. He would disappear for days at a time, showing up bleary eyed and sullen with no explanation for where he had been or what he had been doing.

And worse than that, he was dangling after my daughter who was completely insensible to any warnings I gave her that she was being sucked into a black hole!

It was turning into a nightmare! My dreams of producing a magazine and getting it to the Gulf Breeze conference were rapidly fading, my daughter was being drawn into the clutches of a family that I was beginning to see as Tobacco Road incarnate, and meanwhile S** and her wicked-witch mother lurking like spiders in the background. I resolved to keep my cool, navigate these treacherous waters as best I could, and try to get out of this minefield with as little damage as possible.

Meanwhile, as if things were not crazy enough, another weird element was introduced into the situation. Against all odds and opposition, I finally had all the layout done, the copy was finished on the computer (I should add that I had to learn the program by doing it!), and we were ready to print. At this point, a man came into the print shop talking big money and big print jobs. He was a huge guy, over six-and-a-half feet tall, puffing a cigar and punctuating the verbal dollar signs he was scattering through the atmosphere with smoke rings. Pam and her kids, desperate for more money, hung on his every pronouncement of how he was the answer to their prayers; they were sitting on a gold mine in their print shop, and he was just the guy to turn every ream of paper to riches. I could see my magazine being shoved to the back room with every word.

Not surprisingly, all of a sudden, Pam and her kids were no longer interested in the magazine or anything but the promises of gold and glory being spun by the "mysterious stranger." I couldn't get anyone to answer the phone at the print shop, no one answered the phone at Pam's house and I was feeling desperate again at the thought of all my hard work being locked up and inaccessible to me. At least my daughter seemed to be seeing the light and was distancing herself from Patrick. I counted my blessings on that one.

Then Pam called. Something was not right with the "mysterious stranger." Things were getting totally weird in her life also! She needed to come and talk to me and she needed to ask the Cassiopaeans some questions. Well, finally! The light was shining through and everybody was going to figure out all the issues and start acting like human beings again!

As best I could make out from the very confused tale she recounted to me, this mysterious man was taking control of her son and filling his mind with promises of big money while, at the same time, not coming up with any money of his own to back up his big words. Not only that, but the stories he recounted to all of them about his experiences as an undercover agent were getting stranger and stranger. He claimed to have been a spy against the Nazis in WWII and he also claimed to have been single-handedly responsible for bringing down the Outlaws Motorcycle Gang! (This mention of the Outlaws Motorcycle Gang was a really creepy thing and comes up again. It was just another of the many crazy connections threading through this whole drama.) He also claimed to have been forced to divorce his wife and abandon his family to do this job, which was a great and noble sacrifice on his part, though no reason was ever given as to why this had been necessary. Further, after it was all over (and all this was supposed to have taken place in Tallahassee), he had remarried her, they had a child, and this child had convinced him to give up the cloak-and-dagger life, which was why he was now looking for promising businesses in which to invest lots of money. The only problem was, the money didn't seem to be materializing.

He promised to show up with a large check to put down on a big job for Patrick that was going to be the start of their future moneymaking enterprises; however, this event kept getting put off over and over again. So Pam was becoming suspicious and thought that they were being taken for a ride by a con artist. She expressed this opinion to her son, and Patrick was so taken in by the man that he fell out with his mother and spent more and more time away from the shop, which meant that less and less work was getting done!

I really wanted *out* of this mess. But, I didn't know what to do. I knew that Pam was not in any position to pay back the money I had already paid her to purchase the paper which was sitting unused in the shop. I knew I couldn't just take my paper to another shop and get a similar deal where I could do some of the work for a lower cost. I also knew that I didn't have the money to just go to any print shop and get the whole thing done from scratch. What's more, time was growing short. If we wanted to have a thousand magazines to take to the conference, it had to be done pretty soon!

As it happened, the very day that Pam called me, right after she hung up the phone, the mysterious stranger *did* come in to the shop to reassure her that he would be dropping off some big money in the next few days. *And* he had his wife with him along with the child. The only problem was, as Pam expressed it to me when she called later, the child was only about 8 or 9 years old, and the woman was clearly in her 70s or thereabouts. The man, himself, didn't look to be much over 40, so all the numbers regarding when he was doing what just didn't add up.

Pam was mystified.

I was disgusted with the whole thing. I couldn't figure out why Pam just couldn't see that the guy was a con artist from the word "go," and why did she keep dangling after him when he hadn't put up a single dime?

Well, she came over wanting to discuss every detail of what this man had told her, every thing he had told her son, dates and times and just the whole scenario and it was so bizarre as to baffle the cleverest mind. He couldn't be old enough to do all the things he claimed, and his wife wasn't young enough to be the mother of a preadolescent child! It was perfectly weird!

Well, we decided that the guy was a complete fraud and con artist. I just wanted him gone and my magazine printed. Apparently, Pam had been ashamed to call me for advice without being able to produce something of what was supposed to have already been finished, and she had prevailed on Patrick to print the inside pages. So, Frank and I were invited to the shop the next day to get all the pages of the magazine assembled. Now, all that was left to do was to print the covers.

So the next evening, there we were, in the print shop after closing and the doors were locked. The presses were running in the back, and Patrick seemed to be more stable than usual. He was working hard and doing a very good job. I was thinking that things might work.

A knock came at the door.

It was the "mysterious stranger" just "dropping by" to say that he would be there with the "big check" in the morning. He was full of all kinds of apologies for having had to "leave town on a special assignment that was an emergency." Never mind that he was retired from cloak-and-dagger stuff. They had had an emergency that only he could handle! Now he was back, and all would be well! Then, out of the blue, *in response to no question whatsoever*, he began to, point by point, give explanations for all the difficulties we had found with his story, including the fact that he was from a family that just simply did not show their age, even though he was now claiming to be well into his 60s. So, naturally, that explained how he could have been a spy against the Nazi's and still look young enough to go undercover with the Outlaws Motorcycle Gang! His wife, on the other hand, had been horribly injured because of some of "secret agent" work, and that was why he had had to divorce her – for her safety – and when they remarried, she was still undergoing plastic surgery that "went bad" and that was why she looked so old. But she was really much younger than she looked! But, they had dreamed of a regular family and had gotten help with in vitro conception, even though she was still older than she should have been to have a child, while being younger than she looked, and so on and on.

No problem. Everything was explained. The only thing was: no one had asked any questions about these things or voiced their doubts and questions; at least not to his face!

Yet, he had just stood there and, point by point, in the same order we had discussed them, answered every question we had established as important in our private conversation of the night before. My back was to him as I listened, working on collating pages, and I can tell you that my jaw dropped to the floor when he started on this subject. The hair on the back of my neck stood up and my skin felt like it was going to crawl off my flesh! I had the most bizarre sensation of time stopping and I almost froze in my rhythmic paper stacking motions; I had to force myself to keep working and to show no sign of surprise or curiosity.

Then, just as if he had done what he came to do, he gave everyone a cheerful good night and left! We all turned around and looked at each other with our mouths hanging open, our eyes as big as saucers, and said: What the *heck* just happened here?! The three of us could hardly speak. We could only sit and look at each other and feel like the laws of the universe had been violated somehow.

After a few minutes Pam breathed, "Jesus H. Christ! It was just like he had been listening to us talking last night!" And she was right. We called Patrick out of the press room and told him the story and he looked at all of us with disgust on his face and pronounced us paranoid. Well, maybe we were.

But maybe we had a reason to be. The next night, Frank was at his job, sitting at his desk, when he stood up to go to the water fountain. As he rose from his chair, he turned and looked at the window of the office building where he was employed, and there, standing and staring inside, was the mysterious stranger. As soon as he saw Frank stand up he began to move away as if he had just been "passing by," but it was too late. Frank knew he was being watched.

He called me when he was home and told me. The main thing we couldn't figure out was how did this guy know where Frank worked and what his schedule was? I called Pam to see if she had told the guy anything. It turned out that even Pam didn't know where Frank actually worked! How did this guy know? Why was he watching Frank? Who was he and what did he want? How did he know about our private conversations at *my* house?! What was this deal about the Outlaws?

Pam had become so frightened by the incidents that she had called the local law enforcement offices to inquire and complain. The day after she did this, the man showed up and made vague, threatening remarks about how "traitors" were dealt with "permanently" and that guys in law enforcement always shared information with each other. He didn't say anything specific, but was generally vague and indirect. Nevertheless, Pam nearly had a heart attack!

So, it seemed that some questions were in order. The next session was attended by a number of guests, including a friend that Lilly had brought. The Cassiopaeans were uncharacteristically sharp with S** and I was aware of all kinds of crosscurrents of energy flowing around the room. For some time, S** had been in charge of note-taking, and it was a constant struggle for me to work with her notes because she was careless and easily distracted. It seemed that the Cassiopaeans weren't too happy with this state of affairs either, or they were trying to convey something to me through their remarks to her:

February 3, 1996

Q: (L) We have several questions tonight. Do you have any particular messages for anyone here first?

A: The need to deliver messages flows naturally, there is no way to "choreograph" it by requesting a specific "time" for this procedure. And, please tell S** to relay specifically when we place words in quotes!!!!! It is annoying to not get messages properly transmitted when it is important for each entity receiving to absorb every detail of the given messages as it is intended. We have up until now not said anything about this, in the hopes that she would learn this by herself, but alas, she has not. Therefore, we regret the necessary reprimand. Sorry S**, but now please be aware that you have been told, and do not make this error ever again!

Q: (L) Goodness! All I did was ask if there was a message for anyone!

A: But it is important for you to continue at the same steady pace.

Q: (L) Can I continue with the questions now?

A: Obviously, it is always possible to do all that you desire to attempt.

The following week I declined all requests for guest attendance. I wanted to deal with this issue of corruption of the channel, as I perceived it:

February 8, 1996

Q: (L) Last Saturday night we had a very large group of people here and I experienced very unpleasant sensations. I would like to know the source of these? Was the channel corrupted?

A: Not corrupted, diluted. Static EM discharge from two entity sectors.

Q: (L) Was this due to the presence of any one or more persons in the room?

A: One person but two entities.

Q: (L) Well you said, at the time, that Lilly had an attachment and needed spirit release, is this the same person?

A: You learn by answering, using your own learnings, not from ceaseless confirmations by us.

Q: (L) Well, I am obviously not learning too well, even if you have been telling me about my "amazing abilities" which don't seem to be so amazing lately!

A: All who have amazing abilities must too guard against corruptive forces from within and without having to do with prejudice, assumption, and the anticipatory desires involving patterning presumption. i.e. keep an open mind, always!!! [...]

A: First things first! Please, S**, try to be accurate! You were warned, S**! Please, please, please, please, when you call or cry out for help and or guidance, know that we will always, always, always answer. It is up to you to be aware and then trust and follow. If your deep seated stubbornness prevents this, it will result in nothing short of your total undoing! This is because we never give such warnings, except when Vitally necessary! This applies to all others present equally as well!!

Well, I was still trying to fit that square peg in the round hole! The Cs gave me the clue, and it was coded right into the remarks: "It is up to you to be aware and then trust and follow. If your deep-seated stubbornness prevents this, it will result in nothing short of your total undoing! This is because we never give such warnings, except when Vitally necessary! *This applies to all others present equally as well!!*"

Note that S**'s last name was "Vitale."

Now, the reader has to understand the problem here. Sure, the Cs were telling us all kinds of things about agents and theological struggles between forces and that those forces act through human beings, and that people can be activated as agents and that everybody was controlled to one extent or another by a vast, bizarre system that was basically run by a sort of Evil-Magician complex; but having them tell us this, and apply it in our lives so that we made life decisions based on it was another thing altogether.

However, the situation was becoming unbearable at the time we made the trip to Gulf Breeze. I decided to closely observe S** during this time we were going to be together day and night and see if I could discover what, exactly, the problem was. I certainly did not want to jump to conclusions and exclude her if it was just a matter of personality. I have always believed that people can get along even if they have very different personalities, if they have some things in common, or at least a common goal. The question was: what was S**'s goal? What were her intentions? Why did she so eagerly seek to join our group? It had been gratifying, of course, to think that she was so excited over the

material as she claimed to be; that she was truly being helped by participation; and that she was the most faithful attendee! But, was there a
motive behind this that was *not* so benevolent?

Just prior to this trip, Frank asked me one day didn't I think it was
strange that S** had been involved with the Outlaws Motorcycle gang,
and Pam's agent had also been involved with the Outlaws?

I had never given the matter much thought. S** was adopted and really knew nothing about her biological family, but that was not the
issue. At a young age, she had rebelled, as is generally considered normal, but her mode of rebellion was a little extreme: She became
involved with a member of a notorious motorcycle gang!

Of course, by the time we knew her, all that was in the past. She had
long been disassociated with them, had gone to school to become a
massage therapist and had become actively involved in the local metaphysical community. She had experienced an "awakening" and
"conversion," and her declared form of service was to be a part of our
group.

But still, as Frank pointed out, she could talk about mayhem and
even murder in the most disconnected way imaginable. It was as
though she had no emotion about it at all! This was *very* disturbing.
Frank pointed out how on the several occasions when he had asked her
questions about her experiences, rather than seeing them as dreadful,
she talked and laughed about some of them, and she never seemed
reluctant to talk about it at all! Frank drove home the point that this
simply did *not* mesh with her reformed persona. How could someone
decry the extermination of roaches, and pass off the murder of human
beings as though it were nothing?

I had no answer, but Frank did. He was convinced that this was the
root of any problems with the group. It was S** who was to blame for
attitudes, atmosphere, strange connections that are too numerous to
describe. But, most of all, it was now clear that this was the reason the
Cassiopaeans would not be as forthcoming in her presence as they had
formerly been. It also explained the reason they had changed the subject when I was talking about the Coral Castle and, instead, brought up
the fact that S**'s background was unusual ... all were clues for me to
pick up on, designed to not violate my free will.

And exactly like the guy in Pam's shop, no sooner had we discussed
it, than something manifested to explain it or counteract what we were
thinking and talking about. During the trip up to Gulf Breeze, all of a
sudden, S** was a literal bundle of emotions. She more than made up
for all the emotions she had never displayed before all in a three day
period. It was as though she had been able to hear our thoughts and
was now counteracting them. The thing that never, ever occurred to

me at the time was the fact that Frank was the only one who was physically present at each conversation, following which the Matrix did its little two-step shift.

Tom French and Cherie Diez met us in Gulf Breeze for the conference. When we arrived after a trip that was probably more exhausting than driving up in the van would have been, we settled in our rooms and went looking for Tom and Cherie. There was a bulletin board in the hotel lobby where Tom had left a message for a rendezvous, and we made our way to the vendors to unload a stack of magazines to our friend who promised to distribute them.

Having done that, we attended a few lectures, met Tom and Cherie for lunch, attended a couple more lectures with Tom and Cherie, and at the end of the day, everyone went out on the beach for a UFO watch.

I have read that people who have visited all the most famous beaches in the world say that the beaches along the Florida panhandle are the finest in the world. I have to agree. They are absolutely gorgeous.

But, no UFOs showed up, and we finally retired for the evening, Frank to his private room, and S** and myself to our shared double room. I was soon asleep. And then, the dream.

I dreamed that there was someone far away, in a room full of people who were planning to do something to harm him, only he didn't know it. I tried to get his attention and signaled that he should meet me in the next room. He followed me in there and I told him that I was afraid for his safety. He told me not to worry, that he would be all right, and that I should go back home and wait for him because as soon as he could make the arrangements and extricate himself from this danger, he would come to me. And then he kissed me. I couldn't see his face clearly, but I most definitely felt that kiss.

The only thing I can say about it is that it was like being Sleeping Beauty and being kissed by the Prince, because *I woke up*. Not just figuratively, but literally, too. I woke up and sat bolt upright in bed with the sensation of having been kissed still on my lips. I stared around the unfamiliar hotel room in bewilderment and heard S** snoring lightly. I reached up to touch my lips with my fingers as if by doing so I could detect some trace of who had kissed me. But there was nothing, no clue. Just an incredible feeling that something amazing had just happened. I laid back down and went back to sleep. I dreamed again. This time, I was with the man who had kissed me, though again, I couldn't see his face. In the dream, my then husband came to me to ask me to come back to him, and this other man put his arms around me protectively and said, "She belongs to me. She always belonged to me. You were supposed to protect her until I came, and all you did was hurt her. Now go!"

At breakfast I shared the dream with S** and Frank, and later told it to Tom and Cherie. I still had the sensation on my lips of having been kissed. Now, as so many years have passed and I understand more – even understanding what "We are You in the Future" really means – I realize that this dream, this kiss was the appearance of the Cs at the UFO conference!

The flight back was a real doozie. We went through a major thunderstorm that there was no way to fly under, over or around. We just had to brace ourselves and the plane bucked like a bronco. I had to laugh because this was only the third time I had ever been on a plane in my life, and Frank had spent hours before the trip recounting all his memorable flights and how much he loved to fly. And now, he was popping motion sickness pills, looking as green as a tree frog, and I was having the time of my life.

Curiously, S**, who had been so terrified of getting on a plane on the trip up to Gulf Breeze, just slept through the whole thing. And lest you think I am exaggerating, at the end of the flight, even the Captain was green as he stood there shaking everybody's hand on their way out. They were all thanking him for still being alive!

After we were back from the trip, V** came over and we decided to ask about this situation since she was there to take notes.

March 23, 1996

Q: (L) The first inquiry I have is our situation relating to SV, and the different clues that we have received, and the different observations that I have made myself, and the discussions or the networking interactions that we have had on the subject. Can you tell us anything in a general way, or do we really have to ask specific questions about the subject?

A: SV is storehouse of vital information, clue for you was in name, but you failed to notice!

Q: (L) OK, but SV ...

A: This is why the frustration is for you; nothing of value comes without a price!!

Q: (L) Number one, SV has lied to us. Number two, it seems that she began to demonstrate emotional affect after we had discussed the fact that there was a serious lack of emotional affect after you had told us that these robot people are people who spend a lot of time alone and have ...

A: The price, my dear, continues ...

Q: (V) By continuing the relationship?

A: The Nordic Covenant was a duality.

Q: (L) SV comes from that area where that Nordic covenant, what is it, Minnesota, she's from Minnesota? Oh, I never made that connection! Holy Frijoles! "Nordic Covenant was a duality" ... so, when you made

267

mention of the Nordic Covenant, and the banking scandal, was that a double-layered statement to us?

A: Maybe, but you are missing the point! All persons of Nordic heritage hold secret power centers, can be of darkness, or of light ... SV is of Teutonic bloodline leading directly to such super power source such as Thule Society and others, and she is aware of her powers and mission. It is of positive orientation. However, you are being tested by 4th through 6th-density forces to determine if you have the strength and wisdom for continuance!

Q: (L) The whole thing just doesn't make sense ... I mean, with that nasty red aura she has ...

A: Red aura needs much further study on your part. Your sources for such information could be deceiving you.

Q: (L) Well then ...

A: And we are the Cassiopaeans, but it is of your will to live as you desire.

Q: (L) Well ... Then why was she told by you guys, that if she didn't do certain things that it would lead to her total undoing?

A: Go back and study that message again, with assistance of tape, and with mind open to all angles. Check intent, however, malice is in absence. Notice the difference. The duality of covenant!!!

Q: (L) Well, Frank is of Nordic extraction. Is he a member of this covenant, also?

A: Maybe.

Q: (F) If so, it's news to me. [laughs] (L) Do you say she is aware of her mission?

A: Some are.

Q: (L) Is her mother something in the way to block her from performing her mission?

A: Mother is inconsequential.

Q: (V) Her mother, her adopted mother ... inconsequential. OK, so does ...

A: Curious how background is murky, yes!

Q: (L) Yes, that is curious. (V) Something tells me that this can go further ... (L) Well, yes, but they were also talking about her birth, and her adoption, and all that kind of thing in another session. Stuff that's so unclear, she doesn't know anything about it, and claims she doesn't. So strange ... Is SV a "walk-in?"

A: Not correct terminology.

Q: (L) Well, then what is the correct terminology? What is SV?

A: Birthright.

Q: (L) Now, what does that mean?

A: Discover.

Q: (L) Are you saying that when we make mention of the Nordic Covenant and the Thule Society, that there's some possibility that SV has been programmed, or has layers of programs, and that some part of her program knows what she's doing, and maybe other parts don't?

A: Yes, but this is not a negative thing.

Q: (L) OK, now let me go a little bit deeper. Could SV be what you described as a robot person, but programmed for a positive purpose?

A: No, robot "people" do not have bloodlines.

Q: (L) So, this is something that's programmed genetically in a bloodline?

A: Not exactly, those that have the bloodline have the corresponding soul alignment.

Q: (L) We are talking about a genetic bloodline that activates certain abilities and genes that interface with the corresponding soul that has prepared for this manifestation of the bloodline?

A: Yes.

Q: (L) Is there any significance to the fact that SV spent all of those years living with the Outlaws Motorcycle gang and this covenant?

A: Yes, and that is what has led and is leading to the destruction of the "Outlaws," a group associated directly with 4th-density STS.

Q: (V) Her presence there caused them to break up? This was a good thing. Is this what is meant here? That her presence was uplifting to them? (L) Well, it's not uplifting them, it's breaking them; they are all going to jail!

A: Yes and because of circumstances planted by "Agent SV." This is why the perceived lack of emotion connected with that whole situation. Vitale is the bravest human you have ever known! All evidence to the contrary is veil; part of the testing process.

Q: (L) If we're being tested, why are you telling us? (V) So that you do not fail?

A: Yes.

Q: (L) Is SV aware that this is going on?

A: Vital that you do not fail.

Q: (V) Is SV aware that …

A: Yes.

Q: (V) Is there a pivotal word that might break this open to a clearer understanding?

A: Discover.

Q: (L) Now, when we were flying back home, and we were flying through that storm, was that storm, which began before we left, and we flew through it on the way back, was that a byproduct or bleed through of a battle between the forces?

A: Yes.

Q: (L) Was it trying to harm us in any way, because we had to fly through it, and couldn't fly over it? I mean, even the pilot was worried, and he had been flying for years!

A: Yes.

Q: (L) What brought it to an end?

A: Vitale. Notice how "unaffected" she was?!?

Q: (L) I told you that the whole thing about being scared was a fake! (F) Yes, she was scared on the way up, when there was nothing to be scared of, and on the way back, when we were bouncing around like a pinball in a pinball machine, she's sleeping, I'm getting sick, and Laura's going "Ride 'em, cowboy!!" [all laugh] (L) OK, so how are we supposed to react to this situation?

A: Up to you.

Q: (L) OK, we knew that was coming. It wouldn't have been a good night without it! (V) Some things never change, huh? (L) Well Frank seems to think there's a whole lot more there in terms of background than she was letting on. Is that correct?

A: Maybe.

Q: (L) Well, OK, I'm going to trust you guys, and I'm going to go with the flow, and I'm going to assume that you are right, and I'm going to assume that this is for the best and for the good, and I'm going to stop my knee jerk reactions, and stop worrying about such things.

A: Suggest you look before you leap. All can be wrong in their quick judgments, whether the result be acceptance or rejection. All is not as it seems … Remember, those that come into your group, or your circle of influence can be different than you think.

Q: (L) You said we were being tested. Tested for what?

A: Continuance.

Q: (L) Continuance of what?

A: All.

Q: (L) Continuance of all. OK, and we are being tested through SV?

A: Currently.

Q: (L) Are you saying that what we have been considering attacks were just tests?

A: The ones associated with Vitale. And no, all with that name are not of this orientation, but this clue was installed for you.

Q: (L) Are you saying that SV is our fourth-density Nordic?

A: ?

Q: (V) Maybe just by the purpose of her being, she's vital for you!

After the end of the session, I read over the notes quickly, and noted that, in response to my acquiescence to the idea that S** was a positive being exactly as the Cs were saying, the Cs had said: "Suggest you look before you leap. All can be wrong in their quick judgments, whether the result be acceptance or rejection. All is not as it seems … Remember, those that come into your group, or your circle of influence can be different than you think."

I realized suddenly that their high praise of S** had been so exaggerated that I was supposed to catch the fact that the truth was the exact opposite of what the Cs were saying. I knew that I was so uncomfortable with the situation that I simply wanted to find a way to bring our association to an end amicably and without any ugly confrontations. With those thoughts firmly in mind, I asked for the Cs to come back and comment.

> Q: Hello. Are you there? I am not comfortable with this information about SV. It seems to be contradictory to everything I can observe and feel.
> A: Hiklu Cassiopaea. Worry not further! Discomfort is not necessarily danger, and is indicative of growth and learning. So, proceed and celebrate!!

Apparently, I had passed the test. But there were so many more yet to come!

I was beginning to get the idea that there was a lot being said to me that required study and contemplation. Obviously, getting the truth through the Matrix was not so easy. I was beginning to feel like a spy in enemy territory needing to decode messages that were double and triply encoded.

And it was Vital to succeed.

CHAPTER 46
THE THEOLOGICAL REALITY

This section deals with my growing awareness of the Matrix that conceals the theological reality and how difficult it is to break free of the illusion that our reality is as it presents itself to be. Though I didn't realize it as I went through it, all of the events of this period were simply the results of forces that activate to terrify the awakening individual, to convince them to go back to sleep, or if that is not possible, to wear them out, destroy their health, or otherwise make it impossible to awaken.

The important thing for the reader to remember as they go through this recapitulation of events, relations, and my thoughts regarding same, is that there was no Cassiopaea site for me to read, there was no *Wave Series* for me to read, and there was no real concept of the Matrix, as such, available to me by which I could evaluate my experiences. I was in uncharted territory, slashing through the jungle, and hardly able to fully grasp the nature of the beast, much less articulate it.

It is so easy, looking back, to say, "Oh, well, you should have seen that Frank was this or that," or that "you should have known it was going to turn out that way," or "why did you continue in the relationship so long?" and so on.

If we keep in mind the programs of family, religion and society, which are more or less the same for everyone with only slight variations, we realize that it is not so easy to go against the programs of "give the benefit of the doubt," "turn the other cheek," "forgive and forget," "kiss and make-up," "make it nice," "if you can't say something nice, don't say anything at all," and so forth. We are taught by our culture, via various psychological theories, to "compromise and work it out," or to deal with our own issues so that what other people do won't have any power over us. We are taught to heal our wounded inner child, or blame everything on our parents. We can learn to reframe our experiences and achieve rapport with anyone in three days of neuro-linguistic programming, or, as a last resort, we can solve the problem with a little Prozac or something similar.

The fact is that, even though the Cs were telling me about these theological dynamics, that didn't necessarily mean that I was buying it. Just because the Cs said it, didn't mean I believed it. And that still applies. Sure, there are many things the Cs have said that we have experimented with – "try before you buy" – and have observed results that indicate that they are presenting a view of our reality that is objectively testable. There are many other things that we have researched based on the clues the Cs have given us and have discovered again and again, "Damned if they aren't right!" And very often, these have been things about which we were most skeptical.

But that doesn't mean that everything is true, for sure, nor that we will buy anything that we haven't checked out thoroughly.

Even though I was being given a higher-density view of human relations and dynamics as the medium through which higher-density forces engage and do battle – the Matrix Control System – I was still in it, and still controlled by it to a great extent. In this sense, the Cs were very wise in *not* telling me anything directly as to what I ought or ought not to do in terms of my choices and actions. They were, indeed, giving me a new perspective about higher-density affairs, giving clues about our own level of reality so that I could research these matters and determine the interaction between the two, but if they had just told me the answers or told me what to do, they would have violated my "Free Will Learning Directive." That is to say, it seems that all of existence is for the purpose of gaining knowledge. Hopefully, the reader has read P. D. Ouspensky's *Tertium Organum*, and is familiar with his writings on this subject. The point is that if we are here in this reality to learn, it doesn't do us any good for somebody else to do our homework for us. We can't learn to ride a bicycle by watching somebody else do it, or by reading a book about it. Indeed, we will have clues, and some idea of what we ought to do, but we cannot master it unless we get up and try it. And very often, we may think it looks easier than it is, and we discover on our first try that falling down and scraping our knees is what teaches us how not to fall down!

So it was that, in the places where discussions of the matters of the theological reality were taking place as recorded in the transcripts, that didn't mean that I was ready to get on the bicycle just yet. Even if S** or PZ or any other given person was identified as being an agent or in a close relation with purported STS forces, didn't mean I was going to jump up in their faces and shout, "Lizzie Lover!" or "Gray Hugger!" and ditch them as a friend or associate!

However, after the "kiss", I woke up.

My perceptions had certainly changed, but I was not really able to say how or why. All kinds of thoughts and realizations about reality were shaping themselves in my mind, but as usual, I was keeping it to myself to observe and ponder it before I attempted to explain it to anyone. The first concrete manifestation of this awakening was right after we returned from the conference and I drove to the high school to pick up my daughter as I did every day. I was sitting there in the parking lot watching all the kids pouring out of the different doors of the building onto the school yard. There were kids who were racing to their cars or to their buses, and there were many others who were milling about, congregating in their little groups and cliques. I couldn't hear anything anyone was saying since I was observing from a distance, but I could most definitely see certain dynamics – something like a pecking order – playing out before my eyes.

Each group consisted of about seven or eight people – maybe as many as ten. In each group there was a dominant person who was the focal point of the gathering. Watching the eye contact, the touching, the fawning behavior of the "low man" in the group, was a fascinating study. And as I watched, I noticed something else: the dominant person actually seemed to swell and grow while the submissive persons gathered around him literally seemed to shrink. Of course, this was a trick of posture and the way they were all holding their bodies, but it was definitely clear that there was a form of feeding taking place. And when the submissive persons ran out of "juice," they were dismissed to the outer fringes of the circle and a new submissive moved in to take their place. The eye contact and touching went through the same series of gestures, and the dominant person stood taller and taller, and his or her eyes opened wider and glowed brighter, while the submissives were diminished one by one, shoulders slumped, and they often crept away.

I found myself actually holding my breath as I watched this amazing display. Of course I thought of Jane Goodall and her years of observation of chimpanzees, and I knew I wasn't thinking anything terribly original here. The big difference was that I was seeing it not just in terms of psychological dynamics, but an actual energy transfer – the theological reality. It was this theological reality that had suddenly been opened to my perception as though I had withdrawn into space and was viewing it from a distance.

As human beings, it seems that an essential part of our nature is to feel that there is more to life than the immediately apparent material world. This is the aspect of our make-up that is played upon by religions and philosophies. The different explanations for what is "more" than the material world are what divides us into groups, and separates us one from another. Most of these religions and philosophies tell us how special we are and promise great things if we will believe this or that teaching, follow this or that teacher, or perform a certain set of "salvific" activities. What is most apparent when we examine such teachings is the fact that we don't like to think that our lives are a game of chance played by the gods. Yet, at this moment, after all of the study and experiences of my life, most especially in light of the explanations offered by the Cs on the many and almost endless occasions when the standard teachings collapsed in the face of the hard evidence, I realized with startling clarity that heartless randomness of the world is at odds with the religious views of a loving, caring God. It was as though suddenly, my perspective was no longer that of a human being, immersed in the reality, unable to see the forest for the trees.

All around us in the natural world there are wonders and horrors. On almost every corner of the planet, from the highest mountains to the lowest valleys, from the hottest to the coldest climates, above the oceans and within them, there are populations of interdependent plants and animals. Most of the time this term interdependence really means that they "eat" one another.

I thought about the garden behind my house. There are birds and lizards, insects and plants of all sorts. The lizards eat many insects and they are, in turn, eaten by the birds or the cat, who also eats the birds if she gets a chance. There are roses – beautiful but deadly – which grow in soil composed partly of plant detritus – dead plant matter – converted by earthworms into usable nutrients. There are also grubs and mole crickets that seem to do nothing but destroy what I work so hard to produce and maintain. In the evenings, the bats and mosquitoes both come out in force, the former preying on the latter (thankfully), and the night blooming jasmine opens to feed a particular species of night moth that delights in its nectar.

There is spring, when I spend eight hours a day getting the garden in shape; there is summer, when I relax and watch my efforts grow and blossom; there is fall when I pull up the dead annuals and prune the overgrowth; and there is winter when everything rests and builds strength to burst forth the following spring, to initiate a new cycle; cycles within cycles; birth, growth, maturity, reproduction, decline and death; to everything there is a season.

Now, imagine that you are observing the earth with a high-powered telescope from a point out in space. This telescope gives you detailed close-ups of any point on the planet, but you cannot hear anything. You can only *see*. Forget everything you think you know about the principles of biological life or psychology. Forget that you think you know anything about what living things are or how they are supposed to behave. Now, what do you see?

The first thing you notice is that the surface of the planet is teeming with activity. This includes areas under the soil and deep within the ocean. The activity on the surface of the planet consists of an immense number of different shapes and sizes of living things going about in circles *eating* each other!

Further, you notice that there is a whole class of these living things that are, essentially, immobile; incapable of escaping being eaten. In fact, they don't seem to object being eaten at all. Maybe if they *could* run away, they would, but they can't, so it may only seem that they don't object. But, the fact of the matter is that these immobile beings (call them plants) use this fact of being eaten to their advantage. By being eaten, they are often able to propagate themselves in far distant places that they would otherwise be unable to populate on their own.

However, all the other living things clearly resent being eaten. They very often make strenuous efforts to *not* be eaten.

I began to see a certain pattern emerging: the variations of biological systems have to do with whether or not, under specific and ever-changing conditions, one variety of creatures can survive the competition in the terrifying planetary game of life and death. It was clear that danger is omnipresent and only the most vigorous and adaptable survive.

I also saw that there was a sort of balance. Many of the creatures that are most often considered prey are equipped with elaborate sensing organs that help them to stay out of harm's way. Many of the creatures that are the predators have horrifyingly efficient organs of destruction such as teeth and claws. If predators became too numerous, they quickly devoured all but the cleverest of prey, and then turned on each other. In this way, both populations were culled. What I also was seeing was that populations that existed in herds, where there was sharing and protection of weaker members by stronger ones, had a far better chance of survival in the presence of voracious predation.

I realized with absolute horror that this was exactly the case with human beings, though it occurred at a different level – humans were an interface between the strictly material and ethereal realms, and it was through them that the energies of prey and predator manifested at the theological level. From the strictly human perspective, such a realization was monstrous. The psychological and spiritual environment in which we live is the infrastructure of the theological reality which is accurately represented in the wild world in which animals live out similar dramas. "As above, so below," the ancient teachings have repeated for millennia, and I realized that this was part of what they intended to convey. When they tell us that the Great Secret can be learned from Nature, they weren't kidding!

On the one hand, I was seeing a terrible vista that shattered my illusions of "God in his heaven, and all is right with the world." On the other hand, I could see that it wasn't just mindless cruelty; that it was purposeful activity from another level of being.

My daughter arrived and I told her what I was observing – that the cliques were similar to Jane Goodall's chimpanzees – and she, of course, dryly remarked, "Gee! How long did it take you to figure *that* out?!" The only thing was, she was thinking about it only in psychological terms and not in terms of literal life-force energy transfer.

Because of the many things the Cs had said, my mind immediately made associations. I also recalled a passage from James Redfield's book *The Celestine Prophecy.*

> My field is conflict, looking at why humans treat each other so violently. We've always known that this violence comes from the urge humans feel to control and dominate one another, but only recently have we studied this phenomenon from the inside, from the point of view of the individual's consciousness. We have asked what happens inside a human being that makes him want to control someone else. We have found that when an individual walks up to another person and engages in a conversation, which happens billions of times each day in the world, one of two things can happen. That individual can come away feeling strong or feeling weak, depending on what occurs in the interaction.
>
> For this reason, we humans always seem to take a manipulative posture. No matter what the particulars of the situation, or the subject matter, we prepare ourselves to say whatever we must in order to prevail in the conversation. Each of us seeks to find some way to control and thus to remain on top in the encounter. If we are successful, if our viewpoint prevails, then rather than feel weak, we receive a psychological boost. In other words we humans seek to outwit and control each other not just because of some tangible goal in the outside world that we're trying to achieve, but because of a lift we get psychologically. (Redfield 1993, 71–72)

He then describes an unpleasant encounter between a man and woman and their daughter where the parents are pointed out as dominating the girl, and she lashes out violently in order to gain some control for herself. It is then suggested that when she grows up, she will think that she has to seize control and dominate others with the same intensity. "This same trauma no doubt happened to her parents before her. They have to dominate now because of the way their parents dominated them. That's the means through which psychological violence is passed down from one generation to another."

The only difference in that view and what I was seeing was that I was realizing that it was deeper than that – at the apex of the pyramid of predators, somebody was getting all the energy being passed along through something akin to etheric psychological filaments. It suddenly made sense that the Control System had been set up millennia ago, social and religious programs instituted, to produce this psychological trauma that extended over thousands of generations, in order for somebody, or some thing, to benefit; there was an "ultimate dominator" of the global clique. And guess what? Human beings were *not* at the top of the food chain!

As simple as this insight may seem to the reader, having access to all of the other information that has become available about these matters over the past few years, it was a stunning revelation to me.

I then began to think about S** and the "Vital information" that could be conveyed to me. The first thing I realized was that human beings at a certain point in their development reach a crossroad where they can choose which dynamic they will develop in spiritual terms: predator or prey, and it had nothing to do with material considerations. In fact, I wasn't even sure if it was a choice and not just simply the inherent nature of an individual.

I could see that S** was, indeed, as the Cs had described her: a simple, giving soul. But in her dynamic interaction with her mother she was literally acting out the role of prey to her mother's role of predator. As her mother grew older and less able to hunt on her own, she manipulated S** to engage in interactions whereby she became a sort of lure to induce other prey into her mother's range of operation so that the feeding could continue. In a sense, it was very much like a weakened member of a herd that keeps wandering away into the realm of the predator, and when others would go after her to save her, they become prey as well; they leave the protection of the herd, or the network. In this sense, some individuals become a sort of predator by proxy – a lure to destruction; a decoy. On the other hand, I wasn't too sure if that was exactly accurate either. Perhaps there were predators who stalked their prey in long, slow, silent exercises in patience and concealment?

I could instantly see that nearly all of humanity was in a terrible predicament by being unaware of this infrastructure of theological prey and predation. In the animal kingdom, who was who and what was what in terms of predators and prey was pretty easy to see because they look different and their behaviors are out in plain view. But in the human dynamic, it is masked from us. And it seemed to be masked for a reason: the masking is utilized to separate the herd, to divide and conquer.

Of course, that such a condition could be possible seemed to have no explanation in positivist terms until I thought about the culling factor, and the idea that spiritual vigor might be the objective. Using the animal kingdom as a template, it seemed obvious that those creatures that most correctly assessed and responded to their environment had the best chance of survival and reproduction. Those members of herds that remained in the symbiotic networked environment had strength and safety and numbers on their side. Those that strayed from the herd, those that exposed themselves to danger, were eaten. It was that simple.

It was at this moment that I saw myself as a cog in a vast global mechanism – a feeding machine – and I was nothing more than food. It literally made me sick to see it. What was more: I needed to understand where all this energy was really going. Who was getting it? Who was at the top of the food chain?

A day or so later, my husband came in and initiated another of the endless series of diatribes he habitually generated which always started with him picking at one of the children. I would defend the child, trying to reasonably explain to him that each of them was different, that they had a right to their own opinions, likes and dislikes, and that they were not little clones of him who existed just to reflect what he believed, or to do what he wanted. The other children would join in and try to support my reasonable remarks with examples of their own. They all loved their father and all of us knew that he had a "problem" because of his religious fundamentalism. He was bigoted and judgmental, harsh and even cruel in his judgments, and if the children did not immediately agree with him, they became outcast also, damned and doomed to perdition unless they quickly changed their ways and views – to his ways and views, of course.

As usually happened, the discussion ended up with him becoming more and more antagonistic and harsh and saying many mean things to all of us, couched in Christian theology that was for our own good, of course. As the dynamic progressed, and I tried harder and harder to soothe and make nice, trying to mediate and sustain his parental authority, even though I knew he was completely wrong, and protect the children from this psychological destruction, I saw with horror that what was really happening was that he was feeding on all of us!

I instantly stopped trying to reason with him at all, told him that he was entitled to his beliefs, and I was entitled to mine, the children were entitled to theirs, and I wasn't going to discuss it at all with him anymore. He left in a huff with some parting shots directed at all of us that I can't even remember.

The children were upset, I was upset, and I sat there pondering what I had just seen. As I did, one of my daughters came in to hug me and tell me that she was sorry that I had to go through such things over and over again. Then she said something that nearly knocked me over: "I don't know how you have lived with it for so long; he's just not *like us*. He's like a cat in a house full of dogs."

Out of the mouths of babes.

Actually, he was like a cat in an aviary of birds, but she made her point. He wasn't "like us." At that moment, I realized that I had to *do* something. The Universe had been giving me clues for years, and I had been ignoring them, stubbornly clinging to my self-sacrificing, make-everything-nice, shove-it-under-the-rug, let's-work-it-out view of things. I had read all the pop-psychology books; I had tried all the guaranteed methods of self-help, taking the brunt of the burden of making things work on myself; I had expended untold amounts of energy in trying to compromise, to work it out, to support and sustain this man and to simultaneously protect the children and myself from his clear predation. I had done all of this for years in the firm belief that all could be made right, all could be healed, all could be worked out with sufficient devotion and giving.

But now, suddenly, I was seeing it all in a completely different way. He was a predator, and we were prey. We, the children and myself, were his sources of energy. Where his energy was being drained to, I didn't know, but I had a pretty good idea.

What is important for the reader to understand is that I didn't blame him for being "bad" or for being "wrong," or for anything at all like that. I simply realized that he was not like us in terms of the theological reality, and therefore, something had to be done. It was one thing for me to be aware and willing to sacrifice myself to this energy feeding dynamic. It was something else altogether for me to pass it to my children by example and to oblige them to live in it. A mother's primary role is as advocate and protectress of her children. And in this case, I saw that the one my children needed to be protected from was their own father.

The toughest part is the fact that I also knew that I had to do something *for* my husband as well. Cats that feed on pigeons have as much right to be and exist as the pigeons do. They are not bad because they are cats and because they eat pigeons if given the chance. What was even more difficult was the knowledge that even if I explained to him what I was perceiving, he wouldn't get it; he wouldn't believe it; he wouldn't agree. He would insist to his dying day that his mode of being – his "catness" – was right.

In the end, I knew that I had to bear the burden of doing what was right *for* him – strange as it may seem – because he was neither able nor willing to see it or understand it. I remember thinking that the only way I was going to be able to get through it was to take all the blame, to completely release him from *any* responsibility because, on the many occasions I tried to get him to be responsible for anything he said or did that hurt me or the children, it was a dead end.

For example: if he was being a steamroller toward the children, I would spend hours explaining child psychology to him, and how damaging it was to a child to not be accepted and allowed to have their own likes and dislikes – that he would tell them "that's stupid" or "you'll go to hell for that" and so on was abuse. I tried to engage him in a cooperative work with raising the children. He would seem to listen and I would think I was getting somewhere, and then a glassy look would come into his eyes and he would say, "Well, if nothing I do is right, I'll just not do anything. *You* raise the kids and I'll stay out of it."

Then, I would try to explain the importance of *both* parents being involved and united for the sake of the children and the glassy look would come and he would twist that around and tell me that since he wasn't wanted, his way wasn't accepted, *he* wasn't respected … well, to heck with all of us. And that was *not* what I was saying! I was saying that, as parents, we had to put many of our own things aside for the sake of the children.

He simply could not think beyond him*self*.

So, when the time came, and it came within a day or so, I knew this and I knew that no amount of explaining would be effective in any terms other than just repeating, "I made a mistake when I married you and now I am correcting it," and words to that effect. That put all the blame on me. My objective was not to put him down, to lay blame, to do anything but get myself and the children out of this situation.

And the war began in earnest. He was fighting to retain his position, to reclaim his feeding territory. And I was equally determined that he was not going to feed on any of us any longer.

When he said, "I knew you would do this. All women are alike. Blah blah," I just agreed even though I knew that his view was completely twisted. It was not necessary for me to be "right" because I knew that when I was right, it didn't matter because he was going to see it the way he saw it anyway.

I just kept remembering a funny thing that I had read about how to get proper service from a store clerk who keeps trying to sell you something you don't want: just keep repeating what you *do* want, and when they say, "What about this over here?!" say, "No, I don't want that. I want this."

So, I knew what I wanted to accomplish, I knew I would be subjected to a "sales talk" of some kind, and I knew that I had to keep repeating over and over again what I wanted and insist that the focus stay there. Whenever he tried to engage me in a discussion, I said,

"That's fine. I know you see it that way, but I don't and this is what I want." Over and over.

When he started listing all the things that he had done, I just agreed that he had done them and that it was good that he did, but it didn't change the fact that I had made a mistake, and it needed to be corrected and I was going to do it.

Then came the name-calling and accusations ... and I agreed with everything. "Yes, you are right. I lied to you. I never loved you, blah blah." I just agreed that everything he said was right, but it didn't change the fact that I was going to do what I was going to do and that was that.

In his initial declaration of territorial rights, he made it clear that he wasn't giving an inch. If I didn't want to be around him, if I had decided that it was over, then I was the one who was going to have to leave. If I didn't want to sleep with him, I would have to sleep somewhere else because he wasn't giving up his right to sleep in the master bedroom.

I didn't argue with him. I moved into the baby's bedroom and slept with her. After a day or two of this, of sleeping somewhere other than on the special orthopedic mattress that had been bought after my accident, the children told their father that he was being very selfish to make Mom sleep on a bed that hurt her. Of course, he wanted to appear to be the injured party, so he immediately moved into the playroom and slept on the sofa in there, giving me the bedroom back.

After failing to change my mind with argument, insult and manipulations of the overt kind, he went into the pity-trip mode. He claimed that he had nowhere to go, that he would have to build a camper on his truck and live in the woods somewhere. He then asked for several days to make his preparations.

I just wanted him out of the house. I was hanging onto my resolve by a thread, and I knew I couldn't take much more of the pity me trip because that had always been my weak point. I knew that, for the sake of the children, I had to win this battle. I had already spent too many years teaching my children by example how to be prey and now I needed to teach them by example how *not* to be prey.

It was at this point that something completely bizarre happened. I went to the kitchen to get a drink of water in the middle of the night and had to pass by the door to the playroom. As I did, I heard him talking in there. I wondered who in the world was he was talking to. In the low, ambient light of the house, I could see that he was stretched out on the sofa, alone and apparently asleep. But he was talking. I stood there very quietly and listened. He seemed to be having a long conversation with someone in a dream and I could only hear his end of it. The thing that was so amazing was that in all the years of our marriage, he had never once talked in his sleep. Not once. And now he was saying things like, "Yes, I know I failed in the mission, but I won't fail again." "Please don't punish me! I won't fail again!" There were a long series of "yes" responses as though he were receiving instructions, and the subservient nature of his end of the dialogue gave me the absolute willies. An air of evil emanated from the room and I understood that the subject of discussion was me. Somehow, he had been assigned to do something in regard to me, and the present situation was unacceptable to the overseer of this "mission" he kept mentioning.

If my resolve had been growing weak, it was increased a hundred-fold by this little encounter. I made up my mind that I had to get him out of the house. His physical proximity was dangerous. He was slowly but surely wearing me down, he was playing on the emotions of the children and the situation had to end *now*.

I talked to my friend Sandra about it. She was a supervisor of the Child Support Enforcement Unit of the State Department of Health and Rehabilitative Services. She told me that I needed to apply for assistance and make it clear to him that he had to be out of the house or he would be subject to legal sanctions. I was already receiving a supplemental check from Social Security because I was unable to work due to my health problems, so this seemed the logical thing to do until the insurance case related to the accident was settled. I reasoned that, since our house was paid for, the children and I would be able to survive – though just barely – until he could get himself settled and the court could set a reasonable amount for him to pay as support for the children.

So, that's what I did. I made it a legal matter, and because Sandra was behind me and he knew that he couldn't play any games with the State legal system with Sandra watching, he packed up his things and moved back to his parents' house.

It was at this point that something akin to physical withdrawal began to manifest. Sandra explained to me that I had to keep repeating over and over in my mind why I was doing what I was doing. She told me to make a list of all the times when we had gone through the feeding episodes, and how when I had reached the end of my rope and declared that I couldn't take it anymore, we had gone through the same deal and all the promises that were made and not kept.

I realized that I had to just keep hitting myself over the head to stay awake.

Then there came the fear of not being loved, of being judged a "bad girl" or a "bad wife and mother." This was the program that had kept me in the situation for so many years. It had been inculcated into me (and millions of other women) as a little girl. It is the chief program of women in general: to cover the bad things up, to shove them all under the rug, to make things nice – to be a "good girl" by being a doormat.

I had to keep reminding myself that I was Bluebeard's wife. And Bluebeard had a secret room in the castle with the bodies of all his other wives – symbols of the fact that he was a predator, feeding on our energy because he had none of his own. And he had none of his own because he was inured in the Matrix, a source of energy in the food-chain pyramid of the theological reality of higher-level dark forces that feed on humanity. We can feel sorry for such people, as they may only become Bluebeard because of damage to them as infants or children. But they cannot be fixed, and their damage spreads like an infection to everyone with whom they are in contact.

What was ultimately important to me was the fact that I knew I had to become what I wanted for my daughters. Children do what they see, not what we tell them. And the greatest gift we can give anyone is to become what we would have others be: Free.

At this point, I brought up the matter with the Cassiopaeans:

March 29, 1996

Q: (L) In the past week I have been going through some fairly severe trauma because of certain ideas and realizations I have been forced to face ...

A: Stress, yes, trauma, no.

Q: (L) Well, it has felt traumatic to me. The first question I would like to ask is: in reading and analyzing the Bluebeard fairy tale as a map of consciousness, am I correct in my understanding, that I am basically living the life of Bluebeard's wife?

A: Close enough for now.

Q: (L) My application of this map of consciousness, so to speak, is not only in the area of my marriage, but also a number of other interactions. Is this correct as I understand it?

A: Maybe.

Q: (L) What part is the maybe?

A: Learning is a complex process, answers follow study. [...]

Q: (L) Well, it seems to me that I have a strong tendency to manifest my psychic and emotional state physically; not only in my own body, but also in manifestations and events around me.

A: Yes.

Q: (L) Back when we first moved into this house, we had a burglar break in during the night. I have always been troubled by the fact that a strange man broke into my house, the symbology of it. The other night, I was reading about dreams of people breaking into one's house being a warning that there is extreme danger from the deep subconscious. These dreams always have a strong physiological manifestation. Well, I had an "intruder dream," and it *was* like this. But then, I thought about the actual intruder being a psychically manifested warning in the flesh.

A: Yes.

Q: (L) Was the fact that it could manifest in a physical way any kind of indication of the seriousness of the threat?

A: Yes. [...]

Q: (L) Back to my question: the intruder dream the other night was *very* disturbing. In the dream, I tried to wake my husband to tell him that someone or something was in our house, I discovered that he was paralyzed. He was like my friend Keith ... can you help me with this image?

A: Learning is fun!

Q: (L) Well, it was not fun! My heart was about to pound out of my chest, and I ended up sitting in a chair half the night. There was a realization that I have been being drained by a lot of people for a long time ...

A: Yours to look and discover. Not ours to help you "cheat!"

Q: (L) No cheating, huh. I can't look at the answers in the back of the book. [...]

Q: (L) Well, you are not helping! I have been seeing things so completely differently lately. I even see that you have given all sorts of clues about this that just went over my head ...

A: Laura, please learn just to trust your expanding insights. They will bring you to ever increasing knowledge and ability. But, you want us to lead you by the hand. All this can do is ultimately lead this channel and conduit into an STS vehicle!

Q: (L) That is not what I am trying to do here! I am trying to expand on a learning experience to help other people.

A: You have the ability to do that all on your own!! Cannot you see this yet?

Here, again, the Cs are pointing me in the direction of realizing that the entire purpose of the communication was to prepare me for the task of utilizing what I was learning through this personal initiation process so that it would be of benefit to others. Of course, at this particular moment in time, I was not feeling terribly confident about anything. I was having trouble with my eyes – an inflammation had taken hold and I had to keep medication in them that made it difficult to see.

Q: (L) I am still in the process of making major changes in my life based on such insights ...

A: And, how do you feel when you make a decision to make one of these changes?

Q: (L) It hurts to make some decisions, even if I feel that it is the right thing to do. It can be painful and scary.

A: Relief?

Q: (L) Definitely relief!

A: And ...

Q: (L) I have some little hope that maybe something else will happen to help with the work if I make sure that my own life is clean. I am cutting off my financial support, and that is frightening. [...]

Q: (L) I am between a rock and a hard place.

A: Not really.

Q: (L) Easy for you to say.

A: Wait and see. When you get money, pay someone to transcribe.

Q: (L) I will do it myself as quickly as possible ... SV was supposed to help me with this ... but obviously she is fading from the picture here ...

A: Maybe, maybe not, you are not completely in control of all possible factors.

Q: (L) Well, however things work, I don't really care right now. As soon as I can see again, I will get back to transcribing. I have sent some samples out to a couple of places. I have had some *very* positive responses ...

A: Have fun!

Q: (L) What is that supposed to mean? I don't like the sound of that! The other day when you said "celebrate!" all I did was suffer!

A: Stop suffering!

Q: (L) I can't help it! I feel so sorry for [my soon to be ex-husband]! He is a master at being a victim! It tears me apart! Anything I need to know about my situation? I feel pretty desperate.

A: Has it been "desperate" before?

Q: (L) Yes.

A: Did you turn into dust?

Q: (L) No, but I thought I would!

A: What about your settlement?

Q: (L) God knows when that will happen! You won't tell me!

A: If we did, you'd become a "softie."

Q: (L) It seems that over the course of time, you have turned us more and more in the direction of learning on our own. Does this mean that it is winding down to come to a halt?

A: No.

Q: (L) Can you tell me what this means?

A: You needed more assistance earlier.

Q: (L) Well, am I correct in the MPD idea regarding SV?

A: Pursue with an open mind and cross check all analyses.

At this point, there is almost an entire month between sessions. The reason for this is the fact that my infections became so severe that I was bedridden for almost a month. My ears, eyes and lungs were infected and I had been ordered by the doctor to not read or look at a

286

computer screen for several weeks. I had to spend several periods a day with hot compresses on my eyes. In a funny sort of way it represented my human reaction to what I was literally seeing, hearing and experiencing. I was also depressed almost beyond endurance.

During the same period, one of my elder daughters was also so depressed that she could barely get out of the bed. Even though I was struggling with my own health issues, I was more concerned about her than anything and I took her to the doctor several times to have her checked for any kind of physical illness. Our family doctor had been part of our lives for about seven years at this point, and he was intimately familiar with all of the ups and downs of our situation, and he was concerned as well. He ran every test known to medical science and finally just said that if I was patient and supportive with this most sensitive of children, that she would pull through it. Being of the "old school," he didn't think that medication was the right option. He knew my daughter too well.

The next disaster was that my next-to-youngest daughter broke her ankle on the trampoline in the back yard. I had been gone from the house only long enough to pick up the eldest from school, and when we returned, there was another crisis to deal with.

I struggled on, and during this month something amazing occurred. In the past year I was given a copy of a lecture of Gurdjieff which describes exactly what transpired. Had I read it before the experience, I wouldn't have understood it at all. And I realize that anyone who has not been through it also will probably not fully understand it, which is why I am taking the time to explain the events and experiences so as to provide a platform for understanding some of the more esoteric teachings of different pathways. Ordinary Life itself, properly understood, can indeed be the means by which we are initiated, as Gurdjieff believed. He wrote about the "First Initiation" in the following way:

> You will see that in life you get back exactly what you put in. Your life is the mirror of what you are, it is your image. You are passive, blind, demanding. You take all, you accept all, without ever feeling indebted. Your attitude towards the world and towards life is the attitude of one who has the right to demand and take. Of one who doesn't need to pay or gain. You believe that all things are due to you, only because it's you! All your blindness is there. It doesn't catch your attention. It is however what, in you, separates a world from another.
>
> You have no measure to measure yourself up. You live only between 'I like it' and 'I don't like it'. Which means that you have appreciation only for yourself. You do not allow for anything above you – theoretically or logically maybe, but not in reality. This is why you are demanding and keep on thinking that everything should be cheap, and you can afford to pay for anything you want. You don't recognize any-

thing above yourself, or outside yourself or inside yourself. This is why, I repeat, you have no measure and live only to satisfy your whims.

Yes, your 'self appreciation' makes you blind! It is the biggest obstacle to a new life. One has to be able to pass this obstacle, this threshold, before one can go further. It is the test that separates the 'chaff' from the 'wheat' in people. No matter how intelligent, how endowed, how brilliant a man is, if he doesn't change his opinion about himself, he will be lost for inner development, for the work based on self-knowledge, for a real evolution. He will stay as he is all his life. The first demand, the first condition, the first test for he who wants to work on himself is to change his appreciation of himself. He cannot just imagine, or simply believe or think, but actually *see* things in himself that he did not see before, really see them. Never will his opinion about himself change as long as he will not see inside himself. And in order to see, he has to learn to see: it is the first initiation of man into self-knowledge.

Before anything else, he has to know what to look for. Once he knows it, he has to make efforts, focus his attention, look constantly, with tenacity. By maintaining his attention on it, by not forgetting about looking, one day he may see. If he sees once, he can see a second time, and if this is repeated he cannot ignore seeing. This is the state to look for in our observation; it is from this that the true desire, the desire to evolve, will be born; from cold we're becoming hot, vibrating; we will be deeply touched by our reality.

Today we have only the illusion of what we are. We overestimate ourselves. We do not respect ourselves. To respect myself, I have to have recognized in me a part which is higher than the other parts, and to which I show respect by the attitude I have towards it. In this way I will respect myself. And my relationships with others will be ruled by the same respect.

We have to understand that all other measuring units, talent, erudition, culture, genius, are changing units, units of detail. The only true measure, never changing, objective, the only real one, it is the measure of inner vision. 'I' see – 'I' see myself – and you have measured. With a higher, real part, you have measured a lower one, also real. And this measure, defining by itself the respective roles of each part, will bring you to self-respect. But you will see it is not easy. And it is not a bargain. One has to pay a lot. For the bad payers, the lazy, the losers, no chance. One must pay, pay a lot, pay immediately and pay in advance. Pay from oneself. With sincere efforts, wholeheartedly, without expectations.

The more you will be willing to pay without reticence, without cheating, without falsity, the more you will receive. And from then on, you will meet your true nature. And you will see all the tricks, all the dishonesty it goes to in order to avoid paying cash. Because you have to pay with all the gratuitous theories, all the deeply rooted convictions, all the prejudice, all conventions, all 'I like it' and 'I don't like it'. Without bargaining, honestly, not just make believe. Trying to see while using fake money.

Try for a moment to accept the idea that you are not what you think you are, that you overestimate yourself, therefore that you lie to yourself. That you lie to yourself always, every moment, all day long, your whole life. That the lie rules you to the extent that you cannot control it anymore. You are its victim. You lie everywhere. Your relationships with others, lies. The education you're giving, your petty conventions, lies. Your learning, lies. Your theories, your art, lies. Your social life, your family life, all lies. And what you think of yourself, lies too.

But you don't stop from what you're doing or from what you're saying, because you believe in you. You have to stop inside and observe. Observe without prejudice. While accepting for a time this idea of lies. And if you observe in this manner, paying of yourself, without self-pity, by giving all your false riches for one moment of reality, maybe someday you'll see all of a sudden something you have never seen in you before. You will see you are someone else from what you thought you are. You will see that you are two. One that is not, but takes the place and play the other's role. And the one that is, but so weak, so inconsistent, that just brought forth it disappears immediately. It cannot stand the lies. The smallest lie kills it. It doesn't fight, it does not resist, it is vanquished in advance.

Learn to look until you have observed the difference between your two natures, until you have seen the lies, the impostor in you. When you will see your two natures, that day, in you, the truth will be born. (Gurdjieff, quoted in Michel 1989, 34–35)

And that is what happened during that period from the dream of the Kiss in March, to the moment when I realized that everything I had ever believed in was a lie, and I was being asked by the universe if I was willing to pay everything. And pay I did; in advance. During the period following my separation, as my energy was no longer being drained daily, the manifestation in the body was the evidence of the price I was paying. Everything in my physical system cried out against this view of the world of human affairs, the view of predators and prey, and I wept tears of blood and pus from my eyes to the point that I nearly lost my sight altogether.

There, at that moment, in the middle of my life, mother to five children for whom I had given most of my life, I saw that not only had I been lying to myself by believing lies and deception, but that I had conveyed those same lies to the people I loved the most – my children.

What do you do when you realize that most of your life you have given away your free will and, at the same time, have taken away the free will of those dearest to you? More horrible still, what do you do when you realize it has *all* been done in the name of *love?!*

When the last illusion was stripped away and I was left with nothing but the skeleton of my being, I reached what Kafka describes as "Von einem gewissen Punkt an gibt es keine Rückkehr mehr. Dieser Punkt ist zu erreichen." "There is a point of no return. This point has to be reached."

When you have been stripped of all your illusions, when you have nothing left to believe in, there is no one there at all but yourself. It felt rather like falling endlessly in icy, black, meaningless space. No rhyme nor reason, no truth or beauty, no anything that I had ever believed in could be seen anywhere. I had peeled away the layers of all the warm, fuzzy, comforting beliefs and found that it was all a lie, a deception, a mask for feeding and manipulation.

By believing the lies, I had participated in the feeding and manipulating to so great a degree that my grief and regret became an ocean in which I was drowning. No wonder we resist giving up our beliefs! Without them, we have to face the truth about ourselves! And, as much as we think we are loving, caring, giving beings, when we see the *truth*, when we see that most of our ideas about loving and caring and being have been manipulated to deprive us of our free will and to pass the infection on to those we love the most, it is like looking into the pit of Hell.

And when you look into the pit of Hell and realize that you have been feeding that black and bloody, sucking and gaping and gore filled maw waiting to swallow you, and that you have taught those you love to feed it as well, the horror of the realization is enough to drive you mad with grief and despair.

You search for a meaning, some little point of illumination, and there is no light anywhere, not even a single candle to dispel the darkness.

On a humorous note, it was at this point that Tom French came to visit me one day and asked me what I really thought about the alien reality. Well, it was not a very good time to ask me this question! There I was, wrapped in a blanket to ward off the chill that I couldn't seem to shake, constantly wiping the oozing mess that dripped from my eyes, almost unable to speak above a whisper, and that whisper sounding as much like the croaking of a strangled crow than anything, and Tom French wants to know what I think about the alien reality. Who or what did I think these aliens were? Well, that's like asking the guy who falls out a fourth-floor window and is lying broken and dying on the pavement below, "Are ya hurt?!"

"Spawn of Satan," I managed to croak. At that moment, I could see no light anywhere.

But, while falling in this dark, empty space, something begins to form inside you. In the beginning it is very small, but it catches your attention and, since it is the only thing that is different in the sucking, feeding darkness, you become riveted on it. You cannot be sure exactly what it is at first, but your attention gives it energy and it begins to grow inside you.

What you have found is your will – the spiritual essence of who you are – and once you have found your will you *see* "the *choice*." Choice is a function of will. Where Will exists, Choice comes into being. You *can* choose. What you see is that you can choose the *orientation* of your soul. You cannot change the reality, but you can choose what *you* will personally *do* within it.

The way the thought came to me was, "Well, okay, I don't see any light or love or truth or beauty anywhere; and the universe may just blink out one day without it ever having really existed. But that would be a tragedy."

Desolation overwhelmed me and I felt so great a pity and love for what *might* have been – for what radiant and sublime dreams may be in the Mind of God that might never be fulfilled, because the deceptions are so deep, and the reality is so monstrous – who can really *see* it, and survive?

And I became aware of the feather-like weight of my inclination, my True Will to Be. It was not more than an inclination, a propensity, a preference. But as I noted it and focused on it, it became firmer and purposeful.

And I realized, "I am just one single, solitary, lone being in the darkness, and there really and truly might never, *ever*, be anyone or anything in existence of real love, truth and beauty." And the sadness and despair vaulted from my soul into darkness that enveloped me. But nothing answered except that my attention was drawn back, again, to this small thing that was growing inside me which had now begun to glow and give off warmth in that soul-chilling blackness. Somehow my thoughts were making it grow. My thoughts were aligning me with it.

Resolution and steadfastness began to blossom. And then I realized that it was connected to some greater source of Light and by my penitential love and compassion for the Dream of Love and Truth, the light was increasing. And I understood that the darkness, the predatory nature of our reality, was *also* God!

Disasters, misfortunes, tragedies, ruin, destruction, adversity, suffering, pain, anguish in all the varied manifestations we find them in our world are expressions of the *idea* of nonexistence. I understood that the idea of nonexistence exists *only* as an idea, and *only* because, in a realm of *all* potentials, even the potential of nonexistence exists as non-being. In the two fundamental ideas of Being and Non-being, all creation is manifested. In the act of Creation, the outrush of creative energy, half of the Consciousness of God formed itself into a reflection of this idea of Non-being as part of the Grand Experience. And this reflection of

Non-being is matter – it is only the half of the Consciousness of God gone to sleep to become the clay from which the material cosmos is formed.

I also understood that, in that eternal instant of falling asleep, of compression, there was a sensation of loss in this half of God that became matter, and that this sensation is expressed as a recoil, a contraction upon itself. It is this recoil and contraction in flux interaction with outraying creative consciousness that establishes the tension of polarization that is the dynamic by which the cosmos is manifested. And, in third-density terms, this recoil or contraction is the essence of service-to-self – the Predator – those who choose this mode ultimately recycle into sleeping matter.

The creative-consciousness half of God uses the matter that is formed by the recoil/contraction of the other half of God to take on form, to engage in exploration of all the ideas in the mind of God. This results in an increase of its relative energy. This using of matter to increase energy is felt by the sleeping consciousness/matter as fear of loss of self. To assuage the fear, the matter-oriented consciousness must circumscribe, limit, and restrain. It must believe that the grand constructions of illusion are not only *real*, but *all that exists*. Physicality becomes the standard, the measure, the object of veneration. The Physical Universe is, in effect, God. This is the essential dynamic of all physical or partly physical realities, including the hyperdimensional fourth-density STS reality.

The moment of true initiation. It seems that, as the great masters teach us, it is not a moment of great enlightenment. It is not someone who comes to show us reality. It is not a seeing all the world as a oneness. It is seeing the self as a liar and a feeder on others. It is measuring the self with *truth*. It is seeing that the Predator has been feeding on the self, that the self has been feeding on others and propagating the infection on to all those whom one claims to love and wishes to help. Initiation is not a glorious in-pouring of life and love and tears for the beauty and oneness of the world.

It is sheer terror.

It is a descent into Hell. It is the Shamanic descent into the underworld to do battle with demons. It is the dismemberment of the body, the flaying of the flesh from the bones, and the subsequent rebuilding of the self on a different foundation – a foundation of spiritual verity.

And if I could convey to you that Hell, that sensation, that solitary test in which the soul is weighed, *by the self*, finally and completely and seen for what it has truly done, you would see how little truth there is because of all the beliefs of the Matrix that have been inculcated and promulgated and tended so carefully by our emotions and by the deceptions of the predator within who convinces us that we are "good" and "pure" and there is "oneness."

Indeed, one sees that there is "oneness," but one sees that the aspect of God that is experienced at this level is the black, sucking, feeding maw of STS. One sees how little true Love is actually manifested at this level of being. One sees that all of our illusions about goodness and truth and beauty are *lies*. They are masks for more feeding.

And that is so horrifying an initiation that few survive.

That is "paying everything."

Now, reread what Gurdjieff had to say about the matter; how he pointed out that a person has to "pay in advance," that the key is to accept the idea that one is not what one thinks, that there is a different reality from which our own is projected, and that developing this idea in the realm of pure thought, and then using it as the platform by which one can observe and analyze, is the key to being able to see for a moment, and then again. One must be able to see the interactions of the petty tyrants in our lives, the predators who prey on us in the theological reality. Then, one must be willing to act. It is only after action that the true nature of the Predator reveals itself just as the vampire reacts with violence to being exposed by the presence of a mirror. Because, it must be kept always in mind that there *are* predators who are predators by choice – even if that choice is made at some level, in some part of themselves, that is not available to even their own conscious awareness. They, too, are part of the Matrix, and they wouldn't be able to play their roles if they were not consciously convinced that they are right, that they are good, that they are righteous and long-suffering.

After this month of suffering, of initiation, of *seeing*, I wanted to try to formulate some questions to determine what I ought to do next. Even though the spiritual reality was changed, the physical reality was still in a state of near desperation. I had no idea how the children and I would survive to the extent of not knowing how I would keep food on the table.

April 24, 1996

Q: (L) I would like to deal with certain issues relating to the progress of this "mission" or "project" as you have described it. As you know, we have experienced serious disruptions and "attack" in recent months. I came to a conclusion that my husband is a robot person. But, I am not going to ask you to confirm or deny that. I came to that idea through information in the transcripts. What I do want to know is: is it likely now that much of the attack will cease since that energy has been removed from my environment?

A: Maybe, but not necessarily in the ways you think! Robot or not, all are programmed.

Q: (L) All are programmed including myself and Frank?

A: Yes.

Q: (L) Well, considering a lot of my internal experiences, I had already come to this conclusion. What is the objective of this programming?

A: It is too complex to explain yet. [...]

Q: (L) I was analyzing some of the material regarding the recent episode with SV and her mother. To this point, she still has done none of the things that you advised her to do in response to her requests for advice. I told her that I was very angry that she took so much of my time and energy and still did none of the things advised, resulting in *everyone* being upset. Now, I had someone call me and tell me that SV was involved in some sort of coven or very dark organization. I just have a very difficult time believing this. How can she speak so disparagingly of such things and then, be a part of such? Yet, the source of the information knew things that "clicked" and could not possibly have been said unless this was true. Is it possible that SV could have multiple personalities and one of her other "selves" is doing this? As in Greenbaum?

A: Sure!

Q: (L) Is it possible for either Frank or I to be involved in such and not be aware of it?

A: Yes, but it is not that.

Q: (L) Does that mean that there *is* some other thing that we are involved in, in some other aspects of our selves, that we are not aware of?

A: Close.

Q: (L) Is this something that happens in altered states or in sleep states?

A: Not happens, happened.

Q: (L) Something that happened in the past?

A: Laura, you need to consult a powerful, practiced, effective hypnotherapist to unlock these questions for you.

Q: (L) Is this something I could do for Frank in the meantime? Obviously Frank could have a big piece of the puzzle locked up in there ...

A: Both of you and others. The locks have been installed in such a way that it is literally impossible for you to unlock them, as they were installed with full knowledge of present circumstances.

Q: (L) Who installed these locks?

A: Supremely powerful STS consortium!!

Q: (L) And what circumstances were they aware of, as you have mentioned, when they installed these locks?

A: All.

And right here we have a most interesting series of clues. Note that the reference was clearly to the fact that something was locked away from my awareness and that it had been done with full knowledge of the present circumstances. At the time, it never would have occurred to me that this could mean that Frank was working for the other side to make sure that I was not accessing the information, and if I ever did get to the point where it was possible, to attempt to derail or destroy me. At that point in time Frank was the only one I felt I could talk to freely, and he had been so supportive during the previous month that anything he had ever done prior to that time was completely forgiven.

Q: (L) You are the Cassiopaeans, correct?

A: Yes.

Q: (L) And you are STO?

A: Yes.

Q: (L) And you are telling us that we have locks on knowledge installed in us, installed by supremely powerful STS consortium. Can we not, in our conscious state, reject this programming, and ask you to inform us of this information?

A: Not possible!

Q: (L) What is not possible?

A: What you just asked.

Q: (L) You mean we can't change our minds, or you can't inform us?

A: Incorrect analysis.

Q: (L) Give me the correct analysis.

A: You cannot unlock, and we cannot tell you details of what, or why.

Q: (L) Why can you not tell us?

A: Free will violation, and endangerment of you if done thusly.

Q: (L) Is there some way to do it that does not endanger us?

A: We have told you.

Q: (L) Is it a danger to us to *not* unlock these things?

A: In a sense.

Q: (L) When I was kidnapped at the age of three or four in Jacksonville, how many days was I missing. My mother simply has a blank about it, which amazes her.

A: 12 days.

Q: (L) Who was it that kidnapped me?

A: Jan.

Q: (L) Who was Jan?

A: Corps member.

Q: (L) What corps is this?

A: Select division of economic legion under control of G5.

Q: (L) Economic legion? What is G5?

A: Intel.

Q: (L) What was the purpose of this kidnapping?

A: To install self-destruct programming.

Q: (L) So, this Jan was known to us as "Cecil Brien."

A: Yes.

Q: (L) And he more or less overwhelmed my mother and persuaded her to marry him just to get at me? I find this to be incredible!

A: It was easy at the time. She was vulnerable.

295

Q: (L) So, I have a "self-destruct" program. And Frank has one also?

A: Similar, but not an exact copy so as to mask.

Q: (L) Was Frank abducted in a similar fashion?

A: Close, but not exactly.

Q: (L) Was Frank's pneumonia when he was a child, that nearly killed him, part of this self-destruct program?

A: Yes.

Q: (L) Was Frank's father also programmed?

A: Semi.

Q: (L) Well. I think we can safely assume that every member of our families have had some sort of program installed, if only to facilitate our programming. This whole situation is beginning to sound inexpressibly grim.

A: Grim?!? You have lived decades after these episodes! How many brethren? Multiples of millions!

Q: (L) That is why I am saying it is pretty damn grim …

A: And it is part of a natural process, do not forget.

Q: (L) Well, we need some help from the good guys. Or, is it that unless we can figure it out we are stuck?

A: No.

Q: (L) It sounds so dreadful. We need some help here. I am becoming *very* tired.

A: You only need knowledge. […]

Q: (L) Well, I want to have a little direction here.

A: Concentrate on settlement. This can be a problem solver if handled wisely, a curse if not so! Use some of the funds to locate a "super-hypnotherapist."

Q: (L) Who might this person be? A clue?

A: No.

Q: (L) Is there some progress that we can make on our own?

A: Yes.

Q: (L) Give me a clue … I want something that will blow me off my chair and enrich my life which is so grim … produce knowledge that will protect me …

A: Won't succeed until locks are blown off in proper way.

Q: (L) Well, I hope I survive until then.

A: Refer to previous answer.

Q: (L) If you guys were here, I'd throw something at you!

A: We'd dodge!

Q: (L) Well, you see my problem here … I guess I just want to know that there is someone out there who cares …

A: You should by now.

Q: (L) Then you guys ought to get behind my lawyer and jack him up …

A: We do, through you. […]

Q: (L) So, we have a *lot* of stuff locked up inside and all we have to do is find the key …

A: Yes, exactly.

Q: (L) Anything else …

A: Beware of cardiac concerns. Not what is, what may be.

Q: (L) What specifically?

A: Possible thrombosis in future.

Q: (L) What can I do to avoid such?

A: Many things, but most important is your attitude. You must decrease your anger.

As it turned out, this was the second incident in which the Cs "saw" something in connection with me that was actually related to someone I was interacting with. In this instance, it was Sandra. Within a few days of the above remark, Sandra suffered a thrombosis that stopped her heart. She was in her office when it happened, working after hours, so there was no one there to help her. She fell and a couple of people standing by an elevator out in the hall heard a crash of furniture being knocked over. After some discussion, they decided to investigate, but had to find the janitor to unlock the office. By the time the EMT folks arrived, Sandra had been dead for 20 minutes. She was revived and placed on life support, but her brain was dead.

I was devastated. I also saw it as forces "out there" deliberately depriving me of my closest friend and supporter. Even if Frank was a confidant, he was not a woman and there are things that women talk about that cannot be discussed with a man.

While Sandra was still on life support, I was unable to accept the fact that I couldn't have a miracle. I had had a dream about the event a few weeks earlier. In the dream, I had confronted Sandra's children in a hospital waiting room where she was lying sick. I told them that if they did not give her a reason to live, she wouldn't. When this exact drama actually played out, I decided to ask the Cs if she would be able to be restored to health. Was she, as the doctors said, really already dead? The Cs confirmed this and agreed to step aside so that I could communicate with Sandra directly. It was an amazing conversation, and when it was over, I was convinced that I had, indeed, been talking with Sandra. Her personality had come through so strongly in her use of words, and her memory of events we had experienced together way in the past – things Frank could never have known about – that I was comforted, especially when she remarked that she was finally having some fun. I was able to let go of my hope that she would recover. A week later, after her family had all assembled to say their goodbyes, the respirator was disconnected and her body was allowed to expire.

The most stunning thing about the event was what I saw happening with Sandra's two sons, the ones she had babied and supported all their lives. They had never been required to be responsible for any of their actions, in the same way I had acted as a buffer for my husband. Just as I had always stepped in and made nice to fix things for him, Sandra had been doing it for her sons. In her case, it was slightly different, of course, but still the result of emotional programs. We do these things thinking that it is love, and now I was seeing the result. Her sons (aged 27 and 34) were actually angry at her for dying and depriving them of access to the good money she made that supported all their many ventures, all of which ended in disaster, at which point she poured more money into the situation to get them out of the soup. Now, she wasn't there to do it, and they weren't sad that they hadn't done anything for *her*, they were actually *angry* that she was depriving them of this income! I was stunned. All the love Sandra had felt for these two parasites, that she had expressed by doing so much for them, only made them want more and more and more – right up to her very life! And then they had the nerve to be angry that there wasn't any more to get!

What, I wondered, is this thing we call "love" that is obviously *not* love? How do we get sucked into these traps? How come we believe that giving and helping in every way we can is Love, when it is clearly not? Those two boys were now faced with having to figure out things on their own. Their mother had "loved them so much" that she had never allowed them to learn to walk on their own, and now they were angry at her that they had to walk, that she wasn't there to carry them anymore. And how difficult a road it was going to be for them. So, yes, they were angry, and, in a sense, rightly so. She had deprived them of the incremental lessons of experiencing the consequences of their own mistakes, and now they were going to hit the wall in a big way, starting with having to pay for her funeral!

What I wanted to know was how do we get sucked into these traps of believing something is love, of giving when it is not really giving, of thinking we are doing something good, when all we are doing is setting someone else up for a big fall by not letting them learn their own lessons.

I wanted to know why it was so physically painful to stop this activity when finally we were able to see that we weren't really doing good when we helped others in such ways? What is it that blinds us to the truth? I already knew the answer: emotions. But I wanted to know where and how it all began. What was going on here? How did this start?

THE THEOLOGICAL REALITY

April 28, 1996

Q: (L) We had a little chat with Sandra and we thank you for that. Now, we have been discussing a lot of different things here, and the main thing that I have been focusing on is the trap of emotions. I would like to know if this trap is foisted upon us from external sources?

A: The formula is "foisted."

Q: (L) What is the formula?

A: Set pattern, like a maze.

Q: (L) OK. And what is the most effective way to get out of this maze of emotional control?

A: Calculate.

Q: (L) Is there anything that can be done when one is in process of extricating oneself from an emotional trap to cut off or ease the pain of it? It quite literally hurts.

A: No need to ease.

Q: (L) Well, once you have done it and gone through it, or, more particularly, once you see that it is a trap, it doesn't hurt anymore – or lessens. Another thing is that we all have been affected by being sucked into emotional traps, seemingly since birth. Is this common for all people?

A: All? No, most, yes.

Q: (L) Would it be a fair statement to say that people who have potential to do very positive things in terms of clearing away and understanding the reality in which we exist, might be primary targets for this emotional turmoil?

A: Yes.

Q: (L) Can you tell us what might be the characteristics of a person who is not caught in the emotional trap?

A: Embracing? No. Uniting? Yes.

Q: (L) Ah! So, you are saying that people who can clear the emotional traps can unite in a higher emotional sense?

A: Emotions are chemicals only.

Q: (L) So, if emotions are chemical only, is it true that when one is in physical proximity to certain people, that perhaps their frequency vibrations cause these chemicals to be stimulated or generated within us?

A: Okay.

Q: (L) And, that it takes great force of will and mental power to counteract this physical action?

A: No, just practice.

Q: (L) OK, once you have done it a few times in small ways, you can build up to big ones?

A: Not quite correct concept.

Q: (L) I was reading this piece sent to us on the Internet where this Cosmic Awareness source talks about people who deliberately have come in because, since the good guys really can't interfere from the outside, because it would violate free will, that many of them incarnate and

299

thereby partake of the physical experience, and then wake up and be able to do the things that are needed on the planet. The object being to try to make sure that they will awaken to their purpose, and that emotions and emotional traps are used repeatedly and continuously to try to prevent them from awakening. What I am getting at is: what are the things that we can do to awaken? You have told us many times that we need to awaken. Obviously we are not fully awakened. We are aware of that. Is there some other thing we can do?

A: Let it happen naturally. If you are on a path, do you seek to jump up into the air and fly to the end of the path? If you did, you would regret missing the "rest of the path."

Q: (L) A lot of very strange things have been happening ... Sandra and her heart attack, [my daughter] and her ankle, the terrible sicknesses I have had in the past months, [my other daughter] talking about the things that have happened in her experiences ... it seems like, to me, that the situation in terms of attack is really heating up. Can you comment on this?

A: No.

Q: (L) Well, thanks a lot! Can we ask questions about it?

A: Yes.

Q: (L) Well, my eye infections, the ear problems, the loss of my voice for so long ... were these part of the attack process?

A: Yes.

Q: (L) My mother also fell down and has a black eye. I am trying to find the portal? What is the portal through which all this attack is coming?

A: Discover.

Q: (L) Did we already discover it in part, i.e. SV and her mother and that situation?

A: No.

Q: (L) Are you saying that SV is not a portal?

A: People are not portals!!! They are only victims of the things that come through the portals. Otherwise, many could describe you as a "portal."

Q: (L) Well, I never said that I wasn't. Speaking of that ...

A: When you concentrate on the people as portals, you falsely direct negative energy upon the soul units themselves. Rather like treating acne with the therapy to be found in a shotgun!

Q: (L) What is the appropriate response when you are in a situation and you know that the person is being victimized, yes, by the forces coming through the portal, but their victimization is causing you a great deal of problems? What is the appropriate response here?

A: How do you view those afflicted with disease? Do you throw rocks at them?!?

Q: (L) Well, no, you don't throw rocks at them ...

A: What do you do, then?

Q: (L) Well, a person with a disease: you send or take them to a doctor or suggest that they go to a doctor.

A: For what purpose?

Q: (L) To discover the diagnosis of the disease, to obtain medicine, to either relieve the symptoms or cure the disease.

A: Bingo!

Q: (L) We are talking about people who won't even admit they have a disease! How do you tell someone to go to a doctor when they don't think they are sick? Most people do *not* believe that they are subject to control or manipulation from other densities! You have told a number of people that they were going to be subjected to attack and manipulation and they have blithely said, "Oh, there is nothing in our lives that would permit that ..."

A: Denial is not incurable until you give up. Patience combined with kind invitations to participate in the learning process eventually allows the victim to awaken, thus to be open to cure. This helps you to build the "army" you seek. Isolation cures nothing. Thereby stifling progress, as any and all will ultimately be seen as "portals." Rather like "spinning one's wheels," yes??

Q: (L) So, in other words, you are saying I should remain married to my husband, I should have SV and other disruptive and destructive people over here constantly to "participate" in the learning process?

A: The point is not to rigidly adhere to specific lifestyles, nor maintain exact patterning of behavior, merely to not close doors completely and permanently.

Q: (L) OK, if a person were, say, a robot person, when a person becomes a robot person, what happens to the soul of the robot person?

A: Same process.

Q: (L) As what?

A: Death.

Q: (L) So, a person can die and leave their body, their body can be taken over and reanimated and controlled to function and do a lot of things for a long time. Meanwhile, the original soul has completely departed to fifth density ready to recycle?

A: Yes, but body is replaced, not reanimated.

Q: (L) Is this what happened to [my husband] when he had that surgery back in 1981?

A: We caution that, even though you have met 7 "robots," in your entire lifetime, not to "see" them under every bush or around every corner. You have met so many people in your life. We gave you one, and only one!!

Q: (L) What was the source of the dream where this was stated to me quite clearly?

A: Dreams are the best forum for disinformation that exists.

Q: (L) OK. I can see that. But, at the same time they are also one of the best ways to get information from the subconscious and the higher conscious, is this not true?

A: We have mentioned dualities a lot!!

Q: (L) Skipping the disinformation part, and just getting to the analysis part, the story of Bluebeard ... I am still of the opinion, robot person or not, I am doing the right thing. Is it possible that, even in this situation, that I am caught up in an emotional trap?

A: Sure. This learning thing is anything but easy!

Q: (L) Yes, that's all fine and dandy, but we are talking about breaking up my whole life here ...

A: Maybe, maybe not.

Q: (L) What good is channeling if it does not help you to make decisions once in a while? Once in a while, I say. Not all the time. Or to help clarify things! To put additional light on it instead of muddying the water!

A: We are not "muddying" the water, only you can do that!

Q: (L) Well, enough of that ...

A: No, not enough of that. And a much needed pointer for you: answers to questions of global or universal significance provide for a greater personal learning than direct personal inquiries. If you disagree, check transcripts and especially un-transcribed sessions for validation! You will see, my dear!!

Q: (L) Well, that is why I said that was enough of that because I don't want to talk about my personal stuff anymore. I did think that the thing about the robot people was pretty significant, but obviously it is not that significant or important. There's two million of them on the planet, and I have been told that I have encountered seven. I did think that this was a pretty high ratio of robot people for one person to encounter ...

A: Yes, but your life path has been unusual. And you have met 4588 people personally!

Q: (L) How many people has Frank met?

A: 2754.

Q: (L) How many were robots?

A: 3.

Q: (L) How many has PZ met?

A: 3856.

Q: (L) How many robots?

A: 1.

Q: (L) So, why seven for me – yeah, we know the path is unusual ...

A: Yes.

Q: (L) Can you tell me in what sense it is unusual?

A: Can't you?

Q: (L) Well, I thought I would trick you into telling me ...

A: No tricks, we only treat. [...]

Q: (L) I am so tired now that I cannot formulate a legitimate, reasonable, intelligent or coherent question of global or universal significance, we will say goodnight.

So even though the Cs were telling me many things in the above dialogue, I was still not seeing how to properly connect it all. But again, we see that I was being urged to get all the transcribing done, and to search the transcripts for the clues. It was being hinted that there was an "unusual" aspect to my life, and that there was obviously something that needed to be awakened to, but what it was I couldn't yet see. But the Cs suggested that I concentrate on questions of global and universal significance.

A week later my brother came to give me moral support, and to help with some things around the house. My soon-to-be-ex had never been one to fix anything anyway, and my brother was finally going to fix some of the things that had been driving me batty for the six years we had owned the house. We also decided to have a session, and the majority of this session was, indeed, concentrated on things of "global and universal significance." It was only toward the end that my brother, retired from the Navy, was directed to make some inquiries about his own life situation. He revealed that he had experienced some strange things while onboard ship, the symptoms of which certainly sounded like abduction byproducts.

May 5, 1996

Q: In terms of what we understand – I know you aren't gonna answer it that way – if Tom tries to bring up the memories and understand, the headaches ought to go away … (TK) I haven't had any since I have been out of the Navy.

A: O'Brien is "lyin'"

Q: What is it about O'Brien?

A: Discover. Why is Tom there, of all places?!?

Q: Is there something in that area, some frequency from the earth, some electromagnetics or something, that can tend to …

A: Maybe, maybe, maybe, maybe …

Q: It keeps a person quiescent and in the dark?

A: Stalling frequency … And by the way, can anyone come up with a purpose for the existence of Camp Blanding? Well?? … First, some blockbuster stuff for the Knighted ones … Look upon a detailed map, and reflect, remember lonely journeys from long ago, and begin to unlock shattering mysteries which will lead to revelations opening the door to the greatest learning burst yet!!

Q: (F) Oh, my. A *lot* of questions … (L) Was there more than one journey to Camp Blanding?

A: No.

Q: Only one?

A: For you.

Q: More than one for Tom?

A: ?

Q: You said "knighted ones," as though there were some significance to the name …

A: Discover …

Q: Is there some genetic engineering here?

A: No, not in the sense you are thinking. But, all are in some sense. […]

Q: Why did my mother marry men who kept affecting our lives in such terrible ways?

A: Ask her.

Q: She has no answer. She is baffled herself.

A: So, get her to discover. That is where the clues lie.

Q: So, the clues lie with some of these people … We remember the trip with one of them – to North Carolina – when we were taken to school …

A: Why did he insist you go to boarding school? And why did your mother acquiesce?

Q: All this comes back to the original question, why Tom is in O'Brien, near Camp Blanding …

A: EM waves curdle the mind producing complacency in the face of contrived misery. Numbs the mind through isolationist influences. Why are you there, Tom? Who begged you to stay there? EM waves emanate from?? Suggest you, Laura, go to library and research Camp Blanding. You may find a "black hole," so to speak!!

Well, I was dense as all get out, to say the least. "Camp Blanding." Why was this term being related to a "black hole" in relation to EM waves curdling the mind producing complacency in the face of contrived misery? Why was it being pointed out that such EM waves can "numb the mind through isolationist influences?" Why did they ask "EM waves emanate from?" Well, from whom?

In retrospect, it is easy to see that Frank's ongoing manipulations were designed to isolate me from everyone, and in the above all the clues were given – even the term "Bland-ing" in connection with a "black hole."

To understand the connection of the term "bland," we need to go back to October of 1995 where we had been asking some questions about the UFO crash in 1947, near Roswell. During the course of this discussion, the Cs revealed that there were dead humans aboard the craft, and that these bodies had been retrieved for reanimation as robot-type beings. This was so unsettling an idea that I almost couldn't take it seriously. In recent months, however, Scott Corrales has written an article about this very thing, confirming with witness testimony, that what the Cs were saying here might very likely be true. (If you are interested, read the October, 2001 issue of *Fate Magazine*. Funny that our discussion and Corrales' article both appear in the month of October.)

In any event, it related to the ideas I had come to about my ex-husband, as in the April 28 session above where the Cs were suggesting that I was looking for the robot in the wrong direction. The following remarks contain the clues to the personality of the mechanical individual.

October 21, 1995

A: We gave you one for your own knowledge and protection, but cannot give you others at this juncture. [Laura's note: Does this mean they can be given at another time, after a particular, destined interaction takes place?]

Q: (L) Is it up to me to figure out what characteristics these individuals have, in order to ...

A: Based upon data given, yes.

Q: (L) OK, is one of the, I mean, I'm clicking right now, one of the characteristics I think, that these kind of individuals might have, since they have this projected emotional frequency, would be a repeating emotional pattern, that they just simply, in spite of seeming intelligence, do not seem to learn from anything, that it just repeats over and over again. Is that a clue?

A: Yes.

Q: OK, then, this same inability to get a clue about what's going on ... OK, that's a clue, right there. Is there any kind of instinctual sensation that one would get about these types of individuals?

A: Bland. Spend inordinate amounts of "time" in solitude.

Q: (L) Well, that means Frank's one! Well, Frank's kind of bland! And he spends a lot of time in solitude. (SV) A lot of people do! (L) So, is Frank one?

A: No.

Q: (L) We're teasing you, Frank! I didn't mean it! (SV) He's not bland, though! Frank's anything but bland! (L) Is my husband one?

A: No. Bland is not universal in this situation, just a clue for you to identify individual.

Q: (L) OK, one is a nutritionist, one is very bland. Is that what we're getting at?

A: No.

Q: (L) OK, bland is just part of it.

A: Not key component, more likely to be spreading of disinformation. [...]

Q: Do these beings know what they are?

A: Not conscious beings!

Q: (L) They're not conscious beings, so, they just react to you as though they are being remote controlled. (SV) So, if you told one of them what they were ...

A: Are being remote controlled.

Now, the strangest thing of all is that, in the above remarks, I had the answer. Being "bland" and "spending inordinate amounts of time alone" immediately made me think of Frank, as the reader will notice. Of course, by even voicing it playfully, I felt guilty. But with recent revelations, we begin to see just how clever the Cs really are. All the clues were being given, I just wasn't ready to see everything at once. Camp Blanding and a black hole indeed!

Anyway, I had come back to the subject again a couple months after the October session:

December 2, 1995

Q: (L) When we did the session on October 21st, we were talking about robotoid-type people, or reanimated humans, and that this is what is done rather than cloning and replacing. Then you said I had been in contact with seven of these, and we identified one of them. Then, we talked about profiles, and it was indicated that a "bland" personality might have something to do with identification. You also said that you could not identify the others right at that moment. Can you now do so?

A: Search your "files." Learning is sometimes best accomplished by study and exploration.

Q: (L) Can I have a couple more clues as to what I am looking for? You mentioned being in a hospital …

A: Non-emotive. There are other clues which you can discover by your own study. It would not be advantageous for us to give you further information on this subject. Speculation about this particular subject will throw you off track.

Q: (L) Is the subject as important as I think it might be?

A: Ultimately, but not yet!!

And indeed, we now see how spectacularly important it was, as well as exactly where the clues were leading. Getting back to the session with my brother present in May of 1996:

Q: A black hole. OK. Well, there is sure a lot of stuff that has gone on in our lives for which there is simply no rational explanation. (TK) They sure have been giving a lot of stuff tonight without a lot of questions …

A: Visits through trees, forests, leading to a perfectly square clearing … […]

Q: (L) Well, what I *really* want to know is *why* have we had all of these *crazy* things happen in our lives, and all of these people ranged all around us seemingly placed there, or manipulated deliberately to affect us negatively? I mean, am I wrong, or is this not a *very* unusual and crazy situation?

A: Why do you think?

Q: Well, I have no idea!

A: Because you are of the extremely rare and few who have the abilities to put the puzzle together.

Q: So, what are we supposed to do? (TK) Discover.

A: Yes. And, for tonight, good night.

The important thing to note is that, throughout all of the attacks, Frank had the effect on me of numbing my mind, of "producing complacency in the face of contrived misery." I was so depressed most of the time with his repeated rants on how deaf, dumb and blind I had been for years, that little by little, any and all confidence I had in my ability to accurately perceive anything was fading away. I figured that I was so stupid that there was simply no point in my trying to do anything at all without Frank there to guide me because, after all, he had been "right" all along about my ex-husband, right?

But the Cs were saying something different. They were suggesting that I go to the library and research Camp Blanding. I did. There was nothing significant. The result of their encouragement, however, was to stop me from thinking about my own misery, and stimulate me to think about solving puzzles. Once I had picked myself up out of the hole of the depression, lured by the carrot of a puzzle to solve, I felt better enough to undertake some further study on other issues.

There was a three-week break in sessions at this point because I was ill again. The reader ought to note that Terry and Jan were rarely present during this period, mainly because I was sick most of the time, but also due to Frank's animosity toward them because they were not convinced that he was the channel. Added to this was my own support of Frank's position, to my great regret. It is interesting to notice that after nearly every session when Terry was absent, I became ill again. Fortunately, Terry and Jan understood only too well what kind of game Frank was operating and also knew the stresses I was under, so their perspective is one of acceptance that I had to learn about Frank on my own. They were right, and I am grateful for their understanding.

It was at this point in time that the session (June 1, 1996) occurred where the Cs supposedly accused me of trying to take credit upon myself for the material, and that this resulted in many of the attacks I had experienced. As the reader now suspects, that was altogether untrue, and we can now view this as evidence that, after so long an absence of Terry at the board, as well as along with my deteriorating physical condition, Frank's controllers were seeing their plans coming to fruition and in that session, had made the putsch to try to send me over the edge.

Immediately after this session, I was so depressed that I ended up sick again. As is usual, unless I am completely unable to see or function, I have always tried to make my sick time count for something useful. On this occasion, the only book in the house that I hadn't really read was a new one that had sat on the shelf for a couple of years, untouched, which I now proposed to read. It was William Chittick's translation of the works of the great Sufi Shaykh, Ibn al-'Arabi, *The Sufi Path of Knowledge*. I struggled through the dry introduction, and gradually began to realize that the Shaykh must have been drawing his information from the same source as the Cs were. It was all so familiar, so similar, so full of synchronous passages that described in great detail the many things the Cs were telling us. I was astonished. It was third-party confirmation that what the Cs were saying was derived from a very ancient knowledge exactly as they suggested. But obviously, without the Cs more modern explication, the deeper reality was difficult to see since so much time had transpired since Al-'Arabi had written his *Futuhat*. But taking the loss of understanding that takes place over time, as well as the loss that occurs when something is translated from one language to another, it was stunningly clear that the Cs communication was something more amazing than even I had suspected. I was not only strengthened, I felt that I had made some sort of inner connection to this tradition of knowledge, and I wanted to ask about it.

June 9, 1996

Q: (L) My question is: is the information we are receiving similar to what Al-'Arabi calls an "opening?"

A: Yes.

Q: (L) You say that you are unified thought forms in the realm of knowledge.

A: Yes.

Q: (L) Al-'Arabi describes unified thought forms as being the "names of God." His explication seems to be so identical to things you tell us that I wonder ...

A: We are all the names of God. Remember, this is a conduit. This means that both termination/origination points are of equal value, importance. [...]

Q: (L) What do you mean? Does this mean that we are a part of this?

A: Yes.

Q: (L) So, it has to do with ...

A: Don't deify us. And, be sure all others with which you communicate understand this too!

Q: (L) What quality in us, what thing, enabled us to make contact. Because, obviously a lot of people try and get garbage.

A: You asked.

Q: (L) A lot of people ask!

A: No they don't, they command.

Q: (L) Well, a lot of people do ask or beg or plead, but they get all discombobulated with the answers.

A: No, they command. Think about it. You did not beg or plead ... that is commanding. After J** left, purification began.

Q: (L) This recent "awakening" or period of seeing things with such clarity, as they really were, and the whole picture of the interactions between people and how truly ugly it can be. I plunged into a terrible depression. I needed to get my balance from seeing so much all at once. Can you explain to me what was going on?

A: Growth.

Q: (L) I tried to share this perception with other people, and almost without exception, when I said to people that I was finally seeing things in their true state and it was *not* a pretty picture, they all said, "Well, you are obviously seeing this through the eyes of some major spirit possession!" Why would they say this?

A: First of all, it is not correct to perceive "everything in such darkness and gloom, etc." That is merely the result of a cocoon of falsehood being removed. Celebrate the balance. Don't mourn the death of an illusion of an imbalance.

Q: (L) Where do I go from here? Where do we all go?

A: Everywhere.

Now, notice that above, I am speaking of the very same interactions that I was speaking of before when I had been accused of taking credit on myself (which was obviously Frank's handlers in action). But in the above, the answer is completely different. In retrospect, it seems that when I began to read the Sufi material, balance was restored, and I became sufficiently strong to counteract the negative intentions of Frank and his controllers. It should also be pointed out that the remark, "Remember, this is a conduit. This means that both termination/origination points are of equal value, importance," followed by the answer as to why I was able to make contact, "because you asked," could in no way be construed to refer to Frank. Frank never asked anything. And at the point in time when the so-called aura photos were made, on January 20, 1996, the Cs had made this completely clear:

Q: (L) [looking at aura photo of self] This is very strange, guys. How come I am not in this picture and Frank shows up in his? Why have I physically disappeared?

A: Learning builds spiritual growth, and awareness "solidifies" knowledge.

Q: (L) OK, but that does not explain why I disappeared.

A: Because the energy field enclosure was unifying you with the conduit, as is usual during channeling sessions between 3rd and 6th-density level communications.

Q: [photo of board develops, and geometric figure appears to sounds of amazement from group] (L) What is this geometric figure?

A: Was a visual representation of the conduit, indeed!!! The reason for such clear luminescence is that thought centers were clear and open in you at the moment of the photograph.

Even though, at that point in time, the Cs had clearly pointed out that it was me who was unified with them during channeling, and that the learning I was experiencing was solidifying the knowledge into soul stuff, I was still not ready or able to take the responsibility for any of it, preferring to think that it had just been a sort of fluke. A large part of this was my emotional desire to not diminish Frank's importance. I wanted him have something that was his own, and I aided and abetted him in this belief, thinking that when he became secure enough, he would be able to acknowledge the truth, let it go, and simply be part of a group seeking answers. But Frank never did seek any answers. I was too engaged in trying to save him to notice.

Nevertheless, the reading of the Sufi material and the realization that something was going on in my life that was truly amazing apparently opened some kind of door. All the little hints the Cs had been giving up to now, including the one where they said that the "ending of the attacks" would happen, but not in any way that I suspected at that point, began to coalesce at this point in time. By choosing to end the illusions, to act based on the theological reality, as imperfectly as I may have understood it at that point, I was apparently ready for the next step – and it was a big one!

> June 15, 1996
>
> Q: (L) As you know, I have been studying the Sufi teachings, and I am discovering so many similarities in these Sufi "unveilings" to what we have been receiving through this source, that I am really quite amazed, to say the least. So, my question is: could what we are doing here be considered an ongoing, incremental, "unveiling," as they call it?
> A: Yes.
>
> Q: (L) Now, from what I am reading, in the process of unveiling, at certain points, when the knowledge base has been sufficiently expanded, inner unveilings then begin to occur. Is this part of the present process?
> A: Maybe.
>
> Q: (L) My experience has been, over the past couple of years, that whenever there is a significant increase in knowledge, that it is sort of cyclical – I go through a depression before I can assimilate – and it is like an inner transformation from one level to another. Is there something we can do, and if so, is it desirable, to increase or facilitate this process in some way?
> A: It is a natural process, let it be. [...]
>
> Q: (L) Al-'Arabi presents a very complex analysis and he probably didn't know it all either ... Nevertheless, it almost word-for-word reflects things that have been given directly to us through this source.
> A: Now, learn, read, research all you can about unstable gravity waves.

Say what?! Where in the world did *that* come from?

> Q: (L) OK. Unstable gravity waves. I'll see what I can find. Is there something more about this?
> A: Meditate too!

As usual, I tried to include Frank in everything. But the Cs made it clear that Frank was not the intended recipient of what they were saying. This was the case on many other occasions, but never had they been so clear and adamant about it.

Q: (L) Yes. Well, they have been telling us to meditate. Have you been meditating, Frank? (F) Not lately.

A: We mean for you, Laura, to meditate about unstable gravity waves as part of research. Unstable gravity waves unlock as yet unknown secrets of quantum physics to make the picture crystal clear. [...]

Q: (L) I feel like I am missing a really big point here ...

A: You are, but you can only find it at your own pace.

Q: (L) Well, I think I need to do some reading and research so that I can come back to this.

A: And, on that note, good night.

It was bizarre enough for the Cs to just toss in something like a nudge to do research in the field of quantum physics, but I discovered they really meant business. Sure, I did what I could, I went through the books on my shelves to see if gravity waves were mentioned, and the result was less than successful to say the least. I went on the Internet and tried to find something, which was really a pathetic attempt considering the fact that I was barely capable of doing more than operating my mail program. I didn't have enough power in my computer to do any real web browsing, and everything was so slow that I soon became frustrated and gave up that approach.

Meanwhile, something else really strange was going on, and it wasn't just with me – V** was experiencing it also. It seems that whenever we would begin to talk about what we now call the Matrix, we would suddenly begin to just simply burn up. It didn't seem to matter if we were talking on the phone, or in person, or if we were talking to strangers or each other, the instant other realities were mentioned, the heat would fall on us just as if we had been suddenly shoved into an oven.

As this phenomenon developed, it also became obvious that whenever Frank walked into the house, I started to feel so much heat I could barely stand it. Of course, I was sure that this was a sign that higher levels of being were stimulated by his presence because it was a *good* thing. The fact that Frank never experienced it I attributed to the possibility that he was already an advanced being and didn't need to go through these stages. It never occurred to me that it was a defensive mechanism, or a connection that was protecting me. The funny thing was that this heat never registered on a thermometer nor did it produce perspiration. But it was quite miserable. V** wanted to ask about it.

June 22, 1996

Q: (V) A few weeks ago several of us began to suffer from internal heat, insomnia, and other things. What was this?

A: Image. Deep conjunction of fibrous linkage in DNA structure.

Q: (V) Well, I want to know if it is in my mind that I get so hot, or does my body temperature actually elevate?

A: Only on 4th.

Q: (V) I don't understand.

A: Bleedthrough, get used to those!

Q: (L) Does this mean we are actually experiencing a bleedthrough of fourth density?

A: Image.

Q: (V) Are the little flashes of light I see also a manifestation of this?

A: Maybe so, but try to concentrate on the ethereal significance, rather than the physical.

Q: (L) When you say "deep conjunction of fibrous linkage," does this mean that we are conjoining with a linkage to a fourth-density body that is growing, developing?

A: Slowly, but surely. Now, get ready for a message: We have told you before that the upcoming "changes" relate to the spiritual and awareness factors rather than the much publicized physical. Symbolism is always a necessary tool in teaching. But, the trick is to read the hidden lessons represented by the symbology, not to get hung up on the literal meanings of the symbols!

Q: (L) You say that the symbology has to do with hidden meanings. The symbology that you used was "image" and "deep fibrous linkage" of DNA. Now, is that a physical, symbolic image?

A: Yes.

Q: (L) What is your definition of "image?" We have many.

A: Learning is fun, Laura, as you have repeatedly found!

Q: (L) Well, I am so hot now that I really want to know! And, how come I am always the one who gets assigned the job of figuring everything out?

A: Because you have asked for the "power" to figure out the most important issues in all of reality. And, we have been assisting you in your empowerment.

Q: (L) Image. DNA linkage. (V) "Power" was in quotes.

A: Leave that alone for now, you will know soon enough.

At this point, I was curious about the possibility that I could use acupuncture to "unlock" the secrets that had been mentioned on several prior occasions. My acupuncturist (also named Terry) had shown me a couple of points that were supposed to induce an altered state of consciousness, and I was thinking that I could combine this with self-hypnosis and do the "unlocking" myself.

Q: (L) Terry showed me a couple of acupuncture points that seem to induce an altered state. Is this, as he says, a way to open the door to the subconscious?

A: Stimulates endorphins.

Q: (L) Is there any point on the body that *can* be used to assist in opening the gate to the subconscious?

A: No such assistance is needed. First, we would like to suggest that you seek a "spin" doctor for your quest!!

Q: (L) Would a "spin" doctor be a Sufi master?

A: One example.

Q: (L) Yes. We are supposed to do several things involved with spinning.

A: Hilliard. Leedskalnin. Coral Castle.

Q: (L) Well, they are really pushing on this gravity thing.

Now, when the Cs gave the additional clues that a "spin doctor" was connected in some way to Hilliard, Leedskalnin, the builder of the Coral Castle, and the "discovery" process that was involved in that series of strange events, they were saying something that only became clear much later. You see, as it happens, Hilliard and Leedskalnin and Ark are all from the same area of the world, with the same ethnic background. During the second half of the 18th century the Kingdom of Poland included all of what we now call Lithuania, Belarus and half of contemporary Ukraine. As I was later to learn, all three of them were ethnic White Russians. All three of them had strong ties to Lithuania, Ukraine and Poland.

So I gathered all my "gravity" material together and posted it on Steve Wilson's mail list. Ark was researching gravity waves in Florence, and a correspondent discovered my post, sent it to him, and this brings us around full circle to Ark, the "spin doctor," and the "super-hypnotherapist" whose presence awakened memories and dreams and who was now, at the point where we diverted, on the "quest" with me. And it seems that this very fact – that we had joined forces – was a serious threat to someone or some thing: the Matrix.

CHAPTER 47
SEMIOTICS AND
THE CONTENT PLANE

As I have already described, the suicide of Frank's father opened a door to past-life memories of an extremely unpleasant sort. It was almost as though the old gentleman attempted to give me a warning, and the Cassiopaeans described it as a "steppingstone" or a "milestone," indicating that my "superconsciousness" was telling me something. Of course, as I also noted, based on standard teachings, put together with my emotional thinking that I needed to "save" Frank, resulted in the interpretation that I was intended to integrate these memories, forgive and forget. I created a wonderful theory that all of Frank's issues in the present life were designed to act as atonement for this former life of evil depravity. It never occurred to me that he just may have graduated in terms of the evil pathway as a result of that life and was now assigned to re-institute that control in a different way!

And how often do all human beings have warnings that they disregard, explain away, and later pay a heavy price for ignoring the messages of the higher self?

In any event, the effects of this steppingstone were interesting. As I witnessed repeated scenes in my mind of being subjected to mental, emotional and physical torture at his hands, and experienced all the emotional and psychic horror and suffering all over again, I realized that I had been born with a carryover of submissiveness to the predations of others. I could now see that in my current life, I had acquiesced to domination by both my mother and my husband, and that this was very likely a result of a carryover of this program from the previous life with Frank. Of course, I further reasoned that Frank was now in my life to atone for his sins, and was "helping" me to recover from what he had done, and this was why he was so concerned that I should escape from my marriage and the manipulations of my mother. It never occurred to me that he was intent upon helping me out of the frying pan into the fire – that he might be manipulating the removal of others from the picture so that he could resume his own psychological domination which was his own carryover from the previous life!

But, as it turned out, as I came to see this issue as something that needed work and will in order to *not* perpetuate a karmic burden of allowing myself to be negatively dominated, I also managed to become free of Frank's domination. All the clues that the Cs gave about a mission and a destiny, I am sure he interpreted as referring specifically to him and myself in some sick fantasy where he was again the master and I was the slave. It was another instance of semantic aphasia, wherein the Cs were delivering clues to me right in front of Frank, which he did not even understand because he was so lost in his wishful thinking, the Achilles heel of STS.

At the point in time when Ark found me as a result of the message posted to Steve Wilson's email discussion list, I was as close to dead mentally, psychologically, and even physically, as I had ever been. I had been stripped of everything I ever believed in, my life was basically at an end as far as I could see, and all I wanted was peace for whatever time I had left. There had been a partial revival of my interest in the world as a result of the Cs' hints about gravity waves, and I thought it would be a fairly simple matter of doing some little research, finding the clues, and voila! The Secrets of the Universe would be all laid out for mankind, and then I could die in peace and get some much needed rest. Frank, of course, was happy as a clam that I was getting a divorce. He now had the run of the house, and I was so wounded that it wouldn't have taken much to push me over the edge. Frank's plans are quite evident in the following session, and they included getting his hands on S**'s inheritance, and getting Tom French out of the picture. Nevertheless, in spite of the powerful emotional skewing that Frank was producing, the Cs were still able to utilize his agenda to get a message through to me.

May 27, 1996

Q: (L) Is this pool meant to be built here, on this property?

A: Up to you.

Q: (L) Well … (S) Had you planned on moving? (L) Well, I hadn't planned on it, but that is a strange answer. I guess I will do whatever presents itself as the right thing to do. (S) Well, you have to get the money first …

A: SV, invest now!

Q: (S) What should I invest in?

A: Market.

Q: (S) Penny stocks? Should I sell my gold?

A: No.

Q: (S) I could get advances on my credit cards … What kinds of stocks?

A: All the reference materials you need are at your disposal. Magazines, newsletters, "papers," etc.

Q: (S) I am getting an investment magazine, but I haven't really been reading it because of everything else …

A: Is "everything else" earning you money?

Q: (L) OK guys, you gave advice before that SV did not follow, can you be more specific now that her situation is changed?

A: If we did that, she would balk.

Q: (S) I would not balk!

A: Yes you would!

Q: (S) In order to go to Argus tomorrow …

A: We did not say to go to Argus tomorrow. "Now" means without unreasonable delay. The reference materials as well as networking will provide you with all the answers you need. [This was delivered *very* fast and strong!] Use your mind to find low priced stocks in the areas of conservation, environmental protection and medical, telecommunication and computer technology … Also, information processing, such as software development, etc … Precious metals and related is a good area too.

Q: (S) Well, I was brought up to not borrow money and to keep all the bills paid first … then if there is anything left over …

A: SV, for heaven's sake, why limit yourself? When you exercise your credit lines and use the capital borrowed, as long as you have a steady income, the worst that can happen is you store your money. The best that can happen is that you become wealthy … So, why sell yourself short?!?

Q: (L) Are you saying that she should extend her credit, use the borrowed capital to invest, and that she will make money?

A: Yes. Now: All three of you are uniquely oriented toward generating unearned income at a meteoric level.

Q: (L) Is this something that requires an interaction between the three of us, or is it individual?

A: Are three gold bars worth more than one? Laura! Turn over stones, sell apples, do whatever you have to do to get your computer refitted to accommodate the Internet, including the online market system, as soon as absolutely possible!!!!!!

Q: (L) Well, I am not really in a position to spend that money right now! And what do you mean to "turn over stones and sell apples?"

A: Figures of speech! Do what you have to do … take care of the mechanics, my Dear, the rest will fall into place …

Q: (L) Well, I don't know how we got off onto this thing about making money … what is all of this making of money supposed to do for us? (S) Build the pool …

A: And other … […]

Q: (L) OK. What is going on with PZ … I am just completely baffled by this behavior …

A: She thinks you are "out to lunch."

Q: (L) Well ... why?

A: Her conditioning.

Q: (L) Well, she seems to be going down the tubes fast ...

A: Yes.

Q: (L) And there is nothing I can do about it ... I feel sorry for her.

A: She hoped that you would be a money maker for her, and so, she put up with your "eccentricities ... "

Q: (L) Well, I sort of figured that out finally.

A: Beware! Tom French has a similar thought pattern!

Q: (L) I have been thinking that I ought to write to Tom and ask him to just write me *out* of the whole project ...

A: Suggest you not waste "time" on your suggestion, and make certain it includes all others.

Q: (L) What suggestion? Suggest that I not waste time in contacting Tom?

A: Yes.

Q: (L) Then I will just e-mail him ...

A: And.

Q: (L) What do you mean by "include all others?"

A: Who else has Tom French met through you?

Obviously, the Universe had other plans. We notice that the Cs sent an urgent message in the midst of Frank's favorite subject: stock market investing which he firmly believed would make him rich if he could only get his hands on some money to invest with. The Cs said: "Laura! Turn over stones, sell apples, do whatever you have to do to get your computer refitted to accommodate the Internet, including the online market system, as soon as absolutely possible!!!!!! ... Do what you have to do ... take care of the mechanics, my Dear, the rest will fall into place ..."

Well, since Frank was so taken with the idea of the stock market and being in control of an investment portfolio in real time via the Internet, he persuaded S** to pay for the computer upgrade that made it possible for me to do more than just run a mail program. So we see how the Cs utilized Frank's greed and semantic aphasia to get me online which enabled Ark and me to connect exactly 40 days later.

The initial interaction with Ark was similar in some ways to the interaction with Frank's dad – it opened a huge door in my psyche, and again I began to remember. But it was quite different in flavor, texture and context. All of the memories of lifetimes with Ark centered around the efforts of outside agents to separate us from each other, to make us suffer for our attempts to be together, and repeating scenarios of being horribly and brutally killed for seeking to work together for the betterment and freedom of others. Hopefully, such lessons will help us to avoid similar traps in this life, though it will become clear that the same types of forces have been activated against us.

There was a strange byproduct of this remembering and integration: I began to cry on that first day of the connection with Ark, and cried almost daily for the next year and a half. It was as though an ocean of grief was locked up inside and every single instance of suffering had to be re-experienced and fully mourned in order to integrate it. As a person who seldom cried, who had always had some measure of control over emotions, this inability to stop this flow of soul-deep grief was disconcerting to say the least. But there was another interesting side-effect of this releasing of the waters of life in such copious production of tears: my eyes began to heal.

But I wasn't the only one who was "remembering." This "superhypnotherapist" action of the awakened superconsciousness had also apparently been activated for Ark as well. I am going to skip all the strange instances where this sort of thing manifested with each of us, simultaneously, on opposite sides of the Atlantic for the present. Suffice it to say that these incidents included visions, bilocation, synchronized dreams; effectively, so much strange activation of the inner psyche that Ark once wrote that if we hadn't lived through these experiences, and someone else had recounted them, we wouldn't have believed it.

Ark's physical presence was also obviously very important in the unlocking-of-secrets process. And it wasn't just the dreams that were stimulated, and the way he was able to assist me in bringing information up, it was also his uncanny ability to select books he thought I might be interested in reading. One of the very first he bought for me contained the key to the "3/5 code" that the Cassiopaeans had brought up on 11-11-95 in response to my questions about the true esoteric significance of the number 33. This book, John Gribbin's *In Search of the Double Helix*, about the interface between quantum physics and genetics, actually had a sufficient number of code words given by the Cs that my hair stood up while I was reading it!

When we noticed the strange upsurge in visitors to our little site on the day before the Hale Bopp suicides, and found that one of the repeat visitors was an organization that did genetics research, and the later discovery of the same site while doing the web search on the word "Brana," we really began to get the idea that the Universe was pointing us in the direction of some deep research into genetics.

So it was that the period of research in Gainesville, and Ark's presence had opened a huge door and I could barely keep up with the flow of ideas and information that flooded into me. The "Three Dominoes

Dream" led to a startling series of discoveries which I have yet to chronicle, though much of the information is included in *Secret History*, even if without the background of how the Cs gave the hints that I followed, and when I hit a snag, how they would offer a couple more hints that would clarify the sticking point.

Reading the transcripts directly you may be able to see some of these things from an external point of view, but without this background, you can have very little idea of what is behind the questions, or what was discovered between sessions. It is rather like watching a person who is reading hundreds of books from a distance. You can see them devouring the material on the page, and once in awhile they will talk about one or another point that they are reading, but for the most part, the drama between the reader and the book is inaccessible.

It is, of course, possible for an individual who is reading to attempt to follow the same pathway, and make the same discoveries, but not terribly likely. Because, in point of fact, many of the keys were provided by Ark who now made books and journals and papers available to me in unlimited supply. As he worked through the summer in the universities in Bielefeld, at Dijon, Gottingen, and Florence, it seemed that he was always ideally situated to search the libraries for exactly what I needed when a question arose. The synchronicities between his discoveries as he searched for clues, and my own activity thousands of miles away, aren't always recorded in the transcripts, but are preserved in a series of email exchanges and letters that amount, at the present time, to somewhere around three thousand pages of material that we hope to arrange, edit, and publish at the proper time. This material, correlated to the transcripts is an incredible document of confirmation of not only the clues themselves, but the wisdom of giving the clues as they were delivered: in code.

In some instances, these clues consisted of the use of specific words or phrases that were part of a private discussion between Ark and myself, wherein a certain meaning had already been explored and established, and the Cs would either confirm or expand that meaning by their comments which could seem, to the outside viewer, to be either meaningless, excessively cryptic, or even construed to mean something else. The Cs made it very clear that they used words in a certain way, and that they put in quotes the words that it would help us to further examine. I have an entire notebook full of these word clues and my research findings.

But this story is about the Matrix dynamics, and not the research itself, so except for those issues that will be important in this recapitulation, I won't go into extensive detail on all of the work we were doing. Suffice it to say, while Ark and I were working on gathering the clues pretty much every day, all day, for the next few years, Frank was merely showing up about once a week for a session, and generally managed to do as little as possible even when I repeatedly asked him for assistance. On one occasion I handed him a printed copy of the transcripts and asked him to just go over it in his spare time and highlight or circle the spelling or typographical errors so that I could go in and correct them. He wouldn't even do that. So, because of the fact that Frank never participated in any research, any of the work of the mission, he was completely in the dark when the Cs communicated and remains so to this day.

Semiotics is the study of language or any other symbol system that conveys meaning. The Bible tells us that God spoke before all things, and in this way he created both heaven and earth. It was from the Divine Word that the Cosmos came into being.

One of the great themes of esoterica is that of the alphabet giver and namer of things. Adam is, of course, the one we think of when we think of the giving of names to things. In terms of the study of semiotics, the question is: did he name things based on what they *were*, in *essence*, or did he simply create a convention, and arbitrarily name them whatever appealed to him?

This is an important issue because conveying things in language is very much like the game in which one person whispers something to another, and on down a line of people, and at the end, the last person announces what was said, and it often bears no relationship whatsoever to the original statement. Being able to communicate the *true* meaning of something is of paramount importance not only in terms of the thing being said remaining as clear and undefiled as possible, but also in terms of the rapport between the speaker and the listener.

According to the Pythagoreans, the true language was mathematics, and sounds were simply a transformation of mathematical principles into an exchange medium. In this sense, the sound vibration of a word had a mathematical nature that could convey something much higher than just the ordinary understanding of the world as it applied to objects in our reality.

But this leads to a problem because there are many languages, and they utilize sounds in different ways, which then leads to the question of which language is the one that truly conveys the deepest, or widest meaning of a word?

The theories of semiotics propose that there are two levels, or planes of articulation. At the level of any given language, such as Greek, English, Chinese, or whatever, there is what they call the expression plane that consists of a lexicon, a phonology and syntax. In other words, the expression plane is the selection of words that belong to that language, the sounds that the selection of words produce, and the way they are arranged to convey meaning. That is the first plane. The second plane is called the content plane. This is the array of concepts that the language is capable of expressing. This last is rather important because, as we have all heard at least once in our lives, Eskimos have many words for snow while people who do not live in an environment where snow and ice are the dominant features, may only have one or two words for these phenomena.

So it is that the content plane of a language becomes crucial to what can be discussed in that language. Whatever a group of people experience the most becomes part of their awareness, and thus the content plane of their language is accordingly modified. In order for the sounds of speech to be meaningful, the words formed out of these sounds must have a meaning associated with them. In other words, the sounds relate to the *content*.

This brings us back to the example of the sea slug in which a kind of associative learning could take place when a mild shock was delivered with the puff of water. The slug learned to associate the puff with the shock and when the puff came alone, the slug withdrew. For the slug, the semiotic content of the puff of water was pain. Words are similarly learned. And, as we have also discussed, the pyramidal neurons in the Ammon's horn gather the input of other sensory neurons and fire if two separate inputs arrive at the same time. Once fired, it is easier to fire by one of the two inputs that originally fired it, but not by another input. In this way, we also learn the meanings of words; *we establish the content continuum of our understanding.*

The content continuum represents the Universe or reality to which our words relate as we are capable of conceiving it. Thinking about this factor, we begin to get a glimmer of the idea that our ability to associate words, to derive deeper and broader or multilevel meaning from them in our process of understanding, is directly related to how we, ourselves, interact with the cosmos.

The words we use, individually and collectively, and the way we use them, are very deep clues to our perspective and comprehension of the Universe. Our words and the way we use them reveal the totality of our experiences – mental and physical and emotional – our sensations, perceptions, abstractions and so forth. Keeping in mind, of course, that no purely verbal system ever achieves total communication, how do you express in words the scent of a rose? We are always required to supplement words with helpers, which may include expressive gestures, or even producing a metaphoric example, or finding a basis of comparison to convey meaning. Nevertheless, in our reality, language and words are clearly divine, and are the rungs on which we may climb to the Stars.

As noted in the example of Eskimos and snow, there are experiences recognized by other cultures and capable of being expressed in their languages, which we neither recognize nor can we express. The same problem poses an even greater difficulty when we consider realms of pure thought, or the hyperdimensional reality in which our reality is embedded. In dreams we revert to using words in the universal language, a content continuum wherein the sound is still connected to the object it designates. This is a clue to the phonetic cabala, of which Fulcanelli speaks. This is also the language into which I was initiated by the Cassiopaeans.

As the Cs dropped word clues and encouraged me to search for the mosaic meaning, I discovered many amazing things. At one point, I stumbled on a little book by a gentleman named Abraham Abehsera. He points out that there seem to be two universal dictionaries in which words from all languages are grouped according to their meanings (synonyms) and sounds (homonyms). That is to say, whenever the same or a similar sound is given to different objects in two or more languages, a precise relationship between these objects is being indicated by the Universal language. He theorized that the sum total of languages forms a puzzle in which the image – the true meaning – may only be recovered through reassembling words having the same sound.

> The fact that in English, for instance, morning and mourning have the same sound could have been just a coincidence. When German and English both reproduce this coincidence by using the same sound to say *morgen* (morning) and morgue (chamber where the dead are laid), Hebrew the same group of consonants BQR, to say morning and tomb, and Chinese the same syllable *mu*, to say evening and tomb, we may legitimately ask what lies behind this repetition. What have morning and evening time to do with mourning, tomb and morgue? (Abehsera 1991)

Abehsera then establishes a mathematical model for comparing words, or a "four language unit" that suggests a deep common experience between a certain period of time and death-related themes. And, as it happens, hundreds of other sound-relationships develop these themes, such as dream and drama, *traum* (German for dream), trauma, bed, bad, *mita* in Hebrew which means both death and bed, and so on. Words then *become the mode of access* to the right half of our brain as opposed to the flat and precise use of words typical of the left brain. Speech can then become a synthesis of the "universal content continuum" by a study of the "expression plane."

There are, of course, many so-called "one-way words" that may seem to be sharply defined, and necessarily so for the purpose of describing events in our world. But when dealing with what are called "state vectors" in physics, or all possible events given a certain set of parameters, the phonetic cabala is a similar state vector to thinking multi-dimensionally. Like pieces of a puzzle, words have been inextricably interwoven into our reality since the dawn of human history. To find the living unity behind language, without negating diversity, is like assembling a body with all its different parts, each of which does different things, and without one of which, the body would be lacking. The greater the number of words for any given object, the more precise a definition can be made about it in terms of the content continuum. If there are a thousand ways to say apple, by knowing all the associations, we can access that higher realm of thought from whence the idea of an apple has a deeper meaning for man. In this sense, all languages are necessary because they are all complementary. They all tell us about the extraordinary wealth and diversity and limitless possibilities of the Universe in which we exist. What is more, *such study of words enables us to interact dynamically with the surrounding reality itself.* Word studies develop hyperdimensional awareness which binds us to higher realities.

For the reader to simply read the Cassiopaean Transcripts and to assume that they have received the information that was intended to be conveyed; to read any part of it and assume that one has a grasp of a principle, or that it means this or that in a one-way sort of context, is to miss the important process. The process of initiation consisted, in part, of the encouragement of the creation of a far vaster system of associations than normally prevails, most especially among those who have followed rigid scholastic or ritualized programs. By expanding the associative memory, the very practical result is that synaptic relationships are created in the Ammon's Horn, and they are sensitized to perceive the reality in a multidimensional way. At another level, expanding the associations of things that occur together in time, with other things that do likewise, *the perception of time changes fundamentally.* And we begin to realize why the alchemist Fulcanelli insisted that word studies were the key to unlocking the great secrets.

June 21, 1997

Q: Well, I think that a *huge* key is in the tracking of the languages …

A: The roots of all languages are identical …

Q: What do you mean?

A: Your origin.

Q: You mean Atlantis?

A: Is that your origin?

Q: You mean Orion?

A: Interesting the word root similarity, yes?

Q. Well, the word root similarities of a *lot* of things are *very* interesting! It is *amazing* the things I have discovered by tracking word roots …

A: The architects of your languages left clues aplenty.

It was from these word studies as well as the above remark that I began to realize that the process of expanding associations of words was literally *the process of learning the higher-density language.* And it most certainly was not, as some suppose, a process of memetics or "deriving new meanings" from word associations. Oh no! It was the process of assembling words into mosaic structures through which the mind could access the *original meaning* that was inherent in the structure. It was a process of restoration of the original language of supernatural wisdom that was present in mankind before the Fall. Studying words and myths is a process of archaeologically excavating a marvelously ancient, pre-historic, almost extinct parent language – the language of the gods.

This process began when Ark arrived. It received a major jump start with the "Three Dominoes" dream. And the dreams continued to bring up the keys. On the night of April 15-16, eight days after Ark had returned to Poland, I had a dream. I wrote as soon as I awakened:

Date sent: Wed, 16 Apr 97 16:07:47

To: ajad@physik...."

Had a dream about the Frankenstein monster as depicted on the funny movie ... he was drinking whiskey and mowing the grass!!!! It was funny! And when he was done, he hid his whiskey bottle next to another bottle, on a ledge over a window under the eaves of the roof of a bank!!! He told me "I hide it in plain view so no one will find it. This way, after many centuries, I will return and retrieve it."

The reference to the funny movie we had watched just before Ark had left was *Young Frankenstein,* one of my favorites. The symbolism of Frankenstein was almost transparent: putting a body together from different parts, reassembling clues. And as we began to assemble the clues, the forces of the Matrix heaved into action like a great juggernaut of destruction. My book *Secret History* contains the results of putting together these clues. Here's what I wrote Ark at the time:

Date sent: Thu, 24 Apr 97 06:39:36

[...] Perseus was the slayer of Medusa ... and Medusa was mentioned by Cs in the 11-11-95 session about prime numbers and the phi and 3-5 sequence.

Not only that, but Perseus was the son of Zeus and Danae ... And it was while watching the Perseid meteor shower that the UFO came over the pool ... And Perseus married Andromeda, the daughter of Cassiopaea, after rescuing her from a SEA monster ...

And this brings me around to my funny Frankenstein dream that is having so much meaning in the past week or so. He was mowing. i.e. mowing down opposition. Making a "level playing field. "And he was drinking whiskey while he was doing it. And telling me that this was the special fuel that made him able to mow in such a powerful way. That fuel was needed for him as much as for the mower itself.

Okay, then he put the still over half-full bottle away on the ledge over a window, next to a bottle of vodka, and indicated with a big smile that he was putting it there so he could get it when he "came back to mow again." It was implied that it would be safe and no one would know it was there.... because it was hidden so obviously in the open. And the building that the window was in, the ledge was on, was a bank. And I understood that the period of time was very long and this coming back meant reincarnation and the two liquids were meant to be poured together...

Okay, a few days ago I described money in terms of energy, so that was already in my mind when I had the dream. Whiskey is a Scots-Irish invention, and Vodka is Russian.

The Caucasus Mountains are in Russia. This is considered to be the origin of the Celts. The two places where the Celtic influence was, and may be still, archaeologically strongest were along the Baltic coast and in the Wales...

So, the sources of "life" and "power for mowing" are symbolized by these two items. These two places are represented by these two bottles of liquor. What is liquor often called? Aqua Vitae.

And, that they are stored "in the open," in plain view, which makes them obscure means what? "The secret is hid in plain sight."

And why the bank? Well, it was implied in the dream that the bank was a Swiss one. They are considered to be the "bankers of the world."

And, Switzerland is one of the areas were the Celts developed in Europe for a long time before they began to move outward. They cremated their dead, which was VERY different. They did not believe in the resurrection of the already used body, they believed in getting a new one via reincarnation. This was a far more elegant and abstract idea than any ever held by the Egyptians.

But, the liquor was different from the money in energy terms. What was in the bank was money. It may have just been to symbolize Switzerland, or it may have another meaning having to do with money. But what?

So, trying to understand if there is more to this dream is presently on my mind.

In addition, I think this relates to the issue of prime numbers, "dwellings" of the mystics, primeco, prime rib and primary elections. It has to do with the DNA because that is the "dwelling" of the soul. The more DNA a person has activated, the more of the soul energy is available. The "cellular phone company" refers to the neuron transmission modes and the "orgone" energy and the positive states as we have already discussed. So, the "dwelling" relates to the idea that the neurons are activated in the correct way, which is interrelated with the activation of the DNA, which then causes the suppressor genes to "unplug" because there is "communication" at the "cellular" level. This communication, this neuron stimulation that is similar to "voting," this activation of DNA then activates "power" centers which are available to those with the proper genes to have them.

The 3-5 sequence was a "marker" for recognition as was the phi spiral... and there may yet be MORE to these. But, the phi spiral may also be related to the double helix configuration of the DNA... the clue about phosphorous was related to the phosphate chain which is the 3-5 sequence.

And, the remark that too much phosphorous could make a person "spontaneously combust" would mean that the person had become super-conducting ... So, we can think that a certain amount of additional phosphorous might be useful.

And then we have the Percy-Perseus connection and something else that I thought of...

Did you know that a fellow named Nicolas Poussin painted a famous picture entitled "Et in Arcadia Ego?" I was giving it a lot of thought when you first wrote, which is why it seemed so strange that your name is Arkadia. [...]

On May 1st, 1997, I wrote to Ark:

Date sent: Thu, 01 May 97 06:41:19

On the way home, I had a thought.... I was thinking about the 98% of DNA that isn't used. Then I was thinking about the fact that the pancreas completely replaces itself every 24 hours. And the lining of the stomach every 8 hours or so... And, every cell has the exact same set of DNA as every other one... But, each one replicates only it's own kind of cell....

Now, the C's have said that the 4th density STS wanted to create a "breeding ground" for the reintroduction of the Nephilim. And that a special gene was introduced into the Jews, starting with a "symbolic" Abraham who was told he would be the "father of many nations." The idea being that the Jews were supposed to mix with the other races because they carried a gene that prevented absorption of the Nephilim genes.

But, the bad guys came along and twisted this "specialness" of the Jews around and used it to convince them that they should keep their genes to themselves... made them feel "exclusive." Old Yahweh and Jehovah were probably 4th density STS guys.

So, the bad guys try throughout history to eliminate the Jews. Hitler almost does it, and even starts the project for the STS in a big way. The "Master Race."

So, here we are... they failed with Hitler... to create the "breeding ground" for the Nephilim. So, they have become more subversive...moving back and forth in time, and perhaps even manipulating it to some extent, they have created "bloodlines" so that a LOT of people are carrying these Nephilim genes.

Now, what turns on genes and turns them off? Neurotransmitters and hormones and maybe other factors.

What stimulates hormones?

It has been demonstrated that hormones can be stimulated by "frequencies," particularly ELF. (The Navy did some strange tests that I read about.)

With the right hormone, thinking runs amok – and then there are combinations of hormones or neurotransmitters.

Okay, what if people get abducted to implant a device that will pick up a signal and stimulate production of a specific hormone? Or a thought pattern? Or, what if genes themselves respond to frequency?

Now, this is being done by getting a LOT of people to turn their free will over, thinking they are going to get saved. Through deception etc... But, on the other hand, those who turn over their free will are simply at that point where that is what they do. Eventually they will decide they don't like it or they will contract completely for a long time until they have had enough of that... then they will start to grow.

Now, we also have been told that the 4th density STS also want new bodies for themselves because theirs no longer satisfy them. And that they want to lock the earth into 3rd density where it is easier to control... because on 4th density, it is a "level playing field..."

But, as we well know, STS simply do not see anything that they do not wish to see.

So, they are merrily abducting and implanting, the plan being to TURN ON THE NEPHILIM GENES at a certain point.

What if HAARP is being built for this purpose?

Just imagine .... 98% vs 2%. Who knows what that 98% could do. Especially if there is no Jewish suppressor gene.

Okay, genes can be turned on and off in other ways too, via freewill. And the energies of the coming wave can be utilized in a POSITIVE way also. The good guys can transform also. The only thing is, they have to do it themselves. (With help that is ASKED for...) And, it would certainly help to have the Jewish gene....

So, this is what I thought, going back to the idea that the pancreas can replace itself every 24 hours and the lining of the stomach completely replaces itself about every 8 hours – what IF a signal is broadcast that turns on a "master gene" which begins a "transformation" process that is quite literally similar to the transformation of a man into a werewolf in the movies? In other words, what if literal, material transformation of the physical body in terms of just everything about the body, could be coded into the DNA??? If the stomach lining can replace itself every eight hours, if the pancreas can replace itself every 24 hours, considering the 98 percent of DNA that we don't know anything about at all, there is NO REASON that an entire human body could not be drastically changed in fundamental ways in a period of hours, or days at most!

Well, of course, when that thought occurred to me, I nearly had a heart attack!!

But it also means that it is possible for the "good guys" to transform also!

[...]

But, there is a LOT of evidence and stories referring to a central mystery, and to specifics like severed heads, talking heads and skulls, blood as a substance and a symbol, alchemical wonders and, most importantly, some sort of super-secret group of elders or initiates that guide the destiny of the planet. This central mystery is a LOT older than the Christ legend, because the stories in the Gospels were merely the Osirian legends with the names changed just as the Grail stories were built upon the foundation of Bran the Blessed.

327

Then there is the claim of Lincoln et al claim that there is a secret order that predates other secret orders [...] ITS DECLARED OBJECTIVE IS TO GUARD THE LINEAL DESCENDANTS OF CHRIST.

Which may not be too far off... It just isn't who they think it is, and the Priory of Sion is a red herring.

From the Cassiopaeans: Oct. 5, 1994

Q: Did Jesus have children?

A: Yes.

Q: How many?

A: Three.

Q: Is that, as some people claim, the true meaning of the search for the Holy Grail, that it is not a cup, but the Sang Real, or holy blood line?

A: Yes.

Q: Are there any descendants of Jesus living today?

A: 364,142

Oct. 16, 1994

Q: I would like to know the origin of the Freemasons?

A: The "Osirians.

Q: Can you tell us when the original freemasons formed as a society?

A: 5633 B.C.

Q: Is Freemasonry, as it is practiced today, the same as then?

A: 33rd degree, yes.

Q: Is this an organization with a plan to take over and rule the world via the "New World Order?"

A: Not exactly.

Q: What is their focus?

A: They are overseers.

Q: Overseers of what?

A: The Status of Quorum.

Q: What is the Quorum?

A: Deeper knowledge organization. Totally secret to your kind as of yet. This is very important with regard to your future.

Q: In what way?

A: Changes.

Q: Changes to us personally?

A: Partly. Earth Changes also.

Q: What is the relationship between the Quorum and the Cassiopaeans?

A: They communicate with us regularly. [...]

And then, of course, there were a LOT of other clues that simply blew my mind. But, I will have to do a LOT more work to get it organized so that they can be read sequentially.

What do you think? It is a crazy idea, but it all fits. Itis the most mind boggling series of connections imaginable.

After I had this thought about "turning on" the Nephilim genes, I started to wonder exactly what that would mean... And, by the same token, what would it mean if WE could turn on some specific HELPFUL genes???

So, I think I have found Medusa. Only now we have to figure out how to cut off her head!!!!

From the time Ark came in February of 1997, the session frequency was greatly reduced. There were several reasons for this. One of the first reasons was the fact that the Cs themselves suggested numerous times that I ought to read what had already been delivered already more carefully, contemplate, study and research on my own. As the research progressed, I began to perceive things differently. One of the things I perceived was exactly what they suggested: that I needed to do much more work on my own.

Another factor was that Terry and Jan were becoming quite irritated with Frank's arrogance, control games, and manipulation. Terry kept telling me that Frank was not the channel, and he wanted to experiment without Frank. I couldn't bring myself to agree which probably made the two of them irritated with me. I was having some cognitive dissonance of major proportions about this because on the one hand, I was committed to helping Frank, but on the other hand, I couldn't deny my observations. I flipped and flopped on this issue like a fish on the dock.

Terry and Jan were excusing themselves from many sessions, and I was spending a lot of time doing research and keeping up with Ark's travels. Frank, meanwhile, was complaining all the time that he was sick or tired from the rigors of his telemarketing job. I certainly had a lot of sympathy because that kind of work is soul killing.

At several points Ark and I offered our support to Frank if he would go back to college to get his degree. He was such a gifted mimic and "incidental linguist" that we were sure that he could have a great career as a professional linguist or translator. Frank flatly refused. He was not going to be embarrassed by going to college at his age!

Meanwhile, Frank began to play some heavy duty games with me. Because of the time difference between the U.S. and Europe, I wanted to adjust my schedule so as to be up and about during the times of the day when Ark and I could communicate either by email or phone. Frank seemed to be equally determined that I should operate on his schedule. He started pushing the envelope on this issue, arriving later and later on the nights we had sessions, making it impossible for us to get started at a reasonable hour so that I could get to bed and be up in time for a few hours with Ark. On a few occasions, I simply announced when he arrived that it was too late to have a session, we would chat for a short time, and then seeing that I really meant it, he would yawn and go home. I noticed that my energy was increasing and Frank's was diminishing. He was also showing serious signs of jealousy that there were things I shared with Ark that I did not share with him. He would periodically try to plant seeds of dissent by suggesting I was being "controlled" by Ark, simply because I wanted to spend as much time with him as possible – considering the fact that it was so little, and he was so far away.

All of these confusing issues brought me back to the subject of just how our interactions with others might make us vulnerable to attack. What was the significance of agents and moles and who might be the mole in the group, and did it even matter? At one point, V** had been pronounced to be a mole. At another point, several other individuals whom Frank didn't like were also pronounced to be moles. Just who was on first here? I needed to know! A visit from my brother gave me the opportunity I needed to ask these questions. We discussed the matter and agreed before Frank arrived that we would use my brother's situation as the question model. He did, indeed, want information about his own concerns, but we agreed that I could slip in a question or two about Frank. But before we moved to that issue, I wanted to cover the issue of monitoring and energy exchange in a more open way to see what would come out.

May 3, 1997

Q: I have quite a number of questions this evening. The first one is: is it possible for a person to be used as a monitor, to monitor other people's activities through their eyes and ears?

A: Possible, but hardly necessary.

Q: You once said that PZ was like a monitor, that wherever she went, she monitored aural frequencies for whoever had put the implant into her. Was this an unusual situation?

A: Most likely.

Q: Last week we did not have a session, but went through the notes I have been making since I was in Gainesville. Frank became very tired and went home. I was not tired. Usually, Frank is not tired, and I am the one that is exhausted. I would like to ask about this. Is there some sort of energy exchange that takes place during channeling?

A: Not in that way.

Q: Well, both Terry and Jan commented on this, and I would like to know if there is any relationship of this reversal to the fact that we did not do a session?

A: Terry and Jan's comments in this case should be viewed with caution, as they may be nebulous in their intent.

Q: When you say nebulous ... my perception was that they wanted to develop a separate channel, as before.

A: They wanted to pursue their own idea of casting doubts upon Frank.

Q: Well, not only was that going on, but I was sharing the information that I had gathered in response to clues given in the material, and I had the impression that it was not interesting to them. Yet, I thought that the fact that clues in the material had led to such discoveries was extremely important ...

A: Interesting to some includes only that which casts the spotlight upon themselves.

In this last question above, the term "them" was employed deliberately with the intent of inquiring about Frank, since, as it happens, *it did not apply to Terry and Jan* who were, in fact, most interested in the material. Frank, however, *didn't know that* since he had left early and was not present for our later discussion. In this way, I was able to ask about Frank himself. Next, I began my approach to the question through the medium of asking about my brother.

Q: Reading through the session of May 23, last year, when Tom was also here, and the issue of his being in O'Brien was addressed, you asked who had begged him to stay there, then there was a remark about an EM vector. The way I understood it is that a person can be an EM vector. Is that possible?

A: Vector means focuser of direction.

Q: Could that mean that EM waves can be vectored by a human being simply by their presence? I also noticed that several of us have been involved with persons and relationships that seem designed to confuse, defuse, and otherwise distort our learning, as well as drain our energy. Basically, keeping us so stressed that we cannot fulfill our potential. Is there some significance to this observation?

A: That is elementary, my dear Knight!

Q: One of the things I have learned is that these individuals seem to attach via some sort of psychic hook that enters through our reactions of pity. Can you comment on the nature of pity?

A: Pity those who pity.

Q: But, the ones who are being pitied, who generate sensations of pity, do not really pity anybody but themselves.

A: Yes ... ?

Q: Then, is it true as my son said, when you give pity, when you send love and light to those in darkness, or those who complain and want to be "saved" without effort on their own part, when you are kind in the face of abuse and manipulation, that you essentially are giving power to their further disintegration, or contraction into self-ishness? That you are powering their descent into STS?

A: You know the answer!

Q: Yes. I have seen it over and over again. Were the individuals in our lives selected for the extremely subtle nature of their abilities to evoke pity, or were we programmed to respond to pity so that we were blind to something that was obvious to other people?

A: Neither. You were selected to interact with those who would trigger a hypnotic response that would ultimately lead to a drain of energy.

Q: (T) Well, it is a fact, because my energy is sure drained. (L) What is the purpose of this draining of energy?

A: What do you think?

Q: (T) So you can't concentrate or do anything. You can't get anywhere with anything.

A: Or, at least not the important things.

Q: (T) Is that why my concentration is so low?

A: Yes.

Q: (T) Is L a robot type?

A: You are dealing with a no-win situation!!

Q: It is a no win situation …

A: As you know.

Q: (T) So, if I don't get out, I will just keep going down. Is it the area or the person?

A: Both. One is wrapped within the other.

Q: (L) Why is it that it seems to be one of the primary things about us that prevents us from acting against such situations, is our fear of hurting another person? That was the chief thing that kept me in my marriage for so long. And, only when I knew that it was hurting the kids more to stay, did I have the power to get out. Why are we so afraid of hurting someone's feelings if they are hurting us?

A: Not correct concept. You do not need to "act against them," you need to act in favor of your destiny.

Q: But, when you do that, these persons make you so completely miserable that there seems to be no other choice but a parting of the ways.

A: Yes, but that is not "acting against." Quite the contrary. In fact, remember, it takes two to tango, and if you are both tangoing when the dance hall bursts into flames, you both get burned!!!

Q: Why is it that when one tries to extricate from such a "tango," why is there is such violent resistance to letting you go when it is obvious, clearly obvious, that they do not have any feeling for you as a human being?

A: It is not "they." We are talking about conduits of attack.

Q: What is it that makes them susceptible to becoming conduits of attack?

A: All STS are candidates for this. There are only about 6 billion of you though.

Q: OK, all people can be conduits of attack. (L) Would just coming down and working with us on Saturdays, on a regular basis, help him to get his concentration back?

A: Making the necessary changes would.

The intent of this last question was to determine if channeling with the group was actually something that was helping Frank. The answer was somewhat ambiguous to me. What did "making the necessary changes" mean? Even though the Cs were giving pretty definitive and clear answers that would have suggested to me that Frank was definitely running the program, the pity-me thing and all that, this last remark gave me the straw to hang onto, allowing me to convince myself that it was a simple matter of Frank making the necessary changes, that he would win that battle with the darkness, and everything would be fine.

Q: Is it true that being in the presence of such people, that one is under the influence of an energy, an emanation from them physically, that befuddles the mind and makes it almost impossible to think one's way out of the situation?

A: It is the draining of energy that befuddles the mind.

Q: Where does this energy drain to?

A: 4th-density STS.

Q: They drain our energy from us and fourth-density STS harvests it from them?

A: "They" do nothing!!!! 4th-density STS does it all through them!

Q: (T) Well, I would like to know what is it in us that makes us attracted to such people.

A: It was the idea of 4th-density STS.

Q: That means that they can control your thoughts and emotions, put ideas into your head, and you think it is a good idea to "save" someone. You don't know. It is taught in our religions and culture to give until it hurts, and, in fact, to give because it hurts. The whole situation is designed and controlled from another level. Any further comment on this subject?

A: Once you have truly learned the program, just plug it in.

Q: I guess once you have truly learned what is being said here, just plug it in …

A: No. We mean that all you have to do is learn the patterns of behavior, the subtle signs, and you will always have the ability of avoiding it. Your own as well as others.

Q: So, once you have learned the program from this person, you will be able to avoid getting into another, similar one. (T) But, I should have learned it from H. I did the same thing twice. (L) Well, when you are wounded, it is hard to see clearly.

A: The signs were present, but you did not read them.

Q: You ignored it.

A: No, he did not yet know the program. Anticipate not!

Q: I guess that means that when you are thinking that you can change another person, or that changing something about what you are doing naturally will help them, you are anticipating.

A: Or that it would be different than it turned out to be.

Of course, all of the above was again interpreted by me as justification to continue to work with Frank. Don't even ask how I managed to distort it that way. I decided that since I was "learning the program" I could deal with it effectively. I could prevent Frank from draining my energy. Ark and I had discussed the growing problem with Frank's jealousy, and he did not want me to do anything to rock the boat until he was back in the States. He was sure that we would be able to reassure Frank that he had a place in our lives and that we could all work together.

Q: (L to T) Well, you knew that there was a lot wrong in the beginning, but you thought that it would be different. [At this point, I shifted to another subject that was on my mind. Surprisingly, the Cs continued to relate it to the issue of "attack."] Ark's mother is sick. Will she be better soon?

A: Wait and see.

Q: He is carrying a very heavy burden just now, and I am concerned for him.

A: Does this surprise you? Unfortunately, Ark still does not completely know this program.

Q: Are you suggesting that this sickness of his mother's has been caused from fourth-density STS?

A: Lesson number 1: Always expect attack. Lesson number 2: Know the modes of same. Lesson number 3: Know how to counteract same.

Q: When a person is sick, old and one's mother … the only thing to do is take care of it. But, I guess that it is true that anything that tends to cause interference in doing what one is here to do could be considered attack. Whether it is your mother being sick, or your kid falling off a bicycle and breaking his arm. It is all related to lack of vigilance on the part of the one who is the conduit of attack?

A: When you are under attack, expect the unexpected, if it is going to cause problems …

Q: So, if there is something that can cause problems, expect it to happen.

A: But, if you expect it, you learn how to "head it off," thus neutralizing it. This is called vigilance, which is rooted in knowledge. And, what does knowledge do?

Q: Protects! Is there anything I can do to help?

A: How so?

Q: Well, I don't know. I guess that a person just has to come to the full realization that virtually everything that happens on the planet – no exceptions – is a symbol of some interaction of STS versus STO energy at higher levels.

A: Yes, and that is not as of yet realized. It must be part of a natural learning process.

Q: Well, I guess that all of us tend to keep one or another area sacrosanct and think that it is not subject to attack, or that we can use logic and third-density thinking to explain it. Until a person realizes that attack can come through even one's self, wives and husbands, children and parents, friends, virtually *anybody* – *nobody* is exempt.

A: The block is a lack of faith in the concept. Remember, when one has been indoctrinated by religion, culture and/or science, they are predisposed to view all things in the sense of the measurable physical reality exclusively.

Q: Well, in Ark's case, is something going to happen for him that will give him a view under the surface, so to speak?

A: Please do not anticipate. This is a logjam of "quantum" proportions.

Q: Well, I think he is cured of thinking that certain people can be helped.

A: But he is not cured of his lack of faith in the reality of non-physical attack.

Q: Speaking of non-physical attack, I went through some things this morning that were rather unpleasant. I later discovered that at the same time I was experiencing this, there was communication from the Brana woman. Is there a connection between his correspondence with her and my feeling that an elephant is sitting on my chest? When this happens, I actually feel like my spirit is being compressed in a painful way. Is there a relationship between this and the Brana person.

A: Maybe.

Q: Is there any relationship between the Brana correspondence and the fact that Jim also wrote to him and JW, the spook, called me today?

A: Maybe.

Q: Is there any relationship between all of these portals of attack, and the things I have been discovering in the past week or so?

A: Maybe.

Q: Can you tell me anything about this at all?

A: If it does not need to be answered, that may mean that it has already been answered, simply because, though you have much still to learn, you have learned so much already, my dear. And, on that note, goodnight.

As the reader now notes, the issue with Sue Brana continued to run in the background. In the above session, I was trying to deal strictly with the issue of draining of energy or vectoring of direction by an individual who was physically close to the target. But a vague idea that some sort of subtle filament-like threads of consciousness could be strung between individuals like a network, and that this could be used to drain energy, was forming in my mind. I had noticed that shortly *before* each incident when Ark wrote to me that he had received communication from several individuals, including Sue Brana, I would go through a peculiar experience of feeling compressed and short of breath and even somewhat confused. After several such experiences, I was prompted to ask the above questions about this.

As I thought about it more, and observed things, I realized that when two people have a strong psychic or psychological bond, whatever happens to one of them, affects the other. It may or may not be noticed, depending upon sensitivity. In these instances, I was definitely experiencing sensitivity to those things which drained Ark, even if he wasn't paying a lot of attention to it.

I wrote to Ark and suggested that some of these people were like psychic vampires and that maybe he ought to just stop "dancing" with them since it seemed to be draining me. He thought I was being a little bit overreactive. But all I could go by was what I observed and felt and then the ongoing confirmation that something of this sort was going on. I began to realize that it was not just who you associate with that can make you vulnerable, but who your associates associate with also!

In any event, Ark decided to put my theory to the test and wrote to the individuals in such a way that the manipulations were blocked. This resulted in a strange phenomenon: no sooner had he attempted to "stop dancing" with them, than they began to try even more intensely to sustain contact! They refused to take "no" for an answer!

May 21, 1997

Q: I have a whole bunch of questions: First, in the past week, Dimi, Jim and SJB contacted Ark. I simultaneously had another of those experiences where I felt that an elephant was sitting on me, or compressing me. I have a theory that there is some sort of frequency wave that activates "agents" and their pre-implanted programs to contact their "target," and that the frequency is what I perceive as the "compression." Is this possible?

A: Yes. Notice how contact intensifies post put off?

Q: What? What is "post put off?"

A: After Ark delivered message indicating declining interest.

Q: Oh, I see. Is the sensation I experience strictly related to a frequency? I mean, I was thinking that I was having this feeling because force was being taken by them from me through his bond to me, that his response to them closed the circuit. Would I have suffered whether he responded or not?

A: Waves unify significant events.

Q: Well, what does that mean?

A: It is interrelated.

Q: Would a blank wall, termination of contact, minimize my suffering?

A: Only you can tell.

Q: Well, he knows who and what they are, and there is also the view that by continuing interaction, it prevents *other* portals from being opened. In other words, the devil you know is better than the devil you don't know.

A: Oh yeah?!?

Q: So, this does not prevent others from coming along?

A: Unless one prevents fires by watching only the matches.

Q: What are the matches?

A: That is not the point. Does one prevent sinking just by looking out for icebergs?

Q: No, one steers away from them. Is that what you mean?

A: Oh ... We see ... Then you must mean by inference that the only cause of sinking is icebergs, yes??

Q: Oh. So, there is a lot more that can cause one to sink than icebergs. Well, I was just concerned about the fact that there has been repeated events of this kind. It seems that I get the horrible feeling of being compressed even before they contact him … and then it just snowballs. And, it always seems to come at about the time I have my period, when I am most vulnerable and least capable of coping with such things.

A: When your periods cease, the contacts will not. Yes.

Q: Yes to what?

A: It is soon now. […]

Q: OK, some time ago when I had the "Three Dominoes" dream, or experience, I asked you about this, and you said it was not an important dream. Yet, it led to an incredible series of discoveries. Why did you say it was not important?

A: What was important, the dream or the discoveries?

Q: Well, of course the discoveries … and there really were no dominoes … but it gave me a teensy idea that helped with all the rest … and one thing led to another to another …

A: Dream was not important until fulfilled.

The discoveries referred to above fill three notebooks with notes. It would take us too far from the present subject to detail them, but suffice it to say that using phonetic cabala (even if I didn't know that this was what I was learning) was becoming second nature to me and as my awareness of the hyperdimensional reality expanded, I was just simply stunned at the connections I was seeing.

Q: Does it have anything to do with the Frankenstein dream, which seemed to contain all the basic elements of the following weeks' discoveries. Does it have something to do with putting something in a particular place in one life to come back for it in another? Or, is it that all the clues …

A: You should know by now that all this will be revealed as appropriate.

Q: OK. Now, the 64,000 dollar question … tunnels, longitude of Oak Island, leading to Pointe Perce, Mont Blanc and the St. Bernard Tunnel, and St. Bernard wrote the rules for the Templars … and then, Tenerife, the Canaries and the latitude of 28:30 connected to the spider in the King James version of Proverbs 30:28 … and that leads directly to New Port Richey. Therefore, is there some connection between the location of this house and something on the Canary Islands?

A: You have made much progress, expect more, if vigilant and persistent!

Q: Well, you know I am that! Well, at the time the question was, "could the position of my house over a tunnel be detrimental?" And the answer was "yes." Then, the question was "how?" which led to the answer "That is the 64,000 dollar question." So, is there any further that I can have at this time?

A: Detrimental is subjective, according to unfolding events and choices.

Q: So, it was a question at that time, the *big* question as to what I was going to choose to do …

A: Close.

Q: At that time, it was also said that there was a vortex here that merges levels 1, 2, 3, and 4 with density 5. And, you said that the primary issue about this was "the physical imprint locator." What is this?

A: Forces that tune and influence participants on the various above mentioned density levels.

Q: The other night, I guess at the time that the Jim, Dimi, and SJB thing was brewing, I had a terrible dream of a person trying to break into my house ... that [my youngest daughter] had followed V** out, and I had to get her back, and this put me in danger ... then, I was afraid that he was going to start trying to kill us while we were in the house by shooting through the walls. Ark, Frank and Tom did not seem to be quite as alarmed as I was ... I woke up with my heart nearly beating out of my chest and covered with a cold sweat, and somewhat paralyzed. I recognize this sort of dream from before. Was it just a dream, a warning, a screen memory of some other event? It was very frightening.

A: Choose selection two above. Always be aware of your significance as the possessor and potential purveyor of unusually high level knowledge store. And, what that means to those who would prefer that it not be.

Q: Is there more I could do in terms of protecting my children? That is where I am most vulnerable and I am not sure that they understand the seriousness of the situation.

A: What do signs keep telling you? Who took what positions and behaviors in the dream? Well?

Q: Yes ... I realize that it was because of going out to do something ordinary ... not thinking ... while Ark and Tom and Frank were distracted ... and I was just concerned about [my daughter] ...

A: And what role did V** play?

Q: I see. Like the Pied Piper?

A: Or maybe programmed decoy, due to FRV?

Q: What is FRV?

A: Frequency Resonance Vibration.

Q: Is there any danger to [my son and daughter] with these kids and church people they have been around the past few weeks?

A: What do you think?!? It is a vulnerable age for anyone, much moreso for the children of one on path to superconsciousness, and in contact with those who provide advice and data ...

Q: Well, this church group makes me very uneasy. What can I say to them to make them understand how very vulnerable I am through them?

A: Tell them the truth as you would tell others, of more mature stature.

Q: Any other advice where they are concerned? This whole situation absolutely gives me the willies.

Regarding the above dream and the role played by V**, a very important thing to consider is the fact that, as I was learning to interpret my dreams, I discovered that, very often, when there is something I don't want to look at, the characters playing the different roles are switched in my dream. I also frequently dreamed about a person who represents a type of individual rather than a specific person. This is what the Cs seemed to be indicating; that programmed decoys could lead the children into dangerous situations. As events were later to show, this was indeed the case here. My children were in greater danger than I ever could have imagined. But it wasn't through V**.

Ark was also in danger. By this time he was at the Institute for Theoretical Physics, University of Göttingen. He had been assigned an office overlooking the *Max Planck Institut Fôr Strömungsforschung* (fluid dynamics). He was having a terrible time. No sooner would he sit down to work in his office than he would begin to feel absolutely drugged and unable to hold his eyes open or keep his head upright. His brain wouldn't function, and he was desperate to get his work done. At one point, he decided to go to the basement library just to stretch his legs, and the instant he was in the basement, the sensation just "turned off." He said it was the strangest thing he had experienced in a long time. It was so strange that he began to experiment and observe the effect. He would go in the office, sit down and wait for the sensation and notice how long it took to initiate. It was almost instantaneous. Then he experimented with going outside for a walk, and to the basement library. In the end, he just took his laptop to the basement and worked there. It seemed to be the only solution because he could *not* work in that office.

May 31, 1997

Q: Change gears: Ark has been having a problem sleeping at night and staying awake in the office. The building is a number 9, but there is also the Max Planck Institute across the street. Is it the number 9, or the Max Planck Institute across the street?

A: Well, we vote for Max!

Q: So, what are they doing over there in that building that is affecting him?

A: Better question: What are "they" doing on 4th density that is affecting him?

Q: Since that is a better question, what *are* they doing on fourth density that is affecting Ark?

A: Guess.

Q: Is he being abducted from this building?

A: No.

Q: Are they STS or STO?

A: STS.

Q: Are they zapping him with some kind of frequency modulation?

A: Close.

Q: Why is it more effective in that building than in the basement or at his hotel?

A: Because of Max.

Q: OK, they are using whatever is going on in that building to zap Ark. Anything else they are doing there?

A: Yes.

Q: Could you tell me what?

A: No.

Q: Is there anything else they are doing to Ark?

A: Yes.

Q: Can you tell me?

A: Body chemistry alteration.

Q: In what sense is there body chemistry alteration going on?

A: Brain wave factors.

Q: Is there something he can do for protection?

A: He soon will leave the area.

Q: Well, during the time he is there, how much damage can they do?

A: Probably not much.

Q: Is there any other step he can take other than going to the library or staying in his hotel?

A: Good idea!

Q: Anything else?

A: One shot of whiskey per day will help.

Q: Well, that is a bizarre thing to say! A shot of whiskey?! That will help his brain chemistry?

A: Some.

Q: What is this altering of his brain chemistry designed to do?

A: Befuddle.

Q: Well, I think it is working. Any other suggestion? Come on, we are you in the past! Help us out here!

A: Then you will know in the "future."

Q: Well, then, since I know in the future, why don't I tell me in the past anything else that will help besides staying in the hotel, or the basement, and drinking a shot of whiskey a day?

A: No need.

Q: And you are not going to tell us what they are doing over there in the Max Planck Institute?

A: As Carlos Allende would say: "If you knew, you would die of shock."

Q: That is *not* friendly! I don't want to know things that are not friendly. Now, you have got me so startled that I don't even know if the path I am following in researching the history and the other things is even worthwhile or useful.

A: Oh, you bet it is!!!!!

As it turns out, they are doing a *lot* of curious things in that particular branch of the Max Planck outfit; very interesting work in such things as neural networks, self-organization of neural maps, signal processing, theoretical brain research, spatio-temporal dynamics in the cortex, analysis of neural activity patterns and time series, function of the visual and auditory systems and God only knows what else!

As soon as his work was done in Göttingen, Ark had to rush back to Poland for the divorce hearing described in Chapter 43. On the day of the hearing, he had to leave for Dijon.

Date: Tues, 17 Jun 97 19:43:48

From: "flato@u-bourgogne.fr"

Subject: via Belfort

To: "ajad@physik ... "

Dear Ark,

From Belfort you have, on the 19th: Belfort 17h00 –" (regular train) Besancon 18h06 (could be the same train which takes you to Belfort). then TGV (booking required; buy ticket in advance, possibly in Freiburg) Besancon 18h13 –" Dijon 19h06.

In Dijon you either take a cab or simpler BUS 9 to Campus. The stop is next to the cinemas which you see from the station (it is one end stop), avenue Foch. It costs 5.20 FFR single ticket, and buses run until 21h.

You have a room on Campus and we shall try to get the key in advance. When you arrive we should be in the middle of Reshetikhin's talk in a room (normally first on your left in the corridor). Get in!

If you miss that connection there is a all-regular-train connection: Belfort 18h02 -" Besancon 19h14/19h30 -" Dijon 20h29. Then you should take a cab to the hotel where we shall have dinner (we should be there around 21h; ask for Flato's table). It will presumably be restaurant Chateau Bourgogne in Hotel Mercure next to the Palais des Congres. I'll try to let you know tomorrow.

Have a nice trip!

Since Ark was going to be with his longtime friend and colleague, Moshe Flato, I thought I could relax. But there was a problem. Ark wrote to me:

Date sent: Fri, 20 Jun 97 09:58:04

From: "ajad@physik"

It seems we will have communication problems here and I will not be able to connect with my notebook. But we will see.

These people here close everything on Saturday and Sunday. I do not know whether I will manage to get access to e-mail.

Yesterday there was a dinner – till 2AM, and it was in a VERY FANCY restaurant, 18 people, and Moshe was paying for ALL. Funny. I told him about you, about previous lives, mention of his name, and probable trouble in Israel. He is of course interested as to why his name was being mentioned. Well, I do not remember and did not yet find the file.

Typing this from secretary office computer, and these secretaries here do not speak English so everything is really funny.

Today 5:30 I have a seminar and in fact there are seminars all the day starting 10:30. Moshe and Daniel are normally in Paris and they are scheduled to be here just for two days a week, Thursdays and Fridays.

For us, in our situation, being out of communication was devastating. I suddenly became ill after Ark arrived in Dijon and the pool turned green again against all efforts to kill the algae. Ark wrote to me:

Date sent: Fri, 20 Jun 97 20:32:04

From: "ajad@physik"

Honey,

Seminar is over. It was OK. Now Moshe wants me to go with him to a Chinese restaurant. I will go. Will take care.

In general all is awful. I am sleeping in a room where the bed is awful. But we will manage.

With the green pool and you being sick ... . indeed something is in the air. But we will manage as we did it before. YOU TAKE CARE AND I TAKE CARE. You watch and I watch. We keep 1000 eyes open.

WE WILL MAKE IT WORK!

Ark was able to work out the communication problems, though we didn't have the access we would have liked. We had another session and I announced to the Cs that they had been named as co-respondents in a divorce trial. There was also the most interesting factor that, after Ark had told Sue Brana that he didn't have time to waste discussing endlessly with her his ideas about crop circles, that he was paid for his time, she suddenly wanted to talk turkey.

June 21, 1997

Q: OK, well I guess you know that you have been named as a co-respondent in a divorce trial! I guess that is one claim to fame that was never expected!

A: Divorce is a concept long since conquered here, as you would measure time, that is.

Q: I was just teasing you! Now, let me get Ark's questions first so that I am sure that they get done tonight. It seems that SJB has suddenly become willing to finance crop circle research after hearing a guy on the Art Bell show say that one was a "power plant" for a UFO.

A: Really?!? Then we suggest he write back and demand in writing that there be no "strings" attached, and gauge the response accordingly.

Well, we did. Or Ark did, that is. And of course, when he said that he would not do anything if she was going to breathe down his neck, the whole thing fell flat again. But I was curious about this strange business with Moshe in Dijon:

Q: Back in 1995 when we did a session with RC present, I was re-reading this yesterday because Ark is in Dijon where this guy Moshe is, and the night of that session was when I had the vision of his face, and also when I mentioned the dream where I was getting married and this was so bizarre an idea to me at that time. RC was focused on her agenda about female gods and the Elohim, and it seems that she simply shut off any ability for you to communicate to her at all. So, in re-reading this session, it seems that you were talking on a completely different level, to me alone, and that it was almost in code. She wanted to talk about the French Revolution, and you were talking about my past life in Germany … and now Ark is in France … and there was the vision … and that was when you brought up Moshe … and Moshe is in France … is there a connection?

A: Maybe.

Q: Am I correct that you were talking to me on a level that I was not even aware of at the time?

A: Could be!

Q: Can you help me out here? I would like to know about this Moshe thing. You not only brought up the name, but you brought up a lot of other things. And it seems that this was the opening of a door of moving me in a certain direction. I don't even know how to ask about this because it is so strange …

A: Then it should be shelved.

Q: Is this one of those things you are going to avoid?

A: Alfalfa fields in Rhineland yield as of yet undreamed of treasures.

Q: Where are these alfalfa fields?

A: Near tracks well worn.

Q: Another clue, please?

A: Nope, that is enough for now!!

Q: You guys are gonna drive me crazy! Do you mean Rhineland as in Germany proper?

A: We do not mean Rhinelander, Wisconsin … Or do we?!? Who is to tell?

Q: Who?

A: The searcher, the sepulcher, the one who carries the staff in constant search for greener pastures.

Q: Oh my! You are being *very* obscure tonight! Just the fun things I like, too! Now, I think I will be pretty busy this week on this, but is there anything that can be expanded, or any additional clues for me or Ark?

A: Last clue for tonight: Look for the vibratory frequency light. Good Night.

Q: Good Night.

While many of these clues only made sense recently, and are more fully described in *Secret History*, at that time I was finding connections between certain place names, like the Weser River (*wes* being the Indo-European root of "well" and "worn"), Alfeld (i.e. Alfalfa field), Leiden (i.e. light frequency) and their geographic relation to other places according to latitude and longitude. While researching Alfalfa I discovered that growers can get plants to flower at the "wrong" time by adjusting how much light they received and how this may have parallels with humans in terms of genetics and spiritual development. I asked Ark what the Polish word for light was, and he told me that it was *swiatlo*, from the root *swiat*, meaning world or universe. The verb, to shine, comes from the same root, which is similar to *swiety*, meaning holy, saint, or endowed with light. Interestingly, on the same latitude as Leiden was *Swie*bodzin.

And so we were going along just happily sorting clues and looking for more when the warnings began to come. It turned unseasonably cold in Dijon, and there were thunderstorms here. Communication by Internet was up and down – mostly down. Then it began to rain in Dijon. All the while, Ark was computing, computing, computing.

To: Laura

Date sent: Fri, 27 Jun 1997 01:31:02

So I was trying to send you a message before going to dinner but network was dead. I was worrying if it will work again, but fortunately it does.

Before going out I talked to Moshe and he was funny ... He wanted to know what and how Cs were talking and he was repeating that he is "open". I checked with him that in September 95 he WAS in Israel!

Then I told him about A and the money and that I am looking for a job in Florida ... He said that if we had been for some time in the same university we would do together great things, he said several nasty things about the spook in Wroclaw and then he went on that if I will need a recommendation he will write the best possible for me and not only that he will write it but also that he will give me a copy so that I can see if it is good enough.

Then there was restaurant and funny little things there. Again 17 people and Moshe paying for all. 8 Russians including two wives one daughter and an 11 years old daughter of a French guy from the faculty who divorced his Indian wife and has custody of the girl. The children were on and off Moshe's lap and he was making faces at them and in general the children are loved by the faculty. So this was the story in short.

The weather is awful, it is raining and your honey is rather tired after getting up at six and having seminar and now it is rather late. And tomorrow (that is today) I will discuss with Moshe some physics ...

To: Laura

Date sent: Wed, 2 Jul 1997 17:09:12

Okay, Computer works again ...

Notice that there are long periods when everything works and THEN there are periods when ALL crashes ... even if only for a while. So we are in such a period. I do not like this Dijon anyway. The frequent noise of jet planes does not act in a positive and constructive way on the nervous system. And the base is not far away, perhaps less than two miles.

I am now thinking ONLY about the fact that SOON we are leaving and we will be on the train and we will finally be able TO REST. I am utterly(?) tired.

I am packed and ready. I have some pain in the back since a few days and am in general feeling weaker than usual. Perhaps this is the "aspect", perhaps it was simply TOO chilly. It will be all better in Florence. It is in fact all better now once we know in three hours we will be leaving this place. [...]

And so it went. My mail program crashed, my server suddenly decided to start cutting me off in the middle of sending or receiving mail. We spent days trying to work out those problems so we could continue to communicate. The rain started again in Dijon, and the computer systems were down again and again. But between some few emails and phone calls, we managed and Ark survived the stresses of Dijon. Finally, he was in Florence again.

To: Ark

Date sent: Thu, 03 Jul 97 06:59:39

WELCOME TO FLORENCE!

I so hope that you are feeling better and that Florence works its magic!

But, if you are not feeling well, you need to tell me every little detail. And you must take care of yourself and get rest and exercise and eat properly. Hopefully, Marco will cook some more while you are there and you will have some pleasant "family" type meals in the basement as you did last time!

It is still VERY breezy at night ... and I understand that a volcano has erupted in Mexico now, on top of the one that has erupted in the Caribbean (Montserrat.) So, things are happening and moving all over the place! It is certainly an interesting time to be alive! [...]

To: Laura

Date sent: Thu, 3 Jul 1997 18:15:47

Although last week the weather was bad here, and it was raining all the night, today is a beautiful and sunny day.

Your HB is however somewhat tired after night on the train. Indeed there were three beds on each side ... rather crowdy and I could not sleep well. But now I feel COMPLETELY different than in Dijon.

And now it is okay and alright and we have a VERY nice apartment, with two big beds ... in the center of Florence and, well, quite expensive, five times the price in Dijon, but Dijon was VERY cheap. And Marco claims it is impossible to find something cheaper at this period in Florence. Well ... it is only slightly more expensive than the Apartment in Gainesville.

Well, it is normal that people in Florence own several apartments and rent them. Not necessarily lawyers do that. It is a good way of investing money. Sure way. And you know these rooms are HUGE rooms with high ceilings.

There is a bus. But if I want to walk it is half an hour walk. Perhaps 300 yards from the station. I though perhaps you could come but then perhaps it would not be wise, we leave it for the next year. Marco wants very much me to come also next year.

And now I am sitting in the office and you know from the photo the view outside. The sky and the hills and the little tower with a bell....

Two days later, we discussed these events with the Cs:

July 5, 1997

Q: (L) This couple of weeks that Ark spent in Dijon were miserable. What was the fundamental reason for these conditions and this misery?

A: Near ELF transmitter. Also the water supply is loaded with fluoride.

Q: (L) OK, I did some research on the Emerald Tablets and discovered ...

A: Is this all you want to know about this? We suppose if we told you "Laura, a great big rock is about to fall on your head," then you would say: "okay, now moving right along, about the Emerald tablets ... "

Q: (L) Well, that was about Dijon. He is gone from Dijon now. Whatever it was in Gottingen, you said he would be gone soon and not to worry. So ... he is no longer near the ELF transmitter ... he is no longer drinking the water ...

A: Fluoride is toxic, and deposits in fatty tissues, and lymph system. Aside from the obvious possible negative consequences, it can make one more susceptible to electromagnetic wave frequencies that are designed to make one open to mind alteration!

Q: (L) OK. You have my undivided attention. How does he get the fluoride out of his system?

A: Recommend daily ingestion of Goldenseal root, as well as vinegar and garlic in moderation, along with up to an hour per every two days of light aerobic exercise.

Q: (L) Would half an hour per day be alright?

A: One hour every other day. Light at first.

Q: (L) Well, this sounds serious. Anything else that will help?

A: This is a good start.

Q: (L) Well, now I am all upset.

A: Arkadiusz, or as we like to call him, Arkady, is the primary target of your trio, for now. Great potential dangers lurk ...

Q: (L) So this really is like the Grail hunt. He has to go through a magic forest, chop heads off dragons, keep his eyes open and not be led astray by deceptive images and tricks ... the whole thing!

A: Where to get the influence for the inspiration behind that story?

Q: (L) Are you asking me?

A: Yes.

Q: (L) I don't know. What do you mean. Talk about confused thought patterns!

A: No, not so confusing.

Q: (L) Well, that leads to some of my other questions about what we are doing …

A: Imagine how much your cause would be damaged without him? Where would your ambition for the quest go? You must be extremely vigilant when it comes to him and his safety. He still does not completely fathom the depths of the situation. Until he is here, thus more protected, and it will not be easy to get him here, danger awaits the greeting of each new day. Vigilance! Vigilance! Vigilance!!!!!

Q: (L) That is completely depressing. Help me out here!

A: Now … Calm down! No need for depression. Would you rather be left with a lack of knowledge, and in an ever increasing state of false security oriented oblivion, only to be struck by lightning?!? Of course not!!! So remember … Knowledge protects, ignorance endangers!!

Q: (L) Well, you said that it was going to be difficult to get him here. The arrangements have already been made. Are you saying difficult in a general sense, or is there going to be some major move made, some plan going on at other levels, or behind the scenes, to prevent him?

A: There always is that. Have you not seen the evidence already? Must be aware. Think of it as a war. Expect every possible move/or occurrence. Victory comes from being forewarned, and therefore, forearmed.

Q: (L) Is that, as Frank said, the key? To turn up the vigilance volume to maximum?

A: Always. Don't be like the sentry who fell into a peaceful, pleasure filled, dreamy sleep while on watch! He did not even feel the blade as it pierced his heart!

Q: (L) Well, that is *not* friendly. Now I really *am* depressed! Tell me: is what we are doing so important that this kind of energy has to be concentrated on us?

A: Yes.

Q: (L) Can we quit?

A: No. Too late! Look at it this way: make it your goal to succeed, then you have not to fear.

Q: (L) Is there any connection between the dangers of Dijon, the dangers now, and the interaction with Moshe?

A: Connection? Not exactly, except that Arkadiusz must be made aware that dangers lurk everywhere, potentially. He has spent a lifetime building a strong sense of security, based upon his own natural self assured state of being. But now is the "time" to learn that this is not enough.

Q: (L) Is there any specific danger in Florence that you can point out, or back in Wroclaw?

A: No specific dangers. Just remember: there are forces "out there" that wish to see your project, and you, fail. You two have both previously felt the sting of these forces acutely. He has not so much, until now.

Q: (L) I have the feeling that this has been a recurring drama in other lives, preparing us for this period?

A: Recurrences of this type are usually intermittent in nature.

Q: (L) Anything further on this?

A: We could go on and on. The point is: warn Arkadiusz! Knowledge protects ...

They weren't kidding. And the rain began to fall in earnest.

FACING THE UNKNOWN

CHAPTER 48
THE JUVENILE DICTIONARY

It is now time for a reality check.

I realize that I have been bringing up the idea of "semantic aphasia" somewhat often in this little recapitulation. There is a reason for this aside from the ordinary interpretation that deals with words and our ability to access realms of pure thought via the expansion of associations. It seems that this is a model for our reality as well. In the same way that we expand our awareness of thought realms by increasing our brain capacity by mosaic word associations, so may we increase our awareness of our "hard reality" by expanding our interpretative associations of events and relationships in our lives.

But is that healthy? Is it normal? Is it not, as some might suggest, pathological?

We know that our website and books are full of some of the most far out material imaginable. We admit it freely. We also admit that we don't necessarily believe it. For us, it is an experiment, a working hypothesis to be tested and proven or falsified. Much of what we deal with here is in the realm of pure, speculative thought. As I have said again and again, I have never seen a "Lizzie," nor any other kind of alien except in states of altered awareness such as hypnopompic and hypnagogic sleep states. I *have* seen our reality in a different way more or less spontaneously when a certain "state" has fallen upon me, but as is usual with me, I always want to consider any number of things as being possibly contributory, including blood sugar levels, brain chemistry, different stresses, and so on.

We also know that there are a lot of critics out there who stop in, read a few paragraphs, shake their head in dismay, and move on. Others, with agendas, stop long enough to write and tell us that if we don't call on Jesus, we are going straight to Hell, without passing "Go" or collecting 200 bucks. Still others feel moved to write their own websites devoted to nasty or disparaging remarks about us, in particular, rather than producing any material or theories of their own which they can test. We find this to be a curious phenomenon, but one we certainly understand.

A lot of people draw lines in the sand of their minds and establish very early on what kinds of things they will or will not consider. We have done it ourselves. Not too long ago, proposing the idea of aliens as "real" in *any* sense was so far outside of our own reality that it wasn't even within hailing distance. So we know how this works. Since we had decided, *a priori*, that such a thing was impossible, we simply never exerted any effort really looking into it, much less examining it in a systematic way. That door was firmly closed in our minds.

But it's a curious thing, this Universe we live in. It seems that the doors we close in our minds leave other doors in our lives wide open – and things come through those doors that are not altogether friendly. Just as a particular definition or association of a word may be unknown to an individual, leaving a sort of blank spot in their mind – a point of ignorance which may one day cause them embarrassment if they are challenged in a situation where that particular definition is the right one – so it seems that such blank spots in our awareness of the possible associations of events in our reality leave us open to their effects on us without any ability to define or understand the real meaning.

I wrote *Amazing Grace* for the explicit purpose of describing my life during the many years when my definitions and associations of reality were strictly circumscribed by the "dictionary of life" I was using. When things happened in my life, they were ever and always interpreted by this "dictionary" written by Christianity, and the linear, uniformitarian view of the world. If the interpretation didn't quite fit the event, the event was either distorted in my mind, parts of it covered up, shoved under the rug, or I just ignored it. I didn't realize that whoever writes the dictionaries that we use to understand the events of our lives have written them with only one or two basic definitions, and have left out a whole host of associations or other definitions that more fully explain the word/event. In a sense, the dictionary we use to define our lives is like a children's dictionary where the simplest and most juvenile definition is given. This leads us to interpret our lives and the world around us in a cosmically juvenile way. Even great scholars and "experts" of all kinds continue to use the juvenile version of the cosmic dictionary when it comes to defining and interpreting the facts of their lives and the "real world."

When the average person puts on their power clothes and goes to the workplace, or puts on their Jerry Garcia tee shirt to settle down with a brewski for the big game, intimations of mortality or immortality are not allowed to intrude. Sure, everyone has a little "strange story" to tell maybe once in their life, maybe even an ghostly encounter, and it is always whispered in hushed or embarrassed tones if it is mentioned at all. The very idea that there are layers, or depth and breadth to our reality that may not be part of the dictionary we have been brought up to use is strictly hidden. Everyone has agreed to use the "juvenile dictionary," and anybody who proposes to use one with more definitions, more semiotic content, is attacked.

Why?

Well, because our basic reality is defined by a juvenile dictionary, of course! That means that juvenile reactions are part of the "right" definitions. People who evaluate life based on this juvenile dictionary tend to feel overwhelmed by more semiotic content. It is too much for their brains, too much to think about, too much to handle, and they begin to feel oppressed by their awareness that there may, indeed, be more to the world than they supposed. This awareness of so much unknown territory makes the person who has circumscribed their reality into comfortable zones of what is or is not right and acceptable, feel a terrifying sense of vertigo, and they want, at all costs, to close that door of awareness. So, since they can't destroy the universe that *is*, they seek to get their revenge against the symbolic target of awareness – the individual who has pointed out that there are other definitions and other dictionaries.

Most of ordinary humanity – the vast majority of people – use the juvenile dictionary. They have adopted, internalized, and made real this narrow view of the world, and woe to anyone who points out that there *are* other languages, there *are* other definitions, and there *is* a wider semiotic content plane. But what is important is that no one is born to be forever stuck in a circumscribed semiotic content plane. They are first taught, and then they actively choose to select what definitions of their experiences they will accept and which ones they will edit out.

Gurdjieff was right: People get out of life what they put into it.

Charles Fort, an obsessive collector of anomalous events, once remarked that the only conclusions he could draw from all his research, was that earth was owned by some beings who we could neither see nor comprehend. He said: "I think we're property."

Barbara Marciniak's Pleiadians say, in *Bringers of the Dawn*:

> During Earth's early history, there were wars in space for ownership of this planet ... Skirmishes took place, and Earth became a place of duality ... When this skirmish occurred, a certain group of entities fought in space and won the territory of Earth. These new owners did not want the native Earth species – the humans – to be informed of what took place. Uninformed, the species would be easier to control. This is why light is information and darkness is lack of information ...
>
> These new owners who came here 300,000 years ago are the magnificent beings spoken of in your Bible, in the Babylonian and Sumerian tablets, and in texts all over the world ... Who were these gods from ancient times? They were beings who were able to move reality and to command the spirits of nature to bend to their will ... The creator gods

who have been ruling this planet have the ability to become physical, though mostly they exist in other dimensions. They keep Earth in a certain vibrational frequency while they create emotional trauma to nourish themselves ... In order to have you believe they were Gods with a big G, they rearranged you genetically ... They can do many kinds of manipulations and work with realities in many different ways ... Some of these creator gods married and merged their line ... The creator gods would mix one kind with another to see what they could create. Remember, they understood genetics, and all things were created by manifesting and using the life force and understanding how the life force works ...

Who are these beings ... the Dark T-shirts? Be kind when you speak of the forces of darkness. Do not speak as if they are bad. Simply understand that they are uninformed, and they create systems that are uninformed because that is how they believe they must operate. They fought at one time and separated themselves from knowledge, so now they desperately hold onto their existing knowledge and onto life as they have evolved it into being. It is life based on fear, life that does not honor other life, life that uses other life. Who are these beings? They are the reptiles. These space beings are part human and part reptilian. We call them Lizzies because we like to make things a little less emotional and a little humorous so that you don't take them so seriously and get so upset. (Marciniak, 1992)

The Cassiopaean perspective is slightly different from the Pleiadian perspective, even if there are many terms and concepts that are similar, if not identical. But what I notice particularly in retrospect is the development of the ideas of Quantum Metamorphosis, cyclical time, and other concepts that originated in my mind (from where?) back in 1985 and 1986. As it happens, these are ideas on the cutting edge of physics research. Unfortunately, what physicists think about and develop theoretically is often unavailable to the public for up to 50 years, if at all, so it is not difficult to understand why the material from the Cs is not comprehensible to users of the juvenile dictionary.

One correspondent wrote his objections to the alien reality in the following terms:

Have you ever considered how difficult it would be for an alien species to land here on earth? It is bad enough just traveling from the United States to a place like Bali. The immune system is under a constant attack unless one gets the proper shots and these usually don't help. The immune system of any alien would be under attack almost immediately.

Now, from reading the above, we might have the idea that the writer is averse to spiritual realities. But, not at all! He is, however, trying to grasp spiritual realities in juvenile-dictionary terms. He writes further:

Consider this: How about the idea that it is impossible for a human or any organism to be far removed from its home planet for very long. The organism and the planet are in a symbiotic relationship with each other. When there is a separation they die. It is all a Disneyland show out there to make sure that you are not looking in the right place. That's why the UFO's show up where people can see them. This is not to say that all UFO's are fake. Many are light bodies, the bodies of the luminous ones. One does not need a tin can to get around in time/space.

I certainly would have agreed with him at a certain point in time. As I gradually added more entries to my dictionary, my view expanded into what is called the paranormal. I was open minded enough to talk about ghosts and odd experiences, to study them, to consider them as part of the expanding content plane of the realms of thought I could inhabit. But that's where I drew the line. "Realms of Thought." That's far enough, don't go one step further; I have drawn the line here, and alien realities *as real realities* with some sort of concrete features, are on the other side of that line! We don't need them for a good definition. We have enough with our ideas of observer created reality.

Such a view is the result of the millennia-old program that attempts to sharply divide matter from spirit, and denies any possibility of spiritualized matter, or para-physical realities, such as the alien reality undoubtedly presents. And, in this sense, traveling from distant star systems, aided by technology that is hardly distinguishable from magic to our human understanding, as well as existing in hyperdimensional space becomes not only possible, but altogether likely. Astronomer and UFO researcher Morris Jessup wrote about this problem in the following quotation:

> Flying Saucers are not new! For thousands of years men have seen mysterious objects in the skies ...
>
> Probably the oldest, and almost surely the most prolific of sources bearing on wingless flight, are the records of the Indian and Tibetan monasteries. These in themselves are almost conclusive. Records of 15,000 years ago imply wingless flight at least 70,000 years prior to that. Add this to the recorded visit of a space fleet to the court of Thutmose III, approximately 1500 BC, and we are close to paralleling the sightings of today.
>
> In many ways, the most intriguing data of all comes from the skeptical astronomers. Their observations do tend to be quantitative, timed, and documented. The astronomical data is more than merely qualitative. In other words, the astronomers themselves, being conscientious data hounds, were not content with merely seeing things move in space. Although unaware of the true nature of what they saw, they recorded as much as time and equipment would permit, and, as a result, they have enabled us to locate the habitat of the UFO's.

It may be difficult to see the significance of antiquity in the consideration of space flight or space inhabitance. But failure to consider the sprawling background of the UFO problem is the greatest single factor in the appalling chaos which engulfs this enigma.

Take but one small item: the little piece of meteoric iron which was found deep within a tertiary coal bed. The locale and the finding are authentic. The shape is purely artificial. It is but an inch or so square, practically a cube. Four sides are squarely faced, and the other two are convexly shaped, with complete symmetry. Around the four surfaced sides runs a groove, geometrically contrived. Here are three established facts:

1. Placement in an incipient coal bed some 300,000 years ago.
2. Made of meteoric iron, identifiable by structure and chemical content.
3. Clearly shaped by artificial means.

The number of explanations as to how it got into that coal bed may be few or several, but there is one underlying fact which cannot be scoffed into oblivion: This piece of natural steel was shaped by an intelligent instrumentation at least 300,000 years ago!

We can go on, but somebody has to make a choice, or deny and ignore the entire factual substratum. Science has ignored it. The choice is most galling to face: Was this gadget, created as it was by intelligence, placed there by man indigenous to earth, or was it dropped from space by a space traveler?

You choose to say: placed by Man? Then there was a race of men here 300,000 years ago who knew enough to shape steel, and, by inference, make machinery. If they could do that, they most likely had locomotion of some sort, and there is no good reason to deny that they could have found space flight either by research or accident. At worst there was time to develop a civilization of any pre-assigned refinement. Science doesn't like that. Alternative to that horn of the dilemma, we must contemplate space flight of 300,000 years ago, capable of bringing this little machine part to the earth, or of bringing civilization itself and planting it here within that type of animal life judged most likely and suitable to perpetuate and develop mental capacity. It is indeed a nasty choice for inhibited minds. ...

Throughout the series of modern (after Arnold) sightings of UFO's, there is a thread of frequent references to "Mother Ships" and huge superconstructions. The vast thing chased by Mantell and the ten-mile-long thing over Kansas are examples. There can no longer be serious doubts of their existence. It seems probable that these constructions are the domiciles of the smaller-fry discs, spheres, balls of light, etc., which are so frequently seen in proximity to the earth's surface and to our planes, rockets, airfields and cities.

It is my belief that these constructions are few in number, not many (there is some possibility, in fact, that there may be only two of them) and that *they do not come from distant planets such as Venus, Mars, Jupiter or the vastly more distant stars*. It is my belief that they are usually globular, sometimes spindle-like, and that *they are an indigenous part of the earth-moon binary-planet system*. I make this statement on the basis of hundreds of astronomical observations in which the rough determinations of parallax can be made. Parallax shows these objects to be somewhere between a few hundred miles away and a maximum of something less than the distance of the moon. ...

There seems to be something of *periodicity in events of celestial and spatial origin.* This has been called to our attention by John Philip Bessor in the *Saturday Evening Post* as early as May, 1949; but no one has thus far been able to catalogue and classify enough of this data to determine for certain whether such cycles exist, much less their time period or cause. It is not particularly astonishing that these phenomena should be cyclic, for practically everything astronomical is periodic. If periodicity could be firmly established for these phenomena, that fact alone would be proof of their reality and integration with the organic world about us.

We can conclude that the UFO's are permanent because they have been here for many centuries. That we have so suddenly become aware of them may be due in part to an increased activity, but it is more likely the result of our own slow awakening from intellectual immaturity. Exhaustive research has disclosed records of sightings covering thousands of years, and occasionally actual visits and contacts with our race. More of these incidents are coming to light constantly as research is pursued with UFO's in mind. Now that we are aware of UFO's and know what to look for, the uncorrelated data of our predecessors takes on a meaning hitherto lacking and becomes significant. It is now up to us to discover and analyze all the data, and to correlate it with current observations.

It is no longer necessary to explain them as visitors from Mars, Venus, or Alpha Centauri. They are a part of our own immediate family – a part of the earth-moon, binary-planet system. They didn't have to come all of those millions of miles from anywhere. They have been here for thousands of years. Whether we belong to them by possession, like cattle, or whether we belong to each other by common origin and association is an interesting problem, and one which may soon be settled if we keep our heads.

In final summary, the UFOs have been around us for a long time and probably are a connecting link with the first wave of terrestrial civilization. The UFO's spend most of their time at the neutral points in space.
...

No other set of conclusions will serve as a common denominator for all observable facts. (Jessup, 1955, emphases added)

We further discuss Jessup and the relation of gravitation to psi and hyperdimensional realities in Chapter Four of *Secret History*. These ideas have been adopted by many "alternative science" writers who have related them to buildings, energy fields, light beings, earth grids and all that, and it does, indeed, seem that there may be locations on the planet where one can tap a certain energy with greater or lesser ease. But the phenomenon that these ideas speaks to more directly is that of hyperdimensional realities wherein mental energies or consciousness energies are amplified, and can be interactive with the environment in terms of specific technology. This suggests not only power for transport that is partly physical, partly ethereal, but communication that is also partly physical and partly ethereal, as well as powers of manifestation that might seem impossible to us in our present state of technology. All of these properties *do* belong to hyperdimensional existence, and such a state of being has been being reported for millennia as being the realm of the gods, including dragons, serpents, and critters of all sorts.

Some casual readers have the idea that the Lizzies originated with Barbara Marciniak. Well, perhaps the humorous term did – and we like it – but it is only ignorance that would suppose that these concepts only go back as far as, say, *Star Trek*, or other mass-media forms of promulgation. It has even been conjectured that all of the Cs material is made up out of my head based on movies and TV shows that may have influenced me. Well, it is a certainty that no one can escape the influences to which they are exposed, but since I never liked or read science fiction, and most certainly have never watched more than one or two partial episodes of *Star Trek* (and then only when forced to! Apologies to the Trekkies!), such an influence is not very likely. But then, perhaps individuals who would suggest such have never heard of that most interesting invention of paper and ink and glue called a "book."

Recently, I tried to remember exactly when I first encountered the idea of Reptilian beings as actual, hyperdimensional entities whose technology was so advanced it seemed to human beings not much different from magic, as Arthur C. Clarke suggested.

My copy of *Bringers of the Dawn* is so full of challenges to what is being said there, jotted in the margins with exclamations, that it is a certainty that I didn't take it all that seriously. In actuality, I thought that a whole lot of it was nonsense. At the present time, I have the idea that it wasn't the Cs who liked Marciniak so much as it was Frank.

Nevertheless, the idea of hyperdimensional reptilian beings, even if I think that they are not represented completely accurately by the so-called Pleiadians, certainly fell into place with a bang when one considers physics, history, myth and archaeology.

I described it in my autobiography *Amazing Grace*:

> I was, I admit, a flaming skeptic about aliens. I had spent so much time poking around in people's heads in therapeutic ways, that, with only a cursory examination of the issue, I'd decided that sightings and claims of abductions were strikingly similar to past life dramas. After reading Whitley Strieber's Gothic book *Communion* and Ruth Montgomery's patently ridiculous *Aliens Among Us*, I refused to give any serious consideration to the subject. The stories were so crazy I simply could not consider them to be real in any context other than as useful metaphors. ...

In short, stories of aliens and abductions seemed an archetypal drama of the subconscious mind. I called it the Millennial Disease, and saw it as a form of mass hysteria. I attributed the physical scars and traces of abduction to stigmata-like effects, or poltergeist type events. Clearly, there was very little about UFOs and aliens that couldn't be explained by these theories.

It wasn't until I actually began to study some of the literature about abductions in early 1993 that I even considered the issue with any seriousness. Even then, I decided that there were a lot of better answers for the reported phenomena than "aliens among us."

There were people claiming we had been being visited by aliens since archaic times. There were others who claimed we had been visited a few times, but they were gone now, nothing to worry about! Another group claimed that we had "let them in" by setting off the atomic bomb; they were here to make sure we didn't blow ourselves up along with the rest of the universe. Some claimed they were good guys who were just a little weird because they had followed a different path of evolution, or were further along than we were. Others claimed they were demons from Hell and we had better get ourselves back to church if we expected to survive the invasion.

Sheesh! The only thing certain was that people were seeing and experiencing something singularly strange. Secret government projects? Secret alien-in-cahoots-with-the-government? By the time I finished I was sure of one thing and one thing only: there was a *lot* of smoke!

But smoke obscures the source of the fire. Underneath, there might only be a smoldering mess. I wasn't sure if this was a manipulation by the government to make people think aliens existed, or if aliens did exist and were trying to make the government look guilty.

What a morass of confusion!

It was, of course, as a result of that strangest of hypnosis sessions reported by Tom French in his article in the *Times* ("The Exorcist in Love"), followed by my own sighting, that I began to consider the possibility that the alien solution was the better fit by Occam's Razor. In *Amazing Grace*, I speculated on this problem:

If we conjecture that this "alien phenomenon" is part of some deep government conspiracy designed to experiment on people – perhaps to make them think that they are being abducted by aliens so that they will assiduously seek greater controls and protection from "Big Brother" – we have a curious problem with this case. The problem becomes: how could such a hypothesized group engineer the response to this session that did, in fact, manifest?

I was very careful not to mention the word "alien" or "abduction" to the woman on the phone prior to the session. If phone conversations are being monitored, how did this one get selected for special attention?

Such monitoring, even for key words that would trigger a need for personal attention, suggests a conspiracy of such vast and complex proportions that the logistics of it stagger the mind.

Well, suppose it is a government conspiracy. Suppose that they do have such monitoring capabilities, that they are monitoring my phone, the woman's phone, or the phones of everybody by computer. As a result, suppose they knew I was going to hypnotize her and sent out a flotilla of stealth-type aircraft to beam some wave at her (or something like that) which would prevent her from talking to me.

Why would they go to all that trouble? [Are they really going to send several multimillion-dollar aircraft to scare the bejeebies out of a housewife/part-time hypnotherapist in Florida?]

It seems to me that it would be easier to just send one of those nice white panel trucks we see in the movies to park a block away from my house for their wave-beaming activities.

Well, okay; maybe they just thought it was a handy time to create a UFO flap at that moment for general purposes: to get everyone all excited, to reinforce the alien phenomenon scenario they are creating.

We are still looking at logistics that stagger the mind.

The next question we have to ask is this: since this woman appeared in my life at precisely the moment I had been familiarized with the phenomenon sufficiently to recognize the symptoms, how do we deal with that synchronicity? If it is a government conspiracy that was aiming at taking me in by gradual degrees, by creating a series of events in my life that would lead me to give up my rational explanations of the phenomenon, what kind of surveillance and management does that suggest?

Again, it boggles the mind.

Thinking these thoughts produced a strange feeling in me of being watched in ways hard to describe. It was so strange a synchronicity that I couldn't help but think that the appearance of these craft related to our activities. I tried to sweep this thought under the rug, but it kept coming back.

Nevertheless, I had read so many cases by now of strange events similar to my own that were attributed to aliens. And that was the problem. Who or what were they? Were they literally visitors from deep space? Or were they the perceptions of victims of some vast government mind-control experiment? Most terrifying of all: were they demons?

I detected the signature of a malevolent intelligence working in my life and my experiences in an effort to either destroy or divert me from something. If these evil beings had the power to interfere in my life with malicious intent, even when I was deeply involved with prayer and meditation – which one would suppose should act as a defense – what protection did anyone have? Were we, the human race, defenseless against these creatures?

The words of Gurdjieff came back to haunt me. Were the belief systems of metaphysics and religion useless drivel promulgated by an Evil Magician to convince people they were Lions, Men, Eagles or Magicians instead of sleeping sheep?

What kind of madhouse had I opened my eyes to see? Was the fact that I had seen it the very source of its existence? Was I, by noticing evil, more vulnerable to attack? Surely not: the evidence of the presence of evil threaded its way through the lives of others who denied all the clues. I saw clearly the mechanical or accidental nature of the Universe that Gurdjieff talked about. But now I realized that our own pro-grammed refusal to see reality, our ignorance, was the chief door in our lives through which Evil entered.

Was it possible, as Gurdjieff suggested, to become free of this? To awaken? To see the projector behind the slide show of our lives? And, more important, to see who was running the projector and why?

To consider the idea of malevolent beings in control of our world that could prey on us at will, behind our ordinary reality, was utterly soul shattering.

I began to see the possibility of an interpenetrating reality of more or less physical solidity that interacted with humans as we may interact with wildlife in a forest: the hunters and the hunted. ...

Well, in thinking about it deeply, it does appear that these beings – whatever they turn out to be – can plunder our world, our lives and our very minds at will. But I also have observed that they seem to be going to an awful lot of trouble to conceal their activities and to confuse ob-servers with hundreds of crazy stories of different races and groups of semi-mythological good guys and bad guys.

Many people who think they are psychic, have prophetic dreams or visions, channel "space brothers," or who are contacted by beings who are here to "help" us or to "save us" if only we will let them, or have other psychic experiences are, in fact, being regularly visited by aliens who literally program these ideas into their minds. These stories are spread around, increasing the level of confusion. But the greatest decep-tion of all is the idea that negative forces do not exist. And even if negative forces did exist, there's no need to worry. If we just think nice thoughts, meditate regularly, and repeat our affirmations, nothing icky will ever enter our reality.

We are not dealing with materialistic, earth-based technology here! For God's sake, these guys walk through walls, float people out of their bodies and control minds – the abilities we have historically attributed to angels or demons or vampires.

In the past, we dealt with ghosts and gods and demons. We are deal-ing with the same entities now, only we are calling them aliens. They probably always *were* aliens! And maybe they want to be gods again.

It was a stunning and grotesque prospect for me to consider that humanity, as a whole, has been used and cunningly deceived for millen-nia beyond my wildest imaginings. I realized that the UFO and alien business was truly nothing new. We have historical records of these phenomena stretching back thousands of years. If these beings could get what they want simply by moving in and taking it, would they spend so much time creating terror and confusion? Alternatively, perhaps the ter-ror and confusion is exactly what they want to generate because they feed on it. But that makes me also wonder why they are going to so much trouble to persuade us to accept their total control if they could take it at will? These guys would not be spending so much time terrorizing us and trying to sneak in the back door if it were possible for them to walk in directly. There is something we have that they want. There is some power we have that they don't want us to discover.

The act of facing the pattern of activity behind the events of my own life that bespoke such a hidden reality was absolutely soul searing and mind numbing. You could even say that, of all people who never wanted to know anything at all about UFOs and aliens, I deserve a place at the head of the line. Yet, there it was.

Standing back from my life in overview, there were the hints of some sort of pattern maker, and it wasn't God in any sense that I had ever conceived of Him. Yes, I could see both positive actions and negative actions; a dynamic interplay of forces that related in some direct way to my own thinking, seeking, and growth. But exactly what it was, and precisely how it operated, I couldn't tell yet. It was like a shadow show where the shadows are produced by certain angles of light behind objects which, when finally revealed, may bear no resemblance whatsoever to the form of the shadow. A balled-up fist could as easily be interpreted as a bird or a dog, or – when expanded to its full shape – a hand. Just what was I seeing? What's more, why did it seem that I was being challenged to see it? Why me? I think this question is echoed by thousands, if not millions of others who have had similar experiences.

In the earliest days of my investigation into the phenomena, the enormity of the problem began to overwhelm me. From what I could determine, many, many thousands of people – a cross section of humanity – were coming forward and saying that they had experienced contact with aliens from other worlds. The general response that they get from others, including professionals who are supposed to be providing help and support, is ridicule. In reviewing the cases available to me, I noted that the typical victim was almost frantically worried about a loss of time, and some vague memory of being restrained or trapped. The person becomes almost hyperactive in their irritability, suffers from loss of concentration and short-term memory. An abductee is generally hypersensitive to loud noises, claims to hear things no one else can hear, and to see things no one else can see, including getting feelings about others that are impossible to explain or quantify in any way. No matter what the explanation for their experiences, these people needed to be taken seriously; they needed to be validated; and most of all they needed a support system.

Basically, when considering abductions, there are three choices:

1. They're a hoax, no abduction occurs and all these people are making it up.

2. Abductions really happen, performed by persons or beings unknown.

3. No abductions happen, but all these abductees believe they do for unknown psychological reasons.

I very early gave up the idea that abduction stories were concocted for fame and glory. For most, the event was one of great shame and they most certainly didn't want anybody to know about it. That they were so desperate for help that they overcame tremendous reluctance indicates how severely they were traumatized.

The question of the sanity of people claiming to have been abducted was answered in the negative as far as I could see. If millions of people believed that a guy, 2000 years ago, died on a cross and arose three days later, and were considered sane, then people claiming abductions, with far more direct experience and evidence, were undoubtedly sane also.

Sure, it was fine and dandy for Bob Lazar to say that he worked on alien craft at Area 51 and that endless reports of the phenomenon existed from thousands of years ago; but were the lights in the skies and the stories of fairy abductions the same phenomena that happened here and now in our world? The claims of coverup and conspiracy had a certain appeal. I really got the creeps thinking about alien critters with bug eyes and B.O. No wonder so many people flee in terror to the safety of the government-conspiracy idea. It's a lot more comforting to think that the man behind the curtain is a man, after all, and not a hyperdimensional being who is not only physical, but can manipulate space and time at will. As Morris Jessup said so eloquently:

> *We can conclude that the UFO's are permanent because they have been here for many centuries.* That we have so suddenly become aware of them may be due in part to an increased activity, but it is more likely the result of our own slow awakening from intellectual immaturity. Exhaustive research has disclosed records of sightings covering thousands of years, and occasionally actual visits and contacts with our race. More of these incidents are coming to light constantly as research is pursued with UFO's in mind. *Now that we are aware of UFO's and know what to look for, the uncorrelated data of our predecessors takes on a meaning hitherto lacking and becomes significant. It is now up to us to discover and analyze all the data, and to correlate it with current observations.*

One anonymous writer claimed that until he had hard evidence that it was not the CIA or some maverick secret government experimenting on human beings, he would continue to deny that it could be aliens. This person wrote:

> Until someone kills a real alien and lays its cadaver on my doorstep, I will continue to believe 'Grey Aliens' are USAF or CIA personnel

dressed up in funny costumes. I will continue to believe that our comrades are being abducted and murdered by government agencies [and] that telepathic contact experiments are being conducted by the same government agencies. If aliens are not humans in costumes, they are at least darklings built by human DNA tinkerers in some of those secret underground laboratories.

I have a great deal of trouble accepting the story that aliens have been conducting genetic experiments on humankind for 10,000 years. That would suggest that we are really little more than their livestock, they actually 'own' us, just as we believe we 'own' beasts of the field and fish of the seas and birds of the air. It also suggests they have an extremely long attention span unless they are moving through time and aren't really 'going anywhere!'

We tag sea turtles in the North Atlantic and track them by satellite to see which way they go. We tag birds and fish and elephants to follow their migrations. Are we supposed to believe creatures from Zeta Reticuli are doing the same to humans?

Friends! Why would beings who can travel sixty-six zillion light years through space and time in any direction at any time, want to concern themselves with something as stupid and boring as tagging and following the migration and sexual behavior of humans (who would be the equivalent of primeval slugs to them)? What is the point?

To capture, examine, impregnate and tag human females to carry their crossbred children? If they are as wonderful and advanced as some say, they should be able to grow their children in canning jars on their own planet!

To cultivate us as food? If they are twenty billion years more advanced than we, why haven't they figured out how to grow synthetic protein in culture dishes in their own labs on their own planet in their own star cluster?

If we are nothing more than experiments of an advanced race of beings, no more than bacteria on a cosmic glass slide, that means there is no God, no law, no rules, no leaders, no followers. ... There should be no trials or punishment for "crimes" because the concept of crime and punishment would be null and void if we belong to funny-looking grey creatures from Zeta Reticuli.

If we have no more rights than a common housefly, then we'll have to do away with ownership of property as well. If we believe that, we'll have to do away with governments and public minions, dismantle the military and let anarchy reign supreme, laying about until one of the owners comes round to lop off an arm or leg for dinner or grind us into sausage and stir us up in a big vat somewhere in Nevada, USA.

But wait! Why would creatures who can jump from Earth to Zeta Reticuli in a heartbeat keep their food supply in Nevada? Why don't they take it with them? If you were able to jump from one town to another or one state to another by thinking it, and you wanted to paint a house in say, Texas, would you keep the paint bucket in New York and jump back and forth every time you had to load the brush just because you could jump back and forth? If you could jump to the grocery store, would you jump forty times to buy forty items or would you get everything in one jump so you wouldn't have to bother?

People! That's why we have refrigerators and pantries! So we don't have to get in the car (flying saucer) and drive to the store (Nevada) every day! I can't believe we're more intelligent than our grey owners! They must be humiliated.

But if all this nonsense is being orchestrated by an agency of Earthlings who wants you to believe in UFOs and funny-looking grey aliens, then it all makes sense, doesn't it? Humans are being abducted for medical experiments. Humans are being contacted telepathically to sort out the ESPers. Human females are carrying the seeds of a future race of cosmonauts. They may be producing embryos which are sent into space aboard the shuttle to see if they live or die in a weightless environment, the evidence of which will be applied to the technology of future manned excursions to the planets of this solar system and beyond.

The above is, in a nutshell, the view of the hard-shell skeptics. Putting aside the hyperbole and evangelistic style of writing, the guy has a point. But only for those using the juvenile dictionary.

Such an argument sounds pretty reasonable at first glance. It was only when I thought about it a bit longer that I realized the chief problem with such an idea. If the government is behind all the abductions, surely they would have screwed up at least once in 45 years and we would know that fallible human beings were doing it! The fact that not one single incident, not one single abduction, not one single purported kidnapping event has ever resulted in a screw-up that led to anyone seeing the man behind the curtain, not one, should give us pause to think.

This guy expects me to believe that the U.S. government can pull off an enterprise of this kind, with evidence of worldwide activity, for thousands of years, involving millions of individuals, the logistics of which make the machinations of WWII look like the planning for a picnic? I'm sorry. I can't buy that. And so, even though he has many points about the phenomenon that beg for explanation, I think that we have to look for a hypothesis that explains and predicts the phenomenon better than what he has suggested. And part of that hypothesis may be that *the ideas he is proposing are deliberately planted in the mind of the public for the very purpose of hiding a dreadful and sinister secret.*

We can also see that, even if the government is not involved, then public officials would be most interested in maintaining the coverup. As the guy pointed out: to admit certain possibilities could lead to worldwide chaos and anarchy. If we are, as Charles Fort said, "property," if we belong to some race of advanced beings who use us for food and resources, then there is no point to anything we believe in at all. It is all a lie, a sham, a grand illusion, an enormous cosmic fraud. Who can live with that thought?

All over the world, from time immemorial, gods have been represented with scales. Most analysts have interpreted this to be a symbolic representation of the powers of the gods, or the wisdom of the serpent. But why a serpent would acquire any kind of cachet as wise simply does not compute in any way, shape or form. How do we explain the ubiquitous presence of a serpent race on earth? Perhaps it is because at one time, or at various times, and even still, they are present in our realm, but as hyperdimensional beings – the secret Control System that owns Earth.

And if the reader thinks I *like* such an idea, that I spend ten or more hours a day researching and writing about it because I watched a few episodes of *Star Trek*, or Barbara Marciniak's work just tickled me pink, think again! Our work is devoted to bringing many, many thousands of hours of research and experience to the reader. And for those who wish to speculate wildly upon whether or not any of the ideas are derived from here or there, it might be useful to actually read our material. Then the questions might be answered.

> A little Learning is a dang'rous Thing;
> Drink deep, or taste not the Pierian Spring:
> There shallow Draughts intoxicate the Brain,
> And drinking largely sobers us again.
> —Alexander Pope

Getting back to our narrative, the reader may want to remember that there were several things going on during the summer of 1997, including the necessary work to get all the details of the Xth Max Born Symposium hammered out. The Conference was scheduled for September 24th through the 27th, and Ark already had his date to return to the States scheduled for October 12th. Things had been timed so that he would be able to obtain his return visa – but that depended on him being in Poland long enough in advance to get the paper work done. The divorce hearing was supposed to be held on July 22nd. All the while Ark was working. Threaded throughout all of this was the fact that we were puzzling our way through the transcripts, searching for clues.

Back in the States, I was dealing with the daily issues of house, children, and the ongoing struggles with my health – trying to achieve some sort of stability after all the massive changes of the previous year. The children were struggling to stabilize also. My eldest daughter was being caught up in a fast crowd and was spending all her money for appearances. She was not taking the responsibility of being behind the wheel of a car as seriously as she ought, and I could not figure out what had happened to my serious, responsible child. She was involved in a small accident. She gave me one version of it, and the policeman who took the report gave an altogether different version based on witness testimony. I advised her that if she was going to drive that thing like a 747 that she ought to increase her insurance coverage. She said she would.

Daughter number two had recovered from her depression and was now enthralled with inline skating – to such an extent that her health was suffering from the endless hours she practiced. What was worse was the crowd of kids she was meeting while skating. My son was determined to break every bone in his body on a skateboard. There was a group of Christian Fundamentalists who were always stalking about where the kids were skating, handing out tracts about hellfire and damnation, scaring the kids so they would go to church and get saved, and this concerned me a great deal. This activity ultimately led to a terrible tragedy when my son's best friend was induced to go to a revival by this group, and was in a terrible automobile accident, leaving him permanently crippled and brain-damaged. So, there were Pied Pipers everywhere, and I was trying to find some reasonable activity for the children that would engage them and keep them safe.

I was also trying to get caught up on all the transcribing. I still had a big box stacked with tapes from past sessions that had not been transcribed, and I struggled against the partial paralysis of my hands to get them transcribed so that Ark could read all of them. In this project, I received some assistance from Jan, but *no* help from Frank at all. It was a protracted and painful struggle, but eventually it was finished.

Even though I have decided not to include the massive numbers of emails we exchanged during this period in the narrative, there really is no way to understand the dynamics and flow of energy behind the scenes without them, so I have assembled a selection into a separate file, chronologically, for those who are patient enough to wade through that sort of thing, and who may be interested in discovering exactly what we were discussing at the precise time of the disaster.[11] Many of the clues to the great mysteries on the planet were discussed in these exchanges, and there were a number of dreams that were significant, and later mentioned in the transcripts without being fully explained, as they are in the emails. My guess is that we were getting too close to some things to allow this exchange to continue. These emails also chronicle the beginning of the Cs website.

---

[14] http:// www.cassiopaea.org/cass/julyletters1.htm

The main purpose of publishing this correspondence is both as a sort of map of the areas we were investigating and our thinking about them at the time of the flood in Poland – which I have the idea is sort of synchronous – and as a historical document as to what ideas were discovered at what point in time and how. It also provides some sort of idea of what was going on in our lives, which is part of the process of realizing the Matrix by experiencing it. One of the things I was learning was that anybody in our lives, our children, partners, friends, could and would be used to bring pressure to bear – to whatever level they do not realize that they can be controlled and manipulated and used as an agent of the matrix. This is a tough problem to deal with because, very often, we are very much involved with people who are not yet ready to even consider the idea much less begin the process of observing their own mind to watch for signs of manipulation. And it is particularly difficult when we deal with our children. It's almost fatal if it is our mates or partners – because, in the Biblical sense, we are "one" with that person, and their karma sort of becomes ours.

That the flood in Poland was, most assuredly, a disaster, is without question; it was a flood of sufficient significance that it threw all our plans into confusion. Apparently, it had begun to rain in Poland early in July, and continued to rain daily until the rivers swelled to overflow, and the water was everywhere. The Polish authorities called it the Flood of the Millennium. There had not been such an event in a thousand years. It was a national disaster. The strangest thing about it was the fact that almost nothing was published about it in the U.S. Roads were washed out, railroads and communication lines were cut off. Food and water supplies weren't getting through. There was loss of life, and significant loss of property. Ark was in Florence, and couldn't find out what was going on – if his family was safe or not – for several days.

Obviously, under such conditions it was unsafe to travel, not to mention the fact government buildings were reported to be flooded, documents and files were floating in the streets, and there would certainly be no divorce hearing. It was even possible that he would not be able to obtain his Visa in time. Everything was turning into a disaster.

When all of this began to manifest, I called Frank for an emergency session. In this session we were given several huge clues to exactly how the Matrix illusion was maintained in our reality, as well as some hints that our mission was significant, though again, nothing specific was mentioned.

July 19, 1997

Q: As you know, there is a flood in Poland, and Ark has to go back. There is so much that must be done, but the government offices may be closed, the court session may be delayed indefinitely, God knows what is going to happen. What is the source of this dreadful disaster in Poland?

A: Sopophoric screen alterations of the magnetic belt overlay.

Q: And what is causing these screen alterations of the magnetic belt overlay?

A: Influences of Acquiim.

Q: What is Acquiim?

A: 4th density overseer.

Q: Does that mean sopophoric screen alteration?

A: Soporific/phosphorous.

Q: What is the purpose of this screen alteration?

A: Deterrence of collinear wave reading consciousness units.

Q: What is a "collinear wave reading consciousness unit?"

A: Suggest you "look in the mirror."

Q: Well! I don't know if I like being a collinear wave-reading consciousness unit!

A: Why not?

Q: Because I don't like feeling responsible for all these people who are suffering in this disaster!

A: Responsible? Are you altering the weather?

Q: Well, no. But, if they will go to that extent to thwart us, is it safe for him to go back?

A: If he takes precautions.

Q: Can you suggest some of these precautions?

A: Drive not. Travel by rail only if such travel does not include the possibility of having to evacuate the train and walk on or near live electrical current conduits.

Q: Anything else?

A: Guns do exist in Poland, unlike some other European countries.

Q: What more?

A: Total awareness at all moments is hypercritical.

Q: Are the members of his family all right?

A: So far.

Q: How long will it take before this flood business has come to a halt?

A: Open.

Q: Are all the government offices going to be closed?

A: No.

Q. Will the divorce hearing proceed?

A: Eventually.

Q: How many days will we be out of communication?

A: Not point. Just remember that anticipation is the "mother of preparation," and defense.

Q: So, anticipate or expect to be out of communication for some time
…

369

A: No, it is for Arkady to be prepared!

Q: Are there any good guys who can come in and help? I mean, good grief! A flood no less! How come we haven't been afflicted with that sort of thing here?

A: No need as we have told you, it is Ark who is the vulnerable link, therefore, the attack goeth there.

Q: Is there anything *we* can do to help?

A: Get the message through to expect the unexpected; feel vulnerable, and do not ever assume invincibility. Knowledge protects, and ignorance endangers … does it ever!!!

Q: Well, anything else?

A: Must beware of agents near.

Q: Can you give any clues about these agents near?

A: Have "look," if one is looking.

Q: What kind of look?

A: Consult fiction for the truth.

Q: You mean like spy stories? If they look like a spy, they are one?

A: Close.

Q: Anything else? This is going to be a rough period!

A: Not if aware and prepared, and not caught up in fantasies.

Q: What kind of fantasies?

A: Energy wasted upon unnecessary communiques.

Q: So, he should not exert himself to be in contact with me if it might put him in danger? Is that it?

A: No, for the time being, suggest you cancel the "mushiness."

Q: All right. Anything further?

A: No.

Q: I will be in a bad way through this ordeal until he gets here, so …

A: Better to be in "a bad way," than a pedestrian on the widows walk.

Q: Is there anything that we can do for protection?

A: We have told you! Be forearmed by being forewarned! Be careful that he does not believe the message.

Q: In other words, he needs to really believe what you are saying?

A: More important: what is a false sense of security?

Q: So, if he receives a message that he is secure and that all is okay, then is when he must be most aware?

A: One must not ever feel "secure," but think of it. When is one ever secure?

Q: Well, we notice that things are really heating up. Weather, government exposure and confessions of this and that …

A: Massive alien/UFO coverage, some fictionalized, some not.

Q: OK, I just thought of this: getting back to our earlier questions, would you suggest that Ark avoid going back to Poland altogether?

A: Avoidance may avoid objective also.

Q: OK. That is understood. I want to ask about what, precisely, this soporific/phosphorous screen of the magnetic belt overlay is.

A: And have you communicate it thus? No.

Q: When you said "collinear wave reading consciousness units," and "look in the mirror," was that a clue that Ark and I are mirror image consciousness units?

A: Not exactly.

Q: Well, in a previous session, you said something about being a "half soul," and my assumption was that he was a half-soul and I was a half-soul, and together we made a whole soul. But, since that time, I have wondered about this ...

A: No one is unto themselves a half soul.

Q: OK, what would give me a more clear understanding about "half soul balancing?"

A: The soul as read as a unit of completion. It is the communication which completes the whole in each.

Q: What are the potentials of collinear wave reading consciousness units?

A: Specifics.

Q: Well, if an overseer in fourth density wishes to prevent unification of same, there must be some reason; that there is something that the fourth-density STS would not like to see happen. What is it?

A: Is that not self-evident?

Q: So, does that mean that it is important for us to be physically together to do whatever this is?

A: 'Tis preferable.

The strange series of remarks about Ark's safety, once again, until the events played out, did not make any sense. And, of course, it is difficult to know in retrospect whether our interpretation was correct.

Ark made the decision to return to Poland in the middle of the disaster, and it was quite a journey since what few trains were running were crowded with people trying to get back to take care of their families. It was practically standing room only. All trains to Poland were canceled and he managed to get a train to Wien. From Wien, he had to pay an exorbitant sum to a driver to get him to Poland, and he spent some time sleeping on his luggage before he finally made it. By this time, the waters were receding, and the mud and mess was everywhere. There was no safe drinking water and it had to be brought in by truck, and there were long lines to get water from the trucks. During the period of time right after he returned to Poland in the midst of the flood, there are no emails. We communicated by phone, for the most part — only after the phone lines were back in service.

One of the results of the flood was that Ark's ex-wife began to call repeatedly to ask that he come and help her with taking care of things she had stored in the basement of the apartment building where she lived. It was full of water, and she declared that she simply was not able to manage things.

After our experience with the fact that this woman was perfectly capable of finding a way to remove and then replace a customs seal so that it looked like it had not been disturbed – an item we were never able to figure out unless she had been assisted by someone in the government – in order to steal things from his luggage, neither of us trusted her. We discussed it on the phone and I was concerned that if he went over there and was standing knee deep in water, she could very easily just toss a plugged-in electrical appliance in the water and that would be the end of everything. Whether or not she had a gun, we don't know. But when we considered the warning, "Energy wasted upon unnecessary communiques," and "Be careful that he does not believe the message," this was the only thing that it could apply to – at least up to that point.

She had told Ark when he announced his intention to divorce, "I will destroy you!" and she was spending every waking hour trying to do it. Her violent and vicious acts against him seemed to be her sole reason for existence. At one point while she was claiming psychic stress, she visited the university psychiatrist and told him a complex story about how Ark had become brainwashed by "an alien cult" and was using their brainwashing techniques on her to destroy her mind. In Europe, the Church that teaches such things, but which will remain unnamed, is looked upon with a very dim eye, and this was a serious charge against a department head of a large university. In any event, the story traveled up the chain of command to the Rector of the University who confided to Ark the kinds of lies his ex-wife was spreading about him. It was easily refuted, but the fact that she had embarked upon such a path of lies and defamation gave us a good idea of what other things she might be capable of doing.

The end result was that we decided that it was dangerous for Ark to respond to her repeated requests to come and take care of the water-filled basement. Putting that together with the hint about walking on or near live electrical current conduits, and guns being obtainable in Poland, we finally decided that being "caught up in fantasies" would be to continue to think that this woman was not a direct instrument of fourth-density STS, if not an actual agent who had long ago been given the assignment of preventing Ark from ever leaving Poland to come back to the States.

Of course the divorce hearing was canceled and rescheduled to October 21, which was the date that the ex had asked for previously, knowing that Ark was scheduled to leave Poland on October 12th.

What is more, the "friendly" judge who had sat through the previous hearings where the ex was a repeated no-show, was suddenly replaced! We were debating whether or not we ought to rearrange our schedule in order to accommodate this new date, postponing Ark's departure until after the hearing, so I decided to ask the Cs:

August 22, 1997

Q: (L) OK, now, I have been thinking that since the last series of obstructions are in the process of stabilizing, maybe there are other surprises and unexpected events around the corner ...

A: Maybe for Arkadiusz.

Q: What kind of surprise might this be?

A: Mount "Anna" may erupt. [Anna being the name of Ark's ex-wife, as well as the nickname of my number-two daughter.]

Q: Very cute! And, if so, what kind of eruption?

A: Cataclysmic.

Q: Well, *swell!* How about another clue!

A: Just be vigilant!

Q: Is that it?

A: To be forewarned is to be forearmed.

As it turned out, we discovered via the grapevine strong indications that the ex-wife had something to do with the selection of the date as well as the replacing of the judge. After all, she had all Ark's money and a person gets exactly as much justice as they can pay for. Ark was keeping his ear to the ground and the grapevine produced another interesting item, namely, that the judge might ask for a competency evaluation based on the ex-wife's claims about cults and brainwashing and her claims that she was merely acting as she was to protect Ark from a mind-control cult.

With this bit of intel, we realized exactly what kind of danger he was in. Knowing that, in the past, his ex-wife had hired a private detective to get the goods on the former husband of their daughter, in order to blackmail the young man into divorcing her, Ark had no illusions that she would not also find a doctor who would write any report he was paid to write.

I once knew a woman who was married to a doctor who wanted to divorce her and marry someone else without having to split their property. She had been standing on a chair one night putting ornaments on her Christmas tree when a couple of guys in white coats, accompanied by two policemen, broke in the door and put a straitjacket on her and took her to a psychiatric hospital where she was kept drugged for weeks until she managed to get a message out to her family and friends about what was being done to her. I knew that these kinds of things happened in real life, and Ark knew it too.

After discussing it, we decided that the best course of action would be to just let everyone think that he planned to change his schedule to accommodate the new hearing date, while quietly making his preparations to get out of Poland as we had already scheduled it. We had a very sympathetic firm of international attorneys here who were ready to go into action if necessary, and we were watching for any sign of new developments on the part of whoever it was that was so determined that Ark would never make it back to the States. It seems that somebody wanted him to stay in Poland – dead or alive.

All through August and September Ark worked to get things back to normal after the flood. In addition to all of his regular duties at the University, he had to walk many miles to get to the water trucks, to the market to get food, and to manage all the necessary care for his mother, with whom he lived. He was also assisting in the cleanup effort since the basements of the University had been flooded and many documents and books had to be salvaged, dried and arrangements made for future storage. The entire Max Born Symposium had to be reorganized since the place where it had originally been scheduled to take place was a ruin from the flood. Ark went looking for a new conference center that would meet the needs of twenty or thirty physicists as well as the crowd of attendees. He finally found a resort in the mountains that seemed to suit, and most definitely was not subject to being flooded!

Finally, after two months of backbreaking labor it was all done and the speakers were arriving from around the world. Ark and his fellow organizers had to be there to monitor every detail, to meet every need, and make sure that all proceeded according to schedule. We communicated by phone every day since there simply was no time for email. He would call me just before I went to sleep which was about midnight here and 6 a.m. there. Everything was proceeding just fine – until the unthinkable happened on the last day of the Symposium. I wasn't at home when Ark called. The email exchanges between us will explain why.

To: Ark
Date sent: Sat, 27 Sep 97 09:00:34
Honey, I am back at the house for a few minutes to change my clothes and grab some coffee and go back to the hospital. Anna is stable, but still on life support. It was VERY close for about 7 hours and truly about the most horrifying experience of my life until this point.

She was with her friends, and an older guy gave them some Vodka. Anna drank some and went into insulin shock and then a coma. She stopped breathing right when we got her to the hospital.

I am okay, but I am VERY tired mostly from terror and grief. I will tell you when I am back. She hit her face when she fell and they are doing a CT scan to make sure there is no serious damage and then she will be taken to Intensive care unit where they probably will not allow me to stay with her very long. If she seems better and sleeping okay, I will come home, but I would like to wait until she is no longer on the respirator ...

So, don't worry, Honey ... the worst of it is over. It was terrible, but we just DO the things we have to do.

Take care of YOU for me, please. I told Anna you were worried and she seemed to understand what I was saying.

To: Ark

Date sent: Sat, 27 Sep 97 12:46:58

Okay, Honey, I am home now ... it is about 6:20 in the morning and I left her sleeping ... The nurses think she will sleep for about half a day.

I didn't want the baby to wake up and find me not here.

So, the terrible crisis has passed ... Anna has learned something about Lizzies ... and so have I.

The police were there. The man who bought the liquor for the kids has been arrested and charged with aggravated child abuse, which is a serious offense. All the policemen involved came by to see her before I left to check on her and make sure that she was alright. That was very sweet.

And I survived. It was terrible – horrible – but it is over.

So, now, I think I will try to get some rest.

Good Night, Honey ... I hope that all has gone well and everyone is satisfied with the conference, and that you can get some rest too, soon.

To: Laura

Date sent: Sat, 27 Sep 97 17:49:45

Honey, we knew there will be furious attacks. We could have predicted it. But there will be future and it will be good because we are not alone we do have helpers. We have had car accident one kid was involved with. It should teach us a lesson. We have another accident now; it should teach us a lesson.

The conference is over the last round table discussion was long, much longer than it was planned. It was a smashing success. I gave an overview of EEQT and all these people were happy so EEQT exists and everybody is satisfied and calling this meeting exceptional.

I am VERY tired almost unconscious but all is fine and well and okay we will make it and now REALLY SOON.

IT WAS HARD today because of what has happened to ANNA but it gave me, in fact, even more determination to find the force and energy that was necessary.

To: Ark

Date sent: Sun, 28 Sep 97 05:28:20

Oh, Honey, I feel like I've been hit by a truck. I spent most of the day at the hospital. V** came with me and we gave Anna Reiki for hours.

Finally, in the late afternoon, she talked a little bit and seemed more like herself. So, I came home and tried to rest. But, I couldn't. So, I went back to the hospital and sat with her while she slept. Then I cam home again. I am almost to the point that I think I can sleep.

You know, I wonder about what the Cs said about "Mt. Anna may erupt ... cataclysmically ... " and, indeed this was a cataclysmic "eruption," though more physical than anything, though I would have to say that it must represent something spiritual or psychological.

Well, I am too tired to think about it or analyze it. There are just some images that get frozen in the mind and take forever to go away, and seeing my baby like she was last night is one of them.

I have little red spots all over my legs that look like measles ... they are ruptured capillaries from the hours standing with my legs and back braced, holding that child while she convulsed over and over again – trying to keep her from hurting herself, and fighting to keep her in the body. When I wasn't trying to calm her down and keep her still, I was pleading with her not to leave me.

So, I wish I could cry just now because I think I would feel better faster if I could, but it seems to be stuck in my throat.

I won't feel comfortable until she is home and fine.

Oh, Honey! It is absolutely incredible just now how much I need you ... And so do these poor babies of ours ... Thank God it won't be long.

And, it is still raining, there are flood warnings and it is just very strange right now.

So, Honey, I am going to lie down.

To Ark:

Date sent: Sat, 27 Sep 97 19:17:17

I slept about 5 hours. The lung specialist called and said that he had been called in because Anna had inhaled vomit into her lungs and they are watching for pneumonia.

Then I went back to the hospital for awhile, and now I am back again.

She is sleeping from the medicine that keeps her from vomiting more, the oxygen is still connected, but they felt that they could remove the respirator. She has a tube that empties her stomach constantly, and a bladder catheter. Everybody at the hospital is in love with her because she is so sweet and grateful when she IS conscious. She has certainly had a serious shock, and lesson, as have we all.

You know, it is funny – they put her in the same room Sandra died in.

Well, I expect Sandra is watching out for her a little, if that is possible.

Anyway, I KNEW the conference would be such a success!

So, you sleep as much as you can. I am taking all care. We will survive this as we have all.

And, I DO believe that she lived because I was there giving her Reiki from the very beginning. It was so close. My arms and legs are very sore from bending over the bed and holding her still during the hours of convulsions. It was utterly terrifying. I just want to hold her in my arms and make it all go away.

And, funny – it is the end of September again. And the end of September always seems to be such a rough time.

I will send news when I am here. I will be in and out for the next few days. They say they want to keep her in ICU for another couple of days.

To: Laura

Date sent: Sun, 28 Sep 97 06:24:12

Honey, I was writing a long letter to you and then, at the end, it was all lost ... the connection was lost. So I make it short: I love you I send kisses and you are in my arms.

I am packing now and in the evening I will be sending you kisses from Wroclaw.

Take strength from my love.

To: Laura

Date sent: Tue, 30 Sep 1997 07:37:49

Mother was very much moved by what has happened to Anna. She was praying in the night for Anna to get better. Funny is this mother of mine. Otherwise all is okay and alright.

These Lizzies must have been using the fact that I was so much busy and involved with the conference ... and they have chosen to attack just then! But we must make this event to act against them. I can't help thinking that Anna was supposed to go to school ...

Well, now the most important thing is that soon we will be together and we will be doing all those things that need us being together. And then all will be different. And it's gonna be rather soon. I am watching. You too.

I still haven't fully recovered from the trauma of the near death of my daughter. I knew, at that point, just how down and dirty the attacks could get. The realization that an agent could appear anywhere, at any time, under any guise, had been, up to this point, something of an abstract idea. I now understood what the Cs had meant when they said:

A: Or maybe programmed decoy, due to FRV?

Q: What is FRV?

A: Frequency Resonance Vibration.

Q: Is there any danger to [the children] with these kids and church people they have been around the past few weeks?

A: What do you think?!? It is a vulnerable age for anyone, much more so for the children of one on path to super consciousness, and in contact with those who provide advice and data ...

And the last remark about being "in contact with those who provide advice and data" is clearly meant to refer to Ark as much as the Cs themselves. Indeed, we had suffered attacks before Ark entered the picture, but the forces of the Matrix went into overdrive afterward – mainly to prevent us from being together. And here, an explanation for how this worked was being proposed: that certain individuals with a certain FRV, were susceptible to being programmed and utilized as decoys or Agents of the Matrix.

Over and over again we had told the children that there were forces out there that were going to be targeting them, that they needed to operate at the highest awareness level possible. We told them that they needed to examine their friends and relationships and keep always in mind that people would be brought into their lives whose intent was to do them harm. They revolted against this idea. It was unthinkable for them to hold suspicions about their "friends." They were sure that we had just simply gone over the edge.

Within the next three months, despite my pleas for her to be more careful, my eldest daughter had two more accidents, making a total of three in an 11-month period. The third one totaled her car, and if it had not been a Volvo, she would not have survived. She was hit broadside, on the driver's side, by a man who ran a red light. He claimed that he fell asleep at the wheel. I had been hit by so many shocks in so short a period of time that I was simply not able to assimilate and deal with all of it.

Both girls came to a hard realization that it wasn't a joke, and they struggled with cognitive dissonance. Naturally, they wanted us to give up what we were doing so they could have a normal life like all their friends. We tried to explain to them that we loved them, and because we loved them, because we were concerned about not only their future, but the future of everyone else's children, we could *not* give up our work. We told them that one day they would understand, even if they didn't now. The real solution was for them to understand the level of vigilance that was necessary and to undertake to employ it. They resented that. They wanted to have a normal life, to have fun, to not have to worry about agents of the Matrix around every corner. And that was perfectly understandable. They were both upset with us, and later they both decided that safety lay in distance and they moved out on their own.

I made an appointment with an insurance agent and purchased large insurance policies on each of my children and announced out loud as I put them in the safe: "OK, you sons of bitches! Touch another one of my kids and every damn dime will go to expose you for what you are." And I meant it.

Hell and High Water had come, and we had survived.

CHAPTER 49
FREQUENCY RESONANCE VIBRATION

It would be very easy to just write off the series of attacks I have been describing as just the way things are. My daughters were just kids who made mistakes, and nearly died because of them. Our lives are just like anybody else's lives in the sense that about half the time good things happen and half the time bad things happen. It's just the nature of life, it's the way things are. The same things happen to everybody. This last is most certainly true. And that is the point of the Cs communication: to explain to us the nature of good and evil, the nature of this reality in which we live, where bad things happen to good people, and very often, because of the fact that they are good, and are trying to do good things.

The interwoven themes of the Cassiopaean messages reflect the very things with which I was concerned for many years prior to meeting Frank and undertaking the "channeling" experiment. These two themes: the explanation for the existence of evil in a world created by a purported loving god, and the possibility of metamorphosis into a different world where there is no sting of sin or death, were expounded in the first manuscript version of *The Noah Syndrome*, written in 1985 and 1986. So, in a very real sense, it is altogether possible that the Cs *are* me at some level of consciousness, that I have made it all up to explain the things that concern me in a crucially deep way. One thing is certain: these issues never concerned Frank and his entire consciousness was focused on rejecting and reviling human existence rather than attempting to understand and explain it, and learning to live in the world as it is, successfully and effectively.

It took me years to realize that Frank's contractile nature was not merely the result of being psychologically wounded, but was the fundamental expression of his being: *self*-ishness. I never realized that his almost serpentine lethargy was the way he was, because it was the *way he was*. With my rose-colored glasses, I thought this stillness, this lack of activity was quiet strength. I accepted all his criticisms that I was always getting attacked because I was doing and sharing things. I tried to temper my nature, my natural tendency to share everything I discovered with anyone who asked with sober reflection and caution. Indeed, I am sure that caution would have kept me out of the soup on more than one occasion. But caution should not make a person inactive. One should not be so paralyzed by the fear of attack that they do nothing! I didn't realize that it is the one who accepts the risks of commitment that is the stronger person.

Frank was not just afraid of commitment and creativity, he was repelled by it from the depths of his nature. Commitment and creativity are acts of giving, of sacrifice. It is the Sulphur of Alchemy, the Soul Fire. The Soul Light. It is joy and delight in giving away spiritual energy. And there was no joy or delight in Frank's soul; there was only fear, jealousy, and contempt. These are the emotions of stasis, inaction, or reckless destruction.

A correspondent who is very attached to the government-conspiracy-to-create-the-UFO-phenomenon-as-a-means-of-social-engineering theory, who yet is convinced of the existence of ethereal beings, recently wrote to me, "You are very close. There are UFO's and there are 'aliens.' But the aliens are us and vice versa."

He then went on to propose that our level of reality and the next higher level, have a "symmetry balance" which posits that *we are in control of the Matrix*. The Matrix reflects us and we it. What we become – it becomes. Indeed, this possibility is one that the Cs have proposed in the following exchange:

July 23, 1995

Q: (L) Does it ever happen that individuals who perceive or think they perceive themselves to have experienced an abduction, to actually be interacting with some part of themselves?

A: That would be a very good possibility. Now, before you ask another question, stop and contemplate for a moment: what possibilities does this open up? Is there any limit? And if there is, what is that? Is it not an area worth exploring? For example, just one example for you to digest: What if the abduction scenario could take place where your soul projection, in what you perceive as the future, can come back and abduct your soul projection in what you perceive as the present? Is it one possible future, but not all possible futures? And is the pathway of free will not connected to all of this?

In short, any and all of the manifestations of aliens and so forth are "us" in probable futures. We *can* choose which future manifests: *us* as the creepy reptoids and grays who abduct and violate, torture and torment, or *us* as beings who completely honor free will.

When we first consider this idea, the solution seems to be rather simple: we just choose to do what is good and right and everything will be fine and dandy. If we are being good, then the future will be good, and "as below, so above," the higher "future" reality will reflect our choices of goodness and free will, right?

But here is where we arrive at the sticking point. As I have written numerous times, there is something about this that we don't understand because such a simple solution has never worked, and I wanted to know why. *Think about it.* Throughout history we find one group praying to their god to protect them from the depredations of another group. The other group is praying just as fervently that their depredations will be successful. When one group succeeds in killing another, is that proof that its god is supreme? What then happens if the members of the successful group are then reincarnated into the group that was defeated? This is not a rhetorical question since a rather influential book was written about the great numbers of Jews who died in the Holocaust now being reincarnated as Christians. There has also been some suggestion that many Nazis are now being reincarnated as Jews. What then, does such an idea do to the concept of "my god is the only right one?"

I can assure the reader from my own experience as a hypnotherapist, that every single case I have worked with in terms of past-life therapy, has demonstrated a string of lives in such variety of nationality and religious orientation, that it literally makes a joke of anyone stating with absolute certainty, that their beliefs or orientation now, are the only right ones. It is evident that those who declaim against another group most vehemently will most certainly find themselves a member of that very group in the next round of incarnation. And frankly, it doesn't matter if the reader believes this or not; there is sufficient clinical evidence that it is so, that if presented in a court of law as circumstantial evidence, it would be so overwhelming that the judge and the jury would be persuaded of the truth of it even without a smoking gun.

And that brings us back again to the factor that, for some reason, we are denied access to our greater self. And thus, people continue to kill one another for the conscious beliefs they hold, never realizing the price they may pay for these actions. This begs the question of why people cannot remember the previous lessons in past lives; why the wisdom of the soul is not available to the person. *If humans have souls or spirits, why is the knowledge of past karmic cycles not part of a person's wisdom?*

What can answer the question as to why human beings engage in activities that will only trap them here for a myriad of lifetimes? Is this planet nothing more than a huge recycling bin; no-matter what people do, there will always be new and improved ways for killing other humans?

What would be the payoff for our reality to exist as such a structure that causes the soul to constantly recycle? What would be the reason for such darkness that perpetuates this vast and abyssal ignorance? What is the payoff for all this misery and suffering; the tormented souls and the deaths of innocents? What is this mysterious gap between intent, desire, and physical manifestation? What darkness exists in our subconscious minds that has created a world so hostile and uncaring? What power separates us from knowledge of the true nature of our reality and leaves us exposed to suffering and pain?

No matter how one defines reality – as a self-created manifestation, or as an accomplished fact thrust upon us – the reality of suffering must be seen as a consequence of this separation. And, if the world of matter is created and maintained by us, what brought this blindness into being?

If the world is created by God, is our suffering a consequence of willful disobedience? If so, then man's being is a blight on the cosmos. If that is so, then what shall we do with goodness, nobility and selfless brotherly love and reverent worship? From where has this duality originated?

If we accept that, for whatever reason, some aspect of creation has manifested the limited three dimensions in which our consciousness finds itself, how would we describe this condition and its potential for change? What does it mean that the universe may leave all its options open until the very last instant? If that is the case, then what are we doing when we pray for a specific outcome, or when we believe in the End of the World? The questions about how our beliefs may shape our reality are among the most significant in all of consciousness research.

This leads to another point: it seems that we must accept the objective fact that attempts to change the world spiritually, or to regulate large-scale events, simply do not work. Yes, there does seem to be evidence that individuals or small groups of individuals can make small changes or produce effects with a limited range of influence. But for some reason the world, as it is, seems to operate based on rules or laws that we do not understand. The fundamental nature of the physical world seems to be antithetical to this spiritualization. While we all might like to think we can transform our world by praying and/or thinking positively, we must remember that there is a great deal of evidence that *real transformations of the planet have repeatedly been cataclysmic.* A philosophy which ignores this fact is courting disaster.

It may be that the focus upon creating a new world or a New Age quite literally contributes energy to the dissolution of the present age *in a manner which follows scientific principles.* This brings us back to Einstein's remarks in his 1938 paper:

We have, therefore, to take the fifth dimension seriously although we are not encouraged to do so by plain experience. The most essential point of our theory is the replacing of rigorous cylindricity by the assumption that space is closed (or periodic). Kaluza's five dimensional theory of the physical space provides a unitary representation of gravitation and electromagnetism. It is much more satisfactory to introduce the fifth dimension not only formally, but to assign to it some physical meaning.

In other words: time is cyclical. We live in a time loop. And here is where the Cs material is so important. Over and over again, developing the themes of my lifelong search, they have expressed concepts and ideas that are on the cutting edge of physics research.

January 21, 1995

Q: (L) What is the "ultimate secret" being protected by the Consortium?

A: You are not in control of yourselves, you are an experiment.

Q: (T) When you say this is the ultimate secret that we're being "protected" from by the government, are we talking about the ultimate secret of humans only here?

A: Basically.

Q: (T) The ultimate secret of the human race is that we are an experiment that other humans are conducting on the rest of us?

A: Part.

Q: (T) OK, does the other part have to do with the Lizards?

A: Yes.

Q: (L) Other aliens also?

A: Yes.

Q: (T) OK, so, are the humans who are running the experiment, do they know that they are part of the experiment also?

A: Yes.

Q: (T) And they're doing this willingly?

A: They have no choice.

Q: (L) Why do they have no choice?

A: Already in progress.

Q: (T) What is the experiment about?

A: Too complicated for you to understand.

Q: (J) I hate it when that happens! (T) OK, is this part of, is this about the experiment the Lizzies are doing of dominating us and sucking us dry?

A: Yes, but there's much more than that, you will understand at level 4.

Q: (L) OK, in this Krill document there was a statement made that the Grays and other aliens use glandular substances extracted during physical exams of human beings, what they would call the gynecological and the sperm-extraction exams, that they used these glandular substances to get high or to feed on, that they are addicted to these. Is this a correct assessment?

A: No.

Q: (L) Do they use glandular substances at all?

A: Yes.

Q: (L) What do they use glandular substances for?

A: Medicine.

Q: (L) And what or who do they use this medicine on?

A: Themselves.

Q: (L) And what does this medicine do for them?

A: Helps them cope with 3rd density.

Q: (T) Is this something that they use to help them stay in the third density?

A: Close.

Q: (L) Does it help them to manifest in a more solid physical manner?

A: Yes.

Q: (L) So, in other words, they draw glandular substances; do they also use sexual energy given off by individuals to maintain their status in 3 dimensions?

A: No. That feeds them in 4d, as we told you before.

Q: (L) Yes. OK. How "long", and I put long in quotes, because we know, as you say, there is no time, but how long, as we measure it, have the Grays been interacting with our race? The Grays, not the Lizards, the Grays, the cybergenetic probes?

A: Time travelers, therefore, "Time is ongoing." Do you understand the gravity of [this] response?

Q: (L) They are time travelers, they can move forward and backward in time, they can play games with our heads ... (T) They can set up the past to create a future they want. (D) They can organize things so that they can create the energy that they need ... (L) They can also make things look good, make them feel good, make them seem good, they can make you have an idea one minute, and then the next minute, create some sort of situation that confirms that idea ...

A: When you asked how long, of course it is totally unlimited, is it not?

Q: (L) That's not good. If they were to move back through space-time and alter an event in our past, would that alteration in the past instantaneously alter our present as well?

A: Has over and over and over. You just are not yet aware, and have no idea of the ramifications!!!

Q: (L) We're getting a little glimmer! Yeah, I do, a little! (T) The ramifications of being able to move in and out of time and manipulate it the way you want (L) So, in other words, our only real prayer in this whole damn situation is to get out of this density level. That's what they're saying, that's what it sounds like to me.

A: Close.

Q: (L) Because, otherwise, we're just literally, as in that book, stuck in the replay over and over and over, and the Holocaust could happen over and over, and we could just, you know ... Ghengis Khan, Atilla the Hun ... over and over and over again. (T) We're stuck in a time loop; they're putting us in a time loop. (J) Are we in a time loop?

A: Yes.

Q: (D) I have a question about ... Mankind has found it necessary for some reason or other to appoint time. The only reason I can see is to have a means of telling, like in verbal or written communications ...

A: Control mechanism.

Q: (T) Is there a way for us to break the control mechanism? Besides moving to fourth density?

A: Nope.

Q: (D) When fourth-density beings communicate it's telepathic, right?

A: Yes.

Q: (D) OK, since time doesn't exist, how do you communicate about happenings?

A: Rephrase, please; clarify.

Q: (L) What she means to ask is, if time doesn't exist, how do you communicate about events as one happens now, as opposed to later and the next thing happens, and the next thing happens ... I mean, we talk about 1907 something happened ...

A: Translate. That is how it is done. You translate the experience from 4 to 3. And vice versa.

Q: (L) So, in other words, if you're a fourth-density being, everything is more or less happening, excuse the term happening, everything is simultaneous, and if you wish to discuss or communicate or have any focus upon any particular aspect of this unified dimension, then what you do is you kind of extract it out, project it into 3d ...

A: Close.

Q: (L) ... like a movie.

A: But you will not understand fully until you get there.

Q: (L) Is the only way of getting out of this time loop, so to speak, to move into another density, or is there a loop in the other density as well?

A: No.

Q: (L) No loop in the other density?

A: Yogis can do it. How they control their own physicality.

And so we have a few more clues. We have some idea that our reality is something of a stage upon which the dramas of fourth density are projected. In short, it seems evident that the energies of Creation emanate "downward," and our individuality as human beings is merely an expression of these theological dramas. To attempt to exert our will or to make our voice travel "upward," against Creation, results only in the strengthening of the forces that violate free will, because it is, in essence, an attempt to violate the free will of Creation. This is why praying, rituals designed to change reality, positive thinking with the intent to change something "up there," in order to receive the benefits "down here," is always doomed to produce more strife, misery and suffering.

What we *can* do is to prepare ourselves for the emanations that are traveling "downward" to be better received. So, indeed, my correspondent is correct: "There is a 'symmetry balance' which posits that we are in control of the Matrix. The Matrix reflects us and we it. What we become – it becomes." This is the essential point of Castaneda when he wrote:

> He explained that one of the greatest accomplishments of the seers of the Conquest was a construct he called the three-phase progression. By understanding the nature of man, they were able to reach the incontestable conclusion that if seers can hold their own in facing petty tyrants, they can certainly face the unknown with impunity, and then they can even stand the presence of the unknowable.
>
> "The average man's reaction is to think that the order of that statement should be reversed," he went on. "A seer who can hold his own in the face of the unknown can certainly face petty tyrants. But that's not so. What destroyed the superb seers of ancient times was that assumption. We know better now. We know that nothing can temper the spirit of a warrior as much as the challenge of dealing with impossible people in positions of power. Only under those conditions can warriors acquire the sobriety and serenity to stand the pressure of the unknowable."

All around us we see the results of this error: the idea that we can exert our will and voice upward to change what is "above" us in order to change our reality. This idea is at the root of rites and rituals, demanding, pleading, visualizations, "workings," and so forth. When people think that "meditating on compassion," or "feeling the feelings of all beings," is going to result in the "sonic entrainment of the heart's rhythm [being] braided into more complex and coherent patterns," which will then enable the person to "create a diamond imperishable body for use as a teaching vehicle down here on earth," they have missed the point entirely. To compare such ideas to the true work of the Yogi is simply ignorant.

Yogis don't just sit down one day and meditate on compassion or the feeling of oneness and "boom!" experience an "implosive soul force." Before the Yogi has ever achieved the point of being able to think even momentarily about "the oneness of all beings," or the "feelings of all beings," he has spent many, many years in the struggle between "yes" and "no" – the struggle to master his emotions, his desires, his physicality. It is the work of making the physical vehicle "down here," receptive to whatever may be "up there," as opposed to trying to forcibly create something "up there," in order to have it "down here."

But not everybody can just drop out of life and become a Yogi.

And it seems that those nasty versions of ourselves in the future really wish to continue to exist, to become even more powerful, and as a consequence, they exert a great deal of energy attempting to ensure not only their continued survival, but their ultimate dominance over all Creation! After all, it *is* a time loop, and the last time it looped around, they were the outcome, the choice, the probable future that became the Now. And they want to keep it that way.

And the choice as to which reality we will cycle into for the next round, or whether or not we can step out of the loop at the nexus point, has to be made rather soon. Which is why there is so much effort to conceal, disinform, obfuscate, and disrupt the dissemination of the ideas of free will and true service to others. These future selves of the Reptilian, Gray, and other STS varieties are using time travel to go back and repeatedly change the past, to plant misleading clues, to get folks to make the choices that will strengthen their hold on this density, and consequently, fourth density. The alternate futures: us in the future as the "bad guys," or us in the future as light beings is being decided now. The battle is *now*. It is *through* us.

It seems that one of the chief forms of disinformation that keeps humanity locked into the STS mode of existence, and which is hoped to ensure the ultimate victory of the STS forces at higher levels, is exactly what we have described above: the reversal of the natural order of achieving self-mastery. A very popular form of this disinformation is found in the so-called "Flower of Life" and related "Sacred Geometry" teachings that are very popular in the present time. The stated purpose of the system is:

> Through our teachings of sacred geometry, we introduce the student to ancient esoteric teachings given around the world for thousands of years. These teachings, based on sacred geometry, illustrate for the left brain how there is truly only one consciousness, one spirit, one God, and that we are all part of that oneness. After the mind understands this concept, we then teach the student a 17-breath merkaba meditation that will allow he or she to feel and experience this unity of all life. The left and right brains suddenly awaken to this universal truth and the heart begins to put this truth into action.
>
> Seeing and feeling this unity of life clearly within every aspect of our lives is very important. Both sides of the brain begin to move into harmony and balance, and this kind of balance aids the heart in opening. Experiencing this universal unity also integrates the heart and mind, which weaves peace and balance into all corners of our being. Harmony and balance opens windows in our mind, our heart, and our spirit. Without divine unity inside of us, these windows of inspiration are rarely available. Internal unity opens a doorway within us and allows prana or "divine balanced life force energy" to enter the innermost channels

of our physical being. It begins a process of inner healing and rejuvenation that affects our physical, emotional, and spiritual bodies.[15]

There are many variations on this theme, including "Projecting the Tree of Life on the Celestial Globe," or utilizing the "Meta-Programming Protocol." All of them, as the reader can easily see from the above description, constitute the idea that we can exert our will and voice upward to change what is "above" us in order to change our reality, ourselves, moving our brains into harmony, or aiding the "heart in opening," obtaining "harmony and balance" which is then going to "open windows in our mind, our heart, and our spirit," etc. It is then stated (quite truthfully, I should add, since good disinformation is always wrapped in a warm and fuzzy truth), that, "without Divine Unity inside of us, these windows of inspiration are rarely available." What is left out is the cold, hard fact that this is entirely the bass-ackward way to go about achieving any of the above claimed benefits.

Sure, such activities will temporarily produce chemical changes that will feel *very* good, the same way a good meal satisfies hunger temporarily. It really feels good! But just as the steak and salad are digested and most of the matter excreted in a few hours, and another steak and salad is needed to fill the stomach again, so do such practices fail to so anything more than perpetuate the food chain. And, staying with the analogy, very little of the substance of such practices actually stays with the individual.

A self-proclaimed Enochian Magician of our acquaintance has described such pathways in the following terms: *"The magickal training was great too. I was learning and experiencing faster than I had dreamed possible, and for a sensation junkie like me, this was heaven."*

And that is the key: sensation junkies. As I wrote in *Secret History*, the problem with the whole human potential/consciousness expansion movement is this: in the midst of all these mind-blowing peak experiences of drug-induced spiritual voyages, turning on and tuning in, ecstasy and encountering, many people encountered things that, perhaps, ought not have been awakened. Boundaries were breached into unseeable and terrifying realms of consciousness. Never mind that all of these products of the psychedelic mysticism of the 1960s and 70s *bypassed the vital processes of reason and conscious decision making*. By its very nature, the whole techno-spiritual machine operated completely without critical thinking; it tapped the bottomless pit of feeling – emotion – primal being. Never mind that much of this emotion was negative, confusing, anxious, and fearful! Let's just get it *all* out here in the open and have a party with it!

---

[15] http://www.floweroflife.org/toverview1.htm

So preserve yourselves, my brothers, from the calamities of this place, for distinguishing it is extremely difficult! *Souls find it sweet, and then within it they are duped*, since they become completely enamored of it. (Al-'Arabi, Futuhat, III 38.23, translated by William Chittick)

Nowadays most people interested in the spirituality of the East desire the "experience," though they may call what they are after intimate communion with God. Those familiar with the standards and norms of spiritual experience set down by disciplined paths like Sufism are usually appalled at the way Westerners seize upon any apparition from the domain outside of normal consciousness as a manifestation of the "spiritual." In fact, there are innumerable realms in the unseen world, some of them far more dangerous than the worst jungles of the visible world. (Chittick, 1989)

Thus, by the end of the decade of the '60s, the human potential movement had become a veritable potpourri of religion, science, mysticism, magick and the occult. The drug use got out of hand, the techniques began to show serious flaws in the many tragedies that occurred in any given practice, and the whole idea of human beings becoming "psychic supermen" hit the skids. The promise of the '60s decayed into an aimless lethargy – old hippies living in communes, braiding their gray locks and lusting after the sweet young teeny boppers while they fired up another bong and reminisced about the good old days at Esalen.

But wait! Something else happened here! Remember, this is America! The home of the Free – Market, that is. Big business saw a gold mine in the consciousness raising movement of the '60s and we saw the development of slick, newly packaged psychoanalysis and psychodrama! There was mass-distribution and Madison-Avenue marketing of things like Mind Dynamics, Arica, Silva Mind Control, Transcendental Meditation, and on and on.

And the cults proliferated. Yes, many of the mind-wounded ran straight back into the arms of their childhood faith; but many more became victims of the many up-and-coming cults that were happy to take them in and patch the holes in their psyches, or fix them up for a few weekends of Merkaba Meditations, Equinox Workings, Mystery School Mish-mash, or Pagan Pow-wows. Many of the cults, and even the old time religions, took advantage of the new marketing strategies and polished up their images, sent their people to advertising classes and then out into the world in massive fundraising and recruitment drives. Many of them even have their own ad-men!

So, the race was on again! Only now, it was like buying Coca-Cola! The "pause that refreshes" right here in this very tape set, consciousness-raising course, or cult practice! It had become a form of spiritual masturbation where everyone was "meeting their own needs" in private. You could put on your strobe glasses, listen to your astral travel tape, channel your very own guides, confer with the Ophanic Intelligences, merge with the "Nine Neters," and get high without ever leaving the farm! You could change your beliefs, create your own reality, indulge your inner child/ego, and become One with all Creation, by mail, by golly!

What nobody seems to be talking about, however, are the concomitant changes in our world that very well may be the direct result of this so-called shift in consciousness. Nobody wants to talk about the hard reality of what is really going on out there. One correspondent described it so well that I will reproduce his comments:

> I think I am noticing a vast world of things going on that, just a few short years ago, would never have happened. Almost everywhere I look, when I see circumstances and reactions and goings-on, the thought explodes into my head – "What in the world is going on here?"
>
> -The modern-day Roman circus spectaculars of Elians, O.J.s and Monicas
>
> -The appeal of today's non-music, music that appeals to the most base of human emotion and response
>
> -The opiate of the mindless drone and flicker of constant television
>
> -The dangled carrot of a manipulated and contrived economy
>
> -The apathy toward the government and their meaningless platitudes
>
> -The increase in violence and attacks from close and least expected sources, which appear to be designed by outside forces to both provide an energy feeding frenzy, as well as, divert those seeking awareness and understanding from a path of discovery
>
> -The dark side of Tesla genius
>
> -The easy access of Internet porn and the proliferation of cyber-sex as an option to replace "real life"

And to the above I would like to add:

> -One out of every 100 Americans is living in a prison, a figure unprecedented in our history.
>
> -The numbers of people on prescription, mind-altering drugs is even higher than the number of people in physical prisons.
>
> -We are now diagnosing and drugging even our children for behavior that was once considered to be "normal" for a child!
>
> -Gang proliferation throughout all levels of society, where once such things existed only among the very poor and disadvantaged.
>
> -Violence among children who are becoming violent at younger ages than ever before.
>
> -Mass killings have become so common they aren't even reported on the front page anymore!

And, while I have your ear: what's up with the way kids dress nowadays? Well, it's not even just kids – it's ubiquitous! It seems that human beings, under the influence of Madison Avenue and the motivation masters of greed and degradation, get up real early in the morning in order to figure out how to dress themselves, arrange their hair, and decorate their bodies in as repulsive a way as possible!

I am continuously revolted by clerks in stores with multiply pierced body parts, tattoos that look more like dirt smudges or bruises than art, hair that looks like it was arranged by Atilla the Hun or Torquemada, the Grand Inquisitor; make-up that looks like it was applied by Vlad the Impaler. Young people wear clothing that makes them look like rejects from the Oklahoma dust bowl days. Chains and chunks of metal clank from every part of their person as they saunter about displaying their "cool" to their peers, looking more like a combination of an ancient Mongol warrior and survivor of a death camp than anything else.

And it's *not* what they claim – personal expression – because it is more of a uniform than anything else! The demand to have the same look, the same brand of clothing, the same body parts pierced, or to think of new and more bizarre ways to do it, is overwhelming every parent I know. I have had to draw the line in my own house, telling my kids that they won't eat at my table if the way they look makes my stomach churn!

Who or *what* is inspiring these manifestations of purely barbaric behavior? Who is turning humanity into beings who accept what used to be the trappings of slavery as if it were the latest style? And what's more, to convince them that it is "expressive" or "attractive?" What, in the name of God, is going on when physical self-mutilation and self-defacement, mind-numbing and body-jarring sounds, and things that are just plain *ugly* are considered normal?! And, not just normal, but *attractive*, for God's sake!

Those who have bought into the New Age bonanza seem to have shut off their minds and the effect on their offspring is frightening. They have become part of a reality that is ripe for being taken over by the first "strong man" who comes along with "signs and wonders."

However, based on the information from the Cs, we now have some idea that the fourth density (equivalent to the fifth dimension in mathematical terms), is a para-physical realm of archetypes, and that these archetypal groupings may be the arbiters of human, societal, and national interactions as conceived, and created by mass thought *or vice versa!* We may merely be the actors in an archetypal play that is written, cast, directed and produced from some other layer of reality. It may be that there are set pieces we each play, and perhaps these cumulative events of humans in this world are the energies that express the balance or imbalance of forces or beings at higher levels.

And this brings us to the problem of frequency-resonance vibration. Why did the Cs make a remark about a Pied Piper-type of person as being "programmed decoy, due to FRV??" How does this relate to the Matrix? As it happens, the subject of FRV was brought up on a number of occasions by the Cs, in several contexts that need to be carefully examined.

August 5, 1995

Q: (L) There was a discussion the other day and it made me curious. It seems that some people simply do not have the capacity to understand certain concepts. Is this a function of vibrational frequency?

A: That is not quite hitting at the subject matter in the way in which you desire to answer the question. In other words, it is a parallel understanding pattern. It is not vibrational frequency that determines ability to conceive of any particular notion. Vibrational frequency involves the groove, or pattern, that one has chosen in general terms.

But, to give you an example, there are those who are of very LOW, as you would measure, vibrational frequency, who are able to conceive of extremely complicated issues and have also discovered extremely precise, complicated, and intricate answers to very complex notions and problems from your standpoint in the illusion.

But, the frequency vibrational level has more to do with the emotional path that leads either to Service to Self at its greatest possible expression, or Service to Others at its greatest possible expression, not with intellectual capacity. So it is possible for a completely STS individual at any density level to be completely cognizant of all existence, just as it is possible for a completely STO individual to be completely cognizant of all existence. It has nothing to do with vibrational frequency because that is the emotional pathway.

Think, if you will, in your lifetime have you ever met either a) an individual that you did not perceive to be particularly intellectually developed, who was, nevertheless, of a very kind and loving and giving nature; or b) an individual whom you perceive to have great intellectual capacity who was, nevertheless, extremely selfish and non-giving and not generous and not concerned about anyone's well being but their own?

Naturally, [lesser intellectual capacity] itself, can lead to all sorts of emotional entanglements and frictions. The greater the intellectual capacity, the greater the chance that each and every facet of intellect will be available for use, growth and stimulation. The lesser the intellectual capacity, the greater the chance that some will not be available. [However], it does not require a differential in vibrational frequency level to produce the types of symptoms that you describe. It is merely intellectual capacity that is inferior rather than the vibrational frequency level. Again, this vibrational frequency level involves nature of being and emotion, not intelligence.

The remark the Cs made about FRV, which suggests that a person is amenable to being programmed *because* of their FRV, or, as we understand it now, the "emotional path that leads either to service-to-self at its greatest possible expression, or service-to-others at its greatest possible expression," seems to be related to abductions. The reader will remember the discussion we have already had about frequency of abductions:

Q: (L) Why have they abducted Frank more than me?
A: You fight it.

This was later connected to Frequency-Resonance Vibration in an interesting way. In the following short excerpt, the discussion was about mind programming, in specific, what is referred to as Greenbaum programming, a sort of Nazi/Satanist/Secret government Manchurian Candidate-type of thing. Everyone was asking "what about me?" and reference was made to me:

October 5, 1996
A: Laura had more advanced work done on her.
Q: (V) That opens up a whole new can of worms. (L) And what do you mean by that?
A: Not now.
Q: (L) Who did this work, can I have that? Can I know that?
A: Consortium.
Q: (L) Is there any possibility, to some extent, that I have overcome this influence at the present time?
A: No. Was partial, then aborted, leaving fragments of trigger response programs that have been in remission.
Q: (L) Why was it aborted?
A: Because STO forces intervened.
Q: (L) And when was this?
A: Mid 'fifties.
Q: (L) So it was when I was three or four years old.

At a later time, when there were not so many people present, I came back to the subject, and it was here that the remark about frequency-resonance vibration was inserted which, when taken in conjunction with the remark about fewer abductions because "you fight it," begins to give us some idea of how these things may be related:

October 12, 1996
Q: (L) Well, was I mind programmed? You said once that I was not Greenbaumed, but that something else was done. What was this?
A: The work that was attempted was more intense, but it was aborted because it turned out that your frequency resonance vibration was not proper for that particular type of "experimental" programming.

393

Q: Does this mean that there was something about my vibrations that caused what they were trying to do to result in positive things?

A: Possibly, in an offhand way.

My thought at the time I asked the last question above was that perhaps the fear and trauma I had experienced as a child was what motivated me so powerfully to seek for answers. That would be a positive result from a negative event. In the same way, I think that many of the difficulties we all face, some of us more than others, tend to make us stronger. Of course, the real test that we have learned from our difficulties seems to be not so much that they no longer happen, but that they no longer have any ability to control our responses – we have disconnected from the reaction machine.

Nevertheless, the fact that what was done to me as a child included a major attempt to gain physical control of me – that was obviously an act of desperation or so many risks of exposure would not have been taken – seems to suggest that my life was certainly in danger to the point that protective intervention was necessary.

August 1, 1998

Q: (L) I was also reading in some of the transcripts as I have been going through them getting them ready to print, that you once said that "supremely powerful" STS forces were responsible for kidnapping and programming me. My question is: if they had me, why did they bring me back?

A: Would you expect otherwise?

Q: (L) Well, you said that they tried to do some programming and that it didn't work and that STO forces intervened. So, I am just a little confused. If I was such a threat to them, why did they bring me back. Under the circumstances, I could have just disappeared forever and that would be that!

A: No.

Q: (L) What prevented that?

A: Occlusion.

Q: (L) Occlusion of what?

A: Best to research through meditation and hypnosis.

Occlude: to block or stop up (a passage or opening); obstruct. 2. (tr.) to prevent the passage of. To be occluded is to be veiled, or to be hidden behind a blocking wall or frequency envelope. Apparently, there are parts of myself that do things that the rest of me knows nothing about!

We come back now to that most interesting series of comments about the monitoring of the sessions:

February 1, 1997

Q: (L) Let me ask; is there going to be any attempt to further attack or harm us in any way?

A: Well, let us put it this way: the future is fluid, as you know. Knowledge protects you. But, it would be wise to picture these letters appearing on a screen somewhere, at the same moment that they are uttered!

Q: (L) Is it the uttering that ... ('T') Uttering, or spelled on the board? (L) ... "the moment they are uttered" ... is it the uttering that is the key?

A: Does not matter, in all reality. The key is what the expectation is as to how they are intended to be put to use.

In short, as long as it was just me and a few friends talking about physics and the Matrix reality, there was really nothing terribly threatening to the Control System. But at this point in time, apparently something significant had changed, and that was the fact that Ark was on his way to join us.

Q: (L) Is there an internal configuration or frequency level that makes it so that the persons who are selected to do this monitoring, or to be involved in any of this kind of activity, such as you have described, as in the words appearing on the screen, etc., so that they are definitely selected because of their STS orientation?

A: This process takes place naturally. Now, a warning for you. Frequency resonance modulations of vibration rate can be altered or modified from outside if one is not cautious and/or aware enough, and thus takes necessary precautions.

I know that my question above is really worded in so confusing a way that it is hard to know what I am asking. I had the idea that what was being described was a sort of techno-implant that was used for such monitoring. I realized that the Cs were suggesting that someone in our group was a monitor, and I most definitely wanted to find some excuse for this. Surely it could not be because the person was fundamentally STS. I thought that maybe some people are involved in some of these activities are innocent of any ill intent. Or, maybe they are forced to do things against their will. I was looking for an out for that person.

And the Cs didn't give it to me. They said: "This process takes place naturally." In other words, if somebody is doing it, it is because that is what they are since "the frequency vibrational level has more to do with the emotional path that leads either to service-to-self at its greatest possible expression, or service-to-others at its greatest possible expression," and this was followed by a warning that "Frequency resonance modulations of vibration rate can be altered or modified from outside if one is not cautious and/or aware enough, and thus takes necessary precautions." This is the big humdinger of the thing we are concerned with here. Very STO-oriented individuals can be switched onto a different track if they are not constantly on the alert and if they do not take the necessary precautions! Sometimes, those precautions include divorcing oneself from association with individuals who are vectors if it is realized that continued association will expose one to things that can alter or modify frequency. This was the approach we took with Vincent Bridges. There is also another very important factor relating to FRV: Earth Changes.

February 22, 1997

Q: (J) What causes the change in the axis?

A: By slow-down of rotation, Earth alternately heats up and cools down in interior.

Q: (L) Why does it do that? What's the cause of this?

A: Part of cycle related to energy exerted upon surface by the frequency resonance vibrational profile of humans and others.

July 4, 1998

Q: (A) I understand that the main disaster is going to come from this comet cluster ...

A: Disasters involve cycles in the human experiential cycle which corresponds to the passage of comet cluster.

✳ Keep the above in mind in relation to both the death of Princess Diana (discussed in the next chapter), as well as the September 11 disaster.

The idea of frequency-resonance vibration is intimately connected to what the Cs have referred to as an "EM vector," or "focuser of direction."

May 3, 1997

Q: Reading through the session of May 23, last year, when Tom was also here, and the issue of his being in O'Brien was addressed, you asked who had begged him to stay there, then there was a remark about an EM vector. The way I understood it is that a person can be an EM vector. Is that possible?

A: Vector means focuser of direction.

Q: Could that mean that EM waves can be vectored by a human being simply by their presence? I also noticed that several of us have been involved with persons and relationships that seem designed to confuse, defuse, and otherwise distort our learning, as well as drain our energy. Basically, keeping us so stressed that we cannot fulfill our potential. Is there some significance to this observation?

A: That is elementary, my dear Knight!

Q: One of the things I have learned is that these individuals seem to attach via some sort of psychic hook that enters through our reactions of pity. Can you comment on the nature of pity?

A: Pity those who pity.

Q: But, the ones who are being pitied, who generate sensations of pity, do not really pity anybody but themselves.

A: Yes ... ?

Q: Then, is it true as my son said, when you give pity, when you send love and light to those in darkness, or those who complain and want to be "saved" without effort on their own part, when you are kind in the face of abuse and manipulation, that you essentially are giving power to their further disintegration, or contraction into self-ishness? That you are powering their descent into STS?

A: You know the answer!

Q: Yes. I have seen it over and over again.

What this seems to suggest is that the individuals with whom we associate can vector our direction in terms of thinking as well as emotional pathway. This relates back to the remark about the possibility that "frequency resonance modulations of vibration rate can be altered or modified from outside if one is not cautious and/or aware enough, and thus takes necessary precautions." This is, in fact, something we have had to deal with on a number of occasions, as the reader will soon see.

What all of this seems to signify is that frequency-resonance vibration can be amplified or damped which can have a powerful impact on whether the individual is ready to graduate to the next level or not. The levels of density have been described by the Cs as "slots," and consciousness energy as "marbles."

May 31, 1997

Q: Now you have mentioned these "slots." What are these slots, and how does one move from one slot to another?

A: Picture this: you have 7 sizes of marbles. You have 7 widths of slots. Where do the marbles "fit in."

Q: Do the marbles represent units of consciousness?

A: Close. Or, divisions of consciousness level energy resonance profiles.

Q: Do these divisions of consciousness grow and change?

A: Yes.

Q: And they grow and change through acquiring knowledge; is that correct?

A: Basically.

Q: And acquiring knowledge is akin to acquiring energy? Or light? Light energy?

A: Not exactly. That would be like saying that "filling up" at the gas station is akin to acquiring speed.

Q: So, knowledge and light are like the gas for the car, but speed comes from utilization?

A: Yes.

Q: And utilization means ...

A: Knowledge application which generates energy, which, in turn, generates light.

Please notice that *utilization* of knowledge is what generates light. The Cs have already pointed out that "it is possible for a completely STS individual at any density level to be completely cognizant of all existence, just as it is possible for a completely STO individual to be completely cognizant of all existence." It has nothing to do with vibrational frequency because that is the emotional pathway, and the difference seems to lie between individuals who are of a very kind and loving and giving nature, as opposed to individuals who are extremely selfish and non-giving, and not generous and not concerned about anyone's well being but their own.

August 28, 1999

Q: (A) There are those who are happy in the STS mode; and there are those who are trying to get out of the STS mode ...

A: STO candidate.

Q: (A) These STO candidates cannot just simply *be*, even theoretically, because then, STS would eat them.

A: No.

Q: Why not?

A: STS does not eat according to protocol. STS "eats" whatever it wants to, if it is able.

Q: That's what we said. If you are STO in an STS world, you are basically defenseless and they eat you.

A: No.

Q: Why? What makes STO unavailable or "inedible?"

A: Frequency resonance not in sync.

This last remark takes us back to *utilization* of knowledge. In order for knowledge to protect, it must be utilized. By becoming aware of the theological reality that utilizes the psychological substrate, we are enabled to make choices based on this invisible reality, which greatly enhance our possibilities of avoiding being "eaten" by STS forces. Notice that the Cs said that STS "eats" whatever it wants to, *if it is able*. And what makes STO inedible is frequency resonance of *true* STO, and not STS masquerading as STO which is the majority of what passes for love and light. This leads us to another most enlightening series of remarks:

April 14, 2000

Q: (A) What is interesting is how do those who are trying to get these people, to abduct them, how do they spot them? How do they get the information? By following the bloodline, or by some kind of monitor you can detect from a long distance – and they can note that "here is somebody of interest" or "here is somebody dangerous" or "let's abduct this one" or whatever. How do they select? Do they search the genealogies or is it some kind of remote sensing?

A: Now this is interesting Arkadiusz, as it involves the atomic "signature" of the cellular structure of the individual. In concert with this is the etheric body reading and the frequency resonance vibration. All these are interconnected, and can be read from a distance using remote viewing technology/methodology.

Q: (L) Can it be done in a pure mechanical way without using psychic means?

A: At another level of understanding, the two are blended into one.

Q: (T) Computerized psychic remote viewing, maybe. Like artificial intelligence. Maybe a mind connected to a computer?

A: That is close, yes.

This takes us back to a much earlier remark about the reason that the aliens have been doing their abducting and genetic meddling.

October 7, 1995

Q: (L) But isn't the nature of a person determined by their soul and not the physical body?

A: Partially, remember, aural profile and karmic reference merges with physical structure.

Q: (L) So you are saying that particular genetic conditions are a physical reflection of a spiritual orientation? That the soul must match itself to the genetics, even if only in potential?

A: Yes, precisely.

Q: (L) So a person's potential for spiritual advancement or unfoldment is, to a great extent, dependent upon their genes?

A: Natural process marries with systematic construct when present.

Q: (L) Well, if that is the case, and the aliens are abducting people and altering their genes, can they not alter the genes so that higher level souls simply cannot come in?

A: Not incarnative process, natural biological processes. Incarnative involves strictly ethereal at 5th density and lower, and thus is enveloped in triple cycle "veil" of transfer which is impregnable by any means. However, any and all 1st, 2nd, 3rd, and 4th processes can be manipulated at will and to any degree if technology is sufficient.

Which then leads us to the following:

July 22, 2000

A: We wish to review some things first. The concept of a "master race" put forward by the Nazis was merely a 4th density STS effort to create a physical vehicle with the correct frequency resonance vibration for 4th density STS souls to occupy in 3rd density. It was also a "trial run" for planned events in what you perceive to be your future.

Q: (L) You mean with a strong STS frequency so they can have a "vehicle" in third density, so to speak?

A: Correct. Frequency resonance vibration! Very important.

Q: (L) So, that is why they are programming and experimenting? And all these folks running around who some think are "programmed," could be individuals who are raising their nastiness levels high enough to accommodate the truly negative STS fourth density – sort of like walk-ins or something, only not nice ones?

A: You do not have very many of those present yet, but that was, and still is, the plan of some of the 4th density STS types.

August 5, 2000

Q: OK, last session you brought up the subject of frequency-resonance vibration. You suggested that there are certain STS forces who are developing or creating or managing physical bodies that they are trying to increase the frequency in so that they will have bodies that are wired so that they can manifest directly into third density, since that seems to be the real barrier that prevents an all-out invasion, the fact that we are in third density and they are in fourth. Now, I assumed that the same function could be true for STO individuals. It seems that many individuals who have come into this time period from the future, coming back into the past via the incarnational cycle so as not to violate free will, have carefully selected bodies with particular DNA, which they are, little by little, activating so that their fourth-density selves, or higher, can manifest in this reality. Is it possible for those energies to manifest into such bodies which have been awakened or tuned in third density?

A: STO tends to do the process within the natural flow of things. *STS seeks to alter creation processes to fit their ends.*

Q: This Top Secret document and the Anna Hayes material to some extent, both talk about many abductions being "ourselves from the future" who have come back to the past, or what is for us, the present, to abduct their own bodies to make genetic adjustments so that they can advance and not make the mistakes they made in another timeline. Is that, in fact, part of the scenario?

A: Very close to the truth!

Q: Can you abduct yourself in an STO manner and help yourself in this way? Can that be STO?

A: It is not, because that is not STO.

Q: So, when that is happening, and if it is happening, it is occurring in the STS parameter?

A: Yes.

Q: How do the STO manage?

A: They do not concern themselves with such things.

Q: Well, if the STS guys are genetically tweaking themselves to have some kind of different outcome for some reason that we do not perceive, don't you think there should be a balancing action on the STO side of some sort?

A: You are thinking in STS terms. But that is natural, since human 3rd density is STS.

Q: You say they don't concern themselves with that. What do STO individuals coming back from the future into the past concern themselves with?

A: Answering calls for assistance with knowledge.

Q: What do these STS individuals coming back into the past hope to do by genetically tweaking their ancestors? What happened that they want to have happen differently?

A: Infinite number of possible answers to that question.

Q: So, they are coming from all different timelines with all different kinds of agendas – all designed to serve themselves.

The important thing to think about in all of the above review is the fact that we are talking about emotional pathways when we talk about frequency-resonance vibration. Indeed, as the Cs noted, intellect can serve us well in avoiding emotional traps and entanglements but intellect, in and of itself, is not FRV.

"Emotion that limits is an impediment to progress. Emotion is also necessary to make progress in third density. It is natural. When you begin to separate limiting emotions based on assumptions from emotions that open one to unlimited possibilities, that means you are preparing for the next density."

We come closer to understanding what the Cs meant when they mentioned "programmed decoy, due to FRV," and we have a much better idea of how others can be activated as programmed decoys because of their STS FRV. Apparently we were posing a significant threat to the Matrix's agenda, because once Ark and I joined forces, the attack became almost unrelenting.

With all of the above clues, the reader is going to be able to spot them coming in the remainder of this account. But keep in mind, we were learning as we went. As I said at the beginning of this chapter: it would be very easy to just write off the series of attacks I have been describing as just the way things are. My daughters were just kids who made mistakes, and nearly died because of them. Our lives are just like anybody else's lives in the sense that about half the time good things happen and half the time bad things happen. It's just the nature of life, it's the way things are. The same things happen to everybody. And this last is most certainly true. That is the point of the Cs communication: to explain to us the nature of good and evil, the nature of this reality in which we live, where bad things happen to good people, and very often, because of the fact that they are good, and are trying to do good things.

And things were about to get very weird, and even very scary.

CHAPTER 50
SHIFTS IN THE MATRIX

Coming back now to our narrative, I think I will mention that, at the same time that I was dealing with the near death of my daughter, my year-old, super-duper, large-capacity, top-of-the-line washing machine broke down and the Sears repairman delivered the unpleasant news that it would cost almost as much to fix it as to buy a new one. It was, in fact, only about a week past the end of the warranty, and I was absolutely devastated by the news. Fortunately, my neighbor who worked for the appliance department at Sears also agreed with me that a washer that was so completely dead within a week of warranty end, obviously ought to be replaced, and she made sure that Sears replaced it with a new one at no charge. But, even before that item had been accomplished, my water heater also died – completely – and I was faced with needing to have a new one installed.

The point of this is that when the Matrix begins to shift, all kinds of mechanical things also go kaflooey. My best guess about this factor is that when the program is changed, and the reality is merged, any electronic or electrical devices within the sphere of the targeted individual that have a weakness simply cannot survive the reality bridge. The same conditions seem to apply to plumbing. Noting these things over time, I began to have a deeper understanding of what Gurdjieff, Sufis, Alchemists, and others meant about watching the environment for small clues and messages. Things can be lost or found; objects fall and break for no apparent reason; new batteries go dead; pets can suffer in various ways, even including death; and just a whole host of signals manifest to get our attention, which we normally sweep under the rug and say, "Oh, that's Murphy's Law."

At this point, I want to back up to the end of August. There was a very strange event at the time of the death of Princess Diana that taught me something about the Matrix even if there were many other clues emerging at that time that I missed or ignored. The reader who has perused the series of emails from our July exchanges, prior to the flood in Poland, will see that not only were we coming to some idea of the trans-millennial manipulation of our reality in our digging around the issues of Rennes-le-Château, but it was at this point that the Cassiopaean website was actually born.

Prior to this period, we had a few pages – very condensed – that were posted on Ark's website hosted by the server at the University of Wroclaw. During the month of July, along with everything else, the Internet service I had been using started to get greedy and objected to the fact that I was online so much of the time. So, they decided to change their unlimited access to very limited access, and I was constantly being cut off in the middle of transmissions. Of course, they swore they weren't doing anything, and maybe they weren't – maybe it was something else. But, the end result was that I canceled that provider and signed up for Internet service with the local phone company. As part of the sign-up package, we were notified that we had reserved webspace. Ark decided that it was time to put the Cassiopaean material on the web in a dedicated way. We hoped that it would help bring us into contact with others who also had pieces of the puzzle.

It was ten days before we could come back to this idea, between the time Ark left Florence, and by degrees and a circuitous route, made his way back to Poland. After he had returned and was able to assess the situation there, we decided that we would also use our webspace to try to generate interest in the flood-relief effort. There was over a million dollars in damages to the University of Wroclaw, and Ark was spearheading the drive to obtain funds for repairs and restoration.

So, we had started to work on the dual project of getting some publicity for Flood Relief in Poland as well as getting the Cs material on the Internet. I was working practically night and day to assemble excerpts into chronological subject files. It was right at that moment that Princess Diana was killed.

Frank had come over that night and announced almost gleefully that Princess Diana had been in an auto accident and was not expected to live. "She could be dying as we speak!" he intoned ponderously. I didn't want to believe it, so I quickly logged onto the Internet and went to CNN and discovered that the announcement that she had died had almost that instant been posted. I was too upset to do anything, so I sent Frank home after a short discussion and a cup of coffee. Several thoughts were niggling at the back of my mind, so after Frank had gone, I started digging.

As I dug, I began to get the strange feeling that somehow this event actually related to our own activities, though I was unable to figure out how or why. I found a couple of references in Nostradamus that could have been construed to connect Diana's death to the Flood in Poland as if they were interactive events. If the Cs were correct that the Flood in Poland was directly connected to efforts to thwart our mission, then somehow, everything was part of a huge, global plan, which included the activation of certain archetypes.

I knew how easy it was to fall into the trap of ego, however, so I brushed that absurd feeling aside, and just synopsized my findings in a series of emails to Ark. In the end, I assembled the text of these emails and added a few additional comments, and they became the first "Diana Page." I had the idea that if I was correct, my posting of these ideas would send a signal, and someone would signal back. On my mind was the strange comment the Cs had made the previous May:

May 21, 1997

Q: OK, some time ago when I had the "three-dominos" dream, or experience, I asked you about this, and you said it was not an important dream. Yet, it led to an incredible series of discoveries. Why did you say it was not important?

A: What was important, the dream or the discoveries?

Q: Well, of course the discoveries ... and there really were no dominos ... but it gave me a teensy idea that helped with all the rest ... and one thing led to another to another ...

A: Dream was not important until fulfilled.

Q: Anyway, I found at the same longitude as Oak Island, a place with the name "Percee." This led to Fontainebleau, Chartres, and Coll du Perche and Moulins la Marche. Then, the "blue waters and white skies" led to lake Geneva and Point Perce. And this was the third "Percy" ...

A: Devour newspapers for any recent news re: Percy.

Q: OK. So, then I had the thought that "Percy" was the center of an incredibly complex web. It was like what you had described for me before: mosaic consciousness. I could see connections no matter which way I looked. I mean, literally everything connects ... alchemy, Rosicrucians, Masons, physics, genetics, eschatology, Cassiopaea, prime numbers, Medusa, Perseus ... I mean, it is the most incredible thing I have ever seen in my life ...

A: So far ...

Q: OK. But, that led to the idea of the universe being like a sort of spider web, with the spider being at the center ... kind of an expanded and more complex "perpendicular reality" idea. All the levels connected by the threads, or conduits ... the gravity binder from the spider in the center ... am I onto something here?

A: Stay tuned ...

The following is the text of the original version of my "Diana Page" as bait that was posted later that day, September 2, and was removed five days later on the seventh and replaced with something that was more "vanilla" in flavor.

To Ark

Date sent: Tues, 02 Sep 97 06:44:07

Here is my text:

~~~***~~~

While it is still too early to make a comprehensive esoteric analysis of the death of Princess Diana, lacking certain details and developments; it is obvious that there are certain factors that deserve to be mentioned. And, it is with a heavy heart that I have decided to discuss this subject at the present moment.

Like everyone else, the all too human heart in me grieves at the loss of one so beautiful, young and gracious, in such a tragic and unexpected manner. And, I grieve for those who loved her in a more personal and familial way. Most of all, I grieve for her children. If the love of humanity in general, and the sadness at such a loss were to be counted as legal tender in the next world, Princess Diana would be one of the richest women in the etheric realms. Because, as Edgar Cayce once said: "The only luggage you can take with you out of this world, is the love you have given away." (Words to that effect, in any event.) So, Diana had a LOT of luggage. Being as fashion conscious as she was, she would SMILE at that!

But, she seemed to know the difference between the clothes of the body and the clothes of the soul – and was a shining example of a class act in *any* milieu. She was, indeed, "The People's Princess."

Like nearly everyone else, even though I never met her in person, I felt that I knew and loved her. But, there are now other, very significant reasons, why I mourn her passing. I am going to present a few things here that are FOR THOSE WHO KNOW.

At the time of the death of the Princess, I was (and still am) deeply interested in trying to generate interest in relief efforts for Poland, which has suffered a flood of cataclysmic dimensions, in almost a media vacuum. The disaster is truly remarkable for the LACK of attention given to it by the press. My interest in this flood is related, in large part, to my work with the Cassiopaeans, and their successful efforts to bring me into contact with my "complementary soul," who is now my fiancé – in Poland.

Nevertheless, in the middle of trying to generate some interest and support in a relief effort for the Polish Flood, I learn that Diana has been in an automobile accident, and later, that she has died.

One of the first things I thought about was the astrological aspects that might surround such an event. Having dabbled in astrology for over 30 years, naturally, I had done her chart along with any number of other well-known persons, for the sake of study. I pulled out the file, and entered the data into the computer. I had heard rumors that Diana employed either a psychic or an astrologer to guide her decisions, and I simply could NOT understand how such a set of likely aspects could be missed or ignored.

Yes – indeed – there were some rather dramatic and interesting aspects! But, as expected, they could not be taken as a direct clue to dying in a car crash ... though, it was apparent that there could be troubles while traveling, and her Sun was conjunct the ascendant in direct opposition to the Moon on the descendant, which was a pretty dramatic aspect. But, it DOES look like, if she had been at home, this would have passed without serious physical harm. But, her chart for NEXT month was also VERY disturbing ... so, whatever it was, it was REALLY some powerful energy coming against her.

My experience has taught me that astrological aspects are merely "doorways," if you will, and the energy that enters is more or less like pressing icing through a cake decorating tip on a pastry tube. It has a certain configuration, but HOW it shapes depends on the surface it is being extruded to, either receptive or opposing energy.

Because of certain researches I have been involved in for the past several years, I regularly check numerous sources for implications of connections to other, very mysterious, and unnamable (at this time) situations and activities going on here on Earth. One of these is the Liturgical calendar of the Catholic Church.

Frank had commented on the severe headache I had on the morning of the crash that killed Diana. I often have them before plane crashes and other such things, but I hardly see how the death of just three people could be counted in the same category. On the other hand, I did think that this particular death could have some rather far-reaching ramifications which I will discuss in a general way.

One thing I noted right away was that Diana died in August. For THOSE WHO KNOW, this is immediately significant. Not only in August, but on the feast day of Saint Raymond Nonnatus. And, the page of the mass for this date is 1233! Nonnatus means 9 and 1233 add up to 9 and Diana was 36, which is also a 9!

This was even more significant due to the recent researches I have been doing into the alterations of the Zodiac as well as the changing of the numbers of the degrees on the circle. This action was taken by certain organizations under the influence of beings at higher densities, in order to further conceal certain knowledge and confuse and obfuscate those on the "Quest." Additionally, the actuality of the frequency effect of certain numbers on the essential nature of our reality makes this a particularly nasty event, because the dominant number of our realm is "9," which is the number of sickness, endings, decay and destruction and death. Nothing EVER prospers under the influence of the number 9. And, for the Questors, note that the number 666 adds up to a 9.

So, we have a powerful influence of the number 9 surrounding the death of the Princess. This is, as far as I can determine, the signature of the 4th density beings of STS.

Anyway, this Saint Raymond (c. 1204-40) was a pioneer member of the Order of Our Lady of Mercy for the redemption of Christians enslaved by the Mohammedans! And, she died in company of an Egyptian whose father was named Mohammed. I think that this connection of things present with things past is a little more of the signature of the 4th density.

Another thing that struck me as odd was that Diana is descended from a family which had important players in certain events of history that were very significant in terms of present day speculations about secret societies and bloodlines, though the current literature does not even come close to the solution to the problem. That may be deliberate misleading, or it may be that the authors simply do not know. (See Lincoln, Leigh and Baigent's *Holy Blood, Holy Grail*, and *The Messianic Legacy*.)

Nevertheless, I and my fiancé in Poland also had ancestors involved in these dramas. In fact, my ancestor probably murdered hers if some of the genealogists are correct and her line of Spencers descends from the Despensers. What I do know is that the Spencers and Percys later connected, and by virtue of that connection I am something like 13th cousin to Princess Diana. But then, so are a WHOLE lot of other people – probably half the people in the U.S.! So, if there is anything to the idea that DNA can communicate with other DNA, then it is no wonder that there is so much grief over Diana's death. Probably a lot of people feel it in their very bones because of their literal genetic connections.

But, what is most curious is, Roger de Mortimer, my ancestor, was the lover of Isabella of France, daughter of Philip the Fair who ostensibly brought down the Templars! Searching for the roots and fate of the Templars has become something of a popular pastime in recent years, though it is being done by persons who have little, if any idea, of the true nature of reality and the nature of the manipulations from higher densities. Thus, for every answer they THINK they have, three new questions emerge. So, this is a peculiar thing – even that Diana should die in France, in Paris, in August, the month of the Perseid Meteor Shower, which has played so important a part in all of these mysteries, including the relationship of the name of Perseus to Perceval to Percy, and that a Mortimer married the Granddaughter of Henry III, and their daughter married a Percy! The bloodlines that came together in Henry Percy and Elizabeth Mortimer included all five of the so-called "lines of Odin," including the blood of the last of the Welsh kings, the line of Llewelyn the Great.

And, of course, we notice that, although 4 people were in the vehicle, only 3 died. The dead included an Egyptian, a Spencer, a Frenchman, and ONLY THE WELSHMAN LIVED.

Well, the next thing that I noted was that Diana's accident was immediately compared to the one that killed Princess Grace, whose death was purportedly described by Nostradamus. Just recently the Cs had urged me to be on the lookout for any mention of the name "Ranier," also – in any context, including volcanic! So, I immediately made the connection that Grace was married to Prince Ranier. The Nostradamus quatrain reads:

> With blood and famine even greater calamity;
>
> seven times it approaches the seashore.
>
> Monaco, from hunger, captured in captivity.
>
> The great golden one caught, in an iron cage.

The author of *The Further Prophecies of Nostradamus*, Erika Cheetham, comments:

"Princess Grace, of the Golden Movies, the golden hair and golden life died in the iron cage of her crashed car. However, whether she could really be described as "great" I feel to be in question. Monaco, after all, is a very minor principality, and she achieved nothing that could be honestly called of international worth except for the few films she made in Hollywood. ... But since the death of the Princess, I have received such a remarkable number of letters from readers who were convinced of its meaning, that I include it for the readers' interest, if nothing else." (Cheetham, 1985)

Well, if anything, I would say that Diana would fit *more* the criteria of the "Great Golden One caught in an iron cage," particularly since she died *in a tunnel*, supposedly pursued by *seven* photographers! But, if this is *anything*, I would think it was a prediction that *this event may be the "marker" of the beginning of that which is described in the first three lines*. On the other hand, I think it is stretching to apply it to *either* of these events! However, while flipping through these things, I did note another interesting reference, which may be the reason I was stimulated to search through Nostradamus. The quatrain reads:

Seven times the British nation will be seen to change,

Soaked in blood in two hundred and ninety years.

Not at all free through German connections

Aries fears for the protectorate of Poland.

We have now two quatrains that talk about "seven times" and "blood" and that struck me as curious. Cheetham writes:

"The great problem for this verse is to find the date from which to calculate the 290 years and the seven great changes which affect Britain. If the year 1603 is taken as the starting point, quite arbitrarily, the whole verse fits including the last line which clearly links Poland with Britain in some manner connected with a war." [This is assumption on her part] ...

"Nevertheless, Nostradamus indicates that there will be a critical state of affairs in Poland at the same time as Britain faces a great crisis connected with Germany. It also implies that the royal family on the throne at that time will be the last British dynasty of any note. This may mean that Prince Charles, a Battenberg by origin, will be the last king on the English throne."

It almost seems as though these repetitions of the number seven in the quatrain about the "Golden One," as well as this one that connects the end of the domination of the British nation under the German Usurpers of the British throne (the current royal family) after 290 years, in conjunction with fears for Poland that are connected to Aries, are all part of the same piece of the puzzle. Well, this made me curious. So, I did a little rapid calculation and discovered that 290 years ago from 1997 was 1707. Did *anything* of note happen then that ties all of these elements together?

As it happens, it *does* fit! Queen Anne, in 1707, the *last* Stuart Sovereign, sealed the Act of Union between England and Scotland, thus forming Great Britain, which was immediately given to George I, the first of the German Hanoverian dynasty, which is the origin of the present royal family. This act deliberately passed over the superior hereditary rights of the Stuarts (whose rights were inferior to the rights of the Mortimers and Percys), and gave Great Britain to those who had no real claim to the throne other than statutory. Because Anne signed it over!

So, we have the passage of exactly 290 years from the beginning of the German domination of Britain, to some event that is connected to Poland. Well, as I was flipping through more of Nostradamus, I noted *this*:

Salon, Mansol, Tarascon of six arches

Where is still standing the pyramid,

Shall come to deliver the Prince of Denmark,

A shameful ransom shall be paid into the temple of Artemis.

Well, Nostradamus is funny. It seems to be written in code. But this one again connects us back to the 290-years-ago Act of Union, because Queen Anne was married to the Prince of Denmark, and "Artemis" is another name for Diana. Also, we note the names and the "arches" of the tunnel in which she died. Most interesting is the mention of the "pyramid," or something very like a pyramid – the Eiffel Tower. And, significantly, she was in the company of an *Egyptian!* Was Diana's life paid to ransom England from the action of Queen Anne almost three centuries ago?

If it is so, as it seems to be, that Nostradamus foresaw a connection between the tragic death of Princess Diana as a crisis in the British Monarchy, and the flood in Poland, about which we have heard almost nothing in the media, perhaps there is a deeper reason into which we ought to inquire? It is *most* peculiar that both the Pope and President Clinton paid visits to Poland just prior to this disaster. There was no lack of coverage for *those* events! At this point we cannot know what Nostradamus may have intended, but we can know that there is a symbolic connection.

What about the "Aries fears for the protectorate of Poland" reference? The constellation of Cassiopeia is one of the side-pieces of the zodiacal sign, Aries. The earliest associations we can find are that Cassiopeia is associated with the Celtic Goddess Danu, and also the Goddess Danae, the mother of Perseus. And, as it happens, the Cassiopaeans have made most curious remarks about the flood in Poland!

Well, it is all connected. The truest thing I ever read was something that Franklin Roosevelt was quoted as saying: "Nothing in politics *ever* happens by accident. If it happens, you can bet it was planned that way." And, it is amazing what a different view one can have of things if this is taken as a postulate. It causes one to look at things quite creatively. However, the problem is always assuming that the planners of such events are human ... if one also does away with *that* restriction, then things actually begin to make sense.

This is where so many have a problem. They do not know or understand the different levels of density, and how the events in our world are but a reflection of manipulations at other levels. One who labors under this delusion will *never* find the connections between the clues!

What does the death of Diana, the Beloved Princess of Wales tell us? In my opinion, by her death, she has guaranteed the beginning of the downfall of the British monarchy. *Nothing* Charles *ever* does will redeem him now.

None of us can know what the relationship truly was like. So, we cannot judge. The only thing that is certain is, had there been no divorce, Diana would *not* have been being hounded to *quite* the same extent by the paparazzi while in the company of an Egyptian playboy. Thus, it is *possible* that she would still be alive. And, the point is, a *lot* of people will see it this way. They will think: no divorce, no trip to Paris and riding in fast cars with drunken drivers, therefore, no crash, no death. No matter what he does now, he will never be able to fully redeem himself. Both his public and private lives will play out to the end, in the shadow of a dead princess, forever young and beautiful.

I read a remark in one of the news reports that someone had said that Di was saintly, so I thought that we can expect a *lot* of miracles to soon be attributed to her, and there will be a cult, and probably demands for canonization! And, this leads to the problem of the present dynasty. I am going to quote at some length from the work of Lincoln, Leigh and Baigent, so I humbly request the indulgence of same. No one else has put the subject so clearly.

"For the past century and more, organized religion has suffered increasingly severe blows to its credibility. But the religious sense of 'the sacred,' of 'the numinous,' of a coherent pattern transcending one's personal experience – remains, for a great many people, essentially intact. The traditional custodians of 'the spiritual' may have been compromised or have compromised themselves. ... And yet, for a great many people, 'the spiritual' remains a reality, even if organized religion no longer speaks on its behalf.

"There is an entire facet of twentieth century thought and culture which reflects an aspiration towards meaning and the 'spiritual' outside the context and framework of institutionalized religion. ... Thus, more and more individuals, recognizing the bankruptcy of prevailing systems, have sought one or another valid means of synthesis for reintegrating a fragmented reality.

"[Carl] Jung's overriding concerns were ultimately religious in nature. His concentration on universal experience and his use of the crucial instrument of synthesis, rather than analysis, springs from his desire to reassemble the world, to imbue it again with meaning. What is more, he sought to do so not in purely theoretical (or theological) terms, but in terms which might be directly experienced rather than merely accepted as articles of faith – which translated into psychological dynamics, might be practically viable not just on Sundays, but throughout the individual's life. ...

"Jung did not see psychology and religion as incompatible. On the contrary, he saw them as complementary, each aiding the other to generate a renewed sense of meaning and coherence. And Jung understood religion in its broadest, most profound and most valid sense – not as a mere edifice of conceptual dogma, not as one particular denomination or creed, but as something encompassing all of them, a basic element in the make-up of the human psyche. In consequence, Jung proceeded to synthesize, to compare and establish common sources, common denominators, common psychological dynamics, shared patterns – not only in the world's major religions, but in much of man's other activity as well. The result was something that could indeed function as a viable religious principle for the modern age – a mode of thought and understanding which did indeed confer meaning, while at the same time fostering tolerance, flexibility and humanity.

"Are there any established institutions ... that are genuinely archetypal, that impinge even if only subliminally on the collective unconsciousness and thereby function, at least in some measure, as a repository for meaning? In some of its aspects, at least, monarchy can be seen as such an institution.

"At its worst, as exemplified by numerous autocratic regimes of the past, monarchy can be synonymous with tyranny. At its best, however, monarchy can indeed be seen as a repository of meaning – which, albeit in a circumscribed way, does perform at least a semi-religious function. Certainly monarchy rests on an archetypal basis. Kingship in itself is an archetype. ... Whatever the form of government under which one lives, the psyche, from childhood on, will still be populated by kings and queens, princes and princesses. However 'republican" one may be, such figures are part of a collective cultural heritage, with a psychic validity of their own. In the absence of genuine dynastic royalty, we will endeavour to create a surrogate royalty from, say, film stars, pop singers or from families such as the Kennedys. Yet such surrogates are always pale imitations of the originals on which, deliberately or otherwise, they are based. ...

"The essence of such a monarchy is that it rests on the basis [that] the king ruled but did not govern. In other words, he was ultimately a symbolic figure. To the extent that he remained unsoiled by the tawdry business of politics and government, his symbolic status remained pristine. ... In other words, his currency resides in what he embodies as a symbol, rather than in anything he does, or in any real power he might or might not exercise. The most potent symbols always exert an intangible authority, which can only be compromised by the more tangible forms of power.

"During the German occupation of Denmark in the Second World War, all Danish Jews were ordered to wear yellow stars on their coats, thus facilitating the process of identification and deportation to concentration camps. In contemptuous defiance of the power occupying his country, King Christian took to wearing a yellow star himself, as a gesture of sympathy and solidarity with his Jewish subjects. In support of their king, thousands of non-Jewish Danes followed suit. The effect of the gesture was more than symbolic. Anti-semitism and denunciations of Jews dwindled and countless lives were saved." (Baigent, Leigh, Lincoln, 1986)

This echoes the Arthurian legends, the Grail stories, and, ultimately – the Alchemical Quest for the unveiling of Isis and the restoration of Osiris. But here, in considering Charles and Diana, we have an archetype of a man who may never be king because he has "killed" the queen. And the queen symbolizes the source of knowledge, light and life. Whether it is conscious or not, this is the essential imprint that will form in the minds of the people; to the destruction of the institution of the monarchy in England.

Thus, we see from the clues, the signs, the synchronicities, that the death of the Princess of Wales, Diana-Artemis – was undoubtedly chosen by her before the birth of her soul into the body of Diana Spencer. It was only a potential – but became a reality as each decision was taken by those around her. It is part of a Grand Pattern – a symbol of the stupendously complex Mystery, designed to awaken *those who know*. We are grateful. We wish her God Speed in her flight to the Stars to become a member of the Court – Tuatha de Danaan.

Ark, of course, had his own theory about the death of Princess Diana.

To: Laura

Date sent: Tue, 2 Sep 1997 14:56:13

And after Mother told me the news version of the Diana death I am more convinced that the "Scorpio's theory of Diana death is true".

Scorpio's theory is this: there was a little plot to replace the chauffer by a security man. This security man was totally controlled and chemicals were injected before suggesting he was drunk at the time of the crash. Mind control devices were used to brainwash the car passengers. Who was behind the plot? Perhaps it is better not to know and not to want to know. Why? Too many reasons. Will it cause decline of British monarchy? That I do not know. There are many factors and it is hard to guess which option will win. This is what comes to mind. That there is such a possibility.

To: Ark

Date sent: Tues, 02 Sep 97 16:51:33

> I am more convinced that the "Scorpio's theory of Diana death is true".

Well, I think I agree, now that you put it so plainly. Especially considering the stuff in this book I am reading *The Messianic Legacy*. Also, there was a lot in the Bramley book. Seems that there are a LOT of people who might be interested in the elimination of the British royal family – for varied reasons.

> Who was behind the plot? Perhaps it is better not to know and not to want to know. Why? Too many reasons.

I agree. The point is, I think, that this death is a "marker." It is symbolic and archetypal. I am not exactly sure of the precise dynamics, but it is very deep. And, once again we have an example of how "knowledge protects, ignorance endangers." This poor girl is dead and her poor children are without their mother. And that cowardly nincompoop she was married to simply doesn't have a clue!

> Will it cause decline of British monarchy? That I do not know. There are many factors and it is hard to guess which option will win. This is what comes to mind. That there is such a possibility.

I think it is almost a certainty. Why? I am not sure either. There is whoever is behind the creation of the "Prieure de Sion," which is more of a "front" organization designed to lead people astray; and there is that bunch of Lunatics that Bill Mann is hanging out with – the Sinclairs – who have their agenda which is to say that they think that one of THEM ought to be king ...

I think that the archetypal "Priest-King" is an important concept, but I don't think that it can necessarily be hereditary. The Tibetans have a good idea with the Dalai Lama. He is just a symbol, more or less, but they replace him by searching for the "incarnation." The British royal family has produced so few – if any – significantly beneficial monarchs, that it is almost like a family of idiots. They have been, in general, morally bankrupt and intellectually deficient as a whole, not to mention arrogant and absurd in their eccentricities! The whole concept is, in my opinion, a joke. I even had a dream one night about Queen Elizabeth – I told her that I could not allow my children to play with hers because her children were corrupt!!!

So, this poor Diana was drawn into this nasty mess and it certainly killed her!!!

Anyway, I am still reading this book. Seems these guys came to much the same conclusion about the Prieure de Sion that I did ... though there are some FUNNY elements to the story. Seems they have had a couple of similar experiences to mine, only they know NOTHING about other density manipulation, so they are only baffled and impressed! I see immediately that they are being led astray by this confusion!

Now, I hope you can get our Diana page up today. Now it is a HOT topic and will bring a LOT of people to the Cs pages. If you don't have time, tell me what to do the make a header, change the color ... add a counter and link back to the main page ... etc. I do think we ought to put the Percy Lion on there ... offset the header to the left and put the image of the lion on the right ...

Because, as I am reading this book, the "Scorpio Theory" is making a LOT of sense. Only I can't see the objective yet. I think that we can believe Roosevelt when he said that "nothing happens by accident." And just see things as intended, and then try to extrapolate backwards.

I am even wondering if this Sinclair bunch that Mann is connected to is involved? Even if as only another "false clue" to lead people astray. This is what MOST of this stuff is!

To: Ark

Date sent: Tues, 02 Sep 97 19:26:52

Honey, Do you notice the tail of the Percy lion is like a "spear?"

Very funny. And, I think this is a MUCH better image to use ... for THOSE WHO KNOW. I am not sure who they might be. But, I think this is a somewhat subtle signal to the "others."

Also, the building in the background is Alnwick Castle in Northumberland where the 62 alchemical manuscripts are stored that nobody seems to know anything about.

And green IS the appropriate color for the subject.

There is the Celtic legend of the "Green Man," which was also the "Head of Bran," and the origin of the Holy Grail. The picture of Danae is funny too, if you take any time later and examine it. Note the rose by her hand which is entwined with a fabric ... indicating the concept of the "weaver" or "tentmaker" which is related to the Cathars as well as gnosticism in general. And, the "platter" or "grail" that is raining gold down upon her and that it is spilled about her thighs showing the "transdimensional atomic remolecularization" properties of the genitive organs as well as the creative act itself.

The image is supposed to represent Zeus impregnating Danae with a "shower of gold" or "light" from other densities.

Also, the rose has TWO blooms, note the condition of the two.

This "Green Man" makes me wonder about the mention of "chlorophyll" that they made when I was asking about the "blessing" given to Esau by Jacob. "The leaves of wrath." And the idea that the elimination of the chlorophyll ... means that the harvest is near.

Laura responds to Ark

Date sent: Wed, 03 Sep 97 20:45:14

> Marek told me that there is a theory propagated by Kadaffi that it was a murder because her fiancee was an Arab.

Yes, I heard that in the Sunday paper ... the Iranians are calling her wicked, too. (They will find themselves COMPLETELY without friends if they keep THAT up!)

Anyway, I think the Scorpio theory is the correct one. And, I read some things in this book last night where Poland is STRONGLY connected to this secret society business ... so, I decided to add a couple of things to the page ... just hints and questions!!! But, hopefully, will start people thinking!

In reading all this history of these dynastic battles ... it seems that it is simply an ongoing reflection of the same dynamics over and over again. There seem to be 3 main players and the representatives at the present time could be seen as: 1)The Sinclair/Jacobite group 2)The Hanoverian/Windsor group and 3)The silent Percy/Mortimer group.

One thing I have noticed is: when a person dies by being pierced in the eye, it is almost a certainty that he has been symbolically killed by the "Assassini." So, all these other people are simply on the wrong track with this one! I found another with this symbolic death: William Rufus, the son of William the Conqueror.

And, the time period when the Templars were "destroyed" is the key event that gives the clues to the present dynamics. I have GOT to make a timeline chart so that it will show this. It is all in my head, and I can see it ... but it needs to be demonstrated visually. The series of events at that time are so incredible that no intelligent person would ever deny the "controlling" element from higher densities after having seen it.

And then, the death of Mother Theresa? Two of three of the Triple Goddess image?

To: Ark

Date sent: Sat, 06 Sep 97 07:18:14

I think I caught a fish ...

There was an editorial in today's paper by an English journalist. There are a couple of paragraphs he writes that sound like they were lifted almost verbatim from our Diana page.

But then, he says this: (About Prince Charles) "Both his public and private lives will play out, forever, in the shadow of the dead princess, forever young and beautiful. Imagine a circle of deadly sharp, inward pointing daggers: in the center is Charles."

In this, the quote from our page is almost word for word!!! Is it a message???

Now, this guy's name is Rupert Cornwell, and he writes for the "*Independent*" in London.

This paragraph made the hair on my head stand up because he also used the "buzz words" about circles, daggers etc.

Is it possible that this guy read my piece, and – perhaps this is some sort of message ... or is he just reacting unconsciously?

And, the name "Cornwell?" All the references to "corn," goddesses of the corn, harvest, the woman being the source of the corn, spikenard being like corn ... picking ears of corn on the Sabbath ... and then, "well," and Hagar at the well, the "springs" etc. ...

Well, it was just TOO strange ... So, we will see. I'll see what the Cs have to say.

*

September 6, 1997

Q: We would like to know if there is any significance to the fact that Mother Theresa and Princess Diana both died within a week of each other?

A: Vague.

Q: Why didn't you tell us that Princess Diana was going to get killed in an auto accident? That's pretty big news!

A: You would not have benefited, and, besides, it was not predetermined. Just one possible future.

Q: Why was this particular future the one that manifested?

A: Because it was chosen.

Q: Why?

A: No escape any other way.

Q: For whom?

A: Diana.

Q: Escape from what or who?

A: Judgment.

Q: Judgment by whom?

A: You pick. She was damned if she did and damned if she did not.

Q: (T) Let me ask: is she dead?

A: Yes.

Q: Was there any factor involved in her death that could be connected to any secret groups on the planet that wish to bring down the monarchy?

A: No.

Q: So, this wasn't part of a plot to bring down the monarchy?

A: Soul mates.

Q: She and Dodi were soul mates?

A: Yes.

Q: And they decided to leave together …

A: Yes, at another level.

Q: Is there any special significance to the fact that they were soul mates?

A: No, only way out, and valuable lessons learned by everyone else.

Q: So, this was a gift?

A: And STO. And the same with Mother Theresa who waited for the proper timing, so that others would notice what you did.

Q: (T) Well, things usually happen in threes … who is next?

A: Usually threes is an old wives tale.

Q: So, from one perspective, the death of the Princess is nothing more than a tragic accident?

A: We did not say that.

Q: So, she chose this because it was the only way out … (T) Was she helped along? Was there more to it than choosing the time and the way?

A: There always is.

Q: Can you list some of the other factors involved?

A: Lessons, that is all there is!!

Q: (T) Was she murdered?

A: Would murderer agree to be crushed to death?? What future is there in that line of work?

Q: Well, there are some Middle Easterners who think there is a *lot* of future in that line of work … suicide bombers and so forth as well as persons programmed to do that sort of thing … Was anybody or any other thing behind this?

A: No.

Q: Was the driver drunk?

A: Yes.

Q: (AH) Would she like to tell us something?

A: Statement as such would not benefit this work.

Q: Did Dodi give Diana the purported ring as an engagement ring?

A: Yes, but that is incidental to the "bigger picture."

Q: What *is* the bigger picture?

A: STO.

Q: You are saying that this was an STO act? (T) That's what they said …

A: No.

Q: That's not what they said. They said that this act would make others realize what we did and would start thinking about STO.

A: Yes.

Q: Are you saying that this was done by Diana as a service to others?

A: Part.

Q: I get the feeling that there is something we are not getting here ...

A: Maybe we are waiting for you to figure it out on your own!

Q: When I read the article by Rupert Cornwell and there was a paragraph that was identical to what I had written on the original web-page, and then he made the remark about the circle of daggers surrounding Prince Charles, that he was in the center of a circle of sharp daggers ... that struck me as a rather bizarre thing to say. With all the theories going around about the various families and bloodlines killing each other off from time to time ... and this is connected with all this other underground business, CIA, KGB, God knows what else ... Is the way the press plays the event a capitalizing on a circumstance on behalf of such conspiratorial groups?

A: If so, that is nothing new.

Q: Was this Cornwell saying in this article that the "dagger men" are gathered around Charles and that they are going to use this event to bring him down?

A: No.

Q: (T) Were the deaths, in addition to generating feelings of STO, also to speed up the process of the changing of the systems, the entering the new realms ...

A: Close.

Q: There is still something we are not getting. And, they are waiting for me to figure it out – OK. But, give me a clue!

A: You will do so when it is appropriate.

Q: OK, there is an issue here and it is just not the appropriate time to address it. Jan asked about the significance of the circle of daggers ...

A: Circles are always significant.

Q: (T) Well, the only way out of a circle of daggers is through the center ... (L) Or up ... (T) The daggers may not be pointed at him to take him out but to limit him ... or to move him to the center ... (L) Once before you told ...

A: Seven.

Q: Seven what?

A: Ask your question.

Q: Well, I was going to ask ... once before you told us that the monarchy in England was going to come to a halt and that Charles would never be king ... what are the probabilities that one of the sons will?

A: Are you trying to coerce a response?

Q: No, I'm just trying to be sneaky! [My mental question that was asked when the Cs said "seven" was "how long before the end of the monarchy?]

417

A: Well, forget it!!!

Q: ('I') Does this have to do with getting Charles ... is this whole thing designed to get Charles to take charge the way he is supposed to ... to get his center back ...

A: You are making a mountain where the universe sees a molehill.

Q: OK, change gears: I read the other day that the word "Iscariot" means "from Sikarios," and this connects the Jesus story directly to my Paran Sikarios ... the Percys, piercing, PS, etc. Could you comment on the fact that Judas Iscariot was "from Sikarios." Was he a member of the Paran Sikarios, the Assassini, a dagger man?

A: You are not to be told some things yet, because of your tendency to share before realizing the ramifications it can bring to your doorstep.

I realized that I had found my "Percy" in the newspapers. I also understood that maybe I had gone too far. I had "tested" the Matrix, and found that it was, indeed, paying attention. Or *somebody* was. No point in waving a red cloth in front of the Bull.

I took the Diana page down.

But it was already too late. Within ten days the first attempt was made on my eldest daughter's life, and 20 days later, my second daughter nearly died. And in both cases, it's pretty clear that FRV modulation was at work – that the Matrix had downloaded agent programs and had gone to work.

CHAPTER 51
THE PSYCHOMANTIUM

In the two weeks following the end of the Xth Max Born Symposium, Ark undertook the process of cleaning out his office at the University of Wroclaw, the institution that had been a home to him for thirty years. He began to pack his books and papers into large mail sacks of about one hundred pounds each, hauling them on foot, one by one, to the post office, and shipping them to me. When the process was complete, eleven big canvas bags had been mailed, but after five years, only three of them ever arrived. We were, of course, devastated at this loss, and many forms were filled out, and letters exchanged with the Polish and American postal service in an attempt to locate these bags. We could understand the loss of one or two, but to "misplace" eight out of eleven has just simply never been satisfactorily explained. We suspect that this "loss" was similar to the "loss" of the luggage on the return to Poland.

Apparently, someone was noticing the activity. On the day before he was to leave, Ark received a message from his attorney that his ex-wife had sent word that he could come and she would hand over his property that she had stolen from the luggage. Neither one of us believed it; it was a trap. So Ark left instructions for his attorney to inform her attorney that she must turn it over to him, and he would see that Ark got it. She never did.

After his return, Ark spent four months doing research sponsored by the Kosciuszko Foundation. During this period we drove to the University of Florida in Gainesville, the affiliated institution, once a week for a couple of days of meetings, but most of the work was done at home. There were a number of strange "accidents" during these drives, but nothing that couldn't be explained in normal terms. On one occasion, a truck swerved in front of us, and a huge steel baker's rack just jumped off the back of it and came bouncing violently in our direction with us going 70 mph. We managed to swerve and avoid being hit head on by it, but the tractor trailer just behind us and in the lane to the right wasn't so lucky. In our rearview mirror we witnessed what was almost a multi-car pileup. We had two blowouts of brand new tires, and for some reason, the van suddenly developed an undiagnosible heat regulation problem. This led to a couple of strange incidents.

We were just tooling along and all of a sudden the temperature gauge shot up. Fortunately, an exit was just ahead, and we pulled off into a gas station. We parked to the side to wait for the engine to cool, and as we stood outside, stretching our legs, a tall young blond guy in a mechanic's uniform came strolling up with his hands in his pockets and asked us out of the blue, "Seen any aliens lately?"

I was rather taken aback, to say the least. I had no idea what to say. I was reminded of Terry's experience with the guy who pulled in his driveway with an overheated engine and started talking about electronic ignitions as tracking devices right at the time that he had been discussing it with a friend. Even though the event was probably set up to scare us, all it really did was make us more acutely aware of the truth of what the Cs had said at that time:

November 11, 1994

Q: (T) Can our movements be tracked through the electronic ignition systems in our cars?

A: Not necessary. You are not yet aware of the extent to which humans have been "aided" in technological advancement.

Q: (T) By whom?

A: This requires long and complicated response.

Q: (T) The object behind using the electronic ignitions, from what I have heard, whether the source is true or not I can't say, but I had a strange confirmation of part of it.

A: Beware of disinformation. It diverts your attention away from reality thus leaving you open to capture and conquest and even possible destruction.

Q: (L) Is the information about the electronic ignition systems correct?

A: Disinformation comes from seemingly reliable sources. It is extremely important for you to not gather false knowledge as it is more damaging than no knowledge at all. Remember knowledge protects, ignorance endangers. The information you speak of, Terry, was given to you deliberately because you and Jan and others have been targeted due to your intense interest in level of density 4 through 7 subject matter. You have already been documented as a "threat."

Q: (L) Can you tell Terry what event occurred [referring to "confirmation" of electronic ignition subject] ...

A: Remember, disinformation is very effective when delivered by highly trained sources because hypnotic and transdimensional techniques are used thereby causing electronic anomalies to follow suggestion causing perceived confirmation to occur.

Q: (T) Who was the guy in the Camaro?

A: Diversion.

Q: (T) About two weeks after I saw the video tape where I heard this information, a guy pulled up out of nowhere driving a souped up Camaro … (Jan: No! It was the night we were watching it!) We had watched it before and we were talking about it and decided to watch it again. So, Gary and I had decided to go outside to take the dog around the block and we had just gotten back and put the dog on the porch and we were standing outside smoking a cigarette when the guy in the Camaro pulls into the driveway with steam coming out from under the hood. He asked to use the hose. I told him yes. He gets out wearing jeans, tee shirt and scraggly blond hair. He says, "I overheated. I'm coming back from Gulfport and was going back to Ocala and was on the interstate" when his car overheated. Now, 275 is a little ways from my house and he came all the way, passed a gas station and convenience store, turned off the main drag and then onto my street to get water … then he started talking about how the new electronic ignitions are designed to shut down when the car exceeds a certain speed so he had installed a special racing ignition but ever since his car had been overheating … we had just finished watching this movie about electronic ignitions and we were flabbergasted … What I want to know is who has the power and ability to set up these kinds of "confirmations" or synchronicities?

A: Same forces spreading disinformation: Brotherhood/ consortium/ Illuminati/ New World Order/ "Antichrist"/ Lizards.

Q: (T) But I'm just a nobody. Why would they go to all trouble to send somebody in a Camaro to drive up on my lawn …

A: Several answers follow: Number One, Nobody is a "nobody." Number two, it is no trouble at all for aforementioned forces to give seemingly individualized attention to anybody. Number three, Terry has been targeted and so has Jan and others because you are on the right track. Number four, this area is currently a "hot bed" of activity and extremely rapidly expanding awareness.

But more than anything we marveled at the machinations of the Matrix.

During this period of time, we had a number of discussions with the Cs about the invitation we had received to travel to Mexico. We were becoming more and more aware that the children had become targets – most especially when they felt that extra caution was hampering their social life. The Mexican Gravitational Society was sympathetic to the fact that we could not attend their meeting and leave the children at home, and they graciously agreed to include them in the arrangements. We took the two most vulnerable of the children with us, and following the Cs' advice, managed to have a safe trip even though my eldest daughter's second auto accident occurred while we were gone.

Ark accepted an offer to teach at the University in Gainesville, starting in January and since this meant that he had to be there five days a week, we decided to schedule some planned remodeling of the house during this time. As might be expected, this turned into a nightmare of truly monumental proportions, and we ended up discovering that the contractor we had hired was not licensed and had a police record an inch thick for cocaine abuse and fraud.

It is too horrible and tedious to even describe what this lunatic tried to do to us, how he destroyed our house, and how it took six months to get it put back together. It took quick thinking and work to recover our money from this guy, and I had to negotiate with the bank to take over the job of contractor myself. This meant, of course, that I had to be there every day to estimate, price, and order materials, supervise the work, pay the subcontractors, submit the bills to the escrow agent, and just a whole host of fun activities that made me aware that a good contractor is worth his weight in gold.

I drove Ark to Gainesville every Monday morning, and went to pick him up to come home for the weekend every Friday night. The schedule and workload was crushing, but we managed to have our sessions no matter what room in the house we had to use, though some of them were rather short and personal.

There were a couple of incidents with the van during these long drives down lonely back roads, one of which resulted in a very strange glitch in the time sequence, which we discussed at the session the following night.

I had been driving along State Road 121 that runs between US 19 and Gainesville. It's a two-lane, mostly straight shot through a planted pine forest, with almost no traffic except loggers and hunters. It's a nice drive in the daytime, even if it tends to be a little creepy; but I sure wouldn't want to drive it alone at night! I was just driving along when the temperature problem suddenly kicked in, and I pulled off to the side to let the engine cool and check the coolant level. By this time, we knew that there was nothing wrong with the system, the thermostat had been replaced, and it was just a "personality problem" the van had developed, and we coped as best we could.

I opened the hood to let the air circulate around the motor and the instant I did, the radiator cap exploded off, and boiling green coolant shot into the air. I was lucky to be able to jump out of the way of being scalded.

After a period of cool-down, when not a single car passed, I replaced the coolant from a jug we had gotten in the habit of carrying, and went looking for the cap. It was nowhere to be found. At this point, a truck came along the road and the guy just stopped and got out and found my radiator cap *under* the middle of the van. Don't even ask me how it got there! He then got back in his truck, turned around and went *back* in the direction he had come! Even though it seemed like just an ordinary incident, this act made it clear that he wasn't just "passing by."

I then continued on my way, figuring that I had lost about half an hour. In fact, however, I had lost an hour and a half.

May 16, 1998

Q: We have been talking about this funny incident. Do I really have a problem with the time issue on the way to Gainesville, or was I just simply that late and not aware of it?

A: Awareness is the key to all learning.

Q: What caused my radiator cap to pop off the van?

A: Simply search through the "archives" for the answer.

Q: Well, what do the archives have to do with … uh … all the way up to that point, the temperature needle was fluctuating, though it never overheated exactly. Can you tell me anything at all or am I going to exhaust myself over it? If you are not going to tell me anything, just say so!

A: See the truth recorded.

Q: What do you mean? Recorded where?

A: Look.

Q: Look where? The psychomantium?

A: Archival record.

Q: What archives? And what am I looking for?

A: Clue in response.

Q: What about the guy who stopped to help?

A: How dressed?

Q: He was dressed in work clothes. He had on jeans and a long sleeved shirt – cuffs and buttons – and it seemed like he had on a vest. A hunting vest. Padded.

A: All important events reveal themselves in their construction.

Q: Well … okay. (A) Does it mean that the event was important?

A: Yes.

Q: (A) Was there also something unusual on our way back?

A: Maybe other, look for clues from which to compare.

Q: Alright, when we were leaving, we had to pull over and stop for that machine to be moved. We had to sit on the side of the road …

A: Search and research until "light" goes off.

Q: Off? Remember, when we stopped, there was the strobe on top of the vehicle? Maybe they were *not* moving farm equipment … maybe it was a UFO!? (A) Which light?

A: That is part of the clue.

Q: Did having to stop for that farm equipment – was that part of the important event? Was it a cover for something? Was it not as we perceived it?

A: No.

Q: That was just ordinary?

423

A: No.

Q: Well, what was it?

A: What is "ordinary?"

Q: Well, that was as it seemed to be? They were moving an irrigator across and down the road?

A: Maybe.

Q: This is *not* the time to be cagey! Are you talking about stopping at a traffic light?

A: ?

Q: Well, you are gonna have to help me out here … there are a million tiny details and we could go through every one of them!

A: Not necessary to be that thorough.

Q: (A) The archival record. Is there something in the van that can be recorded? (L) The light on the tape recorder?

A: No.

Q: A light in the van?

A: Not necessarily.

Q: Not necessarily, but it could be. (A) Something in the van?

A: Or around.

Q: (A) What do we have around? A tape recorder? Around here or around the van? (L) The taillights?

A: In magnetic "sphere" of the van.

Q: (A) Are we talking about the way in or way back?

A: Both and others as well.

Q: So, what is the deal with the van here? I want you to know that I am so tired and it is utterly impossible with such a tired brain to figure this out! Help us out here!

A: We are. But you need not know answers today. If you search as usual, they will become apparent.

Q: I know! The van is a time machine!!!! It is a traveling psychomantium, complete with mirrors!!!

A: All is a "time machine."

Q: So, when we get in the van … and that is funny, when I drive the van, it never has that bumpy business. So, when Ark drives the van it must become a time machine! Does this have something to do with the van?

A: Its occupants.

Q: Well, when the light goes out … search and research until light goes off … part of the clue … something about the occupants … search and research …

A: Take "time" to study.

Q: Do you have another clue? (A) There is no point of departure. (L) What is the point of departure for the clue?

A: Look for it.

Q: Is it in what you have given?

A: Yes.

Fortunately, in July, Ark received an offer to work for a Defense Contractor, and we were able to settle down to a more stable level of activity. During this period, I was busy creating files of material to post on the website, each of which was an assembly of text that dealt with a given subject. It seemed more logical to publish it this way because so many follow-up questions had been asked about any given subject at different intervals, that I realized it would be difficult for most readers to have the patience to read through *all* of the text and connect the dots, so to say.

But still, at this point, I was just posting the material, and was not even attempting to explain any of it, except just briefly with an inserted paragraph here and there to set up the background. Doing this made me acutely aware of how much more research I needed to do, and I began to follow the clues given by the Cs in a more dedicated way.

With Ark home and available to help me with the html programming, the website was growing and changing. I experimented with a number of formats, designs, and had a little fun at one point including musical selections on each of the pages. Bit by bit I was learning to make the site as easy to navigate for the reader as possible, considering the complexity of the material we were trying to publish, and I removed all the bells and whistles out of consideration for those who may have had less powerful computers because it took up too much space and required long loading times. I experimented with different size fonts and appearance, trying to find the right look and feel. Readers offered feedback and advice, and I tried to accommodate their requests.

Meanwhile, the readership was growing apace. In the earliest days, we were happy to have 50 visitors in a 24-hour period. At the present, we have a steady stream that averages 5,000 page hits per day. The increase in visitors presented a new problem: correspondence. We were being deluged with email from readers who recognized the truth of the Matrix-reality explanation presented by the Cs. They all had questions, and what's more, they all felt isolated and in need of knowing that they were not alone or crazy for being able to see the unseen. What was most encouraging was the realization that most of our readers – those who got it, so to say – were highly intelligent, articulate, stable and productive members of society. We do, of course, get a few messages from lunatics and people who are clearly unstable. But for the most part, those people who contact us are people who have a well-defined work ethic, a history of success in dealing with "real life," *and* a questing nature that motivates them to look deeper into our reality because, all the while they have been living their "normal lives," they have also experienced things that suggest to them there is more to this world than meets the eye. Also, a significant number of them have spent their lives battling an ongoing series of attacks that seemed designed to wear them out, discourage them, and generally prevent them from having sufficient time and energy to actually do the research they would like to have done on these matters of the soul.

But, they all had questions, and they all felt isolated. I felt then, and continue to feel, that each person who writes is special and their concerns are very likely the concerns of others, so all deserve whatever I can give in response to their asking. But, I also knew that I couldn't spend every waking moment answering all of these emails individually. Ark and I, and the website, were the one point of contact that all of them shared, so I decided that a good thing to do would be to create a discussion group where all of them could be introduced to one another and they could then discuss these many subjects with like-minded people. And so, our egroups were born, though in the beginning, they were just a list of addresses that each person had to paste in, and it was often inconvenient and produced double messages, or someone's address would be omitted.

At this point in time, I was still trying to get Frank to be more involved in this work. I would print stacks of email from readers to share with him before the sessions, and he would avidly read those that praised the Cs, pointing out that *he* was the one to thank for such glowing letters since he was "the channel." I was happy to just let him go on about it in this way since I felt so sorry for him because he had no computer and was out of touch other than what we were able to do for him on Saturday nights.

But when any readers posed questions, or presented problems for discussion, especially if they were questions that posed doubts about the material itself, he would toss those emails aside with contempt and remark that I ought not to waste my time trying to answer such questions. This was a very disturbing thing to observe and I tried to explain to Frank that our philosophy was that sharing what we had learned when we were being asked was one of the more important things we could do as service to others. It was somewhere at this point that Frank began to drop hints to us that we ought to be paying him to attend the sessions because, obviously, he was the channel and if there was going to be public attention, he deserved to be compensated as well as given star billing on the website! I didn't agree. I referred to all of us on the website as "The Group." I did think that it would be alright to have a little page of bios of the different members of the group, and I asked Frank to write whatever he wanted to say about himself, and I would type it up and post it. Month after month I would ask him, "Did you write your bio yet?" And he would deliver the list of excuses as to why he hadn't, and then suggest that I should write it. At this point, since Ark and I were doing literally everything else, I began to resent the fact that Frank did so little, complained so much, and expected to be carried like a baby to fame and glory. I refused to write his bio for him. I told him to come a couple of hours early on one of the session nights, or any other time during the week, and sit down at my computer and write it. He never had time.

The fact that Frank was so resistant to making any kind of contribution was really starting to bother me. All the while he was proclaiming what a high spiritual being he was, that he was most definitely the most STO being on Planet Earth, there was simply no evidence to support it. The Cs had said that an STO being was one who "gives to those who ask." Well, I was asking Frank to help with organizing the material, with spell-checking, with writing a little bio, with answering questions for readers, with editing, and other things that certainly would have taken only an hour of his time a day. But he stubbornly and steadfastly failed to do one single thing. When I would point out that his excuses didn't hold water, he would just laugh and point out that by now, I ought to realize that this was just the way he was, and I had better get used to it.

As a result of all this, I was becoming less and less sure of Frank's exact role in the process. Since I had finally caught up in the transcribing, and was in the process of going through all the sessions and trying to get spelling errors cleaned up, cross-checking them with the notes and sometimes the original tapes, I was becoming more and more aware of just how clever the Cs were in their communications to us. With a broader overview, I was able to begin to see that Frank was *not* the channel in the sense that he "was the Cs." I also realized that the Cs had been gently agitating for a long time for me to disengage from Frank and undertake a more direct form of communication, which excluded trance channeling (which I knew to be iffy at best), one which suited my particular make-up far better – the psychomantium.

The subject of the Psychomanium was first bruited by the Cs, right out of the blue, on January 17, 1997, exactly 25 days before Ark came to the States for the first time. It is always interesting to go back over the sessions and see what the general discussion and flavor is that sets the tone for what sorts of things come out later. Somehow, it always seems to be interconnected.

On this particular evening, we began the session with a discussion of an individual who had been present the previous week. This woman is described in volume two of *The Wave*; the one who experienced the "reptoid rape," and who was later to behave in so strange a way that it was absolutely frightening. The entire group witnessed her bizarre behavior on more than one occasion, and Terry was extremely concerned that she was programmed to be physically violent. The Cs had warned of "grave, grave, danger" when she was present, and we had all thought that it referred to her. In was only later, during the week, after we had a chance to discuss it, that Terry pointed out quite logically that the Cs were warning *us* of danger in this woman's presence.

Q: (L) Also, I am very tired. This has been a very long day.

A: Time to consider construction of psychomantium.

Q: (L) What is a "psychomantium?"

A: Use Latin knowledge. [group discusses possible definitions]

Q: (L) Is it something that you use your mind to direct or control or power?

A: Chamber for viewing other realms, possible futures and entities residing in other densities. Need clear depth … such as large polished mirror on stand, which can be adjusted as to angle … walls must be completely covered in black, so as to eliminate reflection … soft, low, indirect lighting.

Q: (L) Wasn't it Dr. Moody that did the life-after-death thing? (T) He's got a room with the mirror with the black velour walls and the comfortable chair that you can look in the mirror without seeing yourself …

A: Yes, and it is real and it works. In the clear depths, you can even see us, on occasion!

Q: (L) Didn't we ask once about what this guy was doing, having people staring into a mirror, that it was opening them up to attachment, and was that not confirmed?

A: Attachment is merely a function born from a lack of knowledge … something you have enough of now so as not to worry.

Q: (T) This psychomantium, isn't it in essence a way of opening up a doorway to other realities and other levels and densities?

A: Yes.

Q: (T) Is that something you really want to do?

A: Yes.

Q: (T) Why?

A: Because you are ready now … and besides, what do you think you are doing here?!?

Q: (L) Is it a doorway that can be as Castaneda described it, where something can walk in, or walk out?

A: Possible … but … if you recall, what was the missing factor with Castaneda's story?

Q: (L) He didn't have knowledge. Is that it?

A: Not enough.

Q: (L) Is this something that can or ought to be done as a group, or singly … what's the deal?

A: Both.

Q: (T) So we're going to really construct one of those here? (L) Do we really want to do this at this house? Don't we want to buy something out in the country, where people won't be watching our bizarre behavior? (T) It doesn't really matter, we're watching everybody else's bizarre behavior, how bizarre can it be?

A: They won't watch, unless you invite them in.

Q: (L) OK, we've got all of these little things that need to be done; we've got a hole in the cellar that needs to be dug, that's still sitting there, we've got a pool that's supposed to be built, now we're supposed to build a psychomantium.

A: This is not a daunting or costly project ... materials: felt of the type you used for your charts, mirror and soft light, or candles. [TR describes a portable version that can be set up when using, and taken down when not needed.]

Q: (L) Is this basically the way that it is done, as TR has described it?

A: Yes.

Q: (L) How long is it necessary to sit and stare into the mirror before one experiences ...

A: Varies, but not long.

Q: (T) It's going to vary from person to person ... (L) OK, what advantage is there to using a psychomantium to using the board, I mean, is it going to replace the board?

A: No. Visualizations clarify and unite images.

Q: (L) OK, what images would we wish, or would be suggested to unite and clarify, and particularly in the term unite? You've used the term "unite" on a number of occasions, and in unusual ways.

A: Anything and everything in transcripts, for example ... and all else.

Q: (L) OK, so we would be able to see all of the things told about in the transcripts. Would we also be able to, by seeing a fourth-density reality, be able to generate some sort of unification between ourselves, in some sense, and this new reality ?

A: Yes.

Q: (L) Is this part of the way and means of bonding oneself to fourth-density reality.

A: Helps.

Q: (L) Can one also use this to visit other parts of the globe in real time?

A: Yes.

Q: (T) Visit the past and the future?

A: Yes.

Q: (T) There's other things on the other side. Can they come through?

A: Only if used ignorantly.

Q: (L) Is it the mental blocking technique that we are familiar with what prevents entry of something else?

A: Close.

Q: (J) "Knowledge protects!" (T) Well, this is easier than digging out under the pool, and building a reflecting pool, and finding 75 square feet to build a labyrinth. (L) It sounds like a damned amusement park! (J) Yeah, "LauraWorld!!!" (T) It would give a whole new meaning to an "E" ticket ride!

A: "Amusement" denotes fun!

The most significant points about the above remarks were 1) the use of the mirror would clarify all the things in the transcripts that had remained unclear to this point, which obviously meant that there was something about the present process that was unsatisfactory; 2) the use of the mirror would strengthen the bonding with the higher reality, which, as we already knew, would "hasten the receiving of assistance;" and 3) there was no need to be concerned any longer with the possibility of negative experiences because the knowledge energy field had been solidified in me and was, essentially, impenetrable; 4) Frank was not being proposed as the individual who ought to do the work. He was, effectively, excluded.

But, by now, the reader knows me. I had resisted all other suggestions to change the mode of the channeling up to this point, so just because the Cs suggested it, didn't mean I was going to do it! Besides, it wasn't brought up again until that ill-fated August after the flood, and just before the death of Princess Diana. But, the reader may recall that odd remark in the session about the flood, during July of '97:

Q: What is a "collinear wave reading consciousness unit?"
A: Suggest you "look in the mirror."

In retrospect, of course, it is easy to see that once I had been "awakened," to some extent, and once Ark had been brought into the picture, the process of changing gears, advancing the process, and eliminating Frank from the picture had begun. That it was intended to be utilized by Ark and myself was strongly hinted in the following, which included the "carrot" that answers of a personal nature would also be obtainable by this method.

August 9, 1997
Q: OK, I was reading something that related to mirrors. What was said was: "Negative existence is the silence behind the sound, the blank canvas beneath the painting, the darkness into which light shines. Emptiness is the stillness against which time moves. Negative existence enables a man to be what he is. It is the mirror of mirrors. Non-anticipation is non-interference, and allows the most perfect reflection of creation." I thought that this was a nice way to express it. Could you comment on that and how it applies to other things you have told us?
A: Build a psychomantium.
Q: We are going to. As soon as Ark gets here …

A: Answers re: divorce, career, et cetera, come through that medium, as they are personal and thought center reflective.

Q: So, maybe I will build it *before* he gets here ...

A: Or, use the mirror, and Ark too.

Q: Ark could also use the mirror?

A: In a darkened room, mirror pointed away from your reflection, indirect light, preferably candle, meditate ...

Q: Anything further? I can just do it in my room?

A: To start.

Q: How long will I have to meditate?

A: Open.

Q: Approximately? Day after day, or the first time?

A: Try it.

What was hinted at, but not clearly stated, was that the answers regarding the mission would also be "seen" in the mirror. And later in the session, the parameters of the mission itself were somewhat defined. Again, the flavor and texture of the question that was the platform for the introduction of a certain topic is interesting to consider.

This session was right at the point in time that I was still digging into the Templars, the relation of the Templars to my own ancestors, as well as the discovery of the possibility that the first Knight in my line had been the illegitimate offspring of Roger de Mortimer and Isabella of France, the daughter of Philip the Fair, the French King who brought down the Templars.

At this point, I knew only that the child had suddenly appeared in Winchester with a surname that was, at that point in history, a function and not a name. I assumed that he could have been born in France. It was only later that I discovered some documentary evidence that the child had been born in the Tower during the year that Isabella was in residence there, at the same time that Roger was a prisoner. Roger later escaped, being the only person (or one of the few) to *ever* escape from the Tower of London. It was pretty obvious that he had been helped, very likely by Isabella and Adam Orleton, who was later made Bishop of Winchester in 1333. It is even thought that Adam was ultimately the one responsible for having Edward II murdered, so it is evident that his loyalties were with the ancient Welsh bloodline.

So, of course, with all the strange bits and pieces of the puzzle floating around this issue of Perceval of Wales, the Mortimers as the carriers of the Welsh royal line, the Templars as guardians of the Grail, and Adam Orleton being clearly in the camp of the Templars, and right on hand to take charge of an infant born of such a union, I was naturally curious if there was any significance to these clues as being a possible template for present events. I had the idea that Edward II, the first

"English" Prince of Wales had been murdered for symbolic reasons as much as anything. So, that is the doorway that was opened which resulted in the following remarks about the mission.

Q: Next question: is there any relationship between the fact that Roger de Mortimer, the carrier of the last of the line of the Welsh kings, was the lover of Isabella of France, who was the daughter of Philip the Fair, the destroyer of the Templars, and the murder of Edward II, the first of the English Prince of Wales?

A: Templars are a setup, insofar as persecution is concerned. Remember your "historical records" can be distorted, in order to throw off future inquiries, such as your own.

Q: I know that. I have already figured that one out! But, it seems that no one else has made this connection. I mean, the bloodlines that converge in the Percys and the Mortimers are incredible!

A: You should know that these bloodlines become parasitically infected, harassed and tinkered with whenever a quantum leap of awareness is imminent.

Q: Whenever a quantum leap …

A: Such as "now."

Q: Did Isabella and Mortimer have a child while they were in hiding in France?

And it is at this moment that the most bizarre shift of subject took place.

A: No. Here is something for you to digest: Why is it that your scientists have overlooked the obvious when they insist that alien beings cannot travel to earth from a distant system???

Q: And what is this obvious thing?

A: Even if speed of light travel, or "faster," were not possible, and it is, of course, there is no reason why an alien race could not construct a space "ark," living for many generations on it. They could travel great distances through time and space, looking for a suitable world for conquest. Upon finding such, they could then install this ark in a distant orbit, build bases upon various solid planes in that solar system, and proceed to patiently manipulate the chosen civilizations to develop a suitable technological infrastructure. And then, after the instituting of a long, slow, and grand mind programming project, simply step in and take it over once the situation was suitable.

Q: Is this, in fact, what has happened, or is happening?

A: It could well be, and maybe now it is the time for you to learn about the details.

Q: Well, would such a race be third or fourth density in orientation?

A: Why not elements of both?

Q: What is the most likely place that such a race would have originated from?

A: Oh, maybe Orion, for example?

Q: OK. If such a race did, in fact, travel to this location in space-time, how many generations have come and gone on their space ark during this period of travel, assuming, of course, that such a thing has happened?

A: Maybe 12.

Q: OK, that implies that they have rather extended life spans …

A: Yes …

Q: Assuming this to be the case, what are their life spans?

A: 2,000 of your years.

Q: OK, assuming such a bunch have traveled …

A: When in space, that is …

Q: And what is the span when on terra firma?

A: 800 years.

Q: Well, has it not occurred to them that staying in space might not be better?

A: No. Planets are much more "comfortable."

Q: OK … imagining that such a group has traveled here …

A: We told you of upcoming conflicts … Maybe we meant the same as your Bible, and other references. Speak of … The "final" battle between "good and evil … " Sounds a bit cosmic, when you think of it, does it not?

Q: Does this mean that there is more than one group that has traveled here in their space arks?

A: Could well be another approaching, as well as "reinforcements" for either/or, as well as non-involved, but interested observers of various types who appreciate history from the sidelines.

Q: Well, *swell!* There goes my peaceful life!

A: You never had one!

Q: Well, I was planning on one! Is this one of those items we should *not* put on the Net, or are you addressing it because you want it on the Net?

A: We will leave that until a bit later.

Q: Any other comment?

A: You chose to be incarnated now, with some foreknowledge of what was to come. Reference your dreams of space attack.

Q: OK, what racial types are we talking about relating to these hypothetical aliens?

A: Three basic constructs. Nordic, Reptilian, and Greys. Many variations of type 3, and 3 variations of type 1 and 2.

Q: Well, what racial types are the "good guys?"

A: Nordics, in affiliation with 6th density "guides."

Q: And that's the only good guys?

A: That's all you need.

Q: Wonderful! So, if it is a Grey or Lizzie, you know they aren't the nice guys. But, if it is tall and blond, you need to ask questions!

A: All is subjective when it comes to nice and not nice. Some on 2nd density would think of you as "not nice," to say the least!!!

Q: That's for sure! Especially the roaches! Maybe we ought to get in touch with some of these good guys ...

A: When the "time" is right.

Q: Speaking of time – any further comments?

A: Just pay attention to the signs, please! It is not helpful to place yourself in a vacuum of awareness.

Q: I don't think I am in a vacuum of awareness. Now, this Jason Dunlap is printing a lot of stuff that reminds me of the Hale Bopp incident. There is a lot being said about the sightings out in the Southwest area. They are saying that this is the "new" imminent invasion or mass landing. Can you comment on this activity?

A: Prelude to the biggest "flap" ever.

Q: And where will this flap be located?

A: Earth.

Q: When is it going to begin?

A: Starting already.

Q: Is this biggest flap going to be just a flap, or is it going to be an invasion?

A: Not yet.

Q: Not an invasion?

A: Yes.

Q: So, it will just be inciting people to frenzies of speculation ...

A: Invasion happens when programming is complete ...

Q: What programming?

A: See Bible, "Lucid" book, Matrix Material, "Bringers of the Dawn," and many other sources, then cross reference ...

Q: Well, if something is fairly imminent, we are not gonna have time to do all the things you have suggested that we do!

A: Yes you will, most likely.

Q: Well, we are supposed to build a pool, a maze, a psychomantium, to build a database, get a Nobel Prize ... a *lot* of things in the works here ... This just sort of takes the heart right out of me!

A: Not so!

Q: Well, are we going to have time to do all these things?

A: All these things were suggested for this reason, among others.

Q: So, all the things you have suggested are to get us ready for this event?

A: Yes.

Q: Well, we better get moving! We don't have time to mess around!

A: You will proceed as needed, you cannot force these events or alter the Grand Destiny.

Q: I do *not* like the sound of that! I want to go home!

A: The alternative is less appetizing.

Q: Sure! I don't want to be lunch!

A: Reincarnation on a 3rd density earth as a "cave person" amidst rubble and a glowing red sky, as the perpetual cold wind whistles …

Q: Why is the sky glowing red?

A: Contemplate.

Q: Of course! Comet dust! Sure, everybody knows *that!* Wonderful!!! Anything further?

A: Stay tuned for all pertinent information.

The question, of course, is why did the consideration of the events of that period in history open the door to information about a group of beings who had traveled here to "patiently manipulate the chosen civilizations to develop a suitable technological infrastructure. And then, after the instituting of a long, slow, and grand mind programming project, simply step in and take it over once the situation was suitable"?

I was already getting the idea that time loops were somehow important, and that there were big loops and sub-loops, and that there were periods of history that gave evidence of manipulation by virtue of their connections to other periods in history, but how it all connected I wasn't sure. All of this thinking went back to the three-dominoes dream. I could see that, at certain points in history, an event had been changed or manipulated in some way, and this change acted liked a domino in a long chain of events. I had even discovered that there was some sort of mathematical law that related to the third domino. This law posits that in a row of dominoes where the first one is knocked over to hit the second and third and so on, that no matter how fast or slowly the first domino falls, the rate of fall of the third domino is the same as the rate of fall of all the rest. Somehow, I had the emerging idea that this was connected to three periods in history that were the "dominoes." But there were many other connections as well, that was just the one that worried me.

I started to think a bit more about the psychomantium, though obviously not a whole lot. I remembered that Nostradamus had used a similar method, looking into a bowl of water or something, that Jakob Boehme had used a polished brass bowl, and that Dr. John Dee had utilized a polished stone. I read a magazine account of this event and my question was based on the information in this account.

November 22, 1997

Q: John Dee supposedly had a vision of the Angel Uriel who gave him a highly polished black stone which was convex, and into which he gazed to communicate with other realms. This sounds very much like a psychomantium. OK, these beings would appear on the surface of the stone and reveal all the secrets of the future. This was not an imaginary stone because it now resides in the British Museum. However, he later hooked up with Edward Kelley who was, apparently, a complete con artist. What kind of beings did Dee and Kelley conjure through their polished stone?

A: Fourth Density.

Q: STS or STO?

A: Both.

I wasn't particularly interested in following this up because the history of the contact was such that it was pretty clear that the STS entities were dominant. John Dee was led on a merry chase by these beings, and the fact that the material was later used by MacGregor Mathers and Aleister Crowley was sufficient to indicate to me that the fruits of the work weren't what I would consider positive by any stretch of the imagination. Interestingly, much later the issue of Dr. Dee was brought up in a most unusual way. Vincent told me that he believed he was the reincarnation of Dr. Dee and it was *his* job to finish Dee's work, which Crowley and later Mathers were was unable to do. However, at that point, I did take the trouble to read his material and realized that poor Dr. Dee was as duped by Edward Kelley as I had been by Frank and later, others. But, we will come to that.

The next mention of the psychomantium (the Cs were really hitting it hard, considering the fact that they kept coming back to it again and again), was at the time I have described above, when we were in the midst of the house renovation disaster which had followed directly on the heels of my daughter's third auto accident, the one that had totaled her car. It was another shock and, after having had so many in so short a time, I wasn't sure how much more I could tolerate. On top of the psychological trauma of the very fact that my child had been in an automobile that was now completely destroyed, but which she had walked away from, thank God, was the fact that she had not increased her insurance coverage as she said she would, and we were faced with absorbing the loss. Curiously, again the date was January 17, exactly one year after the psychomantium had first been mentioned.

January 17, 1998

Q: First question: why are we in the middle of such a horrible mess? Things were supposed to get better?!

A: Do you not expect there to be turmoil in accompaniment with a level one quantum life change?

Q: A level-one quantum life change? Do you mean the change we have already effected, or the change we *hope* to effect?

A: Both and transition between.

Q: So, this is a level-one quantum life change of some sort. […]

Q: Now, on Ali's car. What happened to this guy who hit her car? It destroyed her car and thereby her life.

A: Did no such thing.

Q: Well, I know that! But she is crying and thinks her life is over. We are completely lucky, in my opinion, to have her still with us. Why three accidents in a year's time?

A: The dark forces always attack the weakest, or most vulnerable, links in the chain.

Q: Did the guy actually fall asleep?

A: Close. Hypnotic state.

Q: Alright. What can I do, any of us, Ali, or whoever, to derive the proper lesson from Ali's car being totaled?

A: Refer to standard response.

Q: Knowledge Protects.

A: Yes.

Q: OK, anything in particular about the line of attack through this construction project?

A: No.

Q: Well, when I fire this guy, is he gonna give me a hard time?

A: Some. […]

Q: OK. Any advice on how to go about getting the permits I need?

A: Look at easement.

Q: What?

A: Reexamine courthouse records for interesting anomalies which should work in your favor.

As it turned out, the Cs were right. The guy had no license, and had a criminal record.

At this point, Ark wanted to ask about the "work" we were supposed to be doing. It was pretty clear that all we were doing was spending our time keeping our balance in the face of repeated assaults from every quarter. While teaching at the University was a blessing, it also took up a *lot* of Ark's time, and we were so tired from the constant traveling back and forth, that what little time we did have was spent trying to catch up, and we were getting very little sleep!

Q: (A) When I was coming here I hoped that I will do some work and you guys will be helping us and that we will doing things that are important, and, until now, with all this teaching that I have, the fact is that all the forces work in such a way that I can do just nothing. Is there any hope?

A: Yes, of course. But you must accept that it will unfold step by step, and you will not have the luxury of knowing well ahead of time what will happen. All is lessons. You may choose to look upon it as adventure or as torture … Have faith and get more sleep!! The lack of this is breeding a chemical imbalance within, thus leading to depression.

Q: (A) Well, I always like to be sure, and maybe I should take some steps before the end of life happens?

A: Sarcasm becomes you not! All will work out well for you, and we would not say this if we did not know it to be so.

Q: There is a meaning and a purpose in this attempt to integrate this into physics, and because the concept of density seems to have something to do with psychic and consciousness, I cannot find, until now, how to put it, how to relate it ...

A: It has to do with perception, and the ability to perceive, which is in larger measure determined by genetic makeup. Your realm is created by your ability to understand it. The Wave comes as so many seek "graduation."

Q: Are you saying that we are actually, in a sense, creating the Wave?

A: And vice versa.

Q: Are these densities something that can be defined in terms of physics, as in divisions of reality that some significant change occurs at, say, the boundary of one density that signifies the beginning of the other?

A: This, as with so much else is so difficult for you to understand because of your limited view point. Remember, you see the densities below yours perfectly well. But they don't perceive you as what you are.

Q: (A) They said that, in physics, we have one seventh of the equation ... (L) When they said that, he was talking about matter and the direction in time of an anti-particle, which was referred to as the one-seventh. (A) But, what I mean is, animals, minerals, they are described by just one physics that we learn in school. We do not see that this is a different density.

A: Only because you know it is there. You cannot measure that which is above your level of perception, when you are using measuring tools which only can measure that which you perceive.

Q: (A) We are the form makers. I mean it's not Nature that is creating, it is us seeing order in potential disorder. And we see more order than animals, so it seems. Is this what is meant by higher density, being able to see more order?

A: Well, close, maybe, but you are attempting to employ a mirror to see outside.

Q: What we are trying to understand is: you have described seven densities. Three physical densities, three ethereal densities, and the one in the middle, the variable density. What we are trying to find out here is some way to express this mathematically. Some way to understand this in the universal language of mathematics. Because, if we could do that, mathematically speaking, that would help our understanding and perceptual abilities.

A: Yes, but first you must unravel the part of the puzzle which has nothing to do with mathematics. You would have your best luck finding the mathematical formula while in a "dream state," or under hypnosis, or in meditation before a psychomantium.

Again, it was made clear that the mission could not proceed until the two of us began to employ the psychomantium. And again, Frank was being excluded. It seems that the true "meeting with the Cs" could only proceed without Frank. But I was still not ready to make so drastic a change. What happened next was very curious.

[At this point a low-flying helicopter apparently begins to circle overhead and this sound continues until the end of the session.]

Q: (A) Now, I want to come back to physics. We have this paper from the French guy who speaks about anti-gravity and relates it to a double structure of the universe; that antimatter is just located, not in our universe, but in another universe ... [sound anomaly on tape for the next few seconds]

A: The two are exchangeable, much like an ion exchanger.

Q: (A) The two are exchangeable, but it's about us. We are apparently made of matter rather than antimatter, or there is another us that is made of antimatter? I don't think that we are exchangeable. We are apparently living in a universe of matter rather than antimatter.

A: Exchangeable.

Q: (A) The loop dimension of Kaluza-Klein ... when I was asking about extra-dimensions, the answer was that there were no "extra" dimensions, but forget terminology, there is this theory of Kaluza-Klein that there is this loop dimension, this fifth dimension and the question is: this is a way toward UFT, and I would like to have a hint if adding this loop, or cylinder dimension, is the right step?

A: Yes.

Q: (A) OK, that is enough.

A: Okay, we sense probing of you now, or interference, so must go, Good Night.

Again and again, the deeper questions were denied in Frank's presence, and we were being urged to undertake a different mode of communication.

The next reference to the psychomantium was, again, in response to questions relating to physics. Over and over again, the idea was being brought back to the original statement about gravity waves: "We mean for you, Laura, to meditate about unstable gravity waves as part of research." It didn't matter how many times I attempted to include Frank in the processes and projects, the Cs kept blocking it.

January 31, 1998

Q: (A) I want to ask about monopoles. Do monopoles exist?

A: Yes.

Q: My thought was that if monopoles exist, the only way they can exist is that if somewhere, under some conditions, the opposite of the pole exists ... I mean they cannot exist in third density without being a duality ... (A) Yes ...

A: And third density cloaks so many truths.

Q: Do you say cloaks in the sense that it cloaks the monopoles from our observation?

A: Measurability.

Q: Cloaks them from our measurability.

A: Psychomantium.

Q: OK, is a psychomantium something that utilizes monopoles? When you use the mirror are you seeing the other "half" of them?

A: Window to many vistas.

Q: Well, I am working on it! I have to get the house put together first! (A) And to get the house put together first we gotta work on these monopoles, get the Nobel Prize for these monopoles ...

A: Spreading yourself too thin.

Q: I know I am spreading myself too thin.

A: But, you are happier now. [...]

Q: (A) Long ago you advised that I should return to something that I was doing long ago, and that I abandoned, like many other things. Monopoles was one of the things, and recently I discovered another, automata. The universe is like a computer and, in the beginning, there was the "word." Should I just do the monopoles temporarily and finish, or is it something that is worthwhile to pursue? Help, please.

A: You need study time.

Q: What is the clue to be derived from "study time?"

A: Both efforts bring results when pursued simultaneously. Weekends provide this, so do evenings soon to be in new environment, if pursue correctly. Basically on the right track, just have patience and faith. Now, we suggest that future sessions delve more fully into matters of universal importance, then personal problems dissolve, or at least ease!

So it seems that study time and the psychomantium were the pathway. But our lives were, at that moment, so disordered that it would have been impossible. The house didn't even have a roof on it at that moment and all our furniture was piled in the centers of all the rooms, covered with plastic sheeting. The walls were torn out, the electrical wiring and A/C ductwork was dangling everywhere, and so on. It was so bad that it had become the final straw that motivated the older girls to move out on their own. Ali had told me, "Mom, I *can't* work and go to school in this environment." And I knew she was right. Even if that was only part of her reasons, it was hard on me when the first chick left the nest. Yes, she was 20 years old already, but to me she was a baby. Everything was a disaster and we were struggling just to survive it, and Ali blamed the whole mess on the Cs. If there had been no Cs, there would be no disasters. From her perspective, the Cs were to blame for the loss of her beloved red Volvo.

Well, not having a roof on the house was a serious issue since it continued to rain in impossible amounts. I brought the strange weather up the following month, and again the issue of the psychomantium is related to some future events of significance.

February 28, 1998

Q: (L) I want to know something about this weird weather. There have been a *lot* of sightings in Gulf Breeze and falling fireballs out in Colorado, strange weather, but, to open the door to this, is there any more to be said about the increased UFO activity and the weather and all the other things going on at present?

A: Review early transcripts and predictions, leaving aside "time" frames.

Q: One of the earlier sessions made the statement "space invasion in 4 to 6 years." That was said in 1994, which is 4 years ago. What is the deal on the space invasion situation?

A: Lessons are to be learned by observation closely.

Q: So, you are not going to give us any more on this idea of the space invasion?

A: See last answer, then wait and see.

Q: Well, I just keep wondering: are we supposed to be *doing* something?

A: What you are doing … Carefully reread transcripts in regard to questions about special efforts and whether they should be undertaken or not.

Q: Well, if you try to force things, you just mess it all up. You are supposed to be patient and let things fall into place …

A: Close.

Q: Well, we are getting close to getting the house ready so we can have our psychomantium in the other room. Hopefully we won't be invaded and wiped out before that happens.

A: Major dramatic change comes with addition of psychomantium.

Q: Well, okay, we are pushing for it. I gotta *really* get this house finished!

A: Will be finished smoothly now … and on that note, Good Night.

The Cs were oh, so right, that a major change would come with the addition of the psychomantium. We just had no idea that it would be the means of revealing the unseen in ways we hadn't yet considered.

The universe gave me a great gift at this point: Danny. This guy was a construction genius. All I had to do was describe what I wanted, point in the direction I wanted it, and he executed it perfectly. He was a master craftsman. Gradually the house started coming back together.

A few days later I found a wonderful cheval mirror in a specialty store that had a ding in the frame and was marked down less than half price! I brought my find home in triumph. In our bedroom, I set up a backdrop of black felt that I could roll up and down like a window shade, placed the mirror so that it reflected the felt, and dragged a chair into place. Voila! Instant psychomantium! But I still didn't have a clue about what I was supposed to be doing with it!

March 13, 1998

Q: And we have purchased the psychomantium mirror. I practiced last night. How long is it gonna be before I see something?

A: As soon as you are content to see or not to see.

Q: Yes, I know that I have to get there – non-anticipation. I was getting close. I was seeing little flashes of light and movement, almost like looking at something going on in a fog. (A) How does one get information using this medium? (L) I don't know! Should you do it with a question in your mind, or just wait to see what comes without direction?

A: Best to experiment for stronger learning.

Q: I don't like the sound of that! My strongest learning comes when I really do something stupid!

A: Not always, and on that note, Good Night.

I wasn't able to really motivate myself to do it, however. I was always so busy, there was so little time, and besides – as long as we were continuing to use the board, I didn't really feel that I needed to apply more than occasional effort to the project. I was gripped by channeling inertia! If it ain't broke, don't fix it!

March 21, 1998

Q: Now, I have tried the psychomantium. So far, no luck. I don't think it is gonna work.

A: Head must be clear, has not been so far.

Q: Well, how can my head be clear when you won't give me the answers about how to take care of this Noah guy and all the other things going on so that I can clear my head?! I have all these worries! I know! I'm just joking!

A: Good!

Q: (A) In my opinion, this mirror is too narrow, it is not the right shape and it will not work even if the head is clear ... (L) I *love* this mirror! (A) I know that you like this mirror ...

A: Mirror is fine.

Q: (L) *See?!* (A) So, the problem is in the head! Too wide a head?! You must narrow the head!

At this point, some strange effects began to manifest. The instant I would sit in the chair before the mirror, I would begin to feel very hot, and a sensation of tremendous pressure – like the barometer was falling – would come over me. I knew something was going on.

April 4, 1998

Q: Alright, I have been practicing with the psychomantium. I once had a little flash of light. Another time there was the sensation of pressure and of course the rising heat. Are there any actions that I can take that will optimize the process?

A: Blacken the room.

Q: So, it will help to be in a completely blackened room?

A: Oh yes!!

Q: So, that will make a difference. You did say that there would be a dramatic change once the psychomantium was in place. Now, I haven't seen any dramatic changes and I am almost afraid to ask because the last time you said something like that I was in an automobile accident!

A: That was not the change we were speaking of ... We suggest you direct your gaze ahead and a little to the left!

At this point, Danny came to the rescue. He built me a large closet to use as a psychomantium. I had decided that Terry's idea of a sort of box lined with felt might work, and I needed closets anyway. So while Danny was building closets, I had him build me a special L-shaped affair around a corner of one of the downstairs rooms that would accommodate a mirror offset to the left, and space for a reasonable chair. I purchased sufficient black felt to completely line the little room (there was no way I was gonna paint any walls in my house black!), and voila again! Psychomantium!

The next few occasions when it was brought up were effort to establish some sort of protocol.

May 2, 1998

Q: We have our psychomantium built. I am of the opinion that the candle must be obscured completely and you should only be able to see the black depth of the mirror. If you put the candle in front, all you see is the candle ... you see the candle light on the walls. You said very plainly: clear depth, indirect lighting only, that nothing ought to be seen, no walls, no reflection, nothing. Frank says that we should put the candle in front.

A: Must be able to distinguish mirror.

Q: OK, that is gonna be difficult.

A: Try the swivel mirror.

Q: Well, Ark says that it is not wide enough – it is too narrow. He didn't like it.

A: Try it. If straight on, and tilted upward, should work.

Q: How long is it gonna take me ... can you give me an estimate? Say, a theoretical person like myself, in my position, condition, and all things considered, how long would it take that person to see something?

A: As soon as their psyche is clear of anticipation/prejudice.

Q: With me, that could be a *long* time!

A: Or it could be a short time.

Q: Yes, but you have given me such a build up over the last couple of years – that seems impossible ...

A: No.

Q: Well, it is gonna be hard ...

A: No.

443

May 14, 1998

Q: Can you give me any advice about the psychomantium? I try to not try and it is pretty hard. I mean, my eyeballs fall out of my head. Should I change my breathing?

A: Meditate, do not anticipate.

Q: When you say that, do you mean that I should not anticipate being able to *see* something?

A: Yes.

Q: Well, I feel pretty stupid doing that. I mean, the obvious reason one goes into a dark room with a mirror and a candle is to *see* something! It's kind of hard to sit there and *not* think about seeing something when you are in a room that is obviously designed to *see* something!

A: No. Meditate; clear head.

May 30, 1998

Q: So, it is not altogether as he is saying. Ark wants to use the psychomantium. Are there any suggestions for him to follow that would be different from instructions for me? But, then I am not an example to follow because I haven't been having a whole heck of a lot of success!

A: Keep experimenting with an open mind ... do not anticipate.

Q: Well, I am really trying to get rid of this anticipation business. (A) I want to know whether this light is important – whether there must be a light or whether it must be total darkness?

A: Must be some light.

Q: (A) Should something be seen in the mirror ... (L) I asked whether I would see something in the mirror or in my mind's eye and they said both ...

A: Yes.

Q: Yes, I didn't know whether it would be a holograph or something in my own head ... any special technique for Ark to use? (A) Yes, because I think that I do everything different from other people. Must I just go into some kind of a trance state, or can I do it my way?

A: Yes, just keep up the experimentation. You will see ...

June 27, 1998

Q: One final question: I have to start scheduling time for the psychomantium. Can you suggest the optimum time or optimum schedule?

A: Mid-evening and nearer to full moon and new moon.

Now, I want to add in this next little clip, even though it is off the subject of the psychomantium. I had been reading Dr. David Jacobs' book, *The Threat*, and based on many clues in there, Frank fit the profile of an alien hybrid. He had always claimed to be special, and this book seemed to confirm that claim. The only problem was, according to

Jacobs, these hybrids were not positive beings at all, even if they could produce that impression.

August 1, 1998

Q: (L) I want to ask about Frank's type B-negative blood. Is Frank an alien hybrid?

A: Open.

Q: (L) Well, that's real encouraging!

A: Best to discover.

Q: (A) What is the test of being an alien hybrid. One is this blood type, what is another?

A: No criteria, but subjects of this nature seem "off-center" by terrestrial standards. However, the truest nature of this subject is as of yet undiscovered.

In this last remark, I wasn't quite sure if the Cs meant the subject of alien hybrids in general, or if they were referring to Frank when they said "this subject." But, since they said "subjects of this nature," meaning individuals that are hybrids, it stands to reason that the following remark, "the truest nature of this subject," was referring to Frank specifically. The instant this was transmitted, a shiver traveled through my body, though I immediately shoved the warning sensation under the rug. In point of fact, I had thought many things about Frank, but the one thing I had *never* thought was that he had been deliberately sent into my life to harm me. The above remark is completed with the remark made on January 10, 2002:

A: He was programmed for the specific purpose of "downloading" from you secrets coded into you before birth of your present body. He failed because you were incorruptible. He is now charged with the mission, in concert with Vincent Bridges, of destroying your ability to accomplish your mission.

Getting back to the psychomantium, finally, after months of trying with no real success, being stuck in a claustrophobic little closet that became hotter than an oven in a very short time with just a single candle, I decided that this was *not* going to work. There was no way I could even get comfortable, much less survive such an ordeal a sufficient number of times for anything to manifest!

August 8, 1998

Q: (A) OK. Now, I want to ask a question about the medium. We have been repeatedly told that we should get a better medium which can convey more information. We were experimenting with psychomantium without success …

A: Because you did not do it correctly.

Q: I thought I was doing everything that had been suggested.

A: Light must be placed properly so as to illuminate black depth sufficiently. Also, chamber must be large enough to stimulate relaxed meditative state. And no seams or ripples must be evident in reflection. Lastly, patience must reign supreme, with as little anticipation as possible.

Q: So, you are saying that the closet we are using is not large enough …

A: We never suggested a closet.

Q: How large should the chamber be?

A: 10 by 10 by 8.

Q: (L) Well, that's almost a whole room!

A: Yes. One room idly sits …

Q: (A) I have the idea that one should go with a given question and then come out with an answer instead of waiting and waiting …

A: My dear Arkadiusz, by now, you know imagination is the bridge to the Akashic.

Q: (L) So, you are saying that his idea is a bridge to the Akashic, and when he gets such ideas, they are important clues?

A: Good!

Well! How about that? Nothing like letting me spin my wheels doing all that closet business when, all the while, it was obvious that it wasn't going to work. But heck, by now I knew that the Cs very often let me do such things just to make a point. And yes, there was an idle room in my house. But I darn sure wasn't going to paint a whole room in my house black! Also important to note was the comment about imagination being a "bridge" to the Akashic records.

In the second half of 1998, after the house was put back together, and our sessions were held in a little more comfort, there was a building tension with Frank. Ark was paying very close attention to his behavior in regard to me, and was noting that any prolonged contact with Frank generally resulted in negative effects on my health. This was not something I had previously paid any attention to, because I had been in such poor health for so many years. The definite relationship between Frank's presence and my physical condition had never been noted. But Ark noticed, and watched for several months before he even mentioned it to me. He began to take action to limit this draining, making sure that Frank was not able to focus his attention on me, redirecting conversations and interactions in a subtle, but firm way.

This cutting off the flow of energy from me to Frank had the most interesting result in the fact that Frank began to become quite rude and obnoxious toward Ark in an attempt to overtly manipulate me to "take his side." At the time, I excused his behavior with the idea that he was just simply so socially backward that he didn't realize that he was being offensive. One night he began a long monologue about Ark's accent. Pontificating at great length about his own masterful command of the

English language, he ended his spiel by saying to Ark, "If you ever want to amount to anything in this country, you had better learn to speak English!"

I couldn't believe what I was hearing. Not only was it rude beyond enduring, but Frank seemed to have completely forgotten the fact that he was employed as a telemarketer, and Ark was employed as a defense subcontractor. Accent or no, Ark's income was much above Frank's. Even more, Ark had endured struggles and attacks that Frank had never even dreamed of, succeeding in his chosen field against many obstacles. Frank couldn't even go through a book and circle spelling errors for me.

Nevertheless, we continued to make nice, and ignore Frank's ever increasing personal attacks on Ark that were becoming less subtle by the day. Ark decided to bring up the issue of monitoring again.

August 15, 1998

Q: (A) I want to ask whether this channel is being monitored, and if so, by whom?

A: Only effective monitoring so far is by direct 3rd density observation and enticing some to share data, then "spill their guts" with "shaky" correspondents.

Q: (L) So, it's only when I get enticed to share what ought not to be shared, or when someone is present who is a monitor, that we have been monitored?

A: Close. It can be monitored in other ways, but so far, these have been only seldom necessary. All STS always seek the path of least resistance first.

Q: (L) You once said when Terry and Jan were here that we should imagine the words appearing on a screen somewhere as they were being delivered on the board. Now you say that this is not necessarily the lengths to which they have gone. Was that because they were present?

A: Seldom does not mean never.

Q: (L) If such a thing was to happen, would it be because of the presence of someone, such as when you said PZ was a monitor?

A: PZ, yes definitely!

In the above remarks, naturally, I felt very guilty because I was always sharing what I was learning with correspondents and on the website. And Frank was constantly telling me that I ought not to be sharing the material so freely because I was going to bring fire down on our heads. It never occurred to me that *he* was the one doing the monitoring. Since Frank was so certain that any monitoring was from Terry and Jan, I decided to ask about the comment that had been made when they were present about the "words appearing on a screen." The answer was noncommittal enough to be taken either way. But what was most significant was the fact that they said that extreme methods of monitoring had not been necessary; that STS seeks the path of least resistance. It completely eluded me that this meant that the reason extreme methods of monitoring had seldom been necessary was because we had our own, built-in mole. In a strange sort of way, this almost suggested that Terry and Jan's presence was what had *necessitated* other methods of monitoring because Frank's monitoring activity had been blocked by their presence.

Getting back to the psychomantium, a new plan evolved: a tent that was the exact dimensions, that could be suspended inside the room like a liner, and taken down when not in use. I went to the fabric store and checked out the felt. I drew my design on paper, figured my cuts and yardage, and ordered two bolts of heavy black felt. I had designed rod pockets into which I could insert rope for suspension, so I purchased that. Then I went to the hardware store for window weights to put at the ends of the ropes at each corner, to be hung over hooks drilled into the ceiling. They didn't have any, so I improvised by using PVC pipe filled with sand and capped.

August 22, 1998

Q: Now, we are in the process of constructing a psychomantium tent, a 10 by 10 by 8 foot tent, to suspend from the ceiling in the bedroom. After what you suggested about the time and mode of meditation, and the fact that "one room stands idle," I thought that trying to use it in the early evening in the back room would be almost impossible. However, setting it up in the bedroom, it will be better all the way around. Lying on the bed to meditate makes for much more comfortable conditions. I would like to know if this is going to be … I know that you don't want to tell me, but it just seemed to be the ideal place to put it, in the bedroom – for comfort and quiet and a lot of different reasons. Can you comment?

A: Good.

Q: Well, would it be better in the back room? There are a lot of reasons why that would be unpleasant …

A: Trial leads to realization.

Q: Any further advice about the psychomantium? I am getting kind of excited about trying it this way. It is going to be so much better and more comfortable …

A: Yes.

It took a couple of months to get it finished. I don't know how many people have ever tried to assemble a rather large tent sewn out of heavy felt, but the fact is, as each panel is added, it sort of grows like the blob in the old Steve McQueen movie. It gets larger and heavier, and more difficult to manage. On top of that, I realized that all of the seams would have to be triple stitched with reinforcement just to support its own weight. I also came to the idea that this was not going to be something that would be easily put up and taken down. It was just too big and unwieldy. So, I made it with overlapping flaps on all four sides, joined in the corners, so that the flaps could be tied up when not in use. As the thing began to acquire its final form, Ark had to gather it up and hold it off the floor while I ran the seams through the machine. In the end, it sort of looked like a medieval tent with a peak in the center.

We erected it in the bedroom, and fell in love with it. It was the neatest sleeping tent imaginable. It was like being in the *Arabian Nights*. Only thing was, sleeping in a black felt tent, with a mirror standing at an angle in the corner, led to some strange events.

One night, some time after we had gone to sleep, I was awakened by an electrical-like explosion. Since it woke me up, I couldn't be exactly sure from which direction it had come. I opened my eyes and stared into the blackness, listening. Again, there were popping and crackling noises just like you hear when an electrical cord is shorting out, snapping and sparking and buzzing. The next thing I knew, an Egyptian guy had stepped out of the mirror, walked around to my side of the bed and kissed my cheek, and then walked around to the other side of the bed and sort of merged with Ark. The incident was so weird that I could hardly credit my senses. Ark woke up right then and I told him what I had seen and he asked me who did I think it was. Well, I told him that I had no idea, and we went back to sleep. I didn't want to talk about this event too plainly in front of Frank.

October 3, 1998

Q: (L) OK, I have been hearing funny popping and crackling sounds in the psychomantium at night. The other night I even saw an Egyptian guy walking back toward the mirror along the side of the bed where I was. He looked exactly like one of those carved images with the funny perspective. It seemed that he must have come out of the mirror, interacted with me in some way, and I was awakened by his presence as he was going back ... We have been sleeping regularly in the psychomantium and there is a *huge* increase in frequency and clarity of dreams. There is an interesting energy in the tent. Who or what was this being I encountered?

A: Find out.

Q: (L) Is there anything we can do to enhance this process? We sleep in it and are trying to just be used to it being there without expectation.

A: Good.

Q: (L) Is it a doorway that can be used while we are sleeping?

A: Yes.

Q: (L) Do we use it while we are sleeping?

A: Probably.

Q: (L) Anything you want to add about the psychomantium?

A: No.

Q: (L) Is everything progressing as it ought to?

A: Oh, Laura!

Q: (L) What does that mean? Are you just frustrated with me for asking a silly question?

A: Close.

I wasn't the only one having remarkable dreams sleeping in the psychomantium. Ark had one so intense one night that he woke me up to tell me about it. In his dream, he had even heard angelic music, and he had been amazed at these celestial sounds. Again, neither of us wanted to describe the dream to Frank. With the growing awareness that the Cs were communicating in code, that there were things that Frank could not know for some reason, we were being ever more careful what we did talk about in front of Frank. So Ark asked his questions about it in a veiled manner.

October 10, 1998

Q: (A) I want to ask about the meaning of my dream, which was so vivid … about Elohim and Seraphim. What was the meaning of this dream?

A: Peace torch.

Q: (A) What is peace torch? From whom?

A: Not from. All considered before decision on judgment.

Q: (L) That makes no sense at all.

A: Yes it does.

Q: (A) Who were the Elohim?

A: Elohim refers to past, as a connection to future as envisioned in your dream. It is the connector that counts, see?? Ruling council of Od; Odiem.

Q: (L) What about the Seraphim?

A: Council in clouds … We are speaking of advanced insight here.

Q: (L) Why were there 300 Elohim and 301 Seraphim?

A: Who is the odd one out?

Q: (A) Who is the odd one out?

A: Check your roots. Od, odiem, odd, could we spell it out any clearer for you? Not without abridging free will!

Q: (L) Who is Sara?

A: Roots.

Q: (L) Who is the "King of the Angels?"

A: No more spoon-feeding. Gerber's is out of stock!

The "odd one out." The dream had been about me, and my name was Sarah, and Ark had added his presence to the 300 Seraphim, becoming my husband, which had resulted in the defeat, or displacement of the Elohim. I knew that the message was that Frank was the "odd man out," and I was beginning to get a glimmer about the "Third Man Theme."

July 19, 1997

Q: Well, I found some connections between some tombs in Rome, Nicolas Poussin, and some tombs in England, the processions of "angels" on the Canary Islands. The connection seems to be these funny lights, or Candles, with "peculiar wicks," as they are described, which are "eternal flames." I am wondering if this is what you meant by connecting them by the frequency of light?

A: "Eternal flame" adorns the tomb of JFK. Connection?

Q: Yes. I also found the Solloi priesthood and the priestesses called Peleiades. They seem to be involved with urns, birds, tinkling bells, urns that can be struck and which then set up a particular resonance in other urns, oak trees, and some other peculiar references that relate to laurel trees ...

A: Siren song.

Q: What about the siren song?

A: Greek mythology.

Q: I know that. What about it? What do the sirens represent?

A: Laura, my dear, if you really want to reveal "many beautiful and amazing things," all you need to do is remember the triad, the trilogy, the trinity, and look always for the triplicative connecting clue profile. Connect the threes ... do not rest until you have found three beautifully balancing meanings!!

Q: So, in everything there are three aspects?

A: And why? Because it is the realm of the three that you occupy. In order to possess the keys to the next level, just master the Third Man Theme, then move on with grace and anticipation.

The Third Man is a classic film noir. The action is set in Vienna's bombed out buildings and underground sewers. Post-war Austria was politically divided into different sectors controlled by the U.S., England, France and Russia. Holly Martins (Joseph Cotten), an American author, arrives in Vienna where he has been promised work by his old school friend Harry Lime (Orson Welles). Upon his arrival, Martins discovers that Lime has been killed in a suspicious car accident, and that his funeral is taking place immediately. At the graveside, Martins meets a Major Calloway (Trevor Howard) and an actress, Anna Schmidt (Alida Valli), who is weeping copiously. When Calloway tells Martins that the late Harry Lime was nothing more or less than a thief and a murderer, the loyal Martins is at first outraged. Gradually, he not only discovers that Calloway was right, but also that Lime faked his own death and is still very much alive (he was the mysterious "third man" at the scene of the fatal accident). Calloway wants help from either Anna or Holly to flush out Lime. Blindly loyal, Anna refuses. Martins does likewise, until Calloway shows him the tragic results of Lime's black market in diluted penicillin. Arranging a rendezvous with

Lime at the huge Ferris wheel in the centre of Vienna, Holly listens in barely concealed disgust as Lime casually dismisses his heinous crimes. Feeling particularly brazen, Lime offers not to kill Holly if the latter will go into business with him. Thus the stage is set for the famous climactic confrontation in the sewers of Vienna – and the even more famous final shot of *The Third Man*, in which Martins pays emotionally for doing the right thing.

It's another of those bizarre things that the plot of this movie so accurately represented our real life dynamics right down to my loyalty to Frank, and Ark's arrival on the scene and his initial refusal to see what Frank was really doing at the deepest levels. Even though Ark and I were now at the point where we *knew* that something was seriously amiss with Frank, we continued to want to try to find ways to help him adjust to the fact that he was valued and accepted, but that he was not going to be allowed to willfully manipulate either of us, and control games were not going to be tolerated. Frank had issues – deep ones – and we knew it. I had always known it. But now we were coming to the realization that the only one who could fix Frank was Frank.

We tried to approach the problem in terms of behavior modification. On all the occasions when I would have been inclined to let rudeness pass, or to make nice when Frank was clearly in the wrong, to agree for the sake of peace even when I knew he was twisting things, Ark was undertaking the process of letting him know when he was rude and behaving unacceptably, as well as clearly pointing out the fallacies in his logic. Frank had been accustomed to dazzling everyone with his fine voice and big words. Frank used words as others use algebraic signs. He was meticulous and precise, sculpting the emotions of the listener with finely tuned reverberations of pain and love and fear.

Over the years, I had noticed that he watched other people carefully while he talked to them, and I often caught him actually peeking to see what effect he was having. If the effect was satisfactory, he continued on a given approach. If the effect was not what he wanted – and I wasn't sure what it was – then he would adjust his word choices until they achieved the desired effect. His ability to mimic was obviously very useful in this way because he could make his words and vocabulary resemble that of his target so that they were very quickly entrained. There were only a very few people he was not able to manipulate this way. He did it to me, but I knew he was doing it to some extent, and because I cared for him, I allowed it.

The only emotions that seemed to be really "real" to Frank, the only emotions he expressed, were rage and hurt and inordinate humiliation and fear, which he expressed in reaction to slights and injuries, real or imagined. I guess it could be said that his emotions were reactive, and not active. The curious thing about it was that even though he could rant for hours in rage at his parents, someone who had insulted him when he was a child in school, a stranger who had offended him, his sister (one of his favorite rants), he disdained feelings and emotions in other people. He pronounced anyone with healthy emotions to be "weak" and therefore to be derided. He would pontificate for hours about how superior his own approach to life was because he, *only he*, was completely free of petty human emotions!

Frank was obsessively afraid of sickness and pain. For Frank, any experience of pain brought on an onslaught of memories of every other pain he had ever experienced, and the listener was forced to endure hours of recitation of the multiple levels of agony he had experienced at all the different points in his life. This subject of his pains was an inexhaustible source of verbiage, and I had been subjected to it for years. And now, Ark would no longer allow it. When Frank would start on such subjects, Ark would ask him: why are you so focused on your pains of the past when you can see that Laura is so exhausted she can barely sit up?

As much as I hated to admit it, I was slowly beginning to realize that Frank was not just a poor wounded bird; he was overtly pompous, grandiose, repulsive and contradictory. There was a huge discrepancy between who he thought he was, and claimed to be, and what he really was. He didn't just think he was superior to everyone else, it was an accepted fact in his mind, an all-pervasive reality that made him certain that he was entitled to special treatment and outstanding consideration because he was the most unique human being on the planet. He *knew* this to be true just as he knew that he was surrounded by air. This superior identity was more him than his body. And as long as I allowed myself to be controlled by him, I was allowed to breathe this superior air. But when the control was broken, when Ark exerted his protective influence over me, an abyss opened between me and Frank that grew wider every day.

Frank was quite brilliant at insulating himself from the truth about himself versus what he thought he was. His brilliant rhetoric was used to isolate him from the pain of facing reality. It allowed him to continue to inhabit the fantasyland where he was the ideal of perfection and brilliance. Frank wasn't, and isn't evil in any strict sense. In point of fact, what we call the dark side, or STS for the sake of convention, ought not to be reviled. It just simply is. Most people on such a pathway consider themselves to be good and compassionate people. They even help people professionally or voluntarily. But they only do it to gain something, to get attention, adulation, admiration, money, power or whatever.

But Ark wasn't going to let him get away with it anymore. Frank was certainly entitled to be any way he wanted to be, or to just be. But when it created physical, psychological, or psychic problems for us, he wasn't going to be allowed to do it in our house. He had more than met his match, and he didn't like it one bit.

As we became more aware of the problem, we naturally discussed if we ought to do something more about it, what it might be, and came to the conclusion that the simplest solution was to work with the psychomantium for the deeper questions, and continue the board work as the group channel, for simple questions and issues that did not require complex answers. Frank seemed to be aware of this and several times accused us of planning to ditch him. The fact is, that wasn't true, since we hoped that he was going to stabilize so that we could continue on both levels. But it seemed that the more paranoid he became about it, the more he behaved in ways to make it a self-fulfilling prophecy.

As Ark continued to block Frank's attempts to drain energy from me, his health began to deteriorate. Frank had always been a hypochondriac and a germophobe, but now he was having what seemed to be acute gallbladder attacks. He thought it was his heart and his mother paid for him to go and have a complete cardiac work-up. Nothing was found. The next was a complete gall bladder check, including the most advanced testing available. Again, nothing was found to be wrong with him. At the same time, all his teeth were rotting away visibly week by week. Not just one or two of them, but *all* of them.

I have been a fan of Louise Hay for many years, finding her little book, *Heal Your Body*, to be an invaluable resource. The Cs had confirmed on a number of occasions that physical disease does not manifest unless there is a psycho-spiritual cause, and I knew that these causes could be very deep, often relating to past life experiences. I had used Louise Hay's book to examine my own mental and psychological state, and had spent a great deal of the previous four years in physical therapy, including deep tissue massage, acupuncture, and several other Oriental modalities. I knew how valuable this multifaceted approach was for identifying and helping to release deeply buried issues in order to aid the healing process. My own health had been steadily improving as a result of this work, and with the cessation of energy draining I was feeling better than I had felt in 25 years or more.

I wanted Frank to be fixed. I wasn't ready to give up on him. I wanted him to feel good too. I wanted him to stop this grandiose "I am so special; I am the Channel; I am the answer to the world's prayers!" nonsense. I wanted him to just, for God's sake, get real! I was sick of nurturing, giving, feeding him, with no evidence that anything was ever going to change. I thought he could heal all of this; he could heal his body as well as his soul. So I pointed out what Louise Hay had written about dental problems and gallbladder disease. I then suggested a variety of therapies that would have helped to release the blocked energy or psychic trauma that was certainly to be found at the root of his various problems.

He was highly offended that I would think that there was *any* comparison between *him* and ordinary mortals! How could I even suggest that he get on a massage table and allow anyone to touch his hallowed person? Had I lost my mind? Had I learned *nothing* in all my years of association with him? Wasn't I yet fully convinced that he, above all people, was not like anyone else on the planet, and *none* of the rules applied to him!

Well, if you are so damned superior, how come your teeth are falling to pieces in your mouth, and how come you are suffering from that most common of all mortal ailments, gall bladder attacks? We will ask the Cs, I told him! Then you'll see!

October 10, 1998

Q: I would like to ask if there is any significance to the fact that Frank is being afflicted in the area of his gallbladder, considering the relation to the word "gall?"

A: Only significance is that this is an unnecessary organ, much like the appendix.

Q: You say it is unnecessary. Was it ever necessary?

A: In earlier models … When one receives message of pain there, could it be symbolic of advancement of neo-physicality?

Q: Are you asking me? I have known a lot of people who had pain there who are just unhappy people.

A: But why unhappy? Think, my dear … And remember, your consciousness operates on four levels, not just one!

Q: And what are these four levels?

A: Physical body, consciousness, genetic body and spirit-etheric body.

Q: Are those the four composites of the human manifestation in third density?

A: 3rd and 4th. One leads oneself, through physical actions, as well as psychic ones, to develop these "problems" when one is preparing to "bump it up" a notch.

Q: Very interesting …

A: Now, a gentle warning: soon you too, Laura, will experience something similar!

Q: How similar?

A: Exactly similar!

Q: Is Ark going to be sick too?

A: Not likely, as his chemistry bypasses it. In other words, his gallbladder is functionally obsolete, it is comatose, as a result of diet and psychic nature.

Q: Alright now, anymore on this before we go in another direction?

A: Well, what do you think of that?!?

Q: I think that he must have bumped up a notch or two already.

A: Maybe … but you are all advanced … Why do you suppose you have adopted the dietary practices you have?

Q: Because they seem to be the only ones that work to keep me from being sick. I can't eat like other people … never have been able to.

A: It will be interesting to see what happens post removal …

Q: After the removal of Frank's gallbladder?

A: Yes, and …

Q: Now, listen here! I don't want to go in the hospital! I'm scared of hospitals! I'm scared of doctors. I don't want needles stuck in my veins. I don't want to be put to sleep, and I don't want anybody cutting on me! I swore I would *never* do it again!

A: That will change when nature starts singing her song. We suggest you start now to concentrate on weight-loss, as this will make the process much easier on you!!!

Well, that was interesting. As it happens, I have had no gallbladder problems, and probably won't. However, the Cs certainly confirmed that Frank was unhappy. They were also conveying some deep information about Frank when they said that he was preparing to "bump it up a notch" that meshes exactly with what was later said on January 10, 2002:

Q: Quite a few years ago, there were several remarks made on two or three occasions regarding Frank's battle with the dark forces, and the issue of whether or not he would be able to resist their domination. Was it always known that he would fail?

A: He is not a failure.

Q: What do you mean?

A: From the perspective of STS he is a success.

We had been told on enough occasions that advancement could be made as STS or STO. So we may assume that the higher self in STS terms was activating his program for success. Another thing that strikes me in retrospect was the remark about Ark: it seems that the Cs were indicating that he was already operating from neophysicality. We can certainly see the Cs giving warnings in the above, wrapped in Frank's wishful thinking which directed a warning at me. He was indeed advancing to his new state of being. It just didn't happen to be STO.

We moved onto other subjects and he settled down; until Ark began pressing the physics questions again.

Q: (A) When I was asking about UFT, you said I should go back to 1969. I went back to 1969, but I don't have any notes from then, so the only thing I can remember that I was doing then which could relate, was that I was thinking about certain algebraic machinery which tells us that there is a kind of perfect symmetry between matter and antimatter. Was this the clue?

A: Yes!

Q: (A) I was looking for the connection between the square root of 13 and phi, and I couldn't find any. So, my question is, when you say square root of 13, do you mean an ordinary square root, or using one of these p-adic number fields?

A: Latter.

Q: (A) But, if so, then last time I took the calculator and computed the ordinary square root of thirteen; yet you did not stop me at this point, but ask me to subtract from this ordinary square root, the number phi. So, if it is not an ordinary square root, as you suggest, I would expect that you would not ask me to subtract from the wrong number!

A: We did not ask you to subtract from the "wrong" number. Besides, you did what you are supposed to do; think!! This quest is for you. Our prime channel is becoming weak and fatigued, so we must now go!

"This quest is for you!" And the instant that had been transmitted, Frank "woke up" and we see the manipulation of his wishful thinking. Again, we see the fact that the real answers were not to be delivered in Frank's presence. The answers to such questions, locked away from him and his vacuum operation, only came when Ark and I were working alone. And somehow, since he could not access them, he realized that he was not the "Prime Channel," though he had to maintain the fiction right to the end.

A couple of weeks after this, I had a dream. Keep in mind that, at this point, we are sleeping in the psychomantium. The dream was very disturbing. As you read this, just remember the dream about V** where it turned out that my subconscious was sending my conscious mind a message, but my conscious mind didn't want to hear it, so the characters were switched. Of course, in this following discussion, the reader ought to also keep in mind that it is likely that some of Frank's prejudices against Terry and Jan were present. But still, the Cs managed to do a pretty good job telling me something in code. And pay very close attention to the mention of the "used soap." It was the key.

October 31, 1998

Q: I would like to address a couple of things before Ark gets on to his questions if any. First of all, I had a dream the other night about Terry and Jan. In the dream, Terry was at my house and it was the old house up in Hudson. He was going through the house claiming that I had things that belonged to them, such as books, which I did not have. In fact, they *do* have books which belong to me. Nevertheless, since he could not find anything that was theirs, and I spent some time allowing him to look through everything to prove the point, he began collecting all sorts of little things such as bars of soap, even used soap, cosmetics, and an old book that he claimed because I could not identify it as mine, and it was damaged by water and useless. He kept going around the house saying, "Isn't that mine? Isn't that mine?" and on and on. Finally, I got mad at my time being endlessly wasted and the fact that he did not believe me, and I ordered him to leave my house and never come back. He left reluctantly and soon was back with Jan. Jan was then trying to placate me and being all sweet and huggy and said, "I heard you had a little tiff with Terry," and she did not realize that it was *not* a little "tiff," I had simply *had* it with *both* of them. I was boiling mad, and she was saying, "I know you have stuff that belongs to us," and *she* started poking around here and there, and they even went to the opening to the attic and started pulling down the insulation in the roof to see if I had hidden stuff that belonged to them up there! They just couldn't find anything, but they kept saying that they were *sure* that I had something that belonged to them, and it seemed to be mainly books. Could you tell me what this dream represents?

A: Your reflection of them.

Q: My reflection of them?

A: Yes.

Q: In what sense? I don't understand what you mean?

A: Your view.

Q: So, my view of them is that they are trying to take something from me that doesn't belong to them and insisting that it does?

A: Close. Maybe something you do have.

Q: Trying to take something from me that is mine by claiming that it is theirs?

A: Yes.

Q: Any other comment on this dream? This was rather threatening to me and I thought I ought to examine it because it was so realistic.

A: There is a karmic "twist" between you and them.

Q: What is the karmic twist?

A: Just as it is … Unresolved issues, like kids playing in the sand box.

Q: Is there any indication from this dream that they are going to swoop back into our lives?

A: Well, they probably will, will they not?

Q: I don't know. I thought it was singularly unpleasant.

A: You fascinate and frustrate them.

Q: It is pretty bizarre. Now, the other night, in front of the psychomantium, I did not exactly have a vision, but something came into my head, and the idea was that prime numbers are important because the principle that they are only divisible by themselves and by one is indicative of

the fact that they are direct links, channels, or conduits to seventh density, or first density, or something ...

A: How about all densities?

Q: OK, that is sort of what I mean, that they are, in a sense, gateways –
would that be a good term?

A: Close.

Q: How does one utilize the energies inherent in prime numbers in this
respect? Do they represent frequencies or frequency relationships?

A: Verities.

Q: Is there any formula, or any thing about prime numbers that makes it
easier to find them ... anything about them that is unique?

A: Pyramidal.

Q: Pyramid relationships would help one find prime numbers?

A: Graph.

Q: A pyramid-type graph. OK, anything else about prime numbers?
When you said that they were the "dwellings of the mystics" I had an
idea that a prime number could be a dwelling of a mystic because the
individual would express in some manner a frequency that related in
some way to a prime number. Is that somewhere along the line ... ?
That mystics can traverse all densities because of frequency?

A: Something like that.

Q: My next thought was that it could indicate actual places or locations
in space-time on the planet that would be represented by coordinates.

A: Zuber.

Q: What does *that* mean?

A: Research. [*Die Zauberflaute* – the "magic flute" by Mozart. So perhaps
it is related to sound and "magic".]

At this point, because I was still disturbed by my dream, I decided to
come back to the subject of Terry. After the months and months of
Frank's repeated derogatory remarks about Terry, and now with the
dream on top of it, I just wanted a straight answer. Was Frank right?
Was Terry the bad guy? After all, the dream had been about Terry, right?

Q: Now, I have long wondered about something you said to Terry,
about him being connected to a thought center called Neormm, and
that it was related to orimulsion, and this is some kind of a fuel. I wonder if you could clarify that remark. What is Neormm?

A: Not yet.

Q: You also made a remark to Terry once, "Oh Terry, the battle is always, it's when you choose that counts." What do you mean by "when
you choose." I thought that time did not exist, so why did you make this
remark to him?

A: Remark was for him.

Q: Did that indicate that he was not choosing something, or that he
ought to choose? I know I am poking into his business.

A: Yes, you are.

Q: But in the sense of his interaction with us, it would be useful to know if he was a robot person, programmed to disrupt, a psychic vampire, or something other.

A: The issue here is not him per se, but the blend in a karmic sense. Obviously, these people hold an inordinate level of your consciousness. So why is this? If you seek answers, it is wise to not leave doors unopened.

Q: What kind of doors? Leave the door open to Terry and Jan?

A: No, it is the quest we speak of. One cannot find clues without understanding the interpreter.

Q: Could you be a little bit clearer? I am just not grasping this!

A: Why do Terry and Jan enter your dreams? Do you suppose it is because you have no interest?!? We think not!

Q: What doors ... am I leaving some doors closed?

A: Yes.

Q: What could I do to open these doors in a practical sense?

A: Look within.

Q: Is there something I can or should do to disconnect?

A: Explore the issues.

"Obviously, these people hold an inordinate level of your consciousness. So why is this? If you seek answers, it is wise to not leave doors unopened." In fact, the only issue that had been left unexplored was the idea that Frank could have been deliberately sent into my life to vacuum information out of me and drain me of my life force. Every single other possibility had been considered. I had gone from thinking that Frank was a sixth-density STO being sent to help me, to thinking he was a wounded fourth-density STO being, to thinking that he was just a guy with problems, and those problems made him uniquely suited to be a well pipe in a channeling experiment. The Cs couldn't have said it any plainer when they said, "One cannot find clues without understanding the interpreter." Without having the understanding of what Frank really was, I was unable to see so many, many things that later became crystal clear. I was refusing to open the door to the possibility that Frank was just simply on the STS path, and that it was his free-will choice, and none of the fixing I was trying to do was going to work.

Fortunately, however, with Terry so nicely disposed of, Frank's control issues went quiescent and we managed to continue in a reasonable way.

Q: (A) I was trying meditate and I have discovered that I don't think it will work for me. I don't know how to do it ...

A: Remove ripples, adjust light.

Q: Do we need to move the light backward, forward, or dim it?

A: Back it up and dim.

Q: In general, is the structure as we have it adequate? It seems to have really good energy.

A: Getting there.

Q: Well, it has the size, and the lines of the structure seem to concentrate energy, and there have been a few interesting experiences in there …

A: Sparks, yes, but no flame yet.

Q: (A) I was thinking that for me it will not work at all unless I can write something down, because otherwise, it is not recorded … (L) I think that is a good idea to take a pad and pen and write whatever comes to you …

A: Yes.

Q: (L) You don't have to see what you are writing …

A: Writing has always worked for Ark.

Q: (A) Well, if it is true that writing has always worked for me, is it also true that this psychomantium environment will help?

A: Yes.

Q: (L) Just write in bed, in the tent, every night before you go to sleep. (A) Is there any way we can improve or change the way we are having our sessions with the board?

A: Room.

Q: We are working on changing the room.

A: Okay.

Q: I know that back room is a better room, and maybe I should just clean it out so we can use it. (A) Why is the other room better?

A: Energy vector.

Q: (A) Why is the energy vector in the other room better than in this room?

A: It is conduit.

Q: Where does the conduit extend from, above or below?

A: Both. Like static electrical charge.

Q: (A) What about conduit in the bedroom where we have put this psychomantium?

A: Psychomantium utilizes one's own psychic body, thus is portable to a greater extent. But, if you were to place the structure there, it would enhance things …

Q: It would enhance things psychomantium-wise or board-wise?

A: Each.

Q. Well, the only problem with putting the psychomantium there is there is nothing to sit in as comfortable as it ought to be …

A: As of now.

Q: What are we supposed to do? Have a whole complete room for it?

A: That is how it is generally done. Just ask Michel de Notredame.

Q: Then, I just need a different house! I need a dining room and new kitchen!

A: Have you had this since 1990?

Q: No, and it is a real pain!

A: Oh, the pain, the pain.

Q: So, what you are saying is that you want me to take the psychomantium, set it up in the back room, put the table back there, get some comfortable chairs ...

A: We don't "want" anything. Suggest? Oh yes, we do this. [...]

Q: (A) Now, apparently, everything is going well, and for a while, I think I will have more time to start some real research, and I would like some advice because we don't know how long I will have this time. What would be the first priority for me to work on for now?

A: The journal, to start with. One's objectives should be outlined. The scientist usually begins with this for "fine tuning." We see more opportunities coming though. We led you to the garden, and you planted the beanstalk. Now watch it grow, Jack!

For those who keep writing to me saying, "I'm Jack!" please notice that the Cs were addressing Ark in this last remark.

Q: (L) That doesn't mean there is going to be a giant going around saying "fee, fie, foe, fum" does it?

A: The giant is in the meaning.

Q: You mean we gotta kill a giant?

A: No.

Q: (A) I also wanted to ask if I should be more active and ask more questions in future sessions, or to ask less questions and work more on my own?

A: Questions open the doors, Arkadiusz.

Q: (L) I want to go back to this beanstalk!

A: Well, what of the fable?

Q: (L) Well, Jack got these beans and planted them and they grew. He climbed the beanstalk and figured out how to transform or kill the giant, and got the treasure, and ran away and chopped the beanstalk down so the giant couldn't get him. (F) I remember that he used the beanstalk to get to the same level with the giant. (L) Well, which does it mean? Does he use the beanstalk to rise to the level of the giant, get the treasure and live there, or does he run away with the treasure and chop down the beanstalk?

A: Take your pick.

Q: (L) Well, the essence of the story is that Jack was successful. He planted these magic beans and they *really* grew, like *overnight!* He woke up the next day and the beanstalk reached all the way to the clouds – that is how fast it was. I guess that what you have been doing in this job is planting magic beans that are gonna take off and grow like crazy and be a ladder you can climb to some giant success! If I remember correctly, there was a harp involved.

At this point, Ark decided to try and get the subject right out in the open.

> Q: (A) I want to ask if these sessions we are having are affecting Frank's health in a negative way?
>
> A: No, but as always, the channeling is a wee bit draining. No harm done, but the following hours provide a needed regeneration sequence.
>
> Q: (A) It seems to me that I notice that when I ask some difficult or mathematical question, that Frank becomes instantly very tired. Is there anything to this? How should I ask these questions to get answers and not to make Frank sick?
>
> A: This does not make Frank sick.
>
> Q: (L) We notice also that when we hang out without doing the channeling. The last couple of weeks when we did not do a session, we all became very tired, so that even the next day, it was like being completely drained. Was this because of his recent sickness, or because we weren't channeling and we were supposed to … (A) Or because there were some energies around?
>
> A: A, B, C.
>
> Q: What were the other energies?
>
> A: There are always other energies near you because your work attracts them.

Since the Cs had suggested that the energy in the back room was better, and since I was having trouble staying awake in the psychomantium, we decided to move it, and that way, we could just have our regular sessions inside it, though without dropping the side panels. I had the idea that it would accumulate energy this way.

Now, I love thrift shops. I stalk bargains the way big game hunters stalk their prey. When I find a good one, I am sure that no successful stalker on safari is more ecstatic than I am. So, what happened was that I found a really fine old organ in a thrift shop for practically nothing. I bought it, and after the shop manager and helper loaded it in the van, I drove home in triumph with my great buy.

Ark looked at it, looked at me and asked the obvious question, "Where are we going to put it?" Well, we already had a piano and a big electronic keyboard. We have wall-to-wall book cases, and there was just nowhere to put this thing but in the back room where the psychomantium was. So, that's where it went.

Not too long after, we bought a treadmill and it ended up in the back room also. (This room used to be a dining room and we call it the back room because it is in the back of the house.) A few days later, Tom French came to visit and wanted to know if I had finished my psychomantium. "Indeed!" I proudly told him. After all the trouble it took to make the blasted thing, I was enormously proud of it! I started to lead him to it, and as I reached the door I realized that I had a room in my house where there was a 10-by-10-foot black felt tent, a six-foot cheval mirror, a silver candelabra on a pedestal behind the mirror, an organ, a treadmill, and a table in the middle with a spirit board on it covered with plexiglass. It did *not* look good!

Tom took one look at the set-up and burst into hilarious laughter. As it happened, there were also Barbie dolls, clothes, furniture, and other signs of the girls taking over the room to play, along with the vacuum cleaner standing on the treadmill with the cord dumped in a pile beside it.

"I know you aren't doing anything weird in here," Tom gasped out. "There's a vacuum cleaner!" And he collapsed into laughter again.

November 14, 1998

Q: (L) OK, you notice that we have the psychomantium up. Do you have any suggestions for improvement of this marvel of engineering?

A: Try it.

Q: (L) Well, of course we are. Are we supposed to do it all together, or what? What's the deal on this thing?

A: When needed.

Q: (L) What would be the clue that one needs it?

A: Pangs of psychic hunger. […]

Q: (L) Let me insert another question here. If part of the use of this psychomantium is to bring the earth to the point of fourth-density transitional adjustment, is part of that project also an opening of a doorway for Jesus, who is in the state of suspended animation as you have previously described, to reemerge into the world?

A: Or reemerge into the consciousness.

Q: (L) Of who or what?

A: All 4th density inductees.

Q: (L) Well, you once said that he was actually in a flesh body in this "time warp" in a state of suspended animation, so to speak, or a place of no time …

A: Yes.

Q: (L) Is something going to happen where this singular individual, Jesus, is going to …

A: No need for that.

Q: (L) So, at the point of this fourth-density transitional adjustment, what will Jesus, in his state of suspended animation be doing? Will he continue in that state forever, or will he make some shift of his own?

A: The shift is yours. Afterwards, you can see that which you cannot yet see.

Q: (L) Sure! But, the big problem seems to be getting to the point of that shift! That seems to be the mission, the quest, the objective of all of this … or am I off base here?

A: Not "objective," just is.

Q: (L) Why does it seem that you indicate from time to time that the three of us here, and perhaps others, play some sort of role in this activity? Is that not true for many people?

A: Not true for most.

The astute reader of the session files will note that we faithfully held our sessions once a week all through 1998. In spite of our awareness of the Frank issue, we were willing to maintain the schedule in hopes that the regular contact would be of benefit to him. But in 1999, the frequency was reduced to once a month. We almost terminated the sessions altogether because something very strange happened.

Remember the dream about Terry and Jan, the searching for books, and the bar of used soap?

Well, Frank arrived one evening for the regular session, and he began to examine the books in the bookcases. He was pulling out one book after another saying, "Isn't this mine? Didn't I lend this to you? I had this exact book and now I can't find my copy. Are you sure this is yours?" and so on and on.

I nearly froze with the sensation of déjá vu. Now, one thing I am very faithful about is returning other people's books. In fact, I would prefer to buy my own copy than borrow a book. Unfortunately, not everyone is this way and I have many, many books that are still missing because I will lend them out to someone who swears that they will return them, and then I forget who has them, and until I look for the book later, I don't even realize that it was never returned.

Every single book Frank pulled off the shelf and suggested was his, was not. And in fact, most of them had stickers on them from the two or three used book stores I like to sweep through now and again to pick up copies of things that I think will be useful for research, and if they are good, an extra copy to give away.

Well, Frank finally found an old tatty book that he *insisted* was his. By this time, his rudeness had just simply gone beyond endurance and I just said, "Sure! It might be yours! Keep it." He seemed satisfied, and gave up the hunt. I was disturbed by this little display that was so like my dream. But I brushed it aside, and we settled down for the session.

January 2, 1999

Q: (A) My first question is: I was thinking about what could be the optimal situation for us, for me to work and to proceed, and I decided that the best situation is to have a lot of money, so that we are independent. So, I started to think about how to make a lot of money, and it came to me that the best thing is to get the Nobel Prize next year. So, I started to think about how to get a Nobel Prize, and the best possibility is through computing this Fine Structure Constant. This is in my reach, and it can be done in one year, and it is safe to get a Nobel Prize for this. Am I hallucinating here?

A: Your goals are reachable, but the Nobel Prize is politically charged.

Q: (L) Yes, but it gives sufficient influence that one can do what one likes, and it certainly is not the money that you get as the prize that is so significant, as it is the offers you get after you have it that are significant. I don't think that, in and of itself, it is such a huge amount of dough. It is a chunk of change, but not to set one up for life unless one is very frugal and careful. (F) One bar of soap every nine months.

Right when Frank made the above remark, after the whole scene of searching my bookcases for anything that he could claim as his own, and now the mention of the used soap, the hair stood up on my head and I *knew*.

Q: So, my view of them is that they are trying to take something from me that doesn't belong to them and insisting that it does?

A: Close. Maybe something you do have.

Q: Trying to take something from me that is mine by claiming that it is theirs?

A: Yes.

But I didn't want to believe it.

The dream was not about Terry and Jan; it was about Frank.

CHAPTER 52
THE CRYPTOGEOGRAPHIC BEING

In response to the original online publication of this material, I received a number of communications from readers who wanted to know how they could develop the ability to see the unseen in terms of perceiving the activity of the fourth-density reality. They wanted to know how to expand the semiotic content of their perceptual reality. I also received messages from those who just didn't get it. But by far, the majority of communications have been from people who have been having "Ahah!" experiences right and left.

One reader wrote to me regarding the used-soap clue of the previous chapter, which was the key that unlocked my understanding about many puzzling things over a long period of time. She described a very similar event in her own life which is not pertinent here. What was so interesting was the way she described how it feels when these connections are made, when one finally realizes that the Universe *does* speak to us in these little connections that are so small that, if we were not on the lookout for them, if we did not have some idea that there is a different dictionary, we would miss them altogether – we would sweep them under the rug. She described the realization that the Universe interacts with us dynamically in a way that is truly stupendous, as a feeling that is rather like shooting down a tall water-slide. She wrote:

> You slide so slick, so fast, straight to the bottom and you sit there for a moment collecting yourself from the ride. Don't you think this is the part that makes most people smile even if they're grimacing and gritting their teeth on the way down due to the gravitational plunge, the extreme sensation of near free-falling, landing, finally, intact; a whole new sensation … And no longer speaking metaphorically, at the end of the slide there is a whole new reality/perception, or maybe, finally, the acceptance of the para-perception that was being avoided.
>
> I was, of course, concerned with the deception I had seen through; but more than that I was overjoyed at my ability to cope with watching the truth manifest right before my very eyes! My para-perception was no

longer para, it was a full bloom perception. I had *no doubt* about manipulating forces.

I have learned that the narratives of these types of incidents, when related to people who haven't experienced it, only provokes a rolling of the eyes and a demeaning comment about our sanity or grip on reality.

I know nothing new has been uncovered here, we've all had these experiences before. But it seems important to talk about it. But, doesn't it seem to be so that these experiences of direct interaction with the Universe seem to get bigger and more obvious with time? Maybe the sharing of these types of stories builds solidarity, and this energy of solidarity helps more and more people to pierce the veil.

Funny, when I think about it, the energy of the word solidarity is something I have longed for in my life – familial, personal, global, universal. It is like impenetrable strength of truly cosmic proportions. Solidarity.

As noted above, we have, of course, received a few complaints from folks thinking that the "Adventures Series" would "never end," and who found the subject of dealing with petty tyrants as a means of learning to stand in the presence of the Unknown and Unknowable to be tedious, or even petty. One person suggested that it is a "very large tale of pain and suffering" which is going to take "a long time to process," implying that such time would be wasted. At the same time, another reader said, "Please, keep it coming hard and fast. You're on a roll (once again) with many excellent insights and some of your deepest, most personal material."

Of course, the critics always make me stop and reexamine my process and ask myself just exactly what am I doing, and why am I doing it? And, as usually happens whenever I am involved in writing anything, the Universe continuously responds to my requests for answers with additional clues and information and directions. In this particular instance two things came along that were particularly significant in view of the subject matter of this series: the hyperdimensional reality as a Matrix Control System, and how we can become *free*.

The first item that came along was the most recent issue of *Fortean Times* magazine which is devoted to the Mothman of John Keel fame, and the second is a SETI article shared by one of the egroup members on the same day. The Mothman articles were very timely contributions to the subject of unmasking the Matrix as a hyperdimensional reality, and the SETI article is an example of how the Matrix operates to control people. In a funny sort of way, they are related, and I want to make some comments about them both, starting with the SETI article.

The article, by a Mr. Doug Vakoch of the SETI Institute, says that "alienated people are more likely to think that ET will be hostile." Conversely, of course, anyone who thinks that ET will be hostile is "alienated!" The article then goes on to tell us that *"When someone is confronted with ambiguous information, what he or she makes of the information can sometimes say a lot about the person."* He then suggests that this connection demonstrates that people who hold a dim view of extraterrestrials have negative feelings about how meaningful life is. Right at this point, there is a problem. It seems that it has been arbitrarily decided that seeing life as meaningful can only be possible if an individual believes in the idea that "everything is beautiful and God is in his heaven and all is right with the world." The article tells us:

> We tested the hypothesis that if people feel like the world is cold and cruel, they're more likely than other people to imagine extraterrestrials as being cold and cruel as well. Thus, we set up the survey so we could measure two things. First, to what extent do people feel "alienated," and second, how hostile do these people imagine extraterrestrials would be?

Now, notice one very important thing: neither of these criteria have anything to do with the conclusion drawn as to the meaningfulness of the world. In fact, it is very likely that the exact opposite is true. But we are witnessing an example of the use of the juvenile dictionary in defining reality, as well as the establishing of an authority-base from which to attack anyone who has the idea that the world, *as it is*, is not just peachy keen and strawberry bright. For example, let us have a look at the statements that establish whether a person is alienated or not. This little test, we are told, was described by Robert Travis in the journal *Social Indicators Research*, and is called "The Margins of Society Alienation Scale."

> I feel all alone these days.
> My whole world feels like it's falling apart.
> I wish I were somebody important.
> It's hard for me to tell just what is right and wrong these days.
> I don't like to live by society's rules.
> I often feel discriminated against.
> I'll never find the right person to care enough about me.

What a loaded test! Notice how slyly the statements are mixed. Nearly everybody on the planet who is sitting up and taking nourishment will answer "yes" to all except statements 3 and 5, and possibly the last one. But those two are inserted in there to justify the definition of the test as something that establishes an alienated person as an antisocial one as well! Based upon how strongly the participant agreed or disagreed with each statement, they were identified as people who were feeling very alienated, those who didn't feel alienated at all, and those who fell somewhere between those extremes. And based on their identification as alienated, they were judged as viewing life as *more or less meaningful.*

Another way of putting it is: if you notice the things that are wrong with our reality, that means you view the world around you as cold, cruel and hostile, which then means that you just aren't seeing objectively! You are not giving proper value to this marvelous world in which we live! You aren't fully appreciating the wars and plagues and disasters and man's inhumanity to man properly! You are not giving the proper spin on cosmic catastrophes, military onslaughts, social injustice, personal and familial misfortunes, and a host of assaults too numerous to list.

In short, if you are not living in the warm and fuzzy illusion that the Control System wants you to erect as your personal myth, or at least pretending that you do, then you are clearly deficient and incapable of perceiving meaning to life. Because, note that most important assumption in the study cited above: those who are alienated are being judged about their feelings as to how meaningful life is. In other words, "how meaningful" is a quantitative judgment that is replacing the qualitative value of *what* the meaning of life might be.

As the great Historian of Religion, Mircea Eliade pointed out, the study of history, through its various disciplines, offers a view of mankind that is almost insupportable. The rapacious movements of hungry tribes, invading, conquering and destroying in the darkness of prehistory; the barbarian invaders of the civilized world during medieval times; the bloodbaths of the crusades of Catholic Europe against the infidels of the Middle East; the stalking noonday terror of the Inquisition where martyrs quenched the flames with their blood; and the raging holocaust of modern genocide. Wars, famine, pestilence; all produce an intolerable sense of indefensibility against what Mircea Eliade calls the Terror of History.

As I have written elsewhere, when man contemplates history, *as it is*, he is forced to realize that he is in the iron grip of an existence that seems to have no real care or concern for his pain and suffering. Over and over again, the same sufferings fall upon mankind multiplied millions upon millions of times over millennia. The totality of human suffering is a dreadful thing. I could write until the end of the world using oceans of ink and forests of paper, and never fully convey this terrible condition in which mankind finds his existence.

The beast of arbitrary calamity has always been with us. For as long as human hearts have pumped hot blood through their too-fragile bodies and glowed with the inexpressible sweetness of life and yearning for all that is good and right and loving, the sneering, stalking, drooling and scheming beast of real life has licked its lips in anticipation of its next feast of terror and suffering. Since the beginning of time, this mystery of the estate of man, this Curse of Cain has existed. And, since the Ancient of Days, the cry has been: "My punishment is greater than I can bear!" But if you find yourself saying this, you are "alienated," antisocial, and incapable of finding any meaning in life. You are just simply not with the program, according to the SETI study cited above.

One of the authorities trotted out is astronomer Frank Drake, the father of SETI. Drake argues that ET will very likely be altruistic, rather than malevolent because if extraterrestrials are hostile, then their civilizations won't last very long, and we're unlikely to make contact with them. Only extraterrestrials with a long-lasting, stable society will be around long enough to be detected by our SETI programs.

Unfortunately, Drake's views are those of an astronomer who must not have read much history or many anthropological studies about what really happens when a superior culture encounters an inferior one, or even why superior cultures begin to expand and spread out, and seek new lands to conquer and dominate. Drake probably forgot Hitler's idea of *Lebensraum* as well as the ancient archetypal story of the Trojan Horse. In short, Drake's hypothesis is all wet.

With that idea in mind, let's look at the questions that were asked of the participants in the SETI study as to how we ought to respond to the receiving of a signal from an extraterrestrial civilization.

> ETs are probably looking for planets they can take over for themselves.
>
> We should not reply to the message from ETs because they might be hostile.
>
> ETs would probably look at humans like we are nothing more than animals that belong in their zoos.
>
> Humans would probably not be able to understand the message from ETs because humans and ETs are just too different.
>
> If we reply to the message from ETs, they might come to Earth and take over our world.
>
> We should not believe what the message says, because the ETs may be lying
>
> ETs would probably want to make humans their slaves.
>
> The message from ETs may contain a hidden message that could be harmful to humans.

Aside from the fact that nearly all of the above statements are redundancies, most of them are based on the idea of suspecting that ETs might be liars. For some reason, that strikes me as peculiar. It's almost as though the issue that is really being tested is a person's gullibility index. Nevertheless, if a person has thought long and hard about history – *as it is* – and has made some assessment about it based on the objective facts, then he may, indeed, extrapolate those facts into considerations of ET civilizations that may contact us. This then will lead him to the objective speculation that any ET civilization that goes out looking for New Worlds to conquer does not have our best interests at heart!

The SETI study has told us, "The pattern is clear: people who feel alienated are much more likely to be concerned that ET has evil intentions." You're darn skippy!

But the SETI study has attempted to establish that such an *objective assessment is pathological.* The SETI folks are suggesting that the relationship between alienation and the perception that ET might not be friendly is evidence of a personal prejudice, as opposed to an objective perception of the world. The study suggests that alienation is a personal bias, that is not in synch with reality. Reciprocally, this means that they are suggesting that our world is just hunky dory; that two billion people meeting their deaths in a century of wars and famines is just the cost of doing business in this reality.

Most of our problems as a species come from an inability to agree on our conclusions which are generally based on a misinterpretation of the basic events of life. For this reason we are always fighting over symbolism and definitions, the very things that are supposed to help us understand each other better. It seems that the ability to see reality without any illusions is a very difficult perspective to acquire. It consists of viewing the world without the denial that plagues our understanding of basic events, as opposed to the illusory values imposed on it by society.

As we might suspect from the cited work of Robert Travis in the journal *Social Indicators Research*, entitled "The Margins of Society Alienation Scale," society has a very dim view of alienation. The fact is, however, that where alienation occurs, feedback loops exist between the individual resistance to a system and the system's response. Overall this resistance is very costly for the system. A good example of this is the varying persecutions which have been instituted to chase down relatively harmless people chosen as scapegoats for the cause. Any time one or another group is being labeled as "alienated," you can be sure that it is a smokescreen for other activities. And when there is smoke, there is usually a war; if there's a war, someone is making money churning out weapons or medical care or news or insurance against fear in another form.

The questions "what is an alienated person?" and "what is the philosophical significance of alienation?" are two entirely different orders of questions, and a failure to recognize this fact breeds confusion. What is this thing that SETI is calling alienation? How does it come about? What is its constitution, origin and history? What is the importance of alienation?

First of all, we want to exclude what may be truly pathological alien-ation, which expresses itself as destructive acts undertaken against the shortcomings of our culture. These destructive acts can include feloni-ous behavior as well as self-destructive processes, including self-medicated escape into drugs and alcohol, magical thinking, etc. Here, *we are interested in alienation as a process of expanding the dictionary of reality from the juvenile one that defines our environment.* Do we view reality as a Cartoon World where all the characters suffer all kinds of dreadful experiences which are instantly erased from view and memory in the next frame, or, have we acquired a more spiritually adult perception of the realities of life that tell us that when a huge boulder is dropped on the character, he will be crushed and will not reappear in the next frame without a wrinkle or a bruise. Are we living our lives as comicbook characters, or as *response-able perceivers* of a broader reality?

The answer to the first question – what is an alienated person – amounts to an existential judgment. How a person becomes alienated can simply be a matter of historical fact. We can learn the facts of that person's life, and we can learn what that person thinks from what they say or write. Based on this information, we may decide that they are alienated because they have suffered trauma.

The answer to the second – what is the philosophical significance – is a proposition of *value*; in other words, a spiritual judgment. What alienation ultimately means in this sense can only be deduced in terms of the record of the inner experiences of the soul wrestling with the crises of fate.

Neither judgment can be deduced from the other! They proceed from different perspectives, and it is entirely arbitrary to add them to-gether as the cited SETI study has done. As a matter of fact, there are many people who have had alien encounters who do not qualify as alienated. The individuals who tend to view the alien reality in a posi-tive way, those who think that aliens are here to help mankind, would naturally score very positively on the SETI test.

As I described in the *High Strangeness*, Kenneth Ring discovered what seems to be a direct relationship between people reporting "positive" alien interactions and dissociative personality disorder. While the skep-tics used these findings to debunk "paranormal experiences" as simply fantasies and daydreams, it may be that people who are *not* alienated in the terms in which we are discussing the word (like those subjects in Ring's study), might very well be viewing reality in a dissociated state: dissociated from the objective world. Whether they are promoting the alien reality as a positive experience, or the SETI reality, or any other reality that does not take into account the broadest range of observable facts, such individuals may be operating in pathological states of dissociation. In this sense, the idea that "God is in heaven and all is right with the world" is as much a fantasy as the idea that mankind is the result of mindless evolution.

A very simple way of looking at it is in terms of what is popularly called Stockholm syndrome. A person who is *not* alienated from a world run amok, a system that is clearly operating based on manipulation and terror tactics has dissociated and identified with the oppressor; he or she has sold out in order to survive. The dynamics of Stockholm syndrome directly address the issue of those who view life as meaningful in the terms described in the SETI study as "desirable." Victims have to concentrate on survival, becoming highly attuned to the approval or disapproval of the social norms and requiring avoidance of direct, honest reaction to destructive treatment.

But the alienated person is one who does not succumb to the system, the terrorists, the Matrix. To be alienated, in the terms of the SETI study, is to be *free* of Stockholm syndrome. And this, of course, poses its own set of problems.

There can be no doubt that the alienated person, when they actively pursue the "lights" of alienation, do become exceptional and even eccentric. Most people follow rules that are made for them by others, communicated to them by traditions, shaped into fixed forms by imitation, and continued by force of habit. The alienated person does nothing of the kind. For the alienated person, the perception of the world is not according to the rules of the Control System. And there is indeed something singularly feverish about such individuals that can be perceived as nervous instability. They are generally geniuses and are often commemorated – posthumously, I should add – even though they generally have led discordant lives; and most likely they have suffered melancholy at some point in their career. As a result of their struggles against the system, driven by their inner light of resistance against external controls that they assess – most often objectively – as hostile, alienated people often suffer a great deal and in many ways. This suffering, instead of breaking them, builds in them a single-pointed focus that would be viewed by the people who have sold out as obsessions and fixed ideas. This suffering may induce chemical changes in their physiology; they can fall into trances, hear voices, see visions, and manifest all kinds of peculiarities that are commonly classed as pathological.

We cannot ignore these so-called pathological aspects. We must describe and name them. Even if the psyche recoils from such a laying bare of the causes from which a thing originates, we must still consider our passions and their properties. However, as with everything else, there is a process of naming involved, and this naming relates to the dictionary we use.

It is all too easy to utilize the juvenile dictionary and say that Vinnie believes in magic because he is overly emotional; Nellie is overly conscientious because she is obsessive-compulsive, and that is due to congenital hypertonic nerves; Bertha is melancholy because she suffers from liver problems; Jojo is attracted to religious groups because she is a histrionic personality; Geoff wouldn't be so worried about his soul if he would go to the gym more often, and so on and on.

After spending some time attempting to prove that the ET hypothesis was essentially a psychic contagion, a meme, a "Millennial Disease," and failing, I came to the realization that the reality of the phenomenon of psychic contagion was an important part of the process, but in a completely opposite way of what was being suggested by the "experts." What I noticed was the fact that it seemed to be significantly present *in the context of obscuring the issue.* What seems to happen is that false ideas about what is really happening spread from core "authorities," such as the SETI report cited above, and this is seemingly designed to create attitudes, perceptual controls, reinterpretations of personal experiences *by the act of implanting doubts about oneself and about the nature of experiences* which, due to their hyperdimensional nature, are ambiguous. In short, memes are the essence of societal Stockholm syndrome!

Just as with the alienated people who begin to view the world as it is, defying the memes that are generated and released on society like a form of bio-semiotic warfare, we find that the same types of juvenile explanations are used to reduce or macerate those who suggest a reality to the UFO phenomenon as were typically used historically against anyone who perceived a higher reality, including great saints and mystics of all kinds. In this way, a connection between the physical or sexual life and religious emotions is often drawn; conversion is a "crisis of puberty," St. Paul had an epileptic seizure on the Road to Damascus, Saint Teresa was a hysteric, George Fox suffered a disordered colon, Carlyle had an ulcer. When you dig to the bottom of alienation, you will find all sorts of disordered glandular functions, and voila! All spiritual verities will be successfully disposed of and skepticism and the Blind Watchmaker will reign supreme! By now, we are becoming rather familiar with the tactics of discrediting states of mind that produce nonlinear shifts in the psychic landscape.

The problem with these reductionist explanations is this: even if it is true that St. Paul had epilepsy, and that is the existential account of his vision on the road to Damascus, does that then negate the spiritual significance of the event? Because, in point of fact, every single spiritual condition – positive or negative – probably does have an expression in physiology.

We would also like to note that the hard-core skeptic is as likely to be skeptical because he suffers liver disease as the born again Christian is likely to be converted because his ulcer drives him to seek relief. The evil magician can have a dirty colon and the psychic vampire can have false teeth. In short, raptures and rants can be equally represented by organic conditions. And if this is taken *as the model of verity*, then none of our ideas, our thoughts, feelings, scientific doctrines, beliefs or disbeliefs, have any value at all. If such an idea is the theory upon which we are to evaluate our reality, then we must theorize that *every* idea emanates from the state of the body of the originator. What is sauce for the goose is sauce for the gander.

On the other hand, we *can* take these existential clues and apply the "adult dictionary" to them and utilize them as stepping stones to higher knowledge! We can see them as part of the clue system. We can understand them as part of a wider semiotic content plane.

The scientific/psychological theories do, of course, have favored states of mind that are considered to be inwardly superior to others and which reveal to us more truth than others. Unfortunately, there is no physiological theory of the production of these favored states – such as a peripatetic pancreas, a limpid liver, a static stomach, or genial genitals.

How often do we hear it said that a scientist won a Nobel prize because he was neurotic as all get-out? Or that an Enochian magician is successful due to the fact that his sexual desire is sublimated in reaction to the fact that his first girlfriend laughed at the miniscule size of his genitalia? Do we dare to suggest that the author of the SETI article cited above suffers from Stockholm syndrome? And, of course, it could all be due to the fact that he has suffered all his life from the heartbreak of psoriasis!

The point is: the value of the theory of the scientist and the value of the ideas of those who are alienated can *only* be evaluated based upon philosophical reasonableness, moral helpfulness, and immediate luminosity. Saint Paul could have been an Olympic Ironman champion and it wouldn't mean a thing if his ideas were beneath contempt.

In the end, we are thrown back again to the fact that any and all ideas about truth must be evaluated based on principles, and principles can only be discerned by thinking as objectively as possible, and by gathering as much data as possible. We would all like to be insured against making mistakes in evaluating what we take as true or not. We would like to have some basic criteria that will protect us immediately from such errors. We would like to know the *origin* of an idea, and thereby be able to accept it or discard it either because we have decided the origin is intuition, the authority of the pope, supernatural revelation, direct communication via a spirit, or any of several sources that are variously determined to be true sources. In this sense, the materialists who attempt to reduce any such phenomena to pathological states simply invalidates their own position by using origin as a destructive criterion.

> "What right have we to believe Nature is under any obligation to do her work by means of complete minds only? She may find an incomplete mind a more suitable instrument for a particular purpose. It is the work that is done, and the quality in the worker by which it was done, that is alone of moment." (Maudsley, 1886, pp. 256-257)

In other words: "By their fruits you shall know them." The roots of a person's virtue are inaccessible to us.

The alienated person has extraordinary emotional susceptibility. His conceptions tend to pass immediately into action; and when he gets a new idea, he has no rest until he either tells it, or works it off. The ordinary person asks, "What shall I think of this?" The alienated person asks, "What must I *do* about it?" Such people are not critics and commentators; their ideas take hold of them, and they *do* something.

In the alienated person, we find the emotionality that is the *condito sine qua non* of moral perception; there is intensity and a tendency to emphasis which are the essence of moral vigor and virtue; and we find the love of mysticism and metaphysics that lift the person beyond the surface of the ordinary world of the five senses. In short, *the alienated temperament furnishes the chief condition of receptivity to higher states of being*.

> Cassiopaeans: Emotion that limits is an impediment to progress. Emotion is also necessary to make progress in 3rd density. It is natural. When you begin to separate limiting emotions based on assumptions from emotions that open one to unlimited possibilities, that means you are preparing for the next density.

Charles Fort was an eccentric, alienated personality. After receiving an inheritance from his family which meant he didn't have to work for a living, he devoted his life to an idea: he traveled to the major metropolitan libraries where he would read through the various scientific journals of the day, looking for "damned data."

Damned data includes strange phenomena and experiences such as reports of falls of strange things from the sky, strange things seen in the heavens, and strange disappearances. Fort was not just critical of the efforts of science to explain our reality, he was downright contemptuous of it. He would gleefully and fiendishly mock astronomers, meteorologists, and other scientists and their efforts to either deny or explain away anomalous occurrences. He derided their pompous attempts to deny what they could neither understand nor explain. His notes were published as *The Book of the Damned*.

Fort's condition of alienation was expressed frequently in his repeated remarks that <u>the more dogmatic and authoritarian a system, the more likely it is to be wrong</u>. What was more, the ideas that he formulated after years of collecting data are quite expressive of the Cassiopaean description of densities especially in the idea that our real world is more or less a projection of an intermediate, "excluded-middle" realm of existence that was partly physical and partly ethereal.

I conceive of one inter-continuous nexus, in which and of which all seeming things are only different expressions, but in which all things are localizations of one attempt to break away and become real things, or to establish entity or positive difference or final demarcation or unmodified independence—or personality or soul, as it is called in human phenomena—...

Our general expression [is that] the state that is commonly and absurdly called "existence," is a flow, or a current, or an attempt, from negativeness to positiveness, and is intermediate to both.

By positiveness we mean Harmony, equilibrium, order, regularity, stability, consistency, unity, realness, system, government, organization, liberty, independence, soul, self, personality, entity, individuality, truth, beauty, justice, perfection, definiteness—

That all that is called development, progress, or evolution is movement toward, or attempt toward, this state for which, or for aspects of which, there are so many names, all of which are summed up in the one word "positiveness." ...

I conceive of one inter-continuous nexus, which expresses itself in astronomic phenomena, and chemic, biologic, psychic, sociologic: that it is everywhere striving to localize positiveness: that to this attempt in various fields of phenomena—which are only quasidifferent—we give different names. We speak of the "system" of the planets, and not of their "government": but in considering a store, for instance, and its management, we see that the words are interchangeable. It used to be customary to speak of chemic equilibrium, but not of social equilibrium: that false demarcation has been broken down. We shall see that by all these words we mean the same state. As everyday conveniences, or in terms of common illusions, of course, they are not synonyms. ...

So then: That all phenomena in our intermediate state, or quasi-state, represent this one attempt to organize, stabilize, harmonize, individualize—or to positivize, or to become real: That only to have seeming is to express failure or intermediateness to final failure and final success; That every attempt—that is observable—is defeated by Continuity, or by outside forces—or by the excluded that are continuous with the included: That our whole "existence" is an attempt by the relative to be the absolute, or by the local to be the universal.

In this book, my interest is in this attempt as manifested in modern science: That it has attempted to be real, true, final, complete, absolute: That, if the seeming of being, here, in our quasi-state, is the product of exclusion that is always false and arbitrary, if always are included and excluded continuous, the whole seeming system, or entity, of modern science is only quasi-system, or quasi-entity, wrought by the same false and arbitrary process as that by which the still less positive system that preceded it, or the theological system, wrought the illusion of its being.

In this book, I assemble some of the data that I think are of the falsely and arbitrarily excluded.

The data of the damned.

I have gone into the outer darkness of scientific and philosophical transactions and proceedings, ultra-respectable, but covered with the dust of disregard. I have descended into journalism. I have come back with the quasi-souls of lost data. ...

We substitute acceptance for belief.

Cells of an embryo take on different appearances in different eras.

The more firmly established, the more difficult to change.

That social organism is embryonic.

That firmly to believe is to impede development.

That only temporarily to accept is to facilitate.

But: Except that we substitute acceptance for belief, our methods will be the conventional methods; the means by which every belief has been formulated and supported: or our methods will be the methods of theologians and savages and scientists and children. Because, if all phenomena are continuous, there can be no positively different methods. By the inconclusive means and methods of cardinals and fortune tellers and evolutionists and peasants, methods which must be inconclusive, if they relate always to the local, and if there is nothing local to conclude, we shall write this book.

If it function as an expression of its era, it will prevail. ...

We conceive of all "things" as occupying gradations, or steps in series between positiveness and negativeness, or realness and unrealness: that some seeming things are more nearly consistent, just, beautiful, unified, individual, harmonious, stable—than others.

We are not realists. We are not idealists. We are intermediatists—that nothing is real, but that nothing is unreal: that all phenomena are approximations one way or the other between realness and unrealness.

So then: That our whole quasi-existence is an intermediate stage between positiveness and negativeness or realness and unrealness.

Like purgatory, I think.

But in our summing up, which was very sketchily done, we omitted to make clear that Realness is an aspect of the positive state.

By Realness, I mean that which does not merge away into something else, and that which is not partly something else: that which is not a reaction to, or an imitation of, something else. By a real hero, we mean one who is not partly a coward, or whose actions and motives do not merge away into cowardice. But, if in Continuity, all things do merge, by Realness, I mean the Universal, besides which there is nothing with which to merge. ...

479

So, then, in general metaphysical terms, our expression is that, like a purgatory, all that is commonly called "existence," which we call Intermediateness, is quasi-existence, neither real nor unreal, but expression of attempt to become real, or to generate for or recruit a real existence.

Our acceptance is that Science, though usually thought of so specifically, or in its own local terms, usually supposed to be a prying into old bones, bugs, unsavory messes, is an expression of this one spirit animating all Intermediateness: that, if Science could absolutely exclude all data but its own present data, or that which is assimilable with the present quasi-organization, it would be a real system, with positively definite outlines—it would be real.

Its seeming approximation to consistency, stability, system—positiveness or realness—is sustained by damning the irreconcilable or the unassimilable—

All would be well.

All would be heavenly—

If the damned would only stay damned. (Fort, 1974)

And all would be well if "alienated people" would get with the social Stockholm syndrome program and quit thinking that ET might not have our best interests at heart!

Now, we come to the second line of information that has popped up in the past few days. The new movie, *The Mothman Prophecies* is out now, and there is a great deal of commentary being made in various metaphysical/paranormal research circles. Both *Fortean Times* and *Fate* magazines have articles on Mothman. John Keel, the original investigator of the Mothman case writes in the recent issue of *Fate* (Jan–Feb 2002):

In 1966–68, over 100 people in Point Pleasant, West Virginia, and the surrounding area reported seeing a giant, winged creature. This critter was usually described as being taller than a big man, with blazing red eyes and a wingspan of only ten feet. Yet it was able to fly faster than a speeding car.

Yet the creature failed to leave footprints, feces, or other physical evidence. After a flurry of sightings over a two-year period, it seemed to vanish forever. This proved once again that eyewitness testimony is of little value when you are dealing with fortean events. A thousand people could all see the same thing at the same time and it still isn't proof that the object or entity is a real, physical, corporeal resident *of our dimension.* (*Fate Magazine*, p. 8)

The most fascinating article in the present offerings is about journalist Rick Moran's 1978 investigation of the Mothman phenomenon. Mr. Moran points out in his article that the protocols of "writers," in generic terms, and "journalists" are not the same. He had the idea that *"field researchers looking into cases of the unexplained should adopt the tenets of investigative journalism; to look at the human stories together with the unvarnished facts*

480

(insofar as they could be discovered). This might better help us understand strange events than either the logical data and natural skepticism of scientists or the effort of so-called paranormal researchers looking for proof of their pre-existing beliefs."

We couldn't agree more. The Cs' comments on Mothman connected it to a broader phenomenon-base which, as we will see, is supported by lateral evidence:

June 9, 1995

Q: (L) I read in a book about a monster called the Beast of Gevaudan which appeared first in 1764 and was supposedly done away with in 1767. Who or what was this beast?

A: Other dimensional "window faller."

Q: (L) You mean it fell into our dimension from another through a dimensional window?

A: Yes.

Q: (L) Well, that would explain a lot of things about it. What about the creature known as "Spring Heel Jack" who terrorized England some time ago?

A: Same.

Q: (L) What about the Mothman in West Virginia?

A: Same.

Q: (L) So, windows to other dimensions are the explanation for a whole host of strange things?

A: Yes.

Which leads to a related series of questions:

November 19, 1994

Q: (L) In the Ann Haywood case which is supposed to be a case of demonic possession or obsession, who or what are the beings that are afflicting this woman and her family?

A: 3rd density section "B" energy anomalies same as "poltergeist."

Q: (L) The case that is described in the book *The Haunted*, about the Smurl family, with quite a bit of phenomena occurring in their house including the sighting of a big-foot-type creature, what is the source of the phenomena in that case?

A: Same.

Q: (L) So, neither of those cases are "alien" related?

A: Correct.

Q: (L) Why are there such marked similarities between those two cases and the case described by Karla Turner and other alien abductions?

A: Similarities are open to interpretation. Turner household was opened to multiple types of phenomena due to interaction with Grays and others.

Q: (L) Does that occur frequently in interactions with Grays?

A: When there is excessive activity of this sort it leaves open channels or "windows" which allows all sorts of things to come through.

After reading John Keel's *Mothman Prophecies*, Moran just assumed that Keel had followed the protocols of the author of popular books and not the more stringent journalistic rules. He was warned that he ought not to compare Keel with other writers because he was a good researcher and not prone to hyping his subject.

Rick Moran decided to put this to the test. Ten years after the Mothman incidents, he went to West Virginia and retraced as many of John Keel's steps as he could. He tells us:

> I was hoping to find a witness who might further embellish their testimony as reported in the book, or even recant. The deeper our questions got, the more we were convinced that the witness had indeed seen or interacted with something. Nearly everyone I spoke to remembered 'the year of the UFOs' and had a theory about it. Most seemed to know someone directly connected to the phenomenon and were willing to vouch for their veracity. Most residents had seen something, whether it was strange lights in the sky or 'abnormal' activity on the outskirts of town during that period. Even the more spectacular claims, they said, were made by people who were not otherwise prone to telling tall tales. (*Fortean Times* 156, April 2002)

Mr. Moran was quite impressed by the fact that even the police department and local newspaper staff verified the sincerity and veracity of those who had experienced the phenomena. Many of the reports are part of the public record, in police reports, and they became so frequent that the newspaper actually stopped reporting them due to overabundance of material. *"The entire community became desensitized to the phenomenon and spoke matter-of-factly about nightly sightings of UFOs or the latest news on the creature"* (Moran, *FT* 156).

Then, along came the Men in Black. They passed themselves off as government investigators, and the stories about those encounters are the strangest parts of the book. Here, Mr. Moran makes a rather interesting observation:

> Unlike Mothman, the MIBs sent a shockwave of fear through their contactees. Their aura of menace was combined with an absurd fascination for quite mundane objects. They asked questions about common food items and their speech seemed somehow odd and disjointed. Most importantly, witnesses noticed the MIB had no ears, or seemed to talk without moving their lips. You'd think the witnesses would be terrified, having seen such obvious warning signs, but a strange calm prevailed until after the visitors left; only then did people realize how odd, even horrifying, their visitors were.
>
> Our team conducted interviews, looked for deviations from the original stories and then departed. One witness told us, as we were leaving her home, that she believed the MIBs veiled threats were very real and

that anyone looking seriously into the phenomenon was placing themselves in harm's way. (Moran, *FT* 156)

These remarks about the sinister nature of MIBs is quite telling in light of what the Cs had to say about them:

November 6, 1994
Q: (L) All the UFO sightings in Gulf Breeze, are these aliens or government experiments?
A: Some are and some are projections.
Q: (L) And who is responsible?
A: Multiple sources.
Q: (L) Positive or negative?
A: Both.

November 19, 1994
Q: (L) Who or what are the individuals called Men in Black?
A: Lizard projections.
Q: (T) Does that mean that they are just projecting an image of a being?
A: Yes.
Q: (T) The MIBs are not real, then, in our physical terms?
A: Partly correct. You do not understand technology but we will describe it if you like.
Q: (L) We like. Please describe this.
A: Okay. Get ready. First we must explain further time "travel" because the two concepts are closely related. The first step is to artificially induce an electromagnetic field. This opens the door between dimensions of reality. Next, thoughts must be channeled by participant in order to access reality bonding channel. They must then focus the energy to the proper dimensional bridge. The electrons must be arranged in correct frequency wave. Then the triage must be sent through realm "curtain" in order to balance perceptions at all density levels.
Q: (L) Information in the event that has to be balanced or taken into consideration as to importance so that the program runs correctly. Is this the correct interpretation of triage as you have used it?
A: Sort of. Triage is as follows: 1. Matter, 2. Energy, 3. Perception of reality. That is it folks. […]
Q: (L) Several times I have heard reference to big flying rectangular boxes. I would like to know who these belong to?
A: Lizard projections.
Q: (L) Why do they have so many different types of craft?
A: Not all are theirs. […]
Q: (L) What or who are the South American aliens I have read about who are described as being gray with thick lips, rudimentary features, gray uniforms, and are called by the South Americans "Malos"?
A: Lizard projections.

Q: (L) Were these also the clay-like beings seen by Betty Andreasson only she saw them wearing blue suits?

A: Yes.

Q: (L) Where was Betty Andreasson taken to when she saw the Phoenix in her abduction?

A: Another dimension of reality.

Q: (L) Is Betty Andreasson correct in believing that her experiences are positive and are bringing her closer to God?

A: No.

Q: (L) Is Betty Andreasson deluded?

A: No. She is a victim.

January 11, 1995

Q: (B) What is the proper protocol when meeting a Lizard?

A: Up to you!

Q: (F) I don't think I'll repeat that, Barry. (L) Did he use the "F" word? (F) No, he referred to a part of the anatomy. (B) Are Lizards shape shifters?

A: All on 4th level of density have that ability.

Q: (B) Do they have the ability to block their true appearance?

A: Yes.

Q: (B) Are they walking around amongst us now?

A: Infrequently, they use "agents" to do most of their tasks on 3rd level.

Q: (B) Are these agents the Men in Black or are they the Grays?

A: Both and many others. Men in Black are often Lizards cloaked as human types, and can remain on 3rd density level for limited periods called short wave cycle. Men in Black claim to be government in order to have excuse to have direct contact with selected humans.

Q: (B) Have these Men in Black killed humans?

A: No.

Q: (F) They just threaten?

A: Yes.

Q: (B) Have the Lizards killed humans?

A: Oh yes!!!

January 21, 1995

Q: (L) OK, that's good enough. Who are the oriental-appearing person-nel that have been seen manning the helicopters and the white vans that have been sighted all over the country?

A: MIB. And government copycats. Copy, in order to throw off investi-gation. They do it to protect the public from knowing that which would explode society if discovered. [...]

Q: (L) OK, I want to ask this one, because this is one I haven't hit lately. Wendelle Stevens, who was associated with Billy Meier, and also Gene-sis 2 or 3, put out the Billy Meier book on the Billy Meier sightings ...

A: Some too, are projections. This phenomenon is multifaceted.

July 23, 1995

Q: (L) I also seemed to be aware of several dark, spider-like figures lined up by the side of the bed, was this an accurate impression.

A: Those could be described as specific thought center projections.

October 23, 1998

Q: (L) Keel also talks about Serpent people integrated in our society with holographic images superimposed over their faces. Is this ever the case?

A: Maybe.

Q: (L) As in Men in Black?

A: Maybe.

November 21, 1998

Q: (M) He says: I've had three experiences with aliens, who kindly provided me with silicone beads of some kind. Were these physical abductions or just projections?

A: One begets the other. A projection involves trans-dimensional atomic remolecularization.

At the end of their investigation, Moran's team discussed the evidence, concluding reluctantly that the only explanation that had a broad enough theoretical base for the entire situation was the UFO-as-ultraterrestrials hypothesis proposed by John Keel, Jacques Vallee, *et al.* Their conclusion was that they had failed to find a chink in the Mothman armor. In short, they didn't have an investigative journalism exposé to publish. And there the matter would have remained if not for a series of frightening interference-type events that began to occur in Rick Moran's personal life right after his return to New York. These occurrences more or less pushed him off the fence.

The reader is going to have to get a copy of *FT* to read this account which accurately represents the very kinds of weirdness so many other people experience when delving into these matters, including ourselves and many members of our discussion group. The question is, of course, how to view it: in terms of Stockholm syndrome, or as an "alienated" individual?

In the week following truly bizarre, threatening phone calls, the involvement of the phone company in tracing these calls with startling results that served only to unnerve the journalist even more, Mr. Moran was scheduled to be a guest on Joel Martin's talk show on WBAB on Long Island. The topic had nothing at all to do with UFOs or anything weird; it was about Agent Orange and its use in Vietnam. When Moran arrived at the station, the DJ met him in the lobby, obviously shaken. He, too, had received a visit from a MIB who warned him against doing shows on the subject of UFOs. After a brief "war council," Mr.

Moran and the DJ both agreed that when a journalist feels threatened, the best response is to put everything he knows before the public because, once it is public knowledge, there is no longer any reason to threaten the source. He was right. Neither he nor the DJ were ever threatened again.

What is most interesting is the fact that Mr. Moran points out that throughout his career of reporting on criminals, the mob, and other questionable elements of our society, neither he nor his family had never, ever been threatened before this diversion into the world of Mothman. And this begs the question: what is it about such investigations into hyperdimensional matters that invites a response that seeks to repress, twist, suppress, and otherwise employ Stockholm syndrome to shove everything back under the rug? Moran speculates in retrospect that the entire Mothman phenomenon had the flavor of an experiment.

And here we come to an item that ties it all together here. Colin Bennett brings to our attention the ancient magical connections between Mind and Landscape which is in opposition to the sterile materialist view of reality. The only question, of course, is whose mind? Bennett writes:

> Forster's Marabar caves, Hamlet's castle at Elsinore, and Thomas Hardy's Egdon Heath are all aspects of *crypto-geographic personalities;* they live and breathe *as huge animated forms and penetrate human awareness the way ivy weaves through an old house.* These suprahuman forms are *quite conscious, aware, and active.* In West Virginia, Keel found the local 'system-animal' had its own agenda; it 'spoke' through simulacra and weather, atmosphere and geology, coincidence and dream. Before the coming of Christianity and science, such forms as Keel describes were a fully understood part of an integrated world image that linked Mind to sacred sites, landscape, ideas and evolving culture. *We might have to return to the ancient Greek view that the truth is scandalous beyond all belief, and the gods are neither respectable nor sensible entities at all.*
>
> In the fortean sense, scientific objectivity has 'banned' our recognition of any participants in our conscious life other than fellow humans. Shakespeare shows that there are unnamed *dramatis personae* implicit in the human situation, showing that *humans are not lords of creation but part of an evolving chain of being, shading from 'solid' to almost nothing.* This chain consists of animal, vegetable and mineral domains, all of which have dynamic anthropomorphic elements that we ignore at our peril. Like Shakespeare's *The Tempest, The Mothman Prophecies* depicts humans as poised between the animal kingdoms and the realms of the gods. The Greek Tragedians understood completely such connections between environment and social character, motivation and *supra-human agendas.* Meantime, fallen moderns grate their teeth on the mechanical and wonder that they cannot explain events in Dallas 1963, the assassination of Princess Diana, or the murder of little Jon Benet.

> Like many who return from the magic landscape of *Magonia*, Keel, as wounded initiate, is sick and exhausted. Occult initiation is always a near-death experience. (Bennett, *FT* 156, my emphases)

I hope the reader remembers the remark about "gritting of teeth" from my correspondent quoted at the beginning of this chapter. Put that together with this last remark of Mr. Bennett about "fallen moderns" who "grate their teeth on the mechanical," as well as the mention of the death of Princess Diana and my perception of it as part of a fourth-density, time-looped clue system, and the comments I wrote in the previous chapter about Frank's dental problems, and we have a perfect, living example of a semiotic content plane that is expanding exponentially.

We also begin to see that the so-called "scientific objectivity," including that of the SETI study quoted at the beginning, may actually be more subjective than they would like to think, and "alienated" people do not, in fact, assign less meaning to life; because they are more truly objective, they assign more meaning; and this more meaning indicates, objectively, that ET does not have our best interests at heart.

At the end of this little episode of the revealing of a wider semiotic content plane, of connections to our "living landscape," the action of the crypto-geographic personalities, the huge animated forms that penetrate human consciousness, the suprahuman forms that are *quite conscious, aware, and active*, we become even more acutely aware of the fourth-density Matrix Control System in real time. And when it reveals itself to us, when it touches us, it can be stunning. As my correspondent wrote:

> You slide so slick, so fast, straight to the bottom and you sit there for a moment collecting yourself from the ride. Don't you think this is the part that makes most people smile even if they're grimacing and gritting their teeth on the way down due to the gravitational plunge, the extreme sensation of near free-falling, landing, finally, intact; a whole new sensation ... And no longer speaking metaphorically, at the end of the slide there is a whole new reality/perception, or maybe, finally, the acceptance of the para-perception that was being avoided. ...
>
> I know nothing new has been uncovered here, we've all had these experiences before. But it seems important to talk about it. But, doesn't it seem to be so that these experiences of direct interaction with the Universe seem to get bigger and more obvious with time? Maybe the sharing of these types of stories builds solidarity, and this energy of solidarity helps more and more people to pierce the veil?

Are the "alienated" beginning to build a Network of Freedom?

All would be well.
All would be heavenly–
If the damned would only stay damned.

CHAPTER 53
STRANGE BIRDS

As I have already noted, after the used-soap clue played out, Ark and I were so shocked that we almost decided upon the instant to entirely terminate any future interactions with Frank. We realized at that point what the many clues throughout the years had meant, and that the Cassiopaeans were communicating with me directly in my dreams, and providing me with a series of green-language clues about future actions of Frank that would enable me to "see through." However, there was still sufficient blocking from my conscious mind so that the drama of the dream had to be expressed in terms of Terry and Jan rather than Frank. In this way, a partner at the board was emphasized, only the future event was actually played out by Frank, the point being to show me from the dream Frank's true role. But, at the time of the dream, I was simply not ready to consider the idea that Frank was a mole.

Of course, at the present time it relates to the fact that Frank is illegally and fraudulently trying to claim ownership of the Cs material based on his claim that there would have been no Cs without him. That is clearly not true, as the Cs themselves have made clear. Frank never was the channel. The Cs were not connected to him in any way; the overwhelming evidence is that he was actually incidental to the process, the channeling was done on enough occasions without him present to make this clear, and has continued without him. But for a long time, in my ongoing effort to try to give to Frank some sense of accomplishment, to try to use positive reinforcement to stimulate activity on his own, I would post material with the header: "Channeled by Frank Scott and [myself]." I always put myself in second place and tried to give Frank the honors because he was always ranting about how completely he had been ignored and pushed into a corner by his parents. I never dreamed that this simple act of courtesy, of effort to help him feel better about himself, would be seen by him as proof that he was the channel. But, as the Cs had already confirmed, <u>any "energy of giving"</u>

that is given to those of the STS persuasion only fuels their descent into STS. It never converts them to STO. Never.

After many long discussions about the "Frank problem," Ark and I both saw rather plainly that any continued interaction with him would be under the exact same conditions as we had each continued in our respective marriages even after realizing that there never was and could never be any real meeting of the mind or colinearity of souls with our former partners. The Cassiopaeans had told us over and over again that there was a mission of some sort, even if only that of sharing our information, and that it could not move to the next level as long as Frank was involved. We had observed evidence and clues galore that Frank's path was not just different, but rather diametrically opposed to our own. It was, indeed, a real twist.

The fact is, as one reader has pointed out, manipulation and betrayal of trust is a constant in human dynamics. But in another sense, it is our choice to experience it. The Cs have said we were lured to the threshold, and once we had gone for the gold of third-density experience, we, in some sense, agreed to have our genes altered. But, in the end, it still comes down to the fact that free will cannot be abridged unless we oblige.

This then brings us to the point where we are required to address the unresolved issues in ourselves that make us vulnerable to manipulation and betrayal of trust. Indeed, as innocent children, we are programmed to feel unworthy, and because of this unworthiness programming, we repeatedly accept manipulation and betrayal of trust as our due. Another reader has written so eloquently:

> I noticed very early in my life that people seemed to experience the same emotional entanglements the world over. Over and over again. (I was also painfully aware of how miserable I was on this earth at a very early age.) I wanted to know why, what was at work, how it occurred, and if there was a way out of going through such a meaningless-seeming, endless-seeming loop myself.
>
> Naturally, I had to first experience most of these "set patterns of emotional entanglements" myself, so I could understand them from the inside-out, I suppose. Abuse of every kind, serious and life threatening traumas, intimate relationships wrought with difficulties and codependency, etc. These were the main course of my earlier life.
>
> Anyway, from that dark and painful abyss I learned and grew beyond what seemed possible to my woeful child imaginings, and I couldn't be more tickled in my pleasant surprise of that. I've come to see that the "dark and self-serving" actually serve the "light and other-serving" quite beautifully, and in ways nothing else likely could. If, of course, one chooses to heed the call and learn from the experiences.

The Cassiopaeans have said: all there is is lessons, and until we go deep within and clear these issues, we will continue to face these lessons, and they generally escalate in order to get our attention. But again, it is our own unresolved issues that make us open to these predations. At the point when we replace our feelings of unworthiness with self-worth, we will then understand Don Juan's remarks about right use of energy.

This right use of energy has to do with don Juan's description of a division of seers into two categories:

> "The first one is made up of those who are willing to exercise self-restraint and can channel their activities toward pragmatic goals, which would benefit other seers and man in general. The other category consists of those who don't care about self-restraint or about any pragmatic goals. It is the consensus among seers that the latter have failed to resolve the problem of self-importance."

At the present time, there is a gang of petty tyrants who are so overwhelmingly concerned with their own self-importance, that they seem to have no life other than to spend inordinate amounts of time and energy attacking what we are doing, trying to steal our work for their own twisted purposes, and thereby demonstrating in the clearest of terms that they are unable and unwilling to exert their energy toward pragmatic goals designed to benefit other seers or humanity.

They have no apparent interest in creating their own website where they can share *useful* information that they have produced themselves. Rather than spending their lives studying, creating a theory, implementing it by doing the actual work, and then publishing something original and *helpful to others*, they spend their time violating free will by riding on the coattails of others, stealing the fruits of other people's work and money,[16] plagiarizing other people's work, falsifying credentials, and then attacking anyone who calls them on it.

As don Juan says, "Impeccability is nothing else but the proper use of energy. ... To understand this, you have to save enough energy yourself." Here we aren't talking about just ordinary energy such as is used to run around the block or cut the grass. The energy being discussed is something different, though it can be expressed in the physical body. The energy don Juan is talking about is the energy of awareness.

---

[16] This includes hacking into other people's computers, stealing their user names and passwords, and then utilizing a "roaming number" to run up enormous charges in Internet fees – precisely $795.74 according to Bellsouth's investigators who are compiling the info for the FBI – on the account of an innocent, single mother, who works hard for her money as a nurse in a free clinic for the indigent, but who happens to be a member of our egroup, and therefore, in their eyes is fair game for abuse.

As I have previously written, the most important principles that the Cassiopaeans have given us are free will and "knowledge protects." These two concepts are inseparable. The more knowledge you have, the more awareness you have; and the more awareness you have, the more free will you have as to whether or not you will receive and disseminate lies or truth. With increase of knowledge, there *can* be an increase in awareness, but not always. A person can have a great deal of knowledge, but since he defines what he knows with the juvenile dictionary, he only can have "juvenile awareness."

Knowledge is understanding of or information about a subject which has been obtained by experience or study, and which is either in a person's mind or possessed by people generally. Awareness is a bit different. It is the fact or state of being aware, or conscious, *especially of matters that are particularly relevant*. So, we can understand that relevance in the present context depends upon one's knowledge of the universe, and/or beliefs about same. A person can have a great deal of knowledge based on what is generally accepted by society at large, and based on this, he decides what is relevant and what is not. As we have already seen, this can even lead to Stockholm syndrome.

Acquiring even more and deeper knowledge of the universe, that which goes beyond what is commonly accepted, depends upon openness of the mind to observe reality, to forebear forming hypotheses until a sufficient number of facts become evident, and to then be constantly open to change the hypothesis based on new facts and evidence, rather than trying to force the facts or evidence to fit the hypothesis. In this way, relevance can change dramatically. We can become aware, or conscious, of matters that are relevant to a higher sphere of existence even if it is not part of the knowledge that is possessed by people generally. One reader pointed out a very important point about knowledge and awareness:

> The two words are similar but are not of the degree of intensity. For example, I could have awareness of aliens, but not "direct" knowledge. I could be aware of physics (in my case, true) but not have knowledge of physics. If I have knowledge, I have awareness. However, one could have awareness, but not knowledge.
>
> I know this may seem like hair splitting to some of you, but I think this is an important distinction of just how we can be led astray. Many of us – once we are aware – stop our quest for knowledge because we think we know and that is all that is necessary.

So, even though I had awareness of the higher levels of being, and *some* knowledge of same, as well as the workings of psychic vampires and petty tyrants, it is clear that I still did not have sufficient knowledge at the time of the realization about Frank. We knew that we had to conserve our energy, but we did not yet know that there would come a point when we would actually begin to understand impeccability in a much deeper way. "Impeccability is nothing else but the proper use of energy. ... To understand this, you have to save enough energy yourself."

We come back again to the idea that it is our own lessons that we are experiencing; that we are, in a sense, open to the predations of a petty tyrant because we feel, in some sense, that we deserve it. And yes, we may be programmed to feel that we deserve it due to simple, social and familial programming – no alien interference is necessary here. Even more, we may be carrying programs from past lives, as I was, and probably most other people as well. All of that is the bad news. The good news is this: the instant you come to the full awareness of these factors, you have the right to change your mind. You have the right to stop, right there and then, being used and subjected to manipulation and betrayal. As Clarissa Pinkola Estes writes:

> Dark man dreams are wake-up calls. They say: Pay attention! Something has gone radically amiss in the outer world. ... The threat of the 'dark man dreams' serves as a warning to all of us – if you don't pay attention, something will be stolen from you! The dreamer needs to be initiated so that *whatever has been robbing her can be recognized, apprehended, and dealt with.*
>
> In the Bluebeard story we see how a woman who falls under the spell of the predator rouses herself and escapes him, *wiser for the experience.* The story is about *transformation through knowledge, insight, voice, decisive action.* We must unlock the secrets and use our abilities to be able to stand what we see. And then, we must *use our voice and our wits to do what needs to be done about what we see.* When instincts are strong, we intuitively recognize the innate predator by scent, sight, and hearing ... We anticipate its presence, hear it approaching, and take steps to turn it away. In the instinct-injured (i.e. nuts and bolts person) the predator is upon them before they register its presence. We have been taught to be nice, to behave, to be blind, and to be misused.
>
> The young and the injured are uninitiated. Neither knows much about the dark predator and are, therefore, credulous. But, fortunately, when the predator is on the move, it leaves behind unmistakable tracks in dreams. These tracks eventually lead to its discovery, capture and containment.
>
> Wild Ways teaches people when not to act 'nice' about protecting their souls. The instinctive nature knows that being 'sweet' in these instances only makes the predator smile. When the soul is being threatened, it is not only acceptable to draw the line and mean it, it is required. (Estes, 1997)

The remark about using one's voice struck me and I did a search of the transcripts with this term and found several most interesting things:

February 22, 1995

Q: (L) Any information for us in general?

A: Listen: Now is point where all can learn more information by searching within more, rather than from without. One or two of you are already very adept at this, *this way you access universal truths directly, where there is less likelihood of corruption if done properly, see?*

Q: (L) Does this mean you want us to start using a direct channeling method? (DM) Do you want us to use one of us as a voice?

A: All.

Q: (DM) Do you mean simultaneously?

A: As you wish.

Q: (L) Do you mean that you want us to, for example, gather as a group, meditate together …

A: Just ask yourselves questions, and receive answers.

Q: (L) In other words, no hypnosis, just sit and discuss and ask back and forth among ourselves and let the energy of the group interact?

A: Or in solitude as well. Then network and exchange lessons, one does this often.

The above is obviously the Cs trying, very early in the process, to move me to channeling without Frank, as well as strongly hinting that this would be the mode of less corruption. It was clearly directed at me because of the remark about doing it in solitude, and then network and exchange lessons. Then, as now, my chief activity has been networking and sharing. It's just what I do naturally. What was also clear was the remark about "ask yourselves questions and receive answers." That was already happening, the only problem was, as the Cs were hinting, with Frank at the board, the likelihood of corruption was ever present.

And then, another very strange reference to voice: I was discussing the dreadful situation that existed in late 1995, during which time the pressure of my ex-husband to simply give up the whole experiment was becoming unbearable. He was using every means at his disposal to make me absolutely as miserable as possible, and I was sorely tempted to just throw in the towel and go back to sleep.

December 9, 1995

Q: (L) What are the objectives of this attack aside from crushing me?

A: Secession at an inappropriate juncture to throw plans askew.

Q: (L) What plans would be thrown askew by secession at this point?

A. Voice.

Q: (L) What?

A: And all other.

The strange way the word "voice" was used made absolutely no sense to me at the time. But later, another hint was given:

June 13, 1998

Q: This Medusa idea, as I have recently learned, is part of a triad of female figures. And in this triad, the other two female figures are Cassiopeia and Andromeda, or Cassiopeia and Danae. I don't know which set to select.

A: Select that which fits.

Q: I think that Danae and Cassiopeia could be the same entity in the mythical sense …

A: Who speaks for Andromeda?

Q: Cassiopeia … or Perseus? What do you mean who "speaks" for her?

A: If you do not know, you need more pieces before you can advance. You see, ask the mathematics teacher what happens if students fail to maintain the progression of study? But why?

Q: Because, if you fall behind, you miss a piece and can never catch up because other pieces don't fit, so you have to find the piece that fits.

A: Is this true Arkadiusz?

Q: (A) What happens is just that they stop understanding what follows next. (L) OK, the story says that Perseus has slain Medusa and he is on his way back and came to Ethiopia. He found that a lovely maiden had been given up to be devoured by a horrible sea serpent, and her name was Andromeda. She was the daughter of a "silly, vain woman named Cassiopeia." She had boasted that she was more beautiful than the daughters of the Sea God. The punishment for the arrogance of Cassiopeia fell not on her, but on her daughter, Andromeda. The Ethiopians were being devoured in huge numbers by the serpent – sounds a little bit like what the Lizzies are doing today – and learning from the oracle that they could be freed from the pest only if Andromeda could be offered up to the beast – they forced Cephus, her father, to offer her up. So, her mother got her into the soup and her father turned on the heat. Anyway, Perseus arrived and the maiden was chained to a rocky ledge waiting for the monster. He saw her and fell instantly in love. So, he waited beside her until the great snake came and cut off its head. They sailed away and lived happily ever after. So, who spoke for Andromeda, her mother and father, is that what you mean?

A: It is a beginning.

Q: OK, so what is the point of who spoke for Andromeda? What does that have to do with the 1/3 of 33?

A: Your searches sooner or later "net" results.

I know that many of the readers instantly see the connection, nd I know that many of you are frustrated to read some of these transcripts that demonstrate how totally dense I can be. And I realize that there has probably never been so reluctant a channel, who spent so much time trying to give her power and energy away to others because she was always putting everyone else first, even to the point of personal harm. But those of you who have read *Amazing Grace* will have some understanding of why I have always been reluctant to attribute any special ability or quality to myself. I apologize for frustrating the reader this way. I was certainly programmed to not protect myself, and to be "nice" and I was definitely bait for the Sea Monster. But, as the reader quoted above points out: "I've come to see that the 'dark and self-serving' actually serve the 'light and other-serving' quite beautifully, and in ways nothing else likely could. If, of course, one chooses to heed the call and learn from the experiences."

Right use of energy, or impeccability, is learning *when* not to act nice about protecting our souls. It is learning that when the soul is being threatened, it is not only acceptable to draw a line and mean it, it is required.

In the Bluebeard story, as soon as Bluebeard realizes that his wife has discovered his dark secrets, he informs her that he is going to kill her. She pleads with him for time to make her confession, to pray for her soul, and to generally prepare to die. This is, of course, a ruse. Secretly, she has sent word to her brothers that Bluebeard is going to kill her, and she is buying time until their arrival.

This is an allegory of the need to recoup one's soul energy. Once one has become aware of the secrets of Bluebeard, one has to acquire energy to deal with him. The arrival of the "brothers" on the scene is nothing more than the reviving of the psychic, warrior energies. It is with the energy, skill and forbearance of the warrior aspect of the soul that we deal with petty tyrants – when the time is right.

At the same time, we must be aware that there can be a distinction between the persona of Bluebeard and the actual human being who is playing the role. As Ms. Estes has pointed out, "the young and the injured are uninitiated. Neither knows much about the dark predator and are, therefore, credulous." This is an important point because it might indicate that one is dealing with a soul that is simply in the process of learning the same lessons, but is at a different point on the learning cycle. Perhaps such a soul has not chosen as many incarnations, or a different lesson path has been followed. Perhaps such a soul is one that is "new" in human form, though it has spent other incarnations in other forms. In such a case, it is wise to consider this, and to realize that such a soul may not have any evil intent – they are just learning about the predator by experiencing control by it. And it may require many lifetimes for them to come to that moment when they realize that they have been manipulated and betrayed by their own choices, and they can then change their mind and begin to conserve their own energy for escape.

In other cases, a different dynamic may be in play: an apparent human being may quite simply be an incarnated natural predator. Such an individual may look human, smell human, speak as a human, and have access to the storage capacity of a human brain which allows them to collect data and facts, assemble them, and even to present a very scholarly front. But initiated awareness sees that such a being acts in human form as an animal, twisting human principles and potentials, because such a being has no multiple assemblage points, to use Castaneda's terminology.

There seems to be still another type of human: an extension of a higher-density negative crypto-geographic being. As the Cassiopaeans have pointed out, fourth density most often acts through its human agents, and sometimes these are like dedicated phone lines – there is no human potential present. Don Juan speaks about such petty tyrants: "According to the new seers, a perfect petty tyrant has no redeeming feature." We will discuss these almost-humans in more depth further on in this series.

Nevertheless, whatever factors are in play, the most useful approach to these lessons about predators is a combination of right use of energy, as well as clearing the unworthiness programming. We know that the program is clear when there is no more self-importance left in us, when we are no longer personally offended by their actions. This, of course, does not mean that we no longer seek to discover, capture, and contain such predators when they appear in our lives. We are still aware that there are always going to be instances where we know that acting nice is not going to protect our souls. We must always be on guard against threats to the soul, theft of energy or free will, and just because we are no longer personally offended, it does not mean that we do not draw the line and mean it. But, as Castaneda points out, when self-importance is effaced, all of this can be done with a sense of joy and in a spirit of humor.

When our unworthiness issues are clear, we can look upon petty tyrants with compassion, we can understand that it is quite possible that they have become petty tyrants because they have suffered their own torments and programming. We can thank them for teaching us, and joyfully release them from such an agreement. And, of course, if it is a human soul that we are dealing with, they will go on their way, and both will be the richer for the experience.

However, if the achieving of understanding, the psychic releasing of the contract, has no effect, we have to consider that we may be dealing with either a natural predator incarnated into a human body, or an extension of a fourth-density STS being.

But still, even in such a case, at some level we have asked for the experience in order to learn the lesson that our soul was seeking. So we find that, again, having some compassion for robotic or predatory beings is a deeper level of healing the self. We need to understand that even fourth-density robots and predators in human form are only trying to survive by feeding on us. It is all "nature," and it's not our job to fix them. It is, however, our job and our right to protect ourselves.

> "The instinctive nature knows that being 'sweet' in these instances only makes the predator smile. When the soul is being threatened, it is not only acceptable to draw the line and mean it, it is required.
>
> "Warriors take strategic inventories," he said. "They list everything they do. Then they decide which of those things can be changed in order to allow themselves a respite, in terms of expending their energy."
> … Don Juan said then that in the strategic inventories of warriors, self-importance figures as the activity that consumes the greatest amount of energy, hence, their effort to eradicate it.
>
> "One of the first concerns of warriors is to free that energy in order to face the unknown with it," don Juan went on. "The action of rechanneling that energy is impeccability."

And we come back to the present recapitulation. Is it a right use of energy? Or is it a distraction, as some would suggest? Don Juan has explained what he called a "three-phase progression." This is the mode of approach to becoming a warrior who is *free*. This three-step program consists of:

1. Holding your own in facing petty tyrants.
2. Facing the unknown with courage.
3. Standing in the presence of the unknowable.

> "The average man's reaction is to think that the order … should be reversed," he went on. "A seer who can hold his own in the face of the unknown can certainly face petty tyrants. But that's not so. What destroyed the superb seers of ancient times was that assumption. We know better now. We know that nothing can temper the spirit of a warrior as much as the challenge of dealing with impossible people in positions of power. Only under those conditions can warriors acquire the sobriety and serenity to stand the pressure of the unknowable."
>
> "The seers of [the Conquest] couldn't have found a better ground. The Spaniards were the petty tyrants who tested the seers' skills to the limit; after dealing with the conquerors, the seers were capable of facing anything. They were the lucky ones. At that time there were petty tyrants everywhere."

As we have written in our online article, "The Taste for Things That Are True":

> There is another factor involved here: the Internet as both a boon and a bane to mankind.
>
> On the one hand, the world wide web is a marvelous opportunity for open exchange of ideas, experiences, growth and harmony. On the oth-

er hand, it is a mask behind which some of the most atrocious predation I never hoped to witness takes place.

In recent weeks, we have heard many remarks from readers and members of our egroup about other groups that have been "invaded" by these predators. A fruitful and worthwhile discussion among a hundred or so people from around the world, taking place in almost real time, can be utterly destroyed by one or two bad apples. We have watched one discussion group after another close its doors and fade into oblivion because of this factor, and we simply cannot understand what drives a person to behave like pure embodied hate.

Would these people behave this way if they met each other in the flesh? Does the Internet just simply enable psychosis and neurosis to thrive and multiply? Is it going to become the den of cyber-mafia and virtual vampires? Are decent, hardworking, honest people going to be driven off the Internet?

Or is it just because we are engaged in paranormal research? Is it only in the effort to bridge science and metaphysics that we find ourselves the objects of abuse by cyber-trash?

During the past week or so, we have had to sit down with our children, show them the terrible, hurtful lies that are being written about us by these contemptible, solipsistic, malignant, and lawless people. We have had to show them that these people have no compunction about writing about the children themselves, using their names, possibly endangering them, certainly embarrassing them, and most definitely hurting them psychologically and emotionally. We have had to explain to them about people who choose conscious evil; people who are malicious, evil-minded, envious, obnoxious, and loathsome. We have had to explain to them about people who are so twisted that they derive gratification from deceiving other people and hurting other people. And we have had to explain to them that these people pose as "good and helpful and friendly" when they meet you and when you have something they want, or something they wish to destroy, whether they are being directed by some nebulous Control System, or their own internal deficiencies and general failure at life. What is more, we have had to explain it to ourselves.

And of course, the children have asked us: Why do you even do it? Why not just walk away from the world such people inhabit? Why not just go back to "normal life," and forget about it. Let the world do what it wants to do, let everybody just go away and leave us alone?

And frankly, as I write this, I am hard pressed to answer that question. Why, indeed?

I was most certainly giving a lot of energy to my own self-importance. My emotions were in motion, my programs were running amok, and more than anything I was just purely and simply hurt that people could behave in such vicious and manipulative ways. Not only was I asking myself "why?" I was asking, "What is the proper action to take?" The standard teaching is to "ignore it, rise above it, turn the other cheek, don't waste your energy on such trash." But as members of our egroup combed the Internet, as we read messages from readers of the site, we realized that there was, indeed, a concerted effort being made to connect the word "Cassiopaea" to "doomsday cult" in such a way that many people who might be helped by reading these pages would not venture to even visit the site because of this vicious propaganda. And, in fact, one reader made this crystal clear by writing that she had almost decided *not* to have a look based upon such rumors, but was now glad she had the second thought to just take a peek, because she found that not only was the rumor not true, but that she had never before experienced such a profound relief to realize that others were spiritually skeptical, and bringing powers of reason and research to issues of the soul.[17]

At that moment, I picked up and reread Castaneda's passage about petty tyrants and I knew the answer: why indeed? Because this lesson is going to keep coming until you learn to hold your own. I knew also that the right use of my energy at this point would be to not only explore the lesson for myself, but to share it with others. In this way, I could fully activate my choice of what kind of seer I wish to be. Remember, don Juan said there are two kinds: those who are willing to exercise self-restraint and can channel their activities toward pragmatic goals, which would benefit other seers and man in general, or those who don't care about self-restraint or about any pragmatic goals.

In short, by exercising self-restraint, by refusing to engage in a flame war or giving any direct energy or response to the petty tyrants, and by re-channeling this energy into sharing of my recapitulation, my taking of inventory, recounting the events, the people, the thoughts, the facts, all the while attempting to remove my subjective judgments – or at the very least, clearly identifying them when they were present – I could transform the entire situation into something pragmatically useful to not only other seers, but humanity at large.

At the same time that one exercises restraint, one must also draw the line and mean it. In dealing with petty tyrants and predators, one has to learn not to act nice, to forget about being sweet, and to discover, capture and contain the predator.

And so it is that the present strategy is that I am using my energy in a very pragmatic way, designed to rid myself of my own self importance, and to share the process with other seers who are on the same path of *becoming free*. Don Juan tells us that utilizing this strategy is not only crucial for getting rid of self-importance, it also prepares us

---

[17] For more testimonials of this type, visit http://cassiopaea-cult.com/.

for the final realization of impeccability. And in the end, that is what counts. Impeccability is simply another term for respecting free will.

As don Juan suggested, the present series is also a "deadly maneuver." The petty tyrants are "like a mountain peak" and the attributes of the warrior – control, discipline, forbearance, timing – are the climbers who meet at the summit.

Finally, I'm having a lot of fun writing this series! When don Juan wrote about his own experience with the petty tyrant, and how the maneuver was directed by his benefactor, he made some rather amazing remarks:

> "I'm sure that I could have done it myself, although I have always doubted that I would have carried it off with flair and joyfulness. My benefactor was simply enjoying the encounter by directing it. The idea of using a petty tyrant is not only for perfecting the warrior's spirit, but also for enjoyment and happiness."
>
> "How could anyone enjoy the monster you described?"
>
> "He was nothing in comparison to the real monsters that the new seers faced during the Conquest. By all indications those seers enjoyed themselves blue dealing with them. They proved that even the worst tyrants can bring delight, provided, of course, that one is a warrior."

And this was another of my realizations about my hurt feelings. I wouldn't be having hurt feelings if it wasn't for the fact that I was just simply taking myself too seriously. Because, of course, when we take ourselves too seriously, we also have to take the petty tyrant seriously as well. We worry all the time about saying this or doing that because it might hurt their feelings, or it isn't nice, or isn't love and light, or it doesn't look compassionate!

Notice that all of these concerns are actually based on our worries about how someone else will perceive us!

We worry about someone else's hurt feelings because if we hurt their feelings, *they will think* we are bad. We worry about just simply speaking honestly from the greatest truth we know, because *they might think* we are not "nice" or "sweet" or "Christian" or "compassionate." And all of that is related to self-importance!

We may be having the strongest instinctive reaction of our lives that just screams that someone is a predator, but we shove it under the rug because it's "not nice." And then, when they are poking a stick directly into our eye, we are constrained to say, "Please, I'd like to bring it to your attention, if it is not too much trouble, that you have a stick in your hand, and somehow (and I am sure it is not intentional), the stick has managed to find its way into my eye. It is causing me considerable difficulty – even pain – but I have tried to restrain myself from pointing it out because I am sure that you are just being yourself and have every right to be yourself, and if in the course of being yourself, you have accidentally poked a stick in my eye, perhaps it is *my* fault for having my eye annoyingly in your way. Having said all of that, the fact remains that the stick is in my eye, and if it wouldn't be *too* much trouble, would you kindly see if it would be possible to withdraw it – assuming that it doesn't violate your right to be yourself, that is – because I am, naturally, very compassionate toward others, and being yourself is okay by me … but still … the stick … my eye … "

Acting from natural instinct, the instant the stick begins to approach our eye, we would slap it away and be damned to the niceties. And so it should be in matters of the soul.

Don Juan explained that the mistake average men make in confronting petty tyrants is that they do not understand that reality is an interpretation we make, and that interpretation is based on knowledge and awareness. The plain fact is: petty tyrants interpret reality according to the juvenile dictionary. Petty tyrants take themselves with deadly seriousness while warriors do not. Warriors interpret reality according to the theological dynamic, and utilize the psychological substrate as the instrument of implementation of the four attributes: control, discipline, forbearance, timing.

What always exhausts a petty tyrant is the wear and tear on his self-importance. He is so full of it, and false pride, that he is internally ripped apart by being made to feel worthless, which he only feels because of his self-importance and his need to feed and sustain it. It is self-importance that will drive a man to falsify his credentials, to claim knowledge and experience he doesn't have; and it is self-importance that will drive such a man to fight to his last gasp to preserve that false self.

And this last is the clincher. The petty tyrant is so concerned about what other people think that they will spend endless energy trying to maintain a false image, to continue to act the role, to attack that which threatens their self-importance either violently or with subtle viciousness.

The object of the warrior is, of course, to utilize whatever is necessary to stand against such attacks, to draw the line and hold it, and – if necessary – to strategically and systematically harass the petty tyrant until they are drained of energy, and with their last, desperate burst, they do something so stupid, so destructive, that finally, due to the forbearance of the warrior who knows the nature of the predator, the petty tyrants receive their due – generally at their own hands. And thus the dynamic ends.

One of the chief things I am realizing about self-importance, with each grueling confession about my own ignorance and stupidity that I must make in public, is that we are controlled by our fear of admitting that we have made stupid mistakes, that we allowed ourselves to be used and manipulated – whether at a human level or from a hyperdimensional level – that we are in the process of learning. We are ashamed to discuss these things publicly. We are exhausted by trying to keep it quiet or shove it under the rug or trying to find a way to rationalize it, to think that we deserve it, that we are not free to simply change our mind, and learn a new strategy for dealing with such things. We are programmed to be so concerned about our self-aggrandizing feelings, and the self-aggrandizing feelings of others that we commit the fatal flaw – we take ourselves too seriously! We think that our emotional reactions to the cruelties of others is evidence of our spiritual nature. We think that our concern for the feelings of others who are hurting us is evidence of our superior spirituality. We think that saying something like, "Well, consider the source and ignore it," or "One should not get the messenger and the message mixed up," is some sort of pronouncement of great spiritual wisdom.

We are so terrified by our fear of taking the bull by the horns, that we exhaust ourselves trying to think of ways *not* to do it.

And it is really quite simple: just *do* it.

At the present moment, the above mentioned gang of petty tyrants, consisting of Vincent Bridges, Jeff "Storm Bear" Williams, Frank Scott, and a support team of clappers, as well as assorted others with whom we have had no significant interaction, but who, nevertheless, feel moved to contribute their energy to the activity, are engaged in many and varied activities designed to provoke our self-importance.

In a very real sense, this is a Tempest in a Teapot in global terms, but in another sense, understanding nonlinear dynamics, to refuse to draw the line and hold it could have far-reaching effects. As don Juan pointed out, to act in anger, without control and discipline, to have no forbearance, is to be defeated, and the most important thing of all is to feel joy throughout the exercise.

And so it is, this present series that consists of recapitulation, sharing the process with others, and utilization of the strategy of the warrior, is one of the most effective uses of my energy I could ever have dreamed of – and I certainly cannot take the credit for having thought of the unique combination of features myself – well, at least not myself in the *present*. And I will certainly admit here and now that it is astonishingly effective in rooting out any of my own self-importance, which has resulted in an enormous feeling of true joy!

But now, we must return to that period of time when I was still in the process of acquiring the knowledge about this process: the period of time when there was the realization that Frank was, indeed, a petty tyrant, albeit a very teensy weensy one.

I was, of course, extremely upset about this realization. I was very attached to Frank – at least I was attached to the image of Frank I had created in my mind – and I began to go through a grieving process that was exactly as painful as if Frank had died. Because, in truth, my illusion had died. For so long I had done so much to make it easy for him to blossom as the great soul-friend I wanted him to be; and that was the problem: I "wanted." I wanted him to be on the same path we were on; I wanted him to have similar goals and aspirations; I wanted him to be a part of our work and our lives as we rode off into the sunset, so to say. And I was facing the realization that this would never, ever be possible.

As I struggled with my emotions about the loss of Frank, my mind kept trying to find ways and means to rationalize his behavior over the years; to make excuses; to understand what was the proper response; to find my way. I knew that even though it was very much like the illusion of my marriage, at least Frank was not someone I had to interact with every day, and that did put a different slant on the matter. When a person is "one" with another human being, it is crucial that this oneness be of similarity of mind and soul and goals. When there is no colinearity, it is almost impossible to interact intimately without severe draining of energy. But without the complication of intimacy, there did seem to be a possible solution: we would simply severely limit the contact, meanwhile we would begin to work on the new mode of communication: the psychomantium.

Along with the realization about Frank – after putting together of all the clues – there was the realization that Frank was not, and never had been the channel. He was just another body occupying a chair at the table, just as dozens of other people had done. At that point, I realized why it was really pointless to continue channeling with Frank in any serious or significant way: his presence was only blocking the full flow of the Cassiopaean communications.

That led to an even more startling realization: the only reason it *seemed* to work well with Frank was because he would almost literally go to sleep during the sessions, and that meant that only Terry and I had been active in the motion of the planchette. Frank was as inert as a mannequin. The Cassiopaeans were *me;* they were also Terry; but they never were Frank and that was why there was almost *zero interaction between him and the process.* That is why he wasn't interested in the questions. That is why he had almost never asked any questions, and that was why he wasn't interested in any other aspect of the work. He wasn't interested in networking; he wasn't interested in sharing. He wasn't interested, because it wasn't part of *him.*

Of course, that meant I had to ask myself if I was just making it all up? Obviously, the answers that were being spelled out on the board were coming from me, in response to my own questions. But why would I be so suspicious of channeled information from myself in the future, if I was willing to entertain the idea, even only occasionally, that Frank was the channel? Why, if it was supposed to be Frank, was it "channeling," and if it was me, then I had to think I was "making it up?" Why did I have such serious doubts about the level of the contact on the occasions when it had been just Terry and myself at the board? Had Frank managed to brainwash me into believing that we could only channel when he was present? Unfortunately, that seemed to be the case. He had proclaimed it so loud and so often that I had come to think it *might* be true in the face of all the evidence to the contrary. Terry had never believed it, and had expressed this opinion to me time and again. I had found myself in the position of having to defend Frank, when Frank was actually indefensible. I was like a kid who is being told by a parent that hanging out with unsavory persons was not a good thing, and the kid knows it somewhere inside, but because their "friend," who has attached to them via sympathy, is being "attacked," they feel that they have to defend them too, and close their mind and eyes to the truth. And now I saw that Terry had been right all along. (In fact, the clarity and level of coherence of the communication *without* Frank is dramatic evidence that Frank never was the channel, as the reader will see when I present the relevant 2001 and 2002 sessions in the course of this series!)

And then there were the cases where Frank's emotional overlay was involved and I remembered with startling clarity what the Cs had said on April 18, 1995 when I had suspected SV of being the source of the attack:

Q: (L) Have we ever had a person in our group or in our room here, who was sent here deliberately to break up our interaction?

A: If so, that is for you to discover for purposes of learning and growth. … Remember one can be manipulated by another. … We mean that one can appear to be an "agent" when in actuality, control is originating elsewhere, this is especially true when the apparent "agent" is one of a good and simple and seemingly stable nature.

I realize only now that Frank was an FRV pied piper. He was an EM vector. He was a focuser of direction in the sense that he probably sat there in his semi-sleep state at the board, basking like a reptile in the warm energies that he was absorbing, and emitting signals all the while that befuddled the minds of everyone present, unless, of course, they were of the same type, in which case, their energy augmented his, and the corrupting effect was amplified.

May 3, 1997

Q: Reading through the session of May 23, last year, when Tom was also here, and the issue of his being in O'Brien was addressed, you asked who had begged him to stay there, then there was a remark about an EM vector. The way I understood it is that a person can be an EM vector. Is that possible?

A: Vector means focuser of direction.

Q: Could that mean that EM waves can be vectored by a human being simply by their presence? I also noticed that several of us have been involved with persons and relationships that seem designed to confuse, defuse, and otherwise distort our learning, as well as drain our energy. Basically, keeping us so stressed that we cannot fulfill our potential. Is there some significance to this observation?

A: That is elementary, my dear Knight!

Q: One of the things I have learned is that these individuals seem to attach via some sort of psychic hook that enters through our reactions of pity. Can you comment on the nature of pity?

A: Pity those who pity.

Q: But, the ones who are being pitied, who generate sensations of pity, do not really pity anybody but themselves.

A: Yes … ?

Q: Then, is it true as my son said, when you give pity, when you send love and light to those in darkness, or those who complain and want to be "saved" without effort on their own part, when you are kind in the face of abuse and manipulation, that you essentially are giving power to their further disintegration, or contraction into *self*-ishness? That you are powering their descent into STS?

A: You know the answer!

Q: Yes. I have seen it over and over again. Were the individuals in our lives selected for the extremely subtle nature of their abilities to evoke pity, or were we programmed to respond to pity so that we were blind to something that was obvious to other people?

A: Neither. You were selected to interact with those who would trigger a hypnotic response that would ultimately lead to a drain of energy.

When considering how to deal with Frank, we discussed whether or not we ought to just tell him how we felt, what we had noticed, and why we were concerned. We agreed that this would be the most logical thing to do since it would give him a chance to "explain" himself, or to adjust, if possible. So, we decided that we would try to approach the subject a little at a time and gauge his reaction before going the next step. I tried to talk to him about it, and soon found that there was no possible way to do it. Every approach to the subject that I tried, he blocked with his sympathy ploys, resurrection of his suicide ideas, and general energy-draining tactics.

In short, he was poking a stick in my eye, and I was trying to politely ask him to remove it. And when he began to manipulatively assert his right to poke a stick in my eye, I subsided and withdrew my request.

At the same time this was transpiring, the website was growing, and the correspondence was increasing. I was finding myself spending almost every waking moment answering questions from readers, and this usually involved having to research the subjects they were asking about and quoting the long pieces of text that I would find, along with further information on the subject from the Cs.

At this point, the answer of how to deal with Frank became apparent: there was no way we could do the research, get the material posted, and be drained every week at the session. So, we just simply informed Frank when he called and asked if we wanted to do a session that we had decided to cut back to one session a month in order to have time for research and handling the questions of the readers of the website.

We thought that we could balance things by allowing Frank only limited opportunities to poke the stick in our eyes. Yes, I know, that is really stupid, but there it was. That was the program, and that is what we are all taught to do: to compromise, to see free will as a sort of balance of permitting the free-will choice of another to abuse you to continue, but only occasionally!

I continued to want to give Frank opportunities to contribute out of a sort of despairing hope that we were wrong. I would print letters from readers with questions and ask him to do a little research, or write a reply. His uncaring attitude about other human beings in difficulty, people who were writing and asking for help, repeatedly shocked me. I continued to ask him to write a bio for the site. Every month throughout 1999 when we had our monthly session, I would ask him, "Did you get your bio written?" And he never did. At one point, I even thought that I would give the who-is-receiving-the-Cs question a sort of blind trial. I asked Frank to please begin to experiment with channeling on his own, to write his results, that I would type them up and post them. He never did.

This went on month after month in the background of 1999.

Now, I want to go back for a moment to the "used soap" session of January 2, 1999. This comment was made in reference to our thought that a Nobel Prize might provide the necessary cachet to enable us to do the research that the Cs were urging, to share our results widely, and not worry so much about either money or attack. We had the idea that we must always fund everything we did ourselves, and that the only true sharing was if we could just give everything away for free. So, in order to be able to make enough money to do this, we decided that increase of income-potential ratio per hour was advisable. That way,

Ark could work fewer hours for the necessary money to provide enough for us to live on, maintain the website, buy all the books and materials we needed, and maybe even pay someone to help us with keeping track of everything. He would then have free time for the research itself instead of spending every waking moment trying to meet company deadlines in order to keep the bills paid.

It was pretty obvious by this time that we were not going to get the help we needed from Frank, and Terry and Jan had already bought their longed-for home in Tallahassee and had opened their long-dreamed-of antique business. Jan finished the job of formatting the transcripts through 1998, but at this point, they were too busy to continue to give the time to the material that it required. I was swamped with the work, Ark was swamped with his work just to keep the bills paid, including in books and materials needed to deal with the research questions from readers. We wanted to be able to make the material available to as wide an audience as possible, and that required money – a lot of money.

We did not want to try to publish the material through a regular publishing house where some whacked-out editor who didn't have a clue would cut the Cs to ribbons. We wanted to make any printed copies available at cost, and we knew that in order to do this, we would have to make more money, make it faster, and have more time to do all the editing and cleanup work on the transcripts that was needed. It was an enormous job, and we were simply overwhelmed.

And we weren't getting any help from Frank. He wouldn't even go over the text and correct spelling errors or add personal notes.

As I read through the "used soap" session, I see that there is another very strange remark:

January 2, 1999

Q: (A) Are we on the right track with our public activities? [...]

A: Be careful about being overeager to share the information you receive in this communication too widely.

Q: (L) We are being careful. Where this communication is concerned, we have only shared some philosophical things. I don't think we have ...

A: It is you, my dear, that gives us some concern. This will not be a pathway to "fame and fortune," unless and until it is balanced.

Q: (A) Which communication are we not supposed to share? Cassiopaean?

A: Yes, but we did not say: do not share. We mean to be careful. Snakes in the grass lurketh.

Again we are faced with a conundrum. This was not the first warning to be careful not to share too much, too widely. Such warnings are scattered throughout the text. Yet, at the present time, Frank has declared that he is the channel, and has illegally issued permission to Vincent Bridges to freely publish and distribute the unedited transcripts, in direct contradiction of what he has claimed to channel!

There is also the odd remark that the material would not be a "pathway to fame and fortune unless and until it is balanced." This remark is especially strange since neither Ark nor I had any ideas of fame and fortune for any reason at all other than to be able to better perform our perceived mission of researching hyperdimensional realities, and sharing the Cs material and whatever research we had that contributed to the expansion of knowledge. The reader ought to know that, for both of us, interacting with the public is an act of service that constitutes a form of conscious suffering which, all things being equal, we would certainly choose to do otherwise.

So, the question is: why was this remark made? Is it an overlay of Frank's desires? Or, on the other hand, is it another clue the Cs were giving about the fact that Frank was the odd man out and that nothing would proceed until he was out of the picture altogether? Considering the way things have played out, I tend to the latter interpretation, especially considering the added remark about "snakes in the grass." One automatically thinks of "nurturing a serpent in one's bosom," and that certainly seems to be what we were doing with Frank, and later, others.

Another factor in the early months of 1999 was my concern about my two eldest daughters who were completely unhappy about the whole Cassiopaean thing. It was a source of deep embarrassment to them that their mother was publishing the material on the Internet, not to mention their awareness, followed by denial, that there might be something to what the Cs were saying. They just wanted a normal life. Well, I could certainly sympathize with that. I wanted a normal life too.

I just wanted to be able to read and study, and write a little when I felt like it, work in my garden, take care of my beloved husband and children, my house, and for God's sake, have a little peace after all the years of bone-grinding struggle. I didn't want to think about aliens or ultraterrestrials being at the top of the food chain. I didn't want to have to deal with the fact that anybody with a brain could see that something strange and predatory was moving on our planet. I didn't want to have to wake up in the morning and think about all the suffering of humanity for millennia, and that it was very likely only a precursor to what was to come in the not-too-distant future, whether it was due to ultraterrestrial manipulation, or simply human greed and ignorance. I just wanted to dig in the dirt, arrange flowers, comb through thrift stores for rare or unusual books and odd things that I liked, take the girls to the hairdresser or dance class or sewing lessons, and live like a normal human being. Was that too much to ask?

I wept for the world that I would like to live in. I wept for my daughters and the certain pain they felt in facing this same question. I wept for all the others I knew who had faced it as well.

But weeping is not the way of the warrior. Beware of those who cannot stop weeping when they realize their true condition, for they have realized nothing. As don Juan and Gurdjieff tell us, there are untold dangers in the path of knowledge for those without sober understanding. Seers have to be methodical, rational beings; paragons of sobriety and yet free and open to the wonders and mysteries of existence.

> "It is natural to be scared and to control fear is wrong and senseless," don Juan tells us. Fear is the opposite of Love and to be truly balanced one must experience, on a continual basis, equal manifestations of both. True contact with expanded awareness can bring on unspeakable melancholy. It is a mixture of pure longing for the depths of perception plus an absolute fear of their chilling solitude.
>
> Don Juan remarked that in the life of warriors it was extremely natural to be sad for no overt reason. ... Whenever the boundaries of the known are broken, a mere glimpse of the eternity outside is enough to disrupt the coziness of our controlled awareness. The resulting melancholy is sometimes so intense that it can bring about death. ... The best way to get rid of melancholy is to make fun of it.

I realized that there is nothing lonelier than eternity. And this is the human dilemma. There is nothing cozier than to be a human being. We can live forever behind veils of illusion, suffering our blindness, and dying in our ignorance. And, until some aspect of that human has had its fill of suffering and death, there will be no desire to venture into the absolute loneliness of eternity. It is only the soul that is ready for this definitive journey that becomes a warrior, willing to risk the soul-chilling fear and the unspeakable joy of traveling into the unknown. If you can't handle the fear, you cannot know the love at the "higher" levels.

Now, in the next several chapters, we will enter the world of counter-intelligence operations both of the human variety as well as the cryptogeographic, hyperdimensional type. I will begin listing the *dramatis personae* of the years 1999 to the present. The reader will see the "circles within circles" of the Matrix Control System.

In the very earliest days of my Internet experience, I had encountered a web personality who went by the handle of Density 4, and signed all his messages "Blue Resonant Human." It was sort of a humorous dig at those who followed the Mayan calendar. Blue, as I began to call him, and I hit it off immediately, and I have entire disks full of email discussions we carried on through the years 1996 to 1999. In the very early days, when I was attacked by the crowd on Mike Lindemann's ISCNI discussion board for daring to suggest that aliens might not have our best interests at heart, Blue jumped to my defense, and I witnessed words being used in a way I had never thought possible – literally like swords. The Lindemann harpies fled in terror, and I decided that participating in their discussions was a waste of time and energy. But Blue and I chatted on, and I have him to thank for many, many enlightening posts. I was naive in the extreme, and he undertook to protect me and educate me in matters that were crucial to my survival.

Blue was very interested in the strange twists and turns of my life, and when Ark first made contact with me, he was naturally concerned that I was going to be hurt by an Internet predator. We had a number of long phone conversations, and Blue attended a few sessions with Cs via telephone.

During 1997 and most of 1998, Blue was intensely involved in building a massive website, a hub for information on secret government projects, mind control, aliens, secret societies, and all of their connections to black magick and satanism. Very early on, Blue had stumbled on the connections written about in Picknett and Prince's book *The Stargate Conspiracy*, and he was putting all the information together. We discussed his finds at great length, as well as his plans to try to get inside and find out who was really on first. The folks that Blue was particularly interested in included numerous members of what is popularly known as the "Aviary."

The Aviary has been described by Dan Smith and Rosemary Ellen Guiley, directors of the Center for North American Crop Circle Studies, in their article, "The Aquarium Conspiracy," as "An important link in the communication chain between the civilian population and the intelligence community in regards to UFO matters … This is the final link next to the public network, and so it must be heavily disguised by its own surrealistic smoke screen. The Aviary functions best by amplifying people's own misconceptions about the paranormal. It does this by helping to over-inflate individual pieces of the puzzle so that particular investigators get pushed further into their own blind alleys."

According to the popular mythos, this organization was said to hand out disinformation on UFO research. It consisted of various ex-spooks and military types and the following is a general list of those who were claimed to be the interface with the public:

THE SPARROW – Richard Doty – AFOSI agent.
CONDOR – Robert M. Collins – Former Captain USAF.
OWL – Dr. Harold Puthoff – Parapsychologist/Director of Psi-tech.

FALCON – C. B. Jones – Parapsychology/psychotronics, Navy Intel, DIA, MUFON (1989), as a consultant.

PENGUIN – John Alexander – Former Army Intel on the board of Psi-tech.

PELICAN – Ron Pandolphi – CIA.

BLUEJAY – Dr. Chris Green – CIA.

NIGHTINGALE – Dr. Jack Verona – Liaison between Capitol Hill and Los Alamos.

SEAGULL – Bruce Maccabee – Photographic expert, MUFON consultant, MUFON state director 1975.

UNKNOWN – Bill Moore – Alleged intelligence agent.

PARROT – Jacques Vallee, Ph.D. – Formerly an astrophysicist working with Paris Observatory and the Space Committee (nothing to do with UFOs), later moved to U.S. as principal investigator with Defense Department computer network projects; worked with famed astronomer and dear friend Dr. J. Allen Hynek who left and denounced the military's Project Blue Book as a disinformational smokescreen; prolific author on UFO subjects.

The rumors suggested that the Aviary was an actual organization, financed by the U.S. Government or Lawrence Rockefeller who was rumoured to be throwing a lot of money at UFO research. This organization was supposed to be infiltrating UFO groups such as MUFON and spreading disinfo, which, as we will discover, is true – though not in the way that is supposed. The Aviary-inspired disinformation was not (as some suggest) to create the UFO mythology out of whole cloth as a distraction (i.e. UFOs don't really exist except as a government mind control experiment). Rather, it was to cover up what the UFO/alien reality is *really* doing.

Blue, as a growing Internet presence, sought out many of these individuals to interview them, chat with them, and seek answers to the burning questions we both had about who was who and what was what.

I was naturally concerned that he was going to get into some kind of trouble doing these things. The one thing we had never quite agreed on was the nature of the alien presence. He was having a really hard time grasping the hyperdimensional nature of it, and he wanted very much to find that it was all just a mind-control, social-programming experiment. At the very most, if there were any aliens involved, they must be physical creatures like us, and any weird stuff had to be consigned to the etheric realms of spirit possession.

The following clip was the Cs' answer to Blue's questions about several of the above individuals. I'll let the reader guess who is who:

November 7, 1998

Q: (BRH) What about Phil?

A: Try not to be misled.

Q: (BRH) I mean more specifically about his alleged interstitial hood-lums. (This is in reference to a description of aliens that Blue was fond of quoting, Ephesians 6:12, the idea being that the aliens were demons, or strictly ethereal beings. Apparently, this was the theory of someone on the "inside" whose name was Phil.)

A: "Hoodlums" are not leading, they are led.

Q: (BRH) Anything you can tell me about Ron, John and Victoria and Dr. V that would be good for me to know?

A: We see one with a plight. One secretly holds the light. Why not run with his program? Because it is missing some data. But, who supplies the data? Someone reaches out, but if this one grasps your hand, they will not let go.

After a period of very close interaction with some of these people, Blue came to a certain conclusion and posted on his website the opinion that the Aviary was merely an "ad-hoc dysfunctional family of disparate military/intelligence spooks who share an interest in UFOs and parapsychology yet often work at cross-purposes and frankly don't even get along with each other all that well. Extremely weird birds." There were, of course, a few of them he really liked, and considering what was to happen later, one has to wonder if this "liking" was not manipulated.

On December 25, 1998, Blue forwarded an email to me for Ark (see Appendix B). Ark was certainly intrigued at such a discussion and did some websearches on the participants. I was pretty intrigued to see that there were a number of members of the so-called Aviary on board, including Ron Pandolfi, John Alexander, Bruce Macabbee and Hal Puthoff. Also on the Sarfatti discussion list were Joe Firmage, Uri Geller (Involved with Puthoff, Targ and Ingo Swann in SRI research), Stan Krippner, Russel Targ (SRI remote viewing with Puthoff and Swann), Ed Mitchell (Astronaut and Founder of The Institute of Noetic Science), Eric Davis and, of course, Blue.

The reader may also be interested in doing a little research on their own to discover that there are other links between some of these individuals and other organizations. For example, John Alexander and Jacques Vallee work for Billionaire Robert Bigelow who created an organization called the National Institute of Discovery Science (www.nidsci.org/personnel.html) or NIDS for short.

Segue to the present: Additional research by our research team reveals to us that there is a curious New Age/science crossover organization called the Axiom Visiting Faculty (www.greatmystery.org/visitingfaculty.html). Here we find the following:

Drunvalo Melchizedek,
Mitchell (NIDS, Sarfatti),
Castaneda followers,
Deepak Chopra,
Fred Alan Wolfe,
Greg Braden,
Joe Firmage (Sarfatti, on the Institute of Noetic Sciences board),
John Mack (Rockefeller sponsored NDE and Alien abduction hypnosis researcher),
Laurie Monroe (Monroe Institute),
Rabbi Michael Lerner,
Peter Russel (Institute of Noetic Science/Mitchell's (NIDS) private organization),
Russel Targ (Remote Viewing pioneer along with Puthoff and Ingo Swann at SRI in the '70s and '80s),
Steven Greer (Rockefeller funded UFO researcher),
Zecharia Sitchin.

As the reader can see, there is a loose sort of network emerging with some players figuring prominently. What is even more interesting is the fact that there is a link between the Axiom Faculty and something called the Sangraal School of Sacred Geometry.

Back to the past: There were a couple other interesting members of the Sarfatti discussion group: Ira Einhorn and Hank Harrison, father of grunge diva Courtney Love. Hank claims to be the world's expert on the Holy Grail, and he played an interesting part in the drama that year, but not to get ahead of myself, we will leave him for now.

Our own little discussion group was busily discussing the clues the Cs had given about the Grail Quest, a subject which bored Frank to tears, and on February 6 I found that there were several websites devoted to the subject of Rennes-le-Château. By following several links, I found myself on a page about "ancient wisdom." There was a semi-scholarly discussion group that was closed – you had to submit a sort of little résumé to be accepted – so I figured it would be better if I signed up both of us, which I did. A few days later, we were accepted for membership, and I had my first taste of a real Internet egroup.

Meanwhile, on Sarfatti's mail list, all the guys were just tearing poor Ira Einhorn apart. I didn't really know anything about him, or the crime he was accused of committing, or why he was hiding in France, but when he wrote a long explanation that he was set up to take the fall because he had learned "too much" from the insiders, I certainly knew that this was something that was easy enough for regular humans to engineer, not to mention hyperdimensional beings. I expressed these ideas briefly, and found myself having a private chat with the guy on the side. We will also come back to Ira in the next volume.

In mid March, Ark and I took the kids on a little vacation to the Pensacola UFO conference where we attended lectures by Whitley Strieber, Michael Lindemann, Lloyd Pye, and Linda Moulton Howe. We purchased copies of Howe's books, and I have described the events of this conference briefly in volume two of *The Wave*.

After the conference, when we were at home, I had a brief exchange with Lloyd Pye about his strange skull, and the possibility that it could be evidence of an alien presence on the planet. I was doubtful because it did sort of look like the skull of a hydrocephalic child. But I was most interested in any results he obtained by testing.

Right around this time, I received a threatening series of emails from one of the multiple personalities of the woman discussed in the Rep-toid-rape chapter of book two of *The Wave*, but she subsided rather quickly.

Now that I was turned on to this egroup discussion thing, I joined a couple of other lists, thinking that this was the correct way to network and share information. One of them was discussing the history of Atlantis, another was devoted to researching the Priory of Sion (or so they claimed, but really all they wanted to do was talk about drinking Merovingian blood – I unsubbed pretty quickly!).

Meanwhile, I was busiest on the Ancient Wisdom list. Well, it wasn't exactly what I thought it would be, but I found a few opportunities to share some of the Cs information there and to do it exactly the way the Cs had suggested – you know, "Here is what we received, make of it what you will." Of course, I was hoping that this would inspire others who might have pieces of the puzzle to contact me, and we could get down to business solving this problem of why things were the way they were, and what kind of a mess were we in, and how do we get out of it! Mostly, however, I got slammed for even daring to mention channeled material. It was definitely *not* welcome among academic discussions!

Nevertheless, quite a number of people from these various lists began to correspond with us privately, and it was getting to be just a regular circus!

At this point, I noticed that Nick Herbert was on the Sarfatti discussion list, and I thought that this was really synchronous. Back in 1985, when I was doing the research for the first version of *Noah*, I had read Herbert's book *Quantum Reality*. He seemed to be someone who might be able to answer my questions about Cosmic Metamorphosis, so I had written to him, and we exchanged several enlightening letters via snail mail. Several years later, due to my relationship with Keith Laumer, I had occasion to chat with a well-known fantasy writer whose books cover entire walls of book stores. We engaged in a long correspondence that covered all the years prior to, during, and after the Cassiopaean contact, right up to the time of my divorce, at which point I stopped answering his letters because I was just too depressed. Shortly after, Ark found me, and I was too busy to write. At the time of the Santilli session, I wrote to the fantasy author and shared this info with him, and a couple of physics questions came up in our debate. I decided that since Nick Herbert had been so kind as to answer my naïve questions several years before, that he might be a good one to ask to settle the hash. So, I dashed off a letter to him, mentioning the discussion I was having with the writer.

As it happened, Nick was a real fan of this writer, and he was more than happy to help with my questions if only I would help him get an autographed copy of a book to give as a gift! I was more than happy to introduce him to my writer friend, and they had a nice little correspondence, I assume.

So, here was Nick on Sarfatti's list. What a coincidence!

Well, Ark and I were both a bit curious about Jack Sarfatti and just exactly what this list was supposed to accomplish. I figured that Nick wouldn't BS me, and he sort of owed me a favor, so I wrote to him to ask for the inside scoop on Sarfatti, as well as to discuss some other interesting items that had come up in his remarks to the list. Nick wrote back:

On 18 Apr 99, at 16:50, nick herbert wrote:

First: I have been associated with Jack Sarfatti for a very long time. In my opinion he is a third-rate physicist with a tremendously overvalued sense of his own worth plus a lot of passion. He is indeed a con man but one that fervently believes in his own con – hence very persuasive to those who know little physics. I do not think that there is any deeper conspiracy behind him (Jack would like to think so). He is just a childish bozo – charming in short doses, boring after a while. I stay in touch with him because I am in love with novelty and he has sometimes turned me on to new paths I would not otherwise have traveled – including perhaps this one.

Second: thank you for your part in connecting me with [name deleted]. It enabled me to give one of my Muses a unique "magic" gift for her birthday.

Third: My basic general hunch about psychic experiences of the sort you mention is that the self and the environment are not as separate as we usually assume.

I have also had uncanny experiences where the (conventionally) "outside world" seemed to reflect what was going on "inside my mind". Jung writes about similar events under the name of "synchronicities" and by providing such a label perhaps encouraged us to pay more attention to the possibility of such self/other indistinguisabilities. A very good book on this topic (with lots of examples of synchronicities) is "Science, Synchronicy & Soul-Making" By Victor Mansfield.

Fourth: I believe that the really New Science of the 21th century will truly begin when we learn how to AMPLIFY the magnitude and extent of these accidental connections with nature. I call this new science Quantum Tantra and fancy myself its prophet much as Frances Bacon was a forerunner of Newtonian physics.

Fifth: I have not yet written a book on alchemy (tho I believe it features the same assumption as quantum tantra – that the chemist is not separated from the chemistry: are there reactions that only work if you pray?). Perhaps this book is waiting for us somewhere in the future.

Sixth: Some of my work is alluded to on my website. I will be giving a presentation of Quantum Tantra at Henry Dakin's Lab in San Francisco on May 25 Sponsored by the long-running Psychic Research Group. This work is so new and so far removed from conventional notions of science that I mostly keep to myself and my favorite Muse – the Pacific Ocean – trying not to contaminate my thinking with too many old notions.

Let's keep in touch. I'm sure we all have parts of the puzzle but I fear that a very large piece (or pieces) is still missing and at present NO ONE can make a coherent picture – let alone a science of what we know now.

At this point in time, I had finished reading Linda Howe's books, and there were several things in there that I shared with our little discussion group of which Blue was now a member:

Therein lies the rub: knowledge. The "Photon Belt Phiasco" is a prime example. Somebody came up with this idea and it spread like wildfire to channel after channel ... became all the rage, incorporated with the "Mass Landing" theory and the "Alien Rapture" hypothesis, then interwoven with Hale-Bopp ... resulting in a mass suicide as well as a HUGE amount of energy.

When I first read it a number of years ago, in a magazine ... all laid out in pseudo-scientific terms ... I nearly had a gag attack! I mean, if the folks promulgating the idea as well as the ones reading it, had a CLUE about what the intrinsic nature of a photon was, they would not have fallen for this one ... and NEVER MIND about all the "psychic technobabble" about these "special photons" and how the sources had to use terms that were "close" to something we poor ignorant humans could grasp or that were available in the vocabulary of the channel ... the whole thing was poppycock! I said so then, repeatedly, the Cs backed me up when they came along, and so far, the knowledge of what photons are and what they do has held up! I mean, don't these guys know that the earth is bombarded with TONS of photons every day ... it's called LIGHT ... and if there was an increase such as they suggested ... it would REALLY transform the planet ... to a CINDER!

But, on the other hand, on the low side of probabilities, maybe a photon belt DID hit and all the "good folks" WERE airlifted off the planet! Then, I guess we are all in trouble!

So, it is a VERY good idea to have an extensive knowledge base when dealing with this stuff ... BUT, there is a point at which even this sort of "runs out" because we are dealing with levels of reality about which we have no clue whatsoever. Many times the Cs have told me something that just completely and totally OFFENDED what I thought I knew ... I would be outraged with them! And then, some few months down the road, something would come out in "mainstream science," or some new author who had been working on a specific problem, or some work that I had not yet examined would come along verifying to the last comma everything they said. That sort of thing just gives you the "chills" and so forth.

I have to admit that I was completely offended by the idea of aliens "eating" human beings, either emotional energy-wise or literally ... but then, I came across research and documentation of at least a strong circumstantial kind that pretty much supported this.

Also, I was pretty hot on the Velikovsky ideas and I was pretty much unhappy that the Cs did not admire this theory as much as I did.

Most often, with channeled material, one finds that the answers are sort of "confirmations" of what the channel him or herself believe or WANT to hear ... But, in this instance, we can frankly say that the Cs don't seem to care much what we believe or want to hear. They don't coddle us ... but they DO become VERY VAGUE when a person is present or asks a question who is unable to bear the blunt truth. I did an analysis of the "vague" answers once and discovered that there was a direct relationship between the number of them and the personalities of the people present including their pre-formed belief systems.

So, the bottom line seems to be: if a person is EMOTIONALLY tied up with what they WANT to hear ... they are respected and will not be told anything that they cannot handle ...

There is SO MUCH GARBAGE out there ... and much of it is written to evoke and appeal to the emotions, and it is CLEAR that emotions are chemical. Yes, there ARE "soul" emotions, so to speak, but they are so radically different from what one experiences when "interfaced" with the body that there is almost no comparison.

And this is my idea ... to raise awareness of this "battle," so that people can be objective and non-anticipatory and be able to SEE CLEARLY without emotion, thereby reducing the amount of "food" the aliens can milk from us. Each one of us who wakes up and smells the coffee, so to speak, makes it that much easier for others ... Hundredth Monkey Syndrome and all that ... and THEN, there is the possibility of effecting a change. Cs repeatedly say that the future is "open." But, unless one knows what the present conditions are and where they can lead, probabilities and so forth, they have no hope whatsoever of contributing to a group effort to direct our future.

Linda Howe writes:

"An Air Force intelligence officer once told me about an elderly colleague, a Colonel, who supposedly spent time with an extraterrestrial biological entity retrieved from a crashed silver disc in New Mexico. The Colonel said the being explained telepathically that this is not the only universe. He said, 'Imagine a large island of white sand and that each sand grain is a different universe separated from the others by an electronic membrane. And surrounding the island is a cold, dark, sea.'

"I asked the intelligence officer what the dark sea was and he answered, 'You don't want to know. It would change you forever.'"

Now, this may seem "upsetting" to hear, but one has to consider the perspective of the "intelligence" conveying this information. If we take as a given what the Cs said about the STS perspective, that they "worship the physical universe," then we understand that the "cold dark sea" perceived by the being is "non-delimited consciousness," and, to them it IS SCARY! Unlimited creative potential! Pure Creative Consciousness. And this is how they view it ... as a "cold dark sea."

Col. Corso writes in *The Day After Roswell,* "These creatures weren't benevolent aliens who had come to enlighten human beings ... " Linda Howe asks, "What do other intelligences want from humans and our planet? One government agent told me his superiors hoped to be dead before the 'true story' erupted ... " (Howe, 2001) Then, she received a letter via an intermediary, purportedly from some DOD guys which said, in part:

"Our misguided program directors cling to the false belief that we can control or manipulate the [aliens], when in actuality, the reverse is occurring – we are the ones being manipulated and deceived.

" ... forces being utilized by [aliens] to interact with us in a bizarre, confusing manner, designed to divert us and draw our attention from the true purpose of their actions: manipulation and deception.

"People are now busy chasing 'secret-government' projects, satanic cults, and UFOs, while the actual perpetrating agents go unsuspected [i.e. beings from other densities].

"[There are those] within the government hierarchy who [have] convincingly fed [to Linda Howe] the false ET scenario propagated as disinformation by those who are in charge of the [alien] projects. Many variations of this exist, and all who are privy to a particular variation are convinced they have 'the answer.' With our society as it is now, the core truth of the situation is such that the public really could not handle it.

"The ultimate diversionary tactic to this point (and diversions will begin to increase in frequency, degree of strangeness, and in a more overt fashion, visible to greater numbers of observers) is the UFO abduction scenario.

"The concept of these events, real though they are, being the result of extraterrestrial beings, is a masterful piece of disinformation to divert attention away from the real source of the [aliens]. Our information as to the true nature of these events does not negate the possibility of extraterrestrial life, but, the causal source of the UFO and UFO abduction phenomena is NOT EXTRATERRESTRIAL.

"The aliens being dealt with in our psi "mind control" weapons development, and who are apparently allowing themselves to be used for a time, are neither benevolent nor neutral. It was our feeling that very few could understand this concept.

"Your comments and thoughts concerning ancient civilizations and their contacts with the [aliens] need to be considered in light of the bigger picture of the deception of mankind as a whole. If this grand deception is taking the course it seems to be, then it makes sense to analyze the false gods of ancient civilizations in light of the current level of deception. *It is only logical that, given their non-human, other-dimensional nature, the [aliens] would be able to foresee the need to establish a foundational base, the facts of which could be slightly twisted, or distorted by the fog of antiquity and forgotten cultural distinctiveness, to seemingly establish themselves as the bringers of all good things to humanity.*

"Explore Jacques Vallee's 'Passport to Magonia' again, for more close parallels between the 'faerie' manifestation of the [aliens] and current events. And look very closely at 'Messengers of Deception,' Dr. Vallee was so close to the truth of the situation, with the exception that the *ultimate manipulators are not human.*"

On the 4th of May, a fellow named Ray Flowers posted to the aforementioned Ancient Wisdom discussion list:

Alchemy, Fulcanelli and the Great Cross
A Monument to the End of Time reveals the truth behind the mystery of Fulcanelli: The alchemical transmutation of the soul and the most dramatic event in human history – the end of time as we know it. A Monument to the End of Time unveils the greatest alchemical secret of all – that history is an initiatory process. And the final stage of that initiation is about to occur.
Check out Vincent Bridges and Jay Weidner's new research from Southern France.
http://www.sangraal.com/AMET/index.html

Well! Talk about your major Doomsday pronouncement! I wandered over there and had a look. There was a whole lot of historical research, and I read through the ideas of the book and wrote back to the Ancient Wisdom list:

I wonder if this "new research" was in any way stimulated by the most interesting book "Refuge of the Apocalypse: Doorway Into Other Dimensions; Rennes-le-Château, The Key" by Elizabeth Van Buren ??? Certainly a MUST read for anyone "into" the R-L-C business.
This book begins with a discussion of the Cross of Hendaye …
"There is a small town in the Basque country of the Pyrenees called Hendaye. A stone cross stands there, displaying curious symbols which the famous alchemist Fulcanelli states relate to 'millenarianism.' This is the doctrine of belief in the millennium and the cataclysms that are preordained to precede it.

"On the transverse arm of the equi-armed cross is an inscription which consists of two lines of raised letters. These spell out words which are joined together: OCRUXAVES PESUNICA.

"If the 'S' at the end of the first line is taken as the first letter of the second line, the following phrase can be read: 'O CRUX AVE, SPES UNICA' 'HAIL, O CROSS, THE ONLY HOPE.'

"Fulcanelli points out that the rules of Latin grammar have been ignored, for 'pes' is masculine, and therefore requires the adjective 'unicus' which is the masculine, and not 'unica,' the feminine form of the word.

"Because of the misplaced 'S', the inscription can be read as a secret message. By reading the Latin words as phonetic French, and rearranging the words to form another sentence, the following strange statement is arrived at: 'IL EST ECRIT QUE LA VIE SE REFUGIE EN UNSEUL ESPACE' or 'IT IS WRITTEN THAT LIFE TAKES REFUGE IN A SINGLE SPACE.'

"Fulcanelli tells us that this message refers to a place of safety at the time of the terrible catastrophe, a Noah's Ark where death cannot touch one. He told the alchemist Canseliet, 'The time will come, my son, when you will no longer be able to work in alchemy, when it will be necessary for you to search for some country rare and blessed, privileged without doubt, and situated towards the south, beyond the frontiers.' To others, Fulcanelli indicated that the place was Rennes, in the Aude.

" ... Fulcanelli points out that the letter 'S' which has been misplaced, corresponds to the Greek khi (key) (X) and has the same meaning esoterically. Is this the 'key' to the mystery? Can we read the message as 'Spes unice,' or the 'key' is the one-and-only (feminine) foot? Does the 'X' symbolize this 'foot?'" (Van Buren)

I think that it is interesting to note that the name "Plantangenet" is derived from a root meaning "foot" ... and "platter" is similarly related ... the "foundation" of a thing connected to "gene" which goes to the same root from which we get yoga, yogi, joint, jugular, conjugal, knee, and even knight ... the "Desired Knight" of the Grail Stories, Perceval.

And, if no one has ever noticed it, in the Shepherds of Arcadia, there is a rather prominent display of knees and elbows ... JOINTS.

Martha Neyman says that the shadow of the arm on the tomb, when looked at upside down, is the image of a horse ... but it also looks like a heart when taken WITH the arm itself ... but either view is interesting.

It is also interesting that the legends surrounding the origins of the Plantagenets are almost identical to the legends of the Merovingians ...

Merovee is an interesting word in itself ... going back to Mer which can mean both Sea and Horse ...

So, I guess I shall order this book and see what these guys have to say.

Laura

On May 7th, I received an email from one of the guys doing the above mentioned book, Vincent Bridges:

Date sent: Fri, 7 May 1999 11:49:03 -0500
Subject: RE: Hendaye

Dear Laura,

What a nice comment on our AMET website, and so perceptive too!

Yes, we are aware of E. Van Buren's fascinating book, and, as you supposed, are deep into the RLC thing. However, our starting point was Fulcanelli's book *Le Mystere des Cathedrals* and his chapter on the Cyclic Cross of Hendaye, which EVB quotes at great length in her preface to *Refuge*. In fact, EVB does little but quote Fulcanelli, giving only one piece of new information. "He told the alchemist Canseliet, 'The time will come, my son, when you will no longer be able to work in alchemy, when it will be necessary for you to search for some country rare and blessed, privileged without doubt, and situated towards the south, beyond the frontiers.' To others, Fulcanelli indicated that the place was Rennes, in the Aude."

You just don't know the anguish that little teaser has caused us in the past year or so. The problem is that Canseliet, as far as we can determine, never said that in print, so it must be a private conversation between EVB and Canseliet. When and how did they know each other? And who could the "others" be to whom Fulcanelli identified Rennes in the Aude as the refuge? Did EVB know Fulcanelli?

There is of course nothing else in the text of *Refuge* to indicate that EVB understood the monument at Hendaye or its symbolism in any direct way. But whoever told her about it and gave her the information on the Serpent Rouge and the Rennes zodiac certainly did. But why put the information in such a distorted form, why the insistence on Rennes?

Frankly, none of it made any sense. I had been working on RLC for a long time before the Fulcanelli stuff came along. I was interested in King Rene as far back as Grad school in the mid seventies; I thought he was the prime candidate for the author of the classic tarot deck. Still do, even more so with 25 years of research behind me. But EVB and the Fulcanelli connection threw everything that I thought I knew about RLC into a whole new perspective. (Lest ye doubt that I am indeed an RLC freak, let me just note that I own a piece of the original church, circa Bigou's reconstruction.)

So we knew that RLC was important and connected somehow to Fulcanelli and Hendaye, we just didn't know how, exactly. Then another friend, Bill Buehler out in Crestone CO showed me a piece of landscape geometry linking Hendaye, RLC, St. James de Campostella and Edinbourgh Castle in a big T. Hendaye was at the cross point of that T. Wow, things began to click after that.

See, Hendaye is like the loose thread in the Kmart tapestry of history. Keep tugging on it long enough and the whole damn thing unravels right before your eyes. We had already unraveled the astro-alchemical secrets of the Cross, but suddenly there was another whole pattern coming into view. We had always joked about the Cross being the Holy Grail, we just didn't know how close we were to the truth.

On the base of the Cross are four images, reading from west around to north, the sun, the 4 A's, the eight-rayed star and the moon-boat. We found that they also pointed to four locations in southern France directly connected to the true history of the grail family. By simply locating these spots, the story unfolds, if you know what to look for. Going back to Fulcanelli, we found a very sly series of references that supported our theory, and strangely enough, led us directly to Michel Nostradamus, the Seer of Provence, and that renaissance genius, Leonardo di Vinci.

So with the Fulcanelli book 90% done in first draft, we headed out to France to find some answers. The result is our second book, which I am working away on while my co-author, Jay Weidner, is finishing the final draft of the first book.

Without going into the whole story, here is what we feel the truth is about RLC.

Let's work backward. What did Saunier find? He found conclusive proof of the survival of a group of early Christians related to the Holy family whose Christ was another St. John, the son of Mary Magdalene and Jesus. This information had been passed to local families in the early fourth century CE when the refugees from the Jewish Christian province of Glanum Livii arrived in the Aude. Glanum Livii is the Blue Fruit, or Blue Apples of the cypher, and the Mort epee is also a pointer to Glanum through the Black Sword of Tristan and Jason the Argonaut. Glanum, of course, turned out to be the home town of Nostradamus, who alludes to his ancient bloodline in several quatrains.

Why did this make Saunier rich? There seems to have been an ancient treasure, perhaps the gold of the Visigoths or the Merovingians, because Saunier did antiquities deals all over Paris. This supplied some money, but most seems to have come from the Hapsburg-Lorraine heirs, who interestingly enough, would have the best claim to descent from any Provencal connection through King Rene. In the wake of WWI, everything fell apart, until some group in the 1950's revived the mystery of RLC as a way of revealing or deflecting attention from the bigger picture.

Sigisbert IV did return to Rennes and probably was the lost Merovingian heir, so that part of the story is true. We also know that the legend had currency in the Middle Ages, hence Godfrey de Boullion and the Grail legends, but exactly how it all relates together is a carefully obstructed mystery.

But, your guess about the Plantegenets is right on the money. Your word play would make you right at home with Fulcanelli, that old master of the Green Language. The Plantegenet's rise to power was aided by unseen political forces that correspond to the early Priory of Our Lady of Sion, the precursor to the Templar Priory, founded by Pope Sylvestor II and the mad Caliph Hakim in Jerusalem in 1002. Henry II was a Templar, in the sense of Wolfram's Parsival, that is a man of unknown, or at least unspoken, heritage who ruled through a combination of modern power and ancient right. Henry's interest in the legends of King Arthur is no accident, but an attempt to legitimize and [sic] ancient heritage that was essentially heretical. No wonder their origins, Merovingian and Plantegenet are so similar. They were clues for those in the know as to the true heritage of these kings.

But enough obscure medieval history. If you really want to figure this out, I would suggest that, while waiting on our second volume, you find a good translation of Wolfram von Eschenbach's *Parsival* and read it through a few times. Then take a map of southern France and map out the places he mentions, taking him at his word about time and distances, and you will find that whoever Guy of Provence was, he truly knew the story of the Grail. It's all there, and the story itself turns out to be somewhat true and datable to the ninth century.

Well, I've probably confused you worse by trying to hint and condense things. Sorry, I am working on the complete version and I hate to give to much away to soon. But I found your e-mail interesting in that I haven't found to many folks who have even heard of Hendaye, much less make such provocative connections.

Stay tuned to the website. We will be putting more stuff up from time to time and will be announcing the first book in June for a July ship date. Hope you like it, and if you want to chat further on this, just e-mail back.

Thanks

Vincent Bridges

Wow! Was I ever excited! Thank God! At last there is someone who isn't a whacko, someone who could answer all my questions! Somebody who was not only a scholar (must be a scholar, he went to grad school!), but open-minded! Somebody who had done all that research posted on the Sangraal site! I'd better get back over there quick and download all of it and study it!

And so I did. Every scrap, every word, printed and bound in a cover, sitting there on the bookshelf, a monument to my wish that somebody would come along and give me the answers.

Life gives back to you exactly what you put into it.

There is no free lunch.

CHAPTER 54
GLIMPSES OF OTHER REALITIES

Now, just to keep the sequence of events fresh in the readers mind, Vincent Bridges first wrote to me in May of 1999, after one of my posts to the Ancient Wisdom list had been forwarded to him by Ray Flowers of SanGraal.com, a website connected to the Axiom Visiting Faculty, which lists Drunvalo Melchizidek and a few others who can be shown to have links – even if nebulous – to the Aviary. The Aviary was a subject of investigation by Blue, who was on Sarfatti's email group. Blue introduced us to Sarfatti in late 1998, and Ark joined this discussion in February of 1999. Now, remember the strange invitation to the January 1997 conference at the Central European University in Budapest that I have already described in an earlier chapter? Remember the funny event I described where Ark's documents were stolen, and returned under such a bizarre circumstances?

Well, the reader may wish to do some research into something called the United Religions Initiative (URI). This is a project funded by the same Foundations that have been intimately involved with the funding of the CEU in Budapest. Barbara Marx Hubbard, a "futurist," is one of their spokespersons, making many appearances at New Age-type events. In addition to being a member of the Axiom Visiting Faculty, she has a lot of other interesting connections, as we later discovered. For the past couple of months, several members of the egroup have been researching pretty heavily into these areas, and as we go along, we hope that we will be able to present some of their findings. But just now, the atmosphere is pretty heavy, and we feel the hot breath of something rather vicious breathing on our heels.

The very act of writing these pages, exposing these connections, puts our work, our website, and perhaps even our lives, in grave peril. At the present moment, the attacks have escalated, both in the psychic spheres, as well as from the agents of the Matrix through various avenues, including financial institutions.

To understand what we're dealing with here, let me tell you what happened to Blue. Blue was a really tough skeptic, and gleefully tore just about everything and everybody apart, but for some reason, he really loved the Cs and would call to ask a question now and again during a session. His skepticism prevented him from following a couple of pieces of very sharp advice from the Cs and he was ultimately taken out. And I do mean that literally. The dissolution of his marriage and loss of everything he held dear seems, in retrospect, to have been arranged and then, a love bite situation seems to have been set up to entrap him on the rebound, in his misery. This woman who "gave him tea and comfort" during a terrible time also gave him heroin.

In June of 2002, he sent me an email with an attached photograph showing him in a condition that was absolutely shocking. He was totally skeletal. At that point, he was in a halfway house, I believe, but he was later incarcerated and his great work came to an end.

Getting back to the story, at the point in time I am describing, none of the connections that are now apparent were part of our awareness. We had a vague understanding of fourth-density manipulations, and how agents could be activated and used, but we were actually pretty naive about it. I would like to call the readers attention back to the email I wrote to our own little discussion group which, at the time, consisted of only about a dozen members – not even large enough to run it on a regular egroup list. The part I would like to emphasize is the letter I quoted from Linda Moulton Howe's book, *Glimpses of Other Realities*:

> "Your comments and thoughts concerning ancient civilizations and their contacts with the [aliens] need to be considered in light of the bigger picture of the deception of mankind as a whole. If this grand deception is taking the course it seems to be, then it makes sense to analyze the false gods of ancient civilizations in light of the current level of deception. *It is only logical that, given their non-human, other-dimensional nature, the [aliens] would be able to foresee the need to establish a foundational base, the facts of which could be slightly twisted, or distorted by the fog of antiquity and forgotten cultural distinctiveness, to seemingly establish themselves as the bringers of all good things to humanity.*
>
> "Explore Jacques Vallee's 'Passport to Magonia' again, for more close parallels between the 'faerie' manifestation of the [aliens] and current events. And look very closely at 'Messengers of Deception,' Dr. Vallee was so close to the truth of the situation, with the exception that the *ultimate manipulators are not human.*"

And that was precisely what the Cassiopaeans were telling us, though they were giving details of this other reality that we had never before encountered. There were, of course, researchers who had come to very similar conclusions, as we were later to discover, but somehow they never quite made it to the idea of a realm of para-physical existence that was capable of *both physical and ethereal manipulation of consciousness.* This is the *real* Stargate Conspiracy.

What about Lizzies, or Reptilian type beings? When we search through the transcripts, we discover that this term first appears on September 30, 1994, *after* we had read Barbara Marciniak's book *Bringers of the Dawn.* It was introduced by me as a sort of test question. I decided to use it to discover if the Cs would confirm or deny it as a reality. But, the fact was, I had met Reptilian types even before this – before reading *Bringers of the Dawn.*

In a hypnosis session with an abductee on August 3, 1994, the subject was describing her experiences during an abduction that had started out with the standard Gray aliens, but after she was taken to the place of examination, things began to get just a bit stranger:

Q: Is there anybody there with you?

A: Um-hmm.

Q: How many?

A: Oh God, this is weird. [sigh] It's almost like I see a dinosaur or something. With little short arms … and it's, um … it's got funny skin … it's like, it's like … brownish, slickish … it's got a real funny face … it's like a skull but the front of the skull is like going out, real far out …

Q: Like a snout?

A: Yeah. […] It's gone now …

Q: How tall was it?

A: Um …

Q: Taller than you?

A: Oh yeah, it looked bigger than me. It's just funny.

Q: What's funny?

A: Nothing, it's gone.

Q: Where did it go.

A: I don't know. It disappeared.

Q: What do you mean it disappeared?

A: I don't know, it's almost like an image. And then it just vanished.

Q: How many other beings are there with you?

A: Um … they're all busy all over.

Q: About how many are there?

A: Um … five or six.

Q: What do they look like? Do they all look the same?

A: Oh, they're funny looking … they're almost like, um … they remind me of the baby dinosaur … how puffy his face was with the eyes were like … smaller … not big eyes like him … like squinty eyes …

Q: What color are their eyes?

A: Um … I don't know … when I look at their eyes I see a green circle that keeps swirling …

This same glimpse of dinosaur- or reptilian-type beings in the background, who obviously went to great lengths to conceal their presence in abduction scenarios, was to occur a number of other times. I realized that there was something behind the Grays, that there was a higher level of authority, and it was hiding itself to a great extent. I went on a search for information about this matter, calling everyone I knew who had done any research in UFOs and abductions, asking for information about the dinosaur-type creatures. Apparently, I wasn't the only one with clues about their existence, and there were other cases here and there that had described these critters long before Barbara Marciniak wrote her book of messages from Pleiadians.

And, so it was that, after reading Marciniak, even if I was not convinced of the way the Reptilian beings had been presented there, I certainly thought that "Lizzie" was a handy moniker for referring to what most certainly could have been terrifying creatures.

But, as noted, I had been reading a lot of literature that suggested that the Reptilian-type creatures were just a product of *our* perception, that had been foisted on us by ethereal beings, and that so-called aliens were strictly an ethereal manifestation of demonic-type beings. Many researchers write about them this way, and they write about prayers or rituals that can cast them out or banish them, none of which makes any sense if these beings are real in some sort of biophysical sense. I had, as the Cs pointed out, been drifting toward this ethereal-only understanding, and that is when the Cs pulled me up short to declare that there was, indeed, a real nuts-and-bolts aspect to this matter.

December 19, 1998

Q: If, at fourth density, there is variability of physicality, and the Lizzies, as you have previously said, are engineering new bodies for themselves to occupy in some sort of mass transition at the time of this realm-border crossing; in this state of variability of physicality, why do they need to engineer new bodies for themselves? Why, in point of fact, are Lizzies, Lizzies?

A: Too many questions.

Q: Why do they look like Lizards?

A: They do not.

Q: Well, why do we call them Lizard Beings? I mean, *you* named them that?

A: We label in accordance with your familiarity. If we had called them "Drachomonoids," what would be your point of reference??

Q: What do they *really* look like?

A: You can figure as needed.

Q: You said they resemble upright alligators with humanoid features, six to eight feet tall ...

A: Yes.

Q: So, why do they look like that?

A: Biology.

Q: Does biology exist at fourth density?

A: Yes.

Q: Yet, it's a variable physical density, right?

A: Yes, but what is your assumption here?

Q: I don't know what my assumption is. I guess that I am assuming that if it is a variable state, they could have a different biology very easily. Isn't that the case?

A: No.

Q: Can they appear as something else? Change their physicality?

A: Temporarily.

Q: When you say "temporary," what exactly do you mean? Temporal relates to time.

A: We have explained before that the biggest single factor regarding densities is the awareness level.

Q: The awareness level. OK, how does that relate to them only being able to temporarily change their appearance? Is this because they can control *our* awareness?

A: Closer. Are you not yet aware that absolutely everything, we repeat: everything is an illusion?!?

Q: At some level, yes. So, still I ask, why, in the illusion in which we exist, or in which they exist … (A) They say here that everything is an illusion, and on the other hand they say there is consciousness and matter. Everything is an illusion? Even this?

A: Yes.

Q: (A) God is also an illusion?

A: Yes.

Q: (A) Illusion to whom?

A: To those not on level 7. Your learning naturally dictates your experiences. Once you no longer require something, you naturally move beyond it. However, you retain it as a function of understanding.

Q: (A) And I am also an illusion! And understanding is also an illusion! (L) Back to my question: who created Lizzies *as Lizzies?* (A) Our illusion …

A: Everything is real, therefore, illusion is reality.

So, there they were: Drachomonoid beings, similar to the creatures of Arthur Clarke's *Childhood's End*. There they were, the scaley or fish gods of the ancient civilizations. And there was an "insider" telling Linda Moulton Howe that "ancient civilizations and their contacts with the [aliens] need to be considered in light of the bigger picture of the deception of mankind as a whole." This man was telling her almost exactly what the Cs were telling us: that the gods of the ancient civilizations were false gods, that the aliens, or, more precisely, ultra-terrestrials, having time-travel capabilities, had established our religions as the foundational basis for a grand deception, a takeover of humanity, that was scheduled to be finalized in the not-too-distant future. Linda Howe had written, "One government agent told me his superiors hoped to be dead before the 'true story' erupted … "

Meanwhile, Linda Howe's informant told her that there are egotistical groups among our leaders who continue to wishfully think that they can control or manipulate the so-called aliens, when in fact, the opposite is what is really taking place. The Cs had stated precisely the same thing. The Cs had made it absolutely clear the there were forces of which we were completely unaware, and that these forces were being utilized in a "bizarre, confusing manner, designed to divert us and draw our attention from the true purpose of their actions: manipulation and deception." What is more, the Cassiopaeans had also made it absolutely clear in their remarks about Vincent Bridges that the theories he was propagating – whether deliberately or simply because he hadn't fully grasped the nature of the phenomenon – were part of the deception. This, too, was confirmed by Linda Howe's informant when he stated, "People are now busy chasing 'secret-government' projects, satanic cults, and UFOs, *while the actual perpetrating agents go unsuspected.*"

At the present time, of course, we realize clearly why we have experienced so much disruption and attack from so many sources, including the Williams/Bridges gang with their nebulous connections to the same groups that are known to promote disinformation. It is because we are regularly and repeatedly pointing out that aliens are not extraterrestrials in the sense that it is normally understood, and we are focusing on the hyperdimensional nature of the phenomenon as a *real* reality that has nothing to do with demons in any ethereal sense of the word. We are pointing out, again and again, the main problem in research into these matters is that there are those in the government hierarchy who are convincingly propagating false ET scenarios. In addition to the satanic-cult and government-mind-control projects variations, actively and vociferously promoted by Vincent Bridges *et al.*, there are many others, *all designed to conceal the actual perpetrating agents and deceive the public.* And, of course, as noted, the ultimate diversion is the UFO abduction scenario.

Indeed, abductions are taking place. And the Cassiopaeans have given much information about these events, all of which suggest that aliens-as-extraterrestrials is extremely misleading.

And so it was that, with a growing awareness of the deceptive nature of not only our religions being created as foundations for some sort of takeover at some point in the future, I was beginning to realize that such things as the purported *Holy Blood, Holy Grail* secrets of Rennes-le-Château were part of this very disinformation process. How else was it possible to explain the synchronous way such a story took the world by storm? How else to explain why the obviously manufactured scenario of some sort of search for the Ark of the Covenant or the Holy Grail focused on this little French village had become the object of such frenzied speculation? It was clear that it was part of the project designed to lay the foundation for something else ...

At the point in time that Vincent Bridges wrote to me, declaring himself the expert on the subject, I was utterly ecstatic to have someone to talk to about Rennes-le-Château; someone who was approaching the matter in a scholarly way, was a certified open-minded academic, author of an upcoming book on the subject, and who had responded so positively to the little clues I had put on the Ancient Wisdom egroup discussion list. I have assembled the correspondence through the next few months on the subject into separate files[18] for the perusal of the interested reader.

When I was first introduced to this Rennes-le-Château business by RC in the fall of 1995 – though I didn't dig into it a great deal until later – I didn't realize what an impact it was going to have on my life. But, after the strange events of 1996 when I was so focused on the idea of an enclave of alchemists in the Pyrenees, the relationship of alchemy to the Oak Island Mystery and time travel, antigravity, and the "Shepherds of Arcadia," at which point Ark found me (keeping in mind that he had the image of Magritte's "Le Chateau des Pyrenees" on his website, the name Arkadiusz, and the connection of gravity waves), I sat up and paid attention. I ordered every book on the subject that I could find.

After the later strange things that emerged at the time of the Hale Bopp Flopp that turned into a mass suicide, including the bizarre increase in visitors to our little webpage, the connection between Brana and Bran and the Holy Grail, the DNA issues, the genetics research organizations, a strange connection with someone or something at Boeing coming to our site repeatedly, I also began to order and read everything on the subject of the Holy Grail that I could get my hands on.

As I have written elsewhere, like just about everybody, I enjoyed stories about knights in shining armor rescuing damsels in distress, King Arthur, and that sort of thing, as much as the next person – when I had been very young. But as I became an adult, I consigned all those things to the realm of myth and fairy tales, and had thought very little about it in the intervening years.

---

[18] http://cassiopaea-cult.com/the-bridges---jadczyk-correspondence-part-1

I had also done some research in alchemy, scrutinizing alchemical texts, but had come to the conclusion that it was just a bunch of guys who were dreaming about transmuting lead into gold, and they kept everybody going with their mysterious instructions that sounded more like the ravings of lunatics than anything else.

Now, for some reason, through the remarks of the Cassiopaeans, I was being encouraged, led, nudged, or whatever, to connect all these dots together. So, from early 1996, literally right up to the present moment, I was digging through massive amounts of research, catching up with scholars who had studied these matters all their lives rather quickly, and then leaving many of them in the dust due to the fact that the Cs were giving me clues.

To the reader who is not familiar with these subjects, much of the Cassiopaean material will make no sense at all since many of my questions are related to this mystery. The reader familiar with alchemy will be interested to note the many alchemical suggestions in relation to our mission, whatever it turns out to be:

> August 31, 1996
>
> We have helped you build your staircase one step at a time. Because you asked for it. And you asked for it because it was your destiny. We have put you in contact with those of rare ability in order for you to be able to communicate with us. Again, because you desired it, in order to realize your path. By now, you should recognize the signs ... Those who display thinking patterns which in many ways deviate from that which is considered ordinary. The more unusual, the more telling. They have past lives on 3rd density earth, but not recently, but for this one. And they are not oriented to the earth frequency vibrations.

The staircase is an alchemical symbol. And it was to be brought up a time or two again, even in the symbolism of Jack and the Beanstalk, a ladder to heaven if ever there was one!

I, of course, assumed that the Cs meant Frank when they said "we have put you in contact with those of rare ability in order for you to be able to communicate with us." But the Cs not only did *not* confirm that assumption, they suggested quite otherwise.

> Q: (L) Are we not talking about Frank in terms of being put in contact with someone who enables me to communicate with you, so you can put me on my path, which is building the staircase, etc., etc.? Is that not what we've got going here?
> A: He is one, but not the only one, just the one who awakened your sense of recognition.

In fact, it almost seems that they were suggesting that Terry was more important because, as was later revealed, without Terry's presence, according to the Cs, Frank would have soon killed me with his draining. Considering the fact that the further remarks of this session related to being "hand in hand" with Ark, and that this was just a little over a month after Ark found me, it is pretty obvious that the Cs were also referring to him. In other words, the fullest communication would only occur with myself and Ark at the board. And that has proven to be stunningly correct as the reader will see when we present material from the more recent sessions in this series.

In the course of my searching of libraries and bookstores and the Internet for every scrap of information I could find on the subject of Rennes-le-Château, I came across a book entitled *The Horse of God,* by a Ms. Martha Neyman, a lady living in Belgium, who had devoted herself to the Rennes-le-Château mystery. She was so dedicated to it that she was even spending all her vacations there, and making friends with the residents so that they revealed to her things that might not be revealed to other people. Naturally, I was pretty excited, and inquired about her book right away. I discovered that it was only available on CD and that I would have to print it myself if I didn't want to read it online. I sent off the money to Belgium, and a short time later, the CD arrived. In the meantime, we had kept up a lively chat by email, and I restrained myself from asking questions about the material in the book until I had a chance to read it.

All of this was in the late fall of 1998, and I only bring it up now because immediately after Vincent Bridges wrote to me, I decided that the clearest way I could explicate the development of my views on the subject of Rennes-le-Château would be to forward what I called the "Neyman Letters" to him. I figured this would save both of us time. If he thought my ideas were nuts, as Martha Neyman had, then there would simply be no further reason to discuss the matter. On the other hand, if he read the Neyman letters and thought what I had written was worth discussing, then on with the show!

So, here are the Neyman letters in order:

To Martha Neyman

Date sent: Tue, 3 Nov 1998 12:43:56 -0500

Dear Martha,

The CD arrived yesterday, but I didn't get it until this morning and it is still printing. I was reading as I was printing and am well through the first section and have sort of scanned through the other sections.

Having spent so many years studying mythology, symbolism, comparative religion, ancient history (particularly of the Celts and the Arabs because there IS a connection between these "sons of Hagar" and the "refugees from Troy"), philology and semiotics, I can appreciate all the work you have done.

But, for me, the most significant is the fact that you have gone about and observed things and noted them down. This is important, as you know, because one must go "in the field" to get the feel.

I realized a long time ago that this Rennes-le-Château "business" was an "engineered" archetype. Those who have played parts in it have done so for reasons, though, most often, they did not even realize that they were being manipulated to say and do what they did by the "hidden superiors." And, make no mistake about it, these beings DO exist and all the events of our lives and world are "managed" by them from behind the scenes. They create and destroy "secret societies" at will, including Templars, Priory of Sion, Masons, Rosicrucians, etc. These are all "covers" and "smoke screens." And, they have existed, in a continuous line, for many thousands of years.

For this reason, the sequence of events that you have so rationally described, regarding the main players in this "drama" is most important to me. It fit with some of my own assessments which I had already made about Saunier and Boudet and Bigou.

There is a "rule" of espionage which goes: observe the facts, ONLY the facts, and extrapolate backwards to discover WHO benefits from a given situation, and this will give you the key to the underlying truth.

Well, I have been doing this about the events of history and geography for most of my adult life. The world, in its broadest sense, is a projection, if you will, similar to the shadows on Plato's cave. We cannot know fully the origins of these "shadow" images unless we can overcome our fascination with the moving patterns and leave the cave. But, doing that implies that we must first be aware that we CAN leave the cave …

As I said, this business is an "engineered archetype." Rather, it is a holographic projection of a much larger drama. But, figuring out the small scale mystery is the key to projecting the template onto a larger landscape. It does not end, or even begin, in Southern France.

Now, there are certain "key points" on the planet which I have discovered … with strange names and numbers … and "temple" characteristics (in the original sense of the word) that are, apparently, veiled from the awareness of others thus far. There are symbolic and semiotic and philological connections of a substrata of "events" that stagger the mind.

The one thing that few people think about is "WHO IS DOING ALL THIS?" And, connected to this is: what are their capabilities? And this is most important. If I, for one instant, underestimate the capabilities of "them," I will surely be devoured.

It is in this lack of realization of who holds the secrets and the intellect behind it that causes most people to stumble and fall in their analysis.

And since I am convinced it is an EPOCHAL secret which involves the history of mankind, the moving and changing of large masses of energy on the planet itself, then I HAVE to think about the "figures" behind such a thing.

One example I will mention … you remember what you wrote about St. Anthony's day … January 17 … and the number nine … and all that. It is reasonable based on *what is available* … but there are meanings even older than that ... and they pop up in Mayan constructs ... I was in Mexico last year and came across a figure carved in what was once a bas relief of a Mayan temple ... It was a figure of a man with the flesh removed from his thighs and skull ... but with the rest of his body intact ... and his legs were crossed ... I have an excellent photo of it which I have shared with a few people. I'm sure you recognize the symbol ...

And there is the ancient cult of Janus – guardian of the door – to whom January 17 was sacred ... and there was the celebration of St. Augustine on the same day ... and there is the hermit in the grail stories ... whose hero is Perceval ... "he who pierces the valley," or "mummy with the long member," or "pour suivant ... " and so on; take your pick.

Well, let me get back to having a look at this business.

Laura

After reading Martha's book, which began in so promising a way, I was depressed to discover that she had fallen into the same trap as every other researcher. She was certain that she had discovered something new, but so were all of the other researchers who had written books on the subject. They would arrive on the scene, full of the information they had collected from the written sources, they had a theory, and yep – sure enough – their theory would be confirmed by amazing new discoveries. Over and over again this scenario played out, in book after book, with each investigator certain that his was the answer to end all answers. I immediately recognized the high strangeness factor of the UFO/alien abduction phenomenon. There was hyperdimensional manipulation going on here, for sure. And a careful reading of Henry Lincoln's book, *The Key to the Sacred Pattern*, will reveal this most clearly.

Seeing that Martha had done the same thing, that she had used the same types of sources, that she had been led through a series of hyperdimensional hoops, I didn't really know how to tell her that I could instantly see that she had been manipulated by those time-traveling, mind-marauding controllers of our reality. I didn't want to rain on her parade, and I knew that it would be almost impossible for me to discuss it with her because, like everyone else who is hot on the trail of a bunch of synchronicities, there is nothing you can tell them that will convince them that they *might* be being manipulated by hyperdimensional forces. It's a damned unpleasant thought for anyone, much less someone who hasn't probed into the belly of the beast.

But Martha wrote again and asked, and I tried to break it to her gently:

To: Martha Neyman

On 24 Nov 98, at 17:33, Martha Neyman wrote:

> *I never heard from you again, I hope everything is fine ... ?*

Yes. Thank you for asking. We are preparing for the big "Thanksgiving" holiday ... second only to Christmas in its excessive consumption of calories and fat! I have a 22 pound turkey in my refrigerator and stacks of ingredients for pies and cakes ... ready for the baking tomorrow. I swore I wasn't going to do this anymore, but the children would be devastated if I didn't. Ark is happy to eat yogurt and be done with it ... and I don't need anything at all except to stop eating for about a year ...

> *By now you might have finished reading my book, I think ...*

Yes. And lots of marginal notes ...

> *As you are so well experienced in the subject of symbolism and know so much more then I do, I would appreciate it very much if you could let me have your opinion ...*

I am impressed with what you have done, having started with more or less a blank screen. You have had the unique advantage of "being there," which I have not ... but, yes, there is a LOT I would like to discuss and I have been debating how open you would be to this "putting two heads together" on the subject. I know that I am like a mother about anything I write and very sensitive to what might be construed as "criticism," so I have not wanted to say anything that would be offensive. But, at the same time, you are THERE and can answer some questions I have and I think that there are some things that need further work.

> *How is the weather in your country ... ? Here in Belgium temperature is minus 13° centigrade ... However that was not too bad, because the sun was shining and the cold itself was not unpleasant ... But the weather is changing tomorrow, rain is expected and the streets will turn into skating-rinks ... We stay indoors, that is much safer I think and in any case good for a whole day of writing ...*

My husband has been invited to Brussels by some company that is probably connected to NATO ... they want to pay expenses and all that ... we don't yet know how we will respond. As he says, it makes the drama of our life a little more interesting even if we don't follow the "script."

If you are ready to have a little dialogue about this "Rennes etc." business, well, tell me. What I want to do is something like what my husband does ... you get a theory, you build the structure, you see how it behaves as a "working hypothesis," and if there are problems, you tear it apart and start over. That sort of thing is what he does. He will have an idea, spend weeks on page after page of mathematical calculations and then hit a brick wall and have to start all over again.

We sat up one night and analyzed, in a sort of "hard science" way the evidence of the "phenomenon" of Rennes ... it was an interesting exercise with interesting "conclusions." I was thinking at the time that it was too bad you weren't with us as there were a lot of questions we had no answers to because we did not have the opportunity for personal investigation or observation.

I will say that some of the things you have found are fascinating and I am convinced that there is some purpose and reason, and maybe even your ultimate conclusions are correct – or pretty close ... but there are some big gaps in the symbolic appreciation and historical background of same. This is something of a specialty of mine. I have spent so much time buried in these "old times" that I can "shift" into them and think like them.

And, there is also what I call my "Grail File," which consists of all the remarks and clues given via channeling on this specific subject. It was pretty astonishing that, just a few days before your CD arrived, I had been pressing the subject and was given some information that was right there on your pages ... I nearly dropped my teeth! though I don't think you were aware of the significance of certain things you found ... you were focused in another direction!

So, the result is that I am convinced, like you, that there is some great mystery to be solved ... but I am not as sure as you are that your answers are the "right ones." There are many things to be gone over in a sort of "cold" and analytical way – even including this business of "synchronicity" that we both have experienced in this matter.

This "amazing" confluence of "clues and artifacts" tends to convince us that our ideas are correct ... but I have found that, often, the matter is much more complicated – like a chess game. Some of these "synchronous" events are like a move on the chess board by these "unknowns" and they are waiting to see if we will see through the ruse ... We can either make the mistake of "falling into the trap" of taking the piece "offered" while we are being set up for a swift and stunning mate.

NEVER underestimate the cleverness and cunning of the opponent.

Your ideas are framed in much the same terms as the guys who wrote the Holy Grail series and the guy who wrote the Tomb of God ... in the sense that all sorts of "synchronous" and "amazing" correspondences were found in response to the various ideas had by all. This should be taken as a warning that it can occur to just about anybody. All of you were convinced that you were "on the right track" because of these things ... don't forget that. They, as sincerely as yourself, were convinced of the "rightness" of their "path" and conclusions because of the SAME TYPES OF REMARKABLE SYNCHRONICITIES!!!!

And, for an "outsider" who has not been there ... one is left with a welter of "confusing" and contradictory ideas.

So, this is why I think that it is at this point that all must be torn apart and looked at with a somewhat different and more "playful" idea. Remember – NEVER FORGET – that the opponent wants us to come to false conclusions ... And never forget that he/they are so much more clever and practiced at this deception that we can even imagine. This is NOT a secret of a couple hundred years duration. It is THOUSANDS of years old ...

Anyway, enough of this rambling. If you like, if you are prepared to play with it, to tear it apart with me for the sake of possibly solving it ... admitting in the beginning that your solution may turn out to be correct or not ... but maybe for different reasons ... then maybe there is some hope of solving it. With material results.

Do you want to begin?

Laura

After I had sent the above, I realized that I really needed to be more open about what was on my mind. I didn't want to have the poor woman thinking I was critical of her writing, which was not the case.

To: Martha Neyman

Date sent: Tue, 24 Nov 1998 22:03:37 -0500

Dear Martha,

Perhaps it will give you a better idea of how I am thinking if I address some of your book before you decide if you want to "discuss" it.

Remember, this is all "thinking out loud," so to speak, or on paper. It is just a "scenario" to be tried and tested. I don't pretend that it is the "bottom line." So, here goes:

On page 4 you talk about the BBC documentary where the media, which had once "touted" the "mystery," now has pretty much squashed it. You ask a very good question: Why murder a good story?

Well, perhaps, at this point in time, they were NOT murdering a good story because there were already so many adherents to it, that it would be impossible to do so … it was just more controversy. In fact, this move could have been designed to make people ask the very question you did … sort of like the government constantly pooh poohing UFOs … the more they did, the more people believed they were hiding something.

So, this IS a valid point considering "double and triple reverse psychology" commonly in use by the media and whoever runs it.

So, I think that your question goes much deeper than you think.

But, it also puts light in another area … it seems that, these guys who were making money off of this business were being manipulated from start to finish. And making money was, apparently, not the objective – though for them it might have been a lure. Or it might have started for them as a lure, or a farce … and grew very serious later.

Nevertheless, we may deduce that the objective of this pronouncement by the BBC was to do the exact opposite … to breathe new life into the subject by reverse psychology.

So, question about this now is: why? Why do they WANT to keep attention on this area? Why was the attention drawn here to begin with?

Now, let's skip to page 17 where you list the "facts" which can be substantiated and back engineer a bit from there.

The three "facts" – Documents were found in 1886.

We cannot accept this as a fact. It is only hearsay. No matter about the various arguments for, about, against, or whatever, no one, NO ONE, outside of persons whose credibility is in question has EVER SEEN any actual, ancient or even "pretty old" MSS. They have not been submitted to any kind of professional analysis because they have never been produced. To say that "The discovery of the manuscripts is the key to the mystery of Rennes-le- Chateau," is a huge assumption

So, let's set them aside for the moment. (Don't despair, I am ruthless, but it is useful, as you will see.)

Third fact (we will save the second for last, as it is the most interesting.) – That Saunier was digging at night in the cemetery without obvious purpose, aided by his servant.

Now, on this, what verification is there? I am not too clear from the various stories ... but it seems that the primary source of this information was an old guy who "remembered" all this many years later ... and, considering the circumstances of all the rest ... well, it is hearsay. Not admissible as a fact.

Now, there is the second "fact," that Saunier spent more money than his income as a village priest allowed.

At last, we are on firm footing. There are ledger books, apparently, with this information recorded that can be considered "hard evidence." And, there is the evidence of the building projects and so forth which cost more money than the guy could have made. We have a FACT. Only one, so far.

Remember, our BELIEFS are not important here ... our feelings, our responses to our amazing "synchronicities," and all that. We have to clear away the fog of emotion.

Now, in order to know what other "facts" there may be, maybe you can answer the following questions?

You wrote: In 1892, Sauniere is often absent without permission. What he does and where he goes, remains a secret ...

Says WHO?

You wrote: In 1894, together with Marie he makes long walks. They collect stones that are used to adorn the garden with a grotto.

Says WHO?

You wrote: Also in 1894, aided by his trustworthy helpmate, Marie, he starts to dig in his cemetery! At night, under the cover of darkness ...

Says WHO?

Now, the tomb of Marie Negre D'Ables, that he is supposed to have destroyed, but, fantastically, it happened to have been "copied" ... are you aware of the investigation into the "background" of that little book where it was supposedly reproduced? That it was, very likely, at the hands of the very same persons who deposited the "Dossiers Secrets" and all that in the Biblioteque Nationale?

This is pretty shaky stuff here.

The very idea that the Abbe was "searching for something" could be all rumor.

But, why? Where could such a rumor come from?

The story about Marie in her old age is highly instructive: I am sure you have a few "old people" in your family and are familiar with their little "manipulations" and feelings of "helplessness" as they age.

Now, just suppose there WAS some secret of the Abbe ... but it had NOTHING to do with a "treasure" at all ... and whatever it was, died with him as a source of income.

But, Marie, in her old age, desperate to ensure her comfort, knowing that all she has is this property that is expensive to maintain, and no money coming in anymore, hints to the people who have undertaken to care for her that there is a "secret" that she will tell them before she dies ... Obviously, this is to keep her "control" over her life to what little extent she can. It sounds like the old "if you are nice to me, I'll remember you in my will," routine so common among old people ... From the descriptions I have heard, the people who were caring for her had a hard time making ends meet. Do you think that if she had some secret that would enable access to financial aid, that she would not have acted upon it herself and thereby enabled herself to PAY for her own care in old age, rather than having to depend on strangers that she controlled with the promise of a secret?

It is so typical of something an old lady would do, that I am completely struck by the likelihood of it being so.

But, what happens? She dies without telling anything! Supposedly. Well, the guy spends some time looking for a possible treasure which he hopes is there ... because the old lady told him so ... but, no luck ... maybe he realizes that he was duped ... and the story you have described, about the hints to the papers about a treasure to create business for a hotel ... well, the guy was just playing with the cards he was dealt, and I believe that this is the source of the whole "Rennes-le-Château" cottage industry in "treasure hunting."

BUT, that STILL DOES NOT EXPLAIN THE ABBE'S MONEY!

Okay, the guy had some bucks. Not only that, but his bishop had some bucks ... and both were getting paid by another priest ... and, not only that, there was a third priest who was murdered.

These FACTS are of EXTREME interest! The rest is just rumor, smokescreen, hearsay, and all that.

Now, clearly, as you have revealed to me, the cash flow came from Henri Boudet who wrote the strange book about language ... (and I would very much like to get my hands on a copy of it complete! There may, indeed, be a code in there ... but not what anybody thinks ...)

Now, on pages 19, 20 and 21 you give some very interesting facts OUT OF SEQUENCE. I wonder if it was a subconscious oversight? Because, placing them IN SEQUENCE makes for very interesting reading: Here they are:

1852, Sauniere is born.

1878, The abbe of Rennes, Pons, dies.

1881, Charles Mocquin is appointed, but leaves after just a few months. (Any reason given for his leaving???)

1885, May 5, Antoine Croc leaves Rennes ... (When was he appointed? How long was he there? This is curious. Any reason given for leaving?) Two priests in a short time, appointed, and then leave??? Did anybody ask why???

1885, July 1, Sauniere is appointed cure at Rennes .

1886, Sauniere purportedly receives a "gift of cash from Comtesse de Chambord." (Or was it really a "first payment" from Boudet? We see that Sauniere isn't going to leave after just a few months ... wonder why? The previous two priests left pretty quick.)

1886, According to the ledgers you cite, it was at about this time that Abbe Boudet began paying money to Sauniere. Was this also the time he began paying money to Mrs. Billard in Carcassonne? Any dates on this? The bishop was getting twice as much as Sauniere according to the figures you gave. Was it for the same period? The bishop gave most of his to charity. (Was this because of a guilty conscience?)

1887, July, the new altar is placed in the church at Rennes. This is curious. Was this a completely NEW altar, or was it a re-placing of the old one? If the former, what happened to the OLD one?

1889, Bishop Felix Billard visits Rennes for the first time ... (There may have been some sort of "meeting" amongst these guys. They discuss who is to get what, who is to do what, and so on ...)

1891, major restoration is begun on the church ... (This does not sound too strange, since there is obviously some source of money – Sauniere bargained for enough to make his church the way he wanted. If he is stuck in this out of the way place, he is gonna enjoy it!)

1891, Sept 21, entry in Sauniere's diary – "letter from Granes – discovery of a sepulchral vault, rain in the evening." (Does not sound like anything unusual since he is doing a major restoration on his church. AND, he does not seem too interested in it since he did not list it first.)

1892, hearsay that Sauniere was absent without permission. (unless there are documents to confirm this)

1894, hearsay, unless documented, collecting of stones for grotto.

1894, hearsay, unless documented, digging in graveyard.

1896, restoration of church mostly finished. Sauniere buys more land.

1897, June 6, Mgr Billard visits and the garden is unveiled. (Perhaps another "meeting" between the "guys" takes place now.)

1897, Abbe Gelis was murdered. Reportedly tortured before his death. Was supposed to retire the next day. The magistrate found money hidden at various places in the vicarage ... so, he may have been on the "payroll" as well or ... He was an intimate of Sauniere and Boudet and had been there since 1857. How long was Boudet in the region? Was Gelis the "source" of the money to Boudet? He had been there a long time ... he was going to retire ... perhaps take the secret of the source of income with him, or threatened to do something else at the meeting ... or, being retired, he would have been a threat in some way. This needs more examination.

1898, One year after the death of Abbe Gelis, Sauniere buys the land on which he builds his villa. Doesn't anybody find this odd?

1902, the Bishop dies.

1902, Sauniere was told to give an explanation on the origin of his wealth to the new bishop ... Seems that the old bishop was "protecting" the other "guys" in some way, so it does not seem that it could be a "secret" of the church or the church would continue to preserve it ...

1902, Sauniere argues with his friend Henri Boudet. The friendly relations between Sauniere and Boudet are broken off ... Funny that this comes *right after the Bishop dies* and the new one demands explanation. *This is the strangest thing of all.* If there is some secret between them and Sauniere is under pressure to reveal it, it does not seem very wise for Boudet to break off relations with Sauniere if Sauniere KNOWS something about Boudet that he could tell. This point needs some consideration. Something funny here.

1910, July 23, Sauniere is suspended from his official duties. Seems that if Boudet was worried that Sauniere would reveal something, he would come to his rescue. What was happening to Boudet at this time? Was he getting along just fine, or was he being questioned also?

1915, Boudet sends a message to Sauniere to meet and reconcile ... shortly after the reconciliation, Boudet dies. This is funny, that Boudet sends this message ... is it documented? Or, is it documented BY Sauniere? Did he go to visit Boudet uninvited? How soon after the visit does Boudet die? Five years of no contact, then Boudet sees Sauniere and dies right after????

1916, Sauniere decides to build on a REALLY grand scale ... Exactly one year after the death of Boudet. Strange that he has done this twice ... A year after the death of another priest, Sauniere embarks on more building projects.

1917, January 22, Sauniere dies suddenly.

Now, of all the interesting facts above, the two that strike me most forcibly are the facts that, in the year following the death of Gelis, Sauniere buys the land on which he plans to build his villa – but holds off the building for three years ... and in the year following the death of Boudet, Sauniere decides to really go "whole hog" with his building projects ...

So, what we have, after getting rid of the story of the parchments, treasure and all that mess ... is still a VERY strange story ...

AND, it seems to me, that once certain attention had been brought to the area due to the financial needs of Mr. Corbu and family, there was a DESPERATE need to confuse the issue ... to draw attention away from the situation involving the priests ... and their friendship and their finances.

The question would be WHY would this be so important at such a remove in time? Evidence indicates that it is NOT a secret of the church ... the "treasure" idea is kaput, too, as far as I can see ... all the elements of the "Shepherds of Arcadia" painting as related to this area have pretty much been shown to be "cooked up." But, there IS something going on!!!

Is there a connection between the facts that Abbe Gelis was murdered and Sauniere bought land for his villa soon after?

Is there a connection between the fact that Boudet died "suddenly" and Sauniere made big plans to build soon after?

What could be the REAL source of money being shared among these guys? Two, possibly THREE priests and a bishop ...

Was Sauniere's sudden death natural, considering the funny business around the deaths of the other two?

What or who was it that supplied the money? Obviously, Sauniere had access to it *after* Boudet died, but NOT when he and Boudet were on bad terms ... hmmmm? Funny? What was the connection of Gelis to the money – so that he had to die for it, as it seems?

But, whatever the source, it was NOT accessible to Marie ... She only used the suggestion of a "secret" as bait to ensure her well-being until death ...

So, having ripped away all the smokescreen, we are left with a real mystery. But nothing at all like what all the "researchers" suggest.

But, that is not to say that there is not some purpose in the smokescreen, that is another subject altogether. There IS some great mystery about the Shepherds of Arcadia, but, it may be far wider and more intriguing than just the area around Rennes-le-Château.

But, this is enough for now.

Laura

Along with the last of the Neyman letters that I forwarded to Vincent Bridges, I wrote some comments:

To: Vincent Bridges
Date sent: Fri, 7 May 1999 17:01:33 -0400

This is the last of the Neyman letters ... after this, she wrote and told me she did not see any point in "discussing" it further as she KNEW the truth because she had been "led" by "amazing synchronicities" and all that. Same song, different verse.

My point is: I can see that there is a HUGE thing going on here ... and it seems that everybody, including yours truly, has had so amazing a series of "confirmations" of ideas – one leading to another ... and work, work, work on the research and digging and all that ... BUT each one has come to a somewhat different conclusion and has been led down a somewhat different path.

I want to get to the very bottom of the blasted thing!

I have some pieces to this pie, I think ... and Martha found some interesting things ... and I am still waiting for my printer to finish your pages so I can settle down and read and see what pieces you have found ...

Anyway, this will give you SOME idea of how I am looking at it. I am a strange mixture of "intuitive" and ruthlessly scientific – even toward myself. And, when I get emotionally attached to my ideas, my husband straightens me out pretty quick!

I guess I have a couple of axioms I live by: one is "get results." The other is: "when all the lies are stripped away, what remains is the truth."

To Martha Neyman
Date sent: Wed, 25 Nov 1998 13:23:49 -0500

On 25 Nov 98, at 16:26, Martha Neyman wrote:

> *You are a busy lady ... When is the big "Thanksgiving" day..? I thought this was the 14th of November, but I am not sure and you know better..!*

In USA it is the last Thursday in November – whatever that happens to be. Don't know why they picked a Thursday ... all sorts of symbolic things about Thor and all that could come to mind, but ...

> *Sounds great and finger-licking good that turkey of yours ... Today for us; a bit sliced cabbage will do, we have to watch our diet ...*

So do we ... which is why it is going to be difficult ... I will be sick if I eat things that I ought not to eat!

> *Of course I will answer the questions you have and I do not see this as a criticism of the work I did, because I feel, what I did was good and not done before by anyone ... Even not by the writers of the Tomb of God ... The book they wrote, has at first sight a "certain" resemblance with my work, but it is totally different and the "Horse of God" is not a railway, that is for sure..!*

Precisely. It is such a vast subject, that it is difficult to get into without writing reams. The very important thing you were doing was just going about with an open mind and observing and checking things out.

Yes, the railway part nearly had me laughing off my chair. And those poor guys missed some of the most amazing clues ...

> *Dear Laura, do not be angry with me because I am honest to you and straight to the point ... In a way, I am thinking in the same direction as you ...*

Only way it can all be solved ...

> *I think, where you talk about WHY the BBC is "murdering" the story of RLC, you dig too deep. I can well imagine the US government keeping the truth about UFO's from the people, but to believe that the respectable BBC of England is part of a plot to hide the truth of Rennes-le-Château in a sort of double psychology game, I think is going a bit too far.*

Possibly. It is all too easy to get into a conspiracy mind-set. But, you DID ask the question, and I could see that there was another answer besides these guys just tossing the whole thing out the window.

> *You asked me a lot of questions ... But ... You started to ask questions about the "Preface" and the "Introduction".*

Yes. There are certain foundational facts that I think are necessary. You gave quite a few that I have not noticed in other works ... so, I am asking for more about the "basic story."

> *Please take "This" information at "face value"..! This section is not of any importance to the rest of my book. The information in the introduction is common knowledge, mostly it came from the locals, and they are used by every book-writer ...*

Yes, I know that – but, I want to know WHY and HOW such things were generated. I want to know if anybody ever actually documented any of these things. And these are questions that DO occur to me for whatever reason. If the only answer is "the locals said so ... " well, that IS the answer. If there is an old diary where someone wrote about it, that is a different kind of answer.

And, the point is: somehow, for some reason, stimulated by some "raison," these so-called Priory of Sion fellows played on this story and the painting (which I believe is important because of the facts of Poussin's life) got connected to this area ... Is it because there was some sort of "rumor" that floated about in esoteric circles that this painting was connected to this place? Who came up with the idea in the first place?

> *When you start writing some kind of a book, you have to start some-where ...*

Oh, indeed. And getting from point A to point B is very difficult because there are so many corollary paths that might need to be included that it becomes an agony deciding how to choose what to include and what to leave out – or it could become so lengthy and confusing that no one could understand it! Believe me, I KNOW.

> *I do not have to tell you ... I did start with general information. So readers who are not so well informed, but want to know more about the whole story Rennes-le-Château, can get this general information.*

Yes, but you also did some "investigating" on your own. You observed. A lot of things you mention are not mentioned by other writers, even apart from your discoveries.

> *That is why, in the INTRODUCTION, I wrote: Quote: At the risk of bor-ing those readers, who know all about the history of Rennes-le-Château and its obstinate priest, I would like to repeat briefly, the "original" ver-sion, for those new to the story ... Unquote.*

Yes, but hopefully, you checked some of these things???? After all, the previous writers may have had an agenda ... and it seems that they did not check things out as thoroughly as one might wish.

> *Dear Laura, those inverted commas at the word ORIGINAL were placed there on purpose ... To the real initiated it means the story as it is usually told, as mysterious and uncanny as possible, without actually having completely checked out, who did what and why and who saw him doing it ... This is just the "common" Rennes-le-Château story, only meant as "proof" that something weird was going on in this village and that the priest behaved strangely ...*

Yes, but if none of those things are true ... if they only "developed" AF-TER the fact of the initial "rumor" of treasure was started, which I think you pinpointed in your description of the folks who were caring for Ma-rie, well, then there is nothing to support the "treasure" hypothesis. There is nothing to look for ... at least not in that sense.

Thus, if the story about treasure, the connection to the painting, which seems to have evolved from the rumors about treasure, all are "manu-factured," then one has to start looking in a different way.

> *Because as you will find out later, as you read on, you will see that Sauniere's doings have (very) little impact on the solution I found.*

But, Sauniere's doings seem to be the very thing that the "story" masks ... My point is that the story seems to be a smokescreen for what was going on with those priests.

I can see that I am going to have to start telling you about some of the things I discovered ... in much the same way you discovered things ... in this way you will understand that I am saying that there is SOME-THING HUGE going on here, because what I have discovered dovetails with your "findings" only there are some other implications and corre-spondences that make the picture a lot larger ...

> *I hope you do not mind, I am so straight to the point..?*

No. This has got to be analyzed to pieces I think.

> *What I meant by writing : You are so well informed is: Experienced in symbolism ...*

We will get to that later. I cannot formulate without data. There are some significant symbolic images that are far more ancient and "in your face" in that painting than what you described. Every thing has multiple layers ... question is: which layer do we extract from?

An example is your use of the "knee" as a means of selecting the number "seven." Well, the knee has some very deep meanings and is used symbolically in a rather different way in numerous sources, the oldest I have found being the Egyptian Pyramid Texts ... And it is not chance that "knee" is from the same root as "knead (as in bread), knight, juga, yogi, conjugal, genes, genetic, gonads, etc.)

Also, the hand positions ... there was in use, at the time of the painting, a "hand alphabet" which could signify either letters or numbers or both ... it could also symbolize a mathematical "operation."

> *I started to give an explanation of the perceptible and searching for the truth in the invisible words of symbolism in "Chapter I" ... So let we [sic] start from this first part ... And ... Do not forget I only used A SMALL part of the Christian Church symbolism to explain, sometimes "just enough" to make clear how I came to my conclusions in a logical way..! Otherwise for most of the people "absolute unknown" with this material it would have been much too complicated, long-winded and even boring.*

Agreed. But I am still trying to "connect" the painting to the area and it is difficult.

> *So my dear if you are ready for it ... I am ... But no hurry, take your time..!*

Well, it is going to take some time because the "rest of the story" is yet to be told. And, by that, I mean certain other correspondences that no one knows, I don't think, but myself.

> *This was only a short reply, because I feel the strong desire to write a whole day on my second book ... Which has nothing to do with symbolism ... It is the true story of the "Shepherds" the real "Shepherds": the church-shepherds..! THAT is the story of the painting of Poussin ... "Popes-Crusades-Templars", it starts with the Oriental Schism in 1054 ... For the "Latin Church of Rome" this was a large loss. It ended with a second huge loss: The reformation in 1618.*

Well, if you haven't done so already ... look at the King Rene painting reproduced in the "Tomb of God" book alongside the "Shepherds" painting ... just look at them casually and see what things you note that correspond ... Note the lance and the horse head and compare it to the "horse head" and shepherd's staff in the Arcadia painting ... Note the position of the sun and the mountain peak in both paintings ... note the posture of the Shepherdess and King Rene ... note the ditch and flow of water exiting from the stone in the two paintings ... note the funny leaning tree in the Rene painting ... the funny hand gestures ...

Then look at the Teniers painting and note the shape of the "window" and compare it to the "chink" in the tomb in the Shepherd's painting ...

Then, have a look at Bacchus and Ariadne by Titian ... half-close your eyes and see what you can see ... note the funny overturned vessel on the drapery ... the dog ... go back to Teniers and note the vessel in the window ... the bird ...

In the Shepherds painting, note the drapery of the figures ... the crossed shins, the bared breasts of the figures ... count the numbers of knees, hands displayed ... Note the positions ... it is not as simple as the "finger of Jupiter, Venus or whatever ... "

The system of codes being transmitted via hand signals was widespread in both the Orient and the Occident. There are allusions to it in the writings of several Greek and Latin writers, such as Plutarch, who attributes these words to orontes, son-in-law of King Artaxerxes of Persia: "Just as in calculating, fingers sometimes have a value of ten thousand and sometimes of only one, the favorites of kings may be either everything or almost nothing." (Hmm ... a connection to Persia again?)

Apuleius married a rich widow named Aemilia Pudentialla and was accused of having used magic to win her favor. He defended himself before Proconsul Claudius Maximus in the presence of Emilianus, his main accuser, who had unkindly said that Aemilia was sixty years old, when she was actually only forty. Here is the record of how Apuleius addressed his accuser:

"How dare you, Emilianus, increase the real number of Aemilia Pudentilla's age by half, or even a third? If you had said 'thirty' for 'ten' it might have been thought that your mistake CAME FROM HOLDING YOUR FINGERS OPEN WHEN YOU SHOULD HAVE HELD THEM CURVED. But, forty is THE EASIEST NUMBER TO INDICATE, SINCE IT IS EXPRESSED WITH THE HAND OPEN."

Saint Jerome wrote:

"Thirty corresponds to marriage, FOR THE CONJUNCTION OF THE FINGERS AS THOUGH IN A SWEET KISS REPRESENTS THE HUSBAND AND THE WIFE. [...] AND THE GESTURE FOR A HUNDRED, TRANSFERRED FROM THE LEFT HAND TO THE RIGHT, ON THE SAME FINGERS, EXPRESSES ON THE RIGHT HAND THE CROWN OF VIRGINITY."

The Venerable Bede gives many examples of how the system can be used for silent communication.

In Islamic religions, finger counting and signing was used extensively (remember the "contamination" of the Templars by Sufism ... which is so similar to what is known of the Cathars that one cannot help but think that there is a connection ... and, also, what is known of the Druids ...)

There are a LOT of quotes I can cite about this "finger and hand" signaling system ... but, it would get tedious.

The meanings of these things were obvious to people of the time, (which may be why the painting was hidden), and the citations from old MSS so common that it shows that such allusions were used both in paintings and in written references ... otherwise, the readers could not have been expected to understand them, but it is very obscure to those of us in the 20th century who are not familiar with the method, and casually pass over such references as being "unimportant."

Thus, this may be an important consideration in evaluating the message of this and other paintings.

The mathematical angles are another thing altogether. At the time, the "Golden Mean" was a standard of Art ... it was taught in all the art schools that a composition based on this ratio was more aesthetically pleasing ... so, pupils were taught, and masters perfected, the art of compositional placement on the medium according to the Pythagorean principles. It meant, essentially, nothing. It can be found in thousands of paintings. It's presence in art is generally meaningless.

However, your finding of the stone with the ratio figure engraved upon it ... well, that requires some examination, but not necessarily in the precise terms. Or, on the other hand, in the precise terms ...

Well, I have some transcribing to do for my husband who is impatiently pacing about – and I have baking to do this afternoon. Children won't let me NOT do it!

It will take a while to talk about all of these things and I am going to begin to try to describe to you some of the other things that may be significantly related ...

Laura

As noted, Martha Neyman didn't want to discuss it anymore. Because she had begun with assumptions about where to look – in Christian symbolism – and because she found an "answer" based on her assumptions, and the landscape more or less cooperated with her in the same way it had cooperated with so many other people, the idea that there may be something going on in this morphing landscape-treasure story as a means of screening something else, or distracting the attention of the researcher, was not a welcome idea to her at all.

What was more, the very idea that the BBC might have been manipulated rankled with her, and I knew that the idea of manipulation of reality was simply beyond her grasp. She wasn't asking my opinion because she really wanted it; she was asking for confirmation of what she already firmly believed to be true.

I was almost too excited to wait for this Mr. Bridges to declare his opinion. I was so looking forward to discussing the issues with someone who had deeply investigated it, who had been there, and who wasn't subject to the manipulations of the disinformation program that was evident to me. Finally, I received a response to my posts, and thank the Lord! Vincent Bridges wrote encouragingly:

Does seem as if we are working in similar directions. The stuff up on the web is actually smoke and mirrors. We haven't released the good stuff yet either. Very little on the web about some of our discoveries, for obvious reasons. Was very interested in your Neyman letters, and yes EVB is still alive and living in the town next to RLC, but her story is truly bizarre. She was Canseliet's lover, self identified, in the '60s and he told her the whole story which became *Refuge*. It gets stranger from there. Let me know what you think and we will talk more. <u>Fulcanelli is hard to find, but Brotherhood of Light has now published both *Mystery* and *Dwellings of the Philosophers* in English</u>.

What startled me more than anything was learning that Fulcanelli had written a second book entitled *Dwellings of the Philosophers*. My mind flashed back to the Cs remark:

December 14, 1996

Q: (L) OK, let me jump over to this other subject of the number 33 and the number 11. Is there anything beyond what was given on 11-11-95, that you could add at this time, about any of the mathematics or the use of these numbers?

A: <u>Prime numbers are the dwellings of the mystics.</u>

Obviously, Mr. Bridges was the right one to talk to because he had pronounced the secret word! Certainly he would be able to help me to figure out the exact details of the many things the Cs had said on these subjects. <u>I already had figured out that the alchemical transformation, or the Great Work, was simply the activation of DNA that elevated the human being to fourth density</u>. But exactly what the precise process was, I was not yet quite sure. I figured that all I would have to do would be to just send him the excerpts of the transcripts that related to these mysterious matters, and he would be able to fill in some of the blanks. And so, I did. I sent off huge segments of the text for his review and I was gratified to receive confirmation that we were on the same track. He wrote back, "Had time to read your notes more carefully, and yep you are hot! In fact you are so close that I'm gonna tell you a couple of things that haven't left the 'family' circle yet."

He also wrote reassuringly regarding my declaration that the matter must be approached ruthlessly and scientifically:

My point of view exactly. If you knew how many true believers of all kinds I infuriate, well, as the Sufis say you can't be a saint until 400 wise men have reviled you! I 'believe' I am the center of the universe, but, if I seek to prove it, then I am certifiable. Intuition must be backed up by rigorous analysis or it is just wishful thinking, like believing I'm the center of the universe.

So, all through the end of May and early June I was happily posting all my research to Vincent Bridges, and we were just having a great time. The more we discussed it, the more convinced I became, based on his comments, that he was exactly the right person to discuss these things with, and that he would have other pieces of the puzzle. Vincent wrote back about the Cs material such remarks as:

Cassiopaea as a symbol carries a very significant energy; it is the M or W in the sky and therefore is sort of a cosmic icon for the whole mystery. Is it possible that you are talking to the head masters themselves, here on earth?

I designed a true channeling check list. It's an eleven point test, that most of the best channelers score around 3 or 4. From what I have seen of your stuff, you are around 8 or 9.

Baphomet; Do you grok what the Cs are telling you here? "Seer of the passage indeed!"

Wow, the Cs have given you the big secret and pointed out the main "treasure" to be found at RLC.

I can't believe what I'm reading! The Cs are giving you the secret! I read this to my partner, Jay, and he freaked. I don't think anybody but us knows this part of the secret, and to have it being broadcast psychically is a little unnerving. Combined with the alfalfa clues given earlier, you are on top of the wave. I can't help but wonder if this is for you or for us.

Q: Did the Templars discover the secrets of the Ishmaelis, the Assassini, and is this what they carried into Europe, and then underground?

A: Buried in Galle.

OK, this one made my hair stand on end. Galle is the old word for the region around Glanum and Provence in general. We think we found just what was buried in Glanum, but it older than the Templars.

Q: Has this person also been pursuing the secret?

A: Pour suivant.

OH, boy, the real name of the Order. Whom does the Grail serve? It serves those who follow; for, to follow, is to partake of the nature of the Quest.

Jesus Laura, I can't begin to keep up with all this stuff you are sending me! I haven't hit a lick all week on my own work for chewing on yours. But it is so interesting!

As far as I can tell, the Cs are leading you to the same exact conclusions that we have reached. This is spooky. The session about light is plain in terms of the neuro-chemistry involved. I'm just not sure that it is getting through to you, but maybe that's effect of spreading these clues out over time.

The interested reader may wish to peruse the correspondence for this material. There was a lot more going on in other areas at this exact time. I didn't realize it but I was like a frog in a pan of water being slowly heated, and Vincent Bridges was one of the tools whether he knew it or not, then or since.

CHAPTER 55
ALBERT EINSTEIN, FREE ENERGY AND THE STRANGE DEATHS OF MORRIS K. JESSUP AND STEFAN MARINOV

Let's talk about death now. Sure, I know, nobody wants to talk about death; but I have in mind some very interesting deaths that ought to be talked about for a lot of reasons.

The first death I want to talk about is the apparent suicide of Morris K. Jessup. The problem with Morris Jessup's suicide is that it was too obvious. He was found in his station wagon in a Dade County Park, Florida, on the evening of April 29, 1959. A hose had been attached to the exhaust pipe of the station wagon and looped into the closed interior. The whole set-up had been accomplished during daylight hours, in a public park. Ever since, researchers have said that Jessup's death was the price he paid for getting too close to the truth. You see, Jessup's death is *so* apparent a suicide, everyone just *knew* that it was *not* a suicide. Of course, as a consequence, an entire mythos was born about something called the Philadelphia Experiment having to do with time travel.

There has always been an element of high strangeness to the UFO mystery that has been the subject of endless debates among researchers. Anyone who has seriously begun to delve into such matters, or who has experienced certain manifestations, is aware of the weird guys who dress in black, big-foot-type critters, strange, hooded figures, poltergeist-type events, and crazy electronic glitches in telephones, televisions and radios. Often, the type and level of such experiences can become quite frightening, or at the very least, disorienting. Very often, these effects are trotted out as proof that the UFO phenomenon is nothing other than the product of the spirit realm. Others will suggest that this proves that it is observer-created reality flux.

There are cases where UFOs have appeared in conjunction with all kinds of violent and frightening phenomena, and often, those who experience such things screaming into the arms of anything that will offer protection – usually religion of one sort or another, drugs, or psychiatry.

Anybody, under the best (or worst) of such circumstances, may come to the idea that there is some bizarre sort of conspiracy directed at them as an individual, and, according to the Cassiopaeans, they won't be far wrong. As they have said, "nobody is a nobody," and it is "no trouble at all for such forces to give seemingly individualized attention." After all, a single, small group of so-called aliens, with mastery over time, could be responsible for all such phenomena. All they would have to do would be to return to the same time over and over again, selecting only a different place and a different individual to harass, and all of the victims, being *in* time, would have their experiences simultaneously.

In reading cases of abduction, one becomes aware that there are many instances wherein the individual has no missing time, no memory of anything unusual, but has developed something like a phobia and goes to a therapist for help. One case involved a man who suddenly began to experience a serious reaction to a lonely stretch of road he had to travel every day to and from his job. It was a complete mystery to him why he was having panic attacks every time he approached this section of the highway, and he was quite shocked to have a roadside abduction come back to his memory under hypnosis. In other cases, the individual thinks they have experienced a ghostly encounter, or for no apparent reason they have suddenly begun to manifest psychic abilities. (The reader might wish to have a look at Nick Pope's interesting book *The Uninvited* for elements of such cases from UK, along with some astute commentary.)

What this means is that anybody could be an abduction victim and they might never suspect it. Additionally, as Jacques Vallee points out, the numbers who do have awareness of an unusual event who do *not* report it, when extrapolated from those who *do* report encounters, could run into the multiple millions. And of course, there are still those who want us to believe that this is a government mind-control experiment. Yeah, right!

It is possible, of course, with the electronic technology of the present time, that multiplied millions of people could be – in certain respects – programmed via television, radio, music, video games, and so forth; that their subconscious could be taught a binary-code language of electronic signals that are inaudible to the normal range of hearing; and that they could thereby be constantly picking up signals of some sort that are unpacked in their subconscious mind and emerge into their conscious mind as their own thoughts. We have even studied some specific technology of this type, and it is frightening in its implications. Using a binary code, speeding up the signal, entire books of information can be transmitted in almost no time at all, and the percipient would be certain that they were just "thinking it." It can even be individually directed with the addition of a personal activation code. In this way, even memories could be introduced into the mind which would be accepted as the person's own experiences.[19]

So, it is certainly true that human technology could produce a major phenomenon of belief-system modification by simply broadcasting an inaudible signal over the globe, assuming that the recipients know the language and have been involved in activities whereby the code can be subliminally taught.

This does not, of course, address the historical issue of otherworldly beings, and we notice a large effort to distract attention away from those cases, as though there is a program to gradually cover them up and induce belief in the idea that this is an extraterrestrial phenomenon in strictly material terms. We have already mentioned the function of memes as mass-mind viruses introduced by the Matrix in an effort to distract attention away from the true source of the phenomena. In short, all kinds of possibilities exist, even including mass hypnosis via such coded signals. And there are many, many people who prefer such an explanation to that of hyperdimensional realities and mind-marauding, time-traveling critters with B.O. and questionable fashion statements.

I would suggest, of course, that such an explanation, placing the blame on human beings, leaves a lot to be desired since very often the effects of poltergeist-type phenomena can be photographed, leave physical traces, and no one has yet seen the man behind the curtain. I find it hard to believe that the field work of such a conspiracy could be carried out so effectively that no mistakes have been made, and nobody has ever caught any government agents toting Susy Smart out the back door in a state of drug-induced insensibility, nor can any explanation be found for how such a program could operate logistically over such vast areas of space and time without a single leak of insider info. And when people "escape" from mind programming projects, or so they claim, we have to ask why? When we consider the capabilities and ethics of such programmers, the very idea that they would allow such escape and re-

---

[19] While one of the sources describing this technology has been scrubbed from the Internet, the "neurophone" is another example of such technology; *See:* http://www.worldtrans.org/spir/neuro.html

lease of "inside info" raises serious questions about its authenticity. Anybody who has read any serious literature on the subject realizes how easy it is to put a period to the existence of a squealer. Karen Silkwood was only ratting on safety in a nuke facility and she conveniently had an accident on a lonely road.

Having said all of that, there does seem to be a major human interface to the matter, with certain agencies or individuals of agencies, acting in strange ways that suggest either they know what they are doing, or they are some sort of robotoid-type of individual who can be activated at will to perform various functions. The so-called Greenbaum Program (see *Wave 2*) is a case in point. Then, of course, there are cases such as the Cathy O'Brien situation. Did she really escape, or was she allowed to escape? Was her escape designed to emphasize the human elements of the Matrix and distract attention away from the hyperdimensional players? Is her story supposed to suggest that there are glitches in the program that give us an inside view of human mind-control projects that suggest a vast social engineering program?

In September of 1953, Albert K. Bender claimed that he had received certain information that provided the missing pieces for a theory concerning the origin of UFOs. He wrote it all down and sent it to a trusted friend. Shortly after, he received a visit from three men. One of them held the letter he had written in his hand. They told him that he had, indeed, stumbled on the answer, and then they purportedly filled him in on the details. He became so ill he was unable to eat for three days. A couple of other UFO researchers, Dominick Lucchesi and August C. Roberts, tried to persuade Bender to talk. He would only repeat, "I can't answer that."

Finally, in 1962, Bender declared that he would tell the story and wrote a book entitled *Flying Saucers and the Three Men*. It described astral projection to a secret base in Antarctica inhabited by male, female and bisexual creatures. Researchers were perplexed and wondered if the whole thing was just contrived to hide something more sinister. Lucchesi said that Bender was a changed man after the three men had visited him. He said, "*it was as if he had been lobotomized.*" Bender was obviously frightened, and suffered from extreme headaches whenever he even thought about speaking about his experiences and what the three men had told him. He withdrew completely from UFO research, and went to work managing a hotel, refusing to discuss anything about such matters ever again.

Not too many months after Bender's silencing, Edgar R. Jarrold, organizer of the Australian Flying Saucer Bureau, and Harold H. Fulton, head of Civilian Saucer Investigation of New Zealand, had received similar visits and disbanded their organizations. While writing a previous chapter, I was informed of a fascinating case where another UFO discussion group was broken up by the arrival on the scene of a psychopathic "contactee" who later involved the leader of the group and several members in a murder.

Broadcaster Frank Edwards, who wrote a best selling book, *Flying Saucers, Serious Business*, was a highly successful radio host. He was warned to abandon the subject of UFOs, and refused. He was fired. In spite of thousands of letters in protest of his dismissal, his ex-sponsor, the American Federation of Labor, stood firm. George Meany, then president of the AFL said Edwards had been dropped, "Because he talked too much about flying saucers!" It was later suggested that the Defense Department had put pressure on the AFL.

Edwards was only temporarily silenced. He soon had a syndicated show that dealt almost exclusively with UFOs and related phenomena. Shortly after, the news of the sudden death of Frank Edwards on the anniversary of the Kenneth Arnold UFO sighting near Mt. Rainier, Washington was announced. Some people claimed that Edwards had been ill, was overweight, and so forth. Those closest to him said he had never been ill. The obituary said that death was apparently due to a heart attack, and we wonder how many other researchers have died of an apparent problem that had never before been apparent?

This brings us back to the problem of Morris Jessup's apparent suicide. One of the most pervasive UFO–human conspiracy stories is that of the Philadelphia Experiment which explicates that, in 1943, the U.S. Navy secretly accomplished the teleportation of a warship from Philadelphia to a dock near Norfolk by successfully applying Einstein's Unified Field Theory.

The story tells us that the experiment began in an attempt to develop radar invisibility, but something unexpected happened: the ship became invisible, and when it returned, several of the crewmen burst into flames, and others had portions of their bodies melded into the steel structures of the ship. Of those who survived, most of them spent the rest of their lives in psychiatric hospitals. That's handy. I had a guy kidnap me when I was four years old who was conveniently shielded in a Navy psychiatric hospital. Any connection? Possibly.

The Navy denies the reality of the Philadelphia Experiment, but the rumors persist – and they are very powerful rumors. Researchers continue to hear accounts from eyewitnesses or purported family members of those who died or went insane. I was even told a story about the Philadelphia Experiment by my ex-husband who swore he had heard it from a guy in Key West when he was young. And this was long before I ever knew anything about the mythos of the Philadelphia Experiment proper!

It was the death of Morris Jessup that gave credibility to the rumors of the Philadelphia Experiment. In fact, the details of the experiment all began with the series of letters Jessup was purported to have received from a Carlos Allende. When you try to track the story back to its beginnings, you discover that even the story about the purported annotated copy of Jessup's book emerged only *after* his death, as a rumor in Washington social circles. The fact that Allende mentioned sodium pentothal in his letters is quite telling. That he was aware of the existence of sodium pentothal at that early date suggests that he was aware of mind-control research being conducted by the Navy during the war, which suggests that he was a victim, or a handler of such projects.

Gray Barker, editor of *The Saucerian Bulletin*, loved a good mystery. He was author of *They Knew Too Much About Flying Saucers* and *The Silver Bridge*. Barker had become involved in UFOlogy around 1950 when a strange creature with glowing eyes appeared in front of several eyewitnesses, floating about the ground, and giving off a terrible odor. Barker later discovered that there were physical marks in the nearby soil, and became convinced that an alien craft had landed in rural Flatwoods, West Virginia.

Barker tells us that his first contact with Morris Jessup was when he received a letter from him on November 5, 1954. Barker had sent Jessup a copy of his magazine, *The Saucerian*. This was just shortly before Jessup's first book was published. We discover from Jessup's letter that Barker was apprised of his existence and work by John Bessor who was, apparently, a subscriber to the magazine. Jessup wrote:

> Yes, I'm doing a book. It is far along in the final draft stages, and we are hoping to get it in the hands of the publishers sometime next week. It is rather conservative as compared to some of the wild things so far printed, but I have tried to keep it factual, and have confined it to phenomena in the pre-Arnold era – particularly around 1875-1885. Altogether it makes quite a formidable array of proof and background.

Gray Barker describes Jessup as "a most cordial person, and greatly enthusiastic about finding some solution to the UFO mystery – though he indicated that in his professional writing he felt it necessary to take a more conservative approach. This conservative, scientific attitude, demonstrated in his first two books, may have been the reason that his writings were not popular with many saucer 'fans.'"

Jessup wrote to Barker on December 16, 1954:

> There is so damned much nonsense being put out by silly people that one gets disgusted with a lot of it. I do feel that we are in a remarkable phase of human experience and that the waters should not be muddied by stupidity – the problem is tough enough without any Adamski's in the picture.

And then on December 20th, along with two articles he sent to Barker, Jessup wrote:

> The Mexican craters are real – I found them myself, and I've seen the air force negatives. … The extension of the motive-power theme to include some jolts to religion are rather obvious. This space race COULD be our GOD. They COULD have left the Earth millennia ago. Our book will hint at how *Sun-worship may be connected with the space denizens.*
>
> I read your report regarding Albert K. Bender with great interest. Looks like SOMETHING did happen. He probably did stumble onto the truth. I will be glad of any additional information you may uncover.
>
> In my humble opinion, you are absolutely correct in your thought that the power source is the key to the whole UFO deal. I am convinced of it from my own introspection and reading.

Jessup's reference to Bender was made before Bender told his story. Jessup's little book *The UFO and the Bible* did not sell well and is now out of print. It was originally part of his book *The Expanding Case for the UFO*, but the publisher rejected that section. Jessup himself did not complete the final drafts for his books, such as *UFO Annual.* His agent simply took files of clippings and organized them into book form. A short story from a magazine happened to be among the clippings, and the agent included it as fact, resulting in Jessup's critics pointing this out to discredit him.

From the beginning of his research, Jessup evidently thought that UFOs were propelled by antigravity applications. Regarding the early developments of the factors that contributed to the emergence of the myth of the Philadelphia Experiment, Gray Barker tells us:

> According to Riley Crabb, the annotated copy [of Jessup's book] was addressed to Admiral N. Furth, Chief, Office of Naval Research, Washington 25, D.C., and was mailed in a manila envelope postmarked Seminole, Texas, 1955. In July or August of that year the book appeared in the incoming correspondence of Major Darrell L. Ritter, U.S.M.C., Aeronautical Project Office in ONR. When Captain Sidney Sherby reported aboard at ONR he obtained the book from Major Ritter, Captain Sherby and Commander George W. Hoover, Special Projects Officer, ONR, indicated interest in some of the notations the book contained.
>
> I first learned of the annotated copy when I was talking to Mrs. Walton Colcord John, director of the *Little Listening Post*, a UFO and New Age Publication in Washington. Speaking over the telephone, Mrs. John told me of a strange rumor going around to the effect that somebody had sent a marked-up copy to Washington, and that the government had gone to the expense of mimeographing the entire book, so that all the underlinings and notations could be added to the original text. This was being circulated rather widely, she told me, *through military channels.*

She had not, of course, seen a copy of it, and didn't know too much about it, but somehow she seemed to connect it with an alleged Naval experiment wherein a ship had completely disappeared from sight. I couldn't make too much out of all this until later I also heard about the strange Allende Letters, which told of such an experiment in a most horrifying way.

The publication of the mimeographed edition is established, but I have been unable to confirm whether or not it was actually paid for by the government. It is established that the Varo Manufacturing Company, of Garland, Texas, actually produced the mimeographed edition. I have been unable to find out much about this company, except that it has been said that it engaged in "secret government work."

Apparently, Mr. Crabb in some way came into possession of a copy. … In his correspondence with me of September 24, 1962, Crabb clears up the mystery of how he happened to obtain a copy of the original Varo edition. *It was the copy that the Navy originally gave to Jessup, and apparently was given to Crabb by Jessup.* This copy, however, rather mysteriously disappeared in April, 1960, when Crabb mailed it to himself from Washington, and apparently he no longer possesses any copy at all.

Crabb tells us: I understand that 25 copies were reproduced … Michael Ann Dunn, the stenographer who did the editing, explains why in the introduction. She's married now, living in Dallas, and won't answer her phone. … Varo, by the way, is a small manufacturing firm in electronics and up to its neck in space age business. Apparently it has succeeded in developing some kind of a death ray gadget, judging from a guarded press release of last fall when a group of Congressmen visited there for a demonstration.

Now, first of all, we notice that Gray Barker is apprised of the existence of the book via a rumor that is supposed to be coming down from military circles. Jessup never told him about it, and apparently, it was only *after Jessup's death* that the rumor began to be circulated. We notice that *Riley Crabb claims to have had a copy – that this copy was the one the Navy gave to Jessup – but conveniently, it has disappeared in a weird mailing exercise.*

Ivan Sanderson had been a close friend of Morris Jessup, and Barker tried to get some information from him when he ran into him in New York sometime later. He tells us that Ivan would not discuss the suicide at all, but he was more than willing to talk about the Varo edition of Jessup's book. Barker asked Sanderson why Jessup had never publicized the matter of Allende and the annotated book. (It seems that the only evidence we even have for this story is hearsay *after* Jessup's death!) Sanderson apparently told Barker that Jessup was "just dumbfounded" to be called to Annapolis and shown the annotated edition.

The story from Ivan is that six months before his death, Jessup had visited him *bringing along the annotated edition of his book that had come from the Navy.* Ivan claimed that, during the course of the evening, Jessup had requested Ivan to bring three other persons (never identified) into Sanderson's private office where Jessup showed them the Varo edition, to which he had added his own notes. He asked them to read it and then *lock it up in a safe place* "in case something should happen to me." Sanderson never said what the notes were, remarking only that "after having read this material, all of us developed a collective feeling of a most unpleasant nature. And this was horribly confirmed when Jessup was found dead in his car."

What happened to this annotated copy? Sanderson told Gray Barker that it was left in his keeping. Sanderson is dead now, and no one has ever located such a copy in his effects. Yet Riley Crabb *also* claimed to have been the recipient of Jessup's very own annotated copy.

I smell a rat.

In the years following Jessup's "suicide," almost everyone in the UFO field had forgotten him. During his life, Jessup was not a best-selling author. He was mentioned in Charles Berlitz's book *Without a Trace*, and this revived a bit of interest. As a result of this book, Gray Barker received a phone call from a woman in Miami who had the idea that Jessup did not commit suicide. He sent her a copy of the annotated edition which he had acquired by then (as have a lot of other people, though I am not sure how anybody can assume that it is authentic!) along with *The Strange Case of Dr. M.K. Jessup*. This woman, Ann Genzlinger, became obsessed with the matter, and undertook to investigate. Surprisingly, she found "doors eagerly opened for her" and the utmost in cooperation by both the staff and Examiner of the Medical Examiner's office in Dade County. Ordinarily, medical records aren't available to the public, *yet she was allowed complete access to them, and was permitted to voice copy them onto tape.* Strangely, after ten years, when the records should have already been moved to storage, they were right there in the "current section."

The Medical Examiner himself seemed to be interested in Jessup's death since he had written to Barker inquiring if he knew of any in-stances of the use of hallucinogenic drugs as techniques in UFO investigations. This convinced Barker that the examiner might have thought that Jessup had been made to commit suicide.

As it happened, *no autopsy had been performed.* The body had been do-nated to the University of Miami School of Medicine, which was in violation of the Florida State Code that lists instances in which autop-sies are mandated. Apparently, even if the examiner was "interested," he wasn't interested enough to obey the law and perform an autopsy.

The homicide officer who investigated the death, Sgt. Obenchain, commented:

The job was too professional. And I've been on homicide a long time and I feel I can make such a judgment. For example, the ordinary suicide by monoxide poisoning doesn't take the time to wet down all the articles of clothing and to stuff them in the back window to make it more airtight. Most suicides use an ordinary garden hose. But the hose used in Jessup's car was larger in diameter, and similar to one on a washing machine. It was not just shoved into the car's exhaust pipe. It was wired on. *And all this had been done in broad daylight, just off a well-traveled road, at the height of the rush hour when traffic was leaving the park.* The water could hardly have been applied to the rags at the scene, or some second party had removed the evidence. The closest body of water was 200 yards away. There were no containers for carrying water to the car. *Jessup's clothes were not wet, yet the rags used for stuffing the window were saturated with water.*

While the police were trying to revive Jessup, a Dr. Harry Reed just strolled into the park, though it was after closing time, examined Jessup, and pronounced him dead. There was no Dr. Reed in the Miami telephone book, and none listed in the state licensing records.

Jessup's wife, Rubye, refused to view the body because she was so certain that her husband would not have committed suicide. Homicide Sgt. Obenchain's wife stayed with Rubye for three days after the death, and during this time Rubye told her about unusual telephone calls Jessup had been receiving right before his death. She said that these calls upset him, though he would not tell her what they were about. If Jessup was out and she answered the phone, the caller would hang up. The calls ceased immediately upon the death of Jessup. After three days of repeating over and over again that it was not her husband, suddenly Rubye Jessup asked Mrs. Obenchain to leave, stating that she no longer wanted to talk about the matter.

The person who did, eventually, identify Jessup's body was a fellow named Leon A. Seoul who claimed to be a friend of the family. Unfortunately, none of the family ever heard of him.

So, what do we have? We have someone who purportedly sent some weird letters to Morris Jessup, about which he was reportedly curious, but not terribly excited. All the impressions that are attributed to Jessup regarding these letters are from hearsay, *after* his death. We have a story about the Varo edition of his book, that only emerged as a rumor after his death. The rumor was claimed to be from military circles, as though this would give it credibility. The only people who seem to claim any inside info are Riley Crabb and Ivan Sanderson, both of whom claimed to have been in possession of the copy given to Jessup, on which he had made notes of his own. But this copy disappeared, and somehow, there are copies circulated from somewhere because I have two of them. The end result is that, due to this series of rumors, which seem so obviously concocted *after Jessup was no longer alive to refute any of it,* we have people declaring that Jessup was silenced because he was on the verge of proving that the Philadelphia Experiment really did take place exactly as Carlos Allende described it!

Every detail and element of the Allende story, the Varo edition of Jessup's book, and the purported strange events preceding his death just reeks of manipulation; all of it propagated after he was no longer present to deny any part of the story. After looking into the matter carefully, one gets the strange impression that a dead man was used to create a myth. Or at least, the "right" version of the story – the version that the powers-that-be want everyone to believe. At the center of the myth we find Ivan Sanderson and Riley Crabb, who seem to be responsible for spreading the whole story. Later, as a most telling coincidence, a longtime associate of Sanderson, Al Bielek, comes along and breathes new life into the story by creating "Montauk," followed by Phil Schneider, and others.

We come back again to the death of Jessup: a suicide that was so obviously set up to look like suicide, that everyone *knows* it was murder by persons or agencies unknown. Ann Genzlinger concluded: "I was motivated by a strong feeling that Dr. Jessup did not take his own life. But after my long investigation, I have concluded that he did – but not while in possession of his faculties. He was under some sort of control."

That, of course, does *not* explain the problem of the wet rags stuffed in the back window of the station wagon.

Nevertheless, the result of all of this is that the Philadelphia Experiment, as explicated by the Carlos Allende letters, and the story about the Varo edition of Jessup's book, is now firmly ensconced *as fact* in the minds of many people.

On January 17, 1996, Phil Schneider[20] was found dead in his apartment. He had been dead for about a week. After a lot of fooling around by the medical examiner, it was decided that Phil had committed suicide by strangling himself with a rubber hose of the medical type. Yeah, right!

Phil was a well-known speaker on the patriot and UFO lecture circuit. His main shtick was underground base activities. As a geologist, he claimed to have been involved in the construction of secret government bases, including Area 51 and the base at Dulce, New Mexico. As it happened, for two years before his death, Phil had stated in his lectures that there were constant attempts being made on his life. These attempts were described as staged accidents, running gunfights, loos-

---

[20] See: *The Philadelphia Experiment Murder* by Alexandra Bruce (2001).

ened lug nuts on his vehicle and so forth. Phil further claimed that his father was a German U-boat captain who had been captured by the Allies and inducted into the U.S. Navy under the CIA's Operation Paperclip program in which Nazis were given new identities and became U.S. citizens.

Loosened lug nuts?

I read that part to my kids – movie buffs all – and they looked at each other, then at me and said, "Yeah, right! The Secret Government according to Homer Simpson." The reader may wish to read Alexandra Bruce's well-researched book *The Philadelphia Experiment Murder*, for the many confusing details of Schneider's background and claims that were brought to light which cast doubt on his stories, but still raise confusing issues.

In the end, the question is: was Phil Schneider a crank who took his own life because of paranoid hallucinations, or was he murdered by agents of the government for giving out classified information? Was he murdered to shut him up? Or, could there be another reason: the same reason Morris Jessup was murdered? Were they both murdered to give credibility to stories that were, in fact, *false*?

Phil's death is seen by conspiracy buffs as *proof that what he was saying was true*. In the same way, Jessup's death is seen as proof that the claims of Carlos Allende about the Philadelphia Experiment are true. And in both cases, what seems to be an obvious murder poorly disguised as a suicide is the common factor of conviction that persuades the many believers in the stories surrounding the two figures.

The problem is that we all know that those boys in Black Ops can do better than that when they want to! If they want a death to look perfectly natural, if they want to just shut you up, you can be sure that they can do it. By the same token, if they want a death to look like a murder disguised as a suicide, they can do that, too. It is patently absurd for Schneider to have announced on numerous occasions that the secret government had made over a dozen attempts on his life. Such agencies do not make "attempts" on a person's life. They do the deed, and *it looks exactly the way they want it to look*. Don't delude yourself by thinking otherwise. There are occasional leaks and embarrassing stories about such agencies, but I can just about guaran-damn-tee that they are planned. Nothing like creating a reputation for being a bumbling bunch to cover up the fact that, at the deepest levels, very little bumbling takes place.

What this means is that the deaths of Jessup and Schneider were very likely engineered for the express purpose of promoting disinformation to inspire belief in something connected to them either after their death, or promoted by them before their death. And if that is the case, then we have to seriously suspect the stories that are propagated *in connection with their deaths, and assume that they may be disinformation.*

There is another interesting death of recent times: Stefan Marinov. Marinov was a colleague of Ark's with whom he had corresponded on a number of occasions. Around the time that Ark learned of the flood in Poland described in a previous chapter, apparently Stefan was jumping off a fire escape in Graz, Austria. As it happens, Stefan was a political and scientific dissident. He did, indeed, have a history of protest against suppression of truth and the Scientific Thought Police. He did have a history that would suggest that suicide was not unbelievable in his case. His friend and colleague, Panos Pappas wrote:

I knew Stefan Marinov over 20 years. He used to say I am his oldest scientific co-fighter and fellow friend. Stefan was with me in Athens repeating his last experiments, just 15 days before he died. At that time, nothing could make me suspect his early death, two weeks later.

Adopting the Police explanation that Dr Stefan Marinov killed himself, on July 15, 1997, jumping from the University of Graz Bibliotheque (Library) building, I would like to ask: Why there was no official press or news release?

I was the first to inform his son, Marin Marinov two weeks later, on 31/7/1997 in Sophia for the death of his father who asked me a similar question. "Why the police still did not inform me, for two weeks, after the death of my father?"

Stefan Marinov was known all over the world, half of the citizens of city of Graz knew him. Stefan Marinov's death, jumping off a public building, should have been the first news for the city of Graz, for half the people there will now look for Stefan and many more from all over the world. Is it true that there is no press release in this case for the city of Graz? Does it look like a cover up? Even, Mr Deisting who first informed us, found out accidentally about Stefan's death from the librarian on 25/7/1997.

Stefan had attempted unsuccessfully to kill himself in the past, in Paris, in an attempt to make a protest against scientific censorship and the indifference of the scientific community.

Assuming that Stefan had chosen for himself, a public building, as the Library of the University of Graz, instead of his own high elevated balcony, apparently he did so for the same protest, however, not particularly for the University of Graz. He did so to protest against all universities and position-occupying, indifferent-for-the-truth scientists and salary receiving professors.

The authorities of the University, knowing Stefan and his continuous efforts to answer unanswered scientific questions for the last 20 years, apparently managed to cancel an annoying press conference or press release by the police, which they thought would have caused students all over the world to ask more questions which their Professors could not answer and Editors would not publish, like the lists of questions and problems Stefan used to send and never got an answer – other than the typical "Professor's" answer: "I am not a Specialist", "Do not get me involved", "I have no time … ", quoting only the most recent responses to his questions, just one month before his Last Protest.

Whoever controls knowledge for humanity and tries to stop human evolution by confusing the masses and public media should know that whatever they call Stefan Marinov's death – suicide or killing, they committed another killing for Stefan Marinov killed himself, in order to protest against the control of scientific knowledge.

Just before the end of the last century the authority of the USA patent office issued a direction: "No more patents on electromagnetism will be accepted, for whatever is to be invented in electromagnetism, has already been invented!".

At the dawn of the airplane revolution, scientific authorities, like the Academy of Science in France or the Royal Society with Lord Kelvin made the aphorism: "Machines heavier than air may not fly!", presumably based on mathematical proofs!

At the last part of our century for ten years (decade of 1970), scientific institutions and public media were making repetitively clear via all means: "We are facing a disaster, petroleum is coming to an end before the year 2000!" Now, they say "conservation of energy" is perfect!, even they cannot prove this "conservation" better than the degree of error present day technology introduces – at least 1 ppm masking error, remaining in all experiments, which is huge for planetary and astronomical scale. Instead, they want to say: Energy was violated only once in the past, at the beginning, only at the "Big Bang", and that this conservation will never be violated again in the future by all means! (not to allow humans to step to the next scientific evolution). They say the "Perpetual Mobile" is not possible, only a crazy scientist may attempt it, even, they have no scientific proof for its nonexistence, only the assumption that it has not yet been invented. This attitude is not science!

Apparently the sense and politics, for the next step of civilization is coming, dictates these actions in order to stop or delay scientific evolution.

However, it was the Teslas, the Wrights, the Marinovs who did not listen to these politics, and science advances despite the intentionally spread confusion.

Stefan spent a big portion of his life to fight confusion and misinformation in Physics. Theories reducing the Physics of experiments into the Physics of gendaken utopia, such as the relativity theory with observers moving with constant velocity (non-existing). Stefan, however, soon realized it was a waste of his time fighting a dead horse and the politics behind the Physics.

Stefan Marinov was also a strong believer in the non-conservation of energy as the underlying principle of the universe, creation, and life. Soon, the big passion and mission of his life became to prove the non-conservation of energy and to offer it to humanity, as a mechanism of supplying abundant energy for every one, terminating third world starvation and poverty below all elementary living standards and elevating humanity to its next due stage. Stefan Marinov considered, during the last fifteen years of his life, the construction of a self-sustaining energy producing device, the so called "Perpetual Mobile", as the only mission of his life given to him and purpose of living.

When the noble man (correctly or wrongly) believed could not accomplish this last mission of his life, decided to offer his life against his first noble goal, fighting misinformation, censorship and deliberately spread confusion in Physics. He decided his Last Protest.

Stefan you may not have been able (and you would not be able) with your short resources to give us an effective Perpetual Mobile, producing energy out of nothing and sustaining itself, however, you left us many principles and knowledge. You were unable because of another non-conservation Perpetuum that has long been discovered outside the world of Physics and is in operation in human society – the Perpetual Money Machine, producing (issuing and printing) money out of nothing and sustaining itself.

For as long as the second Perpetuum (even unknown to many, but very well known to a few) is in existence, the first is not allowed to exist. For the big truth is (without entering into details for the effective mechanisms): The one Perpetuum excludes and will exclude the other Perpetuum, ... and yours, Stefan, really happens to be the second.

Stefan you left us, though you could work, dig into forgotten and forbidden research, and produce more. However, you considered your Last Protest more important. Be sure, we do not listen, too, to politics and economics. It is only a matter of time. Your example will give more energy to us. It was the best Perpetual Mobile you made – that of energy and knowledge.

Sincerely,

Professor P. T. Pappas

Markopulioti 28, Athens 11744, Greece.

e-mail pappasp@ibm.net

However, there was one tiny little glitch in what might have been a perfect suicide. Panos was so distressed about this sudden "suicide" of his friend, colleague and current research partner, that he went personally to investigate and wrote the following email. Look for the very startling feature that Professor Pappas mentions.

Update on Stefan Marinov's death .

On 18 to 20 of August, I and Dr. Paul LaViolette visited the city of Graz to investigate the accident.

We visited the University of Graz at the back of the Bibliotheque at Universitatsplatz 2, A 8010-Graz, where Stefan Marinov presumably jumped off from the top of the four level outside emergency staircase to the street. According to the librarian only one student show [sic] Stefan actually jumping off. The name of the student is not known to us. The body of Stefan was found lying on the street below the staircase by Professor Ernst Ebermann. Stefan was not bleeding and initially Professor Ebermann thought he was sleeping there. He was still alive. Stefan left no cry or cries. The ambulance was called and Stefan died on his way to the Hospital. The bicycle with which Stefan presumably arrived there, is still there, locked and unnoticed (at least up to 19/9/1997). No body else noticed the accident, except first the assumed student and later Professor Ebermann, and perhaps a few other people later.

According to Professor Ebermann, *a brightly visible fluorescent spot, about the same size and in the same exact position with the body,* was left on the asphalt of the street, for 3 days, after the removal of the body, without an apparent cause for the spot, or without being due to any bleeding of blood or another liquid coming from Stefan's body.

The Police has made no official announcement today. Apparently, they did not investigate the case obviously in depth, since the bike is still by the place of accident, locked and unnoticed. The apartment of Stefan is sealed by the police and nobody is allowed to enter, except for his son Marin Marinov who entered for a brief time on 6 or 7 of August 1997. His belongings were not allowed to be taken and are still sealed there.

Stefan left various letters typed over his typewriter and bearing his signature. In a particular letter, he was asking me to be notified immediately and a few others. The police never made the notification to anybody.

The authorities of Graz refuse any value for the letters and to his last will, for it bears only one signature without witnesses. The case of Stefan Marinov and his letters were given to the city Advocate: Dr Egbert Sprenger, Joanneuming 11, A-8010 Graz.

In the morning of 19/8/1997, we, together with Mr. Jeorg Deisting visited the offices of the city advocate Dr E. Sprenger. The said case and letters were there, but, we were refused of any information. We strongly protested against the refusal, but, eventually, we had to leave without getting any information.

The son of Stefan Marinov, Marin Marinov is currently Deputy Minister of Industry of Bulgaria and is in a delicate situation with respect to the death of his father.

No one knew or was told about the intended and assumed suicide of Stefan Marinov, even his brother who talked to him on the phone one hour before Stefan's death. Stefan had visited his son in Bulgaria 20 days before, myself in Athens 15 days before, had written a letter to me 3 days before, and had written letters to various other people, making appointments or suggesting various future collaborations (to Professor Selleri for example). 10 days before Stefan's death, Stefan had made a Hotel reservation for me and himself for an International Physics Conference to take place in Koln, Germany, on August 25, 1997.

Professor P. T. Pappas

Markopulioti 28, Athens 11744, Greece.

e-mail pappasp@ibm.net

When I read the above description of what Professor Pappas had discovered in his personal investigation of the death of his friend and colleague, the mention of the fluorescent spot on the sidewalk literally made my hair stand up. I immediately thought of a very strange remark made by an abductee under hypnosis:

A: Umm … You know, that's funny! I don't remember getting out of the truck! I see us getting out of the truck … For some reason … I see the lights of the truck on … I see something over the top of the truck

… I see a flash of light … I see us getting out of the truck … I see us walking in the woods.

Q: Where are you going in the woods?

A: I don't want to go in there. Um … I see almost like I'm fighting … like fighting going or something … I'm afraid …

Q: Take a deep breath, let's go deeper … begin to describe what happened. You said you are fighting and resisting …

A: Um-hmm …

Q: What are you fighting? Who are you fighting?

A: No, I don't … I … It's like I'm … nobody's around me but we're all three like walking into the woods … I'm afraid … I don't want to go … there's like a fear somewhere … It's like I know there's something there …

Q: OK, what happens next?

A: It's like I fall … I'm asleep …

Q: OK, well the subconscious mind continues to record even when you are asleep … What happens next?

A: I'm being carried …

Q: By who or what?

A: Umm … I see this large hairy thing with huge hands …

Q: OK. Where is it taking you?

A: It's taking us to a place … I don't know how we get there … I don't know how we get there … but I see this place, and I see … what I see is a cave-like thing but I see at the top of the cave are these yellow lights …

Q: Yellow lights?

A: Big yellow lights … its almost like, um, not bright lights … like covered yellow lights … like, huge … as big as, um … like small swimming pools … they're big … and they are up in the ceiling … and they're yellow …

Q: Up in the ceiling and they're yellow?

A: Yeah, they're in the cave … boy! this is a strange place!

Q: OK. Describe everything. What do you see?

A: Um, I'm just going to tell you what I see … this is strange … I see a cart … almost like a little golf cart …

Q: What is the cart doing?

A: Um … I see it there … I almost see us, um … this is like a conveyor belt-type thing … It's almost like we're put on a silver disk, or like a silver stretcher-type thing …

Q: What happens next and what do you see around you?

A: Umm … I see myself on a table … [signs of distress]

Q: What's the matter?

A: I see this face I don't like.

Q: What face don't you like?

A: Umm …

Q: Describe the face …

A: Let me see it … can't see it … it flashed and then I can't see it …

Q: What feeling do you get from those faces?

A: I don't like them … they are angry …

Q: Why are they angry …

A: 'Cause somebody's snooping around.

Q: Who's snooping around?

A: They're mad about the hypnosis.

Q: Which hypnosis?

A: The one you did before.

Q: OK. What do they propose to do about it? How did they find out about it?

A: They know everything.

Q: OK. What do they propose to do about it?

A: Change things.

Q: What are they going to change and how?

A: It's almost like I'm hearing them say that, um, change the programming.

Q: Whose programming are they going to change?

A: I guess, mine.

Q: OK, what happens next.

A: Too intense, too fast. Knew something like this was gonna happen … then I hear them say that they're behind schedule … running out of time …

Q: Can you tell what they are behind schedule for and what they are running out of time for?

A: Umm … It's funny, I hear them saying that the cleansing time is almost here … something like that …

Q: Why don't you like them?

A: They scare me.

Q: Why do they scare you?

A: Umm … [distress]

Q: What do you see?

A: It's almost like they're pinching me …

Q: Where are they pinching you …

A: My arm …

Q: What are they doing to your arm?

A: Like they are running a tube up my arm … like at the crease of my arm they're running a tube … into my arm.

Q: Alright, now what are they doing?

A: I don't know what the hell they're doing with my arm … Umm … what was that?

Q: What was it?

A: I see a flash …

Q: And then what?

A: I don't know, it's really hard to see …
Q: What color flash? Just a flash of light?
A: Like a green light or something.
Q: Now what … what do you feel … what do you sense … ?
A: I feel like they're putting stuff in my veins …
Q: And what is this stuff doing to you?
A: Changing me …
Q: How is it changing you?
A: I don't know … its funny … its almost like they're putting something in my blood … something that glows …

The hypnosis session above was conducted in August of 1994, three years before Marinov's death. The remark about something that glowed being introduced into the subject's arm had stuck in my mind as an extremely curious detail for which I had no explanation. I tried to contact several other people who were working with abductees to inquire about it, but no one seemed to have the slightest idea what it could mean.

When Professor Pappas wrote about the glowing spot on the pavement where Stefan Marinov's body had fallen, I wondered if there was any connection. Pappas was an academic, not interested in UFOs or aliens or the paranormal. He had no evident agenda in these areas to promote. In November of 1997, we discussed the matter with the Cs. One thing we first wanted to know was if Stefan was really dead, or had the whole scenario been faked.

November 15, 1997
Q: (A) Alright, I would like to know something about the death of this guy, Marinov. Is Marinov dead?
A: Yes.
Q: Did he commit suicide?
A: No.
Q: Was he physically pushed from the fire escape?
A: He was a victim of highly sophisticated post hypnotic suggestion/mind control.
Q: Who was responsible for installing the post hypnotic suggestion?
A: Chain of Command.
Q: OK, the STS chain of command. In human terms, who was involved?
A: M1.
Q: What's M1?
A: British Intelligence.
Q: (A) What was the main reason for his death?
A: Revelations too "sensitive," would cause "instabilities."
Q: Instabilities in what?

A: Power structure/control.

Q: What kind of revelation?

A: Theoretical physics.

Q: In what specific area?

A: "Unified Field Theory."

Q: (A) I am not aware that he was working in this direction. He was more experimental than theoretical, but he was collaborating with other guys. In particular, I would like to know if this Pappas knows the same as Marinov did?

A: Not completely, or he would be dead, too.

Q: (T) What was this guy's breakthrough in Unified Field Theory? I know they are not gonna tell us, but maybe they can point us in the right direction. (L) Well, they put that in quotes, so I don't know …

A: Merger.

Q: (A) I want to know if it is safe for me to contact this Pappas and ask questions?

A: Up to a point. Better to use faculties you possess for your own discoveries.

Q: (T) Did the gentleman who just passed away learn something about the merging of Unified Field Theories? (L) Or merging of factors …

A: The problem is that these scientists are often too eager to share and reveal. Remember: it is most difficult to win a Nobel Prize when one's residence is a tomb.

Q: Is it true that there was a luminous spot on the pavement where Marinov died?

A: Yes.

Q: Why?

A: Residue of substance used in mind control procedure.

Q: What was this substance? And what was it used for?

A: Phosphorescent Sulphate Ammonia Chloride. Ammonium Chloride with correct formulation, can be injected intravascularly in order to induce a state of super-suggestibility when utilized in conjunction with pre-existant hypnotic programming.

Q: Alright, a subject I hypnotized some years ago described being abducted, taken to an underground facility nearby, and having some sort of glowing green fluid introduced intravenously. Was this a similar substance?

A: Close.

Q: I think that I remember something similar being described by Karla Turner.

A: Obviously, the residual on the sidewalk was there as a result of blunt trauma to the skull.

Q: He jumped because of the programming and the blunt trauma was the result of his head hitting the sidewalk …

A: Yes.

Q: (T) Are these ideas, the programming that is carried on this way that is described here, that was described by Laura's subject, that is described in the Karla Turner book, and that is making something of a stir in other arenas, is this within the realm of the military abduction scenario, or covert operation abductions. Are these all related to human abductors rather than alien?

A: Yes, to some extent.

Q: Yes, well S** described her abductors as being military guys and *not* aliens … (T) Yes, and she was taken out there by Anclote to the little base …

A: No coincidence, the former Stauffer Chemical plant nearby!

Q: (A) There was another guy who was in contact with both Marinov and Pappas, and with whom I was also in contact; his name is Assis, does he know essentially the same as Marinov?

A: Close.

Q: (A) The guy whose book we have, Graneau, it seems to me that he knows more than any of them?

A: Ask specifics.

Q: (A) Does Graneau know the details of the Unified Field Theory that is hidden from the rest of us?

A: More …

Q: He knows more … Why don't you guys just quit messing around and give us the UFT?

A: No. Because, then somebody would kill you.

Q: Alright, then, I don't want to know! Sorry I asked!

A: You will discover on your own, when you are ready.

The difference – or similarities – between Marinov's death and the death of Morris Jessup, or even Phil Schneider, have to be carefully considered. In the case of the former two, they were actually working on very similar subjects. Jessup and Marinov were both interested in sources of *free energy*, and they were both talking about things in ways that drew attention to certain ideas that, apparently, are very dangerous to consider. The case of Schneider is more difficult. His "murder" seems to be set up to discredit him in general, or to confirm the Montauk mythos.

But what about this "M1?" Well, have a look at another curious excerpt from the Cs:

April 24, 1996

Q: (L) When I was kidnapped at the age of 3 or 4 in Jacksonville, how many days was I missing? My mother simply has a blank about it, which amazes her.

A: 12 days.

Q: (L) Who was it that kidnapped me?

A: Jan. […] Corps member. […] Select division of economic legion under control of G5. […] Intel.
Q: (L) What was the purpose of this kidnapping?
A: To install self-destruct programming.

Morris Jessup's death can be directly connected to ideas about UFT. "Carlos Allende" begins his initial letter by jumping on Jessup for requesting the public to demand research into UFT. The letter was received on January 13, 1956, with the return address: RD #1, Box 223, New Kensington, Pennsylvania, but which was postmarked *Gainesville, Texas*:

My Dear Dr. Jessup,
Your invocation to the Public that they move en Masse upon their Representatives and have thusly enough Pressure placed at the right & sufficient Number of Places where from a Law demanding Research into Dr. Albert Einstein's Unified Field Theory May be enacted (1925-27) is Not at all Necessary. It May Interest you to know that The Good Doctor Was Not so Much influenced in his retraction of the Work, by Mathematics, as he most assuredly was by Humantics.

These claims about Albert Einstein's UFT were made by Carlos Allende *exactly 8 months after the death of Albert Einstein* on April 18, 1955 at 1:15 a.m. Not only was Morris Jessup not alive when claims were made about what he was up to, Einstein was similarly *conveniently dead.*

As it happens, the UFT that Einstein developed in 1925–27 was the *wrong* one. It was the first "homemade UFT" and, at the time, Einstein publicly expressed optimism that UFT would soon be solved. Einstein realized soon after the publication of the 1925 paper that the results were not impressive. This *has* been repeatedly checked, and is a mathematical fact, contrary to the assertion of Carlos Allende.

Einstein continued to hammer away at the problem, corresponding with friends and colleagues about his ideas, so there is no lack of source material about his thinking, his efforts, his frustrations. Of course, these papers were not published until long after the propagation of the Allende letters. In his paper of 1927, Einstein wrote that the Weyl, Eddington, Einstein road "does not bring us closer to truth." He then returned to consideration of the Kaluza theory, only he discovered that his own work was identical to that of Klein, and Klein did it first.

In 1928, the *New York Times* carried a story headlined: "Einstein on verge of great discovery; resents intrusion," followed by another: "Einstein reticent on new work; will not 'count unlaid eggs.'" These stories erroneously state that Einstein was preparing a book on a new theory. In fact, as his correspondence shows, and his colleagues confirmed, he was at work on a short paper trying out a new version of UFT by means of distant parallelism. At the time, Einstein's name was as magical as a rock star is today and considering the impending stock market crash, it is very likely that these were merely distractions for the public.

Einstein's friend Eddington wrote to him saying, "You may be amused to hear that one of our great department stores in London has posted on its window your paper (the six pages pasted up side by side), so that passersby can read it all through. Large crowds gather around to read it!" So great was the public clamor for a hero that Einstein had to go into hiding. As it turned out, it was much ado about almost nothing. His attempt to derive his equations from a variational principle had to be withdrawn.

But, in 1929, Einstein was again sure he was on the right track. Wolfgang Pauli wrote scathingly: "[Einstein's] never-failing inventiveness as well as his tenacious energy in the pursuit of [unification] guarantees us in recent years, on the average, *one theory per annum* … It is psychologically interesting that for some time the current theory is usually considered by its author to be the 'definitive solution.'"

When he finally gave up the "distant parallelism" approach, Einstein wrote to Pauli, "Sie haben also recht gehabt, Sie Spitzbube," or "You were right after all, you rascal!"

August 17, 2000

Q: (A) OK. UFT. This is one of these things that I don't know what it is good for, because the Wave will erase everything and make everything new. Yet, it is in me, so let me ask. I don't know what it is good for, but I want to do it. Einstein was working on his UFT for like 30 years. Maybe more. He was changing his methods. At some point, did he realize that he found a solution? During all these thirty years, was there a point where he came upon the right solution?

A: Yes, but sadly, his solution for UFT largely erased TOR [Theory of Relativity].

Q: (A) Once he found this solution, did he reject it because it erased TOR?

A: No. His progenitors sealed it, in order to keep intact the status quo.

Q: (L) His progenitors? Isn't that your parents?

A: Other definitions apply. [A source from which something develops. Possibly Einstein's 4D "controllers" or his Zionist connections, e.g. Chaim Weizmann.]

Q: (A) Can we have an idea of which year Einstein found the solution that erases TOR?

A: Sure, it was 1938.

Q: (A) According to what I know, between '35 and '38 there was a period in which Einstein published nothing. In '38, he published a paper with Bergman which was a revival of Kaluza-Klein theory. That was exactly 1938. So, I guess that was the paper that was close.

A: Can you obtain a copy?

Q: (A) Yes, I have a copy.

A: Good!!! Clues abound within.

Q: (A) What I do not understand is why, a few years later, he completely abandoned that and started working very hard on a completely different solution. If he knew …

A: Was under control.

Q: (A) Can you control somebody and make him spend years … Oh! Mind control! They got him!

A: Why do you think he emigrated to the United States in the first place?

Q: (A) Well, that is not a surprise. He was a Nobel Prize winner and America was getting together every possible Nobel Prize winner, and also there was the persecution of the Jews, so it was natural.

A: More to it than that. What about Freud?

Q: (L) I guess they didn't want Freud! He didn't know anything about UFT! (A) Now, apparently Von Neumann was also involved in application of UFT. But, Von Neumann was, as far as we know, doing a completely different kind of mathematics. He didn't even really know geometry, differential geometry. He was doing completely different things. So how come the UFT that was discovered by Einstein, involved Von Neumann. What did Von Neumann contribute to this project?

A: Von Neumann was one of three overseers at Princeton with level 7 security clearance, and a clear budget request permittance.

Q: (L) My question is, about Von Neumann, as I understand it, Von Neumann was supposed to have been involved with the creation of a time machine, right?

A: Yes.

Q: (L) Did he succeed in such a project?

A: Yes.

Q: (L) Well, why was it that, when he developed a brain tumor and realized he was going to die – and I read that he screamed and yelled like a baby when he knew there was no hope – if he was somebody who had access to a time machine, why wasn't he able to do something about it instead of carrying on like a madman? The stories about his screams echoing all over the place, are horrible. He realized that his great mind was going to soon be still; if he had access to a time machine, one would think that he would have used it, would have pulled every string he could, to forestall his own death.

A: No Laura, it does not work that way. And besides, if you had a brain tumor, you could be forgiven for a few mental peculiarities too!

Q: (L) I just don't understand why, when he knew he was sick, that he didn't just use the time machine to go forward in time for a cure, or backward in time to correct something in his past …

A: The time machine was not his property.

Q: (L.) So, they got what they needed from him and let him die. (A) It is not clear. He got this cancer so suddenly, it may even have been induced. (L.) Well, that's a thought. (A) It is said that when he was dying, his brain was working perfectly and that was his tragedy. He could think, he could produce, he was a genius. [...]

Q: (A) Now, Einstein's 1938 paper is a Kaluza-Klein paper – on torsion. What is the story about torsion?

A: Clues hidden in the text.

Of course, we dug out the 1938 paper and began to read and discovered to our amazement that this was the paper where Einstein proposed to take Kaluza's fifth dimension as *real*.

We now come back to the fact that someone wrote some letters to Morris Jessup about his book on UFOs, including specific mention (in the very first paragraph) of a particular paper of Albert Einstein, which, as it happens, is the *wrong* paper to follow, and as soon as Dr. Jessup was discovered to have been "mysteriously killed," the story was off and running! And all the researchers have been misled ever since, following the wrong paper. And it's all about free energy, so to say. *This should give everyone pause when they read the claims of the many purveyors of New Age Free Energy devices. If you really discover it, you're dead.*

When the Philadelphia Experiment story began to lose its appeal because none of the research was panning out, along came the Montauk experiments and the many handy expositors of that scenario, creating new Grail stories to lead the researchers off into wild, endless, and erroneous speculation.

After studying the Grail question itself for a period, I came to the realization that the comparison between the two situations is not just idle speculation. As we have seen and will see repeatedly, the motivations for the coverup seem to relate to the same issues: free energy leads to concepts of time and time travel, or space-time manipulation and shaping.

As it happens, it was at the time of the propagation of the Grail stories that the three major monotheistic religions took over, and the chief thing about all of them is that they seem to be highly motivated to create the taboo on thinking of time as *cyclical*. Scientific materialism has carried this tendency to ultimate heights. "The world must have been born, therefore, it must die." And scientific materialism claims nothingness before birth and nothingness after death.

Scientific philosophies refer to the *accidental mechanicalness* of the universe and teach us that the only meaning to life is no meaning at all. "Eat, drink, and be merry for tomorrow you may die," and then – oblivion.

Mircea Eliade's opinion is that the religious myths of man were created as a "defense against the Terror of History." And we find that, at the deepest level, these defenses against history have to do with Time. The religious myths are numerous and varied, but, when all the trappings are stripped away, the chief point of argument is *which conception of time is being utilized as the foundation of the myth: cyclical or linear?*

There are those who say that the mythical/religious formulas and images through which the "primitives" expressed their reality seem childish and absurd. Eliade, however, sees in religious myths a "desperate effort not to lose contact with being" (justification of existence in the face of the cruel world) and to find meaning – an archaic ontology.

The *Axis Mundi*, or Center, was a point where Heaven, Earth and Hell met and *where passage to one region or another was possible*. At any point where there was a convergence of the three realms, a temple was considered to exist whether one was constructed there or not. This center was the zone of the sacred – of *absolute reality* – and was symbolized by trees, fountains, ladders, ropes, and so forth. Interaction with these symbols was considered initiatory and took place in a timeless state. Thus it is thought that religious rituals were developed in an attempt to connect to this Divine Model or archetype.

One of the most interesting aspects of this archaic ontology was the Abolition of Time through *imitation of the archetypes*. In this way, a sacrifice was not only an imitation of the original sacrifice of the god, it somehow was seen to be an energetic alignment of the three realms, the creating of a passage of some sort along the *Axis Mundi*. So, for a moment, during the ritual or sacrifice, the supplicant was *identifying him or herself with the primordial gesture* and thereby abolishing time, and regenerating him or herself and all the related participants.

> All religious acts are held to have been founded by gods, civilizing heroes, or mythical ancestors. … Not only do rituals have their mythical models, but any human act whatever acquires effectiveness to the extent to which it exactly repeats an act performed at the beginning of time by a god, a hero, or an ancestor.
>
> We encounter in these myths and rites the idea that man only repeats the acts of the gods; his calendar commemorates, in the period of a year or other longer cycles, all the cosmogonic phases which took place in the beginning or which *take place repeatedly at another level of reality*. (Eliade, 1954)

Everywhere there is a conception of the end and the beginning of a *cyclical temporal period*; and, coincidental to this idea is the expulsion of demons, diseases and sins. These ideas are demonstrated by the ubiquitous celebrations of the New Year.

> In the last analysis, what we discover in all these rites and all these atti-
> tudes is the will to devaluate time. ... All the rites and all the behavior
> patterns ... would be comprised in the following statement: 'If we pay
> no attention to it, time does not exist; furthermore, where it becomes
> perceptible – because of man's sins, i.e., when man departs from the ar-
> chetype and falls into duration – time can be annulled.' (Eliade, 1954)

This is, of course, Eliade's interpretation. However, what we begin
to think when we consider the work of Morris Jessup and Einstein's
1938 paper, is that these myths are all speaking about a hyperdimensional reality that is para-physical and *can be accessed via technology*. I would
like to suggest that these rites represent a pale reflection of an ancient
technology of transcending time, of building an Ark that permits passage through the destruction cycle of Time without loss of internal
integrity. They also tell us that Time is not linear; it is cyclical. Further:
It will be renewed as it was in the days of Noah!

We postulate that the original worship of the goddess and of the
principle of cyclical time – which represented this technology in allegory and metaphor – was progressively vilified and destroyed in favor of
introducing a male deity and a linear eschatology, what we have come
to call global pathocracy. Uranus, the father of the Titans, appears to
have originally been the Mother, Ur-Ana. It would be pointless just
now to track all the changes, inversions, corruptions, and adaptations
of the myths since the primary thing we are concerned with is that the
worship of the goddess was based upon a *concept of cyclical time, and a
literal, ancient technology*. All of the symbology of cycles, of birth, death
and renewal, belonged to the goddess. But it is very difficult to penetrate to the original rites, the original technique.

Eliade, of course, posits that these rituals are based on the idea of
abolishing time only ritually. He proposes that the participants in the rites
believed that, by imitating the act of creation, they could absolve themselves from sin, turn away the wrath of the gods, and call down a new
beginning for all the people. What is significant in this ideation is the fact
that such rituals are predicated upon *levels of reality that are extrahuman*.

In all of these myths there is the idea of the cyclical temporal period
from a realm where time does not exist. The New Year celebrations take
place at the end of the old year so that the New Year can be born free
of sin. What is even more interesting is that such rites act out in very
precise terms the conditions of the Days of Noah.

For the most part, the beginnings of these rites comprise a series of
dramatic elements that represent *a condition of universal confusion, the abolition of order and hierarchy, and the ushering in of chaos*. There is a symbolic
Deluge that *annihilates all of humanity in order to prepare the way for a new and
regenerated human species*.

In numerous myths and rites we find the same central idea of the yearly return to chaos, followed by a new creation. The chaos that preceded the rebirth was as essential as the birth itself. Without chaos there could be no rebirth. *"As it was in the days of Noah."*

In many of the more modern ritual versions, the Deluge and the element of water are present in one way or another as either libations or baptism. Baptism is the subjective, microcosmic equivalent of a macrocosmic-level deluge: a return to the formless state! This formlessness, this chaos, was exemplified in many ways: fasting, confession, excess grief, joy, despair or orgy – all of them only seeking to *reproduce a chaotic state* from which a New Creation could emerge. This suggests to us that the chaos of Carnival is essential for renewal. The ancient science revealed in these myths is telling us that the conditions of disorder on our planet are not leading us to the End of the World, they are the dissolution of structure preparatory to the Renewal of Time!

I would like to ask the reader to take particular note that the ideas of "exhaustion of physical resources, invasion by the souls of the dead, and sexual excess" are part of this archaic model in the sense that they are signs of *the approaching suspension and renewal of time.* In my reading of esoteric literature, I have come across the proposal that such a dissolution was merely symbolic of an ideological new beginning. It has even been proposed that anarchy in political terms is what is being represented here. Some theorists propose a deliberate descent into revolution is the way to bring about a New Age. Certain magical schools even have the idea that they are supposed to perform rituals to invoke the gods of destruction as a means of helping the process along. I think that all of them are missing the point.

A recent discovery in science suggests that this may not be just an archaic idea. On August 15, 2001, an article in the *New York Times* was headlined: "Cosmic Laws Like Speed of Light Might Be Changing," by James Glanz and Dennis Overbye. It said, in part:

> An international team of astrophysicists has discovered that the basic laws of nature as understood today may be changing slightly as the universe ages, a surprising finding that could rewrite physics textbooks and challenge fundamental assumptions about the workings of the cosmos ...
>
> If confirmed, the finding could mean that other constants regarded as immutable, like the speed of light, might also have changed over the history of the cosmos ...
>
> Scientists who have examined the paper have not been able to find any obvious flaws. But because the consequences for science would be so far-reaching and because the differences from the expected measurements are so subtle, many scientists are expressing skepticism that the discovery will stand the test of time, and say they will wait for independent evidence before deciding whether the finding is true.

On the other hand, the finding would fit with some theorists' new views of the universe, particularly the prediction that previously unknown dimensions might exist in the fabric of space. Even scientists on the project have been deliberately cautious in presenting their result. Describing the implications of what his team observed, Dr. Webb said, "It's possible that there is a time evolution of the laws of physics." ...

Dr. Steinhardt said most theorists would have expected those changes to have occurred in the first seconds of the universe's life and be virtually unobservable by astronomers today. Still, he pointed out that several years ago, other astronomers unexpectedly found that the present universe is apparently filled with a mysterious kind of energy that counteracts gravity on large scales. Perhaps the two effects are somehow related, Dr. Steinhardt said ...

But a few physicists, like Dr. Jacob D. Bekenstein of Hebrew University in Israel, noted that some theories have long been predicting a change in some of nature's apparent constants. Dr. Bekenstein called the findings "potentially revolutionary" and said he was inclined to believe them.

In light of this small, but possibly significant finding, we think that it is most interesting that such an idea as the cosmos decaying and changing in very real terms, *was part of the archaic ontology.* Where did they get such an idea? Where and how did they come up with the concept that the running down of the cosmic clock brought about a return to chaos, including an infestation of demons and souls of the dead just prior to a deluge?

This may be a very important clue since it seems that, in our present time, there is a veritable invasion of otherworldly visitors masquerading as aliens as well as a rapid descent of morality into a veritable frenzied return to chaos, as it were! Again we see, "as it was in the days of Noah."

Now, what we need to remember about these postulations is the inherently *optimistic* character of them; the consciousness of the *normality of the cyclical catastrophe*, the certainty of its meaning, and, above all, that it is never, *ever* final! The ideas communicate to us that, just as three days of darkness preceding the rebirth of the Moon are necessary, so is the death of an individual and the periodic death and rebirth of humanity necessary. Any material form, by the mere fact of its existence *in time*, loses vigor and becomes formless *if only for an instant*. It *must* return to chaos, to orgy, to darkness, to water; it must be reabsorbed into the primordial unity from which it issued to be reborn. The King is dead; long live the King!

But something changed the world view. Somehow, the perception of the End of the Time became a terrible punishment. Somehow, a god entered the world stage who destroyed the peace of Eden, and tempted man to place his trust in him, and him alone. "I am the Lord your God, and I am a jealous God!" Time became linear and with a prophesied end that was going to be final and complete. And woe to those who were not on the side of the right god who claimed to be the only one who could offer salvation.

The concept of the end being a precursor to a rebirth was lost with the introduction of monotheism. At that point, the End of Time became the End of the World – for everyone except those special chosen ones who were to be saved by a single, specific god to live in some mystical City of God with streets paved with gold, and almond-eyed houris serving dates and wine on every street corner. This single, specific god, has pretty much run the show ever since in any number of disguises. Until this appearance of monotheism, a myth was annually enacted that described a condition of life that was accepted as the way things were: *Time was cyclical.* The world might end, but if it did, it was only because it had run down and needed to be wound up again. All of the elements of the story of Noah are found in these myths: "As it was in the days of Noah."

In order to maintain this control in the present day, if, indeed, anyone thinks about space-time manipulation seriously, they must be misled to look in the wrong direction. Obviously, control would be lost if people were aware of the true nature of time and the fifth mathematical dimension, i.e. fourth density. So we must understand that this is a very great secret. It cannot be allowed to be scientifically revealed and proven.

July 18, 1998

Q: (A) Can we have a UFT which unifies EM and gravity and does not include the concept of other densities? In other words, can we put in a textbook all about the gravity and electromagnetics, and a student could learn all of this and still know nothing about other densities?

A: No. Other densities become apparent when …

Q: (A) So, it means that Einstein and Von Neumann knew about these other densities?

A: Yes, oh yes!!!

Q: (T) Just a thought: having UFT and being able to manipulate different fields within it, creates different effects. So, as we understand it in the apparent present state of science, we have to spin something in space in order to create gravity. But, with the UFT, one small offshoot is that one could create real gravity without spinning anything. So, the problem of weightlessness is really already solved …

A: Elementary my dear Terry, elementary.

Q: (T) So, this whole thing with the space station and all the trouble they are having readapting to gravity when they come back, is all a game …

A: When you "let the cat out of the bag," you create an entire feline "nation."

Unfortunately, anybody who gets close, anyone who is not misled, generally ends up dead. And that's a fact. They die with great regularity. Another half-dozen or so physicists of our acquaintance, working in similar directions, have died in the past few years, in the prime of life, suddenly and unexpectedly. Heart attacks and cerebral hemorrhages seem to be the affliction of choice – never mind that these are healthy guys for the most part, who generally don't smoke, walk a lot and eat moderately.

There's another curious thing: did the reader notice that Paul La Violette was hanging out with Panos Pappas when he went to investigate Marinov's death? As it happens, La Violette has some interesting friends such as Willis Harman, President of the Institute of Noetic Sciences, staffed also by folks with more of those strange, nebulous links to the Aviary. In fact, La Violette, Edgar Mitchell, and Hal Puthoff are listed as witnesses in the Disclosure Project. The reader might be interested in noting connections between La Violette and Tom Bearden, as well as noting that Col. Bearden has been very active in promoting false leads to the free energy ideas for some years now.[21] Strange bedfellows. We would also like to refer the reader to the most interesting fact of that Vincent Bridges has vociferously promoted La Violette's ideas.

> September 25, 1999
> Q: There is also a theory of Paul La Violette, that there is a wave that comes from explosions in the galactic core, and that *this* is what is behind this increased activity.
> A: Such waves exist.
> Q: Are these waves part of the cataclysmic double catastrophes that are predicted to be "on the way?"
> A: Who says?
> Q: Well, Paul La Violette and Vincent Bridges, and Jay Weidner, for example.
> A: You are not capable of predicting such things yet.
> Q: (A) We are not able to predict many things. You are able to predict better than us.
> A: Maybe so, but we do so oh so discreetly.

As we have already noted in several places, there were numerous instances when the Cassiopaeans gave instructions that we *not publish* certain material related to our research because it was dangerous. We can see from just the short examination of the subject above, that this isn't a joke. People really do die when they get too close to things. And often, their deaths are utilized to give credibility to *a corrupted variation of what they were actually thinking or doing* so as to keep the rumor-machine going, and to lead others off the track.

---

[21] http://quantumfuture.net/quantum_future/bearden.htm

Karla Turner is another one who was onto the hyperdimensional nature of the UFO phenomenon and she suddenly developed a particularly virulent form of cancer. The Cs even sent a warning, which I duly delivered. She didn't take it seriously. I really valued our Internet friendship, and when she wrote me for the last time, telling me that she was too weak to continue her correspondence, I wept.

There is another death that still bothers me. The old man I have written about elsewhere who was the insider to the Coral Castle story: Hilliard. He was in an auto accident the day after I first went to visit with him and talk about the Coral Castle. In December of 1996, he came to visit me here, and it was during that visit that he revealed his origins as Polish/Lithuanian when I shared with him the fact that Ark would soon be coming to America. He asked specifically that once Ark had arrived, I was to bring him to visit because *he had something important to tell us together.* We made the plans, and on the morning we were going to make the drive over to Orlando, I called to let him know we were leaving the house so he would know when to look for our arrival. His neighbor answered the phone and informed me that the old man *had just suffered a stroke* and was en route to the hospital as we were speaking. He died shortly after. Whatever he wanted to tell Ark, he never got the chance.

So, if all of this is so dangerous to talk about, why am I talking about it?

As many of you know, the current activities of the Bridges/Williams gang consist of the fact that Frank Scott suddenly, after eight years of the existence of our legal copyright on our research material, has been cranked up to falsely claim rights of joint authorship simply because he was present, as a guest-participant at most of the early sessions. At first, this truly insane behavior puzzled me because Mr. Scott doesn't have the chance of a snowball in Hell of prevailing in court, assuming that suit is filed. His attendance at the sessions for eight years after the publishing of the copyright notice is sufficient evidence of his intent to accept that it was and is solely authored and owned by me, that the likelihood of a summary judgment against him is a certainty – again, assuming that suit is filed.

After I gave the matter some more thought, it seemed pretty clear that by pirating the Cassiopaean Transcripts and posting them on the Internet unedited, the Williams/Bridges gang are deliberately and intentionally putting us in grave danger. And again, it's not a joke. Both Vincent Bridges and Frank Scott knew what was in the transcripts before they committed this outrageous act, violating not only our legal rights, but our privacy, the privacy of dozens of guests, and putting our children in peril by revealing personal information about them. They both knew of the numerous instances of information that the Cs urged us not to publish or share with "snakes in the grass." So, again, if there was ever any doubt about who is the channel, and who has negative intentions toward humanity as a whole, this effort to not only put our lives in grave danger so that it is possible that we will never be able to accomplish whatever it is we are supposed to do to "let the cat out of the bag", that fact ought to clinch it. It's very similar to the story of Solomon and the infant claimed by two mothers: Scott is clearly not the "mother" because he is not only willing to destroy the material itself, he is willing to destroy us.

However, our review of the above cases indicates that it is not quite so simple. Indeed, we have been attempting to make progress in UFT with some shielding in order to simply survive long enough to do it. If we don't survive, we can't do it. If we don't do it, we can't share it and, as the Cs described it, "let the cat out of the bag," producing an "entire feline nation," so to say.

So we see, of course, that in our case, just offing us in such a way that it would look perfectly natural, with the material published *as it is* would not be sufficient to cover up what we have been working on. Oh, no! It is necessary to put Mr. Scott in place as the channel in order to twist, distort, and corrupt the material, with the able assistance of Vincent Bridges, Jeff "Storm Bear" Williams, and the rest of the gang. It would not be enough to just get us killed – there must be preparation to "fill the void." There must be an ongoing effort to defame and diminish any true understanding of the material which is the major part of our work on the website here, and the ongoing channeling, including that which occurs in the very act of writing.

September 23, 2000

Q: OK, I want to find out about this Jack and the Beanstalk and the "giant meaning" you have talked about in the recent past. Not only that, but you have continuously hinted that something is just around the corner, and we are getting to the point where we are thinking that there is just simply not going to be enough time to do anything. Ark's got 800 pages of Maxwell to go through; he can't stop working to do that; 800 pages of equations is a lot of work – like months of hard work – and, time is passing – four years have gone by, and zip! I'm not getting impatient here, but time is going and you guys are sixth density and it means nothing to you … but we're getting older. What we are supposed to do, if we are supposed to do something to make the connection for things to move?

A: You are so anxious. Perhaps you should examine the ground covered, or were you just as close 10 years back?

Q: Well, ten years ago I didn't wear glasses. I didn't need 'em either! I could thread a needle! I mean, this thing called time has a profound effect on physiology whether you guys notice it or not! I know, it's the soul that counts, but my thought is that we are in these bodies, and it has been subtly suggested that we are in these present vehicles to *do* something.

A: But is it not a great adventure?

Q: Well, lately it has been a lot of working and slaving. Working to pay the bills. Then we had to survive this period when the company wasn't paying our invoices, so we had to borrow on our credit cards, now we have to pay that back *and* live at the same time. So, boom! Work, work, work!

A: So maybe you should return to the way things were when we first contacted you?

Q: No! I'm not complaining!

A: Yes, you are, though in a gentle way.

Q: Well, I mean you did so much, you brought us together, did all these things ... and ...

A: And you think there is no more?

Q: Well, no ... but ...

A: But what?!?

Q: Well, we're together and we are happy. And because we are together and happy we feel like we should be getting things accomplished ... that there are ...

A: And you are not?

Q: Not in a big useful way.

A: So say you. Thank goodness you ain't an expert in this judgment arena!

Q: So, you are saying that, even though it appears to us on the surface that nothing is happening, that at some level, something *is* happening?

A: Oh, yeah!! So ... Quit yer bitchin.

Q: Is it too much for me to ask for you to give me just one teensy tinesy little hint about what is going on at these other levels that we are not aware of that is so important?

A: You may ask.

Q: Well, I did. Just give me a little bitty hint ... a three-word clue ... Something to calm me down. Something to make me sleep well at night and that will let me know that all is right with the world ...

A: RAM.

Q: That's the clue?

A: Yes.

Q: Was that an abbreviation or a word?

A: Seek and ye shall find.

Q: (A) RAM. Random Access Memory.

A: Yes.

Q: How does that relate to what is going on at higher levels? Does everything we do, or does the movement of the project, depend upon my pursuit of the psychomantium project?

A: A little.

Q: Is part of this waiting process the completion of the Wave series since that has been consuming my life since May.

A: Yes.

Q: I have to say that the writing of this series has been one of the most educational projects I have ever undertaken. Because, in the writing, I have had to comb through the transcripts and have had to explain it to other people and before I can do that, I have to explain it to myself. It has become a profound mind expansion thing ...

A: Good.

Q: It's almost as much fun to be learning the things I am having to assemble as if I were reading it. And I'm the one writing it. It's really quite amazing.

A: In part you are.

March 18, 1995

Q: (L) Is there anything anyone can do to release persons stuck in these parallel realities and bring them back into the reality of origin?

A: Yes, but the technology is a closely guarded secret.

Q: (L) Do you know the secret?

A: Yes, but you do too!

Q: (L) I do too? [...]

A: Philadelphia Experiment.

Q: (L) Since you mentioned the Philadelphia Experiment, could you tell us in specific detail, how this was done? What kind of machines were used and how can we build one? [general uproar and laughter]

A: Do you intend to sit here for a day or two? [...] In short, build an EM generator.

February 24, 1996

A: Oh Laura, my dear, seems you need a refresher course in the transcripts. Maybe suggest you read them and relax and privately listen to the ones you have not as of yet transcribed a little more. This would be extremely helpful in your many and increasing communications via the "net" as well. Remember, we help you to unlock answers that have been placed in your superconsciousness files from before the "time" of the birth of your physical body. Also, false information is worse than no information at all.

June 7, 1997

Q: In reading the Celtic legends, I discovered that Cassiopeia was equated with Danu, or Don, as in Tuatha de Danaan, or the court of the goddess Danu. So, in other words, the supreme goddess of the Aryans was Cassiopeia. And, Cassiopeia is found in the zodiacal area of Aries, the "lamb," where Cephus the "rock" and "king" is also found, as well as Perseus, "he who breaks" and serpentarius. The image is of Perseus overcoming the serpent, and the ancient Celtic engravings of the horned god show him gripping two serpents by the throat. I would like to understand the symbology here …

A: You are on the right track.

Q: What is the symbology of the "breaking of rocks," as in the alchemical texts, as well as related to Perseus as "he who breaks?"

A: Occurs at a time when rocks break, as in the electromagnetic impulses that emanate from earthbound rocks when sheared by tectonic forces, and much more importantly, the possible utilization of said forces whether naturally or otherwise induced.

Q: Before we take our break, can you say any more about this ubiquitous "she" of the Celts, Cassiopeia, and the relationship to the Aryans?

A: Better continue your search, as this is how you learn and build power!

Q: When you said I needed to find a "superhypnotist" to break the locks on the knowledge placed in my superconsciousness, and then you suggested a "spin" doctor, and now Ark's actions while I was sleeping brought out some of the keys to large pieces of the puzzle and the connections, am I on the right track when I think that the actions we are taking in searching out these pieces of the puzzle, putting them together, and the amazing discoveries that have taken place as we go along, is the action of the "breaking" of these locks?

A: Likely.

Anyone who reads the transcripts can see the focus of the material. Knowing the focus, and realizing that the Williams/Bridges gang are working very hard to both claim *and* discredit the material, the objective becomes obvious.

Cassiopaeans: [Frank] was programmed for the specific purpose of "downloading" from you secrets coded into you before birth of your present body. He failed because you were incorruptible. He is now charged with the mission, in concert with Vincent Bridges, of destroying your ability to accomplish your mission.

When you let the cat out of the bag, you create a whole Feline Nation. RAM.

CHAPTER 56
INTOLERANCE, CRUELTY, AND THE
ECONOMICS OF INTELLIGENCE

There are several curious issues raised by the material in the previous chapter that I would like to review. One of them is that strange remark of the Cassiopaeans that Stefan Marinov was programmed and it was the triggering of this mind-control program that caused him to take the dive from the fire escape of the University library in Graz. The item of interest was the reference to the human agents of this programming as being part of British Intelligence, a section the Cassiopaeans designated as "MI."

MI5 and MI6 are the world's oldest secret intelligence agencies. They began in 1909 with the formation of a military section (MOT, which became MI5) and a naval section (MI-1C, later MI6).

In July 1942, MI5 played a major part in the creation of the American Office of Strategic Services (OSS). The OSS was modeled on MI6/SOE; American personnel received training and instruction from British agents. OSS later came to concentrate predominantly on armed subversion and guerrilla warfare and was the forerunner of the CIA.

Stefan Marinov was a dissident for many years. I have before me volume II of his work entitled *The Thorny Way of Truth*, or "Documents on the invention of the perpetuum mobile, on the centurial blindness of mankind, and on its frantic perseverance in it." Included in this book is a section entitled "Calvario," or Calvary, as a biographical sketch of Marinov. It is illustrated by reproductions of 12 paintings of Cenni, which Marinov declared in his introduction to be "the unique true and exact reflection of the existing social and political reality." These very disturbing images portray humanity as a prisoner of obviously fascist soldiers, refused help by the Church, proceeding through the Stations of the Cross, so to say, to the final image of crucifixion.

We cannot comment on Marinov's psychological state. He was clearly alienated to an extreme degree. We can only point out that his views reflect a reality that no one seems to want to either acknowledge or address. It is the same reality that caused psychiatrist Wilhelm Reich to write, "Why did man, through thousands of years, wherever he built scientific, philosophic, or religious systems, go astray with such persistence and with such catastrophic consequences?" He then goes on to ask:

Is human erring necessary? Is it rational? Is all error rationally explainable and necessary? If we examine the sources of human error, we find that they fall into several groups:

Gaps in the knowledge of nature form a wide sector of human erring. Medical errors prior to the knowledge of anatomy and infectious diseases were necessary errors. *But we must ask if the mortal threat to the first investigators of animal anatomy was a necessary error too.*

The belief that the earth was fixed in space was a necessary error, rooted in the ignorance of natural laws. *But was it an equally necessary error to burn Giordano Bruno at the stake and to incarcerate Galileo? ...* We understand that human thinking can penetrate only to a given limit at a given time. What we fail to understand is why the human intellect does not stop at this point and say: "this is the present limit of my understanding. Let us wait until new vistas open up." This would be rational, comprehensible, purposeful thinking. What amazes us is the sudden turn from the rational beginning to the irrational illusion. *Irrationality and illusion are revealed by the intolerance and cruelty with which they are expressed.* We observe that human thought systems show tolerance as long as they adhere to reality. *The more the thought process is removed from reality, the more intolerance and cruelty are needed to guarantee its continued existence ...*

The search for truth is closely connected with the natural organization of the human animal. Hence, we may conclude that the evasion of truth and *the adherence to the surface of phenomena must also have a certain connection with the structure of the human animal.* The function of natural research must be buried somehow *if the tendency to evade obvious facts is that powerful.*

With this thought, I found the key to the riddle of why man could err so consistently, so cruelly, for so long, and so much *to his own disadvantage: needless* human erring is a pathological quality of human character ...

I know human erring from my own experience. I, too, have joined in shouting "Guilty! Guilty!" ... I began to err when I held religion alone responsible for human suffering. I did not know that the error of *religion was a symptom,* not the cause, of human biopathy. I persisted in my error when I held the personal interests of a social group – parents or educators – responsible for suppressing human love life. I did not know that the suppression of love life is no more than a mechanism ...

When I was under the spell of the great socialist movement and worked for years, as a physician, among the underprivileged strata of the people, I fell into the gross error of thinking that "the capitalist was responsible for human plight." It took the brutal experience of the deteriorating Russian Revolution to free me from this error. They had killed the capitalists, but misery continued to grow; diplomatic intrigues, political maneuvering, spying and informing on others, all of which they had set out to eradicate, were more powerfully at work than ever …

For years, and in harmony with Freud's doctrine, I committed the error of thinking that the unconscious was "evil" and "responsible for all misery." It took a full decade of hard, clinical work among the emotionally ill to free me from this error. This earned me the bitter enmity of many psychiatric businessmen, who enriched themselves at the expense of human emotional misery …

The answer lies somewhere in that area of our existence which has been so heavily obscured by organized religion and put out of our reach. Hence, it probably lies in the relation of the human being to the cosmic energy that governs him. (Reich, 1949)

Reich was moving dangerously close to describing the hyperdimensional reality. He observed and experimented, and devised gadgets, the usefulness of which may or may not be objective. We do know that Reich was an honored and respected scientist who met his death in a strange drama of persecution and defamation, and that what is left of his work is obviously not all he wrote or thought since there was an extraordinary effort to burn his books, as ordered by the United States government.

What is most interesting to us here is Reich's comments about intolerance and cruelty. He noted that "Irrationality and illusion are revealed by the intolerance and cruelty with which they are expressed. … The more the thought process is removed from reality, the more intolerance and cruelty are needed to guarantee its continued existence."

We have certainly been subjected to such intolerance and cruelty. This activity has taken many forms both public and private, and in every case, enormous amounts of time could be spent going over the cruel lies, twists and distortions, the intolerant libel and defamation about us, that are presently being promulgated by Vincent Bridges, Jeff Williams, and others, but it would be simply wasted effort in terms of their own understanding, as well as the understanding of those individuals who are of a similar make-up, and who choose to believe their lies in the face of hard evidence that they are liars. As Reich has pointed out: "we may conclude that *the evasion of truth and the adherence to the surface of phenomena must also have a certain connection with the structure of the human animal.* The function of natural research must be buried somehow *if the tendency to evade obvious facts is that powerful.*"

And, as Reich pointed out, the very fact that anyone would occupy their time attempting to destroy the work of others – the fact that they operate from a position of intolerance and cruelty – is *clear evidence of their irrationality and illusion; their distance from reality.* As Reich said, "needless human erring is a pathological quality of human character."

In exposing the cruelty and intolerance of society, religion, and science itself, perhaps Stefan Marinov was closer to reality than we might suspect. The only difference between Marinov and say, philosophers or teachers of various paths to enlightenment, was the fact that he was a scientist and could, conceivably, produce evidence of that deeper reality that it is forbidden to discuss or know about. The same was true of Reich and possibly even Jessup; also of many other unknown and unsung heroes of the quest for the truth who may have gotten too close, or had too much cachet to allow them to continue to work in such directions. Because, as the Cassiopaeans pointed out, <u>Marinov's ideas might lead to instabilities in the power structure and ability of that power structure to control humanity</u>.

November 15, 1997
Q: (A) What was the main reason for his death?
A: Revelations too "sensitive," would cause "instabilities."
Q: Instabilities in what?
A: Power structure/control.
Q: What kind of revelation?
A: Theoretical physics.
Q: In what specific area?
A: "Unified Field Theory."

This suggests to us that the material that was left behind by Marinov, the material to which attention was directed by his final farewell, is the *wrong* material.

As we have already discovered, good disinformation consists of a lot of truth with the twist at a crucial point. Considering the Carlos Allende letters, which we now suspect to have been produced within disinformation circles, and promulgated on the foundation of Morris Jessup's death, we come to the idea that the Philadelphia Experiment was very likely a real event, and it was realized that because there were leaks, the only way to do damage control was to produce a version of the story based on the facts, but with the crucial element switched. And we realize that the crucial element was Einstein's attempts at formulating a Unified Field Theory. Regarding the Carlos Allende letters, I asked:

May 31, 1997
Q: Here is this purported letter from a Carlos Allende to Dr. Jessup. Now, whether Carlos was a real person or not, what I want to know is if the information is somewhat accurate. Is it a reliable source of information?
A: Is that not obvious?
Q: I thought it was. He said that Einstein did computations on cycles of human civilization and progress, compared to the growth of man's gen-

589

eral character and development, and that this horrified him. Now, this is the very thing you suggested I do to find clues. And, I am doing it. It says here that Einstein was doing the same thing. Is this correct?

A: Yes.

Q: What horrified him?

A: The discovery of variability of physicality, and all that that implies, when one knows all that Einstein knew up to that point.

Q: So, 4th density blew him away!

A: And the other density levels. One begins with the premise that the material realm is the "whole shooting match," discovers it is not, must rethink everything.

Q: So, it hit Einstein like a ton of bricks.

We notice from Reich's comments above that he was very concerned with what he had noted about the cycles of human history. Marinov was also concerned with these matters. We know that, in 1941, Reich met with Albert Einstein and they talked for five hours. However, this was *after* Einstein's 1938 paper in which he proposed to take the fifth mathematical dimension as real. Einstein declined to become involved in Reich's research which dashed Reich's hopes. This was actually very strange considering the other efforts Einstein was making in public regarding his search for UFT. However, if it is true that Einstein had already been coopted as the Cs suggest, then it only makes sense. What also seems to be true is that many physicists and mathematicians have been involved in attempts to utilize mathematics to create pictures of human dynamics in historical and cultural terms, with strange results (e.g., Morozov and Fomenko, whose work I discuss in *Secret History*).

August 17, 2000

Q: Einstein was working on his UFT for like 30 years. Maybe more. He was changing his methods. At some point, did he realize that he found a solution? During all these thirty years, was there a point where he came upon the right solution?

A: Yes, but sadly, his solution for UFT largely erased TOR [Theory Of Relativity].

Q: (A) Once he found this solution, did he reject it because it erased TOR?

A: No. His progenitors sealed it, in order to keep intact the status quo.

Q: (L) His progenitors? Isn't that your parents?

A: Other definitions apply.

At an even earlier time, when Prof. Roger Santilli was present at a session, the Cs commented to him:

A: What is your knowledge quotient regarding following: electromagnetism, Einstein's "unified field theory." And did he ever complete said theory, or was it completed under the supervision of consortium, and suppressed. And if so, what are the ramifications!!! Also, Roger, are you capable of "filling in the blanks," we think so!

At the time of reviewing the transcripts, I made a note in the text that I didn't think that the remark about "filling in the blanks" had to do with the theory itself, but rather the ramifications. The question becomes: what exactly are the ramifications of research in this direction? As the Cs pointed out in our discussion of Stefan Marinov:

Q: (T) Did the gentleman who just passed away learn something about the merging of Unified Field Theories? (L) Or merging of factors ...
A: The problem is that these scientists are often too eager to share and reveal. Remember: it is most difficult to win a Nobel Prize when on's residence is a tomb.

In terms of Marinov's death, again we notice the presence of Paul La Violette, the darling of the Club of Rome, hanging out with Pappas, Marinov, *et al.* The problem here is, again, the ability of the Control System to use innocent people, as we have already described – at the simplest level – via broadcasting signals that are unpacked in the subconscious and emerge as the person's own thoughts.

If the reader has ever seen the movie *The Lady from Shanghai*, they will realize that what we are dealing with here is similar to the hall of mirrors sequence at the end of the film. Rita Hayworth is caught in a house of mirrors with a man who is trying to shoot her. She sees him and he sees her, but what they see are all just reflections. No one is sure what is real and what isn't. This is the world of science and research into the deeper nature of our reality. As Kevin Costner said in *JFK*: "Everything is exactly the opposite of what you think it is. Black is white, up is down. Is what you are examining a reflection, or is it real?"

Paul LaViolette seems to have an instinctive understanding of our galaxy as a higher-dimensional object. He seems to be one of the few experts – even if his field of expertise does not make him an expert in those things he wishes to study and write about – who has even considered the hyperdimensional aspects of our reality. Regarding La Violette, Marinov, and others, it seems that the human agents of the Control System find such people, fund them just enough to be able to get their ideas out of them, and then, when they have extracted as much from them as they can, they bottle them up with mind programming. And that is how it operates. Researchers need funding to work. And in providing the funding, in creating the research environment, the links are established that enable the total takeover of the individual that eventually results in their ideas being corrupted and distorted.

And this brings us to that most curious remark that the Cassiopaeans made about my own physical kidnapping at the age of four:

April 24, 1996

Q: (L) When I was kidnapped at the age of three or four in Jacksonville, how many days was I missing? My mother simply has a blank about it, which amazes her.

A: 12 days.

Q: (L) Who was it that kidnapped me?

A: Jan. […] Corps member. […] Select division of economic legion under control of G5. […] Intel.

Q: (L) What was the purpose of this kidnapping?

A: To install self-destruct programming.

Economics? What the heck does *economics* have to do with anything?

I have to tell the reader that this remark really baffled me for a very long time. In fact, until I was in the act of writing the previous chapter, the relationships that are behind the scenes here didn't really dawn on me. As we will discuss more fully further on, we were visited by an eminent economist in the late summer of 2000, a Professor Emeritus of Economics at a well known University, who was extraordinarily interested in certain aspects of the Cs material. This visit seemed to be the trigger point of a whole host of strange subsequent events. There was, in fact, a veritable all-star cast of players brought in to act their necessary parts in the drama; all of whose appearances on the scene closely followed this visit. It's really amazing that we didn't see the connections earlier. So, keep that in mind for later, but for now, let's continue our review of the whole scenario and what the Cs told us at various points that relate to those matters that seem to get a lot of people killed or locked up in insane asylums.

At the point in time that I finally, really and truly, grasped the nature of fourth-density reality, it nearly killed me. It's no wonder that people flee in terror from the work on this website. At that point in time I became so ill that it is truly a miracle that I didn't die. My ears, eyes and lungs were besieged by a terrible infection simultaneously and I could neither see, hear nor speak for almost a month. This is why there was no session from the end of March in 1996 until almost the end of April. And finally, I was asking for help. I knew I could not survive much longer. What I didn't know was that if I were given the answers then, I would have already been dead.

April 24, 1996

A: Laura, you need to consult a powerful, practiced, effective hypnotherapist to unlock these questions for you. […] The locks have been installed in such a way that it is literally impossible for you to unlock them, as they were installed with full knowledge of present circumstances.

Q: (L) Who installed these locks?

A: Supremely powerful STS consortium!!

Q: (L) And what circumstances were they aware of, as you have mentioned, when they installed these locks?

A: All. [...]

A: You cannot unlock, and we cannot tell you details of what, or why.

Q: (L) Why can you not tell us?

A: Free will violation, and endangerment of you if done thusly.

Q: (L) Is there some way to do it that does not endanger us?

A: We have told you.

Q: (L) Is it a danger to us to *not* unlock these things?

A: In a sense.

Of course, the question at the time was how would it endanger me to know these things if the only other person present was Frank?

But even more pressing are the questions about why locks were placed on something in my superconsciousness, and why did that threaten the "supremely powerful STS consortium" so that they would take the risk of physically kidnapping me as a child in order to make sure that these locks were put on in the most thorough way possible? We already realize that attempts were made via the standard alien abduction and that didn't work because, as the Cs said, "you fight it." So it seems that the physical abduction and direct work via psychological programming was necessary. Of course, another question is: why didn't they just kill me if I was such a threat to them in the future?

August 1, 1998

Q: (L) I was also reading in some of the transcripts as I have been going through them getting them ready to print, that you once said that "supremely powerful" STS forces were responsible for kidnapping and programming me. My question is: if they had me, why did they bring me back?

A: Would you expect otherwise?

Q: (L) Well, you said that they tried to do some programming and that it didn't work and that STO forces intervened. So, I am just a little confused. If I was such a threat to them, why did they bring me back? Under the circumstances, I could have just disappeared forever and that would be that!

A: No.

Q: (L) What prevented that?

A: Occlusion.

Q: (L) Occlusion of what?

A: Best to research through meditation and hypnosis.

Occlusion obviously has something to do with being shielded, as well as the operation of the STS Achilles Heel itself: wishful thinking. STS always takes the path of least resistance, and their confidence that they could do some programming and that would fix the whole problem is apparently part of this occlusion process. It also suggests some sort of rules about violation of free will between densities. It seems that, without some sort of agreement, even if at a deep subconscious level, such things as ongoing abductions, physical harm and violations, cannot occur. If there was no agreement to that at the higher levels of which my subconscious mind and superconscious mind were aware, then the only way to access me was through physicality, while a child, before full seating of consciousness had taken place.

In fact, this is probably why so many abductions do take place at early ages: it is to condition the physical brain to resist the seating of higher consciousness so as to prevent the expression of soul and will that would enable the individual to fully activate free-will choice and refuse violation. And such conditioning can also take place via very ordinary social and familial programs as well. It's altogether likely that individuals with great potential for full activation of higher consciousness and honoring of free will *are primary targets of childhood abduction*. And apparently, from the literature, it is a very effective program.

The Ra Material, which the Cassiopaeans have suggested as a primer for understanding our basic reality, has some interesting things to say about these matters. Ra describes the hyperdimensional mind-control activity as being effected in our reality by first controlling certain human beings who act as their agents. Ra describes people as being of two types: those people on our planet who do exercises and perform disciplines (i.e. rituals) in order to seek contact with negative sources of information and power, and those whose frequency resonance vibration is such that direct contact with total negative energies is accomplished with no training and no controls.

For the most part, it seems that through telepathy the philosophy of manipulating others is promulgated. The individuals who are receptive to this information are then assisted in achieving positions of power and control. This relates back to our discussion of Stockholm syndrome and how, by being in a captive situation, the prisoners learn to love their captors, and then will begin to align with them, and act on their behalf to manipulate still others. Ra points out that there are "many upon your so-called inner planes which are negatively oriented and thus available as inner teachers or guides and so-called possessors of certain souls who seek [to control or manipulate others]."

In addition to the philosophy of manipulation, the negative hyperdimensional controllers also pass technical information to their third-density agents. This technology includes various means of control or manipulation of others. Through this technology, the Controllers of the Matrix began to set up conditions in our world whereby the masses of people will be enslaved *by their free will.*

This is an important point. In the hyperdimensional realms, the name of the game is Consciousness. This simply means that the higher realms of existence, whether positive or negative in orientation, all recognize that the business of all being and existence everywhere is always that of Consciousness – becoming more and more *aware.*

The positive guys seek to increase awareness by the activities of networking and interdependence and sharing and giving. This is a natural function of creativity and empathy. Empathy is that quality of being that allows us to connect to another person's thinking, feeling, experiences, and so forth, as if they were our own. It is that quality that enables us to deeply care about the pain and suffering experienced by others because, in fact, when we are aware of it, it causes us pain, too.

The negative guys, on the other hand, play the game in terms of domination, subjugation and absorption of other consciousnesses with total disregard for the pain and suffering they cause. In fact, they deliberately cause pain and suffering in order to induce the other to choose their domination in order to bring the pain and suffering to an end. Again, we are reminded of Stockholm syndrome. At the hyperdimensional levels of being, negative entities understand certain rules which are that, in order for them to be able to dominate truly, the other must choose to be dominated. In Stockholm-syndrome terms, it is more energy efficient if the prisoner is persuaded to cooperate, and even to help with his captivity, if he is doing so by choice and the captor does not have to spend endless amounts of energy keeping an eye on him, checking the locks on the doors, torturing him, or whatever. It is a simple matter of *economics.*

Ra has some interesting remarks to make about something that may relate to this. He describes something called a quarantine. I am not certain that I agree with this planetary-quarantine idea as it is described here, since historical research into the alien phenomenon rather contradicts it. It sounds rather like wishful thinking; a desire for a global protector. *But*, what it does suggest is the existence of hyperdimensional "future selves" as guardians that sort of protect free will. Ra says that "These guardians sweep reaches of your Earth's energy fields to be aware of any entities approaching. An entity which is approaching is hailed in the name of the One Creator. Any entity thus hailed is bathed in love/light and will of free will obey the quarantine due to the power of the Law of One."

Q: What would happen to the entity if he did not obey the quarantine after being hailed?

Ra: To not obey quarantine after being hailed on the level of which we speak would be equivalent to your *not stopping upon walking into a solid brick wall.*

My guess is that this idea is fairly accurate but that *it may not apply planetarily*, so to say, but rather individually. I am reminded of the Cs' statement that knowledge protects, and that knowledge is love is light. So it would make sense that a future self of the positive variety would have the potential for protecting its "past self" in this way to whatever extent that is accepted by the past self in its conscious or subconscious mind. This also reminds me of the idea of thought centers and eclipsing of realities, wherein the Cs remarked:

Whenever two opposing units of reality intersect, this causes what can be referred to as friction, which, for an immeasurable amount of what you would refer to as time, which is, of course, nonexistent, creates a nonexistence, or a stopping of the movements of all functions. This is what we would know as conflict. In between, or through any intersecting, opposite entities, we always find zero time, zero movement, zero transference, zero exchange. ... Was what happened a conflicting of one energy thought center that was a part of your thought process and another energy thought center that was another part of your thought process? [...] What if the abduction scenario could take place where your soul projection, in what you perceive as the future, can come back and abduct your soul projection in what you perceive as the present? ... [I]s it one possible future, but not all possible futures? And is the pathway of free will not connected to all of this?

What we seem to derive from all of this is that there is some kind of law of gravity, so to say, in the hyperdimensional realms, and this law has to do with free will. The logical extension of this idea is that if the true negative agenda is to dominate our reality, the only way they can really do it from those realms, where this law is the law of gravity, is to manipulate the mass consciousness of our planet to choose this domination à la Stockholm syndrome. This also explains clearly why there has not been an overt takeover or invasion – and never will be in the terms we think of it – up to this point in time. If the people of earth were to be fully aware of an invasion or a takeover in literal, physical terms, that would mean that the veil would be lifted and all people would see the man behind the curtain and would instantly reject the domination! In short, just as in the *Wizard of Oz*, those Ruby Slippers have to be obtained *very carefully!*

We now begin to see the agenda and mode of operation of the hyperdimensional Controllers of the Matrix. It is to create a completely controlled artificial environment composed of thoroughly predictable human behaviors – made predictable because they have been programmed to respond to cues of conditioning inculcated through centuries of lies and obfuscations presented in the form of religions, and all of this revolves around a "story" that is actually untrue, and wholly misrepresentative of the real negative aim.

For centuries these programming signals have been being set up – either because of time travel capabilities, or because of actual historical presence. Various prophets or religious leaders have been influenced to preach, or teach or prophesy philosophies designed to lay a foundation for later takeover – possibly in our present time. When people begin to get wise, the Negatives simply go back into the past, add something more to the soup to cover up the new awareness. This then acts as a domino effect and influences our present – time loops and all that. A lot of people think that the alien invasion scenario is a ruse concocted by the government to create the impression that there is a forming threat, thereby enabling the institution of a New World Order. But, this idea is based on a misrepresentation of the process just described.

The important thing to remember is this: there is *not* a unified conspiratorial activity going on here in the hierarchy of our visible governments. The divide and conquer effect is also manifest at this level and suits the alien purposes to a "T." Such activity at *all* levels is consistent with their program, in which confusion and cross-purpose prevent a clear perception on the part of the victims.

At some deep level there *is* a direct conspiratorial interaction between the secret government and the negative aliens; but it is unlikely that any name of those involved would be recognized by anyone, no matter how "in the know" regarding the subject. These secret superiors are just that: *secret*. Any organizations you can name, or about which you are *aware*, are merely outer circles.

It seems that the process of this takeover is exactly that of Stockholm syndrome. Little by little, different groups are consolidated into a negative mode which, on the surface, may seem to be very positive or STO (i.e. save the world because it is "wrong" or flawed, or blighted with original sin or whatever). *But*, the very fact that it is formed in the dominator mode of perceiving salvation "outside," means that it can more easily be taken over body, mind and soul at a level that is unseen and unseeable. In other words: Satan *can* and most often *does* appear as an Angel of Light!

It is only at the lower levels of the power structure that many still believe they are playing out the basic "antagonism" and "self-protection" roles. They believe that sending love and light to those "in need" is appropriate, without realizing that this activity is predicated upon a deep belief that there is something wrong, in error, in rebellion, and thus becomes us vs them.

There is evidence that extensive implant technology may be used to ensure influenced obedience; yet, a degree of freedom must be conserved through the consciousness due to the essential fact that the valued commodity *is* consciousness. A totally drugged, surgically altered and thoroughly programmed psyche is only good for robotic slave-service (and this may also be going on, by the way). It is in this understanding that we find our way out of the trap. It isn't easy, but it is a way.

The primary mode of inducing Stockholm syndrome is, obviously, to persuade through strongly influenced, but not robotic, behavior patterns, the free choice of the targeted consciousness to align with negative hyperdimensional existence. Because, in the long run, the *economics* of dominating functioning units of consciousness by the negative hierarchy, is a major concern, because the defining element of true consciousness is the irreducible value of free will. Free will is what distinguishes consciousness as consciousness. A simple way of thinking about it is: what has more value, to achieve domination and control of an animal, or a human being? A pauper or a king? Thus, we can also see that the level of free-will consciousness of the victim is also important. It is far more gratifying to hyperdimensional beings to co-opt someone with greater will and positive potential, than someone who is weak.

Just remember Renfield in Bram Stoker's book *Dracula*. He was dominated so easily, and therefore, was contemptible in the eyes of the Count. However, the virtuous and noble Mina was seen as a highly desirable target. And, those who give in so easily to such manipulations ought to notice the fate of Renfield – he was promised much in order to use him as a tool, but in the end, he was discarded like a used tissue.

In hyperdimensional spheres, a consciousness that has acceded to domination has agreed to be absorbed. This means that it is effectively food for the negative hierarchy. It does not matter one whit if the agreement is a result of being lied to, if the agreement has come because a grand deception has been played out, such as a negative being appearing as the Virgin Mary and demanding that an altar be built, or penance be done, or it the chosen deception is the goddess Sekhmet. The instant compliance is given by the worshipper, they are "eaten" as consciousness. It's that simple. And the same is true in our human relationships. When we allow another to manipulate us or deceive us into being dominated, no matter how subtly, we become part of the chain of domination to whomever, or whatever is dominating them, and on up the line.

The modes of persuasion are many and varied. Inducing choice is the objective, and it is immaterial whether or not this is done via deception, persuasive misrepresentation, or other conditioning. Confusion, physical and/or emotional/mental pain, exhaustion, blackmail, and even forms of torture are legitimate modes of persuasion. Exhausting or terrifying a person so that they will run screaming to the arms of that Old-Time Religion is a favored ploy. Of course, the more subtle the means used, the more free will value is retained. A tortured consciousness is the equivalent to being overcooked. Many higher-level Beings of Darkness are veritable *connoisseurs*! They particularly relish the subversion of those who are truly pure and strong willed by clever employment of great truths with only a small lie embedded about a crucial element such as we find in most religions.

Ra tells us, and the Cs have repeatedly confirmed this, that much channeled information is distorted in exactly this way. This happens because the channels are internally oriented toward STO, but become confused and self-destructive in their desire for proof. The seeking of proof makes an individual open to lying information, and once they have oriented themselves this way, their effectiveness as a positive channel is neutralized.

February 24, 1996

Q: (L) Mike Lindeman has proposed that we submit the channeling to "rigorous testing."

A: Mike Lindemann does not channel, now does he? What sort of rigorous testing does he propose?

Q: (L) He didn't say. I guess they want short-term predictions and all sorts of little tests …

A: Precisely, now what does this tell you?

Q: It tells us that he wants proof.

A: Third density "proof" does not apply, as we have explained again and again. Now, listen very carefully: if proof of that type were possible, what do you suppose would happen to free will, and thusly to learning, Karmic Directive Level One?

Q: (L) Well, I guess that if there is proof, you are believing in the proof and not the spirit of the thing. You are placing your reliance upon a material thing. You have lost your free will. Someone has violated your free will by the act of *proving* something to you.

A: If anyone CHOOSES to believe, that is their prerogative!

Q: (PZ) [unintelligible remark]

A: You did not completely understand the previous response, Pat. And what would constitute proof?

Q: (L) Predictions that came true, answers that were verifiable about a number of things.

A: Those would still be dismissed by a great many as mere coincidences. We have already given predictions, will continue to do so, but, remember, "time" does not exist. This is a 3rd density illusion. We do not play in that sandbox and cannot and never will. The primary reason for our communication is to help you to learn by teaching yourselves to learn, thereby strengthening your soul energy, and assisting your advancement.

Q: (L) Are you saying that your primary reason is just to teach us? This small group?

A: Because you asked for help.

Q: (L) So, you came through because we asked. Is this material being given to others, or is it designed to or intended to be shared with others?

A: If they ask in the necessary way. Otherwise, the sharing of the messages we give to you will teach millions of others.

In addition to disseminating their own negative philosophy directly to those whose internal nature is naturally STS, the greater work of the hyperdimensional controllers seems to be the distortion and corruption of positive information. This takes numerous forms, but the most general is that confusion is induced in the conscious mind, or emotional triggers are utilized to produce "proof" that certain information is – or *must* be – true.

Ra tells us about "wanderers," or higher dimensional-beings who have incarnated for the purpose of assisting humanity without violating free will. This "service to others" is described as a "dispassionate attempt to share information without concern for numbers or growth among others." The *attempt* to make the information available *is the service*. There are no shortcuts to enlightenment. It cannot be taught. It cannot be achieved with rituals or formulas. The only thing that can be shared is information, stories of inspiration, love and mystery, and experiences that may spark another person to reach out and begin seeking on their own.

Ra warns that the challenge and danger of the wanderer is that he or she will forget the mission, become karmically involved, and thus be swept into the maelstrom. The question here is, of course, how does one become karmically involved? Ra answers: By acting in a *consciously* unloving manner in action with other beings.

As the readers have discovered, what is or is not "love" is a huge issue. And it is in this subject that the most intensive disinformation has been promulgated, or so it seems.

Ra describes wanderers as possessing certain qualities of what might be seen as foolhardiness or bravery, depending on the orientation of the perceiver. He adds that they also have a certain purity of mind. This purity of mind presents a certain set of problems that are evident in our experiences, as well as the experiences of many of the readers who have been corresponding with us as we present this series of articles. We aren't the only ones who are dense and have difficulty seeing the games and manipulations of those with negative agendas.

William March wrote in *The Bad Seed*:

> [G]ood people are rarely suspicious: *they cannot imagine others doing the things they themselves are incapable of doing* ... Then too, the normal are inclined to visualize the [psychopath] as one who's as monstrous in appearance as he is in mind, which is about as far from the truth as one could well get ...
>
> These monsters of real life usually looked and behaved in a more normal manner than their actually normal brothers and sisters; they presented a more convincing picture of virtue than virtue presented of itself – just as the wax rosebud or the plastic peach seemed more perfect to the eye, more what the mind thought a rosebud or a peach should be, than the imperfect, original from which it had been modeled.

So, indeed, this series – in fact, my whole life – is a veritable soap opera of events wherein I am perceived as dense, and even a little slow, because, in fact, I still have difficulty attributing negative intentions to anybody. I cannot imagine anybody doing anything to me that I would not do myself. I cannot predict the actions of evil people. Sure, I write about it, I research it, I seek to examine and understand it so as to find the means of protecting myself and others, because this seems to be crucial information for all of us to get, but damned if it isn't so that no matter how hard I try, I still cannot fathom deliberate deception, manipulation, cruelty, and insensitivity to the feelings of others.

Ra tells us that wanderers are vulnerable because they become completely the creature of third density in mind and body, and are, by nature, less inclined to deviousness and manipulation. For this reason, they often do not recognize as easily the negative nature of other beings or thoughts before they become involved with them. Then, very often, because of this very lack of perception of negativity, they often persist in relationships that are negative because they repeatedly attribute to the other person their own benevolent motives and perceptions.

Additionally, there is just as much chance of negative hyperdimensional telepathic mind control influence being brought to bear on a wanderer as anyone else. The only difference occurs in what Ra calls the "spirit complex" which, if it wishes, has an armor of light which enables it to *recognize* more clearly that which is not appropriately desired. This is not more than a *bias*, and cannot be called an understanding. So, in other words, you just have an instinct about things that are not right. But then, with all our be-nice programming, we generally override the instinct and shove such signals under the rug, or search endlessly for reasons to excuse bad behavior.

As the reader might guess, Ra and the Cs both confirm that wanderers, however they are defined, are most definitely high-priority targets of the Matrix Controllers. And this bears on the issue of the physical kidnapping at the age of four that I have described in *Amazing Grace*. Ra was asked if wanderers ever had "close encounters" with the hyperdimensional controllers. I am assuming that the question implied an abduction.

Ra's answer was interesting. He noted that such abductions are, first of all rare. But, when it does occur it is generally for one of two reasons: either the abducting entities made a mistake in failing to perceive the deeply positive nature of the individual, in which case they suffered a loss of polarity, or they are fully aware of the nature of the individual but are willing to risk it in order to attempt to remove this positive being from this plane of existence.

Which, of course, brings us back around to such individuals being high-priority targets. Obviously, they can't abduct them so freely as they would like, and therefore, must make other arrangements or seek other methods to accomplish their aims in order to prevent the loss of polarity, or the "hitting of a brick wall" upon attempting to violate the powerful will of a guardian, or superconsciousness, as Ra described it above. Thus it seems that human agents have to be used in such cases because it seems that the negative hyperdimensional beings often come off badly in these encounters.

As the Cs commented when I asked why I had only been abducted a few times: "you fight it." And we see the nature of that fighting in the eclipsing of realities comments. We also have a glimpse of the "guardian" as the self-in-the-future concept.

Just to finish off these remarks before we move on, Ra also points out that wanderers, due to the extreme variance between the vibrations of third density and those of the density of origin, often have some form of handicap, difficulty, or feeling of alienation which is severe. He remarks that the most common effect is a reaction against the planetary vibrations through what are commonly known as personality disorders, generally "alienation." He also suggests allergies as a common problem, and the Cs have added to the list by including dietary and nutritional deficiencies. My guess is that the soul complex of a higher-density being that incarnates in third density will produce all sorts of strange glitches. Many of them tend to be overweight, as though the physical body is seeking to accommodate a more intense soul manifestation. They also seem to have unusual nutritional imbalances and blood sugar problems due to the possible greater energy needs perceived by the physical body in its attempt to accommodate higher energy output.

So, I think we now have a much better understanding of some aspects of "occlusion" which the Cs gave as the answer as to why I wasn't just killed outright, either by human agents or hyperdimensional agents. What is more, this discussion will help us to understand the nature of many other manipulations involving other people and other situations that we will be looking at further on. It also makes us aware that there *are* rules to the game, though they may not necessarily follow the rules of logic of the material reality. It also seems that learning these rules of hyperdimensional constructs, from which our own reality is mirrored and in which it is embedded, is crucial to finding one's way through the maze of mirrors.

Now, let's go in a slightly different direction and see if we can come to some idea of *why* I was physically kidnapped. Of course, just sharing information as many others are also doing doesn't seem to warrant having such special attention, now does it? This brings us to the repeated remarks by the Cs about answers that are locked up inside me. Just to review, we already noted that, according to the Cs, one of these secrets is the technology employed in the *real* Philadelphia Experiment:

March 18, 1995

A: Yes, but the technology is a closely guarded secret.

Q: (L) Do you know the secret?

A: Yes, but you do too!

Q: (L) I do too? [...]

A: Philadelphia Experiment.

Another clue to this matter, and the essence of Frank as an agent who was present to divert the information to STS uses, was delivered in the following excerpt in which a question was asked for someone else, but the answer was directed at me:

February 24, 1996

Q: (L) Well, what can she do to maximize the STO presence and minimize the STS use of the conduit?

A: Oh Laura, my dear, seems you need a refresher course in the transcripts. Maybe suggest you read them and relax and privately listen to the ones you have not as of yet transcribed a little more. This would be extremely helpful in your many and increasing communications via the "net" as well. Remember, we help you to unlock answers that have been placed in your superconsciousness files from before the "time" of the birth of your physical body. Also, false information is worse than no information at all.

The very fact that the Cassiopaeans suggested that this be done in private, excluding Frank, was a telling remark when we remember that this information had been locked up by the STS Consortium with full knowledge of the present circumstances, which included the process of communication with the Cassiopaeans.

This produces an interesting conundrum. If Frank was a mole sent in to vacuum the information out of me, why would it be locked so that he couldn't get it, assuming that his controllers are the same ones who placed the locks?

Looking back over the relationship with Frank and the many discussions between us regarding channeling, it's pretty obvious now that his primary agenda was to induce me to agree to his role as "the Prime Channel," and to interact with him while he was under hypnosis in such a way that he *could* have accessed this information. Very soon, I will give a most fascinating example of another similar individual and his own vacuum operation and how it got him a Nobel Prize!

In short, if I had given in to Frank's repeated manipulations, I would have been in a state of Stockholm syndrome, and at some deep level, this might have permitted the accessing of the locked information. In fact, it may have been part of the plan for Frank to channel, via trance, entirely different information from what is presented by the Cs. Based on small clues that can be connected to corrupting static, he had some sort of save-the-world agenda in certain terms that were later to be more fully explicated in the manipulations of Vincent Bridges along a similar line. (These manipulations became apparent during and after the mirror session and discussion included in Appendix C.)

It is obvious that the locks were put in place to prevent me from accessing whatever information is buried myself. But, naturally, if I were convinced by corrupted information channeled by Frank that I needed to do something to save the world, I would be far more likely to allow my psyche and subconscious to be manipulated. It is even possible that, given Frank's status as an empty pipe, a sort of black-hole consciousness, he could have accessed the information in my deep subconscious while he was under hypnosis, without me even being aware of it – providing a period of bonding had been gone through in this mode of communication.

So, we conclude that, 1) by refusing to be manipulated into the Frank-as-the-Prime-Channel ruse, I avoided the manipulations of the forces controlling him; 2) by insisting on utilization of the board as a means of accessing deep levels of consciousness, I grooved a channel through the first layer of locks in my own subconscious – as the Cs described it, "awakening self-recognition;" 3) the Cassiopaeans endeavored to make it clear that communicating in this way, with Frank present, was *not* the way to the deeper information. Repeatedly they gave clues and made non-directive suggestions including coming right out and saying:

April 24, 1996

Q: (L) Well, I want to have a little direction here.

A: Concentrate on settlement. This can be a problem solver if handled wisely, a curse if not so! Use some of the funds to locate a "superhypnotherapist."

Of course, the immediate thought about such a statement is to think of somebody who quite simply *is* a hypnotherapist! You know, the guy with the swinging watch and the deep voice intoning, "You vill go deeper!" But it is obvious that the Cs had something altogether different in mind. There was also the additional clue about the "net," which clearly indicates that the Cassiopaeans knew that Ark was going to find me via the Net exactly 72 days following the above quoted remarks about the retrieval of answers placed in my superconsciousness files. What is more, the need for funds was directly related to the fact that my computer needed serious upgrading before I could even connect to the Internet effectively.

May 27, 1996

A: Laura! Turn over stones, sell apples, do whatever you have to do to get your computer refitted to accommodate the Internet, including the online market system, as soon as absolutely possible!!!!!!

Q: (L) Well, I am not really in a position to spend that money right now! And what do you mean to "turn over stones and sell apples?"

A: Figures of speech! Do what you have to do … take care of the mechanics, my Dear, the rest will fall into place …

Funny that they used the words "stones" and "apples," considering the part they play in the Rennes-le-Château affair as well as mythical and alchemical matters! The point was, at that moment in time, I was only 29 days away from my husband, Ark, finding me via the Internet. The nexus point was moving inexorably, and the Cs were most anxious that I not miss the rendezvous!

What is totally bizarre is that Ark's colleague in Florence sent him an email just two days before the Cs' remarks about the superhypnotherapist, which included the words "spin" and "stones."

Date sent: Mon, 22 Apr 1996 15:54:23 +0100 (MET)

From: M*** M****

Subject: spin spin

To: ajad@ifl….

Dear Arkadiusz,

Did you receive my form? did you return it with your signature? do you commute or do you still anticommute? how is your harmonic attitude? I am looking forward to receiving good news of a new life full of positive energy and precious little stones for your feet. […]

Ark replied on the day after the above-mentioned session with the following banter that revealed his state of desperation:

From: "Arkadiusz Jadczyk"

To: m****

Subject: Re: spin spin

Date sent: Thu, 25 Apr 1996 11:06:34 +1

Dear M*****,

I received your form. I signed it and I am sending it back to you.

I am afraid I am still fermionic. Anti-commuting nilpotent (www-home.univer.kharkov.ua/duplij/susy/susy2000.htm). Being alone means in this case being linear. Being linear means being flat. Being flat excludes being sharp. Mio mondo e fragile.

Ciao,

ark

On June 15th, 19 days later, the issue of gravity waves was brought up, dangled like a carrot to my inquisitive mind, with the suggestion that I research it. Of course they knew I would find nothing in local sources, and that I would realize that the Internet was the logical place to search for answers.

Another suggestion/clue about the nature of this "super hypnotherapist" who was supposed to help me access this knowledge of gravity waves and UFT was given 7 days later, as I continued to struggle to find the answers, or to find a way to access them:

June 22, 1996

Q: (L) Is there any point on the body that *can* be used to assist in opening the gate to the subconscious?

A: No such assistance is needed. First, we would like to suggest that you seek a "spin" doctor for your quest!!

So, we have a whole series of clues building until finally the Cs practically give the whole thing away! Putting the word "spin" in quotes indicated that a very special meaning was intended. Then they added: "Hilliard. Leedskalnin. Coral Castle." These were additional clues to what they meant by "spin" doctor, and they all related back to gravity, antigravity, moving stones with sound, and those matters *having to do with physics.* "Spin," of course, with these additional clues, indicated a physicist – or a "doctor of gravity." And as it turned out, Ark shares his roots and origin with Hilliard and Edward Leedskalnin.

So, we come to some idea that Ark, as a physicist, was part of the circumstances of which the Supreme STS Consortium was aware when they placed locks on the knowledge files in my superconsciousness. And that raises the all-important question: what is there about the relationship between a channel and a physicist that such efforts must be undertaken to prevent their meeting and all that would naturally follow from such an association?

Somehow, I don't think that it's just sharing information.

When Ark finally did find me, when the connection with the spin-doctor was finally made, I did attempt to discover in advance what was going on. As usual, the Cs would not give me the answers since it was absolutely essential for my choices to remain fully free to preserve the STO dynamic. However, they did make a very strange remark that is a huge clue to the idea of the locks placed on the knowledge in my superconsciousness. Now, with the connection to Ark established, they begin to talk about *keys*:

> July 27, 1996
> Q: (L) Well, you have answered this kind of question before! You have told me about so many other people! How come you won't answer me about him?
> A: It is not appropriate.
> Q: (L) Why is it not appropriate? I am just trying to understand! I am in such a whirlwind inside ... pleeeeeease ...
> A: Wait and see.
> Q: (L) Does that mean good or bad?
> A: It means what is Anna doing with those keys?
> Q: (L) What are you talking about? Anna doesn't have any keys!? I am exhausted, and you are being too obscure.

Now, the strange thing about this remark is the fact that Ark's ex-wife's name is Anna. It is also a nickname we use for one of my daughters, so the remark about "keys" was, at the moment, so ambiguous that it only caused confusion. Since my daughter didn't have any "keys," and since the question was about Ark, the only conclusion that could be drawn was that the "keys" that the Cassiopaeans were referring to was Ark himself. What was his ex-wife "doing with those keys?" It was pretty simple: she was trying to destroy him. For thirty years, he recorded this struggle in his journals. His desperation to find his way reached a crescendo in 1989 when he wrote:

> April 10, 1989
> I am losing my life (...)

A year later, after intensive work on himself:

> Marseille, March 15, 1990
> Lord, help me. Lord, please help me. I am only a channel. I do not know why, I do not know for how long I am sent here. What else remains than to serve you, oh Lord. (...)

Marseille, April 1, 1990

My plan for life.

First of all I realized that in the sun I see quite well. If I relax myself, then I see quite well. Which is wonderful. I have no problems with even the smallest letters.

Ergo – look into the sun. Ergo – take care about a proper lighting.

On the other hand – this is a sign!

If I see in the sun, that means I need the sun to see clearly what I am doing.

What is this "sun"?

Sun is light which does not come from me. I cannot bring the sun here. I must GO FOR IT. I must find a source of light. (…)

What is this light? Is it FAITH? Is that YOU LORD? (…)

Ark shared his journal entries with me almost immediately. These words were so like my own lifelong search for the light that would show the way that they actually acted like "keys" unlocking something inside me. I understood that such light, if found, may never illuminate anything more than one's own family or friends; but in the grand scheme of things, even such a small effect can have long-term results over vast eons of time. Ark and I both understood this, but we also understood that *there was potential for some truly valuable contribution to humanity*, if only in the realm of discovery and sharing those discoveries. With these thoughts in mind, I continued the questioning, trying not to reveal too much about our private discussions:

Q: Is there some clue as to how to conduct myself? Is he in any danger by talking about coming here?

A: No more than usual.

Q: (L) He believes that we can do things, that they can be done, that we can have a positive effect.

A: Then focus on that! […]

Q: (L) Well, I don't want to put him in any danger.

A: There are ways.

Q: (L) Is there anything we can do with this gravity-wave business? He is also very interested in this.

A: Then work on that with him!! Review the transcripts and that which has not yet been transcribed.

With every answer, the Cassiopaeans were confirming our private discussions on these things, this dream of leaving some legacy to others that would make some positive difference in the world.

Perhaps the reader who is familiar with my own story in *Amazing Grace*, as well as some parts of Ark's story, and how he struggled against growing up under a suppressive political regime that threatened his career because he refused to cooperate with scientific controls and suppression, as well as a control-freak drama-queen wife at home, will have some idea of how amazing it was for us to finally meet our other half, and also how difficult and painful it was to realize that it needed slow and careful preparation in order to ensure that our future together would be stable. Neither of us could just jump on a plane and fly over to meet with the other. Neither of us was of a nature to abandon our responsibilities or to give into emotion without thinking and due caution.

Since our main mode of contact was via the computer in Ark's office, when he went home at night, which was usually around nine o'clock his time, and three in the afternoon my time, both of us would experience a momentary loss of equilibrium at the apparent termination of communication. After so many long and painful years of being alone, we had so little – just words on a screen – and it never was easy to say goodnight. We developed strategies for being together at a distance, including imagining that we were together throughout the day, each of us viewing our activities through the eyes of the other. When he went home at night, to ease the momentary panic, we would both pretend that I was there with him, walking home hand in hand.

On one particular day, we discussed our ideas of possibilities, the questions to be answered, the research to be done, the contribution to humanity that we both had dreamed of making. We discussed the fact that we both had the same dreams, the same ideals, the same drive to serve others at the highest level of which we were capable. We analyzed why it had never been possible to achieve any of these things in the fullest way, and we realized that it was because of the fact that we were alone; our fundamental natures require total sharing to be fully functional. We had both given up hope, but now hope was renewed, and we thought that it was likely that all of our lives up to that point had been just the preparation for combining our energies, sharing the burden, symbolized by being "hand in hand."

That night, at the session, the Cassiopaeans again brought up the "keys" issue with the "secret handshake" as if to confirm our private discussions:

August 31, 1996

A: Appreciate the fact that you have been given the keys to end all this pain.

Q: (L) When you say, "end all this pain," it sounds a little more inclusive than just my shoulder hurting! I mean, that sounds rather suggestive.

A: Yes.

Q: (L) To end all this pain …

A: It all goes hand in hand.

It was quite a while before the realization of these things began to dawn on me. Not only was Ark the spin-doctor, he was the superhypnotherapist *with the keys*.

June 7, 1997

Q: When you said I needed to find a "superhypnotist" to break the locks on the knowledge placed in my superconsciousness, and then you suggested a "spin" doctor, and now Ark's actions while I was sleeping brought out some of the keys to large pieces of the puzzle and the connections, am I on the right track when I think that the actions we are taking in searching out these pieces of the puzzle, putting them together, and the amazing discoveries that have taken place as we go along, is the action of the "breaking" of these locks?

A: Likely.

Which, of course, brings us back to *why* the locks were put there to begin with, and what specific situation was in their awareness when they did this.

If we speculate that there are time-traveling, mind-marauding, controllers of our reality who exist at a frequency that is blocked from our perception via genetic manipulation of our wave-reading faculties, i.e. our brains, and they have an agenda to produce a certain outcome at a certain point in "time," and there is something or someone whose activities or work acts in a nonlinear way to prevent that outcome, it would be only natural for them to attempt to manipulate events by traveling into the past and changing something in some way that stacks the cards in their favor.

But time traveling is an iffy business, according to Ra. There are rules to the game.

As I have been collecting together the evidence – or the chronological reminders from emails and such – for the events of the past few years, the one thing that stands out is that a lot of very strange people have been after us – contacting us repeatedly – for the primary purpose of obtaining information about time travel.

This started almost immediately as soon as we had gotten the Cs site up and running. There were emails from dabbler types who were just curious, and we didn't think too much about it; there were emails from folks who claimed that they had invented a time machine, and wanted some scientific support to get funding for their ideas; there were hotshot physics students gunning for a showdown at high noon so they could prove they had figured the whole thing out, and then … then there was "Greg."

Greg wrote to us, and worked very hard to present a major case for why we should work with him on time travel. I was bleeding all over myself in sympathy until Ark tracked his visits to an IP in Langley, VA.

Well, based on the many glitches in the story, we just figured he was a minor spook. We also figured it was a warning of sorts. But, I patiently undertook to address replies to his emails, and they became part of the website, on some of the earlier discussion page archives.

No sooner had we dealt with Greg, along came a couple from "South Africa" with a similar story. The whole set-up was designed to push all our sympathy buttons and get us to focus on the time-travel issue. As we discussed their terrible story with them (I was really sorry for this woman who claimed to have lost her two children in an auto accident), certain glitches began popping up and when we asked questions about these confusing elements, suddenly the correspondence stopped. We realized that we were being toyed with – that the story was bait.

Not long after this, Greg had another go at it under a different name, though it was the same IP he was posting from. The story was slightly different, but essentially it was designed to lure us into giving him information out of sympathy. You know, "Oh, if I had only done thus and so, my beloved (girlfriend, wife, child, pet schnauzer) would be here today! Please help me go back in time and save a life!"

Then, along came the above-mentioned economist, who came to visit us, and, during the course of two days of talks, revealed that his agenda was time travel. He also revealed very interesting other connections, as we will discover further on.

One after the other, an almost endless parade of folks trying one way or the other to wring from us, trick from us, coerce from us, manipulate or even force from us, the "secret" of time travel. *A secret we don't have – at least not consciously.*

So, there we are trying to figure out what the heck is going on. Why are all these people interested in time travel? Why are they focusing their attention on us, one way or another?

It took me a long time to put the pieces together. After all, we just assumed that they had all the Aces. But, apparently not. You see, it seems that they are all *looking for something.*

The question then arises: Why, if they have time travel, are they looking for something? Did they lose something?

The next thing we discussed was the issue of why they were so desperate that they were willing to physically kidnap me when I was four years old? Sure, all kinds of weird stories of abductions are out there, but apparently that was not the option here. And apparently, something was so important that they literally risked exposure by doing this.[22]

---

[22] I've talked more about this event in my interview with Kerry Cassidy of Project Camelot, which can be viewed here: http://www.sott.net/articles/show/207748-Kerry-Cassidy-of-Project-Camelot-Interviews-Laura-Knight-Jadczyk

So, we came to the idea that the STS forces, lost in their wishful thinking, had somehow screwed up and lost the artifact: Something that is crucial to their plans – something that they are desperately trying to retrieve – and maybe something that they are convinced I can find for them.

And as it happens, during a recent session the Cs said that realms are "Frequency Resonance Envelopes", which made total sense based on certain computer simulations the research team have done. And this leads us to: "why me?"

One hypothesis is that the controllers, those who are deep in the STS Frequency Envelope, literally can't see the artifact due to frequency-resonance problems. The simulations the research team have done with Ark's EEQT make this clear, since it seems a wave can be deconstructed into parts that may or may not be in phase (but this only becomes apparent if you view the wave using all available information about the wave, and Ark says that pretty much no one does that). If they are out of phase, resonance forces the parts to come into phase, seemingly because that's the only stable state of the system. Standing waves are the two-dimensional projection of stable rotating spirals, i.e. *the only motion is rotation.*

What this means is that only individuals who are resonating (literally, not the New Age concept) with it, can *see* it. And things finally began to make sense. They *need* me to find it, because they cannot *see* it.

But note: as a member of the research team said: "This is one of the current ideas anyway, and I guess time will tell how on the mark we are."

So we come back to the circumstances surrounding the locks being "put on knowledge in my superconsciousness" by a "supremely powerful STS consortium," with full knowledge of the present circumstances. We begin to understand that it was crucial to lock it away from *me*, and then, at some point in time to retrieve the information. Frank failed because the Cs were too shrewd, and because of this failure, he was taken out of the project. Vincent Bridges was sent in to make a more direct attempt to retrieve the information, and an entire drama was set up to drive me into an emotional corral – a state of belief that he was part of the mission – and that it would be safe to allow him to attempt to retrieve the information about the object. And he damn near did it, except that, again, the Cs nudged the situation sufficiently so that this attempt failed. (See Appendix C for the full account.)

Of course, we recall that STS always takes the path of least resistance, and rather than waste a couple of perfectly good agents, they just changed their programs, and voila! Energizer Bunny Attack-bots.

January 10, 2002

A: [Frank] was programmed for the specific purpose of "downloading" from you secrets coded into you before birth of your present body. He failed because you were incorruptible. He is now charged with the mission, in concert with Vincent Bridges, of destroying your ability to accomplish your mission.

And we find ourselves again considering kidnapping done by a "select division of economic legion under control of G5." What does economics have to do with it?

You might be very surprised to learn that "economics" of a very special kind is the template for controlling the world. But for that vast subject, we continue in the next volume ...

APPENDIX A

APPENDIX A

22 025 9032

SOSID: 617993
Date Filed: 1/28/2002 12:29 PM
Elaine F. Marshall
North Carolina Secretary of State

State of North Carolina
Department of the Secretary of State

Limited Liability Company
ARTICLES OF ORGANIZATION

Pursuant to §57C-2-20 of the General Statutes of North Carolina, the undersigned does hereby submit these Articles of Organization for the purpose of forming a limited liability company.

1. The name of the limited liability company is: **Aethyrea Books, LLC**

2. If the limited liability company is to dissolve by a specific date, the latest date on which the limited liability company is to dissolve: *(If no date for dissolution is specified, there shall be no limit on the duration of the limited liability company.)* _____

3. The name and address of each person executing these articles of organization is as follows: *(State whether each person is executing these articles of organization in the capacity of a member, organizer or both).*

    Jay Weidner   both member/organizer
    PO Box 1853
    Buellton, CA. 93427

4. The street address and county of the initial registered office of the limited liability company is:

    Number and Street **327 Hillsborough St**

    City, State, Zip Code **Raleigh, NC 27603** County **Wake**

5. The mailing address, *if different from the street address*, of the initial registered office is:

6. The name of the initial registered agent is: **Corporation Service Company**

7. Principal office information. *(Select either a or b.)*

    a. ☐ The limited liability company has a principal office.

    The street address and county of the principal office of the limited liability company is:

    Number and Street _____
    City, State, Zip Code _____ County _____

    The mailing address, *if different from the street address*, of the principal office of the corporation is: _____

    b. ☑ The limited liability company does not have a principal office.

615

8   Check one of the following:

   ✓ (i) **Member-managed LLC**: all members by virtue of their status as members shall be managers of this limited liability company.

   _____ (ii) **Manager-managed LLC**: except as provided by N.C.G.S. Section 57C-3-20(a), the members of this limited liability company shall not be managers by virtue of their status as members.

9   Any other provisions which the limited liability company elects to include are attached

10   These articles will be effective upon filing, unless a date and/or time is specified:

This is the 24 day of January, 20 02

Jay Weidner 01/24/02
Signature

JAY WEIDNER member/organizer
Type or Print Name and Title

NOTES:
1   **Filing fee is $125. This document must be filed with the Secretary of State.**

CORPORATIONS DIVISION   P.O. Box 29622   RALEIGH, NC 27626-0622
(Revised January 2002)   *(Form L-01)*

APPENDIX B

Date sent: Fri, 25 Dec 1998 11:19:20 -0800 (PST)

From: Blue Resonant Human [...]

Subject: For Ark from Sarfatti

Hi L,

Again, ain't my cup-o-tea but Ark may like it.

-Blue

- - - - -

Memorandum For The Record

Subject: Reverse Engineering Alleged Alien Super-Technology

-------- Original Message --------

Subject: Ryazanov Replies #2

Date: Thu, 24 Dec 1998 14:22:17 -0600

From: "Gary S. Bekkum"

To: "Sarfatti, Jack"

Note I have edited this to remove confusing tag lines.

GSB

[Jack]

Note George Ryazanov is a physicist from Moscow who worked with Sakharov. The San Francisco Art Institute is running a show "Angels and Aliens".

George Ryazanov Re: The Philosophy of Alien Science – From the Biological to the Angelic

[Gary]

George Ryazanov says: "There is a common saying that the setting of experimental procedures is determined mostly by the theory that we want to prove or disprove ... we have here a cycle that must be broken."

[George] The "Alien Science" – It is better to name it "the science of future" – it is the next step in our science.

[Gary] (the) simulations by synthesis of reality goes beyond this cycle of informational dependence. It is "alien" in the sense that it is foreign to our normal thought processing. It may be "alien" in the sense that Jack Sarfatti means if the new dynamic is a result of an interaction with intelligence that is not of this world. It may also be a result of a future human reality in the multiverse.

[George] It is the dependence on some unconscious cliché.

[Gary] Ryazanov says that to go beyond mere experimental procedure, we must apply "principles that are above the existing theory and existing experiments."

Regarding human thought as applied to physics, which seeks the precision of "truth" by the application of mathematics, Ryazanov writes " … new physics cannot be described by (the) language of mathematics. The trust in mathematics is the third sin (of physicists). (The first sin is to assume that only retarded causal waves are physical. The second is trust in experimental procedure).

[George] In more concrete form it is the trust in local dynamics that did not depend on motion of distant matter of Universe.

[Jack Sarfatti] Note my conjecture for a new law of nature

$T(\text{orch}) = T_{ao}/N$

T_{ao} = Cosmological Hubble Time = $O(10$ billion years) where $T(\text{orch})$ is the duration of an "occasion of conscious experience" in an entangled N q-bit coherent switching network protected against decoherence for at least time $T(\text{orch})$. Note the universal Machian global character of this hypothetical post-quantum principle like the no-hair theorem of classical black hole physics.

[Gary] Is this an intellectual trust, or an emotional dependence?

[George] It is the erroneous receipt of solving the equations of classical physics.

[Gary] George goes on to say that in his new physics "the most interesting result is the derivation of numbers and geometry from dynamics of pure emotions."

[Jack] Like QM curvature fluctuation/classical curvature = (Planck distance/Classical wormhole radius) (Compton wavelength/scale of fluctuation)^3 in Wheeler far-field (1a) QM curvature fluctuation/classical curvature = (Planck distance^2/Classical wormhole radius) Compton wavelength^3/scale of fluctuation^4 in Sidharth near-field (1b)

$T(\text{orch})$ = (Hubble time) /N (2a)

T(OR) = (spatial separation of coherent q-bit)(Planck's quantum of action)/(Newton's gravity constant)(mass of q-bit)^2 N^5/3 (2b)

$T(\text{orch}) " T(OR)$ (2c)

(Hubble time)/Nmax = (spatial separation of coherent q-bit)(Planck's quantum of action)/(Newton's gravity constant)(mass of q-bit)^2 Nmax^5/3 (2d) threshold crossing point condition

Tmin = Hubble time/Nmax (2e)

Quale(N,T) exists when N " Nmax, T " Tmin all forms of decoherence screened except self-gravity (2f)

Now this is all different from what Hameroff proposes though it is partly based on his ideas and the ideas of many others.

[Gary] In order to understand such an "alien paradigm" one must do as the "aliens" do and learn to think like an "alien".

[George] Yes, I have here the detailed technique.

[Gary] Will the details of your technique be made available?

[George] In near future I shall sent you some details.

[Gary] The primary paradigm shift required to understand the "new alien physics" is to reassess the meaning of "information" and 'knowledge" in human thought. The first step in making this paradigm shift is to reconsider the dynamics of learning in terms of the symmetry of meaning.

[George] Do you mean the mutual influence of angelic and existential levels of dynamics? Laws of physics are norms of angelic translation of one Name into another.

[Gary] Perhaps. I mean that there is a symmetry of meaning between the object of knowledge and the experience of that object. To say that we have meaning in our knowledge of physics is to say that there is a representational simulation taking place within the dynamics of the "fifth phase of matter" – that is, within the Sarfatti PQM backaction of matter on the mind that is guiding it.

[George] Examples: two-signs-of-time-symmetry, two-signs-of-causality-symmetry, part-whole symmetry.

[Gary] What is the fundamental symmetry between matter and mind for Sarfatti back action?

[George] It is the complex procedure of transforming our state of mind to some mathematical structures and our emotions to physical forces.

[Gary] The human approach to learning is technologically primitive. It is based on trial and error exploration of our environment. To transfer this learning we spend a great deal of our lives in classrooms, repeating the trials of those before us. An analogy is in order here. "Alien knowledge" is self-reproducing.

[George] But if we want to feed this self-reproducing entity we must spend our life on this feeding.

[Gary] Can you explain this in more detail?

[George] I have in mind the history of my search of understanding this entity and the ways to interact with it.

[Gary] It is imprinted on the existing order (like a "digital copy" is made on a recording medium). The application of this synthetic dynamic upon the medium of reality produces a change in that reality. The dynamic that results is unique, it bears aspects of the "alien order" and the order upon which it has been imprinted.

[George] Example: my derivation of quantum mechanics.

[Gary] Yes, this is what I had in mind, a transfer of order between organized systems. The core of this issue is found by examining the structure of the physical non-material reality (the fifth phase of matter) that is produced as a result of the strange loops of dynamic interaction between a thought and the physical representation of that thought.

[George] Those loops can be seen in the history of our basic traditions. "Fifth phase of matter" can be revealed through those traditions – I have technique of this revealing.

[Gary] I am interested in the transfer to the present moment of "new dynamics of future (alien) science". In particular the possibility of learning from future to past as a process in our experience of time's arrow from past to future.

[Jack] "That's a nice rendition", Gary. :-) (Kubrick's 2001)

[George] It is learning a program (as DNA), the future is created here.

[Gary] Within this fifth phase is a new set of orders which are not apparent to us from our temporal perspective. Loops of interaction organize this fifth phase product of biological systems from the material brain to the cosmic orders of the angelic realm.

[George] In learning. But in evolution we have inverse order.

[Gary] Yes. It is not that the "dead" material physical matter of the universe has conscious or unconscious mental processes.

[George] But in new physics matter interact with mental processes. – I have a detailed description of this interaction.

[Gary] This is Sarfatti's $Q^{*"}$-"(X). We are anxious to see the details of this interaction.

[George] I shall send. Rather, it is the fact that our minds representational capacity) supply such matter with a corresponding "fifth phase" dynamic. Indeed,what is truly astounding is to consider that the fifth phase of matter is in a state of such incredible dynamic interaction, shaped as it is by the very forces of our mental imagery and emotional states of mind.

[George] So as by imaginary of angels and Creator.

[Gary] Yes, I understand this better now. Our minds are corrupted by errors in the "programming" of our "fallen world"?

[George] Yes. Some of those errors I have deleted.

[Gary] The secret of the "alien scientists" is that they have recognized that this dynamic is intimately interwoven with the material physical world.

[George] And have transformed this knowledge to his apparatus and procedures.

[Gary] Indeed, the totality of their scientific pursuit is based on the manipulation of the physical non-material fifth phase matter, in order to synthesize new properties and order. One might even speculate on the possible "harvesting" of human fifth phase dynamics for raw material to imprint.

[George] Human beings are only a means for regulation from "fifth dynamics".

[Gary] Please explain how we regulate the "fifth phase dynamics". Is there a benefit to the "alien technology" to generate intense human emotion and symbolic imagery?

[George] It is the only way to redemption.

[Gary] Perhaps at the "angelic level", but there is a dangerous application of this technology for psychotronic warfare.

[George] This technology have strong demands on the moral level of "observer", then there is no danger here.

[Gary] Perhaps there are certain qualities that are aesthetically better suited to the "alien purpose"?

[George] These qualities are the most valuable in art, religion, mysticism.

APPENDIX C

After many months of interaction with Vincent Bridges during which time he slowly and carefully spun his web of lies to convince me that he was the "superhypnotherapist" I needed to "unlock secrets hidden in my subconscious", we finally made arrangements for him to visit with us and perform several hypnosis sessions on me ostensibly to "undo" possible negative programming that he was convinced had been put in place by "nazi-satanic ritual abuse." I had my doubts about any of it, but I was willing to check it out just to make sure.

Bridges came to our home in March of 2001. After we had done a couple of sessions, during which no evidence of the alleged satanic abuse, sexual abuse, or any other kind of similar activity came forth, we decided to try a session with the Cassiopaeans with Vincent at the board with me. I was doubtful that anything would happen with a strange sitter, but again, I was willing to give it a try. Vincent was so convinced that he was the one who knew how things ought to be done and that a "big breakthrough" would occur with him present, who was I to reject such claims out of hand? The following is the result of the first attempt:

March 17, 2001 (Ark, Laura, Vincent Bridges; Reconstructed from notes.)

Q: Is anyone there?

A: Yes.

Q: What is your name?

A: Oxajil.

Q: Is that your name?

A: Yes.

Q: Do you transmit via Cassiopaea?

A: Yes.

Q: Do you have any messages for us?

A: Open other door.

Q: What does that mean?

A: Look mirror now Laura.

Q: Does this mean we should use the mirror for communication?

A: Yes.

Q: Is there anything Vincent can do to help this process?

A: Open.

Q: (VB) If it would be my free will to do something along this line, would it help to facilitate communication?

A: Work on Laura.

Q: (VB) That means we should have done the work on Laura before the session, as Ark suggested?

A: Listen to Ark.

Q: (VB) So, we screwed up by not listening to Ark earlier?

A: No. Listen to Ark.

Q: (VB) Something else Ark said today?

A: Yes.

Q: (VB) Can you give us a keyword for this work on Laura that we need to do?

A: Number Five.

Q: (VB) What does number five have to do with anything?

A: Laura. Listen to Ark. […]

Q: (VB) Back to the number five clue. How does this relate?

A: Open other door.

Q: (VB) Door as in the mirror?

A: Open now.

Q: (VB) You mean we should try the mirror right now?

A: Yes.

Q: (VB) Is this related to what I was told in 1987?

A: Yes. More.

Q: Can we have another clue?

A: L V …

Q: We don't understand.

A: Knowledge protects.

Q: But what is this L V?

A: Process of L V. Source.

Q: (VB) Does this mean that the process of deprogramming will lead to the source?

A: L V I 3 5 Ark.

Q: (Confusion expressed about this last "clue.")

A: L 5 I 3 for more. Mirror.

Q: (VB) So we will know more or be able to get more via the mirror?

A: Yes. Goodbye. [End of Session]

It's pretty easy to see in retrospect that the C's seemed very determined to get me to look in the mirror and see something and that they were not inclined – or were unable – to communicate with Vincent at the board. We did a mirror session at that time which is lengthy and has not yet been transcribed, but the major portion of it consisted of Vincent trying to direct me to "see" the "Ark of the Covenant" or the "Holy Grail." He was extremely anxious that I locate this object in space-time.

One thing about the mirror work that really surprised me was Vincent's obvious terror in the presence of a doorway to higher dimensions. This was a strange state of affairs for someone who claimed to be so knowledgeable and experienced in "occult" matters. Ark later described his behavior as totally bizarre. As I perceived myself flying through a tunnel to emerge into the light of a different reality, Vincent was literally throwing up his arms before his face, making signs and gestures, and trying to ward off what he thought were horrible creatures that were going to jump out of the mirror and "get him."

Indeed, I saw such creatures as I passed them on this psychic journey, but I pointed out that one only had to look at them and the light from the soul projected through the eyes caused them to flee in terror. It never occurred to me at the time that I was experiencing this phenomenon that Bridges was not "with me" so to speak, and had no idea of what one sees and experiences on such an excursion. That was another strange thing about him, considering that he claimed to be so knowledgeable and experienced.

Since Vincent was so terrified of the mirror work (all the while claiming that he was the "expert guide" and that I was in terrible danger without his rituals and guidance), we decided to try the board again the next day.

March 19, 2001 (Ark, Laura, Vincent Bridges)

Q: Hello.

A: Hello.

Q: Is someone with us?

A: Air. Cassiopaea.

Q: Do we have the Cassiopaeans with us?

A: To U.

Q: Do you have a name?

A: Faitij. [Curious name; almost an Arabic flavor.]

Q: (L) OK, we had a hypnosis session today. Did we do all that was necessary to blow off the locks?

A: Close.

Q: (VB) Did we do what was necessary for now?

A: Close.

Q: (A) What percentage of what was necessary to do did we accomplish?

A: 49 percent.

Q: (VB) Was 49 the right number?

A: Yes. Laura has open window in more keys. ["keys" as in sound?]

Q: (L) Did we utilize the clues from last night properly?

A: Yes. Now must look us up to talk to us.

Q: (L) Look us up as in the phone book? (VB) Look them up in the mirror. (L) Is there …

A: Key FI 3

Q: (VB) Key "phi 3?" You jokers! (L) What is phi 3? (VB) Phi to the third power? (L) A phi circle with 3 turns?

A: Route.

Q: (VB) Is this phi 3 a path or something?

A: Open your.

Q: (VB) Open "your" phi 3? (A) Now route is French for road, and "F" could be for France; and "I-3" could be a number of a road in France.

A: Yes.

Q: (VB) Are you pointing us to somewhere in France?

A: Yes.

Q: (VB) Is it a place that either Ark or I have been to?

A: No.

Q: (VB) Is it a place we should go to?

A: Yes. O T

Q: (VB) Operating Thetan? I can't make any sense out of this because I am trying so hard to stay out of it. (A) We know the route number. O T must be the initials of something. It might even be in the little book you just bought. (VB) Are we correct in our suppositions so far?

A: Yes.

Q: (VB) Tell us more about O T.

A: O T.

Q: (L) Well, that was real clear! [We get book and look at it.] Does O T mean Operating Thetan?

A: No.

Q: (L) Let's go back … You say "route." (VB) Is it a place in France?

A: Yes.

Q: (L) Is it the name of a place?

A: No. Laura can see.

Q: (L) Do we need to do more hypnosis to enhance the seeing process?

A: Yes.

Q: (L) Do we need to do it as soon as possible, like right away?

A: Open.

Q: (L) Is there a couple word clue … [begins to sweep the alphabet as though gathering energy]

A: Key is not number mix F,

Q: (VB) What?!

A: Yes. Five 3

Q: (L) So, you are saying that it may not be a number mixed with a letter, but that the key is Five 3 O T.

A: Yes. Not key F I 3. Route I 3.

Q: (L) Not "phi," but a route with an F somehow. This is not making a whole lot of sense here. I realize you are trying to tell us something, but you are going to have to come at it another way because we just aren't getting it this way. (VB) Are we understanding what we think we are getting?

A: Yes.

Q: (VB) Can you be more clear because we aren't understanding something here?

A: Titus lair.

Q: (VB) Titus was an emperor, but that's all I remember off the top of my head. [We stop and look Titus up in a book and discover that he was the one who sacked Jerusalem and was commemorated on the "Arch of Titus." It was then suggested that the temple treasure was taken to Rome, and stolen from Rome by the Visigoths.] (L) OK, are we onto something with this Titus and the Temple treasure? Is O T the Old Temple?

A: Yes.

Q: (VB) Does this have to do with Perseus' purpose?

A: Just told you. Place Laura must go to slow F I 3.

Q: (L) To "slow F I 3?" What is F I 3 that it must be slowed?

A: Sneak attack.

Q: (L) So, this is some kind of code for the route of entry of a "sneak attack?" (A) And we must go there to slow this attack? (VB) Can you tell us more about this attack?

A: STS 4 D.

Q: (VB) And what are the STS 4D things attacking?

A: Earth.

Q: (L) So, you are saying that there is a doorway there that they can come through, or do through, or plan to come through, or through which they can send energy, or something along this line?

A: No.

Q: (L) There is something buried there that we must find to use to slow this attack?

A: Yes.

Q: (VB) If we find it, that will slow the attack?

A: Not just slow. Jump up the protection required in order to survive slam by meteors in 2010 space war.

Q: (L) Well, I want to know … why do I have to be there? (VB) Do all three of us in this room have to be there?

A: Yes.

Q: (VB) Why?

A: Must create conduit.

Q: (L) So, we are back to the seven people that must assemble?

A: No.

Q: (L) Doesn't have to be seven. (VB) But it has to be the three of us?

A: Yes.

Q: (VB) Can we bring others with us?

A: Yes.

Q: (VB) Just checking. (L) I'm not leaving my kids! (VB) Bring the whole family?

A: It is humanity's hope for survival what lures you to the quest here Perceval 3.

Q: (L) Well, we have one slight little factor that we are going to have to deal with, and that is the money factor. Obviously, we are going to have to have a lot of money to carry out this mission. I mean, do we need to just pack up, sell the house, and move?

A: To save the world you will vote for knowledge protection rite, Laura; instincts not knowledge abandonment. Move when time is right.

Q: (VB) That strikes me as a really odd note, for some reason. (L) Well, that's their whole thing. Knowledge protection "rite" is "awareness." Do you mean some kind of actual ritual?

A: Be prepared.

Q: (L) Yes. How does knowledge protect? By awareness and being prepared. Being prepared is the "rite" of "knowledge protects." (VB) Is there something we need to do or know to be prepared?

A: Yes. Sell books.

Q: (VB) So, what you guys are saying is that it is not exactly a ritual, but being prepared is having all the books out.

A: Yes.

Q: (VB) Do we have to have all the books out?

A: Yes.

Q: (VB) So, that means it is not on the slate for this May. Are we all supposed to be there this May?

A: No. Just knowledge is must. [tape ends; pause while new one inserted] Quest.

Q: (L) So, knowledge is a must, and for this we must continue to quest. (A) To sell books, one must write books. Writing books is an opportunity to get knowledge and spread knowledge, and that is the most essential thing here. (L) Do we need to do another hypnosis session before Vincent leaves tomorrow? Would it be advantageous?

A: Okay, yes. Not urgent now.

Q: (VB) Yes, it would be advantageous. Is that what you are saying, that we've done as much as we can?

A: Not.

Q: (A) It wouldn't harm, is that what you are saying?

A: Spade up the sleeve.

Q: (VB) Ace in the hole. (L) Spade. Can also be a shovel. A double meaning. An ace in the hole; turn something up, dig. They could have just as easily said "ace." If we were to do another session, what would be the key words to guide the focus?

A: Safety gate.

Q: (A) Define "safety gate?" (VB) A back door they can access you? A secure entrance? What?

A: Post-hypnotic gate pre-text.

Q: (L) Maybe they are saying that we need to install a post hypnotic gate pre-text? Is Vincent supposed to install a post-hypnotic suggestion series of words that I or Ark can use to open or close a gate?

A: Yes.

Q: (VB) What kind of gate? (L) One that can be opened or closed. (VB) Somehow connected to the knowledge protection rite. What is a pretext? A pretext? (L) Should we put in a suggestion for viewing the mirror, a series of words, to open the gate for viewing, and then a series of words for closing the gate?

A: Yes. Precisely. Just a few words.

Q: (L) In Polish?

A: No.

Q: (A) What is this "spade up the sleeve?" (L) Well, applying it here would mean to have it open and close at will. (VB) Does "spade up the sleeve" mean our "secret weapon?"

A: Yes.

Q: (VB) Do we have to develop this secret weapon?

A: Yes.

Q: (VB) Is that what we are supposed to do with the hypnotic safety gate?

A: Yes.

Q: (VB) Is there any more information you can give us?

A: Yes.

Q: (VB) Can you give it now?

A: Puns or slogans.

Q: (VB) The Green Language?

A: Yes.

Q: (L) So we are supposed to come up with some puns or slogans to install as triggers of our own ...

A: Yes.

Q: (VB) And that will facilitate Laura's ability to open the mirror seeing at will?

A: Yes.

Q: (VB) But this is not urgent, it just must be done before we take off on the quest?

A: Yes. Must follow lots of paths.

Q: (L) So, we still have a lot to learn coming up before us here. [And only now are we beginning to move into the stage where we can literally get to the bottom of the matter, I think.] (L) So, we cannot just rely on

the mirror. That's an ace up the sleeve. We have a lot of work to do. (VB) We are talking about a situation in which Laura is going to need ...
A: Yes.
Q: (VB) ... a system in which Laura can "turn on" unknown to anyone else, that we can use in public without anyone else knowing ...
A: Yes. Use to home in on right level of log u to snse [sense] fight ...
[End of Session.]

The energy fell off. Whether this was a remark that reflected a sensing of a "fight" that was present at this point, blocking the transmission, or was an instruction that we were to be able to learn to sense "fighting," we don't know.

The above session was troubling for a lot of reasons. The first one was the fact that the C's seemed to be revealing our "mission" in a plainer way than they ever had done before. This was entirely out of keeping with their mode. They had always told us that we must discover certain things – such as "Level One Destiny Profile" issues on our own, that they could not tell us. Aside from the paradoxes that might be produced when one changes the past, there is the simpler issue of violation of free will.

Another point was the designation of the "Perceval Three." This was also in direct contradiction to the mode of the C's activity, as well as previous information that had been given in abundance.

Something was wrong.

My initial response was that I was very happy that the C's were now speaking more plainly. I was open to the idea that this was because we were now hooked up with the "right" person – i.e. Vincent Bridges. I can even say that I wanted to believe that Vincent was all he claimed to be and because of this, I initially brushed aside all the hints, the urgent clues that suggested I needed to look at this situation more deeply. It wasn't until the mirror session that is the subject of this article, that the C's managed to get through to me what they had been trying to get me to see without violating my free will or learning process. At the end of the mirror session, I will add some more data from later sessions that will help to explain exactly what was going on in the above two sessions with Vincent Bridges at the board.

Also, before reading the session, I would like to bring some other important matters to the reader's attention. As even the most casual observer will note, when listening to the sound clips from the hypnosis/mirror session conducted by Mr. Vincent Bridges, his lapses of professional demeanor in relation to a subject in a state of hypnosis induced and controlled by him, are not merely reprehensible, they are legally actionable.

Mr. Bridges has recently written and posted the following on a public message board where he is active defaming me and my work:

> Note on the practice of hypnosis in Florida – The state of Florida has strict laws concerning hypnosis. Florida Statute 456 outlines who can practice, and who cannot: Florida Statute 456 on the Practice of Hypnosis, LIMITS this therapy to LICENSED practitioners of the healing arts, including physicians, psychiatrists, dentists, chiropractors, podiatrists, and optometrists "within the perview of the statutes applicable to his respective profession." A patient may be referred to a "qualified practitioner" by a licensed practitioner of the healing arts, but that "qualified practitioner" must employ hypnotic techniques under the SUPERVISION, DIRECTION, 'PRESCRIPTION', and RESPONSIBILITY of such referring practitioner. (66) FLORIDA STATUTE 456 Practice of Hypnosis 456.005 Penalities: Misdemeanor of the second degree: (456).

Mr. Bridges is quite correct. Perhaps Mr. Bridges should have checked out the above statute before traveling to the State of Florida to perform therapeutic hypnosis on me – which I ought to add, was taped and the tapes are in our possession and can be produced when the situation warrants. After all, Mr. Bridges is the one claiming to be a "psychotherapist," not me. And thus far, we have been unable to discover a single piece of evidence or validation for his training and claims.

Mr. Bridges goes on to say:

> In the second volume of her voluminous and on-going autobiography, Adventures with the Cassiopaeans, Ms. Knight-Jadczyk informs us that she has no training in hypnotherapy, or any other kind of therapy. 'I admit that I have none freely. Well, that's not entirely true. I have certification in hypnosis; until I quit in 1996, I was listed in the directories of The American Counselors Society and The National Society of Clinical Hypnotherapists, neither of which is any kind of major endorsement.'

What Mr. Bridges fails to note is that the above quoted remark from me (Laura) is a footnote to the following statement: "So, on the one hand, we have six respectable people, none of whom has ever even "fudged" their credentials … "

The reference was to "credentials" in terms of college degrees and other claims, including publishing credits, such as those falsely made by Mr. Vincent Bridges. It made no reference whatsoever to any lack of training in hypnotherapy or any other kind of therapy. In fact, I described quite clearly the training I received in those areas through the years in *Amazing Grace*.[23]

---

[23] The reader may like to view my certification at http://cassiopaea-cult.com/lauras-hypnosis-certification

In short, in Bridges' defamatory and manipulative words above, what we are seeing is another example of the semantic aphasia of the psychopath who, as one expert put it: "knows many words, but not the meanings." He goes on with his defamation:

> Indeed, since the first organization no longer exists, and seems to have had a very small and completely non-professional membership, and the second has no record of a Laura Knight or a Laura Martin ever taking any sort of training or receiving any kind of certification, then we must ask just what does this certification consist of?

This is a case of deliberate falsification since I have on my desk the directory which includes many professional members in all 50 states.

> A Laura Martin was indeed a member of the Society in 1994 and 1995, but simple membership and directory listing explicitly carries with it no certification or even a recommendation.

Unfortunately, Mr. Bridges is incorrect again. The societies named above, are composed of members who have graduated from the training programs of St. John's University, an accredited institution formed long after I received my training from its founder, Dr. Arthur Winkler. As it happens, over the many years since I took the courses, I had lost my certificates and wrote to Dr. Winkler to ask if it could be replaced. My certificates were replaced.

> If therefore Ms. Knight-Jadczyk has any type of certification in hypnosis, which is doubtful as no positive evidence of such certification has been presented or can be found in the records of the institutions cited by her, it does not in the state of Florida entitle her to practice Hypnotherapy without the direct supervision of a licensed practitioner of the healing arts, as listed above. If she has been practicing such hypnotherapy without any supervision, then it is a violation of Florida law, and is a second-degree misdemeanor as noted above.

Since we have dealt with the issue of *my* certification, perhaps Mr. Bridges ought to apply these standards to himself since, as noted, I have never claimed to be a "psychotherapist" as he has done, repeatedly.

Furthermore, Spirit Release Therapy and Past Life Therapy, and exorcism, are not accepted as "therapeutic modalities" by standard psychological therapy and are not even covered under the above statute. However, therapeutic hypnosis that deals with child abuse issues, including sexual abuse, as Mr. Bridges claims is his specialty, is indeed covered under the above statute. Mr. Bridges wrote to a member of our group:

Dear S***,

Well, it sounds like you are a classical client of mine. My specialty was early childhood trauma abreaction, and I mainly focused on incest, sexual abuse, etc. [...] In the course of all that, I've come across many "Greenbaum" cases. Corey's [sic] lecture, quoted by Laura in the Wave I think, is partly taken from my research. I talked at length to him a few months before the conference where he gave the lecture and my then partner was in the audience.

[...] I am Dr. Mack and Bud [sic] Hopkins' worst enemies. Hopkins refused to speak at the same Fortean convention a few years ago, because I had attacked his work so strongly the night before at the party. So it goes. . . These guys are shameful. [...] I studied with Milton Ericson [sic] years ago, and he stressed the value of conscious participation in the trance state as the only way to insure the value of the trance's contents. [...] I had a semi-famous abductee, one of the above's "clients," whose experience turned about to be, with enough carefully unfoldment, her father masturbating at her bedside. [...] Feel like visiting the beautiful piedmont one weekend? I can do a simple evaluation, and see if there is work we can profitably do together. It is possible to do it in one day, I've a few other semi-detached clients in Asheville who do occasionally, so ... Are you game? Anyway, let me know what you feel,

Vincent

What are the statutes regarding such practice in North Carolina?

A more pressing question, however, is when, precisely, did Vincent Bridges study with Milton Erickson? After all, the good doctor died in 1980 at the age of 79. We already have a pretty full schedule for those years according to Bridges' own account. Nevertheless, we have sent inquiries to the related institutes to discover if anyone who did actually study with Erickson remembers Mr. Bridges.

In any event, I do hope that Vincent Bridges clearly remembers every word spoken in the several sessions in which he hypnotized me "therapeutically," as he most certainly is in violation of the law in Florida he has cited. I do thank him for researching this matter for me since it now adds to the list of frauds he has perpetrated on me and others which can be submitted for review to the State Attorney of Florida.

Now, on with the Mirror session itself, which began with the board:

July 5, 2001 (Ark, Laura, VB, OE, BT; Laura and Vincent Bridges at the board)

Q: Testing. (L to VB) Warm up your fingers. You're not going to go flaky on me are you? (VB) You never know. I'll try not to make it go around the board 8 times between letters. I have a terrible time when I start. (L) Hello, is anyone there? Hello, hello. [extremely long pause] Well. We are just sitting here with no action. (A) A** just walked by. Maybe we wait. They don't like kids. (L) They love kids; they just don't want them around. It's not healthy for them. (VB makes inaudible remark) (L) You nonbeliever! [laughter] (VB) It didn't stop them the last time. (L) They were desperate. They had something to say, too. Maybe they thought they told us all we needed to know. [long pause] [L gives VB instruction on how to suspend the arm from the shoulder. Planchette begins to move in circles and stops on Capricorn.] (L) Hello. Is anyone there?

A: 1

Q: (L) Do you have a name?

A: UC !

Q: U I C ?

A: O U Look. [The word "look" is a whole word on the board and was not spelled out.]

Q: (L) 1 U seek, O U look?

A: S A R Wait. [This last is a whole word on the board and was not spelled out.] Listen. [Another whole word on the board was indicated.]

Q: Listen?

A: Yes. [Another whole word on the board.] M

Q: [planchette stops, long pause] (VB) It stopped. (L) It's like in between Sagittarius and Capricorn.

A: Look. [Again indicating a whole word.]

Q: (L) So, what have they said so far? (A) Once "U C." (VB) What are we supposed to be looking for, or looking at?

A: Lara look. [Spelled "Lara," whole word "look."]

Q: (VB) Well, they spelled your name. (L) Yeah, but they left out a letter.

A: Laura look. [Spelled name, whole word "look."]

Q: (VB) Is there some reason why you left the "u" out?

A: Yes. Lara L U C.

Q: (L) What is "Lara Luc?" (VB) OK, are we talking to the Cassiopaeans? Or are we just scooting around in astral space here?

A: Cassiopaea, Laura.. [planchette begins to spiral slowly]

Q: (VB) OK, what is this? (L) It's still turning. We did that in the beginning a lot. It builds energy. [planchette continues to spiral]

A: Aura lock.

Q: (VB) OK guys, don't make it fly off the board, alright? [planchette spiraling faster and faster] (A) It is spiraling very fast. (VB) In my mind's eye I see a little green flame planchette. I can follow it around the board with my eyes closed. (L) You're not supposed to have your eyes closed. They're supposed to be open. (VB) I'm actually doing better with them closed. Um, is there something to that little green flame I'm seeing guys? Anything you want to tell me about it? [No answer. Planchette flies out from under VB's fingers.] (VB) OK, thank you for flying out from under my hand. And it stopped on that same spot. (L) OK, they said they were doing an "aura lock?" (VB) Yes. That's why I asked about the green flame.

A: 3 body junctim ground rail motqetuh.

Q: (L) I don't know what they are saying.

A: o s e over k o r e 5 k

Q: (L) It stopped. What did they say? (VB) [unintelligible remark] (L) We have to start somewhere until it's grooved. It's called "grooving."

A: New groove. [planchette spirals]

Q: (L) That's why they're spiraling. And they just want to spiral. [pause while planchette continues to move in circles] And it makes your arm tired. (VB) Maybe that's the point? [long silence while planchette continues to spiral] I'm getting in the groove here. (BT) It will wear out your muscle response. (L) Yeah. That may be so because of ... (VB) Brother skeptic's desire to make things go a certain way? [planchette continues to spiral] (L) Busy, busy, busy. Boy, they are just busy, aren't they? (BT) Pretty energetic spiraling. (L) My arm is about ready to fall off. All right! Maybe ask some questions, even if we stick with some simple ones here in the beginning.

A: Time to urge everyo [spiraling] ne to under [L sighs] (VB) Come on. [L sighs] stand ri ri ri de.

Q: [VB rubbing shoulder] (L to VB) You hurting? (VB) Yeah. (L) That's good. Something's happening. (VB) Well yeah. The thing's flying around the board so fast I can't ... (L) No, it's doing other stuff, just trust me. (VB) What did we get? (BT) "Time to urge everyone to understand ride." (L) In other words, that you're supposed to ride, not drive. I think they're having trouble doing things because you like to drive, not ride. (VB) Well, I'm doing my best ... (L) I know. (VB) This is so much better than the last time. (L) OK. Well, I'm just telling you. There's probably unconscious reasons for this. (VB) [talking seemingly to air] My mistake. Leave me out of it [irritated]. (L) Well, just stop pressing hard, Just enjoy it. You're supposed to enjoy the ride. (VB) Does your shoulder hurt as much as mine? [laughter] (L) No, but it used to. And it probably hurt a whole helluva lot more.

A: Other method other purpose board is good for grooving so enjoy ride!

Q: (L to VB) Well, you need to be grooved. (VB) Well what's the other method, other purpose? (A) It's open to you to ask. (L) Is it advisable to continue to work with the board? In addition to the other method? [long pause, spiraling]

A: Do it here right now.

Q: (L) Do what here right now?

A: Mirror.

Q: (L) Damn it! (VB) I tell you, you may be grooving me ... (A) Are we having fun? (L) "Do it here right now?" Why? Sorry guys, I had to ask.

A: See 4 density.

Q: (L) They aren't gonna let me out of it, are they?

A: Laura now!

Q: (L) Will I see our $300,000 bux?

A: Open maybe gain insight about funds look

Q: (BT to L) OK, is that just you, or with the moon full or what? (L to BT) Well, I don't think it makes any difference. We did it before with Ark and VB. [long pause] Any other words of wisdom before we set the mirror up? (VB) Uh, actually guys, I've got a couple of questions. Would you kind of help me out here, since I'm the "newbie?" I know she needs to look in the mirror, but you, what can you tell me about all this weird stuff? Like what do I need to know?

A: Laura look

Q: (VB) alright, come on, come on. I'm not through yet! I am the stubborn one guys, I'm sorry. If Laura looks, is there anything we need to know about her looking to help her do it?

A: Hypnosis laura future time new look deed ok not much human toil to funds

Q: (A) What does this mean? (VB Peremptorily) OK, the "deed ok" is, I was silently asking, "I don't want to hypnotize Laura; I'm afraid of being another Dr. Puharich" So I think the "deed ok" was, they were answering me in the middle, which may have thrown off the "much human," because I was resisting … Oh, no, no, I don't want to do this; you guys really don't want to do this do you? (L) Well, you've got to remember, VB, all the work that was done to prevent me from being able to do it naturally, it has to be overcome, and we don't have a lot of time left. (VB) OK. I would prefer to do it another way, but I suppose they're not helping me much, though, are they? (L) Well, why don't you ask a question to the mirror? (VB) Well, this is very interesting isn't it? (L) It's a full moon. [long pause] (VB) OK guys, I'm getting the feeling that you're telling us … [tape ends, VB restates lost question on next side] Are you telling me the only reason I'm here is to make sure she can actually get deep enough to see through the mirror? If not the only reason, maybe a big part of the reason?

A: [long silence, no response]

Q: (VB) Say something guys.

A: Percival.

Q: (VB) OK, there's five of us at the moment. Is this making a difference?

A: Yes.

Q: (VB) Should we cut back down to three for the mirror?

A: No. T iu e t h u l t o i t

Q: (L) What was that? Try again, guys. (VB) Wait, wait, wait, wait. (L) What was this word? This "tiue" whatever?

A. Ties you to it guide Laura mirror look room is mirage.

Q: (L) What is it? (VB) They don't usually spell that bad. OK, more clarity please, on "room is mirage." What do you mean by that?

A: People in room perceive mirage

Q: (L) Oh, I get it. The people in the room add energy to the viewing so it enables it to come through better and clearer, is that what you are saying?

A: Yes.

635

Q: (VB) OK, we're going to look in the mirror. We're going to do it right after you finish this next question. But you need to tell us the steps. You need to tell us exactly how you want it done.

A: point out perception is just mirage and only look for what is real

Q: (VB) What the hell is that? (BT reads back) That was a direct response to you asking for steps. (VB) Guys that really doesn't help. (A) Point out that perception, yes? Is just a mirage, right? (VB) But they're saying that the perception of everyone in the room should be a mirage, that we're giving energy to the mirage, so how do we see through it?

A: people help move perception satisfactorily jump start

Q: (VB) OK. Is there anything else, and if not, we'll go right to the mirror. Anything else we need to know?

A: [no response, long pause.]

Q: (VB) Absolutely nobody just moved close to me right now. Nobody moved? (A & B) No. (L) Why? (VB) Ooooh, nothing. (A) Something touched you? (VB) That's right. So what, I need another pat on the shoulder. (B) It was your right shoulder? (VB) Yeah. [end of tape]

Mirror Session

VB: As you breathe, stay focused on the mirror. And, at the corners of your eyes, allow yourself to become aware of the room. You can see almost all of the room out of the corners of your eyes. Stay focused on the mirror. Take a deep breath, release, again deep breath, release. As you breathe, allow the perceptions of the room to fade. The room we are sitting in is a mirage. It's empty. There's nothing here but you and the mirror. Focus your eyes deep into the mirror, and let your perceptions of everything in the room, except the mirror, let them fade. As if it was a mirage in the desert, waving, disappearing, until nothing is left but the mirror. You can see the surface of the mirror, you can perceive a boundary or surface to the mirror. Everything else is fading out. As you look into the mirror, it's like looking into a very still piece of water. Look deep into that surface, allowing everything else in the room to fade away. Breathing comfortably, relaxing thoroughly, focusing on the mirror. Allowing the room to fade away until nothing remains but the mirror. I want you to focus on the mirror; feel the room fading. Allow yourself to become completely focused; all of your awareness, all of your energy; focused on the mirror; feeling that boundary, the surface of the mirror. In just a moment I'm going to count from ten to one. With each count you will feel your body getting very light, your body fading away like the rest of the mirage. With each count, as your body fades, feel your awareness going through the boundary, until at the count of one, you will be looking with your eyes open deep into the mirror, past the boundary, and deep within the mirror, you will see only that which is real. As we count back now from ten to one, feeling your body fading away, until nothing is left but your focus on the mirror. As you focus on the mirror, look deep into its surface, until at the count of one you will be deep within the mirror, seeing only that which is real. Now, counting back: [countdown]

Deeply focused into the mirror, just allow the energies to come. Focusing on the mirror. Beneath the surface. Just allow the energies to surface. Keeping your eyes open now, stay focused on the mirror, begin to feel or see or sense what is deep within the mirror. Staying focused on the mirror; just feel your body; staying focused on the mirror, just allow the sensations in your body to drift away.

Deep, slow breaths. Focused on the mirror. Allow any bodily sensations just to fade away. Any discomfort, any tension, just allow it to fade away. Staying focused on the mirror. Allowing the energies to emerge. Looking deep within the mirror.

Just describe what you see and what it is. [long pause] Whatever you see – start – just allow it to emerge. [long pause] Whatever it is, just describe what you are seeing in the mirror.

Laura: Lights.

VB: Good. Just keep looking. All the lights. Just keep describing what you see.

Laura: Plasma clouds.

VB: Just stay focused on the mirror. On the clouds. Just tell me what you see. Just describe what you see.

Laura: [mostly inaudible, seems to be descriptions of amorphous cloud shapes that move and come and go]

VB: Stay focused on the mirror. Take a deep breath and allow all bodily sensation to fade away. You can talk easily and without effort. The awareness of your body is fading away as you gaze deep within the mirror. Just describe what you see.

Laura: Nothing in particular. Just amorphous lights and clouds. Shapes. Geometric figures.

VB: Pick one of these figures and look very closely; just describe what you see.

Laura: [descriptions of shapes and colors, clouds of light, coming and going]

VB: Keep looking. Can you follow one figure?

Laura: Well, it's like amorphous. Moving clouds. Some of them billow slowly, some of them are just flitting by.

VB: As you see one flit past, reach out and slow it down.

Laura: Oh, you can't slow them down.

VB: Speed up to their level to look very closely. What do you see?

Laura: Nothing but lights and clouds.

VB: Take a deep breath. Again a deep breath. And release. With every exhale, every exhale, you become more and more focused on the depths of the mirror. Breathe in, as you release, allow your awareness to go deeper into the mirror. Deep into the mirror. Good. What do you see?
[long pause]

VB: Deeper into the mirror. Nothing but the images in the mirror. Deep into the mirror. Breathing deep into the mirror. This room and your body are the mirage. What you see in the mirror is reality. Open yourself to it. Feel it as real, and describe what you see. On the count of three, you will let go of all awareness except for the images deep within the mirror. [countdown] Just describe what you see.

Laura: Indefinite shapes and colors and lights. Figures waiting to take form.

VB: Describe what you see.

Laura: Geometric light. That's the only way I can describe it.

VB: Just let go and move deep into the mirror. Go deep into the mirror, so that you're in the space of the mirror. You're in the space of the geometrical lights. With your mind's eye you can look around in the space; just tell me what you see.

Laura: The problem is, a specific question has to be asked in order for anything to form. [sound of beating heart on tape] Vague directions don't seem to go anywhere except into vague amorphous representations.

VB: OK. You need to ask a question to see something. Relax completely. Stay open and focus deep within the mirror. Ask your question.

Laura: I am not the one to ask.

VB: Why not?

Laura: It's not appropriate.

VB: Why not? OK! What are you experiencing right now?

Laura: Sensations of constriction.

VB: What is constricting?

Laura: Asking for the self, serves only the self. I cannot be the one to ask. It is inward directed, and constricts.

VB: [loud smacking noise] Just keep looking. What are you feeling now?

Laura: It's better now. Some danger was passed.

VB: Breathe deep. As you release the exhale, sink back into that space. Deep into the space. See the clouds. We would like for Laura to see an image of the C's. Can we see an image of the Cassiopaeans?

Laura: In the mind's eye.

VB: You're looking in the mirror. Watch it form. Tell me what you see?

Laura: Shapes, light.

VB: Keep looking. Relax into it. Can you show Laura more about this image?

Laura: I see an image of a spiral galaxy spinning in space.

VB: Can you show Laura fourth density?

Laura: That is inappropriate phrasing. It causes constriction; constriction in my chest.

VB: Why?

Laura: Because it is phrased so as to be a question from self to self.

VB: On the board, you said that Laura could see fourth density if we looked in the mirror. What did you mean? Can you show Laura what you meant?

Laura: What about fourth density do you wish to see?

VB: Try not to merge with the mirror. What does Laura need to see about fourth density that is so important that we do it now? Show that to her.

Laura: That's an inappropriate request.

VB: On the board, you suggested that there was a reason why Laura needed to look now, and that it involved seeing fourth density.

Laura: There are many questions.

VB: Go on.

Laura: Why don't you ask them?

VB: [voice becoming tense and hard] Laura, I want you to make sure that you see or hear C's and that you repeat what they say to you. Don't just answer in your voice. Do you understand?

Laura: I understand that it comes through me.

VB: OK. That's what I'm saying. See it or hear it in the mirror. OK? See it, hear it, coming from the mirror. Connect through the mirror. And let the being in the mirror speak. Why does Laura need to see fourth density now?

Laura: The answers to the questions can be obtained by seeing when the questions are phrased properly.

VB: [obviously irritated] OK now Laura, just look in the mirror, keep your eyes on the mirror, and literally what do you see?

Laura: I see shafts of light to the left, billowing lights at the upper right, fluctuations of light in the central depths, flashing lights that are random throughout, amorphous images coming and going.

VB: [very authoritative] OK. Show Laura what she needs to see NOW.

Laura: The question must be asked specifically in proper terms.

VB: What, in fourth density, does she need to see now?

Laura: Answers to the questions.

VB: How will she see these answers?

Laura: When the question is asked.

VB: How will she see these answers?

Laura: When the questions are asked, the answers appear. Vague questions receive vague answers.

VB: So there is nothing that you need to communicate, other than what we ask?

Laura: Only if you ask, can you receive an answer.

[long silence]

VB: OK, Laura, take a deep, deep breath. Feel where you are, feel your psychic state, feel the openness in the mirror. Now I want you to just leave that behind, and I want you to consciously step out. I want you to look at your connection to the mirror, between the chair and the mirror; and what do you see?

Laura: I see a silhouette like shape.

VB: In the mirror?

Laura: Yes. It's like a silhouette-like cut-out.

VB: OK, keep looking at the cut-out.

[end of 45 minute tape, continuation on reverse begins mid-sentence][24]

VB: The figure is beginning to change. As you watch, you will be able to see more and more. What do you see happening to the figure?

Laura: The figure is there, and there are flitting images in the depths. Amorphous.

VB: What do you see in the blackness?

Laura: Lights, emerging and receding.

VB: Follow the lights. Follow the lights. Just keep watching the lights. What are they doing? Where are they going?

Laura: They come from the center and sparkle out in all directions.

VB: Focus on the center. Allow your awareness to move through that center. Keep looking. Describe what you see when you move through the center.

Laura: It's moving, waving.

VB: Now stay in contact with the waving. Feel that waving.

Laura: Ooh! Look at that!

VB: What did you see? Describe it.

Laura: Living light. Iridescent light. Iridescent shapes. Like shimmering eggs.

VB: Can you see them now?

Laura: No. They emerged and receded.

VB: Feel that waving darkness.

Laura: Yes. It's purple.

VB: [voice very sharp] What's the purpose of doing the mirror work?

Laura: To bond with another reality.

VB: What reality?

Laura: Fourth density.

VB: And what in fourth density do you need to bond with?

Laura: Awareness. When you see, you become more aware. And the more aware you are, the more you are able to operate in that reality, to become more free of restriction and deception.

VB: Can you see the eggs again?

Laura: Now I see a shaft of light coming down from the upper left to the lower right, like a light beam.

VB: I want you to imagine that you're moving into that light. See yourself in the mirror moving into that light beam. Does anything change?

Laura: Everything's brighter.

VB: How do you feel in the light beam?

Laura: Fine. It pulsates.

VB: Will you allow Laura to see – or can Laura see …

Laura: If the appropriate question is asked.

---

[24] You can listen to the tape in mp3 format (the file is almost 6MB) at http://cassiopaea.com/audio/mirror1.mp3. The file is almost 6MB.

VB: Can Laura see what's happening through the mirror?

Laura: If the appropriate question is asked.

VB: Can you show Laura where the artifact is?

Laura: What artifact?

VB: The artifact that was discussed on the board, in the past.

Laura: At the appropriate time.

VB: So that means you could show it but you're not going to show it now?

Laura: There are several steps that must precede such.

VB: Can you tell us about those steps?

Laura: You have to ask a simple question. It has to be phrased simply and specifically.

VB: [sharp and impatient] Anybody *else* want to give it a try with a question?

Ark: Can you see kabbalah tree? Its real structure? Through all the densities?

Laura: Umm! As close a representation as there is, it seems is ...

VB: [interrupting] Can you allow yourself to see it by looking through the mirror ...

Laura: [apparently ignoring VB] Now this is very strange.

VB: Describe it.

Laura: Aaaah! This is a very fluid place! Whooo!

VB: Describe it. How do you mean "fluid?"

Laura: Ahh! Well, light doesn't go in straight beams here. It ... it ... it's like ropes or strings. You ask about kaballah tree and suddenly I see ropes and strings, structures ... the object that we draw as the kaballah tree is very structured and static and has nothing to do with the real thing! Here it is – and it's almost indescribable.

VB: Keep looking. What happens as you just watch? Can you still see the tree?

Laura: Yes, it's living light that moves and connects like a vast network with infinite ...

VB: [interrupts] Can you show Laura the time machine?

Laura: Would *you* like to see the time machine?

VB: Sure. Can you show Laura the time machine?

Laura: That's an inappropriate request.

VB: Why so?

Laura: It's not phrased properly.

VB: Can Laura see the time machine?

Laura: Would *you* like to see the time machine?

VB: I would like for Laura to see the time machine and describe it to us.

Laura: It seems to be an object about the size of a very large breadbox. It emanates a field, or a glowing beam. I'm not sure if you only have to be in contact with it, or stand in the beam, or if you just stand near it. It's clear that one does not get "inside" it, like in the movies. The field it produces is the important thing. The beam is like in the movie where they shine the beams up in the sky and wave them around; it's like that, only it has a shape. It's not long, straight and tubular, it's more cone shaped. So yes, there it is, it's …

VB: [interrupts] Now I want you to stay focused …

Laura [ignoring the interruption] … it has angles to it, metal plates, and the structure itself is like some sort of geometric tubing …

VB: Will Laura be able to remember and draw it?

Laura: Actually, in a funny sort of way, it's similar to the shape of the static tree of life on its side, doubled and inverted like having a mobius twist …

VB: Is this the Ark?

Laura: Yeah … it …

VB: Ark. Noah's Ark. The Ark of the covenant … the Ark of Time …

Laura: The object of which you speak, goes inside … it's the field …

VB: Now, keep looking, and stay outside the mirror; could you show Laura, so she can describe it for us, where, in time, this machine originates?

Laura: Ah! That's odd. The answer comes as 10,000 BC.

VB: Where is it in our immediate future?

Laura: Yes.

VB: Can you show Laura where it is in the immediate future?

Laura: In the immediate future.

VB: Can you show her where on the planet it is, when it enters our future?

Laura: At the appropriate time.

VB: Why is this not the appropriate time?

Laura: Because there would be danger.

VB: Stay on your side … 10,000 BC. Where has it been between then and the immediate future?

Laura: It's been found and used numerous times. It was used for very negative purposes, and it was deemed appropriate to retrieve it and …

VB: [interrupts] Now don't get pulled in the mirror … stay on this side!

Laura: [inaudible remarks]

VB: Can you show Laura so she can describe to us, the catastrophic situation in our future, our near future?

Laura: It seems as though it will be a progression. Like the beginning of rain, when the first few big, cold drops fall; and then a pause followed by a few more drops; and then, a downpour.

VB: Describe what you are seeing?

Laura: I see rocks – but they aren't very large. They are like the size of your fist. Just a few. And they make something of a stir. An uproar. People will be excited … very upset. It looks like just two – two small rocks. And then nothing else happens for a while, and then they forget about it. It all dies down. And then, a third, a fourth, a fifth and a sixth –

and maybe even a seventh ... isolated events, or so it seems. Still small. And then, a big one. All this will go on over a period of months.

VB: Take a deep breath, stay on this side of the mirror ... looking through. Keep looking; look through the mirror. Would you show Laura, so that she can describe for us, the situation concerning Percival, Percival Three.

Laura: The previously mentioned time machine, placed precisely at a specific location – and it's not exactly clear whether the action – there's a choice at that point in time, you know ...

VB: What kind of choice?

Laura: A group can leave with the machine, or a group can bond their awareness, and utilize the device to shift the earth out of the path of destruction. It's not a shift in material terms, it's a shift in time.

VB: So that the comet will hit where the earth isn't anymore?

Laura: Right.

VB: How, much of a jump does this require?

Laura: Oh! Well, in terms of time, a miss is as good as a mile!

VB: How much of a jump in time is required?

Laura: A day.

VB: The space that the earth travels during one revolution on its axis, is enough to avoid a direct hit?

Laura: Yes.

VB: What would the effects be of moving the planet and everyone on it back or forward a day?

Laura: If you can do it, most people, after the shift, will forget that there was ever a danger.

VB: Is that a good thing?

Laura: [sighs]

VB: Yeah, I know. Trick question. Now take a deep breath. Pull back, come out just a little. Let Laura's consciousness hear me clearly. Is there anything bothering you about this contact? Anything you can consciously feel while maintaining your connection? Anything at all disturbing you.

Laura: There's only a disturbance in the questioning. The questioning is constricting and directing consciousness. Questioning needs to be open and it's as though the answer can only come through uncorrupted if the question is framed in a non-assumption way. For me to act as the intermediary of what is being viewed, for others to ask questions, the questions must not restrict. This restriction is felt physically. There is some constriction – instantly, when the question is phrased so as to shift it from me asking myself – me asking the other me – rather than holding the responsibility for the question yourself. Do you understand?

VB: Well, my next question is why does Laura keep slipping into the mirror? Why is it so hard for her to stay on this side?

Laura: Ahhh ... There is a formation of a bond of awareness. There is another self in that not-too-distant future time that is me. It's me communicating with me; it's the C's approaching me; and because it's closer from fourth density, its easier to communicate back and forth if I merge with myself in the future. It's like bringing two soap bubbles close to each other – they just become one. It's not the negative thing you …

VB: It seems to me that we want to avoid that happening.

Laura: Not necessarily. Each and every one of us needs to begin merging with the higher self in terms of awareness … [inaudible]

VB: Why am I sensing negativity?

Laura: Insecurity.

VB: I'm quite comfortable with my own energy. Is that all that is at work here?

Laura: Oooh! [sees something in mirror, apparently]

VB: What are you seeing?

Laura: Well, they are like combination puppies and flowers … [tape ends, new tape starts][25] … something that was with you; I can't say that it was in you or around you; something that you still carry with you, it's almost like a very heavy suitcase. It actually looks like you have to force it to close by standing on it and shoving stuff in the cracks and tying it closed with straps because it is ready to burst open.

VB: OK, now look deeper in the mirror, through the mirror. Just keep describing what you see.

Laura: Ummmm. Now I see amorphous moving lights and clouds.

VB: Keep moving through that waving, purple darkness. In that space, just look around very carefully and tell me what you see.

Laura: [inaudible]

VB: Will you allow Laura to look around in the space so she can describe it for us.

Laura: Well, this is funny, have you ever seen a cartoon with a pencil being? [laughs] Oh, that's funny. That's what it's like.

VB: The stick figure is like dowsing rods?

Laura: No. That's … that's … [laughter] What a play on words! They are so funny! Core. You know the words "core being?" Well, it's not a joke! [laughter] Just think of yourself as a light being, in a sense, and in another, as not so amorphous as some people would think. There is some plasticity. You know how in this reality, the solid substance seems to be what it is and we have no control over it? Well, in fourth density, there is amorphous substance all around, and there is the "core being," who can assemble this substance by an act of will. It then becomes more structured in the same way food, in our reality, becomes your body, though here it takes a long period of assimilating and converting. There, it is rather quick. There is the core being – and it's really a core!

VB: Like an apple core?

---

[25] You can listen to the tape in mp3 format (the file is almost 4MB) at http://cassiopaea.com/audio/mirror2.mp3.

Laura: No, a core – like tubular almost. But you know, most people don't utilize it as such, because they like to play with the materials available. It's more fun. But, it's not necessary, and under different circumstance, they can remove all those things exactly the same way we take off our clothes. [inaudible] It's just more valuable.

VB: Now, you are using "you." Is that a general term, or is the stick figure me?

Laura: Anybody in fourth density.

VB: Are we in fourth density?

Laura: I am.

VB: So that's *you*, you are seeing in fourth density?

Laura: Me and others.

VB: So the stick figure is you in fourth density?

Laura: It is the visual representation of the core being of any fourth density individual. It is the essence.

VB: Take a deep breath. There are mechanisms at work that I, personally, am uncertain of. Is there anything you can tell me to make this easier?

Laura: Can you ask more specific questions? What, specifically are you uncertain about?

VB: I'm uncertain of the nature of the contact. I am uncertain of the nature of the perception. I'm uncertain of why I'm involved the way that I am. I'm uncertain why it's necessary to do this at all.

Laura: OK.

VB: Any response?

Laura: Ask the question. I cannot answer if you do not ask.

VB: Why am I having these uncertainties I just listed? What can we do to make this whole process easier?

Laura: The uncertainty relates to – it's difficult to answer the way you have asked it "why are you having these uncertainties."

VB: Are the uncertainties part of the process?

Laura: How do you perceive the uncertainties?

VB: I perceive the uncertainties … Is the uncertainty an artifact of how I'm having to do this? Does the artifact come from our clumsiness in doing the process?

Laura: It is unfamiliar territory; it is an unfamiliar process to you, in particular, because the essential nature of it requires as much openness …

VB: [interrupts sharply] OKAY! Why am I seeing what Laura is seeing?

Laura: That has to do a great deal with why you are part of the process at the moment.

VB: Why am I part of the process?

Laura: That has to do with genetic linkages, and choices made at other levels to do certain things at a certain point in time, both at a future point in time …

VB: If I decided *not* to do this, what would be the effect?

Laura: Someone else would step up and fill your shoes. The Universe is infinitely capable of taking care of itself.

VB: Is that what is going on here? Is the universe trying to take care of itself?

Laura: Oh, yes! That's …

VB: What do you see?!

Laura: I'm just seeing that you, me, we *are* the universe. It acts through us.

VB: What should we do – we need to know – in order to get funding for our research?

Laura: [laughter] Well, I have to say that the first thing that pops up is a series of numbers and I'll just tell them – 6,14, 25, 48, 52.

VB: Are these dates?

Laura: I don't know.

VB: Well ask 'em, are they dates?

Laura: You ask them.

VB: [yells] Are they dates?![26]

Laura: No.

VB: What are they?

Laura: Numbers to use as you choose.

VB: And what should we do with these numbers?

Laura: Whatever you choose.

Ark: I think I know what to do with these numbers.

VB: Is that a question?

Ark: No. [inaudible]

VB: Well, I don't follow you. Say that again?

Ark: I think they are probably lottery numbers.

VB: Are these lottery numbers?

Laura: They could be.

VB: Why won't you be more specific? I'm asking a very specific question?

Laura: They could be lottery numbers; they could be used in any number of ways. They could apply to choices that are taken over the next three months. You may encounter someone who has these numbers involved with them in some way; you may find these numbers on a page in a book which will then tell you something you need to know. These things come in so many layers; there is any number of applications; so don't close off other possibilities and say they are just "lottery numbers." They could be, but they could also be so much more.

VB: [sighs with exasperation] It's suspicious to me that gave 52. Am I just exercising my suspicions?

Laura: You can reverse.

---

[26] This section can be heard in mp3 format at http://cassiopaea.com/audio/aretheydates.mp3

VB: We already have a 25.

Laura: Then you have two 52's.

VB: OK. Let's go in a different direction. Take a deep breath. Can you show Laura, so she can describe for us, what we need to do, to get the next step started?

Laura: Ask without limits, and everything will fall into place. Do not worry, there are things moving in areas that we don't even know about, that will converge in amazing ways, and it's better not to even know, because then you will anticipate and block it.

VB: [sharply] OK! Why was Ari here today? Can you tell me what that is?

Laura: He has a very strong interest; he wishes he could be as bold as he used to be; and as free. However, it may not be possible for him to get free of the bonds that restrict him. However, the energy exerted in any direction, even exerted toward an individual who does not respond to it the way you wish, when they leave your presence, may carry that energy with them into the rest of the reality. And it is there available to someone else. Any energy put into a goal, even if you talk to 25 people who are the wrong people, the fact that you are putting energy into a goal openly ...

VB: [interrupts sharply] What was that image you just saw?!

Laura: Well, just lights and geometric figures ...

VB: OK, these lights have some sort of function. What's the function?

Laura: They are like the substance from images will ultimately coalesce in a very solid and realistic form. These are incipient image formation stuff.

VB: I get the feeling that some of these lights, some of these seed thoughts, whatever, want to come through the mirror into this reality. Is that a correct assumption?

Laura: I don't see that at all, no.

VB: What's giving me that impression?

Laura: Well, you said it: assumption. You have a lot of assumptions. It's very hard to work with all those assumptions. [inaudible descriptions of mirror images]

VB: And that's *not* crossing over into our reality?

Laura: No. They are just looking. Like friendly puppies; energy forms. They are cute.

VB: Anybody else got a question?

Ark: What was this thing when Vincent felt something touch his arm?

Laura: Vincent has some friends who travel with him, and they try to keep him out of trouble. It seems like, in this particular instance, somebody was banging on his shoulder just to let him know he was okay.

VB: And what kind of friends travel with me?

Laura: Actually, one of them looks like – he has a suit on, with a watch chain dangling from his waistcoat – but he doesn't have the time, which is funny. Brown suit, shoe boots, average height, he points his finger a lot; glasses. He's fond of you. Can't say that he is an "attachment," but he likes to be around you.

VB: Where's he from?

Laura: Actually, what I am seeing is obviously a projection. He is projecting this image, and I almost feel like, in a funny sort of way, he's maybe even you in another life.

VB: OK, he's not the one who patted me on the shoulder. [very strong voice effect] Did the C's pat me on the shoulder, both then, and did they burn the hand print on my shoulder back in the past?

Laura: [feeling extreme constriction and unable to resist the command/assumption, very low and weak voice] Yes. [immediate sensations of choking]

VB: OK. Now, the C's are quite aware of all the different things that are in my luggage. Will you ask them to show you what is in my luggage?

Laura: Dirty underwear!! [laughter] [Constriction released suddenly and the answer erupts almost before VB finishes speaking. The instant the question was asked, the large, overstuffed, strapped suitcase mentioned earlier was seen to spring open and hundreds of pairs of dirty underwear flew everywhere. They weren't just normally soiled, but were stained with fecal matter and it was as though, instead of washing them, or admitting that they needed washing, each pair was hidden away and new ones were added until they were soiled and added to the collection. However, all of this visual imagery was not requested, so it was not given in words. For a better understanding of this imagery, see Mouravieff's Gnosis. In particular, this passage: "Until lying stops, man drags along the defects of his past: lying, weakness, self-pity, inner compromise. Generally, it takes time, the opportunity and the possibility to rid himself of his baggage before committing himself to the fourth step is met. Many individuals, because of the weight of their past, waste time and allow many opportunities which present themselves to go by."]

VB: Keep looking! What else? Come on!

Laura: [strong voice] There is some real funny old fashioned clothes. I swear, this pair of pants – if you ever wore them out in public don't say you know me, they are awful pants – and they have suspenders. [They were huge, baggy, candy striped clown pants.] There's a leather case.

VB: Open the leather case. What do you see?

Laura: In the leather case there is a bunch of little bottles; they are bottles of pills; they are blue. There's a shaving kit, a comb; the comb has missing teeth …

VB: Do you see anything else in there?

Laura: There's handkerchiefs, an old mirror, and there are clean, white shirts, that have never been taken out of the packages. You have never worn these shirts.

VB: Now, you're doing real good. Now, if the C's would be so kind as to explain to Laura why I carry this luggage …

Laura: Why do you carry it? Because you can't let go.

VB: Why can't I let go?

Laura: Because you always want to be prepared.

VB: And what am I prepared for?

Laura: You're prepared for a trip, that's one thing. And you're afraid that something is going to make you get on the wrong train.

VB: Yep. Can you translate that "wrong train" into more direct terms?

Laura: Well, there's a funny thing about that. It's like the real problem is you think you don't have any money to buy what you need when you get there.

VB: [sharply] OK, this is funny but we're wasting time. Anybody else got another question?

O***: [asks question about health issue] Is there a particular course of study to follow to be of greater service to the process of furthering free will?

Laura: [comments on the health issue] [tape ends, large section missing from the beginning of the next tape]

VB: If the C's will be so kind as to give Laura a symbol that she can see in her mind's eye, that will allow her to quickly establish this contact ...

Laura: I've got it.

VB: Do you need to describe it?

Laura: No.

VB: See it very clearly. Now, you will break the contact by seeing this image fade. And as it fades, the mirror will come back to just being a mirror. Coming back into your body. Take a deep breath. [countdown to awaken]

The important thing about the mirror session was that it revealed to those who were present that Vincent Bridges was in no way any of the things he claimed to be, least of all an expert on hypnosis and/or occult matters.

When we began to try to work with Vincent to try to sort the matter out, he became very confrontational. We realized rather quickly that Vincent was "something strange" and had wormed his way into our confidence and group. We weren't sure exactly what we were dealing with, but for the moment, until we could gather more data, his posting privileges were revoked. I wrote a long email to our private discussion group about the matter and why it was disturbing to us. Vincent then wrote a lengthy rebuttal, and, finding that he could not post to the group, accused us of censorship and sent it to many people both on our private discussion group, and outside of it. He did this with full awareness that forwarding *any* emails from QFG private discussions is forbidden. Here is that email (I've included some notes in square brackets to help indicate who is saying what in the various emails, responses, and commentaries Bridges included in this email):

Date sent: Tue, 07 Aug 2001 12:50:56 -0400
Subject: Re: censorship and other issues
From: "Vincent Bridges" <abooks@ac.net>
To: [snipped list of about 120 recipients]

I don't know how you guys feel about censorship, but if you've been reading the cassiopaean list, and my apologies to those who are no longer connected, and don't have a clue what is going on, well, these censored emails should have fill you in. I would appreciate it someone would see that everyone not included in this mailing get a chance to see it as well. maybe someone will one brave enough to re-post on the list.

Thanks,

Vincent

And here's the censored email to the big list:

Greetings group,

My previous announcement of a return was unfortunately premature. My thanks to all for the good vibes...

Thought I would start with the backed up comments on AMET [*A Monument at the End of Time*], as we call it for short. Bruce's summary [Bruce being a member of the Cassipaea discussion group] was very interesting indeed, but not the whole story. Of course, if an intelligent reader can get that much out of, well, guess we did as good as could be expected.

Keep in mind that AMET is meant to be a general reader kind of book, one that presents the basic concepts to people who probably haven't heard of any of it before as well as the more advanced reader in search of new ideas. That's a delicate balance and in places, such as the lack of footnotes, we erred on the side of simplicity. Also, while I am responsible for the final draft of the book, the Dr. LaViolette chapter and most of all the Peru chapter is the work of my co-author, Jay Weidner.

Not passing the buck though. I think that Dr. LaViolette has very interesting ideas, even though he's off in places. The Peru connection is however more problematic.

When Jay brought the project to me, he had already "decoded" the inscription on the Hendaye Cross and had the Cuzco/Urcos connection. Investigation on the ground revealed that there was probably some connection in Peru to the Atlantian culture and even possible survivals from the last catastrophe. The Nazis however had been there long before, and in an earlier version of AMET we covered this part of the story in detail. However we were advised to leave that part out as detracting from the thrust of our argument.

However, I came away from the whole Peru thing convinced that it was at best a half correct red herring designed to lead the materially inclined investigator on a dead end, such as all the Nazis in Peru. Hence chapter ten of AMET, which while simplistic, is at least attempting to address the basic issue of cosmology and immortality.

But a curious thing happened while we were driving madly around southern France. I glimpsed a second interpretation of the Hendaye

Cross. At a conference that August, another friend, David Tresemer, the guy who first spotted the crossing comets on the Gorgon's head, spontaneously hit on the solution that I had roughed out in France. Originally, as seen by our very inconclusive conclusion, we planned to plunge on with this second interpretation right to the heart of RLC business and beyond.

Many things have intervened since. Including my protracted involvement with all things Cassiopaean. From which I have learned: Trust No One.

And on that note:

[Here, within the email being cited, Bridges quotes the email I sent to the Cass discussion group regarding issues with Bridges.]

Laura wrote: Because, the fact is, we are vulnerable here and Stan is moving very close to that point of vulnerability – the fact that we agreed to appear at the Fifth Way Mystery School conference in September – which would connect us almost directly to his "satanist/nazi" conspiracy. [This is in reference to Stan Tenen whom Vincent is accusing of being part of a Satanic group. Whether Tenen is or not is unknown.]

Stan undoubtedly knows of the long relationship between Dan Winter and our own Doc Strange, Vincent Bridges. He probably also knows that Vincent is no friend of Jirka's [Jirka Rysavy who Vincent claimed was a CIA front] because Vincent knew about Jirka's connection to the Ramsey's and that is how he "saw" beneath the surface of the Ramsey case. Jirka and his pals REALLY ARE into Satanism. It's not a joke. And Vincent wrote about it as plainly as he could without risking going on a hit-list. It's clear that Vincent is NOT one of them, but who will care? He does "enochian magic."

The fact is, Jirka tried to "buy" Dan Winter, and couldn't. And the fact is, Stan knows that Dan was connected to Vincent, that Vincent was supposed to publish Dan's book. So, the thread is leading to denounce us here as Satanists, Nazis and funded by Jirka.

We all know that Vincent's own dabbling in things enochian are intended in quite another direction, however, that doesn't matter. A connection is a connection. And it is, in this case, a serious weakness in our defenses.

So it is, with regret, that Ark and I have decided that, for the safety of the group, for the preservation of all we have worked so hard for, for so many years, that we must cancel our appearance at the conference in Zaca Lake.

We have walked a careful path, attempting to build a bridge between science and mysticism. We have made tremendous progress. And, we are certain that Vincent will understand the necessity for this move, and will agreeably refund the pre- paid reservations for all of you who were going to attend simply to hang out with us.

And to make it up to all of you, we will arrange our own "symposium" in the very near future. I am sure that there is enough talent here on the group that we could have a nice series of lectures on varous topics from some of you!

Laura

[Vincent replied as follows.]

> Well isn't that just grand! Things get rough and you decide to dump the person working overtime to get your material in print, to get you an income for your efforts and to give you a venue, a credible venue, in which to present your ideas...

[Keep in mind that he is writing this all the while knowing he does not even have a legally registered company nor are his claimed publishing credentials even partly true.]

> Sorry, but I don't understand. First you trash the conference with your disclaimer on the site, and then when its too late for a refund on the deposit and you're the only speaker left, you decide not to do it. So, you have your symposium, already scheduled, booked and paid for entirely by people who came to hear you guys anyway. Might be a good idea to take advantage of it. Don't worry, there won't be any one else there but the staff. Perhaps you'd care to explain why that's not acceptable?

[All this turned out to be lies.]

> As for the rest of the above, well, let me say directly that I never asked, suggested or encouraged you in any way to write anything on Stan Tenen, nor did I give you permission to use my research on the case in your article, although I can't stop you because it is in the public domain as part of the court proceedings. If you had asked, I would have told you that it was a bad idea for the reasons you have just experienced.

> And I have never said anything on the record, or given permission for any private communications to be shared, concerning Mr. Jirka Rysavy and "satanism" or the JonBenet Ramsey case.

> Having said that, and I hope everyone understands why, I do wish Laura and Ark all the best, as I do think that the Cs material has much of vital interest to us all.

> I will continue lurking unless I am purged completely, in which I case I take this opportunity to say good bye to you all.

> Vincent

> Below are some comments I [Vincent] was working on in reply to AMET [the thread subject of a discussion on the Cass group]:

> on 7/27/01 12:18 PM, three@onelight.org at three@onelight.org wrote:

> >>> 4. From such a catastrophe, a place of refuge is earmarked, taken from inscriptions, symbols, etc.= Cusco, Peru. Personally, I doubt that anything would survive this, so I tend to believe that something just as important is in Cusco, something buried there. It is also interesting that the BCCI scandal ended up being traced back to Peru.

> >> This is probably one of the most effective statements I've read by the C's and it helps to consider it, especially when contemplating/interpreting Alchemy-related writing: They said, "3D thinking is 3D thinking."

> > So much for moving to Cusco. I'd rather go to 4D and realize it :-)

> V: That's how I feel about. Way too many Nazis in Peru for my comfort. But this very clever red herring is not without value, on several levels.

> *4. Fulcanelli speaks of making glass'??*

> *Spiritual Alchemy is the art of making glass, as quoted in the "Mystere" book. I forget who said that, but Fulcanelli was quoting an older philosopher in that passage. It's clearly true--pun intended. Glass making is work upon the soul; to crystalize, so to speak.*

V: The glass making metaphor is very profound and relates directly to brain chemistry.

And then a couple of key comments from me [Bridges]:

>> *"The circumstantial evidence suggests that there really was a person behind the Fulcanelli mask, whose intermittent visits seemed to produce change and upheaval in Canseliet's life. Each appearance marked a major turning point, from his first encounter to his last. Fulcanelli would also seem to be virtually immortal, appearing to be roughly half his probably age, the last time Canseliet saw him. As for the gender-bending androgyny of the completed Great Work, well, the jury is still out on that one. It could have been Fulcanelli's daughter or grand-daughter. It could have been a dream or an initiation, or even some fantasy of Canseliet's long held love for his Master."*

> *[Laura:] This is a pretty tame comment on one of the most significant clues in the entire story. Just like Parzival didn't ask questions, Vincent did not see this for the clue that it was as to the nature of the 4th density reality as described over and over again by the C's.*

V: Nope didn't miss that possibility, just trying to stay with the credible boundaries we set for the work. Notice that not much is made on the possibility that Fulcanelli was over two hundred years old at the time either.

Laura: *From this we can deduce that when a person "completes" the work, they more or less "disappear." By the time they get close to it, they already begin to understand what it is they are doing and what is going to happen. So, they may put off the final activity to accomplish a few necessary tasks... such as Fulcanelli getting his books published. And he may have known that he might need to add a chapter and made arrangements for the "signal" for Canseliet. He was taken in a car to the Chateau in the Pyrenees... it is NOT a 3rd density location, for sure.*

V: I don't get this one. Why is a car trip a sure sign of non-3D locality? I do think that Canseliet went to the Pyrennes, and then turned left into the 4D Twilight Zone, or whatever. This I can readily grasp from my own experience.

Laura: *So, we see that in addition to "knowing the handshake" of the "11 house zodiac," the C's have given many, many other clues about the "Great Work," and the many phenomena associated with it. They have pretty much removed the veils of lies and mystery created around it by all the secret societies through the ages, and have given us direct, initiatory information, and evidence that their information is valid.*

And most of all, they say that ritual is NOT the way to get there... it is the way to NOT get there.

V: I think a distinction should be made between rituals and spiritual practices or yannas. Otherwise you are in danger of missing the point. However any ritual or practice, even chatting with the Cs, if done in ig-

FACING THE UNKNOWN

norance or without a good STO context, can end up feeding the lower astral, 4th density lizard types.

As for the Cs and their prohibition on rituals, well I recommend taking a look at the complete transcripts and read the entire session in which a reference to ritual is made. Some very interesting points emerge when looked at in this light. Here's a list of session in which rituals are mentioned: 00-09-09.txt 94-07-16.TXT 94-10-22.TXT 94-10-28.TXT 94-11-19.TXT 94-12-01.TXT 94-12-23.TXT 95-01-07.TXT 95-01-21.TXT 95-02-25.TXT 95-05-20.TXT 95-07-08.TXT 95-07-23.TXT 95-08-12.TXT 96-03-29.TXT 98-06-20.TXT 98-08-22.TXT 98-12-26.TXT 99-06-19.TXT 99-07-31.TXT

As a general idea for any one really interested in the Cs and the related issues, I recommend sending Perseus some money and getting your very own set of transcripts on CD. Well worth it.

Laura: *Fulcanelli gives clues all over the place that the "double catastrophe" related to the sun is literally that: a Twin Sun... a binary system, the "planet of the crossing" of Sumerian fame, the reason for the "cross" in the circle... the circle represents the Sun and the cross represents that there are TWO of them.*

V: I don't get this one either. Where does Fulcanelli suggest a double sun? How exactly is a cross related to the double sun?

And here's the background emails, starting with email of 8/4/01:

[Vincent:] Well, so much to talk about and so little time...

Firstly, the book – By now you've seen the rough dummies for Noah and if you like the way its going, and given everything else, then take a look at the attached contract. If everything is OK, you can just sign and send it back.

If not, well, we can talk about it...

Secondly, the conference – With your disclaimer, and other things posted on the cassiopaea site, I think it best that FWMS, et al., withdraw our support from the conference.

Which means that the conference is all yours. I'll handle the folks who were interested in the other parts of the program, and it will be a weekend with Laura and the cassiopaeans, exclusively. I'm sure the folks from the group who have signed up would prefer that anyway. I'll take care of the zaca lake details for handling your reduced group, and your plane tickets out there. Anything over the expenses you are welcome to keep.

Which brings us to the money issue. If everything is fine with book and contract, I'll gladly pay your share of any pre-sale, such as distributor purchases, immediately the check clears the bank. That and an aggressive internet campaign should result in some income almost from day one of publication. Better than that, I can not do.

As for the other issues, how would you like to handle it? In person by phone? By email, and if so, privately, inner group or big group? Your choice entirely.

Vincent

APPENDIX C

Another email from Vincent, 4 Aug 2001, at 11:57:

Consultation on Saturday, August 4, 2001 at 11:50 AM.

Present: 62 Attention to Detail

Question: What should I know about the Laura situation?

Ambitious undertakings are not in order now, but attention to small matters brings progress. Such is the case of a person whose resources are meager, but who, through modesty and perseverance, rises to accomplish great things.

The key to success when the small potential dominates the large scene is to avoid pretentious ambitions and grandiose goals. The power of the small is served by slow and steady advancement, and succeeds through an honest awareness of its own limitations, without reservation.

Modesty stemming from recognizing your limitations is a fine quality, but it can be seen as weakness if it is not accompanied by conscientiousness. It is very important, therefore, to understand the demands of your situation, and not to expect success in big things right now. The wise person recognizes the nature of the time. So, know your own role, carefully attend to details and act with humility, and you can achieve success even with few resources.

There are two changing lines. Either one or the other or some combination of both of them will be relevant.

The first changing line is Line 3:

When danger lurks, the wise take precautions, and do not consider even the smallest matters above their concern. Attention to small, even petty, details is often what paves the way for escape during a time of crisis. If you venture into the heart of the city at night, it pays to know the shortest, safest way out before you enter.

The second changing line is Line 5:

When assembling a team to undertake a difficult task, emphasize achievement and talent over status and reputation. Only by assembling solid individual elements can the small be transformed into the great. Keep the group chemistry in mind, for harmonious working relationships are essential to the success of exceptional undertakings begun with meager resources.

Future: 45 Gathering Together

This hexagram represents the quality of likely opportunities and challenges arising from changes that are in process now:

The power of gathering together is represented by a rally, where each individual's strength is magnified by the power of the community as a whole. History has shown that mass movements can bring about stable, ordered and durable conditions for the better. This reading may be pointing to an auspicious time for large undertakings. But the guiding force of a shared vision is essential to hold the forces of unity together, and keep them advancing toward a common goal.

Another image for this situation is that of a lake filling with water. Just as the fullness of the lake can bring good fortune to all in its sphere, it can also overflow, leading to calamity. Thus in a time of gathering together it is essential that precautions against unforeseen danger be considered along with efforts to advance along a clearly-charted course. Much of human misfortune comes from unexpected events for which we are ill prepared; when gathered together with others, we are both more powerful and, in some ways, more vulnerable.

Any time of unity is a time of potential greatness. But that greatness can be both positive and negative. Everything is magnified when masses of people unite for a single purpose. When many people unite behind a single goal or strong vision, it is wise to take personal precautions, and to protect your own reasonable self-interests, because these can easily be lost in the crowd.

I replied:

On 4 Aug 2001, at 11:57, Vincent Bridges wrote:

> > *Question: What should I know about the Laura situation?*

You should know that Laura adores you for many reasons, not the least of which is that you are you.

Also, that she is dedicated to what she does to the point that personal feelings are of secondary importance if they conflict with perceived correct and careful approach to the goal. i.e. "attention to detail."

This means that, all aspects of associations and how they may promote or hinder, whether they can help or hurt, are considered in the approach to the "goal."

"The power of the small is served by slow and steady advancement, and succeeds through an honest awareness of its own limitations, without reservation."

Indeed. And when any enterprise is undertaken, such things as how it begins, and on what foundations it is laid, and who are the associates, and what they practice and believe.

> *The first changing line is Line 3:* > > *When danger lurks, the wise take precautions, and do not consider even the* > *smallest matters above their concern. Attention to small, even petty,* > *details is often what paves the way for escape during a time of crisis. If you* > *venture into the heart of the city at night, it pays to know the shortest,* > *safest way out before you enter.*

That is precisely our position. We cannot fail to observe the fact that our associations, who they are, what they practice, what they believe as evidenced by what they practice, could come back to haunt us.

> *The second changing line is Line 5:* > > *When assembling a team to undertake a difficult task, emphasize achievement and* > *talent over status and reputation. Only by assembling solid individual elements* > *can the small be transformed into the great. Keep the group chemistry in mind,* > *for harmonious working relationships are essential to the success of exceptional* > *undertakings begun with meager resources.*

Again: an accurate rendering. Your professional status is immaterial. But what you do is most material. What you say, how it may be perceived in the eyes and mind of the public, and what reflection it may have on our own work and presentation thereof.

> *Future: 45 Gathering Together > > This hexagram represents the quality of likely opportunities and challenges > arising from changes that are in process now: > > The power of gathering together is represented by a rally, where each > individual's strength is magnified by the power of the community as a whole. > History has shown that mass movements can bring about stable, ordered and > durable conditions for the better. This reading may be pointing to an > auspicious time for large undertakings. But the guiding force of a shared > vision is essential to hold the forces of unity together, and keep them > advancing toward a common goal.*

Note: the "guiding force of a shared vision." This is uppermost in my mind. There is no way a team of horses can be harnessed to pull a wagon if one of them is constantly pulling in a direction opposite to the others. It is not a question of whether or not people are entitled to their own opinions and beliefs – that is a given. But when people are "harnessed together," with a goal in mind, it becomes crucial that the vision is a shared one. And clearly, it is not.

> *> > Another image for this situation is that of a lake filling with water. Just as > the fullness of the lake can bring good fortune to all in its sphere, it can > also overflow, leading to calamity. Thus in a time of gathering together it is > essential that precautions against unforeseen danger be considered along with > efforts to advance along a clearly-charted course. Much of human misfortune > comes from unexpected events for which we are ill prepared; when gathered > together with others, we are both more powerful and, in some ways, more > vulnerable.*

Exactly so. We are indeed very vulnerable when gathered together with those whose beliefs and practices are so widely divergent that there is simply no way to advance along a "clearly charted course." We must expect the unexpected, and that includes accusations far worse than "anti-semite." It is so easy for me to go through and bring up the issues of black magick and its relation to control systems and the negative connotations of Mathers and Dee and Enochian stuff, that any close association with same is a pit just waiting to swallow us up. It doesn't matter whether it is true or not, what matters is the eye of the beholder as to whether or not the presenters of information are "clean" in all their practices, and honest to a fault about presenting them in a clear light.

And, in point of fact, from our own perspective, such practices are not only counter to what we believe to be useful and valid and worthy of teaching, they are a huge detriment in the eyes of the larger public.

> *> Any time of unity is a time of potential greatness. But that greatness can be > both positive and negative. Everything is magnified when masses of people unite > for a single purpose. When many people unite behind a single goal or strong > vision, it is wise to take personal precautions, and to protect your own > reasonable self-interests, because these can easily be lost in the crowd.*

See above.

In the most specific terms I can say it: I was truly not aware of the extent and continuation of the "enochian" theme you have talked about on many occasions. That is my own fault – being so busy that the only pages on your site that I read were related to subjects in which I was interested. I didn't bother to look at or read you "enochian working" business until it was brought to my attention by a member of the group who was distressed by the references to rituals (as many of them were.) When I read it, I will say that I went "through the roof."

I couldn't believe that a person who claims such a rational and skeptical point of view could even do such things, much less write about them and publish them. And this was, of course, after viewing a whole suitcase full of attachments. (Don't for a minute think that it was merely my perception of your "accoutrements," it was and is attachments. That is one thing in which I am so experienced that I don't think you have any idea. And it also presented itself in a shocking way... I was NOT expecting it. But you asked, and I saw. There was a great deal more that I saw, and part of it was that you are simply not prepared to accept it.)

So, seeing these attachments, followed by reading about these 'workings,' right at the very time I am writing a chapter on the very subject itself, and my occasional brushes with the GD [Golden Dawn] folks – well, it was sure a message.

Follow this with reading the Dan Winter book and your essay on magic in the back with the giveaway phrases about "control," which is NOT what we are about, and is exactly that which we seek to expose... as well as your admission of rewriting some of Winter's stuff, and the use of so blatant a series of words designed to hypnotized, or trigger emotions, and the whole deal with that book – well... I hope you are beginning to have some idea of my perceptions here. Just who is on first here?

There is, indeed, more – all of which relates to the bottom line: at this point of our "small beginning," I don't think we can afford to be associated with those things that we know, from experience, can be detrimental in two ways: 1) the very fact of being "in harness" with one whose direction is different leads to a drain of energy, and opens a door to negative energies. It doesn't matter that you are the one doing the "workings" and we are not. If we are united in any kind of effort, it will never succeed, just as I described in chapter 42. 2) The public perception is extremely important, as well as Ark's reputation. It's one thing to engage in a channeling experiment as a scientific exercise – he can do that, and while it may be thought that he has "fringe" extramural interests, it is nothing that unusual; many scientists are studying similar things. However, it is beyond the pale to be associated with ritual magic, enochian stuff that is connected (however you may protest that it is "intent" that counts) to Parsons, Crowley, Hubbard, and a host of negative activities and bizarre activities of those who were clearly either failures, or succeeded in instituting more mind control programs.

Vincent, it's just too much.

Regarding Noah, I can only say that the conditions under which it might be published by you are very narrow at present. If it can be gotten into print ASAP and thereby produce income, it is possible. But most of the illustrations have to go. It looks like a supermarket tabloid, not a serious book. Many, many things about it have to be covered in a serious and business-like way.

Again, I do most sincerely adore you; I have received much in the way of delight and stimulation in our many exchanges. Friends can have conversations and exchanges and agree to disagree on many things. But getting in harness with others is a whole different level of involvement and "attention to detail" is crucial. To leave a shoe-lace untied is to invite a fall. And this is a loooong shoelace!

Much affection, Laura

Bridges then replied to my exhortation to cease and desist his magick activities above so that we could continue to work together as follows:

Well, all this would be fascinating if it weren't so sad, unnecessary and obviously manipulated by the other side. Perhaps that why it's so fascinating.

Anyway, a few comments and clarifications:

> On 4 Aug 2001, at 11:57, Vincent Bridges wrote: > >> >> Question: What should I know about the Laura situation? > > You should know that Laura adores you for many reasons, not the least of which > is that you are you.

And then the rest of it is extremely judgmental, without any real understanding on which to base any sort of judgment. Pure knee jerk reaction.

>> Future: 45 Gathering Together >> >> This hexagram represents the quality of likely opportunities and challenges >> arising from changes that are in process now: >> >> The power of gathering together is represented by a rally, where each >> individual's strength is magnified by the power of the community as a whole. >> History has shown that mass movements can bring about stable, ordered and >> durable conditions for the better. This reading may be pointing to an >> auspicious time for large undertakings. But the guiding force of a shared >> vision is essential to hold the forces of unity together, and keep them >> advancing toward a common goal. > > Note: the "guiding force of a shared vision." This is uppermost in my mind. > There is no way a team of horses can be harnessed to pull a wagon if one of > them is constantly pulling in a direction opposite to the others. It is not a > question of whether or not people are entitled to their own opinions and > beliefs – that is a given. But when people are "harnessed together," with a > goal in mind, it becomes crucial that the vision is a shared one. And > clearly, > it is not.

OK, so when have I done anything but try to help? No, seriously, when have I ever rocked the boat, preached a separate agenda or created any kind of waves on any of the groups that I didn't discuss with you before hand? So we are not in harmony because of what exactly? Your new understanding of some of my ideas?

> >> >> Another image for this situation is that of a lake filling with water. Just >> as >> the fullness of the lake can bring good fortune to all in its sphere, it can >> also overflow, leading to calamity. Thus in a time of gathering together it >> is >> essential that precautions against unforeseen danger be considered along with >> efforts to advance along a clearly-charted course. Much of human misfortune >> comes from unexpected events for which we are ill prepared; when gathered >>

together with others, we are both more powerful and, in some ways, more >> vulnerable. > > Exactly so. We are indeed very vulnerable when gathered together with those > whose beliefs and practices are so widely divergent that there is simply no > way > to advance along a "clearly charted course." We must expect the unexpected, > and that includes accusations far worse than "anti-semite." It is so easy for > me to go through and bring up the issues of black magick and its relation to > control systems and the negative connotations of Mathers and Dee and Enochian > stuff, that any close association with same is a pit just waiting to swallow > us > up. It doesn't matter whether it is true or not, what matters is the eye of > the beholder as to whether or not the pre- senters of information are "clean" in > all their practices, and honest to a fault about presenting them in a clear > light. > > And, in point of fact, from our own perspective, such practices are not only > counter to what we believe to be useful and valid and worthy of teaching, they > are a huge detriment in the eyes of the larger public.

Oh that's a good one! Sounding like a RA retread is OK, but heaven forbid that you have anyone around with real information on such topics. Ouiji boards and black mirrors and psychomantiums are fine, just make sure that no one is around who might understand the mechanism.

> > >> Any time of unity is a time of potential greatness. But that great- ness can >> be >> both positive and negative. Everything is magnified when masses of people >> unite >> for a single purpose. When many people unite behind a single goal or strong >> vision, it is wise to take personal precautions, and to protect your own >> reasonable self- interests, because these can easily be lost in the crowd. > > See above. > > In the most specific terms I can say it: I was truly not aware of the extent > and continuation of the "enochian" theme you have talked about on many > occasions. That is my own fault – being so busy that the only pages on your > site that I read were related to subjects in which I was interested. I didn't > bother to look at or read you "enochian working" business until it was brought > to my attention by a member of the group who was distressed by the references > to rituals (as many of them were.) When I read it, I will say that I went > "through the roof."

Emotional reaction demonstrating programming implant. Probably done during the last mirror session and you didn't even notice.

> > I couldn't believe that a person who claims such a rational and skeptical > point > of view could even do such things, much less write about them and publish > them. > > And this was, of course, after view- ing a whole suitcase full of attachments. > (Don't for a minute think that it was merely my perception of your > "accoutrements," it was and is at- tachments. That is one thing in which I am > so > experienced that I don't think you have any idea. And it also presented > itself > in a shocking way... I was NOT expecting it. But you asked, and I saw. There > was a great deal more that I saw, and part of it was that you are simply not > prepared to accept it.)

Indeed, except what you were viewing didn't have anything to do with me. You were seeing the programming bundle that you had just ac- quired on the other side, astrally. It was obviously a screen, and so perplexing in origin that it plausibly could have been mine. That got me thinking, right there on the spot.

By the time I got to Gainesville on the way home, I had it roughed out in my mind, and it wasn't pretty. We had been set up, big time. So I waited for the other shoe to drop, and it didn't take long. Just who suggested reading DW out loud? And who was there at the time? After a couple of conversations, I could feel it building. What could I do? Tell you? What kind of reaction would that trigger? See where it was going and try to minimize the damage?

And then, conveniently, communications went down on my end. I couldn't even do damage control. And then things got worse, your disclaimer, flame wars that you probably haven't even heard reports of yet, your posts and articles on the site, speakers dropping out of the conference and so on. Through it all, I'm as sick as I've ever been, literally as you pointed out, at death's door and still moving, and the books are getting done.

And now this...

> > *So, seeing these attachments, followed by reading about these 'workings,' > right > at the very time I am writing a chapter on the very subject itself, and my > occasional brushes with the GD folks – well, it was sure a message. > > Follow this with reading the Dan Winter book and your essay on magic in the > back with the giveaway phrases about "control," which is NOT what we are > about, > and is exactly that which we seek to expose... as well as your admission of > rewriting some of Winter's stuff, and the use of so blatant a series of words > designed to hypnotized, or trigger emotions, and the whole deal with that book > – > well... I hope you are beginning to have some idea of my perceptions here. > Just who is on first here?*

Indeed, that's the whole point, against your better judgment and experience, against all the evidence available, you still came up with that perception. Where did it really come from? Pandora's portmanteau?

> > *There is, indeed, more – all of which relates to the bottom line: at this > point > of our "small beginning," I don't think we can afford to be associated with > those things that we know, from experience, can be detrimental in two ways: 1) > the very fact of being "in harness" with one whose direction is different > leads > to a drain of energy, and opens a door to negative energies. It doesn't > matter > that you are the one doing the "workings" and we are not. If we are united in > any kind of effort, it will never succeed, just as I described in chapter 42. > 2) The public perception is extremely important, as well as Ark's reputation. > It's one thing to engage in a channeling experiment as a scientific exercise – > he can do that, and while it may be thought that he has "fringe" extramural > interests, it is nothing that unusual; many scientists are studying similar > things. However, it is beyond the pale to be associated with ritual magic, > onochian stuff that is connected (however you may protest that it is "intent" > that counts) to Parsons, Crowley, Hubbard, and a host of negative activities > and bizarre activities of those who were clearly either failures, or succeeded > in instituting more mind control programs. > > Vincent, it's just too much.*

Sorry, just don't buy it. The energy drain started with the break, back at the mirror, and not through me or any of my associations, which by the way you have been given ample evidence by the Cs themselves of my involvement and associations, if you care to look at it clearly. Lord knows, you sent most of it to me in emails through the years!

Again, a ouiji board, black mirror and psychomantium are OK, but knowing anything about to use them is not?

> > *Regarding Noah, I can only say that the conditions under which it might be > published by you are very narrow at present. If it can be gotten into print > ASAP and thereby produce income, it is possible. But most of the > illustrations > have to go. It looks like a supermarket tabloid, not a serious book. Many, > many things about it have to be covered in a serious and business-like way.*

I assume from your next email that even this is off. Too bad, because we are a day or so away from serious contract talks with distributor. I have a significantly less chance of making the sale without Noah Syndrome, which is very bad news all around. As I said before, if they buy in bulk, I'll pay your share as soon as the check clears the bank. I have a new site, aethyrea.com, just about ready to go as major commerce site, but of course that doesn't matter.

[The reader should keep in mind that Vincent is lying through his teeth here; he did not even have a legally registered publishing company so talks with a distributor would have been impossible.]

> > Again, I do most sincerely adore you; I have received much in the way of > delight and stimulation in our many exchanges. Friends can have conversations > and exchanges and agree to disagree on many things. But getting in harness > with others is a whole different level of involvement and "attention to > detail" > is crucial. To leave a shoe-lace untied is to invite a fall. And this is a > loooong shoelace! > > Much affection, > Laura

So who untied the shoe lace...

Look, I obviously like you guys, and deeply respect your work and efforts. So what, really, is the problem.

Vincent

I replied:

Hi, You have missed the entire point.

Our understanding about you was that you were a student of, and expert on, esoteric phenomena, secret schools, GD stuff, and so forth. The fact that you are an ongoing PRACTITIONER and BELIEVER in same, was somehow not really emphasized.

Teaching about such things as an intellectual exercise is one thing. This is what I understood you to be doing.

Practicing, advocating, publishing clear descriptions of such which promote adherence to such practices as being useful and positive is also fine. Nobody can tell anybody else how to view their world, or how to interact with it.

However, it is contrary to everything we think and do and say.

What I am saying here is, the realization that this is your position, what you advocate, what you teach was slow in dawning. If it had been a full part of awareness on our part, the problem would never have arisen. We would never have been associated.

We aren't even suggesting that we think you are wrong. We just simply see the pitfalls of association and how they will affect what we think, do and say.

The fault is, of course, ours. We should have investigated you more thoroughly before any public links were established.

I remember writing to Johan [a member of the Cass group who wrote numerous emails telling me that Bridges was an agent, bad news, connected to evil people and groups, and I simply did not believe him], answering his accusation that you practiced ritual magic, that, yes, you talk about all that sort of thing on your site, but that you didn't really believe that stuff or practice it – it was just part of your ongoing research. And I thought it was. And you knew that I thought it was because I forwarded that letter to you. That was your cue to say: "oops, wait a minute... I really think that this stuff is the cat's miaou and I do it all the time..."

You didn't. Was that overt manipulation? Or was it merely strategic omission? Is there an agenda on your part? Or is it merely a comedy of errors? I tend to think the latter, though I am aware that such comedies can be written from other realms...

Many people on the group wrote to me privately with some concern when you posted your information about an exercise relating to kundalini. I ignored it. My mistake. I should have gone to read it and the other pages relating to such things. I didn't because I was trusting your statements that you were a "researcher." Heck, I researched all that stuff too... I just figured that you did it deeper than I did by infiltrating all those groups and pretending so you could find out what they knew. It never dawned on me (no pun intended) that you actually bought into any of that sort of thing.

You kept saying that "free will" was your goal. I believed that without checking to see what your real definition was.

Well, from what I have read so far, I don't think that you really perceive free will the way we do.

And from our perspective, any such practices designed to engage any forces whatsoever, to have them do anything whatsoever, is a violation of free will. It is one thing to ask for knowledge for the self, and then to listen for a reply. It is something else altogether to ask, or perform a ritual designed to induce, a change in the reality. The external reality only changes when the internal reality changes. And it can only change via reception of knowledge, and application to one's own life.

So, the bottom line is: our actions are directed at one thing, and one thing only: to protect our years of work and effort. My experience, my education and efforts have brought me to an understanding that any close association with such activities is a huge portal for entry of negative energies.

And simple consideration and thoughtful reflection on your part would bring an awareness of what I have said regarding public awareness, and the potential for attack from any and all directions when one is engaged in, or associated with, such activities.

If you can't see that, then there is nothing I can say. We live in the real world, and we have history to teach us many things. The history of those activities and the people involved in them are fruitful lines of inquiry as to what NOT to do.

Again, let me repeat: we are concerned only with our years of work and effort. Personal considerations simply cannot rule in these matters. If you were concerned about this work, this association, the future, you would not only cease your own participation in those things, but you would publicly repudiate it, change the format of your "Mystery School" to reflect such concern, and otherwise close the holes in your own defenses against such forces which are clearly acting in your life right now.

You try to shift the blame onto us, saying we are rude, we are thoughtless, we are any number of things that have brought this issue to a pass. However, if you were paying attention to the objective reality, you would clearly see what was coming, how it would come, and take certain and effective actions to "head it off."

If the situation is not to your liking, how about an experiment? Do a "working," call on the "Ophanic Intelligences," perform three rituals or more a day to change the reality – and see what happens.

If it was useful, it would be working. See?

Laura

[Vincent:] And then I learned that I was being censored on the list, so I posted the above to another smaller group and got this response [from Laura]:

Some notes for you here.

On 6 Aug 2001, at 11:01, aethyrea [Vincent] wrote:

> [Laura wrote:] Because, the fact is, we are vulnerable here and Stan is moving very close to > that point of vulnerability – the fact that we agreed to appear at the Fifth > Way Mystery School conference in September – which would connect us almost > directly to his "satanist/nazi" conspiracy. > > Stan undoubtedly knows of the long relationship between Dan Winter and our own > Doc Strange, Vincent Bridges. He probably also knows that Vincent is no > friend of Jirka's because Vincent knew about Jirka's connection to the > Ramsey's and that is how he "saw" beneath the surface of the Ramsey case. > Jirka and his pals REALLY ARE into Satanism. It's not a joke. And Vincent > wrote about it as plainly as he could without risking going on a hit-list. > It's clear that Vincent is NOT one of them, but who will care? He does > "enochian magic."

[Laura:] Here you have been offered a platform to speak about your perspective on this, to clarify it. I have said that you are NOT one of them... because it is clearly coming from outside sources, and it is only a matter of time, that somebody is going to make this claim. You could see Stan going there, but pulling up short at the last minute. This was your opportunity to prevent any possibility of that occurrence having ability to harm you. Giving knowledge to others about it, before the slanted versions appear – and you can be sure they will if WE continue in any association – is the ONLY defense. I gave you this platform, but you ignored it.

> > *The fact is, Jirka tried to "buy" Dan Winter, and couldn't. And the fact is, > Stan knows that Dan was connected to Vincent, that Vincent was supposed to > publish Dan's book. So, the thread is leading to denounce us here as > Satanists, Nazis and funded by Jirka. > > We all know that Vincent's own dabbling in things enochian are intended in > quite another direction, however, that doesn't matter. A connection is a > connection. And it is, in this case, a serious weakness in our defenses.*

Here you had another platform... one where you could say "well, it was the best thing I could see up to recent times, but my experiences and exchanges with the group here have brought me to question the value of such things. I will be taking such and such action.... blah blah... and therefore, we have learned from this experience and maybe we can work this out. And, had you said that you were willing to reconsider your position, we would have been most happy to reconsider our position. We have no problem admitting when we are wrong and have made bad choices. But as the situation stood at the moment of this choice, it was the right choice. Had the situation changed, it could all be reconsidered.]

> > *So it is, with regret, that Ark and I have decided that, for the safety of the > group, for the preservation of all we have worked so hard for, for so many > years, that we must cancel our appearance at the conference in Zaca Lake. > > We have walked a careful path, attempting to build a bridge between science > and mysticism. We have made tremendous progress. And, we are certain that > Vincent will understand the necessity for this move, and will agreeably refund > the pre- paid reservations for all of you who were going to attend simply to > hang out with us. > > And to make it up to all of you, we will arrange our own "symposium" in the > very near future. I am sure that there is enough talent here on the group > that we could have a nice series of lectures on varous topics from some of > you!*

Again, you had a platform of learning/teaching and demonstrating growth practices of self-examination, reviewing situations, making course adjustments, and so forth. Is that so hard to do?

> *Well isn't that just grand! Things get rough and you decide to dump the > person working overtime to get your material in print, to get you an income > for your efforts and to give you a venue, a credible venue, in which to > present your ideas...*

Vincent, you have spent most of the past four months doing anything BUT working on our book to get it in print. As for a credible venue, don't you get it yet? A sponsorship by Fifth Way and SanGraal is NOT a credible venue... it is a recipe for disaster!

> > *Sorry, but I don't understand. First you trash the conference with your > disclaimer on the site, and then when its too late for a refund on the > deposit*

I don't get the "too late for a refund." Your statement was that your friend, Jay, was the operator of the conference center. If he was running

665

it like a business, six weeks is adequate time for a refund from any credible conference center. Are you saying that all the money has been spent?

and you're the only speaker left, you decide not to do it.

When did you plan to inform anyone that we were the only speaker left? What about the people who were coming to hear the other speakers? And why did THEY cancel? Something is wrong with this picture.

So, you have > your symposium, already scheduled, booked and paid for entirely by people who > came to hear you guys anyway. Might be a good idea to take advantage of it. > Don't worry, there won't be any one else there but the staff. Perhaps you'd > care to explain why that's not acceptable?

The issue is, and I will repeat it again, the sponsorship by Fifth Way and San Graal, and the fact that both are publicly associated with practices and teachings that can be connected to what is perceived as Satanism, and no amount of declaiming that you are not a Satanist will cure that fact. YOU could cure it by repudiating it. But it would be unreasonable for us to even suggest it. If it were in your heart to do it, that would be one thing, but to do it for political reasons would not be sincere.

> > As for the rest of the above, well, let me say directly that I never asked, > suggested or encouraged you in any way to write anything on Stan Tenen, nor > did I give you permission to use my research on the case in your article, > although I can't stop you because it is in the public domain as part of the > court proceedings. If you had asked, I would have told you that it was a bad > idea for the reasons you have just experienced.

I guess it is a bad idea to talk about things that are necessary to expose the Matrix? That's what we do here. That's the whole deal.

> > And I have never said anything on the record, or given permission for any > private communications to be shared, concerning Mr. Jirka Rysavy and > "satanism" or the JonBenet Ramsey case.

If you don't see this coming, you had better look again. The very fact that you perceived issues under the surface in this connection and wrote about it, is the clearest proof of your good intentions in the whole mess. Again, a platform was prepared for you, but you either didn't see it, or declined to utilize it to your benefit.

Vincent, from the very beginning of our interaction, you had every opportunity to "come clean," to use knowledge in a way that would change your life. You think I am joking, I guess, when I say this. I am not.

You are an expert on many things and a brilliant thinker. But just like the rest of us, you seem to have a big blind spot in your mind that may be self- destructive. As usual, this is generally a symptom of narcissism – an essential STS program. It's very easy for all of us to see the programs in others, but extremely difficult to see them in ourselves, to say: "yes, I have a program, it was running when I made this or that decision, and now, having spotted it, I am dealing with it."

Well, in this case, I was certainly running a program myself. I was not taking the proper precautions because I was quite lulled into a sense of security by your brilliance and your assurances. I didn't do my homework. Having been hit by forces of a certain type, from a certain direction, it was time to search and analyze the issue. Fortunately, I had a clue given to me from the viewing when you were here. It puzzled me, and upset me, and I didn't like it. But, it seems that once it occurred, once the door to perception was slightly opened, the shaft of light that entered into my own wishful thinking was enough to show me many other things, and to show them to me just in the nick of time to take corrective action.

That's what we are all about: knowing that ALL of us have programs – no one is excepted, no one is immune, and one of the most dangerous of programs is to think that one IS immune, or that rituals or certain practices will protect from this running of a program.

And to be able to stand up in public and say: I was programmed (even if we are only talking about socio-cultural programs and not deep, dark, satanic programs) takes a certain amount of courage. To say "I was wrong" takes courage, also. To expose our foibles takes courage. To turn our brilliant minds on our own issues takes courage.

And I can almost guarantee that you, with your mind and talents, are one of the prime targets of programming from any number of sources. To think that you would escape is almost ludicrous. And to think that it will be easy to face it and overcome it is also absurd.

But, again, there is a platform, and I will preserve it for you as long as possible. It ain't over 'til it's over.

Laura

LKJ wrote to the Cass InnerCircle group, the group of original members:

> *[Vincent wrote:] I fail to see how censoring my access to the list is giving me any kind of platform, but apparently the plan was to make sure I couldn't reply.*

The process continued in subsequent emails to the small group:

Laura here: And that is my point. I have no intention of censoring. But, still being 3D enough to wishfully think about what COULD STILL BE an extraordinary collaboration, I would like to leave the door open to that possibility just a little bit longer. If it becomes a billboard falling over my head that the door must be forever closed, then I will release the post, and the door will slam shut. Of that you can be sure.

But, I would like to make a few points here:

We can always sense the wolf sniffing around the perimeter, looking for an opening. If he finds only a small one, he will begin to dig and shove and work his way in.

In this case it was, of course, Vincent's ongoing participation in the Enochian stuff which, I was actually unaware that he DID it himself. My understanding from him was that he had researched it, had even gotten inside the organizations to do so, but that his intereest was purely intellectual and speculative.

Well, in reading Dan Winter's book and during the discussions of "sacred geometry," I knew we had a problem... but it was more than just knowing it.

I knew things were not right because certain plans had not materialized, and certain signs were appearing here, and I always pay attention to signs.

What should I do? Go out and perform a ritual?

Here is the one C's propose: always expect attack, anticipate source of same, take action to head it off.

I was asking the universe, where is the hole? What is the portal of attack. And, just as I asked, a post came from Vincent proposing a ritual, and I decided that here and now we will open this sacred geometry subject up and see what comes out from networking rather than following the same old crap that has been coming down for ages, mostly from the ritual magic sources.

Meanwhile, on the subject of sacred geometry, a post came from Terri pointing out a certain page on Vincent's site which I casually went over to read....

To be pointed to a page on his website where he is clearly not only DO-ING that stuff – believing in it – but advocating it as "the way," just nearly gave me a heart attack.

And, when I realized that, and the fact that Vincent actually gave a copy of his book containing this ritual to a potential funding source who we all knew was a sincere Mormon, well – talk about shooting yourself and the whole group in the foot, damn it. That guy will NEVER give a dime to anything after reading that chapter, and if you don't realize it, you need to wake up and smell the coffee here.

Which chapter, by the way, completely invalidates the "rational" excuse for AMET – that the 4D aspect of it was "known" but that it was not brought up because it was too off the wall. Because, at the end of AMET, that whole chapter on the Equinox working is included.

Well, I saw the portal. And I knew that I immediately had to make our position clear to the big group as well as on the conference announcement. I figured that was enough. Just deal with that, and deal with the issues of ritual, make the position clear. We can agree to disagree, but it has to be public because we don't hide those things.

I figured Vincent could enter the discussion and I was – wishfully thinking, I admit – hoping that he would give it a "theoretical" or "experimental" spin as an act of courtesy. You know "hey, we tried that stuff for the sake of experiment, etc, etc," but we don't really believe or teach that stuff... except as an intellectual and historical exercise...

That he could not, or did not, see the position we were in – from the very beginning – knowing far better than I did, his own involvement in some truly fringe and irrational elements – all the while claiming rationality and research, and serious application of thinking – well, you see my point here? There was a serious lack of consideration about what we are about, our years of work and effort, and even a seeming effort to undermine that very work with the introduction of rituals into the group, which I am supposed to not comment on, thereby giving tacit acceptance or approval to them???

Get real.

But then, as the wolf made the hole bigger, and came in through those anti-semitic rantings against us, and then Stan Tenen posted his deal to Sarfatti's VERY LONG list of scientists... and others, I saw the handwriting on the wall.

Always expect attack, anticipate the mode of same, take action to head it off.

That's the formula. That is the ONLY formula that works. But it necessitates seeing reality OBJECTIVELY.

It was time to stop waffling and waiting for Vincent to get with the program.

So, we not only removed any mention of his Fifth Way mystery school from our site, so as not to leave a trail for the hounds of hell that were now picking up the scent, but also decided that we had to create even more distance. This way, if it ever gets thrown in our face – which you can be sure it will (always expect attack, anticipate source of same, take action to head it off) we will be able to point out that once we were fully aware of the situation, we disconnected.

Because that is the truth.

Well, as you see from Vincent's post here on the crucible, he just simply does not see any perspective but his own. He does not see the danger. He is not looking at what can, and will happen if these things are NOT anticipated and dealt with swiftly and cleanly. His practices and public posting of same, are a HUGE hole in our defenses. And if he does not see this, then he is not seeing reality.

Knowing the C's perspective, knowing the vulnerabilities, Vincent could have put the same sequence of thoughts into action (always expect attack, anticipate modes of same, take action to head it off) at any time. But did he do that? Nope. I guess he did a "working" and communed with the Ophanic Intelligences.

What is even more amazing is the fact that it is all blamed on us because we are so ungrateful, so unappreciative, so uncaring, and most of all sneaky and untrustworthy.

Well, from my point of view, that is fine. I will take the blame. In fact, I deserve it. I should never have taken Vincent's word for anything but should have investigated deep and far and wide and should have paid more attention and been more aware.

Next, in the post to the big group, Vincent makes that most amazing statement about giving us a "credible venue."

Excuse me? Are we forgetting something here? Has it eluded our awareness that Ark is a scientist, a winner of a Humboldt prize, with 80 some published papers (in mainstream journals, I might add) to his credit, and a still existing position with a major European university? Has it been forgotten that our whole work and effort is to build an edifice of real scientific mysticism? That we labor long and hard to that end? And here we are on the point of being connected, in public, to Satanism – never mind whether Vincent himself thinks what he is doing is Satanic – it is the public perception that counts, and its effect on our ability to present the work that is important.

And it is supposed to be a credible venue to be sponsored by Fifth Way and SanGraal who also promote Drunvalo Melchizidek, were big on Dan Winter, and have articles about calling down Ophanic intelligences and rituals and all that?

GET REAL!!!!

That's why we are supposed to use our brains, not rituals. Always expect attack, anticipate source of same, take action to head it off. That's the formula. Works every time.

What really hurts here is that when you like somebody so much, you see so much value in them, so much out and out brilliance, and you would really like to work with them because it could be so much fun – but the reality is that if you do, their beliefs and practices, their blind spot, are openings for attack onto you. It's that simple.

I should never have made the mistake of thinking that we could ever go beyond friendly discussion on any of a number of subjects. You can't be harnessed with a horse that is pulling in the opposite direction. So, most definitely, the fault is mine.

Can that horse turn around and pull in the same direction?

Is it wishful thinking for me to think so? Probably. But heck, I was able to break out of the shell, to look at my history, my track record, and see that there was something not right in my life. If I could do it, anybody can. Yeah, it takes guts like you wouldn't believe... but I am keeping the door open because I think that Vincent has the courage of a lion.

Laura

Bridges responded:

I like the idea of keeping the door open, I just don't see how shutting me out without a response is doing anything of the kind.

So, here's my final response:

Well group, I hardly know what to say. My sudden vilification is quite unnerving and perplexing. Hey look, I'm still me. I haven't changed or even done anything but try to help, and suddenly I'm the villain of the piece programmed for a search and destroy mission. And nobody disagrees with that depiction!

Wow! Talk about control and the power of spin...

Nothing has changed but Laura's perception. And that is so rooted in assumption, ignorance and prejudice as to be suspect in and of itself. Where did this opinion come from? An emotional reaction triggered by some very suspect astral visioning. Oh well...

[He totally ignores the entire list of events I have cited as evidence that the direction being followed is one leading to disaster. Instead, he makes a ridiculous, ad hominem remark about it being an "emotional reaction".]

I don't know why I bother, since Laura's mind is made up and that's good enough for everybody else. But here goes:

I have been initiated into five different traditions. I hold a 3rd degree in traditional Wicca, I am a Christian minister of a gnostic and non-demoninational variety, and I am one of the highest ranking initiates of anything that passes for the Golden Dawn, also I have the barakah of the founder of the Abu Al Hagagg Sufis of Luxor Egypt and I am part of the Medicine Buddha and Kalachakra lineage of Tibetan Buddhism as well as a terton or terma treasure holder, of the Nyngma-pa tradition.

I learned a great deal from all of them. I have been fortunate to meet several real adepts within living traditions who have corrected my mistakes and validated my attainments. For this, I am very grateful.

My personal practices at the moment are Tibetan Buddhist and the last 'ritual' I did was to read the Bardo for the father of a former client who made his transition last Monday.

As I said before, in the censored email to big group, any ritual or spiritual practice that is done without complete understanding and an STO framework is liable to attract unwanted 4d critters and worse. And believe me, that includes ouiji board channeling and mirror work. And of course, using "magick" to curtail anyone's free will, in any way, is very much STS black magic.

What is so funny about all this, is that I have been thrown out of many occult groups because of my insistence on some of the things concerning "ritual" that Laura espouses. I do think that most Wiccan and ritual magick workings are useless and worse than useless, and have said so. I called up an old friend and long time FWMS member and read her some of Laura's rants about the GD, Dee and rituals in general. She thought it was mine and wanted to know what group I was about to get thrown out of. When I told her that it was directed at me, and that yes I was going to get thrown out, we both had a good laugh.

So just to set the record straight, I am not a satanist, I do not do magick of a control oriented STS type, ever, and I have not been programmed to search out and destroy the Cs. Sort of feels like testifying at the anti-amercian hearings of McCarthy or facing the inquisition, doesn't it?

Anyway, there is the conference...

My contract with Zaca Lake Foundation reads: "Deposit is non-refundable 60 days prior to retreat." Sixty days was July 21. You guys canceled on August 5, barely giving even six weeks notice. [This turns out to have been another lie.] Other folks involved with the conference started telling me about your disclaimer, and their discomfort concerning it, around the middle of July. I of course wasn't informed about the disclaimer, and you guys certainly didn't choose to drop out at that point, the reasonable thing to do if you felt that way about the conference and its sponsors. By the time I got back from Kid's camp [he fails to mention that he attended this kids camp during a period when he had his partner write to me that he couldn't get the book ready in time because he was sick], it was a situation. Still no word from Laura and Ark on backing out, so since a majority of the paid attendees were from the cassiopaea list, I stupidly tried to fix it by making the conference all Cassiopaea, withdrawing any support or sponsorship so as not to embarrass anyone's sensibilities, and even offered to spring for the plane tickets. [All completely untrue.]

If you don't want to take advantage of the opportunity, and that's all it is, no nefarious plot, well that's fine. Free will of course. Since I am responsible for the conference, my name on the bottom line and all that, I will do what I can to get as much of the deposit returned as possible. And we will of course just eat the loss if we have to and return everyone's money. [He didn't, to this day.] But it would be nice if everyone understood that this is totally your choice, your call from trashing the conference initially to not wanting to do it period because of paranoia.

As for the book, well, if we wanted to pull together on this we could still make our deadlines. [Impossible. The deadline had passed while he was at "kids camp", while claiming to be in bed with flu.] But of course, in the face of your scrupulous paranoia what does the time, energy and effort already expended on the project matter? You guys didn't have to do anything, right? Just be demanding and incredibly naive about the process and the work involved, and then, when it is finally coming together, trash it and back out. Free will of course... [Never mind that Vincent did not even have a legally registered company.] But I wonder if you are ever going to take responsibility for the damage these Free Will choices inflict on others. Sometimes Service to Self takes some strange forms.

Here's a Sufi story to close out:

A sufi was walking through the suk of a small town and noticed a large group of people paying close attention to a man reading from a book. The sufi walked over and noticed that the book the man was reading from was upside down. "Well," the reader argued, "if you know how to read, you can read upside down." The group listening, having no knowledge of letters or reading themselves, agreed with the reader and expressed that they were quite happy with the story as read. The sufi, having no reply to such certainty, walked away.

Thanks for listening,

Vincent

Sometime later, after this episode had been discussed among the QFG members, one of them, a Terri Burns wanted the other people present at the mirror session to write their impressions of what was happening. These were posted to the discussion group as follows:

From: "Arkadiusz Jadczyk"

Date sent: Tue, 7 Aug 2001 10:19:57 -0400

Subject: Re: Question for O*, Ark, and B*****

On 7 Aug 2001, at 12:13, Terri wrote:

> *We have read Laura and Vincent's account of a certain mirror session in Florida. O***, Ark, and B***, were't you there also? What was your take on that situation?*

Terri,

Here are my impressions. I will present them not in any order.

1) Vincent was very tense, as never before

2) He was acting like under some external imperative

3) He didn't see himself

4) He was forcibly, repeatedly trying to get from Laura "where is the Ark?"

5) But he didn't dare to ask "Laura, tell me where is the Ark" He was addressing his question to some "spirit" as "Show Laura where is it!" in a commanding way.

6) Of course I knew that this is putting Laura in danger. He didn't realize or didn't care.

7) He was unable to ask a simple question. He was trying forcibly to perform a ritual. Nothing was coming. I could see Laura suffering under this pressure.

8) I do not do it usually, but this time I had to interrupt his questioning, because I saw it plainly that leads nowhere, that this Laura is physically suffering. I asked a simple straightforward question about the Kabbalah tree, and we got an instant answer. The key was to ask Laura directly, not to command via "Show Laura ... ".

9) It is significant to observe how the session has ended. Something came from Vincent that struck me like never before. He asked about his "psychic luggage". Laura started to describe what she is seeing. At some point he suddenly interrupted: "Let's stop it and don't waste our time any more." Or something similar. He was angry. "Don't waste our time." Notice, he ASKED for it. But could not bear what was coming. Somehow Laura did not notice how rude he was at that moment. I noticed it, and I was coming back to this again and again for several days. Finally, after few days, I took the tape and played this part to Laura. She was surprised.

These are the main points that come to my mind.

Best,

ark

From: c***@...

Date sent: Tue, 7 Aug 2001 17:56:31 EDT

Subject: Re: [cass] Re: censorship and other issues

The following is a copy of my response to a Cass member who questioned me privately about the "final" session with Vincent and my impressions about the evening. Perhaps it will lend some illumination, both as to what this was all about and the quiet tone of "off list" communication.....Barry

>>Good Morning [xxxx], ...sorry for the delay in my responses – I just regained email access and have been going through the threads to get up to speed. I am responding privately for a reason which I will get into in a minute.

Laura has already heard some/most of this. Let me preface everything by saying my response may be slanted and this stems from some of the previous attacks that have been directed against the group's efforts. I have been involved in ferreting out leaks, moles and thefts by the hundreds over the years, primarily in the business world. A generalized rule in doing this is to bracket your attention.

By bracketing, I mean you look first at the person most likely to have created a breach AND you look first also at the person least likely to have created a breach. If both come up "clean", you move down the line to the second most and least likely, etc. until you zero in on the offender. The process concentrates on access and potential, rather than "personal dislike" and allows for a more objective method of elimination.

With the (xxxx) and (xxxx) disruptions, the nature of attack as we know it, seems to indicate that lesser interruptions are often a smokescreen for something a little more subtle in operation behind the scene. Having launched that "ferret out the problem" mode, I naturally carried it a step further to the extent that it was obvious that Vincent filled the role of "least likely" magnificently.

I am not picking on Vincent and at the time, it was NOTHING personal. I have even cast myself into the role of fitting the "least likely" side of the balance sheet. I don't mean from a conscious intent to do damage to the effort, but simply someone who is geographically convenient to the day to day efforts of Laura & Ark and I realize that if 4th density wants to launch an attack, most of us could be unwitting vehicles. To this end, I have told Laura that she knows my intent and if something I say or do appears to be at variance, holler at me and make me aware of a possibly being cast in the role of a trojan horse.

Enough background on the situation, let me just add that like Laura, my "wishful thinking" kicked into gear also as far as Vincent is concerned. Obviously the man is well-versed and intelligent and if that is the kick-in-the-pants that Cass needs to really bring home the esoteric bacon, I would be all for it. The day of the session was my first meeting with Vincent in person. I mentioned the above most/least process as eliminating the "subjective" aspects when trying to ferret moles, well – the subjective aspect kicked into high gear the whole time I was there, with only brief moments of "wishful thinking" over-ride.

(xxxx), you have been the recipient of comments by Vincent that I was the dross in the mix and that I was beseiged with attachments which hampered the flow of things. What the heck, I don't know, I am open to the possibility, but at the same time, I am being as introspective as possible because I want to contribute, not detract. So during the afternoon and early evening, there was a visible tension or barrier between the two of us.

Now to the part you specifically inquired about. The session started with boardwork around 9pm as usual. The "groove" on the board was pretty good and there was little or no hesitation. Almost immediately, the C's, almost demanded that the session be stopped and mirror-work be commenced with the enhancement of trance induction by Vincent.

It seemed to be a very out of character insistence coming from the board, but in a burst of "wishful thinking" I thought that perhaps the communication which hit some dead ends with Frank, was going to be more overt. We took a short break and rearranged the room to facilitate the mirror-work and trance. Ark is the only person other than Laura who had a clear view of the mirror. Vincent whould have had some periferal visability and then (xxxx) and I were off to the side on an angle. The mirror work portion went evidently very well as far as Laura's participation. The participation by Vincent was just simply "wrong".

674

Some 3-4 decades ago, I did some hypnosis work. I am self-taught, NOT schooled and probably didn't have a clue about what was really happening at the time. I am not talking about serious involvement, maybe 15-20 inductees and perhaps a hundred or so self-inductions. I was prepared to cast Vincent in the role of resident expert in these matters, (that ole wishful thinking thing again). HE WAS NOT. The induction process was smooth enough, although fairly standard with a resonant voice quality. But I would venture to say that it was Laura who was facilitating the induction on her end much more than being led or guided by Vincent.

As the level deepened and Laura began her visualization(s), Vincent became almost paranoid, jerking her awareness around with poorly disguising attempts at protection. Now that is the role (a protector) of the inducer. He is the lifeline to the person in trance. But Vincents attempts at protection were not in response to Laura's being in difficulty, they were in response to Vincents fears from moment to moment...and yes, the protection aspect seemed in retrospect, to be heavily dependant upon a a ritualistic foundation.

Then there reached a stage or depth sufficent for Laura to provide some answers and insight, but Vincent could not formulate a question in a manner which would allow a response. Here, we were watching Laura flounder, listening to her reiterate over and over that the question must be asked in an STO manner and that the answer would be forthcoming adn Vincent simply could not grast the concept, much less get it into words within that framework. I was silently screaming at him, even with my "beginners' knowledge of hypnosis to make corrections and adjustments to his proceedure. Ark was sitting next to me doing much the same.

I didn't want to jump in and risk degradation of the inductor/inductee relationship, I suspect that Ark was quiet for a long time for much the same reasons. Finally Ark could not let things to on and interjected a presence into the session. Things smoothed out some and he handed "control" back to Vincent.

Vincent still did not grok what had and was happening, but continued in the same manner. The culmination of events was when he asked Laura to "tell" the physical/geographical location and identity of a buried energy source.

As Laura has written afterwards, this was something which put her directly in harm's way of any and all that oppose. The fact that the location is yet unknown (or unrevealed), is her lifeline and protection.

It was not a comfortable session, I can give Vincent the benefit of the doubt and attribute it to his being unable to break out of the ritual of protection and mumbo-jumbo he is schooled and acquainted with. I can extend that benefit of doubt to include the possibility that he was unwittingly being used. I cannot excuse the manner in which he conducted and participated in the session.

This is not a "sour grapes" reply and review of the session. From a wishful thinking standpoint, I wanted Vincent's involvement, even if there was a "friction" between us. I wanted the conference to go ahead as planned and be successful, if for no other reason, than it would have given me a perfect venue to do some digital video of the conference and pro-bono video presentation work to justify my spending several thousand dollars on computers and equipment to do just that. So much for wishful thinking. .....B***

From: "O* E****" E***@...**

Date sent: Wed, 8 Aug 2001 10:40:50 +0200

Subject: [cass] V and Mirror

Hi Group

OK, I will testify, although little will be added:

The mirror session has been covered and I don't have anything substantial to add. Vincent was tense all along and specially annoyed when his baggage was described, however he was drawn in by some curiosity, apparently, so it was a while before he said: 'This is all funny, but we're wasting time here.'

Now using the mirror was not his idea, actually he was not eager at all, so if the contact was affected by him then at least the use of the mirror which led to the viewing later was not an artifact of his expectations. Or if so, the effect was not the expected one.

My principal misgivings regarding Vincent had to do with the high esteem/import he seemed to place on Crowley's Book of the Law, which is an STS document if there ever was one. He further indicated in conversation that he considered Parson's and Hubbard's Babylon Working as an event of high import in opening presently unfolding futures, which I also found odd. This is not to say that whoever gave the Book of the Law was not as clever as filled with hate but rather to ask if anybody had ever come to anything except harm from association with same.

Now Vincent's magical track record and rituals and views were not exactly held in secret, although precise details were scarce, except for the Millennial Working and other Ophanic business which he discusses in some detail on his site. A work of learning and intellect, to be sure, but what for? Suffice it to say that I considered that the information that was so openly available had been considered.

In hindsight I had some fleeting questions about the contracts and publishing business arrangements, but took it as a matter of course that these would be regular, so I would not insert myself where not requested.

I met Vincent once and he certainly was fascinating to converse with, erudite and clever and quick and with an air of a world traveler who had seen everything. Fine presentation, no question. OK, but we all have talked of past glories and Vincent has even written about these, so what's next?

Regards O***

Now, regarding all of the above, it is clear that the C's kept insisting on the mirror work so that I would be able to "see" Vincent Bridges as he was. But, as I have written elsewhere, I was so persuaded by him, that it took days for the fog in my mind to lift so that I could begin to put *all* the pieces together. And, even then, I didn't want to believe it. So, at the point in time when Ark and I knew that we had to make some decisions and take a course of action that was, effectively, extremely distasteful to us – i.e. a challenge to Vincent to try to come to some understanding, and if that was impossible, to simply part company, we had another session and inquired about the many puzzling aspects we were now beginning to see.

July 28, 2001

Q: Am I right to be so upset with Vincent and his damned ritual magic stuff?

A: Yes.

Q: Am I right in my thinking that even if he is not conscious of it, he was sent as an agent to extract information from me?

A: Yes.

Q: Are the Cassiopaeans the ones that got in contact with him in his childhood and then when he was older [as he claims]?

A: No. Q: Is he consciously working as an agent?

A: No. [...]

Q: Are we going to have future dealings with Vincent?

A: Looks bad.

Q: Well, that's what I expected. Did the [hypnosis] work that Vincent did with me – was that beneficial?

A: OK

Q: Do I still need more work done?

A: Yes, 5 turns.

Q: (A) By whom?

A: Ark. [...]

Q: Where did that stuff about the "Percival 3" come from when Vincent was here?

A: Vincent.

Q: Is there really something hidden in the "Lair of Titus?"

A: No.

Q: Is there really going to be a 2010 Space war?

A: No.

Q: Are we really supposed to build some kind of thing to shield the earth in 2010?

A: No.

Q: Are we supposed to build some kind of technology for SOME reason? A: Yes. Later.

Q: Can you tell us what our mission is?

A: Keep learning.

Q: It must be the C's! Only they would say that! [...] Well, what else can I ask to get a non-answer?

A: Yes. 5 million.

Q: 5 million questions I can ask to get a non-answer. I see.

A: Voila! Joy! Now Learn!

Q: (A) Was that a joke? (L) In other words, learning is fun?

A: FUN! [...] Q: Are we supposed to move to France?

A: Yes.

Q: Are you sure?

A: Yes.

Q: When will we move to France?

A: 2003. [...]

Q: Are we supposed to DO something in France?

A: Yes.

Q: What?

A: More work.

Q: Well, SWELL! [...]

Q: OK. So we're going to move to France and do more work?

A: U 5.

Q: "U 5?!" Us and the three kids?

A: 8835 million.

Q: (A) What does that mean? (L) Hmm. Do you have any particular messages tonight? To warm up our connection?

A: Hope and glory is coming close!

Q: Anything else?

A: Point the way to love in realms of light. Trust on it.

August 7, 2001

Q: What was behind ... what forces were behind Vincent's action? Were they simply fourth density manipulation?

A: Close.

Q: Was there any satanic cult activity behind his activities?

A: No.

Q: Was there any ... was he, in fact, loaded with attachments, as I saw him in the viewing?

A: Yes.

Q: What was the source of these attachments?

A: Rituals.

Q: All right. What is the motivating factor behind his pushing for me to discover where the "grail" is buried? Was it simply his own desire to discover it?

A: Yes.

Q: Was he programmed to ask this question or to seek this?

A: Yes.

Q: What would have been the consequences if he had been able to squeeze the answer out of me?

A: Death to you. Q: Sh ... was he even remotely aware of that possibility?

A: Yes. Q: Apparently he wasn't sufficiently aware of it to really believe it, I would think. He thinks it's still a game.

A: Yes.

Q: He doesn't really understand how serious it is, that if you really get close to the secret, you die. A: Yes. Nor have you.

Q: So that's why you guys don't answer a lot of questions?

A: Yes.

Q: Well, that's a good enough reason, I reckon – to keep us alive. (A to L) Who gave the orders ... (L) Who gave the orders to Vincent? (A) Who is behind ... We know he was programmed. fourth density? (L) Let me ask this, since he was programmed, and that was the information he wanted to obtain, is it in fact true that fourth density STS either doesn't know or cannot access this secret?

A: Yes.

Q: And they are as anxious for it to be discovered ... in fact, they are the MOST anxious?

A: Yes.

August 10, 2001

Q: I would like to ask if we can ask some questions about Vincent Bridges and Jay Weidner.

A: Yes.

Q: What are their intentions toward us?

A: Bad. [...]

Q: What are their plans?

A: Sip pout gag.

Q: (A) What? What do you ... (L) Sip? Pout? Gag? (A) What is sip? (L) Sip means to take a drink of something – sip something. Sip? Out? Gag? What are they going to sip?

A: Knowledge.

Q: Oh, they took a sip of knowledge – or they're going to take a sip of knowledge?

A: Yes.

Q: And this sip of knowledge is going to make them pout and gag? (A) What is pout? (L) To just ... (demonstrates). Who are they going to get this sip of knowledge from that is going to make them pout and gag?

A: Lawyer.

Q: In other words, they're going to find they do not have a leg to stand on?

A: Yes.

Q: Well, is Vincent really connected to these satanic people?

A: Yes.

Q: Is he connected to them close to the inner circle?

A: No.

Q: Is he really an initiated Sufi?

A: No. Karma is coming.

Q: Do we have anything to be concerned about where they are concerned?

A: No.

Q: Do we need to take any further actions like putting more information on the website, any other things than what we are currently doing or have already done?

A: Yes.

Q: What?

A: Some more web info.

Q: What, in specific, on the web?

A: Files make him sick move to gag.

Q: (L) In other words, I should put something else that would drive him to go to an attorney? Make him madder?

A: Yes.

Q: Should I post Jay Weidner's letter from this morning?

A: Yes.

Q: (A) What's the point? (L) To make him go to an attorney? I don't know. What's the point – I don't get it? (A) What's the point of making them go to an attorney? (L) Well, an attorney may tell them that they are crossing dangerously close over the lines of being subject to a lawsuit themselves.

A: Yes.

Q: And I could also post Vincent's article or the letter he wrote himself about slander and libel.

A: Yes.

Q: Well, I don't like the idea of doing any of those things. They make me feel yucky. So why are you telling me to do them?

A: How do you think Vincent will feel?

Q: Well, he'll obviously feel more yucky that I will. I'll think about it and see how I feel in the morning. [...] Is all this just a con job to put themselves in a position to take people's money?

A: In part.

Q: Well, I just can't imagine what was going through that man's mind when he wrote that E-mail. I mean, that man is like ... I mean, I simply can't conceive of the type of consciousness that could occupy a physical body that could write that type of an E-mail. You know, it passes my understanding.

A: STS love.

Q: Service to Self love. Well, boy, he must be exploding on himself, or imploding or whatever. [...]

Q: Are we going to be able to survive this flame war and attack from Vincent and Jay Weidner?

A: No.

Q: Why not?

A: They will open the door to fame.

Q: What?! HOW can that be possible? Huh? (A) From slandering us?!

A: No, but have contacts who will be interested.

Q: (A) They have ... who? (L) They have contacts that will be interested. That's weird. [...] (L) When, I saw this thing in the mirror, this gadget that shot out this beam or whatever, was that the true image of some kind of a time machine or time-transiting device, or was that something that Vincent was projecting into my mind?

A: Good catch.

Q: Yeah, when I saw that picture on his webpage, I knew he'd been projecting that. He was sitting there focusing on it so I would see it. I told you, I showed it to you, didn't I? That was what I saw, that twisted up figure 8 thing. [laughter] I couldn't figure it out, what in the world it was. Is there an object buried in France I'm supposed to find?

A: Yes.

Q: Are we going to find it?

A: Yes.

Q: Can you tell us what year we'll be finding it.

A: Two (tape ended and was blank for some time then picked back up with a segment of what sounded like a heartbeat)

Q: What is the object?

A: Holy grail.

Q: What is the holy grail? [tape noise gets very, very loud here – planchette was spinning around and drawing figures] Huh. I don't know if they were drawing something or just playing. Guess they're not going to answer that one. [...] Well, is Vincent doing any of his "workings" to try to harm us? I mean, is he out there with his robes on, and drawing his pentagrams, and chanting, and calling to the Ophanic intelligences to slam lightning and thunder down upon our heads?

A: Close.

Q: Is he getting frustrated that it isn't working?

A: Yes.

August 20, 2001

Q: How many times has Vincent been abducted? [laughter]

A: 136. [...]

Q: (T) How recently has he been abducted? Yesterday? Last week?

A: Hot popper.

Q: (L) What is a "hot popper?"

A: Recently.

Q: In other words, he's still hot. He's been there so recently he's still popping.

Considering the uncanny correlation between each new expansion of knowledge and the subsequent reaction from the Control System, I want to call the reader's attention back to the remarks of Mr. Colin Bennett who described the crypto-geographic personalities as "living, breathing, huge animated forms which have the ability to penetrate human awareness the way ivy weaves through an old house." These suprahuman forms are "quite conscious, aware, and active." These unnamed dramatis personae demonstrate over and over again that humans are not lords of creation but part of an evolving chain of being, shading from "solid" to almost nothing. This chain consists of animal, vegetable and mineral domains, all of which have dynamic anthropomorphic elements that we ignore at our peril. Bennett rightly observed that such beings "speak" through simulacra and weather, atmosphere and geology, coincidence and dream, and that human beings are poised between the animal kingdoms and the realms of the gods. He also noted that these connections between environment and social character, motivation, etc., are evidence of supra-human agendas.

It seems that Bennett is aware of something that many others do not seem to consider as a possibility: the evidence of hyperdimensional beings. And, of course, if this hypothesis is correct, without such a theoretical understanding of it, there is no possibility of man becoming free of this Control System. What Mr. Bennett does not, however, address, is the manner in which these hyperdimensional beings create and utilize seemingly ordinary human beings as simulacra, and they "speak" through these agents of the Matrix the same way they speak through weather, geological events, dreams, and so forth. And through these simulated humans they manifest their *supra-human agendas*.

I have discussed the fact that the materialistic human mind, operating with the juvenile dictionary, has great difficulty grasping these concepts because when hundreds or thousands of people are simultaneously experiencing such phenomena that obviously defy our presently accepted laws of time and space, the mind simply boggles at what seems to be a program that *must* be a logistical nightmare. So I began to think of the whole problem in strictly ethereal terms, something that also traps a lot of researchers. The Cassiopaeans disabused me of that notion!

May 25, 1996

Q: (L.) So, out of every 1,000 people, there are 20 that are programmed, and 12% of these [or 2.4 out of 1000] are programmed by aliens, as in fourth density STS?

A: Understand that 4th density is physical, indeed. You are drifting further and further toward an ethereal only perception/theoretical position.

Q: (L) You are saying that the humans working on these kinds of things … and …

A: No, Laura, we are saying that there is really a very strong "nuts and bolts" reality to this phenomenon, and don't ignore it!

Q: (L) Gotcha!

One has to wonder why the Cassiopaeans put "nuts and bolts" in quotes? It was only much later, as I was gathering this material together for this series, that I realized the connection. You see, May 25th is Vincent Bridges' birthday. Four years later, just prior to a series of events leading us towards research on the issue of organic portals and psychopaths, on the Feast Day of St. Mary Magdalen, Penitent, at a session attended by six women members of our discussion group (seven, including myself), Mr. Bridges was discussed specifically, and here we discover another clue that relates to the "nuts and bolts" remark that was put in quotes to set it apart for special notice.

July 22, 2000

Q: I had a call from Vincent Bridges who informed me that the Wave Series was really creating a stir. It seems that he has had a connection to this Dr. Hammond of the Greenbaum lecture fame [this turned out to be another of Vincent Bridges false claims] and also had a number of exchanges with Andrija Puharich [another of Vincent Bridges' fraudulent claims] and it is Vincent's contention that the UFO phenomenon, the alien abduction phenomenon, and the many and varied other things we talk about and study and discuss, are a product of super advanced technological, human controlled mind-programming projects using the technology of Puharich and Tesla. Yes, it is supposed to be so advanced that they can not only read minds and can control minds, but that it is, in the end, merely human engineered programming. Is he, even in part, correct?

A: Well, there are elements of the phenomenon which may be connected to human, 3rd density STS engineering, but by and large, this is not the case.

Q: (L) He also said that it was his opinion, that the center of the web of all of this mind programming conspiracy, is in Tyler, Texas. Is that correct?

A: The what?!?

Q: (L) Well, what about the center of the human branch of the programming conspiracy?

A: *We feel that Vincent needs to recharge his batteries a bit.*

Q: (L) He also said that the area we are living is the center of a particular programming experiment, something like Nazi/Black magick cultists or something like that.

A: Better not to get too carried away. Remember, the root of all "negative" energies directed at 3rd density STS subjects, coming from 4th density, is essentially the same.

"Nuts and bolts?" "Recharge his batteries?" Just exactly what are the Cassiopaeans getting at here? It is astonishing in retrospect, that at the '96 session we were discussing the exact theory proposed by Vincent Bridges as the only acceptable explanation for alien abductions, and the remark about "nuts and bolts" was made as a clue for the future time when we would come back to the subject again, as a result of the remarks of Vincent Bridges. Were the Cs suggesting that Vincent Bridges is the Energizer Bunny of Attack robots?

Many so-called occultists or gurus or purveyors of mystic wisdom in the present day are being guided, controlled, directed, and otherwise misled by these crypto-geographic personalities with supra-human agendas. As a result of this disinformation process, as described by the Cs, there is something rather like a "thought war" going on at present, the agenda being both to control humanity and to set up a certain dynamic to both increase that control in the present realm, and also to ensure that any transitions to higher realms will remain under the Matrix Control System that is presently in place.

In the early days of our contact, Vincent Bridges mentioned the *Stargate Conspiracy* on numerous occasions. He was interested in the fact that Ark was chatting with Jack Sarfatti, named as an insider in the book. Most obviously assumed from this connection that Ark and I were *part* of the Stargate Conspiracy. It is even more obvious, reviewing his emails and the way he wound up his story, that he was very interested in becoming part of that group.

Now, why would Vincent Bridges want to be inside such a group? Why would he want to claim expertise in Satanic Ritual Abuse, in government mind programming? Why would he want to claim that he was in possession of the papers and journals of Andrija Puharich, which – if it is true, and we doubt it – could only have been obtained by purloining them?

The one question that really bothered me while listening to or reading all these claims was: if Vincent Bridges is so much an "insider" as he claims to be, why didn't Picknett and Prince interview *him* when they were writing their book?

Well, I have heard from several people that Vincent Bridges was rather impressed that Ark was "in with Sarfatti." Don't get too excited here; Jack is exactly what he claims to be: a "theatrical physicist." Whether or not that is a cover for a vacuum cleaner operation, we have no idea. We have some observations, but no conclusions. And we will present them in due course.

The fact is, the *real* members of the Stargate Conspiracy are desperate men who have given their souls over to a crypto-geographic being who does not have anyone's best interests at heart. Such people are behind the creation of the "program" that beams channeling signals out over the airwaves to be picked up by selected channels such as Frank Scott – when he is doing his "direct channeling."

It is obvious in retrospect that Vincent Bridges thought that I was channeling a "spirit" that would give him some kind of advantage, or entree into this world of the Stargate Conspiracy. If this group thought that Frank Scott was the "real channel," he would already be residing in a secret enclave, probably hooked to some machine that keeps him in a pre-orgasmic state for hours on end, channeling Set or Atum or whoever is the Neter of Necessity for the day.

But that is not what they have done. The guys in the suits haven't arrived at his door saying, "Please come with us!" In fact, the only contact that is being made with Mr. Scott is via Vincent Bridges, and is clear that this is a very low level contact – a miniscule petty tyrant, if you will – and Scott is playing right into their hands. We have to remember that the forces that serve self always seek the path of least resistance.

In this sense, Vincent Bridges is very much like the rest of us: a useful idiot. He is being carefully watched and tapped to see what he is coming up with. The only thing about him is that it seems he was *actively trying to get into the Satanist club!* He thought I would give him a map to the gold of Satan. He thought I would help him find something that he would then give to the Dark Masters in order to purchase entree into their club.

In this sense, Vincent Bridges, Jeff Williams, Frank Scott, *et al.*, provide us with a unique opportunity. As Carlos Castaneda wrote, if you don't have a petty tyrant, if you want to achieve anything, you will have to go out and find one. In another sense, the Williams/Bridges gang have presented our discussion group with something very much like a bacteria culture isolated in a petrie dish; through their small-scale operation, we are afforded a real time glimpse into the activity of the Crypto-geographic personality, an almost vegetative system that grows and multiplies, acts and reacts, according to very precise rules of mechanical life – the Control System – the Matrix. I'm sure that everyone has heard the old joke, "There's a fungus among us." Well, it's not a joke. As I wrote in my review of Picknett and Prince's *The Stargate Conspiracy*:

> The Control System does not inculcate belief by lying – at least not all the time. The lies – the subtle twists on the truth – are generally buried deeply in a soft cushion of warm and tender concern for their "chosen ones." The Control System proceeds by the method of imitation. It *apes* the expression of the positive, and *all the more carefully when it wishes to be mistaken altogether for truly benevolent intentions.*

The strategy of the Control System is to begin its work by adhering so closely to the letter of the positive as to be virtually indistinguishable to all but the most perspicacious individuals. It installs belief through a sort of rhythmic lull of entrainment which then permits acceptance of all that is said when it finally diverges slightly or greatly from the set pattern and pulls the mind of the believer along with it.

It's one thing to pursue conspiracy theories and to find them and track them and think that there are some very naughty folks here on the Big Blue Marble. It's an altogether different thing, after one has tracked enough of these theories, to come to the realization that they are all just different parts of the same elephant, and that the critter is really thousands of years old. When that fact smacks you in the face, either you run screaming in denial, or you begin to step back from the truly *big* picture, the global-millennial picture, and you see that there is a very stinky rat somewhere. Having arrived at that point, you realize that such a conspiracy could not be carried out by human beings – at least not alone. And then you have to face the most difficult task of all: asking yourself who or what could be behind it.

Having asked that question, you realize that you simply cannot answer it unless you open your mind to a whole constellation of possibilities that you would formerly never, ever, in your wildest dreams have considered. Then, if you work very, very hard, you may discover the "truth" that *they* want you to believe.

But, if you are very lucky, and you seek help based on the knowledge you have acquired that such help can and does exist – only we generally do not have access to it because we are too easily duped and manipulated – then you might begin to learn the rules of communicating with higher minds than our own. And doing that, then there is some hope of sorting out the mess. But it isn't easy, and it can't be easy.

This is extremely unfortunate because many good people are being led down the primrose path, and end up falling under this control, as well as promulgating it. Some people, of course, know exactly what they are doing. But others are innocent dupes. The only problem is, it is difficult to tell who is operating from a position of consciousness, and who is just a manipulated robot, or agent in the Matrix, so to say. And we are brought full circle to our clue about Vincent Bridges. The clue, of course, was in the word "batteries."

BIBLIOGRAPHY

Abehsera, Abraham A. *Babel: The Language of the 21st Century.* Jerusalem: EQEV Publishing House, 1991.

Baigent, Michael; Leigh, Richard; Lincoln, Henry. *The Holy Blood and the Holy Grail.* London: Jonathan Cape, 1982.

_____. *The Messianic Legacy.* New York: Dell, 1986.

Baigent, Michael and Leigh, Richard. *The Temple and the Lodge.* London: Corgi Books, 1990.

Barker, Gray. *They Knew Too Much About Flying Saucers.* New York: Tower Publications, 1967.

_____. *The Strange Case of Dr. M.K. Jessup.* Kitchener, Ont.: Galaxy Press, 1973.

_____. *The Silver Bridge.* Clarksburg, WV: Saucerian Books, 1970.

Begich, Nick; Manning, Jeanne. *Angels don't play this HAARP: Advances in Tesla Technology.* Anchorage: Earthpulse Press, 1995.

Bender, Albert K. *Flying Saucers and the Three Men.* New York: Paperback Library, Inc. 1968.

Berlitz, Charles and Valentine, J. Manson. *Without a Trace.* New York: Ballantine Books, 1977.

Berlitz, Charles and Moore, William. *The Philadelphia Experiment: Project Invisibility.* Fawcett, 1981.

Bruce, Alexandra. *The Philadelphia Experiment Murder: Parallel Universes and the Physics of Insanity.* Sky Books, 2001.

Castaneda, Carlos. *The Fire From Within.* New York: Simon and Shuster, 1984.

Cheetham, Erika. *The Further Prophecies of Nostradamus* Corgi, 1985.

Chittick, William C. *The Sufi Path of Knowledge.* Albany: State University of New York Press, 1989.

Corso, Col. Philip J., with William J. Birnes. *The Day After Roswell.* New York: Pocket Books, 1998.

Edwards, Frank. *Flying Saucers, Serious Business.* New York: Bantam, 1966.

Eliade, Mircea. *The Myth of the Eternal Return.* Princeton: Princeton University Press, 1954.

Einstein, Albert and P. Bergmann. *Annals of Mathematics* Vol. 38, No. 3, July 1938.

Fort, Charles. The Complete Books of Charles Fort. New York: Dover Publications, Inc., 1974

Fulcanelli. *The Mystery of the Cathedrals.* Las Vegas: Brotherhood of Life, 1984.

_____. *The Dwellings of the Philosophers.* Boulder: Archive Press, 1999.

Gribbin, John. *In Search of the Double Helix.* Bantam, 1985.

Gurdjieff, G. I. *Beelzebub's Tales to His Grandson.* E.P. Dutton & Co., Inc., 1973.
_____. *Life is Real Only Then, When "I Am".* New York: Elsevier-Dutton Publishing Company, Inc., 1981.

Hay, Louise. *You Can Heal Your Body.* Hay House, 1984.

Herbert, Nick. *Quantum Reality: Beyond the New Physics.* New York: Doubleday, 1985.

Hort, Barbara E. *Unholy Hungers.* Boston & London: Shambhala, 1996.

Howe, Linda Moulton. *An Alien Harvest. Littleton.* Colorado: Linda Moulton Howe Productions; 1989.
_____. *Glimpses of Other Realities Vol. 1: Facts and Eyewitnesses. Huntingdon Valley.* PA: LMH Productions; 1993.
_____. *Glimpses of Other Realities Vol. 2: High Strangeness.* New Orleans, Louisiana: Paper Chase Press; 1998.

Jacobs, David M. *The Threat.* New York: Simon & Schuster, 1998.

Jessup, Morris K. *The Case for the UFO.* New York: Bantam Books, 1955.
_____. *The UFO and the Bible.* Washington: Library Research Group, 1955.
_____. *UFO Annual.* New York: Citadel Press, 1956.
_____. *The Expanding Case for the UFO.* New York: Citadel Press, 1957.

Keel, John A. *The Mothman Prophecies.* Avondale Estates, GA: IllumiNet Press, 1991.

Lincoln, Henry. *The Key to the Secret Pattern.* The Windrush Press, 1997.

Marciniak, Barbara. *Bringers of the Dawn: Teachings from the Pleiadians.* Bear and Co., 1992.

Marinov, Stefan. *The Thorny Way of Truth.* Graz: East-West Publishers, 1991.

Maudsley, Henry. *Natural Causes and Supernatural Seemings.* London: Kegan Paul and Co., 1886.

Michel, Albin, ed. "Intro to a meeting from September, 1941: Premiere Initiation, par G.I. Gurdjieff," *Question de Gurdjieff* (no 50). 1989.

Mouravieff, Boris M. *Gnosis Book One: The Exoteric Cycle.* Praxis Institute Press, 2002.

Ouspensky, P. D. *In Search of the Miraculous: Fragments of an Unknown Teaching.* San Diego: Harvest/HBJ, 1977.
_____. *Tertium Organum: A Key to the Enigmas of the World.* New York: Vintage Books, 1981.

Picknett, Lynn, and Clive Prince. *The Stargate Conspiracy: The Truth About Extraterrestrial Life and the Mysteries of Ancient Egypt.* New York, Berkley, 1999.

Pinkola Estes, Clarissa. *Women Who Run With the Wolves: Myths and Stories of the Wild Woman Archetype.* New York. Ballantine Books, 1997.

Pope, Nick. *The Uninvited: An Exposé of the Alien Abduction Phenomenon.* London: Simon & Schuster, 1997.

Redfield, James. *The Celestine Prophecy.* New York: Warner Books, 1993.

Reich, Wilhelm. *Ether, God, and Devil.* NY: Orgone Institute Press, 1949.